Technology Integration in Higher Education:

Social and Organizational Aspects

Daniel W. Surry
University of South Alabama, USA

James "Tres" Stefurak
University of South Alabama, USA

Robert M. Gray, Jr.
University of South Alabama, USA

Information Science REFERENCE

INFORMATION SCIENCE REFERENCE

Hershey · New York

Senior Editorial Director:	Kristin Klinger
Director of Book Publications:	Julia Mosemann
Editorial Director:	Lindsay Johnston
Acquisitions Editor:	Erika Carter
Development Editor:	Myla Harty
Production Coordinator:	Jamie Snavely
Typesetters:	Keith Glazewski & Natalie Pronio
Cover Design:	Nick Newcomer

Published in the United States of America by
Information Science Reference (an imprint of IGI Global)
701 E. Chocolate Avenue
Hershey PA 17033
Tel: 717-533-8845
Fax: 717-533-8661
E-mail: cust@igi-global.com
Web site: http://www.igi-global.com

Library of Congress Cataloging-in-Publication Data

Technology integration in higher education : social and organizational aspects / Daniel W. Surry, James R. Stefurak, and Robert M. Gray, Jr., Editors.
p. cm.
Includes bibliographical references and index.
Summary: "This book provides a sound overview of the ways that technology influences the human and organizational aspects of higher education and how technology is changing the relationship between faculty and students, higher education experience, and the role of colleges and universities within society as a whole"-- Provided by publisher.
ISBN 978-1-60960-147-8 (hardcover) -- ISBN 978-1-60960-149-2 (ebook) 1. Education, Higher--Computer-assisted instruction. 2. Education, Higher--Effect of technological innovations on. 3. Educational technology--Social aspects. I. Surry, Daniel W., 1962- II. Stefurak, James R., 1974- III. Gray, Robert M., 1965-
LB2395.7.T46 2011
378.1'734--dc22
2010051814

British Cataloguing in Publication Data
A Cataloguing in Publication record for this book is available from the British Library.

Editorial Advisory Board

Table of Contents

Detailed Table of Contents

Universities currently face urgent demands to facilitate both lifelong learning and widening participation in an era of increasing global competition combined with cost reductions. To cope with rising numbers of students, educationalists are rethinking teaching strategies to consider the potential of e-learning for academic delivery to an ever more diverse student population. However, there is a relative dearth of research examining the role of strategic management and the impact of organizational factors when considering the implementation of Information and Communication Technology (ICT) for administrative/management purposes and learning technologies to support teaching activities. This chapter analyses organizational ICT processes and e-learning in higher education (HE) through the use of a theoretical "rich picture." "Soft systems methodology" (SSM) is applied to argue that since institutional settings, organizational vision, strategy and top-level support are critical to the success (or failure) of e-learning initiatives, these factors should equally be considered in planning for the implementation of integrated uses of ICT and e-learning.

Institutions of higher education must be aware of how students employ technology, and must consider student perspectives regarding how technology can best be integrated for instruction and communication. Student issues must be understood when integrating technology in higher education. This chapter discusses students as digital natives, recreational technologies, digital communication, and multicultural concerns related to technology use in higher education.

Many experienced college faculty who have achieved the reputation of being a good teacher are now faced with the task of moving their teaching to online environments, and some find themselves very unprepared. The purpose of this chapter is to tell the story of one faculty's transition from face-to-face teacher to online teacher with the hope that it will give other experienced college instructors a useful case with which to compare as they make similar transitions.

As institutions of higher education increase access to and support the use of educational technologies, there is a need to examine how to best support faculty's integration of technology into their courses.

and frustrations seen generally in higher education. There are promising areas of investigation such as high-fidelity patient simulators and incorporation of wireless handheld devices for point-of-care reference information and best practices. Widespread adoption of electronic medical records may allow medical education researchers to link instructional practices to eventual patient outcomes, with implications for higher education.

This chapter examines current research on mobile learning, its impacts in academia, and the technologies being used as mobile learning devices. The chapter begins by describing and defining mobile learning. Then, the technologies, research, and specific examples for each mobile technology are presented. The chapter concludes with a discussion of implications of mobile computing on social and organizational aspects in higher education.

The question addressed by the authors in this chapter is how significant of an impact Web 2.0 will have on higher education institutions. More specifically, is Web 2.0 a sustaining innovation that is creating incremental changes in higher education practices as older technologies have, or, is Web 2.0 a disruptive innovation that is slowly easing its way to meet the needs of specialized audiences but ultimately may drive out the conventional education model or turn it on its head? To tackle this question, the authors briefly review the current state of Web 2.0 in higher education, discuss related issues and controversies, and then focus on the impact of Web 2.0 on human, social, and organizational aspects of higher education institutions.

This chapter explores how the use of assistive technology in higher education offers students with disabilities opportunities to participate and benefit from an education. While access to the college is enhanced by assistive technology, there are potential barriers that must be addressed in the academic environment. Solutions to access include implementing universal design in instruction, designing accessible information technology and e-learning, and delivering professional development. Finally, innovations and trends in assistive technology will raise the bar and continue to challenge higher education

This chapter describes the design and development of both software to create social interaction modules on a Virtual Standardized Patient (VSP) platform and individualized affective models for affect recognition. The author describes clinically relevant scenarios for affect elicitation and protocols for reliable affect recognition. Further, there is an elucidation of a VSP interface system that has the capacity to monitor the trainee's affective response using physiological signals. Research findings are summarized from studies on 1) the usability and applicability of VSPs with training clinicians on various mental health disorders (e.g., adolescent male with conduct disorder; adolescent female who has recently been physically traumatized); and 2) preliminary use of the affect-sensitive system to systematically assess and manipulate aspects of VSPs to more fully develop cognitive and affective models of virtual humans with pathological characteristics.

This chapter is organized into two sections. The first section examines classroom assessment and the second section examines program and institutional assessment. Although these are discussed separately, they are becoming more and more connected. For example student performance on capstone projects (often viewed as a program learning outcome), provides information to students about their competency, but also provides feedback to the program about what students did or did not learn from program coursework. Within each section, impacts created by using technology for activities that have been part and parcel of assessment at universities are explored. Then, the transformative impacts of technology on assessment activities are discussed.

In this chapter, enterprise resource planning systems are defined and the benefits to the various constituents of the institution are described. Barriers (and strategies for overcoming them) are identified, specifically administration-related barriers, resource allocation barriers, time barriers, barriers related to campus policies, human barriers, and product specific barriers. Leaders of institutions at the crossroads, who are determining whether or not to implement an integrated ERP, can better understand the social implications of such projects as a result of consideration of the key issues raised within this chapter.

Foreword

Universities have always been at the forefront of the use of technology for teaching and research. *Arpanet*, the pre-cursor to the Internet was initially developed by a consortium of four Universities, SRI (in Stanford), the University of California at Los Angeles, the University of California at Santa Barbara, and the University of Utah. At first the Internet itself was what was being researched and developed. Later it became the key communication and knowledge-sharing source of academics with the development of email, search engines and protocols such as Archie, Veronica, Gopher. In the early nineties it was commonplace to hear of academics collaborating across vast distances and sharing data across networks.

In the mid-nineties things changed with the colonization of the Internet by corporate business. Although the development of the World Wide Web meant that academics could communicate more easily, university technology bills skyrocketed, and, suddenly business cases had to be developed for new or even continued use of technology. This increase of cost of technology to universities coincided with a push for a more business-like approach to the very nature of the university itself. Universities were forced to move away from their role as custodians of knowledge, and move towards strategic plans and business models. A complex relationship now exists between universities and technology. However, what is necessary now is the *integration* of technology into the fibre of the university. The learners of the 21st Century live technologically integrated lives. They do not distinguish between cellular telephones, text messaging devices, cameras, Internet browsers, email readers, music players, and satellite navigation systems. They just carry them in their pockets. Technology is already smoothly integrated with their everyday lives. Thus technology should be fully integrated with their academic lives. We need to recognize the diversification of the student population and consider the value of technology for students, and be aware of how students use technology.

There are two schools of thought regarding the use of Information and Communication Technology (ICT) in higher education. On the one hand technology is seen as the great liberator – an enabler that will deliver a new age of enlightenment with knowledge once again being set free – much as Gutenberg revolutionized university teaching in the mid 1400s with the development of the printing press. In a world with free knowledge the university can once again resume its position as the provider of a liberal education. On the other hand technology is being used to advance the business and entrench the current autocratic, business-driven structures that universities have become. Learning management systems such as *Blackboard* and *Moodle* have the potential to liberate knowledge and make it available at any time and any place. They enable online classrooms and social spaces where students can roam freely and explore intellectual activities. However these technologies are often used to bolster the monolithic university business structure. They are used to support the concept that the university is the sole font of knowledge that is stored and protected by a username and password, and that universities run according to tight schedules with strict deadlines that are strictly enforced by the learning management system. Gone is the concept of a liberal education, enter the world of the digital diploma machine.

It is against the background of this dual nature of technology in higher education that this book becomes significant. It contributes to improved pedagogy for deeper learning, as well as increased efficiency for improved performance. Improved pedagogy involves aligning teaching and learning with learner needs and with what we know about how people learn. But this cannot be done in isolation. Equally important are lecturer or instructor issues as well as institutional issues. How does the institution support its staff when they make the transition from face-to-face to online teaching? Technology in education, however, is more than just the online delivery of courseware. There are augmentative and assistive technologies for students with disabilities as well as software to automate testing and evaluation. Furthermore, the technology itself needs to be studied, developed, and improved not only as universities engage in research about technology in higher education, but also since technology forms the primary tools of many modern sciences. Thus medical research, for instance, cannot be divorced from research on medical information technology.

The university, of course, is also an enterprise such as any other, and enterprise resource planning software forms the backbone of the administration, leading to issues of security, data preservation and disaster recovery. The use of technology in higher education represents a significant investment and regardless of whether the underlying institutional philosophy tends towards liberalisation or regulation, it remains essential that careful planning be done to ensure an effective use of an expensive resource. Aspects regarding technology adoption, sustainability, and technology transfer support universities' need to invest wisely, to obtain user buy-in and develop a long-term perspective, in order to benefit from their innovation. Finally, as businesses, universities need to assess the impact of technology not just on their business model, but also on the quality of the service that they deliver.

Regardless of one's position, either as an instructor or as an administrator, it is essential to remember that the key function of the university is to prepare its students for the future – a future which those very students will be creating, and thus a volume such as this cannot be compete without a glimpse of what can be expected in a while from now. The editors and contributors of this volume can be commended for their valuable input into the field of technology in higher education.

Johannes Cronjé
Cape Peninsula University of Technology
May, 2010

Johannes Cronjé *is the Dean of the Faculty of Informatics and Design at the Cape Peninsula University of Technology in Cape Town, South Africa. He obtained a Doctorate in Afrikaans Literature in 1990 and then a Masters Degree in Computer-Assisted Education from the University of Pretoria. From 1994 to 2007 he was a professor of computers in education with the University of Pretoria. He has also been visiting professor at Sudan University of Science and Technology, Addis Ababa University, Ethiopia; the University of Joensuu, Finland, and the University of Bergen, Norway. He has supervised more than 70 Masters and 35 doctoral students and has published more than 40 academic articles and chapters in books. His hobbies include public speaking, road running, and playing the CD Player. He is married to Franci and they have 3 children, and two dogs.*

Preface

It is difficult to think of two topics more critically important to the modern world than technology and higher education. If pressed, we might mention health care, economic stability, justice, individual liberty, or national security as other critically important topics. While those topics are, of course, important, the advancement of each of those topics relies in large part on technology and higher education. Technology is widely seen as a source for improving and extending life, for expanding economic opportunity, for providing access to information and empowering individuals, and for responding to security threats. Higher education is the main training ground for physicians, economists, attorneys, social workers, teachers, military leaders, and national security experts as well as many other fields. Colleges and universities are also a major source of research and development in medicine, engineering, natural sciences, and technology.

While technology and higher education are each fascinating and important topics in their own right, we believe the interaction between technology and higher education is an even more fascinating and important topic. Technology is changing how colleges and universities function and organize themselves, how students learn and earn degrees, how faculty teach and conduct research, how institutional knowledge is collected, organized, and disseminated, and how universities, governments, and corporations interact. In turn, higher education is driving technological development, identifying and creating new markets, producing technology innovators and entrepreneurs, and developing new models for conceptualizing, marketing, and implementing innovative technologies.

Our intention in developing this book was to explore the complex interaction between technology and higher education. In looking at many of the available books on the topic of technology in higher education, we saw that most books focused on the relatively narrow topic of technology as a tool for accomplishing a specific task. From the beginning of this project we wanted to develop a book that was less about technology and more about the impact of technology. We wanted to create a resource that would help a broad range of stakeholder groups in higher education understand how technology is shaping the organizational and human aspects of higher education. While it is obviously impossible to develop a book that thoroughly explores all the ways that technology is impacting higher education, we believe the chapters included in this book provide an important and often engrossing starting point for understanding technology's impact.

ORGANIZATION OF THE BOOK

This book is organized in three sections. The first section, *Fundamental Issues*, includes eight chapters. In each of those chapters, the authors discuss topics that are central to understanding technology's impact on the social and organizational aspects of higher education. The second section, *Contexts of Social and Organizational Impact*, includes nine chapters. The authors of the chapters in this section describe the impact of specific technologies or discuss the affect of technology on specific areas within higher education. The third section, *Evolving Impacts of Technology*, includes six chapters. The authors in the final section discuss critical issues related to the future of technology in higher education.

The first section, *Fundamental Issues*, begins with an analysis by Surry, Stefurak, and Kowch of the key questions universities must ask during the technology integration process. In their analysis they describe questions that range from relatively simple "first order" questions to highly complex and contextualized "third order" questions. The second chapter, by McPherson and Jameson, presents an interesting framework for implementing information and communications technology in higher education through change management, shared vision, support, and commitment. The third chapter, by Ensminger and Lewis, describes the central role that students play in the integration of technology in higher education. In the fourth chapter Rieber, Francom, and Jensen offer fascinating personal perspectives of teaching and learning in an online environment in order to guide college faculty who may be moving to online teaching.

The fifth chapter in the first section, by Polly, Grant, and Gikas, describes two cases of university support for technology integration and offers a series of useful questions to guide the planning and design of technology integration in higher education. The sixth chapter, by Guest and Guest, provides an overview of vital issues related to copyright and privacy in higher education and discusses important recent legislation and legal cases related to those issues. In the seventh chapter, Rodriguez discusses the important topic of infrastructure development in higher education, describes a case study in infrastructure development, and offers 12 recommendations for effectively planning for infrastructure development. The first section concludes with Lea's interesting chapter on the topic of technology transfer. He describes an example of faculty entrepreneurship and uses the case to highlight challenges universities and faculty face in bringing their innovations to the marketplace.

The second section of the book, *Contexts of Social and Organizational Impact*, begins with a chapter by Stefurak, Surry, and Hayes on the topic of technology's emerging role in the clinical supervision of mental health professionals. Perhaps most notably, they offer an astute discussion of technology's impact on the crucial interpersonal relationships involved in clinical supervision. In the second chapter of this section, Reeves, and Reeves discuss the roles of pedagogy and advanced technology in the reform and redesign of clinical education within higher education. They also discuss the importance of design research both for improving clinical education and for developing guiding principles upon which to base further research and development. Following this, Hopper and Johns describe applications of technology in the medical industry. As part of their description, they include a particularly interesting analysis of the use of simulators in the clinical training and continuing education of medical professionals. The fourth chapter of this section, by Pastore, Land, and Jung, discusses mobile computing in higher education. The authors of that chapter provide an overview of the most common current applications of mobile learning technologies and include a keen discussion of how those technologies impact the social and organizational aspects of higher education. Dabbagh and Reo then provide an overview of the issues and controversies related to Web 2.0 as well as a discussion of its impact on higher education. Their chapter includes a fascinating discussion of several cutting edge topics including "Faculty 2.0", "Student 2.0", and "Classroom 2.0".

The sixth chapter of the second section, by Asselin, is a discussion of assistive technologies in higher education. This chapter includes a thoughtful overview of universal design for instruction and stresses the necessity of professional development to allow educators to make full use of assistive technologies. Following this, Parsons provides a fascinating description of virtual standardized patients that can aid in the diagnosis of psychiatric disorders and help to enhance the interpersonal skills of clinicians. In addition, he discusses the results of several studies that provide important insights into the usability and applicability of the new technology. In the eighth chapter in this section, Van Haneghan discusses the impact of technology on the vital processes of assessment and evaluation in higher education. He skillfully describes both classroom and institutional assessments and discusses technology's impact on the continuous improvement of higher education organizations. The ninth and final chapter in this section, by Haab and Cramer, describes enterprise resource planning (ERP) systems and their benefits to all key stakeholder groups in higher education. Most importantly, their chapter describes potential barriers to the implementation of ERPs in higher education and offers specific strategies for overcoming those barriers.

The third section of the book, *Evolving Impacts of Technology*, begins with a chapter by Gray and Dwight in which the authors apply the concept of "writerly" texts to online learning. This results in an interesting strategy for increasing interaction and creating more powerful online learning experiences. Following this, Plumb provides an insightful perspective of technology's role in higher education. He writes that despite much recent rhetoric championing technology's power to allow students to expand and customize their learning, technology is still widely used in higher education as a tool for transmitting a narrowly defined and highly controlled set of objectives. The third chapter in the section, by Jones and Harmon, looks at the future of online learning in higher education. Among the most interesting aspects of their chapter is an intriguing discussion of how technology may impact higher education in the long term.

In the fourth chapter of the final section, Smyth, Vale, Andrews, and Caladine describe the implementation of rich media technologies in Australian universities. The two year study described in their chapter resulted in important findings related to the funding, utilization, adoption, and implementation of rich media in higher education. Following this, Nworie provides a thoughtful synthesis of adoption and diffusion theories as they apply to technology in higher education. His chapter includes notable discussions of specific areas in which technology has been effectively adopted and of how technology has affected social relationships on university campuses. In the book's final chapter, Rasmussen, Davidson-Shivers, and Savenye offer a compelling look at how technology will likely impact higher education in the near future. Of particular interest in the chapter is the authors' description of four components that will most effectively facilitate technology integration in higher education.

We believe each of the 23 chapters included in this book adds interesting and important perspectives to the existing literature on the topic of technology in higher education. As Editors, we were extremely impressed and gratified that each author attempted to move beyond superficial statements of technological capabilities and sought to describe technology's impact on higher education in unique and meaningful ways. We believe this emphasis on the more nuanced and complex aspects of technology represents the main achievement of the book.

We hope the chapters in this book will inspire greater discussion on the topic of technology's impact on the social and organizational aspects of higher education. We hope future volumes on the topic will follow our lead and expand on the ideas and concepts included in this book. The greatest power of technology is not its technical capability, but rather its potential to fundamentally change individuals, organizations, and societies. We will need ongoing, honest, inclusive, and intelligent discussion to ensure that the power of technology is used to fundamentally change higher education in positive ways.

Daniel W. Surry
University of South Alabama, USA

James "Tres" Stefurak
University of South Alabama, USA

Robert M. Gray, Jr.
University of South Alabama, USA

Acknowledgment

We would like to thank everyone who contributed to the conceptualization, development, revision, and publication of this book. First and foremost, we want to sincerely thank the authors who wrote chapters. The time, talent, and expertise that they devoted to this project resulted in an important collection of well written, interesting, and thoughtful discussions of technology's impact on the social and organizational aspects of higher education. Each of the authors demonstrated a high degree of professionalism, commitment, enthusiasm, and attention to detail throughout the entire process. We want to especially thank Dr. Johannes Cronje from Cape Peninsula University of Technology for writing the Foreward. Obviously, without Dr. Cronje and the other authors, this book would not have been written. We are deeply grateful to each of them.

We would also like to thank the members of the Editorial Advisory Board who reviewed chapters, provided feedback, and assisted in the development of the book in many important ways. They each made significant contributions to the quality of the book and made our jobs as editors much easier and more enjoyable. We are also extremely grateful to IGI Global for believing in and supporting this book. Special thanks to Dave DeRicco and Myla Harty for their kindness, organizational skills, encouragement, and timely support.

We would like to acknowledge our friends and colleagues at the University of South Alabama. Thanks also to all of our mentors and academic role models who have guided and supported us over the years, most notably Kent Gustafson, Tom Reeves, Steve Yuen, Jerry Rosiek, Stephen Tomlinson, and Burke Johnson. Most importantly, we would like to thank our wives, Melinda Surry, Robin Stefurak, and Kim Gray, for their endless reservoirs of love, support, intelligence, humor, and patience.

Daniel W. Surry
University of South Alabama, USA

James "Tres" Stefurak
University of South Alabama, USA

Robert M. Gray, Jr.
University of South Alabama, USA

Section 1
Fundamental Issues

Chapter 1
Technology in Higher Education:
Asking the Right Questions

Daniel W. Surry
University of South Alabama, USA

James "Tres" Stefurak
University of South Alabama, USA

Eugene G. Kowch
University of Calgary, Canada

ABSTRACT

Leading technology integration in higher education requires an inquisitive, reflective approach. This chapter discusses key questions that university administrators, policy makers, faculty, and other stakeholders must address in order to effectively integrate technology into higher education. The questions are divided into three categories. First order questions are conceptually simple questions that can be answered with basic information and little controversy. First order questions primarily relate to the cost, availability, and capabilities of technology. Second order questions build on first order questions and require more data, greater participation, and deeper analysis to be effectively answered. Examples of second order questions include how to effectively implement technology, the costs and benefits of technology, the unintended consequences of technology, and how to move from operational to strategic planning. Third order questions involve the most complex, controversial, and profound issues of technology and higher education. These questions will likely never be definitively answered but force us to continually reassess and evaluate our fundamental beliefs about higher education. Third order questions relate to the role of higher education in society, the control and ultimate impact of technology, and how technology affects the essential elements of the higher education experience.

DOI: 10.4018/978-1-60960-147-8.ch001

INTRODUCTION

The ability to conceptualize, develop, and effectively employ tools is one of the defining characteristics of human beings. Beginning in the earliest days of pre-history, tool use has had a tremendous impact on the biological and social development of humankind (Watson, 2005). Even today, technology continues to play a central role in the development of our world. The tools we develop and employ drive the social and economic development of the human race and are the basis for humanity's hope for a better future (Arthur, 2009). It would be difficult to think of any area of human activity in which technology is not viewed as an essential aspect of future growth. As a society, we expect technology will improve our health care, lengthen our life expectancy and that of future generations, reduce crime, protect us from natural disasters, and improve our economic condition.

Technology also plays a central role in the development and growth of organizations. Technology allows organizations to reduce costs, increase productivity, improve efficiency, develop new products, and reach new customers. Technology links people to processes and vice-versa, and it is often an artifact demonstrating humanity's expression of how we want to work, communicate and exist as an organization. The long term success of any organization, from a small local business to a multi-national corporation, depends on that organization's ability to continually adapt to the ever expanding power of technology. Colleges and universities are no exception. The most successful higher education organizations in the future will be those that most effectively plan for, implement, utilize, and manage technology.

While most people would agree that technology plays a vital role in the development of societies and organizations, there is a great deal of debate about the specific role that technology plays. People disagree about virtually every aspect of technology. There is intense disagreement on such fundamental questions as the meaning of the word "technology" (Kline, 2003), whether technology is autonomous or under human control (Ellul, 1967), whether technology's impact has been generally positive or generally negative (Surry, 2008a), what role the market should play in technological development (Nye, 2006), and even the best way to categorize the various characteristics of technology (Surry, 2008b). Because there is such widespread disagreement about technology, individuals, organizations, and societies have an obligation to be intelligent developers and consumers of technology. If technology use is an inherently human activity, then we have an inherent responsibility to develop and employ technologies in a critical, thoughtful, rational, and humane manner.

In this chapter, we will discuss a number of key questions that colleges and universities must address if they wish to be intelligent developers and consumers of technology. Our goal for this chapter is not to answer the questions. That would be an impossible task. Our goal is to present the key questions and briefly describe the important associated issues related to each question. We hope university administrators, policy makers, faculty members, change agents, students, and other stakeholders in higher education will use these questions as a framework for discussion and debate on their own campuses. The answers to each question will likely vary, and probably should vary, widely from campus to campus.

THE KEY QUESTIONS

In this section, we will discuss key questions related to the integration of technology in higher education. We have organized the questions into three categories. First order questions are the least complex, easiest to answer, and least controversial questions. Second order questions are more complex, more difficult to answer, and more open to interpretation than first order questions. Third order questions are extremely complex, highly controversial, highly contextualized, and open to the most interpretation.

First Order Questions

As mentioned above, first order questions about technology in higher education are relatively simple or well defined. We do not intend to imply that first order questions are unimportant or even that first order questions are less important than other questions. First order questions are, in fact, extremely important because higher education organizations will have to adequately address these questions before moving on to more complex and compelling questions.

The most basic first order question that colleges and universities should ask is what technology options are available? It is important to determine all the options that are currently available as well as those that will likely be available in the near future. New technologies for both instructional and administrative purposes are continually being developed and introduced into the marketplace. Because of this, it is essential that higher education organizations continually stay informed about the current state of technology options. Closely associated with the question of technology options is, of course, the question of cost. Determining the cost for any technology, especially large scale technologies that will impact multiple areas of a university or technologies that are expected to have a relative long period of utilization, is an extremely difficult process. However, at a basic level, higher education organizations should have a realistic understanding of the initial costs of acquiring and implementing a technology as well as an understanding of the most likely continuing or recurring costs during the lifecycle of the technology.

Another basic first order question is to determine which tasks a technology will be required to perform. Technology is most effectively integrated when it is employed to perform a specific task or set of tasks. It is crucial that higher education organizations avoid integrating technology to address ill defined or unrealistic tasks. Associated with this is the question of the underlying need for technology integration. It is common for organizations to acquire and use technology when the root causes of a problem are not technological. For example, an organization may purchase an accounting information system to reduce accounting errors when the root cause of the problem actually is a lack of skills and knowledge among workers in the accounting department. Before making any large investments with technology, colleges and universities should conduct a thorough performance analysis (Rossett, 1999) to determine if the performance problem being addressed by a technology lends itself to a technological solution. For example, a problem involving HR policy exclusively will not likely lend to a purely technological solution.

Once questions about available technologies, costs, and required tasks have been addressed, it will be possible for universities to effectively address questions related to the utility value of technology. Utility value is the level to which the capabilities of a technology seem to be appropriate for completing a specific task (Lin & Ha, 2009). A technology that is very effective for completing a task is said to have high utility value. Determining an accurate estimate of a given technology's utility value requires knowledge of both the capabilities of a technology and the desired task performance and may be the most important first order question that higher education organizations should address. The question of utility value is complicated by the high levels of task heterogeneity (Lin & Ha) common to higher education institutions. No single technology will likely have high utility value for a large number of the varied tasks found in higher education. This often leads to competing task priorities and often results in incomplete or imperfect technological solutions.

Closely related to utility value is the question of the relative advantage of a technology. Relative advantage is the extent to which one technology offers greater potential for addressing a need than another technology or the status quo (Rogers, 2003). Criteria for relative advantage with technology can include cost, functionality, ease of use, compatibility, configurability, support, and stability among others. It is important to ensure that relative advantage is determined from both an organizational perspective and from an end user perspective. It is not uncommon for a technology to have high relative advantage for an organization but low relative advantage for end users.

Another key first order question is to determine people's reactions to technology in a higher education setting. This is a concept analogous to the first level of Kirkpatrick's four level evaluation model (Kirkpatrick, 2006; Kirkpatrick & Kirkpatrick, 2006). It is essential to ensure that the reactions of all stakeholder groups in regard to the technology integration process are taken into consideration. These reactions should be measured both prior to and post implementation. Determining the reaction of stakeholders prior to implementation can identify possible feelings of resistance or facilitate technology integration by fostering a sense of participation in the process and ownership of the technology (Ely, 1999). Determining reaction after implementation can provide valuable insights into the implementation process and improve subsequent implementation efforts.

The questions discussed above do not represent an exhaustive list of all first order questions related to technology in higher education. Other first order questions include critical questions about the sources and sustainability of funding for technology (both initially and continuing), how those funds will be procured, which technology vendors or suppliers offer the best prices and support, who will be the intended users of the technology, which technologies are being used effectively by competing educational organizations, and which technologies are likely to viable for an extended period of time. Each higher education organization will have to identify the most important first order questions for their unique situation and address those questions in a meaningful way before moving on to second order questions.

Second Order Questions

Second order questions about technology in higher education are more complex, more difficult to answer, and more open to interpretation than first order questions. Second order questions build on and extend the discussion and inquiry of first order questions. While first order questions can be often be answered by a small group of people with basic fact finding methods, second order questions typically require a deeper and more inclusive process in order to be addressed effectively.

A common second order question is how to most effectively plan for and implement technology within an educational organization. Implementation is the process by which an innovation is introduced into an organizational or social system after the initial adoption decision (Ely, 1999; Surry & Ely, 2006; Surry, 2002). There are numerous models of implementation and change specific to education (Ellsworth, 2000). One of the most widely cited proposes that there are eight conditions that facilitate the implementation of innovations in educational settings. These conditions are dissatisfaction with the status quo, skills and knowledge, resources, time, rewards and incentives, participation, commitment, and leadership (Ely, 1999). Another model (Surry, 2002) proposes that resources, infrastructure, human issues, policies, a focus on learning outcomes, evaluation, and support are the key factors in technology implementation in higher education. A common goal of most implementation models is to ensure that the use of a technology becomes effectively institutionalized within an organization or social system. Because implementation is a highly contextualized process, each college or university will have to carefully develop an implementation plan that is tailored to their unique environment and circumstances.

Related to implementation is the question of how effectively end users of the technology are employing specific technologies. Even if a new technology is widely implemented and used by a majority of intended users, there can still be problems associated with superficial or inconsistent use. Hall and Hord (1987) describe 6 main levels of use ranging from level 0 (non-use) to level VI (renewal). Universities will have to continually monitor the level of use and the institution's concerns about technology and provide ongoing post-adoption support to ensure technology is being used in meaningful ways by end users. Closely related to Hall and Hord's concept of levels of use is the concept of non-users. Non-users (Wyatt, 2003) include those who have never used a technology ("resisters") as well as former users of a technology ("dropouts"). Any college or university that hopes to effectively implement technology must ask itself why intended users are resisting use of a technology or dropping out after initial use. There is a natural tendency to base the success of an implementation purely on feedback from users of the technology. However, indentifying non-users and understanding the causes of resistance and dropout is crucial to determining the ultimate utilitization and eventual success of an implementation and to facilitating the eventual institutionalization of a technology.

One of the most difficult questions to answer is how a certain technology that is implemented in one area of a university will impact other areas. The various units of a university, the technologies they use, and the social aspects of each unit are not discrete, separate entities, but are all part of a complex sociotechnical system. A new technology in one area will likely impact other areas in unexpected ways. The unintended consequences of technology are difficult to predict and often result in profound changes to an organization or society (Tenner, 1996). Higher education administrators should develop a more complex, ecological perspective of technology integration when planning for and implementing new technological solutions. Just as the introduction of a foreign species often has dramatic and far reaching consequences for an entire ecosystem, the introduction of a new technology has dramatic and far reaching consequences for an organization (Zhao & Frank, 2003). University administrators will have to understand and anticipate the possible consequences of a new technology in an extremely holistic and ecological way in order to prevent potentially disastrous results.

As mentioned earlier, basic questions about the initial cost of a technology are a type of first order question. However, a key second order question is how to understand much more advanced and complicated issues related to the benefits of a technology compared to costs. While determining the initial, direct, and fixed costs of a technology is a relatively simple process, other types of costs can be extremely difficult to effectively measure. Indirect and variable costs (Prowle & Morgan, 2005) are often based on subjective assumptions and can be hidden or nearly impossible to anticipate. As a result, technology planners often do not account for these costs until they result in significant costs.

Another extremely difficult issue for higher education administrators is the question of the benefits of a technology to the fundamental work (or activity) in a higher education setting. As with costs, there are also direct and indirect benefits. Direct benefits for a university are often defined as increased tuition revenue, reduced waste or repair costs, and reduced salary or benefits. Like indirect costs, indirect benefits are much more difficult to calculate. Because of the difficulty in determining indirect and long term costs, higher education institutions of rely on very superficial measures when conducting a cost benefit analysis (Gupta, 2002). Closely related to the question of cost and benefits is the important second order question of whether or not a certain technology enhanced student learning. Not all technologies in higher education are intended to have a direct impact on student learning, of course. However, it would be useful for universities to know if expenditures on instructional technologies had an impact on learning. Because of the mixed impact of technology on learning (Schmid et al., 2009), it can be very difficult justify instructional technology expenditures based on student learning outcomes alone. Compounding this difficulty is the fact that the benefits of instructional technologies are often intangible and occur long after the initial costs are incurred. New models of benefit cost analysis are needed to explore the key questions of how to adequately measure and account for instructional technology expenditures (Surry, 2008a).

As with the first order questions, the questions discussed above do not represent an exhaustive list of all second order questions related to technology in higher education. Universities will have to face key questions related to the opportunity costs of technology, which policies will need to be modified, removed, or created to facilitate the use of new technologies, how professional development and support issues will be addressed, which upgrades to infrastructure will be required by new technologies, how new technologies will impact future budgetary decisions, how data about the effectiveness of the technology will be collected and analyzed, and whether there are any legal, regulatory, accreditation, moral, or ethical issues created (or solved) by the new technologies. Indeed, the basic questions all leaders ask during operational planning and budgeting involve these concerns. Each higher education institution will have to identify the second order questions that are most important to them and develop a plan for effectively answering the questions.

While effectively answering these questions will be extremely difficult, the good news is that adequately identifying and addressing these second order questions will allow universities to make the vital transition from operational levels of technology planning to strategic levels of planning (Kowch, 2005). Planning for *how* we will do things in higher education is *operational* planning. It is the basis for budgeting and resource allocation, underpinning operating budgets for resources (e.g, human resources, information technology, and physical plant). Operational planning is relatively linear, programmatic and reductionist work. Planning for the *what* or *why* of an organization is more difficult and requires *strategic* planning. This is critically important, vanguard thinking that can help leadership in higher education think and act beyond the traditional three year budget cycle. New models for strategic decision making in higher education do exist, but they are new and evolving quickly. For example, Bates (2000) offers a good strategic planning model for information and learning technologies in a learning organization.

Third Order Questions

The final category of questions about technology in higher education are extremely complex and ill defined but address the most fundamental and profound issues related to higher education. Because third order questions are so complex and fundamental, they defy easy solutions, require participation from all stakeholder groups to be meaningfully addressed, and demand ongoing discussion and debate. While first and second order questions have a technological focus, third order questions have an organizational or societal focus. There are many profoundly important and fundamental questions related to technology in higher education, of course, but we attempted to organize them into four broad groups of questions.

The first broad group of third order questions relate to the role of higher education in modern society. One of the most compelling questions in this group is whether a university serves society best by preparing skilled workers for specific job markets or by preparing creative critical thinkers whose educational experiences may not prepare them for specific jobs. The debate about liberal and practical education has gone on for years, of course (e.g., Carnochan, 1993). However, the increased use of technology in higher education has once again brought the debate to the fore. Other third order questions in this group relate to technology's role in helping universities address social issues including poverty, racism, drug abuse, and environmental concerns, the role of technology in the evolving relationship between universities and corporations, and technology's role in increasing diversity and access to higher education.

The second broad group of third order questions relate to the essential elements of the higher education experience for students, faculty, staff, and administrators. The most compelling contemporary question in this group is probably whether "place" is an essential element of the university experience. With the dramatic rise in the number of universities using web-based courses, students are beginning to view a university not as a place but as a technologically mediated entity. This will force universities to rethink how cultural and social experiences such as fraternities and sororities, athletic and academic clubs, and other student and alumni organizations that have traditionally played such a vital role in university life can be fostered in an increasingly virtual environment (Surry & Ensminger, 2009). Associated with this, universities will have to rethink the role of the faculty member and to reconsider ideas, policies and union concerns about how faculty will be hired, evaluated, retained, tenured, and promoted in an increasingly virtual environment. Each university will have to determine the consequences of this ever increasing devaluation of the physical presence of a university for its students, faculty, staff, administrators, alumni, community, and other stakeholders.

The next broad group of third order questions relate to who controls technology in higher education. In general, there are two theoretical perspectives about the relationship between technology and society. The first is perspective can be defined as technological determinism (Ellul, 1967). Under this perspective, technology is seen as the driving forces in societal change. The ever expanding power and complexity of technology force societies and organizations to increasingly rely on technology, to minimize non-technological options, and to devote increasingly large amounts of resources to maintaining and using technology. While technological determinism is not the prevailing philosophical perspective, the current state of technology in higher education can be seen as directly analogous to a state of technological determinism (Surry, 2008c). The second perspective related to the control of technology can be defined as social construction (Pinch & Bijker, 2003). Under this utilitarian perspective, technology is seen as a tool that societies develop and employ. Technology is not seen as an autonomous force, but rather a byproduct of societal needs, ambitions, desires, and market forces. Universities will have to determine and continually reassess how technology is controlled on their campuses, resist being pushed into decisions by the power of technology, and take proactive steps to ensure technology is a tool for furthering the goals of the university.

The fourth broad group of third order questions relate to the ultimate impact of technology in higher education. As with the question of control, there are two theoretical perspectives about the impact of technology on society. The first perspective can be defined as Utopianism. Under this perspective, technology is seen as gradually improving the quality of human existence. Utopianists in higher education see the use of technology as improving educational quality, reducing costs, increasing opportunity, reducing demands on the physical plant, and allowing for a dramatic reimagining of higher education. To a utopianist, these changes are gradually leading to a utopian, or nearly utopian, educational experience. The second perspective about the ultimate impact of technology can be defined as Dystopianism. Under this perspective, technology is seen as gradually destroying the quality of human existence. Dystopianists in higher education see technology as dehumanizing learning, reducing educational quality, crowding out non-technical fields of study, homogenizing the cultural and social aspects of education, and increasing economic disparities. To a dystopian, technology is leading inevitably to a nightmarish future for higher education. Universities will have to seek out multiple perspectives to come to a conclusion about the ultimate impact of technology on their campuses. It is likely that technology integration will have both positive and negative impacts in higher education. Both utopian and dystopian futures can easily be envisioned. The process of determining the impacts of technology, both positive and negative, will have to be an ongoing part of higher education planning in the future.

The questions described in this section are, obviously, impossible to definitively answer. Each university will have to determine which third order questions are most important to their future. Perhaps the ultimate third order question is when should we use technology in higher education and when should we not? Arthur (2009) writes that we should make a clear distinction between the possible uses of technology and the desirable uses of technology. While first and second order questions relate to the possible uses of technology, third order questions center on the vital issue of what uses of technology in higher education are desirable.

RECOMMENDATIONS

Based on our discussion of the three orders of questions, we have five recommendations related to technology in higher education. Our first recommendation is for colleges and universities to embrace technology and to think critically about its place in the work, value and benefit of our institutions. Technology is always changing and constant innovation will likely be needed in order for any higher education organization to remain financially and intellectually viable in the future. We believe a complete rejection of technology in higher education is neither practical nor desirable. The central question is not should higher education use technology, but how can technology be planned, implemented, assessed and used most effectively to improve higher education without destroying the essential elements of higher education that have served our society so well for centuries.

Our second recommendation is for colleges and universities to avoid the trap of technological determinism. It is very easy for any organization to see the potential of technology to address important problems. There is a danger, however, that technology will come to be seen as the best answer to every problem. In addition, as we have seen, technology often causes new, unanticipated, and unique problems. Ironically, the problems caused by technology are often solved by the addition of even more technologies which, in turn, cause even more unanticipated and unique problems. This is the trap of technological determinism. University administrators, faculty, leaders and students have to be aware of this potential trap, develop a plan for avoiding it, and continually seek feedback from all stakeholder groups to ensure technology has not become an autonomous force on their campus.

Our third recommendation is to view technology integration in higher education in more holistic terms. Universities are not simple organizations but complex, interconnected sociotechnical systems. The introduction of any technology will have consequences throughout the entire university. Administrators will need to avoid a superficial analysis of technology and think about technology integration in ecological terms if they want to effectively introduce and manage new technologies. This will likely involve the development and application of innovative, holistic, and interdisciplinary models of institutional research.

Higher education research done by combining interdisciplinary or multiple conceptual lenses like "leadership" and "education technology" is virtually non-existent (Kowch, 2003). This is a pity, because the essence of organization processes, structures, planning and finance in concert with the organization of instruction, technologies, learning and learners describes a larger complex system or mélange contributing to a higher education that improves the well-being and futures of students (Hellewell, 2002). We must go beyond piecemeal change ideas to see larger, holistic systems as we plan system reform (Reigeluth & Duffy, 2008). Complexity theorists suggest that this more ecological approach will be an essential shift in how we understand "parts" or "functions" of education systems in the future (Davis & Sumara, 2007). When a complex education system visions beyond classical approaches to consider an integrated understanding of how we teach, how we use technology to consider *what* and *why* we exist when we lead education "with computers", we ponder strategic, future-oriented questions planning sensitive to not just the *how*, but also to the *what* and *why* of our higher education organization (Kowch, 2009). If we are to truly lead entire higher education systems that are inclusive of macro and meso (internal) environmental change (including government, economic and political change), we're going to need to use complexity thinking and strategic planning knowledge inclusive of all kinds of disciplinary concepts.

Our fourth recommendation is to focus on second and third order questions as much as first order questions. No one would argue that first order questions are tremendously important and have to be effectively addressed. However, the mistake that many universities make is to stop their discussion of technology at first order questions without ever moving on to second and third order questions. Universities focus on first order questions because they are the least complex and are often the most pressing practical and utilitarian questions for administrators. However, universities should focus on second and third order question precisely because they are the most difficult and hardest to address. The complexity, subtlety, breadth, and importance of the second, and third order questions demand extensive time and effort in order to be addressed effectively.

It seems that higher education leaders can well answer first order questions on how to operate universities with better thought about some information technology mechanics (Green, 2002), but that our ability to plan strategically for change by answering second and third order questions remains largely non-existent. Falling well behind other organization transformation agilities, higher education organization leaders today face important global shifts that they can no longer ignore. Evidence on planning in large organizations in the social science domain is telling us that the world's increasingly co-dependent, networked organizations must operate well, plan better, and measurably contribute to social well-being, or risk perishing altogether.

Our fifth recommendation is for administrators to develop a meaningful process for addressing the questions that works for their university. Just as the answers to each question will likely vary from university to university, the best process for determining the answers will likely vary. Large public research intensive universities will probably employ very different processes for determining the answers than small private liberal arts colleges. Of course, there will be commonalities as well. Among these common approaches must be the identification of all relevant stakeholder groups, a valuing of different voices and perspectives, an ongoing mechanism for gathering and disseminating data, and a strong commitment to shared decision making.

The five recommendations discussed in this section represent the primary steps that higher education administrators should take to ensure they are asking the right questions about technology. It is likely that many other steps will need to be taken to ensure that technology is integrated effectively.

SUMMARY

In this chapter, we have discussed some of the key questions that higher education administrators, policy makers, change agents, faculty, and other stakeholders should attempt to answer during the process of technological development. The goal of this chapter was not to find answers to the questions. Even the most basic first order questions can not be answered for all universities. The most compelling third order questions probably can never be definitively answered. Given the uncertainty inherent with technology and social systems and the changing landscape of higher education, each university has the challenge to determine which questions are most important to them and then establish a process for answering those questions. The process each university chooses is critical. The future of higher education will ultimately be defined more by the process we use to explore, discuss, understand and make sense of the questions than by the answers we generate.

As Heidegger famously wrote "the essence of technology is nothing technological" (p. 264). Understanding the essence of technology in higher education will involve more than mastering the technical aspects of new technologies, it will involve understanding technology's impact on the deeply human aspects of learning, the profoundly social nature of human interaction, and critical role of higher education in the modern world.

REFERENCES

Arthur, W. B. (2009). *The nature of technology: What it is and how it evolves*. New York: Free Press.

Bates, A. (2000). *Managing technological change: Strategies for college and university leaders*. San Francisco: Jossey-Bass.

Carnochan, W. B. (1993). *The battleground of the curriculum: Liberal education and American experience*. Stanford, CA: Stanford University Press.

Davis, B., Sumara, D., & Kapler, R. (2007). *Engaging minds: Changing teaching in complex times* (2nd ed.). Toronto, ON: Routledge.

Ellsworth, J. B. (2000). *Surviving change: A survey of educational change models*. Syracuse, NY: ERIC Clearing House on Information & Technology (ED99CO0005)

Ellul, J. (1967). *The technological society*. New York: Knopf.

Ely, D. P. (1999). Conditions that facilitate the implementation of educational technology innovations. *Educational Technology*, *34*(6), 23–27.

Green, K. (2002). *Campus computing 2002: The campus computing project*. Encino, CA: Author.

Gupta, A. (2002). *Management of higher education*. New Delhi: Anmol Publications.

Hall, G. E., & Hord, S. M. (1987). *Change in schools*. Albany, NY: State University of New York Press.

Heidegger, M. (2003). The question concerning technology. In R. C. Scharff & V, Dusek (Eds.). *Philosophy of technology: The technological condition: An anthology* (pp. 252-264). Malden, MA: Blackwell.

Hellewell, J. F. (2002). *Globalization and well-being*. Vancouver: UBC Press.

Kirkpatrick, D. L. (2006). Seven keys to unlock the four levels of evaluation. *Performance Improvement*, *45*(7), 5–8. doi:10.1002/pfi.2006.4930450702

Kirkpatrick, D. L., & Kirkpatrick, J. D. (2006). *Evaluating training programs: The four levels* (3rd ed.). San Francisco: Berrett-Koehler.

Kline, S. J. (2003). What is technology. In R. C. Scharff & V, Dusek (Eds.). *Philosophy of technology: The technological condition: An anthology* (pp. 210-212). Malden, MA: Blackwell.

Kowch, E. (2003). *Policy networks and communities in three western Canada universities: Neo-institutional responses to a pan-institutional issue.* Unpublished doctoral dissertation, Department of Educational Administration, University of Saskatchewan.

Kowch, E. (2009). New capabilities for cyber charter school leadership: An Emerging imperative for integrating Educational Technology and Educational Leadership knowledge. *TechTrends*, *4*(5), 41–48.

Kowch, E. G. (2005). Do we plan the journey or read the compass? An argument for preparing educational technologists to lead organizational change. *British Journal of Educational Technology*, *36*(6), 1067–1070. doi:10.1111/j.1467-8535.2005.00577.x

Lin, C., & Ha, L. (2009). Subcultures and use of communication information technology in higher education institutions. *The Journal of Higher Education*, *80*(5), 564–590. doi:10.1353/jhe.0.0064

Nye, D. E. (2006). *Technology matters: Questions to live with.* Cambridge, MA: The MIT Press.

Pinch, T. J., & Bijker, W. E. (2003). The social construction of facts and artifacts. In Scharff, R. C., & Dusek, V. (Eds.), *The philosophy of technology: The technological condition: An anthology* (pp. 221–232). Malden, MA: Blackwell.

Prowle, M., & Morgan, E. (2005). *Financial management and control in higher education*. London: RoutledgeGalmer. doi:10.4324/9780203416143

Reigeluth, C. M., & Duffy, F. (2008). The AECT Futureminds initiative: Transforming America's school systems. *Educational Technology*, (May): 45–48.

Rogers, E. M. (2003). *Diffusion of innovations* (5th ed.). New York: Free Press.

Rossett, A. (1999). *First things fast: A handbook for performance analysis*. San Francisco: Jossey-Bass/Pfeiffer.

Schmid, R. F., Bernard, R. M., Borokhovski, E., Tamim, R., Abrami, P. C., & Wade, C. A. (2009). Technology's effect on achievement in higher educaton: A Stage I meta-analysis of classroom applications. *Journal of Computing in Higher Education*, *21*, 95–109. doi:10.1007/s12528-009-9021-8

Surry, D. W. (2002, April). *A model for integrating instructional technology into higher education.* Paper presented at the meeting of the American Educational Research Association (AERA), New Orleans, LA.

Surry, D. W. (2008a). Impact of technology. In Tomei, L. A. (Ed.), *Encyclopedia of information technology curriculum integration* (pp. 389–394). Hershey, PA: Idea Group Reference.

Surry, D. W. (2008b). Innovations in learning technology. In Tomei, L. A. (Ed.), *Encyclopedia of information technology curriculum integration* (pp. 413–417). Hershey, PA: IGI Global.

Surry, D. W. (2008c). Technology and the future of higher education: An Ellulian perspective. In J. Luca and E. R. Weippl (Eds.), *Proceedings of the ED-MEDIA 2008-World Conference on Educational Multimedia, Hypermedia & Telecommunications*. (pp.4901-4906). Chesapeake, VA: Association for Advancement of Computing in Education

Surry, D. W., & Ely, D. P. (2006). Adoption, diffusion, implementation, and institutionalization of educational innovations. In Reiser, R., & Dempsey, J. V. (Eds.), *Trends & issues in instructional design and technology* (2nd ed., pp. 104–111). Upper Saddle River, NJ: Prentice-Hall.

Surry, D. W., & Ensminger, D. C. (2009). University 2.0: Human, social, and societal issues. In Yang, H., & Yuen, S. (Eds.), *Collective Intelligence and E-Learning 2.0: Implications of Web-Based Communities and Networking* (pp. 94–108). Hershey, PA: IGI Global.

Tenner, E. (1996). *Why things bite back: Technology and the revenge of unintended consequences*. New York: Alfred A. Knopf.

Watson, P. (2005). *Ideas: A history of thought and invention from fire to Freud*. New York: HarperCollins.

Wyatt, S. (2003). Non-users also matter: The construction of users and non-users of the Internet. In Oudshoorn, N., & Pinch, T. (Eds.), *How Users Matter: The Co-construction of Users and Technology* (pp. 67–79). Cambridge, MA: The MIT Press.

Zhao, Y., & Frank, K. A. (2003). Factors affecting technology uses in schools: An ecological perspective. *American Educational Research Journal*, *4*(40), 807–840. doi:10.3102/00028312040004807

KEY TERMS AND DEFINITIONS

Dystopian View of Technology: A philosophical perspective in which technology is seen as a destructive force that will ultimately lead to a nightmarish human existence.

Implementation: The process by which a technology is introduced into an organization or social system. Implementation occurs after the initial decision to adopt a new technology.

Institutionalization: The process by which a technology transitions from being viewed as new or innovative to being viewed as a routine part of an organization or social system.

Non-Users: Members of an organization or social system who do not use a technology. Non-users include unintended users, former users, and intended users who have not yet used the technology.

Relative Advantage: The extent to which a technology offers greater benefits compared to competing technologies or to the status quo.

Sociotechnical Systems: A theory that states technology and social systems interact and influence each other's development in a complex variety of ways over time.

Task Heterogeneity: A situation in which members of an organization or social system perform numerous, often unrelated tasks.

Technological Determinism: A theory that states technology has transcended direct human or societal control and has become the driving force in social change.

Utility Value: The extent to which a technology is seen as appropriate for completing a certain task.

Utopian Views of Technology: A philosophical perspective in which technology is seen as a positive force that will ultimately lead to a perfect, or nearly perfect, human existence.

Chapter 2
Strategic Planning for the Integrated Use of Organizational ICT Processes and E-Learning in Higher Education

Maggie McPherson
University of Leeds, UK

Jill Jameson
University of Greenwich, UK

ABSTRACT

Universities currently face urgent demands to facilitate both lifelong learning and widening participation in an era of increasing global competition combined with the need for cost reductions. To cope with rising numbers of students, educators are rethinking teaching strategies to consider the potential of e-learning for academic delivery to an ever more diverse student population. However, there is a relative dearth of research examining the role of strategic management and the impact of organizational factors when considering the implementation of Information and Communication Technology (ICT) for administrative/management purposes and learning technologies to support teaching activities. This chapter analyses organizational ICT processes and e-learning in higher education (HE) through the use of a theoretical "rich picture." "Soft systems methodology" (SSM) is applied to argue that since institutional settings, organizational vision, strategy and top-level support are critical to the success (or failure) of e-learning initiatives, these factors should equally be considered in planning for the implementation of integrated uses of ICT and e-learning. Academic programs are set in particular contexts within university environments and many have their own unique administrative procedures. In addition, numerous factors

DOI: 10.4018/978-1-60960-147-8.ch002

impinge on the implementation of technology enhanced learning solutions, including the roles of tutors, learners, courses, and the processes used to integrate teaching-related ICT. This chapter provides a theoretical "rich picture" of these processes at both program and faculty level to confirm prior research on the implementation of Information System (IS) projects, demonstrating that institutional issues such as strategic thinking and top-level sponsorship are key factors in successful outcomes.

INTRODUCTION

It almost goes without saying that society has been facing unprecedented changes in the 21st century. This is thought to be in no small part due to the influence of technological advances. The advent of 'Information and Communication Technology' (ICT) and the emergence of the Internet have spurred on the notion of international connectedness, now commonly referred to as globalization. The ensuing development of a 'knowledge society' (Drucker, 1994) has led to the ebb and flow of information resources on a worldwide basis. As a consequence, universities are being asked to endow graduates with a very different set of skills from those that they may have previously acquired. The growth of interest and activity in the 'information society' (European Commission, 1996) has led to increased competitiveness within most industrial sectors, including Higher Education (HE). Thus, numerous stakeholders are asking HE to meet the development needs of individuals for the benefit of society at large. While Billing (2003) found that team-work; self-management; and problem-solving skills were in high demand, he also argued that communication appeared to emerge as the most important skill valued by stakeholders in the majority of countries participating in his survey. Since then, this emphasis on communication skills has been steadily building as part of a rich variety of technological developments that have taken place over the past few decades.

Since its advent, ICT and other technological innovations have continued to accelerate in unprecedented ways, radically altering education, training and employment patterns around the world, as prior research demonstrates (McPherson, 2003; McPherson & Nunes, 2006; Jameson, Davies & de Freitas, 2006; Stensaker & Skjerski, 2003). As there is no longer a guarantee of employment for any profession, there is an ongoing need for employees to cope with permanently increasing levels of innovation in skills and knowledge, as well as ongoing professional re-qualification. A few years ago, UK government policy (DfES, 2003) envisaged that the investment of independent learners in ongoing skills improvement would underpin innovation and enterprise in the economy and in society. More recently, with the world facing challenging economic conditions, the UK government has made it clear that it thinks that informal adult learning and skills training can provide a 'way back' into 'further learning, qualifications and more rewarding work' (DIUS, 2009).

As a result of these pressures, faculty and other educators are being challenged to offer flexible and accessible programs to more varied student communities. Yet at the same time they are also required to offer more attractive courses that will nevertheless engage students in a way that makes them take more responsibility for their own learning, thus providing students with the opportunity to acquire new skill-sets that are attractive to employers (McPherson, 2003). Recent government cuts to higher education as a result of the global 'credit crunch' also require that such changes take place within static or reduced budgets. As Middlehurst has observed, the UK government expects higher education simultaneously to '[i]ncrease efficiency, find new sources of income and improve performance across an ever-widening range of activities and services' (Middlehurst,

2004). The combination of demands for lifelong learning, widening participation and cost reduction presented above, together with the advent of increased global connectivity made available by new ICTs and emerging competition for students across international markets, has led most Higher Education Institutions (HEIs) to consider technological methods for supporting learning. For many educators, enthusiastic about seeking improved methods of facilitating the learning process, the answer to increasing flexibility and affordable competitiveness in educational provision seems to lie in the use of e-learning. The recent availability of cost-effective technology, combined with the accelerated proliferation of the Internet, the world wide web (WWW), and the use of online learning and social networking environments, has been seen as one of the most recent universal 'remedies' to this type of educational dilemma. Furthermore, widespread acceptance of constructivist pedagogical philosophies, combined with ICT as a delivery vehicle, has led to an increasing number of e-learning, blended learning and fully online courses being implemented both on-campus and at a distance in a variety of forms. Consequently, to many, the implementation of technology enhanced learning solutions is becoming increasingly attractive as a potential solution to provide flexibility and to widen participation (McPherson, 2003).

At the same time that faculty and educators have been asked to improve teaching and learning, HE administrators now have to deal with increasingly complex problems in achieving effective institutional and financial management, as a result of increasing student numbers and cost restrictions arising in the wake of recent worldwide economic difficulties. Keeping track of these multiple cross-cutting demands requires highly effective university management and administration: functions that are now frequently facilitated by innovations in ICTs and other technological solutions. For instance, despite the global economic downturn, HEIs are not only facing demands that they should deal with issues of lifelong learning, but that they should also make university provision more inclusive. Accordingly, as a response to national and international economic and social change associated with the rise of the knowledge society, governments in many countries such as the United Kingdom, Hong Kong, the United States of America and South Africa have developed policies to increase the participation of diverse groups hitherto under-represented in higher education relative to the population as a whole (Naidoo, 2000). This means that universities are being asked to register increasing student numbers within curtailed budgets, which in turn puts pressure on HEIs to reach progressively more students without raising costs too much. Therefore, within these complex trends towards the globalization and increasingly unpredictable social democratization of knowledge, it is now imperative that managers and administrators improve and integrate support services, which often also requires creative information management.

This chapter provides a critical analysis and reflection on the multi-dimensional dilemmas that HEIs face in planning for successful implementation of ICT for administration and learning. In addition to carrying out a literature review of strategic management in higher education and on the use of ICT in educational settings, selected literature on 'Soft Systems Methodology' (SSM), which focuses on human perspectives of the way in which e-learning strategy, processes and systems are implemented in higher education institutions, is also examined. SSM was originally developed at Lancaster University by Checkland and colleagues as a result of concerns that 'hard' systems approaches could not handle 'ill-structured', complex or 'messy' problems involving human factors where the causes and nature of the problematic factors involved are unresolved and solutions are unclear. SSM enables a complex consideration of potential problems and can be useful for the exploration of management problems in a structured way to examine the points of view of stakeholders involved (Chilvers, 2000). The discussion that follows is based on the aforesaid documentary analysis, drawn from the theoretical and empirical research literature and from the extensive experience of the authors of the operation of e-learning in multiple higher education contexts in the UK and beyond. This is then used to create a 'rich picture', first at program level, then at faculty level, to illustrate some of the organizational and systemic factors involved in the implementation of ICT in higher education contexts.

INTRODUCING INTEGRATED INFORMATION SYSTEMS AND E-LEARNING IN HE

In fact, the introduction of ICT and e-learning innovations within HE represents significant changes in teaching practice, learner engagement and student administration, requiring careful management and resourcing. Research within information systems (IS) contexts (Spil & Salmela, 1999) maintains that the implementation of an improved system requires an innovative type of strategic planning. Such a plan should involve a focused, dynamic and holistic research-informed approach to the management of all aspects of university work that relate to the implementation of the information system (McPherson & Nunes, 2006).

Researchers and educators are aware of the need for further research into the implementation of ICT and technology enhanced learning solutions. Numerous studies have revealed key factors to be considered when introducing and developing ICT and e-learning within academic environments (McPherson & Nunes, 2006; Soong, Chan, Chua & Loh, 2001; Testa and de Freitas, 2003; Volery & Lord, 2000). Yet, to date, most ICT and e-learning research studies continue to focus on technological, systems design, pedagogical, learning-focused or student experience issues. Thus, relatively few researchers have discussed the leadership, management, organizational and institutional issues that are vital to the process of implementing ICT and e-learning at all levels. HE developmental learning and teaching case studies involving an e-learning or online learning solution have also mainly tended to diverge away from consideration of the latter issues.

Senior managers of HE institutions often have decisive power at an organizational level to facilitate or to inhibit the development of an ICT or e-learning initiative. As Middlehurst notes, barriers to change the structure and culture of HE can include: "excessive hierarchy and over-heavy bureaucracy, the comfort of ingrained routines, strong vertical command structures and weak lateral and bottom-up communication, unbalanced and non-integrated authority across professional domains, conservatism and risk aversion, territoriality, defensiveness and insecurity as well as willfulness" (Middlehurst, 2004, p. 277). By taking a stance that blocks innovation (whether done deliberately or not), or leaving initiatives to develop ad hoc with little support or effective strategic planning, strategic decision-makers can impede the advancement of new technological developments with which they are uncomfortable. In the case of e-learning courses, choices made at senior faculty levels may impose institutional views on educators lower down the positional hierarchy, obliging academics to adopt particular course philosophies, learning models and approaches. No matter how inventive and effective the pedagogic, technological and learning design solutions of academics are, if strategic leaders in a university are against the implementation of such solutions, learning technologists at lower hierarchical levels may be frustrated and impeded, despite strenuous efforts to implement innovation.

Sometimes effective institutional networking may be more successful for academics trying to implement innovations than expert knowledge. As the Standish Group Report (2001) indicates, without top-level sponsorship, e-learning faculty and support staff may, despite their expertise, try in vain to put e-learning innovations in place. As Wilson and Velayutham (2009, p. 246) observe, such innovation 'at the practitioner level' [can fail]... 'to take hold in a systemic fashion in the institution, and is often an isolated "Fred In The Shed" activity' (Stiles & Yorke, 2007). Expert e-learning practitioners, recognized by both students and external peers for agile innovations, may sometimes work unrewarded by their own institutions, like prophets without honor in their home town. Wilson and Velayutham recognize that 'in the IT management domain there is a common perception that academics' innovation efforts cause vulnerabilities that lead to system breakdown and increased support workload, and this must be checked by constraining the use of resources such as the network and PC configuration'. These researchers observe that IT managers in HEIs may regard the innovation work of e-learning practitioners as a 'problem', and vice-versa.

Yet, in order to facilitate successful integrated ICT and e-learning implementation, institutions need to achieve commitment to be sufficiently flexible in order for all staff involved to be able to respond appropriately to put into effect required changes at all levels, involving both ICT systems and e-learning developments. Since higher education institutions are legal bodies with particular constitutions, they are, of necessity, required to operate in a fixed way within a specific and recognizable institutional context. Thus, it is important to discuss issues regarded as critical to intrinsic organizational ICT and e-learning change management processes in more detail.

Organizational Issues in the Integration of ICT and E-Learning in HE

The strategic and organizational management of ICT and e-learning strategy and policies formed within HEIs influence those responsible for academic settings through the imposition of administrative procedures. They also strongly influence the availability of finance, staffing, technical and other resources for e-learning activities, which impact on realistic pedagogical models. These in turn affect the design of courses and may restrict possible modes of assessment and evaluation. The transition from more traditional delivery methods to the adoption of new ICT and e-learning environments in HE therefore inevitably involves considerable management of change.

Change Management in HE Institutions

Since the implementation of e-learning involves substantial management of change, at this juncture, it is appropriate to reflect on some important theoretical aspects of change management, such as the relationships between institutional culture, structure and strategic management. Many theorists contend that the concept of organizational culture is of great importance in managing change.

Furthermore, change and culture have also come to be seen as inter-connected. For instance, influential prior voices in the field (Peters & Waterman, 1982), state that organizational culture and institutional performance are inextricably linked. These researchers also assert that the manipulation of organizational culture can facilitate changes in organizational performance, if sufficient attention is paid to its structure. Moreover, organizations are as different and varied as the many nations and societies of the world, as Handy notes, making a linkage between culture and structure as follows:

They have different cultures - sets of values and norms and beliefs - reflected in different structures and systems. And the cultures are affected by the events of the past and by the climate of the present, by the technology of the type of work, by their aims and the kind of people that work in them. (Handy, 1993, p. 79)

According to other literature relating to strategic management (Spender & Grant, 1996), learning, knowledge acquisition and adaptation are important potential facets of organizational competitive advantage. However, the ways in which these advances should be achieved within HE can be a source of heated debate. Increasing and progressively more contradictory demands on higher education institutions, exacerbated by complex funding structures, are creating a conflict of purpose and causing an identity crisis in academia. One of the problems is that most academic staff want to be known for their research activities (knowledge creation), whilst on the other hand, university managers and administrators want to be able to control all institutional processes as well as the people within the system (knowledge management). On the other hand, society appears to view teaching as academics' primary role (knowledge distribution), which is sometimes at odds with a research-led culture. Thus, it is argued that HEI staff and programs are often both supported by and constrained by their own unique organizational setting, in which the above various competing tensions are played out in different ways at local levels. Consequently, when considering the adoption of new technological solutions, whether these are e-learning systems or other IS procedures, it is essential that those either wishing to adopt or impose a change of procedure on others should consider all the potential conflicting views of the stakeholders involved in the process. It is therefore imperative to identify who all the stakeholders are and secure their support before attempting to initiate new IS procedures or insist on the use of learning technologies to support taught courses. However, before such stakeholders can be identified, it is useful to consider issues of organizational culture and structure within the particular sector of HE.

Organizational Culture

Organizational culture can be thought of as the values, beliefs, philosophies, ways of doing things and relating to other people exhibited by members of an organization. The traditional university is often seen as a collegiate institution consisting of scholars who have come together to gather, generate and disseminate knowledge (Cornford & Pollock, 2003). There are many different ways of perceiving such institutions. Thus, on the one hand, academic staff may think of 'the university' as its senior management, senate and central administration. However, on the other hand, for those seeking to govern and administer within HE institutions, 'the university' may be thought of as being 'out there' within the organization, in the form of departments, academics, researchers and students. From a student's perspective, both academics and administrators can be regarded as representatives of 'the university' (Wade, Hodgkinson, Smith, & Arfield, 1994), while senior university managers may seem to be so remote from students as to be almost invisible. Thus, it can be seen that a number of views contribute to the organizational culture of HE institutions, and, since enthusiasm for introducing e-learning is not universal, numerous perspectives need to be aligned if Caffrey's (1970) descriptive vision of 'universities without walls' is to be truly realized.

Organizational Structure

Given the complex structures of universities, higher education is not necessarily an easy, robust and secure environment for technology enhanced learning solutions. Even to those with insider experience, the organizational structure of HE is not always easy to determine. Shurville and Brown (2006), for example, reflect on the 'bewildering' number of different systems in ICT and e-learning that are possible within a university, describing these as a 'jungle of competing systems and processes':

As many universities are typically managed as loosely coupled federations [sic] styles (Weick, 1976) it is very common for there to be a bewildering range of configurations and implemented at different scales, for example from the lone-ranger individual up to the critical service for the whole university. This can result in a jungle of competing technical systems and business processes for e-learning. Thus e-learning necessarily brings change management issues into sharp focus, ranging from early adoption of technology and new approaches to teaching and learning through to consolidation of multiple local projects into an institution-wide service. (Shurville & Brown, 2006, p. 246)

Furthermore, increasing demands for rigorous quality assurance mean that the process of gaining accreditation for new courses and new delivery mechanisms is neither swift nor simple, and requires support at a number of levels within the institution. Even course proposals with sound aims and objectives may, despite appearing on the surface to be commendable, sometimes founder because they lack sponsorship from one quarter of the institution or another. Consequently, in the context of managing the implementation of e-learning within HE, it is critical to determine who the key 'university' decision-makers are and to gain their support.

Organizational Strategic Management

At a strategic level, flexible methods of learning, innovative teaching methods and support for self-paced learning all have implications for the development of educational policies. To achieve a real level of success, innovative teaching initiatives need to be endorsed at an institutional level by senior staff. Therefore, it may be necessary to confront fixed mind-sets and to challenge practices that have been in place for some time in subtle ways (Wade et al., 1994; Luckin, Shurville & Brown, 2006). This is particularly the case if HE organizational structures are unsupportive of ICT and e-learning innovations, or if there are perceived risks or threats to the institution from hasty innovation adoption, such as, for example, from potentially negative reputational risks. As Morrison (2009) observed about the attempt to recruit institutions for the UK e-Learning Benchmarking and Pathfinder programme, universities tend to be watchful about their independence and identity:

[....] the UK HE sector is very heterogeneous with institutions jealously guarding their independence and being much concerned with their profile. Attempting to impose a single methodology for a benchmarking of e-learning as though the sector was a homogenous entity risked stimulating resistance in the very institutions that we wanted to recruit. In reality the UK HE sector is a richly diverse set of, sometimes competing, entities that may not always embrace approaches to easy comparison that are not under their direct control. (Morrison, 2009, p. 33-34)

At a local level (i.e. a department), in addition to academic staff developing new skills, it is necessary for them to make fundamental adjustments to pedagogical and philosophical assumptions. If this is to be achieved, it will be necessary to support staff development through the provision of an appropriately focused skills acquisition process. In view of this, it would be reasonable to assert that the introduction of e-learning into a higher education institution inevitably involves a considerable element of change, both in terms of attitude and in practice.

IMPACT OF INSTITUTIONAL LEADERSHIP AND CENTRAL ADMINISTRATION

Over the last two decades, political and social changes have necessitated extensive change within HE. The role of strategic institutional and academic leadership is to balance these demands and to guide institutions through the development of sound management processes for strategic change. Since all formal university administrative procedures and e-learning programs exist within a specific institutional context, it is clear that the organizational decision-makers in that setting have the power to facilitate, influence or even impede the development of e-learning courses.

Through decision-making at an executive level, organizational leaders have the power to facilitate or impede the development of e-learning courses by imposing administrative or financial procedures that support or stifle innovation. However, bearing in mind the peculiarities of university cultures, driving through any such strategic plans require formal agreement via key committees, which is achieved through widespread consultation (Bargh, Bocock, Scott, & Smith, 2000). Thus, if e-learning initiatives, such as new ICT-enabled programs or courses, are to be successfully implemented, there is a need for strong champions to support them in order to guarantee support and 'buy in' from institutional leadership.

Furthermore, there is a need at a 'macro' organizational level for a wider, whole institutional e-learning strategy and operational plan to be developed which considers the management of e-learning at a number of different levels of the organization's structure and culture. If this is appropriately steered through the institution with both 'top-down' and 'bottom-up' input at macro, meso and micro levels, it can enable a much smoother implementation of new 'micro' course level initiatives than if no such overall strategy exists. The development and implementation of whole institution e-learning strategies and operational plans has been adopted on a widespread basis in higher education during the past decade, though there are still some institutions that are lagging behind in this (Luckin, Sherville, & Browne, 2006). While considerable progress has been made in the introduction and implementation of e-Learning strategies in HEIs, however, a weakness in this has emerged in that many senior managers of HEIs are not sufficiently skilled or knowledgeable in the field of e-learning. Therefore, such strategies have sometimes been introduced at the middle management level, thereby attracting less institutional 'buy-in' and support from top levels of management.

Influence of Departmental Leadership, Strategy and Administration

At a departmental level, strategic management forms the basis of other key approaches to change and innovation. In particular, the local context influences the design of courses through the interpretation of corporate views and the imposition of these views on course philosophies, learning models and strategies. Moreover, the process of departmental management imposition of corporate views can enable or restrict feasible pedagogical models. Departmental management and administrative procedures, as well as decision making regarding the availability of resources, strongly influences the design and delivery of courses and clearly affects modes of assessment and evaluation.

Importance of Faculty and Academic Staff Attitudes

Faculty and individual academic staff also have a significant part to play in the change management process. As mentioned earlier in the discussion relating to organizational culture, the academic sector has, like many other sectors, developed particular traditions and customs. Furthermore, it could be said that individual HE institutions go further in constructing their own mores, which are then interpreted and enacted in terms of 'the way we do things around here' (Trowler, 1998). However, there is a danger of accepting traditional management views of 'culture' and 'change' and oversimplifying the interaction between them.

In addition, when attempting to implement change within academia, a consideration to bear in mind is that academics are less likely to be influenced by corporate ideas of social class background, gender, ethnicity, and commercial experience than by the united commitment to guiding principles, codes and myths as well as to a deeply rooted occupational ethos which transcends divisive elements and integrates the profession of academia (Trowler, 1998). This view is corroborated by other researchers (Henkel, 2000) who state that, despite a decline in status, power and the economic rewards of the job, academics retain values of independence, integrity, intellectual rigor, collegiality, enthusiasm for their discipline and commitment to their profession.

A 'Rich Picture' of the Implementation of E-Learning in HE

Soft Systems Methodology (SSM) includes within its research techniques the notion of creating a 'rich picture diagram' (RPD) to represent the complex information collected in, for example, case studies of information systems operating in organizational settings (Sutrisna and Barrett, 2007; JISC infoNet, 2009). The visual depiction of complex processes in a 'rich picture' is designed to facilitate investigations of the way in which human-related systems operate effectively, or not, in real-life situations. Chilvers (2000, p. 169) cites Checkland (1984, p. 317) in defining a 'rich picture' as the "... expression of a problem situation compiled by an investigator, often by examining elements of the structure, elements of process, and the situation climate." Such a picture can be formative in providing an accessible conceptualization of the complex challenges, barriers and problems that occur in the functioning of systems. Thus, 'rich pictures' may be drawn up to represent the results of empirical data collection or to portray a theoretical representation of the ways in which systems do, can or should operate. Rich pictures analyze and depict complex environments in which problematic situations may arise to which there are no easy solutions. Checkland (1985) himself explains a rich picture as recording 'the elements of *structure* in terms of the situation (relatively static elements such as organization and reporting structures, physical locations and the like) the elements of *process* (the things continually happening through, via or in spite of the structures) and the relation between the two, the *climate* of the situation'.

For the current study, a rich picture was devised at both program and faculty level of the implementation of e-learning in HEIs as a theoretical construct arising from the reflections of the authors based on numerous real-life day to day experiences throughout a number of years in various universities. These have been developed as a fictionalized example of a university setting that does not correspond exactly with any particular institution, as it was derived from a combination of factors in operation in a number of different anonymous institutions across the UK. For ethical reasons, no exact representation of any particular individual or HEI is intended, as the reflections of the authors were drawn on the basis of e-learning work with many different universities. However, it is felt that this provides an interesting representation of many of the issues faced at a program level in different institutions that offer distance learning. The rich pictures, depicted in Figure 1 and Figure 3, were designed to represent two different levels of the operation of e-learning systems as they might affect students and staff in a hypothetical UK university. These indicate who might be involved, the communication channels and where there might be clashes (all symbols are clearly explained in a key, which is provided in Figure 2).

The rich picture provided gives rise to a number of recommendations for the effective implementation of e-learning in higher education organizations.

Figure 1. A 'Rich Picture' of the e-learning systems at MA program level in a hypothetical UK Higher Education Institution

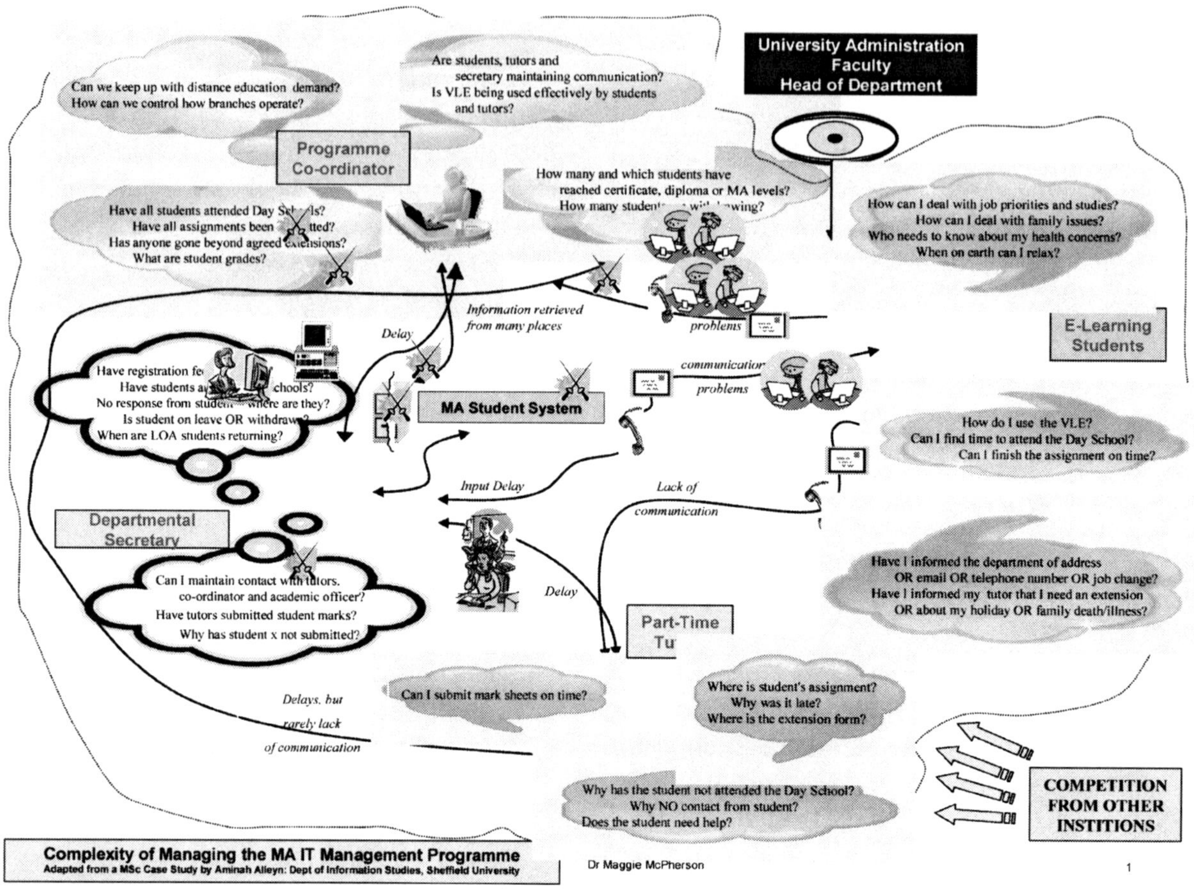

Micro Level: MA Program Rich Picture: Leadership, Strategy and Administration

At a program and individual course level (see Figure 1), complex systems are in operation alongside each other to lead, manage and administer the program (in this case, an MA program with *Part-time Tutors*), on which are registered *e-Learning Students* working relatively independently as part of the program during their hours of study. The *e-Learning Students* exist in various clouds of complexity at the side of the institution on their own. They are remote from many aspects of the university and study more or less independently, positioned alongside each other in groups of students at peer level. The students are primarily concerned with their own personal individual progress on assignments, their use of the Virtual Learning Environment, family issues and their health and time for relaxation. They worry about their attendance, timely submission of assignments and the administration of information about them. They also worry about the communication of their personal issues as well as their interaction with tutors and with the department. There are many lines of communication to and from the students with their tutors, the *Program Coordinator*, the *MA Student System*, and, by extension, with the *Departmental Secretary*. Many of these lines of

Figure 2. Key to 'Rich Pictures' in Figures 1 and 3

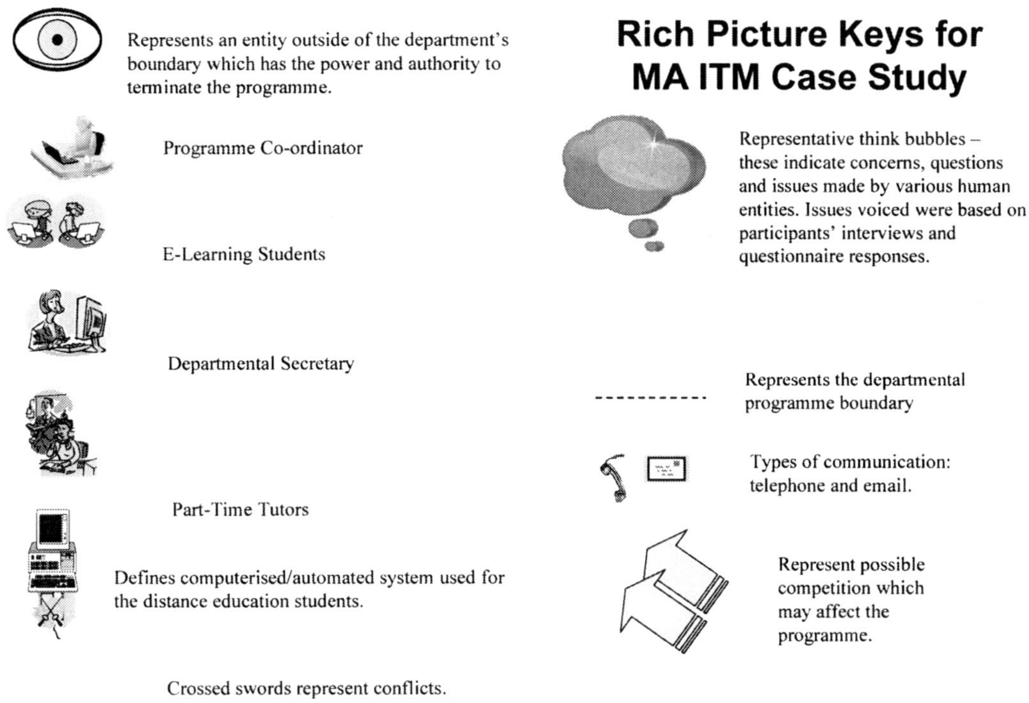

Figure 3. A 'Rich Picture' of the e-learning systems at faculty level in a yypothetical UK Higher Education Institution

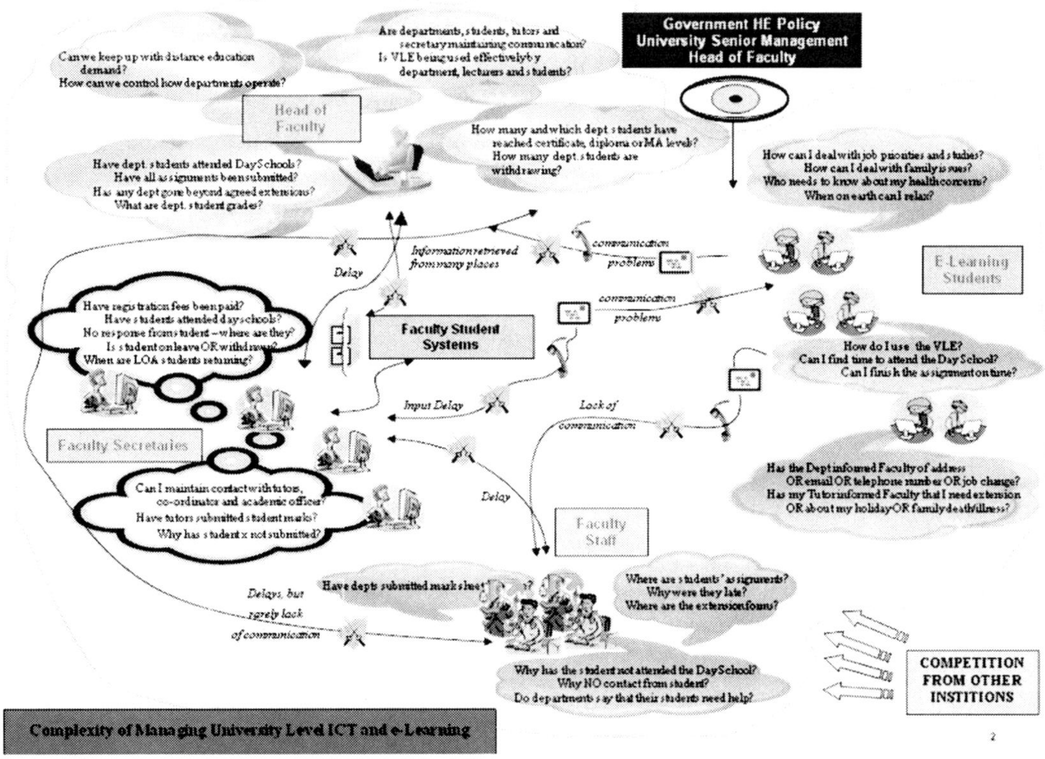

communication, involving telephones, letters by post and emails, are either broken or may suffer delays.

The program is led by the *Coordinator*, who has an overseeing leadership and strategy level role, existing in a cloud of her/his own concerns above the course. S/he leads, outlines strategies for and monitors the program, checking whether the VLE for the course is being used effectively, and whether communication is working between tutors, students and the *Departmental Secretary*. The *Coordinator* is concerned to see whether student systems are in operation, whether students are attending day schools and have submitted their assignments. The *Coordinator* is also keen to monitor how many students are achieving their qualifications and grades or are withdrawing. S/he is concerned to ensure that the program is keeping up with the demand for distance education and queries the ways in which the operation of branches is controlled. S/he is positioned above the *Departmental Secretary* and *Part-time Tutors* in the hierarchy, with her/his back to and well away from the students. The watchful eye of the *Head of Department*, and, above that, the monitoring gaze of *Faculty* and *University administration*, scrutinize what is going on, though that gaze is primarily focused on the program environment overall and the actual results (student achievement, attendance) that the *Coordinator's* work achieves.

The *Part-time Tutors* are engaged on the MA course to teach and assess the students. They exist in a bubble of their own, positioned at the bottom of the hierarchy. They are concerned to monitor student attendance, mark their work and submit their mark sheets and registers. They worry whether they can submit mark sheets on time, why students' assignments are late, whether students have submitted extension forms, whether students are attending Day Schools, why they have had no contact from some students and whether students need help. They are positioned more closely to the students than any other group and their concerns are almost exclusively focused either directly on students or on work relating to them. Their communication to and from the *Coordinator* and *Departmental Secretary* may be delayed but is generally effective. However, there may be many communication problems with students.

The *Departmental Secretary* is positioned directly next to the *MA Student System* and has good communication with this system. On the one hand, her/his focus is on student administration issues such as whether registration fees been paid, whether students have attended day schools, why there has been no response from students, whether students have withdrawn or are on leave. On the other hand, her/his focus is on contact with the tutors, the *Coordinator* and the *Academic Officer*, the submission of marks to the system and the lack of such submission. The secretary is positioned below the *Coordinator* and has good communication with her/him. However, the *MA Student System*, which s/he updates with information, may suffer from input delays and from the confusion of many different kinds of information from different places.

This rich picture outlines some of the complex local concerns of different elements within the MA program, demonstrating some of the communication problems and delays that may occur within the system. Failures and delays in responses between different parts of the program influence the effective implementation of e-learning innovations as well as their assessment and evaluation.

Meso-Level: Faculty Rich Picture: Leadership, Strategy and Administration

At a Faculty and University level (see Figure 3), complex systems are in operation to lead, manage and administer the Faculty. Within this overall environment, the *Departments* with their *Programs* and courses continue to exist as complex systems. The Faculty is an even more complicated, difficult environment, being at a higher level of management that oversees and scrutinizes all Departments and Programs within it.

The Faculty level is more abstracted from students than the Department and Program levels. The *e-Learning Students,* again, work relatively independently within the Faculty's departments and programs. They continue to exist in various clouds of complexity at the side of the institution on their own, even more remote, at this level, from the preoccupations of the Faculty, still primarily concerned with their own personal and individual issues. The lines of communication are more remote, more difficult and distant than they are at Program level. Contact by telephone, letters and emails continue to suffer delays or may be broken and continue to be mediated from the program and tutor level below.

The Faculty is led by the *Head of Faculty*, who has an overseeing leadership and strategy level role, existing in a cloud of her/his own concerns above all departments, programs and courses, assisted by many *Faculty Secretaries* and administrators. The *Head of Faculty* is concerned with the same sorts of preoccupations as the *Program Coordinators*, but at a higher level within the hierarchy, with more complex demands and systems that involve all subordinate parts within the Faculty. S/he is concerned to ensure that the Faculty is keeping up with the demand for good quality distance education and queries how departments and branches are controlled. S/he is positioned above the *Faculty Secretaries* and *Faculty Staff* in the hierarchy, with her/his back to and even further away from the students.

The watchful eye of the *Dean or Pro Vice Chancellor*, and, above that, the monitoring gaze of *the University Top Management* and *Government Higher Education Policy and Funding* bodies, scrutinize what is going on, though their gaze is primarily focused on the university environment overall and the actual results (student achievement, attendance) that the *Head of Faculty's* work achieves.

This rich picture at the Faculty level outlines some of the complex Faculty-wide and overall University concerns of different elements within the HE system, demonstrating some of the communication problems and delays that may occur within the parts and sub-parts of the overall system. Failures and delays in responses between different parts of this environment influence the effective implementation of e-learning innovations as well as their assessment and evaluation.

Issues, Controversies, Problems and Potential Approaches

Significant drivers for change within HEIs over the last few decades include reduced public financial support together with demands to undertake applied research (Gibbons, 1998) as well as demands to widen participation. In an effort to respond to these pressures and to raise vital revenue, universities have begun to undertake a whole range of activities that do not conform to previous views of long-established mainstream academic research and conventional education. According to Davies (2001, p. 25), new activities include "industry related research and development, consultancy, technology transfer, continuing education and lifelong learning in various forms, a considerable influx of non national students to the campuses, substantial overseas delivery of education through offshore campuses, franchise arrangements, and e-learning, and the commercialization of physical campus assets like halls of residence and sports facilities for external use." In addition, (Davies, 2001, p. 27) suggests that attempting to inculcate an entrepreneurial culture challenges the ability of HEIs to respond coherently to change existing bureaucratic processes, norms and traditions. In order to manage the shift towards an increasingly complex organization, more technological solutions have been adopted to address the more diverse nature of these institutions, thereby having a consequent destabilizing effect on traditional structures.

In an effort to illustrate some of the concerns facing HEIs in dealing with information management and systems, this chapter has presented the above two 'rich picture' examples at Program and Faculty level to give the reader a 'balcony view' (as described by Heifetz & Laurie, 1997) of the issues raised by staff and students in interviews for a study of an MA Program. These were adapted from a MSc case study provided by a student within an information systems department at a university in England. Representative think bubbles indicate concerns, questions and issues made by various human entities, based on concerns voiced in participants' interviews and questionnaire responses. The rich picture at each level provides only a glimpse of the complex ICT and e-learning systems in operation in one hypothetical institution. They do not aim to be a full demonstration of all of the many kinds of information and management systems existing within universities, faculties, departments and programs within the UK. The variety and complexity of these is such that it may be impossible accurately to convey, at any level, all and every aspect of a system that is so jungle-like in its manifold intricacy. Therefore the most useful approach is to depict empirical, practical examples of the perspectives of different levels of the university ICT and e-learning systems in operation, in order that greater clarity in strategic planning for more effective and innovative provision can be attempted.

CONCLUSION

HEIs are often too large and too complex to be merely managed top-down, and there is evidence from the literature that collective leadership is required to make sense of this shifting environment. If universities are to survive the onslaught of new demands being brought about by changing demands from society, i.e. students, parents, governmental funding, globalization, increased competition, etc., faculty and other support staff can and need to be able to play a part in forging an adaptive institution. There is abundant evidence in the literature of successful innovative uses of technology to enhance learning. However, although many academics do recognize the need for change, the use of ICT to support student learning is neither universally accepted nor are e-learning initiatives always adequately designed and supported. Academics are unlikely to simply sign up to a corporate 'vision' imposed from the top without real opportunities for discourse. Furthermore, support services too need to understand and work with one another to develop information systems that support academic activities. Therefore, if staff are being asked to undertake new roles, relationships, values and approaches to work, then they need to be convinced of the advantages of innovation for their profession and their own career. Thus, to achieve the goal of successful implementation of technology integration within Higher Education, the way forward is for institutional and academic leadership to manage the change process by proposing and agreeing goals through consensual debate, supporting strategies appropriately and then realizing these through common commitment.

Consensual dialogue between different levels of institutional systems in higher education can be encouraged to foster improvements in the social and organizational aspects of technology integration. The types of engagement in discourse that are needed require a re-commitment at all levels to the collegial and democratic values that were once a strength of academia, but have latterly declined in favour of new public management and commercial practices imported from older business models sometimes inappropriately applied to 'the university'. Universities that are lagging behind in technology innovation and integration need to change to recognise the growing global democratic power of rapid communication and information exchange enabled through the internet and social networking. Academics in higher education can – and in many cases already do - play a vital new role as experts guiding the development of new forms of knowledge creation and exchange, but that innovative role is sometimes impeded by the resistance of some parts of the HE system to facilitate the complex different forces involved in e-learning and ICT implementation. There needs to be a new recognition of the power of consensual dialogue to facilitate integrated social and organizational technological solutions within higher education. The strategic institutional planning of e-learning and ICT needs to encompass the development of shared solutions in democratic structures involving cross-cutting multi-levelled groups of staff to find and implement appropriate technological innovations. Only by working together with all of their staff on the complex problems facing them can universities embrace the new potentials of technological integration in its manifold competitive and challenging aspects.

REFERENCES

Bargh, C., Bocock, J., Scott, P., & Smith, D. (2000). *University Leadership: The Role of the Chief Executive*. Buckingham, UK: SRHE/Open University Press.

Caffrey, J. G. (1970). *Alternative Models for Higher Education*. Paper presented at the 25th national conference of the American Association for Higher Education, March 3, 1970. Chicago, Illinois.

Checkland, P. (1985). Achieving 'Desirable and Feasible' Change: An Application of Soft Systems Methodology. *The Journal of the Operational Research Society, 36*(9), 821-831. Available online at: http://www.jstor.org/stable/2582171 [last accessed 07/04/10].

Chilvers, A. (2000). Critical issues in the use of Soft Systems Methodology: a case study in the long-term management of digital data objects. *Journal of Librarianship and Information Science, 32*(4), 167–177.

Cornford, J., & Pollock, N. (2003). *Putting the University Online: Information Technology and Organizational Change*. Buckingham, UK: The Society for Research into Higher Education.

Davies, J. L. (2001). The Emergence of Entrepreneurial Cultures in European Universities. *Journal of the Programme on Institutional Management in Higher Education, 13*(2), 25–44.

DfES (Department for Education and Skills). (2003). 'Education and Skills: The Future of Higher Education', *UK Government White Paper*, Cabinet Office, Norwich, UK, pp. 1-23.

DIUS. (Department for Innovation, Universities and Skills) (2009). The Learning Revolution. *UK Government White Paper*, The Stationery Office, Norwich, UK, 4.

Drucker, P. (1994). *The Post-Capitalist Society*. New York: Harper-Collins.

European Commission (1996). Living and Working in the Information Society: People First, Directorate-General for Employment and Social Affairs. *Brussels Green Paper, COM(96)*, 389.

Fox, R., & Hermann, A. (2000). Changing Media, Changing Times: Coping with adopting new educational technologies. In Evans, T., & Nation, D. (Eds.), *Changing University Teaching: Reflections on Creating Educational Technologies*. London: Kogan Page.

Gibbons, M. (1998). *Higher Education Relevance in the 21st Century*. World Bank.

Handy, C. (1993). *Understanding Organisations*. Harmondsworth, UK: Penguin.

Heifetz, R. A., & Laurie, D. L. (1997). *The Work of Leadership*. Boston: Harvard Business Review. [reprint 2001 R0111K]

Henkel, M. (2000). *Academic Identities and Policy Change in Higher Education*. London: Jessica Kingsley Publishers Ltd.

Jameson, J., Davies, S., & de Freitas, S. (2006). Collaborative Innovation: Joint Information Systems Committee Distributed E-learning Program. *British Journal of Educational Technology*, *37*(6), 969–972. doi:10.1111/j.1467-8535.2006.00664.x

Jameson, J., Ferrell, G., Kelly, J., Walker, S., & Ryan, M. (2006). Building Trust and Shared Knowledge in Communities of E-learning Practice: Collaborative Leadership in the JISC eLISA and CAMEL Lifelong Learning Projects. *British Journal of Educational Technology*, *37*(6), 949–968. doi:10.1111/j.1467-8535.2006.00669.x

Luckin, R., Shurville, S., & Browne, T. (2006). Initiating E-learning by Stealth, Participation and Consultation in a Late Majority Institution. *Journal of Organizational Transformation & Social Change*, *3*(3), 317–332. doi:10.1386/jots.3.3.317_1

McPherson, M. A. (2003). Organizational Critical Success Factors for Managing the Implementation of eLearning in Higher Education. In McPherson M.A., Henderson, L. & Kinshuk (Eds.) *Proceedings of the Workshop on The Changing Face of HE in the 21st Century: Critical Success Factors for Implementing eLearning*. Massey University, New Zealand, pp.8-14.

McPherson, M. A., & Nunes, M. N. (2006). Organizational Issues for E-learning: Critical Success Factors as identified by HE Practitioners. *International Journal of Educational Management*, *20*(7), 542–558. doi:10.1108/09513540610704645

Middlehurst, R. (2004). Changing Internal Governance: A Discussion of Leadership Roles and Management Structures in UK Universities. *Higher Education Quarterly*, *58*(4), 258–279. doi:10.1111/j.1468-2273.2004.00273.x

Morrison, D. (2009). The Benchmarking and Pathfinder Programme and its Role in Institutional Transformation. In Mayes, T., Morrison, D., Mellar, H., Bullen, P. & Oliver, M. York (eds.): *Transforming Higher Education through Technology-enhanced Learning*. The Higher Education Academy. Online at: http://www.heacademy.ac.uk/technology

Naidoo, R. (2000). The 'Third Way' to Widening Participation and Maintaining Quality in Higher Education: Lessons from the United Kingdom. *Journal of Educational Enquiry*, *1*(2), 24–38.

Peters, T. S., & Waterman, R. H. (1982). *In Search of Excellence: Lessons from America's Best Run Companies*. New York: Harper & Row.

Shurville, S., & Browne, T. (2006). ICT-Driven Change in Higher Education: Learning from E-learning. *Journal of Organizational Transformation and Social Change*, *3*(3), 245–250. doi:10.1386/jots.3.3.245_2

Soong, B. M. H., Chan, H. C., Chua, B. C., & Loh, K. F. (2001). Critical Success Factors for On-Line Course Resources. *Computers & Education*, *36*(2), 101–120. doi:10.1016/S0360-1315(00)00044-0

Spender, J.-C., & Grant, R. M. (Eds.). (1996). Knowledge and the Firm. *Strategic Management Journal*, *17*(Special Issue), 5–9.

Spil, A. A. M., & Salmela, H. (1999). The Fall of Strategic Information Systems Planning and the Rise of a Dynamic IS Strategy. *Proceedings of the 22nd Information Systems Research Seminar in Scandinavia (IRIS 22): 'Enterprise Architectures for Virtual Organisations'*, Keuruu, Finland, 7-10 August, 1999. Online at: http://citeseerx.ist.psu.edu/viewdoc/summary?doi=10.1.1.9.7273 [last visited 13/02/10].

Standish Group. (2001). *Extreme CHAOS*. Online at: http://www.smallfootprint.com/Portals/0/StandishGroupExtremeChaos2001.pdf [last visited 13/02/10].

Stensaker, B., & Skjerski, S. (2003). Organising ICT Initiatives in Higher Education. In Hansson, H.& Holmberg, C. (Eds.) *Eight Contributions on Quality and Flexible Learning, Sweden, Swedish Agency for Flexible Learning Report 3*, 103-115.

Stiles, M., & Yorke, J. (2007). Technology Supported Learning – Tensions between Innovation, and Control and Organizational and Professional Cultures. *Journal of Organizational Transformation and Social Change*, *3*(3), 251–267. doi:10.1386/jots.3.3.251_1

Sutrisna, M., & Barret, P. (2007). Applying Rich Picture Diagrams to Model Case Studies of Construction Projects. *Engineering, Construction, and Architectural Management*, *14*(2), 164–179. doi:10.1108/09699980710731281

Testa, M. G., & de Freitas, H. M. R. (2003). *Critical Success Factors of E-Learning Programmes: An Exploratory Study in The Brazilian Context*. Online at: http://professores.ea.ufrgs.br/hfreitas/revista/arquivos/80AIM.pdf [last visited 13/02/10].

Trowler, P. (1998). *Academics Responding to Change: New Higher Education Frameworks and Academic Cultures*. Buckingham, UK: SRHE and Open University Press.

Volery, T., & Lord, D. (2000). Critical Success Factors In Online Education. *International Journal of Educational Management*, *14*(5), 216–223. doi:10.1108/09513540010344731

Wade, W., Hodgkinson, K., Smith, A., & Arfield, J. (1994). *Flexible Learning in Higher Education*. London: Kogan Page.

Wilson, S., & Velayutham, K. (2009). Creating an Innovation-Oriented Technology Strategy. *Horizon*, *17*(3), 245–255. doi:10.1108/10748120910993277

Chapter 3
Technology in Higher Education:
Understanding Student Issues

David Ensminger
Loyola University Chicago, USA

Joél Lewis
University of South Alabama, USA

ABSTRACT

Technology has played a significant role in changing the face of higher education. In order to successfully use technology, institutions of higher education must recognize that students play a central role in their decision making regarding the application of technology for the purpose of communication, and learning. This chapter addresses several issue related to the student issues and the use of technology in higher education. The notion of a particular type of student (i.e. "digital native") is examined, as well as the current skills and use of technology by college students. The chapter continues on to discuss the concepts of digital recreation, digital communication, and their related issues to instruction in University settings. Finally the chapter explores the need for universities to examine diversity issues when integrating technology. The chapter concludes by recommending a tailoring perspective to technology integration that utilizes a decentralized approach to helping faculty integrate technology.

INTRODUCTION

Technology changes the way we educate, learn, and communicate. Innovations in technology impact higher education in several ways including student issues regarding use, ability, access, and diversity. University students use technology at higher levels than any other generation (Cotton, 2008; Junco & Mastrodicasa, 2007). This increased technology use provides universities with a vehicle to communicate and to instruct in ways not explored previously by institutions of

DOI: 10.4018/978-1-60960-147-8.ch003

higher education. The Internet has transformed higher education, (Robinson & Hullinger, 2008) allowing universities to reach more diverse populations and create new learning environments (Hara & Kiling, 2000). However, institutions of higher education must be aware of how students employ technology, and must consider student perspectives regarding how technology can best be integrated for instruction and communication. Student issues must be understood when integrating technology in higher education. This chapter discusses students as digital natives, recreational technologies, digital communication, and multicultural concerns related to technology use in higher education.

DIGITAL NATIVES OR NOT?

The proliferation of computers and digital peripherals (e.g., video cameras, digital audio recorders, MP3 players) cell phones, smart phones, online resources, online communication applications, and software applications have brought about increased access to information, and new tools for educating, communicating and entertaining our current and future generations of college students. The technological advances in information and communication technologies (ICT) over the last 15 years have allowed individuals to access, share, and create digital "information" more than any other time in our history. The life experiences of individuals growing up in this technological age has led many to claim that they are uniquely different than previous generations, and has even resulted in a variety of labels: "Net generation," (Tapscott, 1999), "Millenials," (Howe & Strauss, 2000), and "Digital Natives" (Prenksy, 2001). The label "Digital Natives" refers to the generations born in or after the 1980s that grew up and were socialized in a rapidly advancing technological society, and describes a generation that embraces new technologies and makes the use of ICT almost a daily occurrence (Prensky, 2001). As a result of growing up in a technological society, it is presumed that this generation possesses significantly more technological knowledge and skills, demonstrates distinctively different means of processing information than previous generations, and creates a unique set of learners, with different needs and expectations.

Essentially, digital natives are perceived as "new learners" whose expectations of the application and integration of technology in their college learning experience uniquely differentiates them from the experience of previous generations. So, what are the suggested differences of these new learners? What makes the digital natives a unique group of students? These students are characterized as being technologically adept, and favoring digital methods (e.g. e-mail, instant messaging, text messaging, and social networking sites) as their means of communicating. They are more interested in learning in groups, and applying technology to their learning, they are rapid processors of information, they are multi-taskers, and are disinterested in the traditional means of learning (Howe & Strauss, 2000; Prensky, 2001; Oblinger, 2003). This perspective of new students purported by Prensky and others appears to suggest that universities, particularly faculty, must change their pedagogical practices in order to meet the expectation of these digital natives. Prensky (2005) goes so far as to suggest that if we do not engage this generation of learners on a technological level, we will enrage them.

Conversely, those born prior to 1980s, make up the majority of university faculty are considered to be "digital immigrants." Digital immigrants are those who were not socialized in a technological society, but instead have had to adapt and learn to live in a digital age (Prensky, 2001). Prensky goes on further to explain that digital immigrants are not responsive to the educational needs of digital natives, "Digital Immigrant instructors, who speak an outdated language (that of the pre-digital age), are struggling to teach a population that speaks an entirely new language" (Prensky,

2001, pg. 2). Others have supported this notion that current faculty do not possess the technological knowledge and skills to meet the needs of the current and future generations of college students (Oblinger, 2003; Frand 2000), and as a result, universities are failing to meet the learning needs of these digital natives. Thus the argument, for engaging in new pedagogy and technology practices in higher education, is founded on the thinking that current college students are uniquely different learners with advanced technology skills and knowledge, and the methods of instruction used by current university faculty do not meet the needs of these new students.

While many have advocated for the shift in the teaching practices at colleges and universities to meet the needs of the current generation of students, others have begun to question the validity of the notion that digital natives are somehow a different group of learners. While much has been written and discussed about digital natives, little empirical evidence exists that supports that as a group these students have a unique learning style and posses significantly more technological knowledge and skills than previous generations (Bennet, Maton, & Kervin, 2008).

Bennet, et al.'s review of the literature indicated that there have been no empirical studies to support the notion that digital natives have a unique learning style that developed from their growing up in a technological society. The authors suggest that much of the thinking that this generation is uniquely different resulted from Cohen's (1972) concept of moral panic, that is, that sensational media focus on a particular issue that leads to the wide social acceptance and claims about a social subgroup even though no empirical evidence supports the claims (Bennet, et al. 2008). Thus, it is the social portrayal of digital natives being raised in a technological society that has contributed to the conceptualization that this generation is a unique and different type of student rather than empirical evidence.

Bennet, et al. (2008) note that little evidence exists indicating that digital natives are a homogenous group in regards to their technology knowledge and skills. In fact, the range of knowledge and skills varies greatly. Research supports the over-generalization of technology knowledge, skills, and use by digital natives (Smith, Salaway, & Caruso, 2009; Kennedy, Judd, Churchwall, & Krause, 2008; Katz 2007; Caruso & Kvavik, 2005; O'Hanlon, 2002). O'Hanlon (2002) assessed college students' information literacy skills and found that only 9% passed the entire test with a score of 70%, with internet search skills being one of the weakest areas. Additionally, the results of this study indicated that an individual's level of information literacy proficiency was associated with variables such as ethnicity, social economic status, gender, and academic background, suggesting that cultural and environmental factors influence one's experience with technology. Caruso and Kvaivk (2005) report similar findings that the inter-group differences among college students knowledge, skills and use of technology can be attributed to factors related to gender, social economics, culture, and major. Kennedy, et al. (2008) surveyed 2000 incoming freshman at a large Australian university. The authors reported that while the use of technologies such as computers, cell phones, and e-mail was common among all incoming freshman, there were vast differences in perceptions, interests, and use of other technologies. Smith et al. (2009) indicated that over half of college students in her study self-reported their technology adoption category as mainstream adopters (i.e. "I usually use technology when most people I know do.") and only a little over a third reported themselves as either innovators, or early adopters. Additionally, Smith notes that college students self rating was influenced by factors such as gender, experiences with technology, and perceived benefit of technology. Furthermore, only 25% of college students prefer an extensive amount or exclusive technology in their courses, while 60% prefer only moderate amounts of technology use in their courses (Smith et al., 2009). The number preferring only moderate amount of technology in their courses in the 2006 ECAR study was 56% and the number wanting an extensive or exclusive amount was still only 25%, (Salaway, et al. 2006). This indicates a pattern of preferences related to the use of technology for educational purposes. Kennedy et al. (2008) also questioned students about the types of technology they wanted to use in their studies. The top rated technologies uses included computers to develop presentations and documents; use of internet to gather information, access learning portals and university services; using text messaging, instant messaging, and, chat for communication. While the technologies students were least interested in using in their studies were, blogs, developing websites, social networking sites, web conferencing, and PDA (Smart Phones).

The empirical evidence does not support the notion of the digital native as a new learner or a homogenous group of technology savvy individuals. Instead it indicates that this generation has a diverse experience with technology, a wide range of knowledge and skills, and moderate expectations regarding the use of technology in their higher education courses.

While the current generation of students has been raised in a digital age, and may favor digital forms of communicating, (e.g. text messaging, e-mail) the research on digital natives indicates that they are not a homogenous group when it comes to their knowledge, skills, and preferences regarding the use of technology for learning. The current research seems to suggest that while this generation has lived in a digital age, factors such a exposure to technology, gender, culture, ethnicity, academic background, and even personal interest in using technology, makes digital natives a heterogeneous group. Therefore universities cannot adopt a one-size fits all view of incoming students when considering technological integration.

However, the question still remains as to the validity of the digital immigrant status being applied to university faculty and the suggestion that university faculty are unable to meet the technological needs of students. This question will be addressed in the next section of this chapter.

DIGITAL USE AND SKILLS AMONG COLLEGE STUDENTS

Since 2004, EDUCAUSE's Center for Applied Research (ECAR) has conducted large scale studies of the technology use, ownership, interests, and academic application among college students. The discussion of all these studies is beyond the scope of this chapter. For this chapter, focus will be placed on the findings from the most recent study completed by Smith et al., (2009) in order to gain an understanding how current college students use technology within United States university settings. The 2009 report indicated that almost all (98%) of students own a computer, with the vast majority owning laptops. The amount of time spent online for school, work or recreational activities varies among students, with approximately one third spending less than 10 hours a week online, one third spending 11-20 hours, and one third spending more than 20 hours. The amount of time spent online was associated with the students' degree major, with those in Engineering and Physical Sciences reporting the most time online, and those in Life Sciences and Education reporting the least. The study does not indicate which of these three activities (school, work, recreation) accounts for the majority of the time spent online.

The highest reported online use was the accesses of library websites, with 94.6% reporting having used their universities' library website. The median frequency of use of library websites was weekly. The second most commonly used university based website was the school's learning management system (LMS), 86% of respondents reported assessing their universities LMS, with the median frequency being several times per week.

However, 90% reported using social networking websites, the median frequency of use of these websites was daily (Smith et al., 2009). While a larger number of students report using their library website, and LMS, the frequency of use of social networking sites is much higher, and suggests that perhaps the amount of time students spend online is associated more with recreational activities than academic activities. Other frequently reported online activities were downloading of video or music files from web, instant messaging, and use of graphic software (Smith et al. 2009). Again, the median frequency of use for these ICT applications favors their use for recreational activities over academic activities.

While accesses of online resources, particularly library websites, is an aspect of the university learning experience, the ability to effectively search, identify, evaluate, and use the information from these resources (i.e. information literacy skills) is a critical part of academic activities associated with technology. Students tended to report their information literacy skills as high, with almost 90% rating their ability to effectively and efficiently search the internet for information at or above the very skilled level. However, approximately only 58% reported their ability to evaluate the reliability and validity of online sources at or above the very skilled level (Smith et al. 2009). This suggests students perceive themselves as adept at "surfing the net" they do not perceive themselves as adept at being able to determine the value of information they find.

Research by Educational Testing Services (ETS) (2006) on students' information literacy skills indicates that many students do not posses adequate skills to effectively search, identify, evaluate and use information accessed through information and communication technologies (ICT). This ETS study supports previous results found by, O'Hanlon (2002) indicating that many college students do not have adequate information literacy skills to use the internet and library websites for academic purposes. While ability to find information may be necessary in a digital age, the ability to evaluate its quality and use it to solve problems is essential. Given these findings, universities need to address the information literacy deficiency of students if instructional activities that rely on these skills are to be successful. Furthermore, universities may soon experience external pressure to ensure that students posses the needed information literacy skills. The results of the ETS assessment has led to the development of the National ICT Literary Policy Council whose charge is to define and develop national information literacy standards (Katz, 2007).

In 2009, ECAR examined the relationship between student academic experience and ICT. Almost half of the respondents agreed or strongly agreed that their learning improves with the use of technology and 37% either agree or strongly agree that the use of technology increases their involvement in a course. Additionally, 47% agree that the use of technology in their courses will have adequately prepared them for their career upon graduating (Smith et al., 2009). This data suggest that students perceive use of technology in their courses as having a positive impact.

While online activities represent one aspect of technology use by college students, specific software applications are also part of the technology related instruction within higher education. Students reported using presentation and spreadsheet software the most; however for both forms of software, the median use was monthly. The frequency of use of these two software packages, suggests that students use the software when required as part of a course assignment. Additionally degree major and academic status (i.e. senior) were significantly associated with amount of use of the software (Smith et al. 2009), suggesting that assignments associated with these packages are related to both the students major and academic status.

During a semester, engineering students were most likely to use a wide variety of technology including computer language software, discipline specific software, spreadsheets, graphic software, and the library website. Physical science majors were most likely to use computer language and discipline specific software during the course of semester. Spreadsheets use was similar for Business, and the Physical and Life Sciences majors. Fine Arts students were most likely to use audio and video creation software along with graphic software. Education students were most likely to use e-portfolios and video creation technology (Smith et al., 2009). This data suggests that the expectation of technology use and the type of technology use varies across departments and may be directly related to the relevance of the technology to the specific assignment, degree major, or future relevance to career.

The reported use of software applications by students in the 2009 ECAR study suggests that faculty do integrate relevant technologies into their courses based on degree program, assignment, and career relevance. This data opposes the view that current faculty lack the technology skills and knowledge as suggested by their digital immigrant status.

Additionally, sixty-six percent of the respondents reported that at least half of their professors effectively used information and communication technologies in the course (Smith et al., 2009). However, the question did not differentiate between the type of technology and how it was used in the course. Since ICT includes e-mail, course management system, as well as specific software and hardware, it is hard to determine the level of each particular form of ICT. It does suggest that the digital immigrant status for faculty may not be accurate, since many faculty seem to require students to use technology for the completion of assignments and faculty are perceived as efficient in their use of technology.

Technology has impacted students' view of instruction in higher education. Students have come to expect some use of technology in their instruction, and to use technology to communicate with faculty and other students (Smith et al. 2009; Marinelli & Pausch, 2004). But, little empirical evidence exists to support the notion that these students are a homogeneous group of technologically savvy and unique learners. However, we must acknowledge that these students have grown up in a technological society. To simply ignore this would be a grave error. All one has to do is observe two students sitting across from each other at a table text messaging each other versus talking, to note that there is something different about this generation. But observations such as these do not warrant global changes in technology integration to meet their learning needs. Rather universities should focus more on selective changes in technology integration that are relevant to the department, degree program, and related career needs of their students.

DIGITAL RECREATION

Information and Communication Technologies (ICT) have infiltrated almost every aspect of our lives. Social and recreational technologies entertain learners by way of music, video games, (Bugeja, 2006), websurfing, email, live chatting, IM listservs, wikis, blogging, gaming, social networking, instant messaging, and texting (Cotton, 2008).

Although the general use of these technologies is recreational, the main purposes of technology in higher education are to educate and communicate. Universities must not mistake the social and recreational use of technology by students as a demand to use these technologies for educational purposes. In 2009, ECAR study 90% of respondents reported sending and receiving text messages, with the median use of this technology being daily (Smith et. al., 2009). However, Kennedy (2008) reported that students favor text messaging, chat and instant messaging for communication purposes over instructional purposes.

While integration of various social and recreational technologies has occurred in higher education, universities must not simply apply these technologies without linking them to educational goals and establishing their relevance to content, degree major or professional career. The research indicates that students' want only moderate levels of technology integration into their courses (Smith et al. 2009) and that students are interested in the integration of specific technologies into instruction. Specifically indicating their disinterest in using blogs, social networking sites, and PDAs in their studies (Kennedy et al., 2008). Universities must consider the value of social and recreational technologies in facilitating learning or communication with students when determining which technologies to implement for instructional purposes. The struggle with technology integration into curricula is not a new phenomenon (Joo, 1999), but if technology is not integrated effectively into instruction, it can evolve from a useful learning tool into a learning distraction (Bugeja, 2006).

DIGITAL COMMUNICATION

The use of Information and Communication Technologies is changing how we communicate, how students relate to each other, and how we disclose information. (Blimling, 2000). Historically, faculty interacted with students during office hour meetings, and discussions before and after class (Stephens, Houser, & Cowan, 2009). These traditional face- to- face interactions are not as common as they were before the widespread inclusion of ICT in higher education. With the implementation of blended, hybrid, and fully online courses, there is less opportunity for in person interaction and an increased reliance on ICT such as e-mail, video conferencing, and text messaging for communicating and building relationships (Stephens, Houser, &Cowan, 2009).

Many students are motivated by interactions with other students and faculty. Virtual learning spaces have decreased face-to-face interactions and have increased the use of technologies to promote interactions (Taylor, 2000). However, these new methods of interacting have brought new challenges related to students' expectations regarding style of communicating and the accessibility to feedback. Technology has also changed the ways we communicate with people. The use of digital communication such as e-mail and text messaging have become major methods of communicating for most college students and has resulted in the use of these forms of communication by universities to their students (Blimling, 2000). Email is widely accepted as a means of communication in higher education (Stephens, Houser, & Cowan, 2009). Institutions use email to communicate important information through student data systems and course management systems. This in turn has created a familiarity among students to communicate with faculty in this way. Although convenient, it has created issues related to the appropriate style of communicating when using these technologies.

Students' frequent use of text messaging for recreational and social communication has brought about concerns regarding appropriate communication etiquette. Some students have mistakenly used recreational text language when communicating with faculty. Text language is considered words without vowels, numbers that sound like words, and abbreviations. The use of text language impacts faculty reaction to students. In a study of faculty, Jessmer and Anderson (2001), found that faculty were more likely to assist students who sent emails using correct grammar and who refrained from using text language. While text language may be acceptable practice for recreational communication, students must be informed of the importance proper grammar and communication etiquette when using ICT to communicate with faculty.

Information and Communication Technologies have also changed the expectations regarding the accessibility to faculty and the receiving of feedback. Students use technology to seek and receive faculty feedback, regarding grades, coursework, professional development, and group projects (Kuh, 2003). ICTs allow learners to have non-existent barriers of time and space to acquire knowledge (Joo, 1999) and communicate with faculty. The increased accessibility and elimination of barriers has resulted in students expecting a faster return on feedback, as well as, an increase in amount. Faculty may need to establish guidelines and communicate to students their policies and practices regarding feedback. Faculty need to inform students of how they personally use ICTs to answer questions, provide learner feedback, and generally communicate to students. This can include expectations regarding length of time a student should wait for a response to e-mails, appropriate types of questions to ask via e-mail and threaded discussion, as well as format for providing learner feedback on assignments.

DIGITAL MULTICULTURALISM

Institutions have for some time sought to find ways to broaden their community of learners (Donahoe, 1995). Now more than ever before in our history, people from different cultures of the world are learning together (Joo, 1999) and creating cross-cultural environments (McNaught & Amory, 2006). Interactions that may not have occurred in the past are now prevalent due to increased diversity in virtual learning environments (Blimling, 2000). Technology provides new ways to reach underrepresented and disadvantaged populations (Joo, 1999), such as rural residents, females, low-socio economic groups, ethnic minorities, global learners, (Ngai, 2003), and students with disabilities (Grabinger, Aplin, & Ponnappa-Brenner, 2008). These opportunities allow for increasingly accessible instruction and learning accessibility for all students that may address issues of multicultural awareness, student technical skill variation, accessibility, and technology reliance.

The culture of technology in learning environments varies based on use, access, ability, context, and accessibility. From limited to extreme use, public venues to home access, beginner to expert ability, use of basic to adaptive technologies, students have a range of technological experiences prior to entering postsecondary education. This variation in experience suggests that institutions must address the needs of those who do not have technological skills as well as students who demonstrate expertise in utilizing various technologies.

It is also increasingly imperative to ensure equal access to persons with disabilities (Buggey, 2000). It is estimated that between, "eight to 12 percent of students in higher education have disabilities that require special attention," (Roach, 2002, p.20). During the last few decades, institutions have attempted to meet the needs of disabled students with additional resources and facility accommodations (Roach, 2002). Reaching students with disabilities can be accomplished through the utilization of universal design for learning and new Web 2.0 applications (Grabinger, Aplin, & Ponnappa-Brenner, 2008).

Possible solutions addressing student multicultural issues using technology according to (Rothstein-Fisch & Trumbull, 2008), include strategies that can be incorporated into virtual and face-to-face learning environments. First, create a shared sense of responsibility in all learning environments is critical. Second, redirect activities to differentiate types of activities (individual, group, collaborative) to transfer focus and allow for increased interactions between different students. Thirdly, integrate transition activities by incorporating technology to add relevance and move from topic to topic. Finally, provide guidelines for appropriate communication regarding respect, communication, and expectations

Other solutions to address multicultural issues according to Rasmussen, Nichols, and Ferguson (2006), include the combination of instructional strategies and appropriate delivery systems as a way to facilitate multiculturalism. Instructional strategies such as "cooperative learning activities, debates, role plays, or group projects," (Rasmussen, Nichols, & Ferguson, 2006, p. 267) are not as common in virtual environments. Different instructional approaches must be used to meet the needs of all learners (Rothstein-Fisch & Trumbull, 2008). With recent technology advancements, these strategies can be integrated to support multiculturalism and learning interactions. Tools that faculty use to increase interaction among students and to support multiculturalism include: threaded discussions (written and audio), chats, video conferencing, and sharing digital resources.

CONCLUSION

Our current understandings of Information and Communication Technologies suggests that universities must act more like tailors when making decisions regarding use of technology for learning purposes rather than taking a one size fits all approach. Universities must take a more systematic approach to determine if or what changes need to be made to curricula and technology infrastructure to promote learning.

Universities cannot assume a standard student profile. The research indicates a wide variation among the digital natives in their knowledge, skills, preferences, and experiences with technology. These differences are associated with gender, ethnicity, social economic status, and academic background. Also, students tend to overestimate their information literacy skills, and may lack the skills to effectively accesses, and evaluate information from both public websites and university libraries.

Additionally, students are not interested in the extensive application of technology in their studies, but prefer moderate and purposeful technology integration. The integrated technology should be connected to the content, degree major and future careers of the students. Finally, students have to be able to overcome the challenges of working with diverse populations (Rasmussen, Nichols, & Ferguson, 2006) and the role of universities is to integrate technological and communication skills in the curriculum in order to facilitate that progress. Given the differences among incoming students, universities, or more specifically departments, may need to assess students' skills, and provide strategic methods for training students on the technology identified as a core part of their curriculum designed to reach indented learning outcomes.

In order for technology integration to be successful, student learning must be at the core of the decision making processes. When student learning is placed at the center, factors such as the application of technology to meet learning outcomes, relevance of technology to the content or subject, value of technology to future professions, learner characteristics, multiculturalism, available resources, and infrastructure can then be considered in order to facilitate student learning. This approach allows for a more idiosyncratic application of technology to the curricula by emphasizing the value of a particular technology and its subsequent changes to curricula to meet educational outcomes. To be successful, faculty need to seek out the empirical evidence in order to effectively use technology to facilitate learning. Using this approach requires an active participation by faculty in decision making regarding the selection and purchase of technology for instructional purposes. It also favors the practice of housing technical and pedagogical support related to instructional technology within schools or departments, instead of university-wide centers.

REFERENCES

Bennet, S., Maton, K., & Kervin, L. (2008). The 'digital natives' debate: A critical review of the evidence. *British Journal of Educational Technology*, *39*(5), 775–786. doi:10.1111/j.1467-8535.2007.00793.x

Blimling, G. S. (2000, September). New technologies: Changing how we work with students. *About Campus*, 3–7.

Bugeja, M. J. (2006). Facing the facebook. *The Chronicle of Higher Education*, *52*(21), C1–C4.

Buggey, T. J. (2000). Accommodating students with special needs in the online classroom. *New Directions for Teaching and Learning*, *84*, 41–46. doi:10.1002/tl.846

Caruso, J. B., Kvavik, R. B., & Nelson, M. R. (2005). *The ECAR Study of undergraduate Students and Information Technology, 2005: Convenience, connection control and learning.* (Research Study, Vol. 6. Boulder, CO: EDUCAUSE http://www.educause.edu/ecar (Retrieved December 2009).

Cotton, S. R. (2008). Students' technology use and the impacts on well-being. *New Directions for Student Services*, *124*, 55–70. doi:10.1002/ss.295

Donahoe, S. S. (1995, February). *Using distance learning and telecommunications to develop strategies of communication for widely diverse populations.* Paper presented at the meeting of American Association of Colleges for Teacher Education, Washington. D.C.

Educational Testing Services. (2006). *2006 ICT Literacy Assessment Preliminary Findings.* http://www.ets.org/Media/Products/ICT_Literacy/pdf/2006_Preliminary_Findings.pdf (Retrieved Jan 2010).

Frand, J. L. (2000). The information –age mindset. Changes in students and implications for higher education. *EDUCASE Review*, *35*(5), 15-24. http://net.educause.edu/ir/library/pdf/erm0051.pdf (Retrieved December 2009).

Grabinger, R. S., Alpin, C., & Ponnappa-Brenner, G. (2008). Supporting learners with cognitive impairments in online environments. *TechTrends*, *52*(1), 63–69. doi:10.1007/s11528-008-0114-4

Hara, N., & Kling, R. (2000). Student distress in a web-based distance education course. *Information Communication and Society*, *3*(4), 557–579. doi:10.1080/13691180010002297

Howe, N., & Strauss, W. (2000). *Millennials rising: The next great generation.* New York: Vintage.

Jessmer, S. L., & Anderson, D. (2001). The effect of politeness and grammar on user perceptions of electronic mail. *North American Journal of Psychology*, *3*(2), 331–346.

Joo, J. E. (1999). Cultural issues of the internet in classrooms. *British Journal of Educational Technology*, *30*(3), 245–250. doi:10.1111/1467-8535.00113

Junco, R., & Mastrodicasa, J. (2007). *Connecting to the net generation.* Washington, DC: National Association of Student Personnel Administrators.

Katz, I. R. (2007). ETS research finds college students fall short in demonstrating ICT literacy: National Policy Council to create national standards. *C&RL News*, *68*(1). http://www.hawaii.edu/lilo/fall09/content/reports/ALA%20_%20ETS%20research.pdf (Retrieved January 2010).

Kennedy, G. E., Judd, T. S., Churhward, A., & Gray, K. (2008). First year students' experiences with technology: Are they really digital natives? Australasian. *Journal of Educational Technology*, *24*(1), 108–122.

Kuh, G. D. (2003). What we're learning about student engagement from NSSE. *Change*, *35*(2), 24–32. doi:10.1080/00091380309604090

Laird, T. F., & Kuh, G. D. (2005). Student experiences with information technology and their relationship to other aspects of student engagement. *Research in Higher Education*, *46*(2), 211–233. doi:10.1007/s11162-004-1600-y

Marinelli, D., & Pausch, R. (2004). Edutainment for the college classroom. *The Chronicle of Higher Education*, *50*(28), B16–B16.

McGill, T. J., & Hobbs, V. J. (2008). How students and instructors using a virtual learning environment perceive the fit between technology and task. *Journal of Computer Assisted Learning*, *24*, 191–202. doi:10.1111/j.1365-2729.2007.00253.x

McNaught, C., & Amory, A. (2006). Multicultural issues in the design of learning technologies. *Research and Practice in Technology Enhanced Learning*, *1*(3), 189–193. doi:10.1142/S1793206806000172

Ngai, P. B. (2003). Linking distance and international education: A strategy for developing multicultural competence among distance learners. *Journal of Studies in International Education*, *7*(2), 157–177. doi:10.1177/1028315303007002004

O' Hanlon, N. O. (2002). Net knowledge: Performance of new college students on an internet skills proficiency test. *The Internet and Higher Education*, *5*, 55–66. doi:10.1016/S1096-7516(02)00066-0

Oblinger, D. (2003, July). Boomers, gen-xers and millennials: Understanding the new students. *EDUCASE Review*, *38*(4), 37–47.

Prensky, M. (2001). Digital natives, digital immigrants. *Horizon*, *9*(5), 1–6. http://www.marcprensky.com/writing/Prensky%20-%20Digital%20Natives,%20Digital%20Immigrants%20-%20Part1.pdf Retrieved December 2009. doi:10.1108/10748120110424816

Prensky, M. (2005). "Engage me or engrage me" What today's learners demand. *EDUCASE Review*, *40*(5), 60–64.

Rasmussen, K. L., Nichols, J. C., & Ferguson, F. (2006). It's a new world: Multiculturalism in a virtual environment. *Distance Education*, *27*(2), 265–278. doi:10.1080/01587910600789696

Roach, R. (2002). Assistive technology comes into focus. *Black Issues in Higher Education*, *19*(11), 20–24.

Robinson, C. C., & Hullinger, H. (2008). New benchmarks in higher education: Student engagement in online learning. *Journal of Education for Business*, *84*(2), 101–109. doi:10.3200/JOEB.84.2.101-109

Rothstein-Fisch, C., & Trumbull, E. (2008). *Managing diverse classrooms: How to build students' cultural strengths*. Alexandria, VA: Association for Supervision and Curriculum Development.

Salaway, G., Katz, R. N., Caruso, J. B., Kvavik, R. B., & Nelson, M. R. (2006). The ECAR Study of Undergraduate Students and Information Technology, 2006. *Research Study, 7*. Boulder, CO: EDUCAUSE http://www.educause.edu/ecar (Retrieved December 2009).

Smith, S., Salaway, G., & Caruso, J. B. (2009). The ECAR Study of Undergraduate Students and Information Technology, 2009. Research *Study, 6*. Boulder, CO: EDUCAUSE http://www.educause.edu/ecar (Retrieved December 2009).

Stephens, K. K., Houser, M. L., & Cowan, R. L. (2009). R U able to meet me: The impact of students' overly casual email messages to instructors. *Communication Education*, *58*(3), 303–326. doi:10.1080/03634520802582598

Tapscott, D. (1999). Educating the net generation. *Educational Leadership*, *56*(5), 6–11.

Taylor, P. G. (2000). Changing expectations: Preparing students for flexible learning. *The International Journal for Academic Development*, *5*(2), 107–115. doi:10.1080/13601440050200716

KEY TERMS AND DEFINITIONS

Digital Native: Label used to describe individuals born in or after the 1980s that grew up in a rapidly advancing technological society, and describes a generation that embraces new technologies and makes the use of ICT almost a daily occurrence (Prensky, 2001).

Digital Immigrant: Label used to describe individuals born prior to 1980 that were not socialized in a technological society, but instead have had to adapt and learn to live in a digital age (Prensky, 2001).

Information Literacy: An individual's skills and abilities to effectively search, identify, evaluate, and use the information from on line resources.

Information and Communication Technologies: Technology tools such as computers, smart phones, MP3 players, text messaging/chat applications, and software applications that facilitate the accessing, sharing, and creating of digital information.

Digital Recreation: The use of information and communication technologies for social and entertainment purposes.

Chapter 4
Feeling Like a First Year Teacher:
Toward Becoming a Successful Online Instructor

Lloyd P. Rieber
University of Georgia, USA

Gregory M. Francom
University of Georgia, USA

Lucas John Jensen
University of Georgia, USA

ABSTRACT

An ever increasing number of college instructors are finding themselves asked or required to teach online. While some embrace this opportunity, others are making this transition with some reluctance. The move from face-to-face to online teaching can be difficult, and unprepared instructors may become discouraged or, even worse, may allow mediocrity to creep into their teaching. In this chapter, a different perspective is offered to instructors who are experienced, but new to online learning to help them make the adjustment—imagining once again themselves as first year teachers. Doing so should help them to revisit the enthusiasm, daring, exhilaration, and yes, even terror that they experienced when they first began teaching. Three fundamental principles are offered to guide college teachers in their earliest online teaching experiences. Examples are provided to show how one instructor found innovative ways to use online technology that were consistent with his teaching style.

INTRODUCTION

Learning to teach well is difficult, yet very rewarding. Becoming a good teacher requires years of hard work combined with a never ending commitment to improvement. However, few things compare to the feeling of pride and satisfaction in knowing that one's students have tackled a difficult concept, principle, or skill. New teach-

DOI: 10.4018/978-1-60960-147-8.ch004

ers encounter many well-documented difficulties in their first few years of teaching (Fry, 2007; Gordon & Maxey, 2000; Martin, Andrews, & Gilbert, 2009). These difficulties can stem from a variety of sources, including inadequate resources, unclear expectations, personal isolation, difficult work, role conflict, and reality shock (Gordon & Maxey, 2000). The transition toward becoming a new online teacher may also result in some of the same difficult experiences. For instance, new online teachers may find themselves without needed digital resources to effectively teach online. They may not know where to find useful learning activities that would be the equivalent to activities done face-to-face. Expectations for online teaching may be different than those in face-to-face classes. A new online teacher may find that the work required to teach a particular online course is more than that required to teach the face-to-face equivalent (Papastergiou, 2006). The role of the teacher might also change, leading to feelings of personal isolation and role conflict in which the teacher does not know what type of person he or she should be while teaching online. Discouragement and frustration can arise when the realities of online teaching interfere with personal teaching preferences. Activities that new online teachers desire to do may not be possible because of the limitations of online teaching tools.

Many experienced college faculty who have achieved the reputation of being a good teacher are now faced with the task of moving their teaching to online environments, and some find themselves very unprepared. The purpose of this chapter is to tell the story of one faculty's transition from face-to-face teacher to online teacher with the hope that it will give other experienced college instructors a useful case with which to compare as they make similar transitions.

A note about how this chapter is written. It is presented largely as a first person account by the lead author – Lloyd Rieber. The other two authors – Greg Francom and Lucas Jensen, doctoral candidates at the University of Georgia – likewise share their first-person experiences of *being students* in online learning environments. All three authors also worked together to extend and integrate these very personal accounts into the broader emerging literature in online learning and education.

BACKGROUND

Before beginning my career in a tenure-track higher education faculty position, I (Rieber) was a public school teacher for five years, with most of that time spent teaching fifth grade. I've often joked over the years that I hoped my students from my first year of teaching received an education somewhere down the line because the only person who probably learned anything that year was me. It was an amazing year, and I never worked harder or learned as much in so short a time. But, with a lot of help and support from my principal and several experienced teachers at the school – combined with a mixture of perseverance, courage, daring, humility, and terror – I slowly found my way. Of course, I also had some skill, knowledge, and a beginning teaching philosophy (however fragile) gained from my teacher education program at the University of Pittsburgh. Over the course of the next five years I think I became a good teacher. Those five years were an incredibly formative time for me as a professional educator, one that has informed and guided me and my university research in the 25 years since I left the public school classroom.

I have thought a lot about my first year of teaching as I have made the transition to teaching online. I earned a reputation of being a good college teacher, yet I knew I was entering into instructional territory for which my past experience had not fully prepared me. There was the same excitement, enthusiasm, and fear that I had when I first started teaching fifth grade. Similarly, I also had the advantage of having colleagues – some in academia and some not – who had been teaching or managing successful online courses for a few years. I found I could turn to these people for help and guidance without threatening my own standing or identity as a "successful teacher." By the end of my first year of teaching online, I made the deliberate decision to take on the attitude and identity of a "first year teacher," just as I had 25 years ago when I began my career as a public school teacher. The identity of a novice gave me the liberty to try new things without fear of making mistakes. Matching my learning curve to becoming a competent public school teacher, I gave myself five years to reach a level of skill and competence with eLearning, and this brought its own sense of freedom and space.

The main message I wish to share with experienced college instructors making the transition to online teaching is also the simplest: Voluntarily embrace the role of a first year teacher, take on this identity fully, and convey to colleagues, students, and administrators that you want them to see you in this way. Consequently, like any first year teacher, you should expect an extra level of support from administration and colleagues. So, if mistakes or not-so-good decisions are made, all should view these as valuable opportunities for reflection and growth.

SOME IMPORTANT LESSONS LEARNED FROM MY FIRST YEAR OF PUBLIC SCHOOL TEACHING

One of the people who inspired me the most when I was a new public school teacher was Ginny Hill. Ginny was one of two second grade teachers at my school. Ginny was an veteran teacher with about 10 years of experience, but she had left the classroom for several years to begin raising a family. She returned to teaching the same year I began. I looked up to Ginny for several reasons. First, I quickly came to admire anyone who had "paid their dues" to become a successful teacher. The curriculum of the teacher education program I went through at the University of Pittsburgh was strongly Piagetian in its focus and structure. The watch word of this program was "empathy," and Ginny exemplified this in the way she viewed her instruction and her students' learning. She was very kind, very humble, and would help anyone who asked. But these are not the reasons she has remained an inspiration to me over all these years. She was also not afraid to be critical of her own teaching style and philosophy and to adopt strategies or ideas that she simply believed were better. I remember that as our school's faculty readied for the approaching first day of school, Ginny told me how she had completed a professional development workshop over the summer in which she was introduced to the "workshop method." And although adopting this approach meant devoting enormous time before the start of the school year, she knew this was the way to go. Through her example, Ginny taught me the principle of "Never be afraid to say, 'yes, that's a better idea'." I think the significance of this principle becomes understood only as one gains experience and reputation. It takes a great deal of humility and courage to admit that what one has been doing for years is inferior to a better idea.

I also began my public school teaching career at exactly the time when the personal computer came on the education scene. Because this was such a formative time for me, everything was new, so the fact that the personal computer was new to education didn't put me at a disadvantage. Also, the administration had little idea of what to do with the computer – it would be many years before school districts would become restrictive and directive as to how teachers should (or should not) use computers in the schools. I also had the wonderful advantage of having Jerry Morris as principal, a very enthusiastic and forward-looking administrator. He campaigned to be one of the first schools in the district to have computers and he was able to secure funding for a small lab of about six Apple II+ computers. I arrived at this school – Bluewater Elementary School in Bluewater,

New Mexico – just as he was hoping his teachers would embrace this technology. I found myself rewarded and encouraged every time I tried using the computers in my teaching. I was particularly recognized when I experimented with computers in my teaching in creative ways. I was also not penalized when all did not go as planned. These first few simple lessons proved quite profound in my journey to become an effective teacher, and they continue to be helpful as I venture into online education.

The lessons I learned are consistent with those found in the teacher education literature. New teachers need to learn a host of new knowledge and skills, such as how to manage the classroom, different ways to obtain instructional resources, how to plan instruction, different methods to assess students, and how to motivate students (Feiman-Nemser, 2001; Gordon & Maxey, 2000) – skills that online teachers also need. In order to enhance or obtain these important skills, induction programs, or programs that are designed to help new teachers learn skills, and succeed in their new job have been proposed and implemented in many schools (Glazerman et al., 2008; Ingersoll, 2004; Kelley, 2004). Research has been conducted to show what effective induction programs offer to teachers and some of these practices might help new online teachers to "induct" themselves into online teaching. Face-to-face teaching induction programs provide new teachers opportunities to observe good teaching, connect with trained mentors, be assessed on their own teaching and effectively teach knowledge, skills, beliefs and attitudes (Berry, Hopkins-Thompson, & Hoke, 2002; Glazerman et al., 2008). Since the transition to online teaching typically does not come with comprehensive systematic induction practices, the new online teacher may have to determine if some of these induction practices are appropriate for their own situation. A new online teacher could find a mentor with online teaching experience and knowledge of the systems that the educational institution uses to support online teaching. This mentor could let a new online teacher observe class sessions and show how to use the tools and systems to teach effectively. New online teachers can also seek out professional development opportunities that focus on teaching improvement in order to learn how to more effectively teach online. Finally, online class-based assessment data can be gathered from students to determine achievement and find out which aspects of the class they found most helpful and which needed improvement.

PRINCIPLES FOR BECOMING A SUCCESSFUL ONLINE TEACHER

The literature is full of books and guides to teaching effectively online (e.g. Dawley, 2007; Farnsworth & Bevis, 2006; Rudestam & Schoenholtz-Read, 2010) so it is important not to confuse what is presented here with similar specific online teaching advice and tips. Instead, this section provides a few general principles for the person who is already a successful teacher in face-to-face contexts and wishes to make the jump to online teaching. These people should also seek out others with online teaching experience at their local site. It is important to take advice from those who have derived their ideas, strategies, and philosophies from extensive experience actually teaching online. Online learning is currently a "hot item" in the professional literature. There are many distance education authors, some actually well known, who have little or no experience with actually teaching online. While much can obviously be gained from any thoughtful writing on a topic, becoming an effective teacher requires extensive professional development, and the best people to provide that guidance are those who have skill resulting from experience. Just as one would want to learn the actual skill of controlling an airplane from an experienced pilot, or learn how to plant and cultivate a garden from a master gardener, so too should the actual craft of online teaching be gained from and supervised by an experienced online teacher. Think of this as similar to the experience of "student teaching," a basic requirement of all professional public school teachers.

Though professional development is an important component in transitioning to a new role as an online teacher, professional development options for online educators are limited and unproven, given that the field of online learning is still in its nascency. Most of the professional development offered to university faculty is technical rather than pedagogical (Oomen-Early & Murphy, 2009). Universities need to offer more professional development and pedagogical training in the field of online education as well as support groups for novice online teachers (Bailey & Card, 2009; Oomen-Early & Murphy, 2009). Because of this, networking and mentorship among online instructors of varied experience should be an essential part of professional development, as it can alleviate the stress, disconnection, and burnout that online teachers encounter (Bailey & Card, 2009; Hogan & McKnight, 2007). Bailey and Card (2009) interviewed experienced online higher education teachers and found that much of what was considered successful teaching in a traditional college classroom made the transition to online education. They identify eight effective practices for successful online teaching: fostering student relationships, engagement, timeliness, good communication, organization, technical competency, flexibility, and setting high expectations (Bailey & Card, 2009). Garnering student feedback is essential to development as an online instructor as well (Brew, 2008). However, Signer (2008) feels that good professional development in online learning is more than transferring traditional practices to an online setting, proposing a model for successful online professional development that derives its success from a confluence of best practices in three areas: teacher education, instructional technology, and online education.

Three principles are offered next to help experienced college instructors successfully make the transition to online teaching. These principles may seem obvious at first, but they serve as important reminders to keep you on track and on course when your online teaching compass begins to spin out of control.

PRINCIPLE 1: WHAT'S GOOD FOR LEARNING IS GOOD FOR ONLINE LEARNING TOO

A good place to start is with the simple reminder that students do not come to online learning versus face-to-face learning as different people. The underlying characteristics of learning, cognition, and motivation remain in force (e.g. Bransford, Brown, & Cocking, 1999; Keller, 2008). This is also a reminder that students come to online learning generally unexperienced and largely unprepared to be successful with the unique demands of online learning (see Box 1 for one student's account of becoming an online student). Even those who report having taken many previous courses online are likely to have experienced the narrowest kinds of online learning, such as those that emphasize participation in asynchronous discussion boards.

Regardless of the course delivery model, the principles of good instruction, and the conditions of learning that underly those principles, remain important and pertinent (Gagné, 1985; Gagné, Wager, Golas, & Keller, 2005; Merrill, 2002). Most college instructors do not have a background in instructional design or education. Those who have achieved success in teaching have largely done so through modeling strategies they found effective when they were undergraduate or graduate students, combined with years of hard work and reflective practice. Some have benefited from professional development workshops and other experiences provided by their host institution (McKeachie, 2002) based on the extensive instructional design literature (e.g. Dick, Carey, & Carey, 2009; Smith & Ragan, 2005). The point is that these apply as much to online learning as they

Box 1. Online learning from the student's point of view: students need to help stay engaged (Lucas Jensen)

When I signed up for my first fully online course, I must admit to being excited at the prospect. The course was administered through the virtual classroom HorizonWimba via WebCT: no class meetings, no face-to-face time, and no trips to campus! My head danced with images of my lounging around on my couch, getting educated on my laptop. And, yes, at first, it was a bit of a thrill. "I'll just make some microwave popcorn!" "I'm wearing my pajamas!" "I can watch baseball on mute!" Distractions piled up. The instructor recessed into the background like that trombone "wah wah wah" adult-speak that populates Charlie Brown cartoons. About two or three classes into the semester, it was clear I had oversold my own multitasking skills. I was behind on the material and unengaged during the class sessions. I was present but not present, and I had to reengage – real active engagement – with the material and the class. I had to push myself to participate in discussion, to ask questions, and to pay serious attention to what was going on. It took work, but I got the hang of it, though I still find myself recalibrating to the online learning environment, even since taking five more online classes.   *The problem here is twofold. Distance learning provided me a good deal of autonomy, and I failed to take ownership of my own engagement. In addition, the professor did little to make sure we were actively engaged, and when intermittent questions to the class were posed, one could practically hear the digital crickets and tumbleweeds.*   *What an instructor might want to take away from this is that students are adjusting to this new learning environment as much as he/she is. If online instructors are to become "first year teachers" again then perhaps they should proceed with the assumption that their students are neophytes as well. Thinking of learners as "first year students" might seem regressive, but learners must be engaged using many of the same techniques employed in the earlier grades: varied activities, frequent breaks, and lots of checking in to make sure the learners are not falling behind. Unfortunately, if left to their own devices, students may end up like me during those first few classes – zoned out and disengaged, with the nearby television flickering on mute.*

do to any other type of instruction. As the field of online learning, or distance education, matures, less significance is given to the technology employed, and more to the learning experience enjoyed (Goodyear & Ellis, 2008).

PRINCIPLE 2: TO THINE OWN ONLINE TEACHING SELF BE TRUE

When I first started paying attention to online learning, the dominant instructional strategy was the use of asynchronous discussion boards. Before I began to teach courses delivered in any significant way online, I tried using discussion boards in my face-to-face courses as a way of augmenting or supplementing the discussions we were having in class. I was not satisfied with these discussions because it appeared that most of the student postings seemed forced or shallow – that is, they did not seem involved in a *discussion*, but instead seemed to be doing the least necessary to get the points. However, I felt that this was my fault as the instructor. I must be honest and say that I've never been very creative, or successful, in leading class discussions even though this was the forte of some of the best college instructors I had as an undergraduate and graduate student. I've tried to improve my skill in this area, but I've come to the conclusion that I just don't have an affinity or disposition for leading class discussions well.

My advice is not to avoid discussion boards, but rather to capitalize on those online learning tools and strategies that take full advantage of your current teaching strengths or dispositions. For many instructors, discussion boards may be exactly the tool that matches your instructional talents. In my case, I love building things for teaching and learning. For example, I have built lots of games and simulations (mostly computer-based) over the years, beginning when I was a fifth grade teacher. I have always received a real thrill out of building something and then giving it to my students to use or explore. My best discussions with students have been through the debriefings that I conduct afterwards.

The temptation is to assume that online learning equates to the exact tools or strategies that the majority of people have used so far and that to become a good online instructor you must mimic their use. I realize I'm on the cusp of contradicting myself here as I have already said that any first year teacher should remain open to new ideas and possibilities, and therefore be open to experimentation. But, as you explore and experiment, be ever mindful of what is best aligned with your own natural teaching abilities and instincts.

I began to fully embrace online teaching upon the arrival of virtual classroom technologies (Horizon Wimba and Elluminate are two current examples). The current state-of-the art in virtual classrooms provides two-way audio with the ability to upload and use PowerPoint presentations. There are many other features as well, of which the most important in helping me to alter my presentation style are the myriad of online polling tools. These polling tools are best thought of as "audience participation tools" – long found on television shows, that allow the studio audience to give their opinions on multiple-choice questions. The current popularity of "clickers" in large sections of live college courses is based on the same concept (Sullivan, 2009; Trees & Jackson, 2007). Although it took time to adjust to the strange feeling of only "talking to my computer" when I used the virtual classroom (which I've affectionately dubbed the "DJ effect," given my guess that becoming a radio disc jockey requires a similar adjustment), I found that the "live" class sessions in the virtual classroom provided me with the opportunity to "meet" my students online periodically in ways that matched my face-to-face teaching experiences, promoting instructor presence (Kanuka & Garrison, 2004; Wise, Chang, Duffy, & Del Valle, 2004) and reducing transactional distance (Moore, 1991; Wheeler, 2007).

However, I made several major mistakes when I first started using a virtual classroom, which took me several semesters to identify and correct, thanks to the honest end-of-course feedback of my students. My most significant mistake was to use the virtual classroom to lecture. Instead, I've learned to make all content available asynchronously, such as through pre-recorded presentations. I use the virtual classroom to probe student understanding of the material and tackle the most difficult concepts and principles for that week. I strive to engage students in highly interactive ways, such as through the use of online polls and breakout room discussions. Our weekly sessions have a very social element to them, which is deliberate. Students need to feel connected to their classmates (Moore, 1989). I always advise new online instructors to invest the time to learn how to use any available live classroom if only because I think they will appreciate how it capitalizes on their ability to prepare and deliver presentations. Then, as they become more acquainted with the affordances of the live classroom and allow themselves to experiment with it, they will likely find it too will help change their teaching in fairly dramatic ways. I consider the virtual classroom a "value added" social experience for students.

PRINCIPLE 3: PREPARE A WELL-ORGANIZED AND EASY TO FOLLOW COURSE LEARNING PLAN FOR STUDENTS

When I began teaching online I was already very skilled at Web design. I had already been supplementing my face-to-face teaching with lots of Web-based resources. I had created my own resources along with using resources and tools available from my university's learning management system (LMS), WebCT. However, I began noticing a pattern to the emails I received from many of my students soon after the online course began. The emails had two parts. The first complimented me on the class Web site and the wealth of resources they found there. The second part of the email asked, basically, "What do I do now?" Students were impressed and kind to notice that I obviously put a lot of work into the course's design, but they were clearly confused as to where to go and what to do.

I eventually came to embrace something called the "course learning plan," an eLearning management strategy I learned from an eLearning

Figure 1. An example of a Web page containing a course learning plan. This shows just the top portion of the Web page. There are approximately 90 individual items listed on the course learning plan.

company called Saber Learning. Our department had contracted with Saber Learning to use their virtual classroom, built on the PlaceWare technology. Saber Learning provided us with the Web infrastructure they had developed for their commercial online courses. A unique aspect to their web design was the course learning plan, which was really nothing more than a big "to do" list. For at least a year I strongly resisted adopting the course learning plan idea because of how it clashed with my constructivist leanings – the idea of providing a linear, sequential list of steps or activities as the plan for learning was anathema to me. Eventually, I came to see the course learning plan as the solution to the disorientation students were experiencing and created my own (see Figure 1 for an example; see Box 2 for a student's perspective on the need for course organization supported by appropriate tools). I also came to see that such a learning plan did not contradict my overall teaching and learning philosophy. There is nothing antithetical to constructivism in providing students with extensive learning materials, carefully designed and organized by an expert in the topic area. And, students could also access the materials from the course learning plan at any time and in any order they wished.

Another seemingly small attribute in Saber Learning's course learning plan that I have found to be extremely important is a recommended due

Box 2. Online learning from the student's point of view: students need organization and tools that make sense (Greg Francom)

I tried to keep using the same "good student" habits I had learned in face-to-face classes in my online classes only to find that things didn't work out as I had hoped. In my first online class experience, I found it very difficult to figure out what assignments, readings, tests, etc. I should be doing today or this week. My face-to-face teachers constantly provided reminders for upcoming assignments and tests in person, but online there were no such "in-person" reminders. I had to actively remind myself to find required activities and dates by reading the syllabus or looking through the online course. Over time, I came to realize that my ideal organization of course activities was very different from most of my teachers'. As a student, I want to quickly and easily see what activities I need to be working on in a chronological format. I found that most online courses put assignments, readings and tests into separate pages making it hard to determine which of these activities I should work on first. The idea of the course learning plan, a single chronological listing of assignments, readings, tests and all other class activities would have been very helpful in order to help me know what I had accomplished and what I needed to do next. As my experience in online courses increased, I tried to determine why the teacher used a specific online technology or feature for a particular learning activity. Students can easily discern if a technology is being used for the purpose of learning or merely for convenience, access or novelty. In one of my hybrid courses, the teacher conducted a class session in Second Life, a virtual world. Despite the fact that we used a cutting edge technology, the pedagogy was still very similar to what we had been doing in the classroom. Our virtual characters gathered together, sat in rows of seats, and viewed a PowerPoint presentation within the virtual world. Sometimes the technology unintentionally shapes the learning activity when the learning activity should instead take precedence over the technology. In one of my online classes, the instructor used only the online discussion board and assignment submission tools. No matter how much each week's subject matter varied from the last week, we were constrained to discussing it only one way and with only a set group of individuals. In contrast, I have experienced online courses in which the instructor explored the use of a wide range of technologies to find the best one for their learning objectives. Such teachers first imagined the ideal learning experience, and only then tried to find technologies to support it. The result was a much more rewarding learning experience for us as students.

date for each of the activities or resources. One of the common complaints students and instructors make about asynchronous online learning approaches is that one always feels a need to work on the course 24 hours a day and seven days a week. It is hard to feel "on track and up-to-date." This is particularly true for students who don't adjust well to the time management of online learning, which is quite different from face-to-face instruction. In face-to-face instruction, we all have come to use the "next class meeting" as a critical milestone and motivation to stay on track. Students who are given access to an entire course's resources, activities, and requirements on the first day of the course not only feel overwhelmed, they can also develop the perception that they will never finish. Students either then develop their own coping strategies or begin to flounder. The small addition of recommended due dates for each item on the course learning plan gives students the knowledge that they are up-to-date, ahead, or falling behind. All three are empowering. I spend considerable time defining the recommended due dates in my course planning.

One final attribute of the course learning plan worth mentioning is that each item on it has a check box for students to check when they have completed the item. Again, this appears at first glance to be a trivial feature. However, students have reported much satisfaction in checking off course tasks as they complete them. Because these check boxes can only be regarded as self-report data (i.e. there is no proof that students have actually done the work), the ability to check activities off as they are completed is best viewed only as a student resource. And, although I had the skill to program these checks into the course database, I think there are many other ways to design a similar checklist activity online. Indeed, there are many free Web 2.0 database tools and resources available to instructors beyond what they might find in their school's provided LMS. For example, Google's suite of tools, including Google Forms, is very conducive to supporting online teaching and learning.

TAKING ADVANTAGE OF THE AFFORDANCES OF ONLINE TEACHING

A tenet of instructional design and instructional technology is to take full advantage of the affordances of the available technology. In this section I present a few of the most notable examples of activities and resources I created to support my online teaching. These examples were ones I designed and programmed given my dissatisfaction with the learning management system I had available to me when I started teaching online. Fortunately, the state-of-the-art in online learning management systems and Web-based tools has improved dramatically in just the past few years, with the expectation that these systems will continue to improve at an equally dramatic pace for the foreseeable future. So, I hope you will consider these examples for the ideas they represent, and not worry about the technological hurdles it would take you to implement them.

NOWHERE ROAD VIDEOS

One of my biggest concerns as I began teaching online was that my students would not get to know me as a human being. Developing a rapport with students was essential in my face-to-face teaching, so much so that I largely took it for granted. As I began teaching online, I immediately felt discomfort in not being able to adequately project my personality to my students. This is another example of the concept of "instructor presence." To fill this void, and in the spirit of being playful with technology, I decided to create some short videos to introduce myself to students, recorded at my home on Nowhere Road in rural Georgia. My wife and I own eight acres on which my wife operates a small farm with some dairy cows, sheep, and chickens. The videos I created playfully used a variety of farm metaphors to introduce students to the course's major topics. In this way, I oriented students to the course organization while at the same time trying to give them a good idea of who I was as a person. I created videos as I gave hay to the cows, gathered eggs from the chickens, and split firewood. Students responded very favorably to this unusual course orientation while getting a tour of my home (and the lifestyle my wife and I try to follow).

It is important to note that I do not have any special video skills or training. Instead, I allowed myself to have some fun with video without worrying too much about the final production results. I thought carefully about the message I wanted to convey in each video and I wrote short scripts for each video to make sure I covered the points I thought most important. I came up with videos that, although lacking in professional video production values, transmitted my playful attitude to students with a few key course ideas underscored.

I encourage you to likewise try some creative and fun ways to convey your personality and attitude to your students, whether your ideas are playful or serious. Students need to know who you are and how you are likely to react to their questions and comments. I created these videos before the advent of YouTube and TeacherTube, so a significant hurdle I faced is now no longer an issue, that is, where to store the videos and how to grant students easy access to them.

ONLINE DESIGN BUDDIES

Like many college instructors in the social sciences, I teach courses in which students must learn unfamiliar and complicated design skills. These skills must be learned and applied in situations which rarely have a definitive "right answer." Instead, data must be amassed to first show that a problem exists, followed by creatively implementing a design skill to solve or mitigate the problem. The more people who review and react to one's design solution, especially early on in the design process, the better. Faculty in my department have come up with very creative ways to do this in face-to-face classes, including some strategies I had developed over the years. A good, simple strategy that emerged in our face-to-face teaching was the use of "design buddies," where each student was paired with a classmate. As new design skills were introduced to students in the course, they would complete first drafts of assignments and exchange these first drafts with their design buddy. Each would then comment or critique the other's first draft for the author to consider when making revisions before turning in a final draft to the instructor for evaluation.

Exchanging papers in a face-to-face class is simple, but doing so online is not, especially if the instructor wants access to the first drafts and the comments made by the design buddies. So, I designed an online design workspace for my teaching which stored all student responses to the activity – first drafts, buddy feedback, and final drafts – along with the eventual instructor feedback in an online database. The system I built managed the entire process for students and instructors. For example, after students finished their first draft of an assignment, they merely clicked a button indicating they were ready for buddy feedback, at which point buddies were sent automated email to let them know. The same thing happened when the buddy feedback was ready for review. Similarly, the system managed the notification of the instructor when the final draft was ready for evaluation as well as letting the student know when the instructor feedback was ready.

However, the biggest advantage of this online design workspace became clear in subsequent semesters because the database became a storehouse of examples for the next crop of students. Interestingly, the best examples were usually those in which previous students had done poorly, thus showing important "non-examples" with detailed instructor feedback about the problem. The database grows with more and more examples as each semester passes.

IN SEARCH OF LOST WISDOM: USING ROLE-PLAYING GAMES TO TEACH ONLINE

Much of my research has been in the area of simulations and games (Rieber, 2005), so I decided to use some of this expertise to design an online game to tackle an instructional design topic that few students liked to learn and, frankly, one that I didn't like to teach. However, the topic – task analysis – is arguably one of the most important skills we teach in instructional design. This game has turned the activity from one of the participants' least favorite to most favorite activities, while at the same time teaching the procedure better with less instructor time as compared to how task analysis was previously taught.

Like almost all good games, this activity begins with a good story:

It is the year 4028 and you are an archaeologist. You are part of a team that has uncovered a lost civilization which appears to be from around the turn of the 21st century, a period for which historians have a huge gap in their understanding. As part of the "dig," you have uncovered a large underground room housing a series of ancient documents, referred to during the time period as "letters." These documents are all fairly intact and the language appears to be a recognizable form of ancient English. Of course, many of the words are completely unknown to you. But, it is clear that each of these letters describe how to perform very specific ancient tasks and rituals. It is your job to identify what task each of the letters describes. By understanding this "lost wisdom" you hope to know more about these ancient people and how they lived their lives. And who knows, perhaps their wisdom can be helpful to us even today!

The game's instructions provide a short tutorial on task analysis. Obviously, the examples of "lost wisdom" found by these future archaeologists are nothing more than task analyses of everyday tasks or topics, such as how to tie your shoes, make a cake, or check email. An online database is also used to manage the game, so, similar to the design workspace, there is now a library of good examples of task analysis for students to consult as they begin playing the game. This pool of examples, which I uncreatively call the "Hall of Fame," is comprised of all past winning entries and also grows a little each time the game is played. As students write their task analysis entry, they must disguise their topic's identity by inventing new words given the assumption, as the game's story suggests, that language would have changed by the year 4028. Students must also provide a translation – a type of "Rosetta Stone" – that is shown to other students as they "play archaeologist."

As an example, try to guess the identity of this everyday task:

1. Grab one bacle in each hand.
2. Pull the bacles tight with a vertical pull.
3. Cross the bacles.
4. Pull the front bacle around the back of the other.
5. Put that bacle through the liger.
6. Tighten the bacle with a horizontal pull.
7. Make a charm.
8. Tighten the charm.

Notice how at first this example sounds vaguely familiar even though many of the words, such as "bacle" and "liger," seem meaningless. Notice also how the familiar word "charm" is used in a confusing way in the last step. These words are used strategically as substitutes for the correct words that, once known, quickly reveal the identity of the skill or task:

bacle = lace
liger = hole
charm = bow

The identity of this task is rather obvious at this point: How to tie one's shoes. Although it is likely you would have guessed it correctly without the code, a more clever example might have led you to believe initially that it could have been some other "tying" skill, such as tying a hook to a fishing line.

My role as the instructor is minimal after the game begins. My main job is to review each task analysis entry submitted to make sure it is a valid example. A student is not allowed to "play archaeologist" until his or her task analysis example (i.e. lost wisdom) is validated by the instructor. If it is not, I give them feedback about what's wrong.

Students are then basically on their own as they play the game. I programmed the game to be scored automatically and continuously as the game unfolds. As students play archaeologist, they must guess the identity of a wide range of task analysis examples and must do so carefully if they hope to be one of the winning archaeologists. Students also critique each example of lost wisdom on the criteria of creativity and "optimal difficulty." By doing so students evaluate whether the task analysis was written with appropriate detail (i.e. granularity) in relation to the intended audience (i.e. their classmates) – two important aspects of any task analysis. By the end of the game, most students have achieved beginning mastery of how to write a good task analysis, if only through the feedback of comparing their task analysis entry with all the others they reviewed. After the game concludes, I conduct a debrief of the game and provide my own critique and review of the winning examples. We end by congratulating the two categories of winners: the best "writers of lost wisdom" and the top "archaeologists." This online game appears to meet the standards of e^3 learning – effectiveness, efficiency, and engagement (Keller, 2008).

SOCIAL AND ORGANIZATIONAL ISSUES

If online and distance education is to provide solid learning, universities must do more than transfer current course materials and classes to staid online environments. Higher education institutions need to grow and support a new culture of online instruction, one that builds upon the affordances of online instruction rather than supplanting tried-and-true face-to-face teaching methods. Universities and colleges need to allow instructors to take on the role of first year teachers when they move online. In fact, they should encourage it, challenging instructors to rethink how they teach to better suit the online classroom. Induction programs should be offered, wherein these new "first year teachers" can observe best practices from more experienced online teachers, who would also act as mentors. Beyond this mentorship system, induction programs need to offer multiple professional development opportunities, from both a pedagogical and technological perspective. Teachers need to learn new ways of teaching with technology and should be able to use the various programs required to teach online. In addition, these induction programs could offer support groups and forums to share stories, struggles, and solutions.

Universities need to prepare students for online learning as well. Just as teachers become "first year teachers" again in an online environment, students also have to adjust to this new paradigm. Students should be given a thorough and honest set of expectations and tips at the onset of their distance learning experience. Good student feedback should be gathered after each course, looking at both cognitive and affective dimensions. If the students feel disengaged with the online setting, then any gains made by the convenience and flexibility of online education are for naught. We should always remember and support the basic human need for relatedness. Online environments can be isolating. The mission here should be to foster the "collegial" feel of a face-to-face class in an online environment, fostering a community of learners and teachers who share and create knowledge together, despite the lack of a common location.

CLOSING

Experienced college instructors faced with the demand to teach online might easily become discouraged. Worse yet, instructors might follow the path of least resistance and approach teaching online without imagination or creativity, such as by restricting themselves to the most archaic of tools available in their university's learning management system. Instead, there is an opportunity to challenge oneself as a teacher, similar to the challenge that came at the start of one's teaching career.

I do not know if my story about becoming an online instructor is typical. Being an instructional technologist, I likely had more technology skills than most instructors. I have tried to present some principles, accompanied by some watershed examples from my slowly emerging online teaching repertoire, that best characterize my transformation from face-to-face to online instruction. If I were to go back to teaching face-to-face those courses that are now delivered totally online, I would integrate most of the activities, resources, and strategies I have created or adopted for online use because they represent improvements to my teaching, not just compromises to accommodate online teaching. The online design workspace and the online game "In Search of Lost Wisdom" are valuable learning and management tools irrespective of the delivery system.

Discovering what works best for you will take time, patience, and a commitment to teaching excellence – traits that all master college instructors have already shown in their teaching careers. As you make the move to online teaching, give yourself the time and the freedom to explore the creative potential of new tools and approaches. Embrace again the identity of a first year teacher and share this attitude with your students, colleagues, and administrators. You will discover new things about yourself and become a better teacher as a result.

REFERENCES

Bailey, C. J., & Card, K. A. (2009). Effective pedagogical practices for online teaching: Perception of experienced instructors. *The Internet and Higher Education, 12*(3-4), 152–155. doi:10.1016/j.iheduc.2009.08.002

Berry, B., Hopkins-Thompson, P., & Hoke, M. (2002). *Assessing and Supporting New Teachers: Lessons from the Southeast*. North Carolina: The Southeast Center for Teaching Quality at the University of North Carolina.

Bransford, J. B., Brown, A. L., & Cocking, R. R. (Eds.). (1999). *How people learn: Brain, mind, experience, and school*. Washington, DC: National Academy Press.

Brew, L. S. (2008). The role of student feedback in evaluating and revising a blended learning course. *The Internet and Higher Education, 11*(2), 98–105. doi:10.1016/j.iheduc.2008.06.002

Dawley, L. (2007). *The tools for successful online teaching*. Hershey, PA: Information Science Publications.

Dick, W., Carey, L., & Carey, J. O. (2009). *The systematic design of instruction* (7th ed.). Upper Saddle River, NJ: Pearson Education, Inc.

Farnsworth, K., & Bevis, T. B. (2006). *A fieldbook for community college online instructors*. Washington, DC: Community College Press.

Feiman-Nemser, S. (2001). From preparation to practice: Designing a continuum to strengthen and sustain teaching. *Teachers College Record, 103*(6), 1013–1055. doi:10.1111/0161-4681.00141

Fry, S. W. (2007). First-Year Teachers and Induction Support: Ups, downs, and in-betweens. *Qualitative Report, 12*(2), 216–237.

Gagné, R. (1985). *The conditions of learning* (4th ed.). New York: Holt, Rinehart, and Winston.

Gagné, R., Wager, W., Golas, K., & Keller, J. (2005). *Principles of instructional design* (5th ed.). Belmont, CA: Wadsworth/Thompson Learning.

Glazerman, S., Dolfin, S., Bleeker, M., Johnson, A., Isenberg, E., & Lugo-Gil, J. (2008). *Impacts of comprehensive teacher induction: Results from the first year of a randomized controlled study*. Washington, DC: U.S. Department of Education National Center for Education Evaluation and Regional Assistance.

Goodyear, P., & Ellis, R. A. (2008). University Students' Approaches to Learning: Rethinking the Place of Technology. *Distance Education, 29*(2), 141–152. doi:10.1080/01587910802154947

Gordon, S. P., & Maxey, S. (2000). *How to help beginning teachers succeed*. Alexandria, VA: Association for Supervision and Curriculum Development.

Hogan, R. L., & McKnight, M. A. (2007). Exploring burnout among university online instructors: An initial investigation. *The Internet and Higher Education, 10*(2), 117–124. doi:10.1016/j.iheduc.2007.03.001

Ingersoll, R. M., & Smith, T. M. (2004). Do teacher induction and mentoring matter? *NASSP Bulletin, 88*(638), 28–40. doi:10.1177/019263650408863803

Kanuka, H., & Garrison, D. R. (2004). Cognitive Presence in Online Learning. *Journal of Computing in Higher Education, 15*(2), 21–39. doi:10.1007/BF02940928

Keller, J. M. (2008). First Principles of Motivation to Learn and e[superscript 3]-Learning. *Distance Education, 29*(2), 175–185. doi:10.1080/01587910802154970

Kelley, L. M. (2004). Why induction matters. *Journal of Teacher Education, 55*(5), 438–448. doi:10.1177/0022487104269653

Martin, E. P., Andrews, S. P., & Gilbert, L. S. (2009). New teachers and support: An examination of ratings of significant agents. *Research in the Schools, 16*(1), 25–31.

McKeachie, W. J. (2002). *McKeachie's teaching tips: Strategies, research, and theory for college and university teachers*. Boston: Houghton Mifflin Company.

Merrill, M. D. (2002). First principles of instruction. *Educational Technology Research and Development, 50*(3), 43–59. doi:10.1007/BF02505024

Moore, M. (1989). Editorial: Three types of interaction. *American Journal of Distance Education, 5*(3), 1–6. doi:10.1080/08923649109526758

Moore, M. (1991). Editorial: Distance education theory. *American Journal of Distance Education, 53*(3), 1–6. doi:10.1080/08923649109526758

Oomen-Early, J., & Murphy, L. (2009). Self-actualization and e-learning: A qualitative investigation of university faculty's perceived barriers to effective online instruction. *International Journal on E-Learning, 8*(2), 223–240.

Papastergiou, M. (2006). Course management systems as tools for the creation of online learning environments: Evaluation from a social constructivist perspective and implications for their design. *International Journal on E-Learning, 5*(4), 593–622.

Rieber, L. P. (2005). Multimedia learning in games, simulations, and microworlds. In Mayer, R. (Ed.), *The Cambridge handbook of multimedia learning* (pp. 549–567). New York: Cambridge University Press.

Rudestam, K. E., & Schoenholtz-Read, J. (Eds.). (2010). *Handbook of online learning* (2nd ed.). Thousand Oaks, CA: SAGE Publications.

Signer, B. (2008). Online professional development: combining best practices from teacher, technology and distance education. *Journal of In-service Education, 34*(2), 205–218. doi:10.1080/13674580801951079

Smith, P. L., & Ragan, T. J. (2005). *Instructional design* (2nd ed.). Hoboken, NJ: John Wiley & Sons.

Sullivan, R. (2009). Principles for Constructing Good Clicker Questions: Going beyond Rote Learning and Stimulating Active Engagement with Course Content. *Journal of Educational Technology Systems, 37*(3), 335–347. doi:10.2190/ET.37.3.i

Trees, A. R., & Jackson, M. H. (2007). The Learning Environment in Clicker Classrooms: Student Processes of Learning and Involvement in Large University-Level Courses Using Student Response Systems. *Learning, Media and Technology, 32*(1), 21–40. doi:10.1080/17439880601141179

Wheeler, S. (2007). The Influence of Communication Technologies and Approaches to Study on Transactional Distance in Blended Learning. *ALT-J: Research in Learning Technology, 15*(2), 103–117.

Wise, A., Chang, J., Duffy, T., & Del Valle, R. (2004). The Effects of Teacher Social Presence on Student Satisfaction, Engagement, and Learning. *Journal of Educational Computing Research, 31*(3), 247–271. doi:10.2190/V0LB-1M37-RNR8-Y2U1

KEY TERMS AND DEFINITIONS

Course Learning Plan: An organized list of all the activities, events, and resources students will use and complete in an online course, presented in the recommended order in which students complete them.

Discussion Forum: An online learning tool in which students engage in asynchronous discussions of topics or questions pertaining to the course.

Instructor Presence: The degree to which students feel engaged with the instructor of a course.

Learning Management System: A software application for the administration and delivery of all aspects of a training or instructional program, such as content organization and delivery, assessment, and communication between and among students and instructors.

Role-Playing Game: A game in which the participants assume the roles of fictional characters.

Teacher Induction Program: Formal practices and resources designed to help new and beginning teachers become competent, effective, and successful professionals in the classroom.

Virtual Classroom: A synchronous online software application that mimics many aspects of a traditional face-to-face classroom, such as the presentation of content and discussion between and among students and the instructor, but augmented with unique tools and resources, such as polling with real-time summaries of student responses, and student grouping tools.

Web 2.0: The second generation of tools and resources found on the World Wide Web characterized by user-generated, shareable content and collaboration among users.

Chapter 5
Supporting Technology Integration in Higher Education:
The Role of Professional Development

Drew Polly
University of North Carolina at Charlotte, USA

Michael G. Grant
University of Memphis, USA

Joanne Gikas
University of Memphis, USA

ABSTRACT

As access to technology becomes prevalent in institutions of higher education, it is critical to find effective ways to support university faculty in the process of integrating technology into their classroom. This chapter surveys the literature on professional development, identifying successful characteristics in higher education. Next, the authors describe two cases in which university faculty have supported their colleagues' attempt to integrate technology into university courses. Finally, promises and challenges of various professional development efforts are also shared.

INTRODUCTION

Technology's Role in Higher Education

As we continue in the 21st Century, access to educational technologies in institutions of higher education is at an all-time high (Bates & Poole, 2003). From previous studies, it is evident that university-level students prefer learning in ways that are supported through technology (e.g., Abrami et al., 2008; Lowerison, Sclater, Schmid, & Abrami, 2006; Milliken & Barnes, 2002). While technology use in university-level courses is appealing to students, technology most effectively supports learning when it is used in ways that support learners' higher-level thinking (e.g., Bransford, Brown, & Cocking, 2000; Mims, Polly, & Grant, 2009; Schacter, 1999). Our views of technology integration speak to these instances

DOI: 10.4018/978-1-60960-147-8.ch005

in which technology is used during instruction to support higher-order thinking processes, such as creating artifacts of knowledge, justifying ideas, and evaluating information.

As institutions of higher education increase access and support the use of educational technologies, there is a need to examine how to best support faculty's integration of technology into their courses. In this chapter we discuss findings and issues related to supporting faculty's integration of technology in university-level courses. We share data from two cases: a university-wide faculty professional development project and a professional development center designed to focus on supporting faculty's integration of technology. Lastly, we provide implications related to faculty professional development.

Professional Development in Higher Education

Faculty development in higher education has been considered through a number of lenses. Caffarella and Zinn (1999) characterize a continuum of professional development over the career of a faculty member. They propose (a) self-directed learning experiences, where "we plan, implement, and evaluate" (p. 243) our learning experiences, (b) formal professional development programs, such as those offered through professional organizations and on-campus teaching centers, and (c) organizational development programs, which are systematic implementations of professional development, usually administratively driven, to impact institutional (i.e., department, college/unit, school, or university) changes.

In contrast, Diaz et al. (2009) consider professional development for faculty based on where and how it occurs. For example, they suggest that faculty professional development is bifurcated: a centralized service and a distributed service. As a centralized service, professional development is driven by an institution-wide unit specific for teaching or faculty development. In the distributed model, services for professional development are organized and offered primarily at the department or college level. In fact, Diaz et al. suggest that as the size of the institution and the geographic distribution of institution increase, the likelihood that professional development will become distributed also increases.

The Technological Pedagogical and Content Knowledge (TPACK) framework has advanced the idea that the effective integration of technology is associated with deep knowledge and skills related to technology (e.g., hardware and software programs), pedagogy, content and the intersections of the three components of knowledge (Mishra & Koehler, 2006; Neiss, 2005). For example, a faculty member in engineering would have to know the content they will teach, pedagogies that best support students' learning of the content, and technologies that most effectively support both the pedagogies and the content. Professional development to support technology integration, through the lens of TPACK, should be connected to both content and pedagogy, and allow faculty to deepen their own knowledge of technology, pedagogy, content, and the intersections of each (Polly & Brantley-Dias, 2009).

Components of Effective Professional Development

Research on the effectiveness of professional development has flourished since the mid 1990s with numerous researchers (e.g., Garet et al., 2001; Penuel et al., 2007; Putnam & Borko, 2000) working to advance what we know about how educators construct knowledge in professional learning opportunities and then enact their new knowledge and skills in their classroom. While the components of professional development are semantically different in various papers, generally all empirically-based lists recommend that professional development include:

- active learning, including hands-on instruction (Garet et al., 2001; Lawless & Pellegrino, 2007; Mouza, 2002-2003);
- alignment with specific curricular content and focus on pedagogy (Penuel et al., 2007; Polly, Mims, Shepherd, & Inan, 2010);
- collaborations, including common planning, team teaching, mentors, discussions and brainstorming and faculty networks (Vescio, Ross, & Adams, 2006; Rogers, 2000);
- on-site support and just-in-time learning (Lawless & Pellegrino, 2007; van Es & Sherin, 2008);
- remunerations, such as recognition and compensation (Cole et al., 2002); and
- sustained learning opportunities over time (Garet et al., 2001; Howland & Wedman, 2004; Polly & Hannafin, 2010).

When coupled together in a comprehensive professional development effort, programs with these factors have the potential to influence substantial change in the ways teachers teach and students learn (Garet, et al., 2001; Penuel et al., 2007). It is important to note, as Scribner (1999) does, that external factors do not ensure engagement with professional development activities and may not encourage active learning. So, faculty may only participate at a surface level, and have no direct influence on their enacted instructional practices.

Professional development through faculty development centers. As identified by Diaz et al. (2009), one of the primary methods technological professional development for university faculty has been implemented is through faculty development centers (Shapiro, 1998). Faculty development centers are housed on-site at institutions and are supported by a single institution. These centers often offer instructional support for university faculty to develop and improve instruction. Some supports and resources can take the form of specialists, such as instructional designers, graphic designers, teaching assistants, library media specialists and audio/video producers (Lee, 2001). Hannon (2008) refers to these individuals as educational developers, where they represent the institution's vehicle for improving teaching and learning.

Instructional technology support from faculty development centers is often implemented through single workshops, often referred to as *one shots*, which lack the comprehensive model found to be effective (Garet et al., 2001). Instructional support may also include course redesign, training in the use and application of distance education technologies, as well as media and technical support (Lee, 2001). As their names imply, these centers have provided a centralized location for professional development. In a variation of the model described by Diaz et al., Grant (2004) described a decentralized model, where services are organized at the university-level and conducted at the department or college level. In nearly all cases, professional development for faculty is voluntary with little extrinsic motivation for faculty to attend.

Barriers to Technology Integration in Higher Education

Research studying higher education reported faculty discussed numerous barriers that inhibit integrating technology in their courses (Al-Senaidi, Lin, & Poirot, 2009; Polly et al., 2010). In a study of anatomy faculty, Weston (2005) found that instructors did not integrate technology since their own skills were not strong; they reported they could not integrate technologies effectively into their courses until their own skills improved. A national study of faculty in Oman found that faculty reported a lack of time to devote to designing and planning technology-rich activities, and a lack of support from university leadership to devote preparation time to teaching (Al-Senaidi et al., 2009). Further, a synthesis of the multi-billion dollar U.S. Department of Education's Preparing Tomorrow's Teachers to Teach with Technology

Initiative found that faculty struggled to transfer what they had learned from a workshop into their classroom without ample follow-up support and mentoring (Polly et al., 2010).

Other barriers to technology integration are the structures at universities, primarily academic freedom and tenure and promotion procedures. In regards to academic freedom, universities have been enculturated with the notion that faculty have flexibility to teach content however they choose, as long as various standards are met (DeGeorge, 1997). In essence, if faculty members choose not to integrate technology in their courses, most universities do not have a system in place to require it. Polly et al. (2010) found that faculty members were more willing to integrate technology when they were given stipends and course release time to develop technology-rich curricula. However, these resources are typically grant-funded (c.f., Schrum, Skeele, & Grant, 2002-2003) and not common in higher education settings. Similarly, tenure processes in higher education are based on a faculty member's work in research, teaching and service. The emphasis of pre-tenure faculty to focus on scholarship and research activities makes it tempting to undervalue time spent on teaching and service activities. As a result, opportunities to learn new technologies and work on integrating them effectively in their courses could be seen as extraneous.

EXAMPLES OF SUPPORTING TECHNOLOGY INTEGRATION IN HIGHER EDUCATION

In this section we present data from two cases relating to technology integration in higher education. The first represents a year-long program offered to faculty across colleges at a large university in the southeastern United States. The second shares data from an interview with two professional developers at a faculty development center at a large university in the southeastern United States. As with any cases (Stake, 1995), these descriptions are used to describe specific phenomena to possibly advance knowledge in supporting faculty's integration of technology in their courses.

Technology Fellowship Program: A Year-long Program of Faculty Development

We (Grant and Gikas) directed a university-wide Technology Fellowship Program (TFP) from 2004 to 2007 at the University of Memphis. Gikas was a staff member in our university's faculty development center, and Grant joined the program for the last two years as a faculty consultant for instructional design and technology integration. This program, modeled after a similar program at Arizona State University, was designed to recognize, encourage, and reward faculty members who were leaders in the innovative use of technology in teaching and learning. Through a competitive-proposal process, five to ten faculty were awarded fellowships for each year, beginning in the summer and lasting through the following spring, approximately May through April.

The overall vision of the TFP was to create a community of practice, following Wenger's (1998) general principles and Cambridge et al.'s recommendations (2005), and to engage faculty in instructional technologies (Chism, 2004) in their fields. The program consisted of a hybrid of instructional strategies, including face-to-face group session, hands on labs, and online learning, as well a discussion, collaboration, and individual opportunities to brainstorm and investigate practical applications for the use of technology in each faculty member's teaching. TFP was one of four communities of practice recognized nationally by the EDUCAUSE National Learning Infrastructure Initiative (NLII), receiving consulting support and the use of iCohere, a virtual collaboration tool.

During the three years of implementation, we conducted one-on-one sessions and collected evaluations, reflections, and artifacts from the participants. Below are selected themes from our lessons learned in implementing this intensive program. The three themes are (a) group and online discussions, (b) instructional design and technology integration, and (c) incentives and motivations.

Group and online discussions. TFP was comprised of many large group, individual meetings and virtual collaborations. While individual sessions were effective, the most interesting and notable changes occurred when faculty members interacted in a group, whether face to face or online. Faculty members were required to participate in an a week-long orientation hosted by our university's faculty development center. This orientation included (a) an overview of the year long program, (b) the demonstration of the collaboration tools that were to be used for whole group communications, (c) presentations on instructional design techniques and instructional technologies and (d) opportunities for preplanning on the redesign of courses. This week provided the opportunity to cultivate the community of practice we hoped to achieve. Faculty members were very forthcoming in these face-to-face sessions about what they hoped to accomplish with their redesigned courses. As one faculty member shared, others were comfortable to ask questions about course organization and technologies to be integrated into the course. This discussion expanded faculty members' visions to what was available and what was possible and appropriate to their disciplines. Many faculty members reconsidered their plans in light of the feedback provided to another.

For example, during the academic year, monthly face to face meetings were scheduled for assistance on instructional design and course redesign questions. During one of these sessions, a faculty member who wanted to code XML for a part of his course shared what he was expecting to achieve with the coding. Other faculty members peppered him with questions and suggestions regarding the purposes of the XML. As such, the feedback from his colleagues allowed him to recognize that the type of interaction he was hoping to create could be implemented without the time and effort of coding XML. These shared discussions provided reflection opportunities for faculty members to rethink their initial ideas. Chism (2005) suggested that peer support scaffolds faculty members' reflection, where colleagues' probing can promote growth.

In contrast one of the most successful online activities was "Star of the Show." At the end of the orientation week, faculty members were asked to select weeks to become Star of the Show — a week where faculty members would share their course redesign ideas with the other Fellows and the faculty development staff in order to receive feedback for their course redesign. This component of TFP continued to use the collaboration tools introduced during orientation. Because of the established community created in the week-long orientation, faculty members were comfortable and willing to post and collaborate with each other. It was exciting to see the connections that were being made with faculty who, prior to this program, had not met and had not previously collaborated but were now open to sharing ideas.

Instructional design and technology integration. One of the goals of the TFP was to emphasize an analysis of teaching practices. In hindsight, we recognized that faculty were typically making instructional decisions reactively to instructional problems in their courses. By infusing the program with principles of instructional design, we felt faculty could move to a proactive approach for planning instruction, particularly using a front-end analysis of content, learners, and curriculum goals (Dick, Carey, & Carey, 2009).

We were reminded afterward, though, that faculty members, like our students, are on a continuum of development. As such, each faculty member tended to appreciate different elements of the instructional design process, but few were prepared to absorb or implement the systems thinking as a whole. For example, one faculty member in the business college became fascinated with performance assessment. In particular, he appreciated how to align criteria in rubrics with course and content objectives. To him, this was new, valid, and valuable.

In contrast, some faculty members were shocked by the time investments required by the analysis of teaching, as well. For example, during a group session on assessments and item analysis, a humanities faculty member commented, "I don't have time for that." She went on to say that she needed to focus on publishing for tenure and promotion, and other junior faculty members in the group nodded in agreement.

Finally, in the field of instructional design and technology, we tend to focus on Taylor's (1980) framework for using technology as a tool, tutor, and tutee, but in all cases these emphasize the support to teaching and learning. We were reminded during TFP that other disciplines and professions value technology differently. In the business college and in technical writing, a small number of faculty emphasized to us that their purposes for learning to use technologies in their courses were to mirror the work of their vocations. One faculty member commented that he wanted his students to learn to use web publishing and desktop publishing software because those are skill sets required in their field. In essence, the technology was the curriculum.

In retrospect, those of us who teach and practice instructional design can become jaded or desensitized to the value of instructional design. On the other hand, we can also be unforgiving or indifferent to other faculty members' undervaluing of instructional design. Gikas described the instructional design and technology integration elements in TFP as a "buffet." We presented a variety of instructional design methods and instructional strategies to faculty members, and faculty members selected those that were meaningful, relevant, and matched their current needs. Overall, faculty members in TFP did not adopt the same framework for instructional design and technology integration that we had intended. But it may be naive to think they would. Faculty members represent different disciplines, different values, different resources, and various professional preparations. We eventually recognized that faculty members represent different stages on the continua of professional development with instructional design and technology integration. We must accommodate professional development to meet these various stages. This is critical because faculty members' work represents, as Caffarella (1998-1999) describes, an intricate mixture of institutional priorities, tasks, and politics. A faculty member's stage of professional development is impacted by his or her own needs and the institution's needs as well.

Incentives and motivations. Cole et al. (2002) and Polly et al. (2010) found and argued that remunerations and external incentives increased the likelihood of faculty choosing to participate in professional development opportunities. TFP offered significant incentives for faculty to participate. The first two years of the program faculty members were provided with laptop computers and a small stipend to use toward equipment, resources, or other professional development in support of their course redesign. The last year faculty members received tablet (slate) computers and a small stipend. (The university was interested in exploring mobile computing, so tablet computers were chosen for the faculty members.) In every year of TFP, there were significant funds remaining from the faculty stipends. In the last year, one faculty member returned the tablet computer, admitting it didn't work for him. Other faculty members during the last year were uncertain on how to make the best use of the tablet computer as well. Still, others explained to us that they did not know what equipment to purchase to significantly aid in their course, and they did not want to waste the money. Many of the faculty members were interested in shifting all or part of their courses online, and they were interested in taking advantage of the university's course management system. So, they felt their resource needs were mostly met. The last year it was evident that the tablet computers were a poor fit for our faculty members. This sentiment has been echoed by other faculty members (see e.g., Weitz, Wachsmuth, & Mirliss, 2006), where use was moderate and some tablet computers remained idle. So, it remains critical for incentives to be relevant and valuable to faculty. We have neither observational nor anecdotal data to suggest that the incentives offered in TFP deterred faculty from applying or participating (Gikas et al., 2005); however, it is disappointing that faculty members were unable to make full use of the incentives offered.

Additionally, as we considered methods to improve TFP, we came to question why faculty members were participating. Our altruistic nature and biases toward improving teaching and learning perhaps offered a myopic vision: We believed all faculty members competed for the opportunity because of a like-minded value in change. However, it became apparent to us that *at least* two faculty members participated in TFP solely to supplement the lack of support for new computers in their departmental budget. In many ways, these faculty members created self-isolation within their TFP cadre, resisting to change their practices and consider others' suggestions. We had numerous discussions as to how to address this seemingly affront to the purpose of the program, and we were left with few answers other than to be aware of the potentiality and to be selective in participants. As mentioned previously, Caffarella (1998-1999; Caffarella & Zinn, 1999) has emphasized that institutional structures and priorities can enhance or impede faculty development efforts. She also recommends that when planning faculty development to identify stakeholders and the power relationships present among them. However, it may difficult or impossible to identify the hidden agendas of participants even if their motives are not visibly detrimental to the program.

CURRENT AND FUTURE DIRECTIONS FOR FACULTY PROFESSIONAL DEVELOPMENT

Overview. Data presented in this section was collected through an hour-long interview with two staff, Steve and Mary, at a faculty professional development center. The purpose of the interview was to better understand two questions:

1. What are the current professional development activities supporting technology integration and what has the impact of these activities?
2. As technology continues to advance how will professional development have to change to meet faculty needs?

During the interview, notes were taken and then analyzed inductively for themes. Themes are presented below.

Current professional development activities. The two professional developers shared information around three major themes: tool-based workshops, follow-up support, and faculty interest. They are each described in detail below.

Tool-based workshops. All of the professional development workshops offered that relate to technology integration center around individual technological tools. Workshops offered in the past two years have included topics, such as Google Documents, wikis, blogs, podcasting, as well as workshops on course management systems and teaching online courses. Mary said, "We've taken the approach to be tool-focused in our workshops with the expectation that faculty will work with the tools and determine how to best integrate these tools into their courses." When asked about the effectiveness of that approach she indicated,

A lot of faculty require individual attention to see how they can be integrated, which is difficult to do in a large workshop. We also have found that faculty need more time and support evaluating

a variety of tools and determining which tool is the best for what they want to accomplish. For example, after working with both blogs and wikis, faculty sometimes struggle with determining which would best support their course activities.

Both professional developers indicated that in the workshop evaluations, faculty reported that most were not yet comfortable enough to use it in their courses. Steve said, "Most faculty will come to our workshops, but not work with it for a few weeks or months and forget what they had covered in the workshops. It is difficult for them to remember things when they don't use the technologies frequently." Consistent with professional development research, ongoing learning opportunities are needed (Polly & Hannafin, in press; van Es & Sherin, 2008).

Follow-up support. While the faculty development center widely advertises workshops, both professional developers are also available to provide faculty follow-up support or individual assistance. Mary stated, "We are seen by faculty as the ones that do workshops, and although we tell faculty in workshops about follow-up support, less than one-fourth call on us for individual help after workshops."

Both professional developers reported success stories of follow-up support. In one case, Mary met with a Dance professor after a Google Docs workshop on setting up a class project. The faculty member and her colleagues had their students create a collaborative group presentation using Google Docs that incorporated video, presentation slides and graphics. Mary's role during follow-up was to work with the faculty member on how the project should be set up and organized using Google Docs. Mary said, "In this case and many others, the faculty member is the subject matter expert, and we can lend our expertise on the technology and work together to design a great project." While follow-up support has contributed to effective technology integration in some instances, only a small percentage of faculty take advantage of this opportunity.

Faculty interest. Faculty members' interest in integrating specific tools in their courses varies, according to Mary. The university's e-mail announcements about podcasts and blog resources sparked interest in both workshops in the past year. However, faculty members interest is largely shaped by their colleagues and their students (Koehler, Mishra, Hershey, & Peruski, 2004). "We have seen many instances of faculty coming to workshops and telling us that their students were asking about Podcasts or other tools. Students' interest in technologies have convinced faculty to learn more about them and consider using them in their classroom. I'm glad that our faculty has taken an interest in learning about technologies that are students are interested in."

Other factors leading to faculty interest include conversations with their colleagues. "I believe that faculty have a desire to use technology more in their courses," Steve said. However, they want things that are easy, and if one of their colleagues convinces them to try something and can prove that it's easy to learn, faculty are more motivated to try it. Many of our workshop members either come with colleagues or tell us that their colleagues have convinced them to learn more about these tools."

Whether faculty interest is increased through conversations with their colleagues or their students, the current structure of higher education will not see increases in technology integration without faculty buy-in. As stated earlier, the tenure and promotion process along with academic freedom have established barriers to technology integration that will only be overcome with faculty interest in integrating technologies into their courses. As Ertmer (2007) concluded, influencing educators beliefs so that they value educational technologies is critical in supporting technology integration.

Future directions of faculty professional development. During the interivew, themes related to the future directions of professional development included: (1) moving beyond just-in-time support, (2) establishing structures for individual faculty support, and (3) support within colleges and department-level structures. Each are described below.

Moving beyond just-in-time support. Faculty, according to Mary and Steve, view the faculty development center as a place where workshops are offered, or a reference for just-in-time help either during or immediately after class when faculty have obstacles while integrating technology. Mary reported, "We get at least a dozen phone calls or e-mails each day from faculty in the midst of using technology in their course that have questions that they want immediate answers for. We would prefer to be involved more in the planning stages to support faculty members before class time, so that there is less of a need for immediate assistance."

Steve added:

Our image has always been one of technical support, and we would prefer to be more like instructional designers, where we focus on the objectives rather than the tools, and spend time with faculty supporting their design of technology-rich activities, and ensure that faculty feel comfortable enough using the tools prior to teaching with them. However, many faculty prefer to jump right in without deeply considering potential problems that may arise.

While just-in-time support is part of the job of both professional developers, both agreed that faculty members would more effectively integrate technology with support and more time invested during the design and planning of technology-rich activities.

Establishing structures for individual faculty support. In order for faculty to be adequately supported for their individual needs, there is a need to reexamine structures in faculty development centers. Steve commented, "It is great if faculty would ask for individual support to co-plan and co-design technology-rich activities. However, it is a double-edged sword if too many faculty seek support. Other than the two of us, who would respond to their requests?"

Mary mentioned one possible solution. "I could see our workshops and initial introductions to these technologies be primarily online through video or other media. Faculty who had a deeper interest in integrating specific technologies would then contact us for assistance designing those activities. However, there would need to be a lot of work trying to convince faculty to participate in these online workshops since many are not comfortable with that way of learning."

The Center has invested both time and resources to increase access to online tutorials to support faculty members' knowledge and skills related to various technologies. However, faculty use of these materials has been scarce. "There are great tutorials that we have linked off our website," Mary said. "However, few faculty make use of those valuable resources."

While individual support and mentorship has been effective in prior projects (Chuang, Thompson, & Schmidt, 2003; Polly et al., 2010), the issues discussed by both Mary and Steve continue to be potential barriers. This model of professional development is difficult to scale-up, and online resources do not provide faculty with as much support as they want.

Support within colleges and department-level structures. As educational technologies continue to emerge, the need for college and department-level support is greater than ever. Steve cited a professional learning community that has developed in the College of Education as one way to support technology integration:

The group in the College of Education is faculty-driven and has developed as a learning community that provides collegial support around various educational technologies. Faculty are able to either attend the monthly meetings to discuss how they are using technologies, explore the resources online, or seek out one of the active faculty mem-

bers for more support. A few of the faculty in the College have emerged as go-to people, and the peer support tends to have a greater impact on faculty than attending a workshop.

Department-Level Supports Can also be Effective

Mary cited another example, "The Google Docs project with the Dance department emerged from conversations among faculty, and one faculty asked me to come work with a few faculty members in her department. The entire department bought in to the idea and supported the faculty that started it."

While university-level reforms have a broader impact, faculty within the same college and department tend to have similar content and pedagogical interests. Faculty are more likely to integrate technology if they have others working towards the same goal (Grant, 2004). However, department and college-level cultures can also impede technology integration. Faculty who are resistant to technology integration and have colleagues that share their opinion tend to spread a culture that does not support technology integration and efforts to try out new technology-rich pedagogies (Keengwe, Onchawari, & Wachira, 2008).

CONCLUSION

It is important to recognize that faculty perspectives on professional development and faculty perspectives on factors influencing technology integration at their institutions are inextricably linked. To this end and building on Lan's (2001) framework, Grant (2004) proposed four components for understanding faculty motivations for professional development:

1. environment, which encompasses the infrastructures necessary to support professional development, as well as the local departmental and institutional culture of the institution;
2. incentives and disincentives, which are the extrinsic factors, similar to Scribner's (1999) classification, that compose "the 'reward' and 'punishment' system" for faculty (Lan, 2001, p. 387);
3. motivations, which represent the intrinsic factors of "an individual's beliefs, value system and confidence" (Lan, 2001, p. 387); and
4. skills/knowledge, which are the competencies necessary to successfully integrate technology into a faculty member's pedagogy.

Some of these characteristics overlap with Caffarella and Zinn's (1999) factors that enhance or impede a faculty members' professional development over a career, including institutional structures, personal commitments, and intellectual characteristics.

Within the two cases presented, some commonalities exist. They are described below.

Technologies v. pedagogy in professional development. In both cases, technology integration was more effective when faculty members' learning were focused on pedagogy along with the technology, rather than just learning about technologies in isolation. The TFP program provided faculty with formal opportunities to redesign courses to integrate technology, but also received support on how to employ the technologies to leverage their teaching and their students' learning. Based on the interviews from the professional development center, both reported higher cases of technology integration when faculty learned about technologies, but received follow-up support in response to pedagogical issues, such as how to teach with the technologies. So, continuing to emphasize appropriate pedagogies with technology integration seems to promote the most value to faculty.

Emergence of PLCs and PLNs. The professional developers indicated successes among faculty who were participating in professional learning communities (PLCs). Faculty from the same College or Department came together to share ideas on how to use technologies in their courses to benefit students' learning. Further, access to blogs, online tutorials and other resources have increased the benefit of faculty's personal learning networks (PLNs). As more Web 2.0 tools and electronic resources develop, faculty will have increased opportunities to develop skills and knowledge related to technology integration. In turn, faculty will need increased information literacy skills so that they can effectively analyze technologies for their value and determine pedagogies that best support students' learning. Pairing these professional networks with the easy-to-learn Web 2.0 tools as described by Grant and Mims (2009) may offer the opportunities, as Steve in the professional development center aspired, for staff members to support instructional design issues primarily with recommendations for technologies to faculty.

Student learning is still the focus. As technology access continues to permeate institutions of higher education, it is essential to keep remembering that student learning needs to be the focus of technology integration and faculty professional development. Based on both the TFP and the interview with professional developers, faculty have had more success impacting student learning when their first question in planning technology instruction centers around, "How can technology support student's learning?" Further, faculty professional development should encompass all aspects of TPACK, developing how teachers' can impact their students' learning by developing knowledge of technology, pedagogy and content, and the intersections of the three domains.

Modifying university structures and organization. This chapter has provided two vignettes about issues related to technology integration in higher education. In the spirit of this book's focus on social and organizational structures, we offer a series of guiding questions to consider during the planning and design of technology integration professional development. What types of instructional support does your faculty require? How can you support technology skills through professional development while also addressing content and pedagogy? Does your university have the resources for a professional development center to focus solely or primarily on supporting technology integration? Is there a mechanism (e.g., website, wiki, blog, newsletter) to communicate to faculty innovative ways to use technology in their teaching? Are there faculty members who have the skill sets and willingness to mentor other faculty about technology integration?

As you consider the answers to these questions keep in mind that there is no one-size-fits-all model for professional development that always works. The research on components of effective professional development and faculty mentoring both describe this idea of learner-centered professional development where faculty are allowed to take ownership of their learning, focus on issues related to the content they teach, and are afforded sustained learning opportunities over time that focus on long-term development of knowledge and skills. From an organizational perspective, universities need to have a mechanism to gauge faculty's perceived needs and interests, and put in a variety of structures (e.g., workshops, mentoring systems, online resources, in class assistance) to support the range of faculty that exists in higher education settings.

REFERENCES

Abrami, P. C., Dehler, C., Schmid, R. F., Bernard, R. M., Lowerison, G., & Tamim, R. M. (2008). Assessing computer use and perceived course effectiveness in post-secondary education. *Journal of Educational Computing Research, 39*(3), 221–234. doi:10.2190/EC.39.3.b

Al-Senaidi, S., Lin, L., & Poirot, J. (2009). Barriers to adopting technology for teaching and learning in Oman. *Computers & Education, 53*(3), 575–590. doi:10.1016/j.compedu.2009.03.015

Bates, A. W., & Poole, G. (2003). *Effective teaching with technology in higher education: Foundations for success*. Indianapolis, IN: Jossey-Bass.

Bransford, J. D., Brown, A., & Cocking, R. (Eds.). (2000). *How people learn: Mind, brain, experience and school, Expanded Edition*. Washington, DC: National Academy Press.

Caffarella, R. S., & Zinn, L. F. (1999). Professional development for faculty: A conceptual framework of barriers and supports. *Innovative Higher Education, 23*(4), 241–254. doi:10.1023/A:1022978806131

Cambridge, D., Kaplan, S., & Suter, V. (2005). *Community of practice design guide A step-by-step guide for designing & cultivating communities of practice in higher education*. Washington, DC: EDUCAUSE National Learning Infrastructure Initiative. Retrieved January 15, 2010 from http://net.educause.edu/ir/library/pdf/NLI0531.pdf

Chism, N. (2004). Using a framework to engage faculty in instructional technologies. *EDUCAUSE Quarterly, 27*(2). Retrieved January 15, 2010 from http://www.educause.edu/EDUCAUSE+Quarterly/EDUCAUSEQuarterlyMagazineVolum/UsingaFrameworktoEngageFaculty/157291

Chuang, H. H., Thompson, A., & Schmidt, D. (2003). Faculty technology mentoring programs: Major trends in the literature. *Journal of Computing in Teacher Education, 19*(4), 101–106.

Cole, K., Simkins, M., & Penuel, W. R. (2002). Learning to teach with technology: Strategies for inservice professional development. *Journal of Technology and Teacher Education, 10*(3), 431–455.

DeGeorge, R. T. (1997). *Academic freedom and tenure: Ethical issues*. Oxford, UK: Rowman & Littlefield.

Diaz, V., Garrett, P. B., Kinley, E. R., Moore, J. F., Schwartz, C. M., & Kohrman, P. (2009). Faculty development for the 21st century. *EDUCAUSE Review, 44*(3), 46–55.

Dick, W., Carey, L., & Carey, J. O. (2009). *The systematic design of instruction*. Upper Saddle River, NJ: Merrill Pearson.

Garet, M., Porter, A., Desimone, L., Briman, B., & Yoon, K. (2001). What makes professional development effective? Analysis of a national sample of teachers. *American Educational Research Journal, 38*(4), 915–945. doi:10.3102/00028312038004915

Gikas, J., Penrod, J., Robertson, J. S., & Schaeffer, S. (2005, January 14). *Final report: NLII community of practice project University of Memphis: Technology Fellows Teaching and Learning Collaboration.* Washington, DC: National Learning Infrastructure Initiative. Retrieved January 15, 2009 from https://umdrive.memphis.edu/g-tfp/www/NLIIFinalReportTFP.pdf?uniq=m5tb9g

Grant, M. M. (2004). Learning to teach with the web: Factors influencing teacher education faculty. *The Internet and Higher Education, 7*, 329–341. doi:10.1016/j.iheduc.2004.09.005

Grant, M. M., & Mims, C. (2009). Web 2.0 in teacher education: Characteristics, implications and limitations. In Kidd, T., & Chen, I. (Eds.), *Wired for learning: An educators guide to Web 2.0* (pp. 343–360). Charlotte, NC: Information Age Publishing.

Howland, J., & Wedman, J. (2004). A process model for faculty development: Individualizing technology learning. *Journal of Technology and Teacher Education, 12*(2), 239–263.

Keengwe, J., Onchwari, G., & Wachira, P. (2008). Computer technology integration and student learning: Barriers and promise. *Journal of Science Education and Technology, 17*(6), 560–565. doi:10.1007/s10956-008-9123-5

Koehler, M. J., Mishra, P., Hershey, K., & Peruski, L. (2004). With a little help from your students: A new model for faculty development and online course design. *Journal of Technology and Teacher Education, 12*(1), 25–55.

Lan, J. (2001). Web-based instruction for education faculty: A needs assessment. *Journal of Research on Computing in Education., 33*(4), 385–399.

Lawless, K. A., & Pellegrino, J. W. (2007). Professional development in integrating technology into teaching and learning: Knowns, unknowns, and ways to pursue better questions and answers. *Review of Educational Research, 77*(4), 575–614. doi:10.3102/0034654307309921

Lee, J. (2001). Instructional support for distance education and faculty motivation, commitment, satisfaction. *British Journal of Educational Technology, 32*(2), 153–160. doi:10.1111/1467-8535.00186

Lowerison, G., Sclater, J., Schmid, R. F., & Abrami, P. C. (2006). Are we using technology for learning? *Journal of Educational Technology Systems, 34*(4), 401–425. doi:10.2190/ER58-3H7P-Y8FK-U8F7

Milliken, J., & Barnes, L. P. (2002). Teaching and technology in higher education: student perceptions and personal reflections. *Computers & Education, 39*(3), 223–235. doi:10.1016/S0360-1315(02)00042-8

Mims, C., Polly, D., & Grant, M. (2009). Technology integration in K-12. In M. K. Barbour & M. Orey (Eds.), *The Foundations of Instructional Technology*. Retrieved June 29, 2009, from http://projects.coe.uga.edu/ITFoundations/index.php?title=Technology_Integration_in_K-12

Mishra, P., & Koehler, M. J. (2006). Technological Pedagogical Content Knowledge: A framework for teacher knowledge. *Teachers College Record, 108*(6), 1017–1054. doi:10.1111/j.1467-9620.2006.00684.x

Mouza, C. (2002-2003). Learning to teach with new technology: Implications for professional development. *Journal of Research on Technology in Education, 35*(2), 272–289.

Niess, M. L. (2005). Preparing teachers to teach science and mathematics with technology: Developing a technology pedagogical content knowledge. *Teaching and Teacher Education, 21*, 509–523. doi:10.1016/j.tate.2005.03.006

Penuel, W., Fishman, B., Yamaguchi, R., & Gallagher, L. (2007). What makes professional development effective? Strategies that foster curriculum implementation. *American Educational Research Journal, 44*(4), 921–958. doi:10.3102/0002831207308221

Polly, D., & Brantley-Dias, L. (2009). TPACK: Where do we go now? *TechTrends, 53*(5), 46–47. doi:10.1007/s11528-009-0324-4

Polly, D., & Hannafin, M. J. (2010). Reexamining technology's role in learner-centered professional development. *Educational Technology Research and Development, 58*(5), 557–571. doi:10.1007/s11423-009-9146-5

Polly, D., Mims, C., Inan, F., & Shepherd, C. E. (2010). Evidence of impact: An analysis of the influence of PT3 Projects designed to transform methods courses and field experiences. *Teaching and Teacher Education, 26*(4), 863–870. doi:10.1016/j.tate.2009.10.024

Putnam, R., & Borko, H. (2000). What do new views of knowledge and thinking have to say about research on teaching? *Educational Researcher, 29*(1), 4–15.

Rogers, D. (2000). A paradigm shift: Technology integration for higher education in the new millenium. *AACE Journal*, *1*(13), 19–33.

Schacter, J. (1999). *The impact of education technology on student achievement: What the most current research has to say*. Santa Monica, CA: Milken Exchange on Education Technology.

Schrum, L., Skeele, R., & Grant, M. (2002-2003, Winter). One college of education's effort to infuse technology: A systematic approach to revisioning teaching and learning. *Journal of Research on Technology in Education*, *35*(2), 256–271.

Scribner, J. P. (1999). Professional development: Untangling the influence of work context on teacher learning. *Educational Administration Quarterly*, *35*(2), 238–266.

Shapiro, W. L. (1998). New ways to link technology and faculty development. *Change*, *30*(5), 50–53. doi:10.1080/00091389809602643

Stake, R. (1995). *The art of case research*. Thousand Oaks, CA: Sage Publications.

Taylor, R. (1980). *The computer in the school: Tutor, tool, tutee*. New York: Teachers College Press.

van Es, E. A., & Sherin, M. G. (2008). Learning to notice in the context of a video club. *Teaching and Teacher Education*, *24*(2), 244–276. doi:10.1016/j.tate.2006.11.005

Vescio, V., Ross, D., & Adams, A. (2006). *A review of research on professional learning communities: What do we know?* Retrieved February 16, 2008 from: http://www.nsrfharmony.org/research.vescio_ross_adams.pdf.

Weitz, R. R., Wachsmuth, B., & Mirliss, D. (2006). The Tablet PC For Faculty: A Pilot Project. *Journal of Educational Technology & Society*, *9*(2), 68–83.

Wenger, E. (1998). *Communities of practice: Learning, meaning, and identity*. Cambridge, UK: Cambridge University Press.

Weston, T. J. (2005). Why faculty did- and did not- integrate instructional software in their undergraduate classrooms. *Innovative Higher Education*, *30*(2), 99–115. doi:10.1007/s10755-005-5013-4

KEY TERMS AND DEFINITIONS

Faculty: Employees at either an institution of higher education or a PK-12 school.

Pedagogy: Instructional practices used in classrooms.

Professional Development: Any experience that leads to learning for current educators.

Technology Integration: The process of using technology as a tool to support the learning of content.

TPACK (Technological Pedagogical and Content Knowledge): A construct describing knowledge associated with effective technology integration (see http://www.tpck.org/)

Chapter 6
Legal Issues in the Use of Technology in Higher Education:
Copyright and Privacy in the Academy

Charles L. Guest Jr.
University of South Alabama, USA

Joyce M. Guest
University of South Alabama, USA

ABSTRACT

In recent years, explosive growth in the use of technology in higher education has resulted in numerous changes to institutional policy and practice. This chapter is focused upon two technology-related issues, copyright and privacy, that have had a significant impact on such policy and practice. The chapter includes a brief review of the historical context, of the legal dimensions, and of current practice related to these issues. As is also reflected in the body of literature on these topics, a heavier emphasis is placed on copyright.

INTRODUCTION

In recent years, innovations have led to exponential growth in the use of technology in higher education. As a result of this explosive and often unpredictable growth in the variety, the availability, and the use of technology, institutions of higher education have been forced to modify existing policies or to develop new policies to maintain legal practices. Policy development is perhaps most difficult when circumstances necessitate haste and when the potential consequences associated with the policies are significant. The rapid nature of technological innovation and the critical role played by technology in every aspect of today's society make for just such difficult

DOI: 10.4018/978-1-60960-147-8.ch006

circumstances. As might be expected under these circumstances, policies have had to be dynamic and change as technology changes. Additionally, issues that should have been addressed with policies may have been overlooked as newer and, perhaps, more important issues arose.

No one chapter could address all of the legal issue policy changes in higher education that were technology-driven in the past year, much less all of them over the past many years. As such, the focus of this chapter will be on two technology-related issues, copyright and privacy, that have had a significant impact on policy and practice in higher education. As is reflected in the literature, a heavier emphasis will be placed on the issues related to copyright.

The internet and World Wide Web are relative newcomers to the Academy but the opportunities they offer for the creation and dissemination of knowledge are virtually boundless. Granted, some of the educational issues related to the use of the internet existed prior to its development but these issues have had to be reassessed in light of the ease of information sharing offered through this medium. Copyright, for example, has been an issue for higher education at least since the development of the printing press. Although an argument can certainly be made that copyright issues only arose because of the use of technology (e.g. the printing press), for the purposes of this chapter, technology will refer to digital age issues such as the electronic storage and transmission of data, etc. In today's world, many copyright issues are specifically related to the use of such technology and were not an issue prior to the use of, for example, the internet and electronic communication. Another technology-related issue that has necessitated the development and/or reassessment of policies in higher education falls in the area of legal practices in electronic communication. Student and faculty privacy issues will be addressed later in this chapter.

COPYRIGHT

Copyright law is that body of law dealing with identifying and securing author rights with respect to writings and other creative works. These rights allow the author or creator to control the use of the work and the creation of derivative works by others. According to the United States Copyright Office (2009), copyright means, literally, "the right to copy" (p. 1) and the concept provides legal protection for "original works of authorship, including literary, dramatic, musical, architectural, cartographic, choreographic, pantomimic, pictorial, graphic, sculptural, and audiovisual creations" (p. 1). Copyright extends to the expression of an idea or discovery in some tangible medium and its protection begins the moment the idea or discovery is fixed in such a medium. Copyright does not extend to the idea itself but, rather, to the expression of the idea. A theory, for example, is not copyrightable but the paper in which the theory is described is copyrightable and may not be used, except in certain limited circumstances, without the author's permission.

The concept of owning the right to use, edit, reproduce, and perform or distribute your work dates, at least as evidenced by the codification of laws protecting such rights, to the period after the development of the printing press. Deazley (2004) indicated that, in England, laws such as the Licensing Act of 1662 protected printers, specifically the Company of Stationers, and granted them a near monopoly on rights related to publishing. Additionally, this act allowed for censorship of the press on the part of the monarch and government. In 1710, however, Parliament passed the Statute of Anne which established an author's ownership for a period of 14 years and, if the author was still alive, renewable for 14 more (Association of Research Libraries, 2009). In the United States, Congress enacted the first copyright law in 1790 and, in 1870, centralized copyright functions in the Library of Congress where they continue to reside (United States Copyright Office, 2009).

Copyright issues were contentious long before the digital era. In the 1700's, Defoe, Addison, and others argued about the rights of authors as opposed to the rights of printers, and the rights of the public. Once the issues were resolved and codified into law, however, copyright remained fairly static until the advent of the electronic age. In fact, "copyright law merited little attention within the academy" prior to the "rapid integration of digital technologies into American life" (Kaplin & Lee, p. 675). In today's digital world, copyright-related issues have once again become contentious and these issues directly impact higher education and the academy's role as a gatherer, creator, and disseminator of knowledge. Kenneth Crews, in a document created for the American Library Association (ALA), included the following pertinent summary of the expansion of copyright protection in the digital age:

Copyright protection vests automatically in nearly all works that are "original works of authorship" and "fixed in any tangible medium of expression" (Section 102(a)). Hence, most writings, images, artworks, videotapes, musical works, sound recordings, motion pictures, computer programs, and other works are protected by copyright law. That protection applies even if the work lacks any form of "copyright notice" and is not registered with the U.S. Copyright Office. Some works are in the "public domain" and do not have copyright protection. For example, works of the U.S. government are generally barred from copyright protection, and the copyrights on other works eventually expire. Copyrights today usually last through the life of the author, plus seventy years. Quite simply, the law protects vast quantities of works for many, many years. (Crews, 2002, p.2)

Copyright is, therefore, a critical issue for educators. Crews goes on to say that "when educators use any of these works in their teaching, they are using copyright-protected materials" (p. 2) but that, in the context of the traditional classroom, they were covered by the Copyright Act of 1976. The meaning of fair use, however, in the digital age is less clear. Materials uploaded to websites, transmitted electronically, altered, etc. pose "threats to the interests of copyright owners" (p. 2).

Fair Use and the TEACH Act

The concept of *Fair use*, sometimes referred to as the "fair use doctrine," is delineated in section 107 of the Copyright Act of 1976 (as amended). Fair use is intended to allow for the use of copyrighted materials without permission or payment when certain circumstances apply in which societal benefits from the use of the information outweigh any potential damages to the holder of the copyright (Bays, et al., 2009). This doctrine states that "notwithstanding the provisions of sections 106 and 106A, the fair use of a copyrighted work, including such use by reproduction in copies or phonorecords or by any other means specified by that section, for purposes such as criticism, comment, news reporting, teaching (including multiple copies for classroom use), scholarship, or research, is not an infringement of copyright" (§ 107). Fair use principles apply to all works protected by copyright. The doctrine also applies four tests in determining fair use: (a) commercial versus non-profit use, (b) the nature of the copyrighted work, (c) the amount used in proportion to the total work, and d) the effect of the use on the value of the work. Although these issues are outlined in the Act, they are broad and vague and interpretation is left to the courts (Kaplin & Lee, 2006). The creator of a faculty guide on fair use at the University of Texas called this concept "a shadowy territory whose boundaries are disputed, more so now that it includes cyberspace than ever before" (Harper, 2009, ¶ 1). Some guidance, however, can be found in subsequent documents related to the Act. Kaplin and Lee (2006) listed the Guidelines for Classroom Copying in Not-for-Profit Educational Institutions (H.R. Rep. No.

94-1476, 1976) and the Guidelines for the Proviso of Subsection 108(g)(2) (Conf. Rep. No. 94-1733, 1976), dealing with interlibrary lending, as helpful in further defining the provisions in section 107 of the Act. These additional guidelines established limits for copying for teaching, including multiple copies, but required the application of tests for brevity, for spontaneity of use, and for the cumulative effect of copying for the entire institution. These guidelines were not, however, universally accepted. In fact, the Association of American Law Schools and the American Association of University Professors "did not endorse the provisions and described them as too restrictive in the university setting" (Kaplin & Lee, 2006, p. 1336). Guidelines established in the 1990s through the Conference on Fair Use had even less consensus among professionals but are still recommended as "useful starting points" (p. 1336) by Kaplin and Lee (2006).

As fair use had its roots, at least in part, in the First Amendment, interpretation is fact and case specific and "taking advantage of fair use in education depends on the application of general principles to specific situations" (Bays et al., p. 3). Application of fair use standards is left to the courts and circumstances must be considered on a case-by-case basis. Guidelines, therefore, must be broad and allow for fact-specific differences in interpretation. Bays et al. (2009) reminded OER course developers that "bright line tests and rules of thumb are not appropriate to fair use analysis" (p. 3). These authors noted that "two common questions have emerged from the case law as core guiding principles for fair use reasoning . . . where material originally created with other goals in mind is being quoted in an educational setting" (p. 4). The question these authors identified were: (a) "Is the use transformative – that is, does it add value to and repurpose preexisting material for a new audience?" (p. 4); and (b) "Is the amount of material taken appropriate to the re-use?" (p. 4). In the context of the development and use of materials consistent with the Open Educational Resources (OER) movement, the authors stated that open resource products, when they appropriately incorporate preexisting materials, "are poised to fare well when these questions are applied to them" (p. 4). The University of Texas (Harper, 2009) publishes a web guide to fair use and, although they make the same argument as Bays et al. that "guidelines" are difficult to apply in fair use, this web guide includes a set of "rules of thumb" for fair use in an attempt to provide faculty with "short, concise, and easy to read" (¶ 4) steps in the application of fair use and recommendations for when to seek author permission.

With the advent of online education and, more recently, with the OER movement, questions have arisen regarding copyright in general and, more specifically, as to whether fair use continues to apply. Several legislative actions have been taken in an attempt to address these concerns. The Digital Millennium Copyright Act (DMCA) (1998) implemented the treaties of the World Intellectual Property Organization and specifically addressed issues related to copyright in the digital age. Among other things, the DMCA (a) added civil and criminal penalties for circumventing technological measures used to protect copyrighted works while including some exemptions for non-profit libraries, archives, and educational institutions, (b) limited liability for copyright infringement for nonprofit institutions of higher education, (c) addressed computer program copying when used for maintenance and repair, and (d) mandated a study of copyright issues in distance education (United States Copyright Office, 1999).

In 2002, the Technology Education and Harmonization (TEACH) Act further specified copyright issues related to educational use. Basically, the TEACH Act repealed Section 110(2) of the Copyright Act, originally drafted with only closed-circuit television in mind, and expanded "performance" beyond the traditional classroom environment. The new language allowed for the expansion of the range of allowed works, the type of receiving location, the ability to copy and store copyrighted content, and the digitizing of some analog works (Crews, 2002). Crews (2002) indicated that the TEACH Act offered significant improvements over section 110(2) of the Copyright Act (1976). Crews warned, however, that if institutions of higher learning wish to enjoy the advantages of the TEACH Act, they "will need to meet the law's rigorous requirements" (p. 1). This author also emphasized the importance of understanding that, although the TEACH Act is a clear indication of the value placed in distance education by Congress, the law is "built around a vision that distance education should occur in discrete installments, each within a confined span of time, and with all elements integrated a cohesive lecture-like package" (p. 3). Additionally, this author warned that the TEACH Act, while allowing fair use in the digital environment, provides important copyright safeguards that do not allow uploading of full works, extended access past that of a conventional teaching format, etc. The TEACH Act only applies to accredited non-profit educational institutions and includes institutional requirements for publicized copyright policies, student notification, access protection, notice of copyright on online materials, and technological measures to ensure copyright policy compliance (e.g. user authentication, print-disabling, copy/paste disabling, content timeouts, etc.) (Copyright Clearance Center, 2009). Additionally, the TEACH Act imposes duties on instructors. Instructors may not use works that are marketed as part of mediated instructional activities and they may not use copies of works that were not made and/or acquired in adherence with existing U.S. copyright law. The instructor must be a part of the planning and delivery of any distance course and must ensure that any display of copyrighted materials is an integrated part of the course and that such displays are directly relevant to teaching the specific material (Crews, 2002).

Universities are not required to use the TEACH Act, it is simply one option for the legal use of copyrighted works (Crews, 2009). The terms of the TEACH Act do not provide for the same generous legal use of copyrighted materials as provided for in section 110(1) of the Copyright Act for the traditional classroom educator but the TEACH Act does expand the scope of these rights in the digital classroom. Crews (2009) predicted that, although some institutions would rely on the provisions within the TEACH Act, others would continue to rely on permissions and the fair use doctrine. The TEACH Act clearly does not give the same rights in the distance environment as those enjoyed by faculty in the face-to-face environment. In fact, an educator moving a course from the on-campus to the digital environment may have to significantly cut down on the use of certain materials such as still images, music, and movies and use them only in limited portions directly applicable to the lesson (Harper, 2010). Because of the limitations of the TEACH Act, Harper (2010) indicated that some educators may conclude that its use is "more trouble than it is worth" (¶ 4). This author went on to say that "fair use is almost always going to be the best source for making copies" (¶ 4) because of its more broad permissions but recommended that, when the TEACH Act applies and you can comply with its conditions and limitations, faculty should use it.

In practice, institutions have everything from policy statements to checklists to online instruction agreements. An internet search for "TEACH Act Checklist" will make it readily apparent that hundreds of non-profit educational institutions have a policy and a checklist specific to the TEACH Act. A few of these seem to stand out and are frequently cited on general information sites. The National Education Association (NEA) directs its members (NEA, 2009) to the University of Texas system, through their Office of General Counsel, for a copyright "crash course" (University of Texas System, 2009; Kaplin & Lee, 2006 p. 1341) developed by Georgia Harper (2001). This "course" includes a review of TEACH Act provisions and a checklist for determining whether a faculty member should use the TEACH Act rather than the fair use test.

Many other institutions have similar policies with decisional checklists. Surprisingly, however, a review of non-profit educational institutional websites also found institutions without specific policies related to copyright. These institutions would not be able to use the provisions of the TEACH Act. Other institutions may have policies but may not be in compliance with the TEACH Act requirements. Faculty attempting to use the TEACH Act provisions at institutions with policies based solely on fair use without the inclusion of the TEACH Act provisions for online education could violate TEACH principles by not identifying how the materials are directly relevant and of material assistance to teaching the content of the course, how access is limited to the students in the class, how protective technologies are used, etc.

Copyright in an Open Educational Environment

With the advent of the Open Educational Resources movement, pioneered by the Massachusetts Institute of Technology in 2002 with its OpenCourseWare (OCW) initiative, and with the growth of this movement, "the problem of using copyrighted material has proliferated" (Bays, et al., 2009, p. 3). Bays, et al. (2009) indicated in their *Best Practices in Fair Use for OpenCourseWare* that citation of the works of others, including direct quotation, is an inherent component of higher education and of most scholarly materials. As such, these authors reminded developers of courses designed for an Open Educational Environment that either a license or the application of fair use will be required in order to incorporate these materials. As materials placed in an open versus a closed educational environment are much more likely to have an impact on the marketability or value of a copyrighted work, the potential for damages is much greater in this environment than in an environment in which a limited number of students would have access. The likelihood of a copyright violation being discovered would also, logically, be much greater in an open environment. With these additional concerns for the OER environment, a consortium of institutions interested in standardizing the delivery of OCW materials (the OCW Consortium) sponsored the development of *Best Practices in Fair Use for OpenCourseWare* (Bays, et al., 2009). As noted earlier, because of the unique nature of fair use and its roots in First Amendment issues, it would be difficult to establish a set of bright-line rules or rules of thumb. As such, the best practices identified by the OCW Consortium do not attempt to identify the limits of fair use in the use of OCW but, rather, describes how these rights apply in "certain recurrent situations" (p. 2). This set of best practices can be useful in guiding copyright decisions in the OER environment.

Bays et al. (2009), through a set of interviews of OCW developers, identified a set of six common copyright misconceptions. Some of those interviewed "expressed concern about showing corporate brand names and symbols in OCW" (p. 5) indicating that these OCW makers were confusing copyright with trademark. In fact, these authors indicated that the re-use of such brands and symbols is not regulated by copyright law but, rather, by trademark law, and, in educational settings, unless the use of such commercial identifiers is misleading or confuses consumers, the use would not be actionable under trademark law.

A second misconception identified by Bays et al. (2009) related to OCW makers hesitancy to incorporate works from the public domain, digitized by others, out of a concern that such use would create a new copyright. In reality, these authors stated that rarely would such preparation of a digitized version of an existing public domain work merit protection any more than would photocopies.

A third misconception identified by these authors related to what they labeled a fear of "secondary liability" (Bays et al., 2009, p. 5). Some OCW makers apparently indicated a concern that they "might be legally responsible for public access uses made of materials they provide" where, in reality, "OCW generally can be distributed safely despite such concerns about so-called 'secondary liability'" and OCW providers will not be liable for public access uses "unless they encourage unlawful uses, have advanced knowledge that materials will be misused, or receive a direct financial benefit from such misuse" (p. 5).

The fourth common misconception that surfaced in the Bays et al. (2009) interviews involved the belief of a few OCW makers that materials found on the Web could be used without copyright concerns. In reality, these authors reminded OCW developers that "much online material is copyright protected" (p. 5). The example used by these authors was of a music snippet from Amazon.com. The presence of the snippet on the Web only indicates that it has been made available for specific use and these snippets "are no less (or more) subject to copyright protection than equivalent passages gleaned from commercial recordings in other formats" (p. 5).

A fifth misconception identified by Bays et al. (2009) was that many OCW makers believed that all copyrights were of equal strength and extent. According to these authors, the reality is that fact-intensive works receive less protection than do creative works. Because of this disparity, the concept of fair use applies more broadly to fact-intensive works and these works can be "used fairly in a wider variety of contexts than more creative ones" (p. 5).

The final misconception identified in the Bays et al. (2009) interviews involved OCW makers misestimating the scope of fair use. Apparently, there was a common misunderstanding among OCW makers that fair use applies differently to text versus music and in the analog versus the digital format. In reality, according to Bays et al., fair use applies to all mediums and formats. Another confusion related to the scope of fair use was that some OCW makers believed that it was automatic for non-profit educational activities but not for commercial activities. These authors stated that, in fact, some commercial uses do qualify as fair use and some non-profit educational uses may not qualify.

Clearly, copyright issues have changed for educational institutions since the beginning of the digital age of instruction. Institutions should be aware of the critical need for clear policies related to the use of copyrighted materials. Non-profit institutions should also follow institutions such as the University of Texas and develop policies that allow for the most flexible legal use of copyrighted materials under both fair use and TEACH Act provisions. Surprisingly, given the court system's strict interpretation of copyright issues, educational institutions have, for the most part, been able to stay out of court (Kaplin & Lee, 2006). According to Kaplin and Lee (2006), this ability to stay off of the radar may be due to efforts by universities to respond quickly and in good faith to infringement allegations. The music industry, specifically the Recording Industry Association of America, began to sue its customers directly for copyright infringement in 2001 (Kaplin & Lee, 2006). In light of this potential for civil liability, educational institutions should continue to act in good faith and in a timely manner in response to allegations of infringement. Additionally, faculty should remain cognizant of the civil penalties but also of the potential criminal penalties for copyright infringement. Public Law Number 102-561 (1992) established criminal penalties for copyright infringement and made certain violations felonies punishable by fines or imprisonment (Kaplin & Lee, 2006; Criminal Infringement of a Copyright, 2008). Although a good faith effort to adhere to fair use and TEACH Act provisions will probably protect faculty members, willful violations of copyright law could lead to PL 102-561 criminal penalties and could bring about career-ending consequences. Extensive Web resources are available to help institutions and faculty avoid copyright violations and, although copyright law is complicated, circumstance-dependent, and ever-changing, the basic principles of fair use and of the TEACH Act are not difficult to understand in the context of educational use.

Copyright Ownership

While policies related the appropriate use of copyrighted materials created by external authors are essential for institutions, internal issues should also be addressed with policy. Institutions vary greatly in their approaches to faculty ownership versus institutional ownership of online materials (Laughlin, 2000). In copyright law, a work is considered a “work-for-hire” when the work is produced by an employee within the scope of their employment. According to Blanchard (2009), within the work-for-hire doctrine, “through *de facto* custom and court dicta, academics may enjoy a ‘teacher exception’ that grants them copyright ownership of publications and course materials” (p. 1). This traditional exception to work-for-hire “has blurred as institutions are investing in distance education and commissioning faculty members to create online courses” (Blanchard, 2009, p. 1). Laughlin (2000) addressed the competing interests of faculty and institutions in light of the new markets created by the use of the internet for education. In his article, he examined the use of technology by educators and the status of copyright law as it applies to works created by faculty. Laughlin stated that, without further amendments to the Copyright Act or clear institutional guidelines, clear answers to copyright ownership of materials created for distance learning may be difficult to find. Additionally, this author warned that, as with other copyright concerns, case law may not provide meaningful guidance as each case will be fact specific. Because case law has not and probably will not settle teacher exception issues, Laughlin recommended that “educators and universities should have policies that clearly spell out the respective rights of the parties so as to avoid litigation and lost opportunities for profit from educator-created works” (p. 581). Laughlin stated that institutions should build these policies to address ownership and licensing to meet the continuing use needs of all parties so the incentives for developing the materials are retained. Additionally, Laughlin recommended that policies, to the extent possible, be created to deal with all forseeable types of work and not be limited to existing media. This author also stated that a separate written agreement for the production of distance works is preferable to reliance solely on employment contracts or faculty policies.

Copyright policies in higher education generally include one of three types of ownership: (a) university ownership, (b) faculty ownership, or (c) joint ownership (Zhang & Carr-Chellman, 2006). Sample policies are available from various sources but two particularly distinct sets of recommendations come from the Association of American Universities (AAU) and the American Association of University Professors (AAUP). According to Zhang and Carr-Chellman, the AAU model “primarily represents the interests of the higher education institution” (p. 177). These authors stated that the AAU argues that, as courseware is a collaborative creation, the university should own the intellectual property. The AAU’s approach views ownership in a similar manner to patent ownership which traditionally remains with the institution in the absence of a specific agreement or policy to the contrary. Zhang and Carr-Chellman cautioned that such an approach could impact academic freedom and the mobility of faculty and, therefore, reduce the motivation for faculty to expend effort in the design and development of courseware. An approach that, according to Zhang and Carr-Chellman, is much more representative of faculty interests is recommended by the AAUP. The AAUP recommends that intellectual property ownership should remain with the faculty creator except as they voluntarily choose to transfer such ownership (AAUP, 2010). The AAUP policy language includes exceptions for made-for-hire works when using extraordinary university resources, for negotiated contractual transfers, and for joint works with the institution as co-author. Regardless of the direction chosen by an institution in developing an ownership policy it is clear that they have a vested interest in protecting the right to use, edit, and revise course materials created with their resources and any policy should clearly protect these interests.

Creative Commons

An option for copyright owners wishing to specify allowed uses of their materials came into existence in 2001 with the creation of Creative Commons (2010). Creative Commons licenses allow authors to clearly indicate which rights they reserve and which rights they waive in reference to their works. Wikipedia, for example, is one of the fairly recent web-based concerns operating under Creative Commons licensing. Though the intent of Creative Commons was to "increase the amount of creativity (cultural, educational, and scientific content) in 'the commons' — the body of work that is available to the public for free and legal sharing, use, repurposing, and remixing" (Creative Commons, 2010, ¶ 1), not all scholars are enamored with the concept and criticism ranges from a view that Creative Commons is unnecessary in light of current copyright law (Toth, 2009), to a view that Creative Commons is only a "quick fix" to copyright law problems and is allowing a delay in properly addressing those problems and a view that Creative Commons could erode the copyright system over time (Dvorak, 2005).

CRITICAL COMMONS

An additional option supporting the use of media for teaching and learning is Critical Commons, a network resource established by John Anderson and Holly Willis through a grant from the John D. and Catherine T. MacArthur Foundation (Critical Commons, 2010.) Critical Commons was designed to "promote, engage and organize academic communities to articulate their needs, models and ethical principles surrounding the 'fair use' of copyrighted materials in teaching and research" (Critical Commons, 2010, ¶ 2). Critical Commons provides information about copyright practices "in order to facilitate the writing and dissemination of best practices and fair use guidelines for scholarly and creative communities" (About Us, 2010, ¶ 1). Critical Commons also serves to showcase innovative forms of electronic scholarship and creative works that are "transformative, culturally enriching and both legally and ethically defensible" (¶ 1). Critical Commons includes an online tool to facilitate "viewing, tagging, sharing, annotating and curating media within the guidelines established by a given community" (¶ 1).

STUDENT AND FACULTY PRIVACY

Student privacy was a concern for institutions of higher education long before the digital age. The Family Educational Rights and Privacy Act (FERPA) (1974) placed significant protections on student records. This Act applies to all public or private educational institutions that receive federal funding from the United States Department of Education or whose students receive federal student aid or loan guarantees (Kaplin & Lee, 2009). FERPA "does not invalidate common law or statutory law applicable to student records" but it has become "the predominant legal consideration in dealing with student records" (Kaplin & Lee, p. 269). FERPA contains provisions that give parents of children under the age of 18 attending school through the high school level access to their educational records. Additionally, eligible students (i.e. those students 18 years of age or older and those attending a school beyond high school) are given access to their educational records. Parents and eligible students also have the right under FERPA to challenge the content of the records and, should the school refuse to amend the record, the right to a formal hearing. FERPA also includes provisions requiring institutions to protect, with certain exceptions, the confidentiality of student records. Allowable exceptions to FERPA's confidentiality provisions include releasing information (a) to other school personnel with a legitimate educational interest, (b) to transfer schools, (c) for audit and evaluation purposes, (d) for financial aid, (e) for certain forms of research, (f) to comply with a court order, (g) for health and safety emergencies, and (h) to State and local authorities according to specific State law (although, under 34 CFR § 99.35 (a) (2) (2009), it is noted that FERPA itself does not provide the authority for disclosing these records and a separate legal basis for such disclosure would be required.) FERPA also requires institutions to notify parents and eligible students of their rights on an annual basis.

Changes in the use of technology by educational institutions (e.g. electronic storage of information, online course delivery, etc.) have led to modifications to FERPA (2009). To include the records of distance forms of learning under FERPA, the definition of "attendance" (34 CFR § 99.3) was redefined to include all types of distance learning. The actual terminology used in the new language is "attendance in person or by paper correspondence, videoconference, satellite, Internet, or other electronic information and telecommunications technologies for students who are not physically present in the classroom" (34 CFR § 99.3, 2009) whereas the old definition was "attendance in person or by correspondence" (34 CFR § 99.3, 1974).

Other technology-related issues, such as identity theft, have also led to modifications to FERPA. FERPA (2009) now explicitly excludes social security numbers and student identity numbers (i.e. those that allow access to student records without an additional password or PIN) from disclosable directory information. Additionally, FERPA now (a) requires educational institutions to obtain written consent before using student social security numbers to search records, (b) has language that includes information such as date or place of birth and mother's maiden name as part of a student's personally identifiable information excluded from directory disclosure, and (c) requires institutions to use "reasonable methods to identify and authenticate the identity of parents, students, school officials, and any other parties to whom the agency or institution discloses personally identifiable information from education records" (34 CFR § 99.31 (c), 2009).

Advances in the use of biometrics to replace passwords have also led to changes in FERPA. The term "biometric record" was added to the definition of "personally identifiable information" and this term was defined as "a record of one or more measurable biological or behavioral characteristics that can be used for automated recognition of an individual" (34 CFR § 99.3, 2009). Examples given in FERPA for biometric information include fingerprints, retinal and iris patterns, voiceprints, DNA sequences, facial features, and handwriting.

The U.S. Patriot Act (2001) has also had an impact on FERPA. This Act, along with many other things, impacts privacy issues for students and for faculty by permitting federal investigators to access private communications (e.g. telephone, computer) (Kaplin & Lee, 2009). The Act amended FERPA to allow access, with an appropriate court order, to student records without consent and without a requirement notify the student or to record the disclosure.

As technology continues to change, FERPA issues will continue to change. Kaplin and Lee (2009) cautioned educational administrators against using secondary sources to interpret FERPA. These authors recommended working with copies of the most current version of the statute to, in conjunction with legal counsel, develop FERPA-related policies.

The prolific use of technology has had an impact on the privacy of faculty as well. The right to privacy and to protection from unreasonable search and seizure, guaranteed under the Fourth Amendment to the U.S. Constitution, was not created with technology in mind. This amendment does provide some expectation of privacy for faculty at public institutions (Euben, 2005). Faculty files stored on computer hard drives and faculty e-mail communication may, however, be a different issue and may depend on the respective institution's computer use policies (Kaplin & Lee, 2009). In *O'Connor v. Ortega* (1987), a case involving the search of the office of the director of a psychiatry residency program, the U.S. Supreme Court ruled that public employees may have reasonable expectations of privacy in their offices, desks, and files and that these expectations may be protected by the Fourth Amendment. The Court, however, also indicated the need for a case-by-case review to determine the application of a Fourth Amendment protection. In fact, several Justices "asserted that an employer's warrantless search of such property would nevertheless be permissible if it is done for non-investigatory, work-related purposes or for investigations of work-related misconduct and if it meets the standard of reasonableness under all the circumstances" (Kaplin & Lee, 2009, p. 203) and that an employee's expectation of privacy may be limited in light of specific office policies or by regulations (Euben, 2005).

In *United States v. Angevine* (2002), a case of a professor at Oklahoma State University who pled guilty to possessing child pornography, a federal appellate court held that a university professor had no reasonable expectation of privacy on an office computer, owned by the institution, because the University had a policy that provided for the inspection of such computers and that explicitly reserved University ownership of such computers and of the data stored on such computers. The appellate court went on to say that, because the computer was issued for work-related purposes, the professor's relationship to the University computer only existed because of his employment. As such, the Court stated that a reasonable person in Professor Angevine's position would not have had the expectation of privacy for the information stored on the University computer. This decision and its lack of discussion of the academic context of the case may suggest that courts are not following the directive of the O'Connor case to consider the context on a case-by-case basis (Euben, 2005). Additionally, the limited case law for private institutions "suggests that private colleges and universities may have even more leeway in restricting employee expectations of computer privacy" (Euben, 2005, p. 126).

Euben (2005) stated that, although "the law may allow a university to restrict faculty privacy in e-mail communications, the law does not require it to do so" (p. 126). Euben went on to note, however, that "many administrations have taken the O'Connor decision to its logical, albeit circular, endpoint: policies asserting that no expectation of privacy exists for faculty establish that faculty have no expectation of privacy" (p. 126). Some institutions, however, such as Rensselaer Polytechnic and the University of Michigan, have policies providing that "electronic mail and computer files are considered private to the fullest extent permitted by law" (Euben, p. 126)

CONCLUSION

In recent years, the explosive growth in the use of technology in institutions of higher education has necessitated numerous changes to institutional policies and practices. As it would take a several volume set to effectively outline all of the issues that have impacted the Academy in the digital age, this chapter focused on only two: copyright and privacy. From a review of these issues, it is clear that institutions of higher education must closely monitor the need for new policies and must monitor the relevance of existing policies related to copyright and privacy. For copyright, it is critical that institutions have policies addressing fair use and, for public institutions wishing to expand their options for the use of copyrighted materials, policies related to the TEACH Act. It is also critical for institutions to maintain policies on copyright ownership that protect the rights of the university with respect to the continued to use of materials developed by faculty while also protecting the rights of the faculty members to their respective work. These policies should clearly specify ownership and usage rights and stipulate when work-for-hire situations apply. In addition to these policies, institutions should invest in regular training for employees on copyright issues. Institutions of higher education need to also be aware of copyright issues in the context of Open Educational Environments and should develop training for faculty to avoid the common misconceptions identified by Bays et al. (2009). As for issues of privacy, institutions should closely monitor FERPA as the law changes to reflect the use of technology and should establish and maintain policies related to faculty privacy that address electronic communication, file storage, video surveillance, and other technology-related issues.

REFERENCES

About Us. (2010). *About us: Critical Commons.* Retrieved April 30, 2010 from http://criticalcommons.org/about-us

American Association of University Professors. (2010). *Sample intellectual property policy and contract language.* Retrieved January 10, 2010 from http://www.aaup.org/AAUP/issues/DE/sampleIP.htm

Association of Research Libraries. (2009). *Influencing public policies: Copyright & intellectual property policies.* Retrieved December 16, 2009, from http://www.arl.org/pp/ppcopyright/copyresources/copytimeline.shtml

Bays, T., Carchidi, D., Carter-Galvan, S., Chambers, P., Fons, G., Gooding, I., et al. (2009). *Code of best practices in fair use for Opencourseware.* Created for the OCW Consortium. Retrieved January 5, 2010 from http://www.centerforsocialmedia.org/files/pdf/10-305-OCW-Oct29.pdf

Blanchard, J. (2009). *The teacher exception under the work for hire doctrine: Safeguard of academic freedom or vehicle for academic free enterprise?* Dordrecht, Netherlands: Springer Netherlands.

H.R. Conf. Rep. No. 94-1733 (1976).

Copyright Act, 17 U.S.C. § 101 *et seq*. (1976).

Copyright Clearance Center. (2009). *The TEACH Act: New roles and responsibilities for academic institutions.* Retrieved December 17, 2009 from http://www.copyright.com/media/pdfs/CR-Teach-Act.pdf

Creative Commons. (2010). *What is creative commons?* Retrieved January 10, 2010 from http://creativecommons.org/about/what-is-cc

Crews, K. (2002). *New copyright law for distance education: The meaning and importance of the TEACH Act.* Created for the American Library Association. Retrieved December 16, 2009 from http://www.ala.org/ala/issuesadvocacy/copyright/activelegislation/distanceed/teachsummary.pdf

Crews, K. (2009). *The TEACH Act and some frequently asked questions.* Created for the American Library Association. Retrieved December 17, 2009 from http://www.ala.org/ala/issuesadvocacy/copyright/activelegislation/distanceed/teachfaq.cfm

Criminal Infringement of a Copyright, 18 U.S.C. § 2319 (2008).

Criminal Penalties for Copyright Infringement, Pub. L. No. 102-561, 106 Stat. 4233 (1992).

Critical Commons. (2010). *Critical Commons: Faculty members receive grant to promote digital fair use.* Retrieved April 30, 2010 from http://cinema.usc.edu/about/news/critical-commons.htm

Deazley, R. (2004). *On the origin of the right to copy: charting the movement of copyright law in eighteenth century Britain (1695-1775).* Oxford, UK: Hart Publishing.

Digital Millennium Copyright Act, Pub. L. No. 105-304, 112 Stat. 2860 (1998).

Dvorak, J. (2005, July 18). Creative commons humbug. *PC Magazine,* Retrieved January 10, 2010 from http://www.pcmag.com/article2/0,2817,1838244,00.asp

Euben, D. (2005). Legal watch: Electronic citizenship. *Academe*, *91*(2), 126. doi:10.2307/40253418

Family Educational Rights and Privacy Act, 20 U.S.C. § 1232g (1974).

Family Educational Rights and Privacy Act, 20 U.S.C. § 1232g (2009 amended) Retrieved December 21, 2009 from http://ecfr.gpoaccess.gov/cgi/t/text/text-idx?c=ecfr;sid=6b7e313020dfabb7caa0216830b2a7d8;rgn=div5;view=text;node=34%3A1.1.1.1.34;idno=34;cc=ecfr

Harper, G. (2001). *Copyright crash course*. Retrieved December 16, 2009 from The University of Texas System, Office of General Counsel Web site: http://www.utsystem.edu/OGC/IntellectualProperty/copypol2.htm

Harper, G. (2009). *Fair use of copyrighted materials*. Retrieved December 16, 2009 from The University of Texas System, Office of General Counsel Web site: http://www.utsystem.edu/OGC/IntellectualProperty/Cprtindx.htm

Harper, G. (2010). *The TEACH Act finally becomes law*. Retrieved January 6, 2010 from The University of Texas System, Office of General Counsel Web site: http://www.utsystem.edu/OGC/IntellectualProperty/teachact.htm

Kaplin, W. A., & Lee, B. A. (2006). *The law of higher education: A comprehensive guide to legal implications of administrative decision making* (4th ed.). San Francisco: Jossey-Bass.

Kaplin, W. A., & Lee, B. A. (2009). *A legal guide for student affairs professionals* (2nd ed.). San Francisco: Jossey-Bass.

Laughlin, G. K. (2000). Who owns the copyright to faculty-created web sites?: The work-for-hire doctrine's applicability to internet resources created for distance learning and traditional classroom courses. *Boston College Law Review. Boston College. Law School*, *41*, 549–583.

National Education Association. (2009). *TEACH Act highlights and resources*. Retrieved December 18, 2009 from http://www.nea.org/home/35377.htm

O'Connor v. Ortega, 480 U.S. 709 (1987).

H.R. Rep. No. 94-1476 (1976).

Technology, Education, and Copyright Harmonization Act, Pub. L. No. 107-273, §13301 116 Stat. 1910 (2002).

Tóth. Péter Benjamin (2009), *Creative humbug*. Retrieved January 10, 2010 from www.indicare.org/tiki-read_article.php?articleld=118

United States Copyright Office. (1999). *Statement of Marybeth Peters the Register of Copyrights before the Committee on the Judiciary.* Retrieved December 16, 2009, from http://www.copyright.gov/docs/regstat52599.html

United States Copyright Office. (2009). *United States Copyright Office: A brief introduction and history, Circular 1a.* Retrieved December 16, 2009, from http://www.copyright.gov/circs/circ1a.html

United States v. Angevine, 281 F.3d 1130 (10th Cir. 2002), cert. denied, 537 U.S. 845 (2002)

University of Texas System. (2009). *Copyright crash course: The TEACH Act finally becomes a law.* Retrieved December 17, 2009 from http://www.utsystem.edu/ogc/intellectualproperty/teachact.htm

USA Patriot Act, Pub. L. No. 107-56, 116 Stat. 272 (2001).

Zhang, K., & Carr-Chellman, A. (2006). Courseware copyrights: Whose rights are right? *Journal of Educational Computing Research, 34*(2), 173–186. doi:10.2190/AM4M-97MF-FJCV-PA1U

KEY TERMS AND DEFINITIONS

Copyright: This concept provides legal protection for original works and extends to the expression of an idea or discovery in some tangible medium.

Creative Commons: An option for copyright owners wishing to specify which rights they reserve and which rights they waive in reference to their works. The intent of Creative Commons was to increase materials available to the public for free and legal use.

Fair Use: Also referred to as the "fair use doctrine," this concept is delineated in section 107 of the Copyright Act of 1976 (as amended). Fair allows for the use of copyrighted materials without permission or payment when certain circumstances apply.

Family Educational Rights and Privacy Act (FERPA) (1974): This Act placed significant protections on student records for all public or private educational institutions that receive federal funding and contains provisions that give parents of children under the age of 18 and eligible students (18 years of age or older or attending a school beyond high school) access to their educational records. Parents and eligible students also have the right under this Act to challenge the content of the records and, should the school refuse to amend the record, the right to a formal hearing.

O'Connor v. Ortega **(1987):** A case involving the search of the office of the director of a psychiatry residency program for which the U.S. Supreme Court ruled that public employees may have reasonable expectations of privacy in their offices, desks, and files and that these expectations may be protected by the Fourth Amendment. The Court indicated the need for a case-by-case review to determine the application of Fourth Amendment protection and asserted that an employee's expectation of privacy could be limited by specific policies or regulations.

Technology Education and Harmonization (TEACH) Act: This Act repealed Section 110(2) of the Copyright Act and expanded "performance" beyond the traditional classroom environment to allow for the expansion of the range of allowed works, the type of receiving location, the ability to copy and store copyrighted content, and the digitizing of some analog works. The TEACH Act only applies to accredited non-profit educational institutions and includes institutional requirements for publicized copyright policies, student notification, access protection, notice of copyright on online materials, and technological measures to ensure copyright policy compliance.

United States v. Angevine **(2002):** A case of a professor at Oklahoma State University who pled guilty to possessing child pornography in which a federal appellate court held that a university professor had no reasonable expectation of privacy on an office computer, owned by the institution, because of the existence of a University policy that provided for the inspection of such computers and that explicitly reserved University ownership of such computers and of the data stored on such computers.

Chapter 7
Growing a University's Technological Infrastructure:
Strategies for Success

Stephen R. Rodriguez
Texas A&M University—Corpus Christi, USA

ABSTRACT

This chapter considers concepts, planning models, and related processes associated with infrastructure growth at institutions of higher learning. The author offers various definitions of infrastructure, describes an infrastructure maturity model, and discusses strategies and models for related strategic planning. In addition, the chapter provides portions of actual strategic plans related to infrastructure. The chapter closes with a description of how the author's home institution has grown its technological infrastructure in order to provide required administrative services, communications, and instruction to a growing student body engaged in an expanding curriculum. The impact of infrastructure growth on the university community is also discussed.

INTRODUCTION

Using technology to administer to nearly 10,000 students at a growing regional institution of higher education such as Texas A&M University-Corpus Christi (TAMUCC) stands as an ongoing challenge. Most all institutions of higher education face the same challenge. The many aspects of university administration that must be addressed include student enrollment and financial management, library services, distance education delivery, telecommunications, smart classrooms, budget management, software licensing, desktop computing, computer lab management, and computer network security, and e-mail among other things. Completing these tasks effectively and efficiently

DOI: 10.4018/978-1-60960-147-8.ch007

requires that a given institution maintain an adequate technological infrastructure. This chapter explores in largely non-technical terms considerations for growing the required infrastructure. Specific objectives for this chapter, then, include the following:

- To define technological infrastructure
- To describe an infrastructure maturity model
- To define strategic planning
- To describe some recommended strategic planning processes
- To provide real-world examples of strategic planning concerning infrastructure
- To describe the general strategy used at TAMUCC to grow its technological infrastructure
- To describe the impact of infrastructure growth on the university community

The chapter's overall purposes are to provide insights, models, examples, and guidance on infrastructure planning to others who are interested in such planning but are not necessarily technology experts. The author's underlying thesis is that infrastructure planning is a critical process for institutions of higher education to complete if they are to deliver required administrative, communication, and instructional service for optimum success and efficiency. So the problem at hand is to describe some planning options and related concepts and to suggest some effective planning approaches and strategies.

WHAT IS INFORMATION TECHNOLOGY INFRASTRUCTURE?

As is often the case, definitions of critical concepts such information technology infrastructure (ITI) vary from author to author. Kling (1992) describes computing infrastructure as the types of resources that are required to effectively operate computerized systems. Kling and others suggest that infrastructure consists of both human resources who deal with professional development and support and technology, dealing with hardware, software, and facilities. Gartner (2007), a technology consulting group, defines ITI as a system of software and service components that supports the delivery of applications and IT-enabled processes. IT infrastructure can also be conceived of as the combined human capabilities and IT resources that a given organization shares in support of the use of technology applications to complete business processes and as a "... distributed technical framework in support of user and enterprise computing" (University of California Davis, 2003, p.1).

GARTNER'S INFRASTRUCTURE MATURITY MODEL

Gartner (2007) developed a six-level infrastructure maturity model. The model's purpose is to enable an organization to conduct self-evaluation and to develop a strategic plan in order to reduce infrastructure costs, increase agility, and improve management of services and staff development. Agility in this context refers to the ability of a given network's software and hardware components to automatically control themselves across varied network devices. The model is not dependent upon specific vendors or products. The model may be modified to any organization's unique goals, including institutions of higher education.

Three concepts are foundational to the Gartner's model: consolidation, virtualization, and real-time infrastructure. Consolidation allows an organization to increase its server utilization by consolidating physical servers and applications. This results in lower hardware, maintenance and electrical costs. Reduced costs are also realized by making better use of technologies by sharing of resources. Related to this concept is virtualization: this allows "The pooling of resources in a way that masks the physical nature and boundaries of those resources from the resource users" (Gartner, 2007, p. 18). The third concept is known as real-time infrastructure. According to Gartner, such an infrastructure is agile, low cost, and highly reliable. It provides for shared access to resources across users, work units, and applications. Dynamic and automatic optimization allows for flexibility and readiness in addressing changing organizational and business needs.

The model's six levels are as follows:

1. **Survival:** At this stage, the ITI is characterized as chaotic and reactive. There are no service-level agreements (SLAS). Little is known about the infrastructure which is run on an ad hoc basis. Changes take weeks to months.

NOTE: A service level agreement (SLA) is a mechanism for outsourcing computing services to an external vendor. Based upon a contract between the vendor and the institution, the SLA specifies that the service provider deliver a particular level of service regarding the software and hardware to be provided. The SLA also includes penalties if services are not delivered as agreed. Examples here would include system downtime or inadequate support for end-users.

2. **Standardized:** The objectives at this level are to reduce complexity and fix costs. There is an effort to centralize control, and some SLAS are used. Management is both proactive and reactive, and changes take weeks.
3. **Rationalized:** The goals here are to employ economies of scale and make rationale use of resources. Classes of SLAS are employed. The organization of the infrastructure is consolidated, and management is proactive and problem-oriented. Changes take weeks to days.
4. **Virtualized:** At this level, resources are pooled in way that hides the physical nature and boundaries of the resources from the end-users (Gartner, 2007). The objectives are to reduce costs and increase flexibility. Costs are fixed and shared, and there is flexible use of SLAS. Resources are pooled in terms of ownership and use. At this level, management is proactive and predictive with dynamic capacity. Change takes from minutes to weeks.
5. **Service-Aligned:** The objective here is to optimize service-level delivery. This level utilizes end-to-end SLAS and resources are organized as service-oriented pools. Management is holistic and focuses upon end-to-end SLAS, and changes can occur within minutes.
6. **Business Partnership:** This level is characterized by dynamic organization and extensive use of SLAS to insure agility. Resources are utilized based upon policy-based sharing and are business-oriented. Management focuses upon value and policy development. Changes can happen in seconds or minutes.

Gartner's maturity model provides a useful self-evaluation tool related to developing a strategic plan for a cost-efficient, effective, flexible, and responsive information technology infrastructure. Since the model is independent of specific vendors and products, it has applicability for the goals and missions of a variety of types of organizations including institutions of higher education. It stands as a useful conceptual planning tool for any organization seeking to strengthen its technology infrastructure regardless of its current status.

THE CRITICALITY OF STRATEGIC PLANNING FOR TECHNOLOGY INFRASTRUCTURE GROWTH

Many universities incorporate infrastructure planning in strategic planning for technology. According to Search for Common Ground (2004), definitions of strategic planning vary. In a general sense, strategic planning is a management tool. Three primary elements are involved:

- Making basic decisions and planning actions to guide an organization toward the future
- Preparing the optimal manner by which to respond to the environment
- Integrating reflection and communication in the developing the actual plan

Titthasiri (2001) offers a cogent raison d'être for strategic technology planning at universities:

Its role in facilitating focused on both administrative and academic areas, where IT is being used in university management, administrative processes, improvement of research, and the teaching learning process. Because IT is rapidly changing with no fixed limits, universities need a strategic plan to guide their future development. (p.153)

The author further argues that a strategic technology plan will assist a given institution in addressing budgetary challenges for IT investments, be more responsive to a changing IT environment, provide adequate technical support, and develop software and tools in support of research, teaching, and administration.

INFRASTRUCTURE PLANNING: SOME EXAMPLES

Most every institution of higher learning has some type of long range plan concerning technology and infrastructure in place. Today's institutions of learning simply cannot achieve their missions, complete required work processes and services, and deliver high quality instruction unless the proper technological tools are in place. The University of California at Davis (UCD) provides but one example of a technology strategic plan which addresses infrastructure development and includes related mission and vision statements. The UCD document notes that technology infrastructure provides the foundation for an increasingly distributed academic and administrative computing environment. "Hidden from the application-based world of end-users, technology infrastructure encompasses the unseen realm of *middleware*, *protocols*, and *networks* that bind the computing enterprise together and facilitate efficient data flows" (UCD, 2003, p. 1). The authors go on to note a critical emerging and recurring perspective: infrastructure involves more than the mechanics of data systems but also includes the people providing related support and services.

The mission for UCD's infrastructure is "To provide a robust technical framework for user and enterprise computing, and to broaden the University's capabilities for applying information technology within the enterprise" (2003, p. 2). The related vision is "To develop a state-of-the-art technical infrastructure, and to support a culture of innovation that expands the campus's technological horizons" (2003, p. 2). It is no doubt a useful exercise for planning groups to go through the exercise of developing such mission and vision statements. Such visionary statements tend to insure that the planning group has thought through and articulated an overarching framework of what is to be developed and why.

UCD developed a number of specific goals in support of their mission and vision. The first goal was to develop a sound, reliable middleware infrastructure in order to mediate between different applications. "It is the essential glue for unifying campus information systems. Its use promotes efficient software design, generates developmental cost-savings, and facilitates consistent interface design by departments" (UCD, 2003, p. 3). Other goals included enhancing coordination among campus information systems; building a reliable security Infrastructure; extending the telecommunications capabilities and bandwidth in support of research and teaching; and enhancing account services and maintaining secured e-mail services. The final UCD goal addressed continuing support services provided by technical staff including training, operating the campus data center, running the campus helpdesk, and coordinating software licensing and distribution.

Before discussing an additional planning model and related advice, it may be helpful to summarize some a goal and related objectives drawn from another university strategic plan addressing infrastructure. The summarized goal and related objectives are from the IT strategic plan of Radford University (2008).

Radford University's goal centers upon building a sound technology infrastructure to support its growing information technology and related communication needs. The University offers nine objectives in support of this goal. In summary, these objectives are as follows:

1. Establish foundational systems to support other services using sustainable maintenance and funding models.
2. Provide a sound technical environment to ensure reliability.
3. Provide options for disaster recovery via multiple data centers.
4. Eliminate single points of failure via enhancements to the campus infrastructure as funding and technology allow.
5. Meet the need of the University community by providing adequate bandwidth.
6. Meet the needs of the University community by maintaining a cost effective telephone system.
7. Provide adequate access and archiving to email via establishment of required systems.
8. Maintain the campus' cable television and radio infrastructure.
9. Leverage partnerships to strengthen delivery of electronic communications and services to the University and the surrounding community.

A number of factors may shape the contents of a given institution's infrastructure plan. These factors include matters such as the status and adequacy of the existing infrastructure, changing needs based upon mission, growth in enrollment or programs, geographic expansion, new buildings or available budget, and the extent to which existing technologies are able meet extant institutional needs. Thus, infrastructure plans are sure to vary from one institution to another based upon these and other factors. The key point is that thoughtful planning is fundamental to the development, maintenance, and growth of a secure, efficient technology infrastructure that effectively supports a given institution's mission and day-to-day computing tasks and services and other technological needs.

GENERAL GUIDANCE ON PLANNING A TECHNOLOGY INFRASTRUCTURE

Gartner (2007) offers five recommendations germane to developing and expanding infrastructure. The first suggestion is to establish an overall infrastructure vision as seen in the UCD example. What return on investment might be expected? What results would produce the biggest positive impact on the institution in the short-term and the long-term? The next recommendation is to evaluate the existing infrastructure against the articulated vision, then conduct discussions based upon existing models and constructs and make required changes. The third recommendation is to plan for regularly scheduled re-evaluation of the infrastructure. This entails evaluating operating technologies, then modifying the strategic plan as appropriate. This evaluation should include measurement of progress toward goals, including matters like cost savings and improved service.

At this point, the planning group may choose to consider alternatives regarding service providers based upon strategic choices. The fourth recommendation is to identify and accomplish additional goals for the next twelve to eighteen months. These goals should be self-funded and accomplished via virtualization, producing rapid return on investment and increased quality and agility. The final recommendation is to consider utilized vendors' relative success in assisting the institution with the evolution of its infrastructure and, presumably, making appropriate changes.

Hubbard, Lucas, Holmes, and Hons (1998) also offer recommendations for infrastructure planning. The first obvious task is to establish a planning committee. The committee's plan should insure that the infrastructure supports the educational plans and philosophies of the institution. They further recommend that the committee will be most effective if it is large enough to represent varied perspectives yet small enough to operate efficiently.

Hubbard et al. go on to recommend that the infrastructure should be designed to be responsive to changing student demographics, curriculum and philosophy, and technological advances. It is further suggested that planning be based upon three critical principles. First, the curriculum should be the prime basis for planning. Student learning is the desired end result: technology provides a tool or means of achieving that end. Second, student bodies differ from one institution to another; therefore, no single plan works for everyone. Finally, flexibility must be inherent in the plan so as to accommodate future technological advances.

Also salient is the importance of security provisions and virus protection (Hubbard et al., 1998). The authors recommend keeping the aesthetic appeal of the resulting environment in mind. Planners should consider the ambiance that will be created by equipment configurations. Efforts should be made to match the school architecture to the vision of the school and the creation of functional and inspiring places that support both work and social life. An appealing environment should lead to improved student motivation.

A MODEL FOR PLANNING A TECHNOLOGY INFRASTRUCTURE

In their provocatively entitled article, *Is Strategic Planning for Technology an Oxymoron?* Ringle and Updergrove (1998) also offer suggestions for successful strategic planning concerning infrastructure. These authors suggest that the likelihood of successful strategic plan may be improved by the following:

- Tying technology to the institution's mission and goals
- Getting the right people involved in the planning process
- Avoiding excessive focus on technical details
- Insuring that the planning group includes an effective leader

These suggestions are well taken. One related suggestion is to include the campus' technology services director on the planning committee. At TAMUCC, the Associate Vice President for Planning and Effectiveness serves as chair of the campus' main information technology planning group. This arrangement has worked well, insuring that the necessary leadership was in place.

Ringle et al. (1998) also provide a thoughtful overview of their adaptable model for conducting strategic planning for technology infrastructure:

It appears there are some common practices that contribute to healthy technology planning processes, regardless of the size and type of institution. The following ten-step method is an effort to fuse these practices into a comprehensive approach. This approach should be viewed as a model—to be adapted to fit the individual needs of a campus—rather than as a blueprint. A guid-

ing principle of this method is to separate the socioeconomic aspects of a technology strategy from the operational aspects, while nevertheless ensuring coherence between the two components. The first five steps of the method focus on the strategic overview, the latter five on the operational dimension. (p. 5)

Following is a summary of the ten steps entailed in Ringle and Updegrove's technology infrastructure planning model:

The first step is to review the institution's objectives. They urge that senior administrators, deans, faculty, and other key people be consulted before planning. It is critical to identify their priorities and obtain input as to how technology will support accomplishment of the institutional objectives they deem most critical.

The second step is to develop a framework of strategic objectives related to technology. In this regard, the authors suggest surveying or conducting focus groups on a five year cycle. They comment: "The outcome should be a brief annotated list of pedagogical, research, administrative, communications, or similar objectives that can be directly enhanced through the application of existing or new technologies (1998, p.5)."

The third step is to prioritize objectives for five years, maximum, according to costs and benefits. The authors suggest that this step is politically sensitive; therefore, it should be completed by the campus technology committee, not the technology director or the information technology department. They also comment that the list should be a memorandum rather than a lengthy treatise and should include discussion of costs and benefits.

The fourth step is to invite key groups to review the framework of strategic objectives. Reviewers should include the institution's senior administrators so that they can consider costs and implications for policy. If such review of objectives is not completed, major obstacles to their implementation may occur. Refinement of the framework may be required to reach consensus.

The fifth step is to make the framework completed in the previous step available to the community at large. Related discussion should focus upon return on investment and added value for institutional functions.

The sixth step is to operationalize the objectives into functional goals. These technical goals should be updated annually by the campus technology department and need not be widely distributed. The goals should be tied to the previously developed strategic objectives.

The seventh recommended step is to discuss the operational goals with appropriate staff members. Financial, academic, and administrative staff should review the goals "... to obtain feedback and support for changes in technology, services, procedures, and policies" (p. 6).

The eighth step is to distribute the operational goals to the community at large to promote awareness of campus technological innovations and related benefits.

The ninth step is to obtain regular input from members of the institution and surrounding community regarding their technology needs. This information may be included in annual assessments on completion of operational goals.

The tenth and final step of this model is to evaluate progress toward annual goals each year before developing goals for the following year. In addition, progress toward strategic objectives should be assessed prior to developing the next five-year strategic plan. Related documents should be brief. In addition, these assessments should indicate which goals have been achieved and explain which goals may have been missed, modified, or abandoned, as appropriate.

One of the described model's major strengths lies in its focus on strategic planning specifically related to technology infrastructure. Another strength is the model's emphasis on keeping senior administrators, "gatekeepers," and the community involved in the planning process. Other strengths include the articulation of goals and objectives and the integration of assessment at regular intervals. Of course, this model is but one of many that technology planners may chose to employ. This particular model, though somewhat dated, still addresses some critical issues that should support successful infrastructure planning. Even if the model is not adopted in toto, many of its underlying strategies are worthy of application.

Tittasiri (2001) also offers a four phase strategic planning process: phase one requires organizing the planning team and determining its organizational structure; phase two entails fact-finding and assessment of trends; this requires determining the current status of IT at the institution as well as related strengths weaknesses, opportunities, and threats; the third phase includes deciding upon and disseminating strategies concerning technology use along with related vision and mission statements; the fourth phase is to implement selected strategies and programs and to gather related feedback. The entire process is subject to ongoing revision based upon feedback and assumes that this condensed planning model occurs within "... a larger institutional strategic planning framework..." (Titthasirir, 2001, p. 157). This basic model provides a logical progression of planning activities and lends itself to expansion and elaboration of a complete infrastructure planning process. It provides a reasonable starting point for institutions lacking extensive experience in infrastructure planning.

A CASE STUDY

This case study describes the fundamental planning strategies utilized at Texas A&M University—Corpus Christi to plan and grow the institution's technology infrastructure. One germane early development was the formation of a University Educational Technology Committee. The provost appointed the author to serve as chairperson for the group: its main charge was to establish a Teaching, Learning, and Technology Roundtable (TLTR).

A TLT Roundtable (The TLT Group, 2010) is a diverse group that meets regularly, considers issues, and (usually) provides advice to the Chief Academic Officer, other leaders, and many constituencies. TLTR is designed to bring together people who would not otherwise work together on educational improvements (for example, technology leaders with faculty who are not yet enthusiastic users of technology for teaching). TLTRs are often asked by Chief Academic Officers for advice on a regular basis, e.g., on new faculty development initiatives, internal grants programs, or budgets that affect resources and support services available to improve teaching and learning with technology. (p.1)

The TLTR initiative at TAMUCC was extremely helpful in identifying faculty members' opinions as to what changes they wanted implemented on campus. Two main concerns emerged: (1) the conversion of classrooms to smart classrooms—that is, the equipping of classrooms with computers with projectors and Internet connectivity; and (2) the need for improved support and resources required to empower faculty to deliver distributed education courses. Senior administrators heard the faculty. Today, nearly all older classrooms have been reborn into smart classrooms with instructor stations, switchers, video playback capability, document cameras, and stereo audio systems. In addition, the University has adopted and implemented a policy of equipping all new classrooms in such a manner. This has greatly expanded the faculty's ability to employ technology on a regular basis in instruction. In addition, the University initiated a Distance Learning Committee and, based upon its work, the University procured a quality course management system to support distance and distributed education offerings. A distance learning training specialist was also employed. Since these events occurred, the institution has greatly increased distance education offerings, maintained a regular schedule of faculty training, and researched and selected a new and improved course management system to improve course delivery via the Internet. Much of the growth in distance education was supported by substantial grants to deliver nursing education across the state.

As time passed, some committees including the Educational Technology Committee and the Distance Learning Committee completed their work and were thus disbanded. Interestingly, the Distance Education Committee was recently re-established. The underlying concept is to establish committees to address specific technology issues such as developing strategic plans, garnering input from faculty, or researching and recommending vendors and new systems and services. Different committees "come and go" based upon specific needs that require addressing at a particular point in time. For instance, a committee was established a few years ago to select a new student information system. The committee spent considerable time and effort in identifying the best vendor to use. This multi-million dollar decision has since been made and the system is operational. Since the committee had completed its work, it was subsequently dissolved.

The major campus technology planning committee has existed for at least sixteen years. It has undergone a few name changes and is today simply called the University Technology Council. Most all major campus technology decisions and expenditures are presented to this council for review and approval. Members of the council include the Associate Vice President (VP) for Planning & Institutional Effectiveness and representatives from the Provost's office, Finance and Administration, Graduate Studies, Student Affairs, the library, Institutional Advancement, and Enrollment Management. Other members include the VP for Technology, as well as representatives from the University's five colleges. The council allocates funds to all University units for the purchase of new computers and peripherals based upon the number of full-time equivalent (FTE) personnel housed in a given unit. Basing allocations based upon FTE personnel data has proven to be a straightforward, equitable way of distributing funding. In addition, should funds be available, the council sometimes funds special projects required by various academic programs that require specialized equipment in order to address curricular requirements.

The University recently implemented a new public web portal. This design of the new portal was the purview of the University's marketing office. It is but another example of how TAMUCC continually strives to maintain up-to-date technology resources to meet the needs of administrators, faculty, staff, and current and potential students.

REFLECTING ON THE IMPACT OF TECHNOLOGY AND ITS INFRASTRUCTURE

As the author has argued, technology is a means to an end. Considering that a single institution many spend many millions of dollars on technology annually, the question of what outcomes and effects on the University community have been achieved looms large. While the question certainly merits asking, answering it is indeed a major challenge.

Each year the University administers an exit survey to graduating students (TAMUCC, 2009). The 2009 survey revealed the following:

- About 9% of students were dissatisfied with the on-line Web registration process. The remaining 91% were either very satisfied or satisfied with the process.
- About 87% of graduates felt that computer labs were adequately equipped. The same percentage agreed that labs were accessible.

These data provide limited evidence to suggest that most graduating students were satisfied with Web registration. A strong majority also indicated satisfaction with computer lab equipment and lab access.

Today, TAMUCC stands as a top-ranked regional university by U.S. News and World Report. The University has expanded its curriculum in the past 15 years adding numerous Masters degree programs and some doctoral programs. Enrollment increases from year to year, and the University recently acquired a large parcel of land from the City of Corpus Christi to accommodate expansion. While these events do not directly speak to the effective use of technology, they are general indicators that, even in these troubled economic times, the University is doing many things "right." The high degrees of effort and expertise that TAMUCC faculty, staff, and administrators have applied in maintaining the campus technology infrastructure appear to have had positive impact on teaching, learning, administration, and the community as a whole. Additional study and evaluation of technology's role in students' experiences at the University would no doubt be useful in verifying this view.

RECOMMENDATIONS

Planning a campus' technology infrastructure is no simple matter. Based upon reviewed literature and the author's experiences serving on the main technology planning committee at TAMUCC, the following twelve recommendations for infrastructure planning are offered:

First, establish a planning group whose members have credibility with the institution's senior administrators and who possess appropriate requisite knowledge of technology (Ringle & Updergrove, 1998). Consider including the chief technology officer, the chief planning officer, a representative from the provost's or president's office, and a representative from each academic unit, the library, and the distance learning area.

Second, to the greatest extent possible, strive to keep senior administrators involved in the planning process (Brooks-Young, 2009; Ringle & Updergrove, 1998). Otherwise, keep them informed of the main planning committee's work and decisions via president's cabinet meetings or other appropriate top-level administrator meetings. Also insure that sub-committees include members who possess first-hand knowledge of the given issue and the right job experience in order to provide required leadership and make effective decisions.

Third, allow adequate time for the main planning group and for sub-committees to do their work and to conduct discussions and research regarding major decisions. Arrange for sub-committee chairs to serve on the main campus planning group or at least request them to report on a regular basis. Apply a workable, explicit planning process whenever possible.

Fourth, insure that decisions are consistent with institutional and university system requirements (Ringle & Updergrove, 1998; Hubbard et al., 1998) especially in regard to security, confidentiality, and fraud issues. Plan to meet auditors' requirements in decision making.

Fifth, when deciding to utilize an external service provider, request in-person presentations and proposals from multiple vendors (Brooks-Young, 2009). Try to utilize vendors with proven track records. Ask for software upgrades and possibly training to be included in the original cost and contract.

Sixth, while intuition and first-hand experiences have a place in planning, strive to utilize a data-driven approach to planning whenever possible (The TLT Group, 2010; Ringle & Updergrove, 1998). Data related to classroom and computer laboratory usage rates, student enrollment projections, help desk logs, network usage, new software systems, and campus expansion plans can assist planners in identifying and addressing future technology and infrastructure needs.

Next, when appropriate, hold open, campus-wide TLTR meetings or similar forums to obtain feedback and identify expressed needs and opinions of faculty and staff regarding technology (The TLT Group, 2010).

Eighth, as done at TAMUCC, when equipment is to be replaced, planners should consider "cascading" or relocating the used equipment to new locations where it can still function adequately.

Ninth, standardize equipment and functions to the greatest extent possible (Novell, 2000). For instance, utilize a single e-mail system and standardize the identification (ID) and the overall e-mail address format. Establish partnerships with computer companies, and consider establishing computer maintenance staff as certified repair staff for one or more companies. Require that computers to be purchased be selected from a limited, approved list and require purchasing of extended warranties. Try to buy in bulk to obtain price breaks.

Tenth, view infrastructure as comprised of both human and physical resources (UCD, 2003). Provide adequate, ongoing support via training, job aids, and a help desk.

Eleventh, when implementing major new systems or software, maintain operation of the system which is being replaced to insure until the new system is operating smoothly and the required transition is successfully completed (Brooks-Young, 2009).

Finally, establish empirically-based mechanisms for regularly evaluating the adequacy of the campus technology infrastructure and make changes as required (The TLT Group, 2010).

The author drew the provided recommendations both from the literature and from his experience serving on TAMUCC's Technology Council. Their implementation has—on the whole—shown them to be appropriate and effective heuristics and procedures for maintaining and managing the seemingly ever growing campus infrastructure.

FUTURE RESEARCH DIRECTIONS

Most of the literature the author unearthed on this chapter's topic took the form of concept papers suggesting strategies for infrastructure planning. Clearly, the topic of planning per se does not lend itself much to experimental approaches. Qualitative research strategies including ethnographic, document review and basic descriptive approaches may be useful in exploring some of the major factors involved in infrastructure planning that emerged from the writing of this chapter. Experimental approaches, however, may have a place in exploring how smart classrooms affect teaching and learning. There is also great opportunity to empirically investigate optimal instructional strategies and faculty-student interactions in distance learning.

A number of specific issues related to infrastructure planning may be worthy of investigation. For example, what planning processes have been employed at various institutions? What comparisons can be made regarding the operational aspects of varied planning approaches and what were the results of employing specific planning processes, especially as concerns outcomes affecting various constituencies of a given institution? Peripherally related to this question is the matter of how the human dimensions of technology infrastructure planning affect the overall conceptualization and implementation of infrastructure specifications. What are these influences and how do they affect infrastructure architecture and overall institutional performance? Also, to what degree are conceptual frameworks such as Gartner's infrastructure maturity model used in higher education, if at all? How have institutions utilized such tools and to what end?

Another area ripe for research concerns smart classrooms. Equipping classrooms with computers, Internet access, and projection and audio systems has surely affected the instructional strategies faculty employ. Related research might focus upon how instruction delivered in such facilities differs from instruction delivered in classrooms devoid of technology. What new instructional strategies do smart classrooms suggest? What are the effects on learning of employing such strategies?

As institutions of higher education are subjected to ongoing pressure to reduce budgets and to maximize value for dollars spent, the question of measuring return on investment looms ever large. Can one planning approach result in greater return than another? What empirical measures can be utilized to answer these questions?

A final research area might explore which aspects of an institution's technology infrastructure current and potential students care about most? Which aspects of technology may most influence potential students' choice of institution? What future trends can be identified in this regard?

Clearly, as the criticality and use of technology continue to expand in higher education, these and other related research questions seem quite worthy of well designed research.

CONCLUSION

Technological advances continue to proliferate, seemingly on a daily basis. The infrastructure that supports each higher education institution's functioning and accomplishment of mission becomes ever more critical in today's highly competitive education market. Every institution must be technologically well equipped and prepared to integrate modern technologies into most every aspect of its operation in order to maintain its competitive edge. Today's potential students have choices regarding which institution they will attend, whether in person or on-line. A sound infrastructure will help insure that required administrative services and instructional delivery will be accomplished successfully. And the human dimension of technology infrastructure must always be remembered.

No single infrastructure planning model will work everywhere. The keys to good technology planning include clarity of mission and vision. In the final analysis, any technology is a tool—a means to an end. Achieving desired end results requires major investments of people's time and commitment as well as the institution's budget. The author hopes that this discussion has provided current and future infrastructure planners with useful ideas and insights regarding this truly complex, multi-faceted and critical process.

REFERENCES

Brooks-Young, S. (2009). *Making technology standards work for you: A guide to the NETS-A for school administrators with self-assessment activities* (2nd ed.). Eugene, OR: International Society for Technology in Education.

Gartner (2007). *Strategic roadmap for your infrastructure — The Gartner infrastructure maturity model*. Retrieved December 1, 2009, from www.microsoft.no/portfolio/Produktivitets-dagen_2007/Gartner_keynote.ppt

Hubbard, G., Lucas, L., Holmes, K., & Hons, P. (1998). Planning the technology infrastructure: General requirements. In *Designing the technology infrastructure for schools,* (2nd. Ed.). (pp. 15-26). Denton, TX: Texas Center for Educational Technology. (Available at http://www.tcet.unt.edu/pubs/telecomm.htm)

Kling, R. (1992). Behind the terminal: the critical role of computing infrastructure in effective information systems development and use. In Cotterman, W. W., & Senn, J. A. (Eds.), *Challenges and strategies for research in systems development* (pp. 365–413). New York, NY: John Wiley & Sons.

Novel (2000). *Standardization of desktops in an enterprise environment*. Retrieved April 1, 2010 from http://www.novell.com/coolsolutions/feature/2940.html

Radford University. (2008). *Information technology strategic plan, 2008-2013*. Accessed October 29, 2009 from, http://cio.asp.radford.edu/about/strategicplan.aspx

Ringle, M., & Updergrove, D. (1998). Is strategic planning an oxymoron? *Cause/Effect, 21(1)* 18-23. Retrieved November 5, 2009, from http://net.educause.edu/ir/library/html/cem/cem98/cem9814.html

Search for Common Ground. (2004). *Resource guide on strategic planning*. Retrieved November 20, 2009, from http://www.sfcg.org/programmes/ilr/stratplan.pdf

The, T. L. T., & the Group. (2010). *Definition and Characteristics of a TLT Roundtable*. Accessed November 11, 2009, from http://www.tltgroup.org/TLTR/Characteristics.htm

Titthasiri, W. (2001). Information technology strategic planning process for institutions of higher education in Thailand. *NECTEC Technical Journal, III*(11), 153–164.

University of California Davis. (2003). *IT strategic plan—Technology infrastructure*. Accessed November 13, 2009, from http://stuaff.ucdavis.edu/reports/ITinfrastructure_plan.html

ADDITIONAL READING

Accessed January 1, 2010, from http://www.mega-planning.com/CaseStudies/Vol18_03_06.pdf

Allison, M., & Kaye, J. (2005) *Strategic planning for nonprofit organizations: A practical guide and workbook,* (*2nd* ed.). New York: Wiley.

Duncan, N. B. (1995). Capturing flexibility of information technology infrastructure: A study of resource characteristics and their measure. *Journal of Management Information Systems, 12*(2), 37–57.

Henricksen, K. Indulska, J., & Rakotonirainy, A. (2001). *Infrastructure for pervasive computing: Challenges*. Accessed November 13, 2009, from http://www.gta.ufrj.br/seminarios/CPE826/doc/ip.pdf

Kaufman, R. (2005). Defining and delivering measurable value: A mega thinking and planning primer. *Performance Improvement Quarterly, 18*(3), 6–16. doi:10.1111/j.1937-8327.2005.tb00337.x

Knowledge Works Foundation. (2010). *See the change*. Accessed April 15, 2010 from http://www.kwfdn.org/

McKay, E. G. (2001). Strategic planning: A ten-step guide. *Mosaica,* 1-14. Retrieved November 13, 2009, from http://siteresources.worldbank.org/INTAFRREGTOPTEIA/Resources/mosaica_10_steps.pdf

Morgado, E., Igarashi, D., & Twani, E. (2007). *Paving the way for a dynamic and mature ICT infrastructure in education: A case for schools in emerging markets.* Accessed December 26, 2009, from download.microsoft.com/.../2/0/.../Paving_the_way_0809.pdf.pdf

National Council of Educational Research and Training. (2006). *Position paper: National focus group on educational technology.* Accessed December 11, 2009, from http://www.ncert.nic.in/html/pdf/schoolcurriculum/position_papers/educational_technology.pdf

North Central Regional Educational Laboratory. (2010). *Technology education*. Accessed October 5, 2009, from http://www.ncrel.org/sdrs/areas/te0cont.htm

Olsen, E. (2006). *Strategic planning for dummies*. New York, NY: Wiley.

Sun Associates. (2006). *Resources for Technology Planning and Evaluation.* Accessed December 22, 2009, from http://www.sun-associates.com/resources/evalpln.html

Wikipedia (2010). *Information technology infrastructure Library*. Accessed October 23, 2009, from, http://en.wikipedia.org/wiki/Information_Technology_Infrastructure_Library

KEY TERMS AND DEFINTIONS

Cascading: The concept of placing or recycling used but functional computing equipment in a new location where it can still perform at a satisfactory level; for example, moving old computers from an advanced lab utilized by a specific academic program to an open use "bullpen" area.

Information Technology Infrastructure: The human and physical resources an organization requires in order to make effective and efficient use of computers and other technologies in order to successfully achieve its mission.

Infrastructure Maturity Model: A conceptual tool which depicts the relative degree of development of a given institution's information technology infrastructure; allows planners to understand their infrastructure's current status and to set goals for growth and improvement.

Smart Classroom: A classroom which is adequately equipped with technological tools to support effective delivery of instruction including an instructor's station with switch box, a computer with Internet access, document projector, "combo" digital video disc and video cassette player, mounted projection unit, projection screen, a stereo audio system, and white boards.

Strategic Planning: The process an organization applies in order to set courses of action from three to ten years in the future in support of appropriately allocating human and physical resources in order to achieve its en-route goals and overall mission.

Teaching, Learning, and Technology Roundtable: An organized group of administrators, faculty, and staff members with varying degrees of expertise concerning instructional and informational technology who provide an institution's lead administrators with data-based insights into campus technology needs pertaining to teaching and learning with technology.

Chapter 8
Technology Transfer:
Are Faculty Entrepreneurs Still Swimming Upstream?

Russ Lea
University of South Alabama, USA

ABSTRACT

Universities and their faculties have long been exalted for the benefits of their innovations on the United States economy, defense, and security. In fact, one of the American public's sustaining beliefs is that the tens of billions of their tax dollars that are provided for university-based research support is important for our country to remain competitive, safe, more energy sufficient, and healthy. However, despite all of the fine examples of regional, state, and individual university responses to supporting innovations, there are still ample examples of faculty who are confused about their roles and responsibilities in the area of technology transfer, entrepreneurship, conflict of interest, and entry into commercial ventures. This chapter will cover technology transfer from a university and faculty perspective and describe key issues that evolve once faculty decide to course through the technology transfer pipeline, which begins with innovations and ends with commercialization.

Universities and their unique resources (high-speed internet, technical workforce, tech-transfer offices, centers of excellence) have proven to be central assets in large regional economic growth spurts. Whether one considers the "Silicon Valley" in the Santa Clara Valley south of San Francisco, "Route 128" outside of Boston, or North Carolina's "Research Triangle Park," these areas have all benefited from the tightly knitted association of university researchers with industry/government scientists in technologies ready to commercially explode. The down side of this association is that universities suffer the criticisms that research programs are being bought out and that commercialization is turning scientists and

DOI: 10.4018/978-1-60960-147-8.ch008

their universities into servants of the industry (Sanger, 1981; Bok, 2003; Press and Washburn, 2000; Greenburg 2007). Although we are almost three decades past the Bayh-Dole Act (1980) in a period where university and industry links have proliferated, there are still many critics among both academia and the public opining that academics should stick to their classrooms and basic science labs and not venture into the technology transfer pipeline.

In the past three decades, economic competitiveness has morphed from an international concern (e.g. outcompete Japan) to a regional concern (e.g. knowledge clusters) to one where individual universities are in an "arms race" with each other for private and public funding (including licensing royalties, retaining star faculty, pursuing academic earmarking, developing technology parks and incubators, etc.). The greatest benefit that Bayh-Dole afforded universities, namely, to promote the utilization of their research for the public good, sometimes seems distant to the perceived objectives whereby universities attempt to maximize their own resources, including commercialization profits from faculty innovations that are ultimately transferred to the economy.

THE SCALE OF U.S. UNIVERSITY R&D

The 2008 R&D expenditures for universities from all sources are just over $50 billion with over two thirds of that amount funded by the government. Altogether, in 2008, industry is responsible for performing over 72%, of the nation's total R&D with academic institutions performing 13% percent, and federal laboratories, nonprofit institutions performing the remainder (NSF, 2009). Although federal agency support seems modest compared to the industry support for R&D investment, this investment supports over 60% of the nation's basic research with over 60% of that basic R&D conducted by universities (AAAS, 2008).

The most telling statistics regarding shifting R&D investment is that the 100 Award-winning US innovations in the 1970s came from corporations acting on their own, whereas the top 100 R&D innovations in the last decade come from collaborative ventures with business, government, and universities (Block and Keller, 2008). This shift is due to many influences, such as, shrinking product life cycles or technological expertise out running the research budgets of industry. With proportionally less research investments made by industry, it is no wonder that they are seeking key relationships with universities who are carrying on the bulk of basic and exploratory research. It is the essence of those university/industry relationships and the faculty tensions of entrepreneurship versus commercialization versus scholarship versus teaching that causes some faculty to feel as if they are swimming upstream against a constantly shifting current of recognition and rewards --and possibly sanctions.

FIRST THINGS FIRST

From a purely academic perspective, there are several key motivators that control faculty recognition and rewards. The first is that that universities have been important sources of knowledge and purveyors of truth as they go about their scholarly activities in teaching, research, and public service. It is through this unfettered compact with the university where faculty and their students have *de facto* become the intellectual center of the entire U.S. research enterprise and where most of the basic intellectual energy is spent. However, this right to conduct scholarship and teaching is not without disciplinary controls, since excellence in one's field is determined by peer review and fierce competition. The goal of peer review is obvious, in that the best is defined by your own colleagues. Not only do your colleagues control your rewards in grant funding, the courses you will teach, and your access to unique university resources, but they also control to what degree your scholarly works will be recognized in publications and/or translated into new products, therapeutics, and technologies.

More recently, as universities attempt to keep their competitive positions with other universities, or attempt to leap-frog over their competitors, universities are generally portrayed as "black holes" for resources. In recent years, this "greed" has become evident to the taxpayers and Congress because of escalating administrative salaries, run-away tuition and fees, some capital campaigns exceeding billions of dollars, and the incessant appetite for modern research facilities, student recreation facilities, and high-cost equipment. Detractors of the academic enterprise are also leveling criticisms at faculty who are supposedly neglecting teaching and research in order to enrich themselves through industry partnerships, external consulting activities, or commercializing their innovations through technology transfer activities. Faculty who used to be rewarded by peers for teaching, research, and public service have found a new avenue where they are rewarded through faculty entrepreneurship. It is the new breed of faculty who recognize their worth to the institution in terms of attracting other key scholars, high-ranking students, selling scientific skills and technologies, starting-up companies, and gaining support of high wealth individuals or foundations. This campus entrepreneur knows the value of his/her know-how and is constantly leveraging it against all intra-and extra-mural donors.

A TATTERED NATIONAL R&D BLUEPRINT?

Faculty are currently dealing with the economic realities of compressed university resources, frozen salaries (or worse!), limited peer-review support, severe industry cuts in R&D, and public attacks against the motives of the professoriate. In the last decade Congress and the White House have also been involved in "micro-managing" science and science funding agencies and have deliberately broken down the public trust of university-based R&D. On top of this, faculty who receive federal research funds are heavily affected by regulatory controls, inadequate recovery of indirect costs, burdensome reporting requirements and little or no financial or administrative support by their departments. The long held national blueprint that the scientific community and the government were in a contract to spawn hope for the nation's future is sufficiently "tattered" making Vannevar Bush's *Science: The Endless Frontier* (1945) now seem like ***Science: The Endless Burden!*** The privileged treatment of university science by the government is over, and science seen as a public good has now morphed into an investment rationale for achieving technological developments and economic growth. Is it any wonder that the faculty are seeking their rewards from more entrepreneurial activities?

As the nation's science blueprint becomes more "tattered" and faculty are seen as more unreliable and unable to guide their own academic affairs, controls are being put in place for all funding agencies to measure the productivity of scientists and their universities. For example, the recent reporting requirements for the American Recovery Act have scientists certifying quarterly; the benefits that their science has had for the nation's economy, tracking jobs creation, accounting for research expenditures, subcontractor activity, etc., etc. Every collateral activity that was once associated with science exploration has now becomes the *raison d'être* for federal mandates, such as, conflict of interest disclosure, patent reporting, responsible conduct of research training, export controls, etc. The "golden age" of the post World War II R&D blueprint when money flowed freely from Congress to federal agencies to peer reviewed faculty researchers who published in peer reviewed journals—driven solely by the interests of scientists and their peers-- is a culture only experienced by the soon to be retired gray haired professors (Guston and Keniston, 1994). Over the last few decades, the golden age of science has yielded to national R&D culture where the common language for the science community is "If you can't count it, it doesn't count" and "What have you done for the economy lately?"

Recognition of a University's capacity to create innovations and commercialize new unique technology products for economic development are metrics that can be counted that translate into government, industry, and international support for R&D. The US and its federal science agencies are not necessarily giving up on its widely distributed knowledge-based resources, but rather it is more likely to fertilize those university environments where faculty exercise their entrepreneurial activities, coupled with geographical proximities, and access to capital, that ultimately ease the transfer of innovations to commercial markets. As Greenberg (2007) writes:

There was a time when many academics would have found puzzlement, if notgrounds for alarm, in this lavishly ambitious undertaking to render, of all things, entrepreneurship—never explicitly defined—into a commonplace aspect of American higher education. (p. 89)

Is the faculty ready to consider the entrepreneurial initiative? Are they willing to assess their science in terms of entrepreneurial ventures, e.g., where one exercises different options under varying conditions of risk and uncertainty (Carayannis, 2008)? It might be suggested that this is the way faculty have always conducted their scientific discovery. But alternatively, have any faculty, as their main entrepreneurial R&D inspiration, sought to drive technological change that accelerated economic development through technology transfer? Not many!

TECHNOLOGY TRANSFER AND THE EARLY ADOPTERS

Following the passage of the Bayh-Dole Act, universities organically grew into their new-found roles as technology transfer agents. This was not a very difficult concept to grasp for publically funded Land Grant Universities, as their roles in state-wide economic development had been exercised for almost one hundred years. Most early adopters had the industry contacts and the region-wide conduits to enable university innovations to be licensed. What markedly changed university technology transfer in the 1980s was the explosive growth in the semi-conductor industry and the biological revolution based on our ability to understand and map genes from various organisms, and the computing power to search for genes of significance. It was also during this time that the "triple helix" of government/industry/university R&D funding (Leydesdorff and Etzkowitz, 1996) was accelerating due to specialized programs such as, Science and Technology Centers, Industry/University Collaborative Research Centers, Engineering Research Centers, the Small Business Innovation Research grant program, and the Advanced Technology Program, among others. Academic researchers, who once disdained commercial involvement, were now rewarded for bridging their academic research projects with those co-funded by industry.

Some university administrations voiced concerns at the proliferation of university-industry collaborations on academic values, but most – pressured by state and federal legislators, joined in the transformation of universities into entrepreneurial alliances. At the same time that universities were struggling to make appropriate ties to industry, many faculty were taking advantage of their new found leverage as inventors on university-held patents. The faculty-entrepreneur was born –not based on consulting activities—but based on founding their own companies (Culliton, 1984). Early success of University of California, San Francisco's Professor Herbert Boyer, founder of Genentech, as well as Nobel Prize winner and Harvard Professor Walter Gilbert, founder of the international biotech firm, Biogen, were inspirational to industry collaborators, venture capitalists, and faculty alike.

One of the downsides of commercialization pressures felt by faculty aspiring to become the next founder of a multi-million dollar company was the degree that they felt free to openly exchange ideas with their colleagues (Fox, 1984). Probably one of the most clearly articulated warnings about the evolving technology transfer culture of the post Bayh-Dole passage was Professor Hotzman at Columbia University who warned, "Unless we find ways of tempering the hectic, get-for-yourself-what-you-can atmosphere that is now flourishing, it will prove difficult to preserve the broadly cooperative structures that have sustained our individual efforts and to protect fragile practices such as an open communication and peer review." (Holtzman, 1984). Similarly in 1981, after Boyer formed Genentech, a UCSF committee investigated the effects of his entrepreneurship on its researchers. It found that "people were loath to ask questions and give suggestions in seminars or across the bench, for there was a feeling that someone might take an idea and patent it, or that an individual's idea might be taken to make money for someone else." (Leskovak, 1985).

Another key obstacle for post Bayh-Dole universities to grapple with was whether the administration was ready to deal with the slight but growing population of campus entrepreneurs. While universities were outwardly pronouncing the many reasons to participate in technology transfer activities, for example -- to commercialize university inventions, facilitate faculty recruitment and retention, engage in economic development, and pursue commercialization on behalf of the faculty and university—it was still hard to contemplate that the university had become a "business" within a peer review environment. This duality of peer review of academic knowledge coupled with the bottom line of tech transfer had many faculty torn between their rewards as traditional academics on one side and purely as capitalists on the other. Another caveat of Bayh-Dole that university administrators had to deal with was that scientific publications could substantially limit the viability for obtaining protection because of the novelty restrictions on patents. The confusion that resulted because of miscommunications between administrators and faculty with regards to publication and patenting, left fractures in the culture of academic science...whereby peer-reviewed journal articles still held sway for promotion and tenure, and patents (irrespective of millions in royalty payments) did not.

Another key area of campus-sea change was the campus research administrators' inability to self-regulate the emerging conflicts of interest that were co-evolving with the new breed of campus capitalists. Conflict of interest, including the mere appearance of a potential conflict, was a sticky issue to deal in the early 1980s especially given the societal views of academic freedoms and abject campus administrators too unsure of themselves to effectively intervene in faculty activities. As most universities did when confronted with serious academic issues, hundreds upon hundreds of hours of committee meetings were called at the top research universities to consider the ramifications of university inventors and faculty having intertwined activities regarding industry contracts, executive positions on start-ups, lucrative consulting contracts, board memberships, stock options, etc. Also remember that during this time, universities were being "pushed" to increase their relevancy to the taxpayers and the economy (GUIRR, Competitiveness Council).

EARLY FACULTY ENTREPRENEUR: PLANT GENETICIST RAY VALENTINE

One of my most inspiring debates of faculty entrepreneurship versus "narrow-minded" university administrators occurred a few years ago during a "happy hour" following a full day of fishing for silver salmon in Southeast Alaska. It just so happened that on this particular salmon fishing trip I met professor emeritus, Ray Valentine, a retired UC Davis plant geneticist. What I was drawn into during that happy hour (playing the role as the narrow-minded administrator) versus Ray (a retired faculty entrepreneur) on the fantail of the wooden yacht, Creole, was a history lesson and debate regarding university technology transfer. Ray, I came to learn, was at the center of one of the earliest and most controversial potential conflict of interest cases involving a spin-out company that ambitiously pursued the commercialization of genetically modified crops for nitrogen fixation and herbicide resistance.

The Setting

The choices and the culture of most major research universities during the early 1980s was simply a case of: you are either an academic committed to the three pillars of research, teaching, and public service, or you had committed yourself to the "dark side" of academic capitalism. In fact, in my role as a research administrator from the mid-1980s to present, faculty still refer to faculty entrepreneurs as being drawn to the "dark side" or away from "pure science." UC Davis was no different from any other major land grant university at that time grappling with not only the accelerated pace of plant biotechnology but with entrepreneurial faculty that could see a future of modifying organisms to perform specific functions. The administrative challenges at my institution, North Carolina State University, were quite similar to those at UC Davis during the same period.

As a young professor in the Department of Agronomy and Range Science, Ray found himself in the swirling debate in the mid 1970s as to whether biologists and/or geneticists should be tweaking DNA to benefit human therapeutics to plants. Inspired by his contacts with other geneticists, Ray proposed an institute at UC Davis to spin out commercializable biotechnology innovations based on recombinant DNA. The institute would gain momentum as royalties and grants were won by institute researchers. Ray encountered the first "dark side" experience when UC administrators struck down the proposal as not having relevance for agriculture (a response more likely born out of the fear of managing conflicts of interest from parochial and very conservative agriculture college administrators).

In 1980, the entrepreneur in Ray was getting closer to understanding plant genetics and the benefits of gene transfer, and the universities – through Bayh-Dole—were also granted the freedom to protect intellectual property arising from federally funded research and to license it to existing companies or spin it out into new companies owned and operated by faculty entrepreneurs or other venture capital players. This perfect confluence of events led to Ray's conflict of interest notoriety.

The Upheaval

Because of his knowledge that plant genetics would ultimately lead to commercializable innovations, Ray was approached by another successful entrepreneur, Norm Golfarb, who funded the university spin-out Genentech and Apple Computer while he was employed by Intel. Norm, a novice to plant science and a brother to one of Ray's Ph.D. candidates, became Ray's new "student" and quickly learned that the plant biotechnology field was getting ready to break wide open. Ray became Norm's student in the study of financing start-ups and structuring industry investments in commercial ventures. No good entrepreneurial activity lasts long on the chalk board when sound innovations and investment come together. Ray and Norm launched Calgene in June 1980 and were well on the way to applying recombinant DNA technology to crops. Ray became the vice president for R&D and began leading the first agriculture biotech start-up in the country. Ray's enthusiasm for the applications of gene manipulations and his new found enthusiasm for entrepreneurship naturally initiated a back-draft of criticism from administrators and faculty who expressed concerns for professors profiting from publically funded research, to graduate students more interested in commercial ventures versus the university lab, to Calgene licensing future innovations, to competing with faculty in the agriculture experiment station for applied solutions. Ray's effusive personality combined with the possibilities that he could seriously profit from his innovations drove the faculty into a froth of criticism--and in some cases jealousy.

The flood gates of campus backlash fully unleashed when Ray and his colleagues won a $2.5 million grant from Allied Chemical to study biological nitrogen fixation. Two days after the grant was awarded, Allied Chemical purchased 20% of the stock in Calgene. The academic upheaval that followed this stock purchase led the dean of the college to offer Ray a choice of several options: end his stake in Calgene, resign his faculty position, or remove himself from the Allied Chemical project. Ray chose to pull out of the Allied Chemical project and also resigned his faculty position and his role on Calgene's science advisory board. Ray is convinced to this day that if the university would have had more experience with faculty entrepreneurs back in the early 1980s, the resentment of his commercial activities with Calgene would have been significantly less and might have also encouraged others entrepreneurial faculty to start up companies. In essence, an early faculty entrepreneur drowned in the act of swimming against the flow of resentment, administrative conservatism, and lack of clearly defined strategies for mitigating potential conflicts of interest at UC Davis.

Postscript

Calgene began working on genes for herbicide resistance, which ultimately led to genetically modified crops resistant to the herbicide 'Roundup'. Monsanto, who purchased Calgene in 1996 and spent hundreds of millions to ensure Roundup-resistant crops' safe use, and now boasts the deployment of their seeds on millions of acres of corn, soybeans, and cotton. As with all major research universities, UC Davis now supports a favorable environment for faculty to spin-out companies by: rewarding faculty in business plan competitions, formalizing the UC Davis Innovation Access program (UC Davis, 2007), supporting a technology park, and engaging the last CEO of Calgene, Roger Salquist, to play an important campus advocacy role for assisting faculty entrepreneurs (Fell, 2004). To date Calgene is the only publically traded company to ever be spun out of UC Davis.

As for professor emeritus Ray, you can find him plying the waters of Southeast Alaska in the summer on his custom lobster boat. He is a prophet regarding the nutritional benefits of Omega-3 Fatty Acids from salmon and other cold water fish. You can read about the benefits of Omega-3 Fatty acids and the DHA Principle in his new book published with his son, David, a professor at UC Santa Barbara (Valentine and Valentine, 2009). His entrepreneurial experiences that I briefly captured above are more fully developed in Chapter 17 of his new book, or you can join Ray and my discussions in Alaska while fishing for Omega-3 that is still swimming!

University Messaging Regarding Conflict of Interest

Ray's eventual technology transfer failure (drowning in the conflict of interest current) was due to a lack of UC Davis' willingness to manage conflict of interest pro-actively. It is understandable why UC Davis took the stance that it did given that, contemporaneously with Ray's situation, there was a substantial movement around the UC campuses led by activists (faculty and public) who were vociferously identifying the down-side of industry ties with academic faculty and programs. There were numerous public hearings regarding faculty conflicts of interest and in June 1982, a revision of the California Administrative Code was adopted requiring faculty at publically supported colleges and universities to disclose financial interests with private entities that sponsored their research (CA Admin. Code, 1982). Following disclosure, it was up to universities to determine to what degree a researcher held an investment interest in, held a position with, or had received income from an outside entity that supports the researcher's university-based research. Of course, the expected backlash from faculty in California was that the privacy and academic freedoms of the faculty were now under attack.

The debate and regulatory environment that evolved from conflict of interest concerns in California was but one "drama" that was playing out in other states, especially those states with significant numbers of publically funded universities. To head the debate off at the pass, one publically funded university, NC State (similar in mission to UC Davis), realized that faculty --and the NC legislature-- needed to receive a clear message that faculty consulting activities, industry relationships, and technology transfer activities were a valuable byproduct of their scholarly works. The mantra that soon developed from NC State's research administration was, "No conflict, no interest!" This simple statement freed up NC State faculty to aggressively pursue federally funded Industry/University centers and institutes that were exploding in the mid 1980s and early 1990s. The freedom allowed faculty to engage with industry and to manage potential conflicts of interest, which were sealed by a compact with administration where faculty would be fully transparent in disclosing their potential conflicts in order to allow the administration to mitigate their activities. Once the faculty recognition and reward system was not burdened with conflict of interest concerns, NC State soon became ranked among the top ten research universities to receive industry funding, and it also led to an explosion of resources from the legislature to be directed at NC State researchers. Probably the most significant gift bestowed on NC State in the mid 1980s was more than 1,000 acres of state property adjacent to the main campus to be developed into an Industry/University/Government research park—Centennial Campus. In 25 years, Centennial Campus has evolved into a world class "technopolis" that is home to more than 130 companies, government agencies, and NC State research and academic units. More than 2,200 corporate and government employees work at the campus alongside more than 3,400 faculty, staff and students. In 2007, the campus was named the Research Science Park of the Year by the Association of University Research Parks.

When the administration came out such an aggressive statement about conflict of interest, NC State faculty quickly learned that their freedom to pursue tech transfer activities was not burdened with the fear of retribution of un-informed department heads, deans, and other academic administrators unsure of mitigating potential conflicts. The collective entrepreneurial spirit led to significant quantities of invention disclosures, patenting, licensing activities, industry/government funded centers, and eventual faculty spin outs.

No matter what modern research university you may consider, internal regulation remains the primary role for managing potential conflicts of interest – especially when dealing with university-industry connections. The balance that is being sought at all research universities is how can conflict of interest regulations be managed to cope with the pressures of universities wanting to demonstrate their role as "economic engines" while holding up to public demands for accountability to students and taxpayers. Based on either positive or negative institutional experiences in technology transfer and commercialization, there are still wide variations in values and norms across institutions and considerable debate is still being waged by university ethicists and administrators on the issue of conflict of interest spawned by tech transfer activities.

What three decades of university debate and regulations regarding conflict of interest have given us is an imperfect system where universities prepare conflict of interest guidelines, require transparency from faculty, set up faculty review committees, communicate responsible conduct of research expectations, and train to ethical standards—and at the end of the day there may still be very little conflict of interest deterrence that is effective given universities are more or less powerless to enforce ethical behavior and accurate disclosures.

Never has the sense of universities being powerless to enforce conflict of interest policies than in the recent cases dug up by Senator Grassley from Iowa. In a letter directed at 23 medical schools in June 2009, Senator Grassley asked the medical schools for information about their policies for conflicts of interest and requirements for disclosure of financial relationships between faculty members and the pharmaceutical industry. "I recently learned from an American Medical Student Association report, AMSA PharmFree Scorecard 2009, that your institution either had "no response" or "declined to submit policies" when asked to supply conflicts of interest policies," he said in the letter.

"There's a lot of skepticism about financial relationships between doctors and drug companies," Grassley said in his press release. "Disclosure of those ties would help to build confidence that there's nothing to hide. Requiring disclosure is a common sense reform based on the public dollars and public trust at stake in medical training, medical research and the practice of medicine," he stated. Enforcement of disclosure requirements were found to be poorly regulated or in outright violation at some universities. His findings were summarized in his letter with the following preamble, "Beginning last summer, I began releasing information that made the point that universities are not managing their professors' financial conflicts of interest and that change is needed at the NIH."

"To bring some greater transparency to this issue, Senator Kohl and I introduced the Physician Payments Sunshine Act (Act)," Grassley said in the letter. Grassley's letter made "poster child" examples of doctors at Emory, Stanford, Harvard, University of Wisconsin, University of Texas, Washington University, and National Public Radio.

In the current climate of increasing federal regulations and mandates involving federally funded research and development at universities, and with the instant success that Senator Grassley has had in up-ending university policies dealing with conflict of interest, it is hard not to imagine that the government will intercede and mandate new conflict of interest policies and enforce them at universities. The days of "no conflict, no interest" might be yielding to days of "no conflict... **period!**"

TECHNOLOGY TRANSFER AND THE "ENGAGED UNIVERSITY"

How often does administration engage the university professors in a discussion of what it means to be an "engaged university?" Ever since the publication of Ernest Boyer's *Scholarship Reconsidered: Priorities of the Professoriate* (1990), most universities have gone out of their way to develop mission and vision statements, support focus groups, change titles of administrative units, institute unit level performance compacts, and develop goal and objective statements to demonstrate to its external stakeholders that their university is involved in their region, state, country, and world. When it comes to regional economic development goals and objectives, most universities have relied heavily on Boyer's writings to convince community leaders and legislators that their campuses are responsive and progressive because they "serve" the public. Although we have grappled with the "service" issue for two decades, it is still difficult for most faculty to understand how they will be rewarded for their individual public service let alone activities related to technology transfer and commercialization.

For technology transfer to work in a university the size of my current university, The University of South Alabama, classified as a Comprehensive University, it needs to make sure that the full diversity of faculty functions are recognized and rewarded. Specifically, the faculty reward system must go out of its way to recognize its prize innovators and to systematically and deliberately support their efforts at commercialization throughout the technology transfer process. This is not to say that the university should diminish its support and recognition of teaching, research and service, but in recognizing technology transfer participation, faculty and students will feel more empowered to bring their innovations to the market. Technology transfer should not be viewed as a hurdle for faculty to jump over, but rather a collegial process, one of team work and commitment, that understands the value of faculty innovations and the satisfaction of seeing those innovations made into something useful in the commercial world.

Technology transfer works at my University because we have made public service a *quid pro quo* proposition where the university serves the public and the public feels a reciprocal need to serve the university. First, we encourage this culture by inviting community leaders, chambers of commerce representatives, local industry, and politicians to our campus to understand the unique attributes of our campus and where we can mutually strengthen areas of innovative excellence. Secondly, we make sure that we invite industry leaders to serve on university boards, occupy our tech park buildings, serve on planning committees, and join licensing review teams and curriculum committees to ensure that we are responsive and sensitive to the needs of industry. Thirdly, we have leadership both in the community and in the university that is willing to pursue concurrent goals of academic excellence and regional economic development based on organizational infrastructures and cultures that enable the external stakeholders and faculty to partner internally across disciplines and/or externally with industry and other research universities (SSTI, 2006). And lastly, we invite into our university those in the community who are willing to expedite commercialization activities including writing SBIR and STTR grants, fund enhancement grants to aid commercialization, provide legal assistance, develop local sources of venture capital, and assist in business plan development. This --inside out and outside in-- operation furthers the position of our university to drive technology transfer activities promoting regional economic growth.

Assuming we have the university and community linked, then my role as a research administrator is to drive technology transfer activities and commercialization by taking the following course of action:

- Invest heavily in targeted and strategic technology areas where core competencies of the university marry up with the local economy.
- Pursue and retain star faculty who have a track record of competing for peer review funds and who know how to leverage basic science into applications that are valuable to a wide spectrum of commercialization interests.

- Link academic researchers with marketplace R&D entrepreneurs and companies that have the desire and ability to commercialize university technologies.
- Set aside funds as part of the technology transfer office's budget to make small strategic investments to develop advanced prototypes, perform commercial assessments, determine freedom of operability, draw in and match seed and venture funding, bring industry teams in for pressure-testing innovations, and provide office or lab space in university tech parks or other specialized facilities for faculty spin-outs and seed stage spin-ins. (SSTI, 2006).

After the above culture and infrastructure is in place, then it is incumbent in my research administration role to identify the technology transfer pipeline for faculty innovations, and to make this process well understood by inside and outside parties. At the University of South Alabama we have defined our priority as technology transfer not patenting. Although invention disclosures might ultimately need to be patented to ensure their commercialization potential (Siegle, et al., 2003), our university has taken the deliberate strategy not to be driven by protecting the potential patent but to first evaluate its commercial marketplace value.

According to Ker Ferguson (2009), the emphasis on evaluating a faculty member's disclosure using market assessment tools have led to numerous benefits, such as:

- The third party marketing assessments provide more credibility to the faculty on the go or no go patenting decision than the in-house judgments.
- Gaps in technology are identified early on so that faculty can focus on developmental research and seeking additional novelty.
- The market assessments set clear and early emphasis for commercialization not patenting.
- Awareness of marketing potential refines future disclosures by serial inventors to concentrate on commercialization.
- The university can make patenting judgments quickly, and for those disclosures returned to the faculty, valuable time as been preserved for faculty to protect disclosures using their own funds. The University of Missouri was recently sued because of lack of commercialization progress on a faculty patent (Zagier, 2009).
- Productivity of our one-man technology transfer office increases due to a reduction in commercialization assessments and cold calling for prospects.

SAME OLD CHALLENGES

The key challenge that remains for universities that are beginning to blossom in their technology transfer expertise and successes is to be able to balance organizational hierarchy and innovation. Most innovative faculty are "big thinkers" and usually think outside of the box of institutional organizations, management hierarchies, and academic unit budgets. It is difficult in my role as a research administrator to confront a dean or department head and campaign for additional resources to be directed at a faculty member who has a promising technology ready for commercialization—but who might be viewed by peers to be more absorbed in commercialization and less in departmental/college affairs (e.g. Ray Valentine's experiences). This acting outside of the box gets even more challenging for research administrators when the faculty innovator is pulling in other faculty and demanding resources from other university academic units and/or from other universities. I have found that technology transfer is best dealt with as a linear process. Not allowing innovators to out-run resources, organizational structures, or the technology transfer office will more likely result in their innovations being properly and more quickly vetted for commercial viability.

Slowly but surely technology transfer activities involving faculty entrepreneurs will chip away at the current culture and reward system in existence at most major universities in the US. Not all universities will be ready to adopt the Texas A&M University recognition that patents and commercialized research will be added to the criteria for tenure (Texas A&M, 2006); more likely faculty involvement with the commercial enterprise will be recognized by other means and backed by codes of behavior and declarations of support. I am looking forward to the day when most faculty entrepreneurs are swimming with the technology transfer current and university research administrators don't have to play lifeguard.

REFERENCES

AAAS. (2008). *Report XXXII: Research and Development FY 2008*. Washington, DC: American Association for the Advancement of Science.

Block, F., & Keller, M. (2008). *Where do innovations come from? Transformations in the U.S. national innovation system, 1970-2006*. The Information Technology & Innovation Foundation. July 2008. 22pp

Bok, D. (2003). *Universities in the marketplace: The commercialization of higher education*. Princeton, NJ: Princeton University Press.

Boyer, E. (1990). *Scholarship reconsidered: Priorities of the professoriate*. New York: The Carnegie Foundation for the Advancement of Teaching. John Wiley & Sons.

Bush, V. (1990) [1945]. *Science: The endless frontier*. Washington, DC: National Science Foundation California Administrative Code. 1982. Title 2, R 18705. Filed June 4, 1982.

Carayannis, E. (2008). Knowledge-driven creative destruction or leveraging knowledge for a competitive advantage. *Industry and Higher Education*, *22*(6), 343–353. doi:10.5367/000000008787225957

Council on Competitiveness. 1986. http://www.compete.org/. Washington, DC

Culliton, B. (1984). Biomedical research enters the marketplace. *Hew Eng. J. Med.*, *304*, 1195. doi:10.1056/NEJM198105143042003

Davis, U. C. (2007). *University of California, Davis Innovation Access: Connecting Research to Market*. http://innovationaccess.ucdavis.edu. Regents of the University of California, Davis, CA.

Fell, A. (2004). Nothing ventured nothing gained. *UC Davis Magazine*, *21*, 3.

Ferguson, K. (2009.) *Personal communication*. Director of University of South Alabama Technology and Research Park.

Fox, J. (1984). Patents encroaching on research freedom. *Science*, *224*, 1080. doi:10.1126/science.224.4653.1080

Greenburg, D. (2007). *Science for sale: The perils, rewards, and delusions of campus capitalism*. Chicago: The University of Chicago Press.

GUIRR. (1984). *The Government University Industry Research Roundtable*. The National Academies. http://sites.nationalacademies.org/pga/guirr/index.htm. Washington, DC.

Guston, D., & Keniston, K. (1994). *The fragile contract: University science and the federal government*. Cambridge, MA: MIT Press.

Holtzman, E. (1984). Competition and the marketplace: The need for balance. *Bioscience*, *34*, 349.

Leskovac, H. (1985). *State governance through conflict of interest rules: The California experience. Monograph 85-8*. Institute for Higher Education Law and Governance. University of Houston.

Leydesdorff, L., & Etzkowitz, H. (1996). Emergence of a triple helix of university-industry-government relations. *Science & Public Policy*, *23*, 279–286.

(August 2009). NSF. 2009. Academic Research and Development Expenditures: Fiscal Year 2008. Washington, DC: National Science Foundation.

Press, E., & Washburn, J. (2000). The kept university. *Atlantic Monthly*, *285*, 39–54.

Sanger, D. (1982). Business rents a lab coat and academia hopes for the best. *New York Times*, 21 March. p. 7

Siegel, D., Waldman, D., & Link, A. (2003). Assessing the impact of organizational practices on the relative productivity of university technology transfer offices: an exploratory study. *Research Policy*, *32*, 27–48. doi:10.1016/S0048-7333(01)00196-2

Texas A&M University System. (2006). *Regents approve Patents and commercialization of research as new considerations for faculty tenure*. Press release. May 26, 2006.

Zagier, A. (2009). *Missouri patent fight shows perils of 'tech transfer.'* Associated Press. Feb. 7, 2009.

Section 2
Contexts of Social and Organizational Impact

Chapter 9
Technology in the Supervision of Mental Health Professionals:
Ethical, Interpersonal, and Epistemological Implications

James "Tres" Stefurak
University of South Alabama, USA

Daniel W. Surry
University of South Alabama, USA

Richard L. Hayes
University of South Alabama, USA

ABSTRACT

As communication technology is increasingly applied to the training and supervision of mental health professionals, a more robust analysis of how such approaches fundamentally change the relationship between supervisor and supervisee and how these approaches both enhance and limit the outcomes of supervision is sorely needed. In this chapter clinical supervision is defined and discussed and the various technology platforms that have been used to conduct supervision at-a-distance are reviewed along with the supervision outcomes observed in the research literature with each method. The potential for technology to reduce geographic and financial barriers to the provision of quality supervision is discussed. However, the chapter also outlines the potential negative impacts technology might have to the supervisory relationship, the ethical dilemmas posed by technology-mediated supervision, and the ways in which technology-mediated supervision may place limits upon the elements of supervision that rely upon a constructivist epistemology.

DOI: 10.4018/978-1-60960-147-8.ch009

INTRODUCTION

Since the advent of telephone technology and later television technology health care providers have sought ways to utilize communication technology to extend the reach of health services and; this approach has come to be known as telemedicine (Strehle & Shabde, 2006). The majority of the research and design in telemedicine has occurred in the last 20-30 years as computer, internet and audio/visual technology have matured and become increasingly available and affordable. Among the forces propelling the interest in telemedicine have been the rising costs of health care and the desire by providers to reach underserved populations (Craig & Patterson, 2005). Similar forces related to shortages of specific health care professional groups and the increased demand for health care services for traditionally underserved populations have promoted the application of technology to the training and supervision of health care providers as well. Such interest in applying technology to enhance both service delivery and training of professionals has certainly been present across the range of medical and allied health professions, and this includes the mental health professions in which the present authors are most interested.

Within the mental health professions a variety of technologies including telephones, email, text messaging, internet chat, web-based groups, virtual reality environments, and videoconferencing have been used to deliver a variety of mental health services including consultation, assessment and diagnosis, and medication evaluations (Hilty et al., 2002), as well as counseling/ psychotherapy (Caspar, 2004; Oravec, 2000). This work has been conducted across the range of mental health professions including applied psychology (Caspar, 2004; Kanz, 2001), social work (Park-Oliver & Demiris, 2006; Parrott & Madoc-Jones, 2008), counselor education (Vaccaro & Lambie, 2007; Myrick & Sabella), and psychiatry (Hilty, et al., 2006).

In addition to aiding the delivery of mental health services to clients, technology, particularly internet-based technology and video conferencing, has also been applied to the task of training and supervising mental health professionals (hereafter MHPs). Scholars across the mental health professions have explored and put forth models of training and supervision that utilize email (Clingerman & Bernard, 2004), web-based supervision groups (Gainor & Constantine, 2002; Yeh et al., 2008), web/computer-based training systems (Berger, 2004; Weingardt, 2004) videoconferencing (Wood, Miller & Hargrove, 2005), and virtual reality technology (Beutler & Harwood, 2004) to enhance the acquisition of knowledge and skills involved in the competent delivery of mental health services such as assessment, diagnosis and psychotherapy. Despite these existing efforts, other authors have noted that the potential of technology-enhanced clinical supervision and training of mental health professionals has yet to be fully tapped (Berger, 2004). It is the area of technology-enhanced clinical supervision of MHPs to which the present chapter applies its focus.

THE MENTAL HEALTH PROFESSIONS

Before proceeding to a discussion of the nature of supervision, a brief discussion of the nature of the mental health service delivery systems and the mental health professions is warranted to comprehend how technology has been adopted differentially to some degree across such professions. First, what are the mental health professions? Answering that question is not as simple as it might seem. Mental health is a field characterized by professions that have different philosophical traditions with sometimes only subtle differences in the scope of clinical practice that separates them. A potential list of these professions is as follows in no particular order:

- Professional Counseling (School, Mental Health, Rehabilitation, etc.)
- Psychology (Clinical, Counseling, School, and Combined-Integrated)
- Clinical Social Work
- Marriage and Family Therapy
- Psychiatry
- Psychiatric Nursing

There are also a variety of specialties within these professions that target a particular age group, e.g. Child-Clinical Psychology, School Counseling; or a particularly type of problem/disorder, e.g. addictions, behavioral medicine, or a particularly modality of intervention, e.g. art therapy, family therapy, prevention work, etc.

Each of these professions and specialties will potentially have somewhat different sets of concerns and priorities in regards to utilizing technology to supervise junior members of the profession. For example Counselor Education as a field has displayed interest in utilizing technology to deliver both didactic classroom instruction as well as clinical supervision. Applied Psychology has focused particular attention on the use of technology to disseminate scientifically-based or evidence based practices to supervisees or to MHPs already in practice and participating in continuing education. Psychiatry has focused the most upon the use of technology for both supervision as well as the assessment of clinical competencies through the use of video conferencing and virtual patients. Social Workers and Marriage and Family Therapists appear to have experienced a more gradual degree of interest and scholarship on this topic and models of technology-enhanced supervision and training are still emerging in these fields. Finally, nursing scholars have explored the application of technology to nurse education in general, though little focus has been applied to the specific nature of technology-enhanced supervision and training of psychiatric nurses as a specialty group. Despite the somewhat unique focus applied by each specialty to technology-enhanced supervision and training, this chapter focuses on a common set of supervisory goals across these professions that generally surround the acquisition of skills in the areas of clinical interviewing and assessment as well as counseling/psychotherapy.

DEFINING CLINICAL SUPERVISION

In order to delineate the vagaries of enhancing clinical supervision with technology, a proper understanding of precisely what MHPs mean by "supervision" is in order. The definition of supervision in these professions is unique and differs significantly from what the terms conveys in other disciplines.

Bernard and Goodyear (2009) offer the following definition of clinical supervision in their widely utilized text:

Supervision is an intervention provided by a more senior member of a profession to a more junior member or members of that same profession. This relationship

- *Is evaluative and hierarchical*
- *Extends over time, and*
- *Has the simultaneous purposes of enhancing the professional functioning of the more junior person(s); monitoring the quality of professional services offered to the clients that she, he, or they see; and serving as a gatekeeper for those who are to enter the particular profession.*

Falender and Shafranske (2004) add the priority of training supervisees in science-based practice, facilitating the supervisee's ability to self-assess and self-correct and encourage supervisee self-efficacy. From these two examples of a definition of supervision we can see that supervision is more than merely a vehicle to promote acquisition of knowledge. Knowledge is but one prerequisite to a MHP becoming competent in any given area of practice. Falender and Shafranske (2004) describe "competence" as embodying knowledge, communication skills, technical skills, clinical reasoning and judgment, emotional awareness and appropriate use of emotions, ethical values, and capacity for regular reflection and self-assessment. In this sense becoming competent is a dynamic process in mental health work that exceeds merely learning objective knowledge. We will later describe how the inculcation of "competence" in supervision is a process that hinges upon an interpersonal alliance between supervisor and supervisee.

Supervision is typically seen as the central and most important mechanism in the education of MHPs (Falender & Shafranske, 2004). Indeed clinical supervision has been referred to as the "signature pedagogy" in the mental health professions (Bernard & Goodyear, 2009). Supervision involves a relationship between a MHP-in-training and a supervisor and typically is provided to the trainee when she or he has reached the point in their degree program where they are required to complete a clinical practicum in which they are delivering services such as assessment and psychotherapy on their own. The supervisor observes and evaluates the trainee's clinical services delivered to clients against professional standards to determine the degree to which the supervisee can practice competently and ethically (Falender & Shafranske, 2004). Just as is the case in the delivery of mental health services to clients the relationship between the supervisor and supervisee has typically been viewed as paramount to successful outcomes in supervision. In fact, when supervisees are asked to identify where important events occurred during the supervision process, they most often cite events related to the supervisory relationship (Ladany, et al, 2005).

Though didactic/teaching tasks are often embedded within the practice of supervision, and supervision and teaching have some similar goals; clinical supervision is distinct from the practice of teaching and didactic training in the mental health professions. Both teaching and supervision share a focus upon evaluating the student. However, teaching within MHP training programs typically involves and explicit pre-set curriculum delivered to a group of students (Bernard & Goodyear, 2009). Programs in higher education that train clinicians of all sorts including MHPs have historically separated didactic instruction from clinical supervision, with the former occurring early in the training program within coursework and the latter occurring when the student ultimately enters a clinical service environment. Though this paradigm may be changing as problem-based learning approaches are increasingly adopted in fields such as clinical psychology (Stedmon et al., 2006). While continued training in specific pieces of knowledge continues during the student's clinical placement through supervision, clinical supervision is distinct in that it involves a more intimate and more individualized approach to teaching, guidance, evaluation and feedback; and the material evaluated in supervision is the supervisees actual clinical work with clients rather than academic product as is produced in classroom settings. It is in supervision's increased individualization of learning and the more intimate relationship that is formed between supervisor and supervisee that a distinction between supervision and teaching can most clearly be discerned (Bernard & Goodyear, 2009). However, as will be explored the distinction may also go beyond this to include differing epistemologies across the task of teaching vs. supervision, a separate distinction which may have important implications for how or when technology should enhance or wholly deliver supervision.

Clinical supervision is typically delivered through a combination of individual and group face-to-face meetings. Supervision may also be provided by both clinical faculty as well as clinicians working at an external site. Supervision meetings that occur at the clinical site may be scheduled simultaneously with a client contact so that the supervisor could observe the supervisee delivering therapeutic services live. Often "bug-in-the-ear" technology is utilized in which the supervisor can communicate with the therapist during the session through an ear bud speaker while watching the supervisee and client either through a one-way mirror or video link. More typically the supervision session consists of either a review of a taped example of the supervisees clinical work and verbal discussion of the work and does not necessarily physically or temporally coincide with the actual service delivery. Usually supervisees would also meet as a group with a supervisor during training concurrent with attending individual supervision. Inherent in this traditional face-to-face approach is the idea that the interpersonal processes that occur in both individual and group supervision are crucial in helping supervisees learn about self, learn to apply knowledge they have gained, and grow in their interpersonal skills necessary to deliver mental health services. However, the traditional supervisory activity described above are bounded by a specific time at which the supervision appointment occurs and by a specific space where the appointment must occur so that all parties can be present together. Technology can remove obstacles associated with time and space, and carries with it unique benefits and deficits relative to the traditional face-to-face model of supervision.

OVERVIEW OF ISSUES IN TECHNOLOGY & SUPERVISION

The role of technology in higher education, in general, and the training of mental health professionals in particular, have received increasing attention since the advent of the internet and other advanced technologies that facilitate human communication and interaction in a manner that removes the obstacles of time and space. Technology has been observed to have three broad uses within clinical supervision: (a) to facilitate the provision of work samples for the supervisor to review, evaluate and provide feedback to the supervisee, (b) to allow the provision of supervision at-a-distance, and (c) to influence the process of supervision in deliberate ways (Bernard & Goodyear, 2009). Additionally there are types of technology that we have selected to highlight; these include: (a) electronic text-based communication such as email, (b) web-based groups, and (c) video-conferencing and other audio/visual media.

ELECTRONIC TEXT COMMUNICATION & SUPERVISION

Early versions of electronic communication technology such as telephone, fax, email, and chat allowed for delivery of aspects of supervision that decreased the impact of distance and allowed for extensions to how a supervisor and supervisee communicate as well as how the supervisee and their peers communicate (Harvey & Carlson, 2003). In addition to reducing the impact of geography and timing, text-based electronic communication such as email and threaded discussions, because they are an asynchronous form of communication the contents of which remain preserved over time, allow for more reflection and thought by the supervisor and supervisee because the text material of email communication is available for repeated review and the asynchronous nature of email allows for more time spent in reflecting upon the information being shared. Also, email and other electronic text communication may foster a larger amount of disclosure on the part of supervisees and therefore promote engagement and intimacy in the supervisory relationship (Clingerman & Bernard, 2004). Such methods build upon older approaches such as journaling and reaction papers that had a similar goal in mind, but without the efficiencies of electronic communication.

Email has been observed to have specific effects upon supervisees reflection and thinking during clinical practicum experiences in counseling graduate training. The two research efforts reviewed here both asked supervisees to regularly send emails to their supervisor in the time between face-to-face individual and group supervision meetings (Graf & Stebnicki, 2002; Clingerman & Bernard, 2004). First, the topics of such emails tend to fall into specific categories: (a) conceptualization and intervention with clients, (b) site supervisor and site issues, and (c) personalization/self-analysis. Clingerman and Bernard (2004) found that the number of emails sent each week declined across the semester, but messages related to personalization issues, involving topics such as self-awareness, self-efficacy and self-reflection, a were consistently the most frequent category. Graf and Stebnicki (2002) limited emails to one per week and observed that emails about personalization/self-reflection issues began with concerns about the supervisee's confidence and self-efficacy, and progressing to an increased sense of responsibility and frustration with a perceived lack of impact, and finally ending in a more balanced realistic perspective on self-as-helper. The two studies differed in that Clingerman and Bernard (2004) observed less emphasis on emails regarding the site supervisor and site than did Graf and Stebnicki (2002). Obviously more research is desperately needed here and these two studies suffer from a lack of a control group and lack of data controlling for the impact of the face-to-face supervision that participants in both studies continued to attend while participating in the email portion of supervision.

WEB-BASED GROUPS

These early electronic text-based communication technologies now sit alongside a host of collaborative technological tools mostly centered on web-based interactive platforms, which further enhance the range of communication options. These newer techniques include the use of threaded discussions, wikis, podcasts, blogs, social networking sites all collectively referred to as Web 2.0 applications (Conn, Roberts, & Powell, 2009). Such applications have allowed for not just communication between supervisor and supervisee at-a-distance, but collaboration between supervisors and between supervisees in regards to acquiring clinical skills and learning new and better ways to best serve clients. Moreover, interactive web technologies have allowed supervisors and supervisees to engage in co-construction of knowledge regarding the needs of a given client as well as facilitating the acquisition of objective knowledge about treatment approaches and specific mental health problems/disorders. We shall discuss this in more detail later.

Now emerging are internet technologies that have been collectively referred to as Web 3.0 or the "Semantic Web" (Ohler, 2010). These web-based endeavors will further allow larger groups of mental health professionals beyond the parameters of MHP graduate training programs or the supervisory relationship to impose meaning structures on bodies of knowledge in the field. Advanced computer software will potentially be able to comprehend the ways in which large groups of MHPs have labeled and organized concepts in a given domain of practice and be able to create detailed and tailored information regarding questions that arise in the process of learning to be a MHP. As Ohler (2010) suggests the semantic web will not link users to "pages" or discrete locations on the internet or within an internal network, but to "reports" of information tailored to the user's specifications and informed by the contributions of a broad audience of users' perceptions of said information.

One intriguing approach is peer-based online supervision and support groups that seek to address supervisee's needs for support, identity development and skill development. Given that supervisees have generally been shown to benefit more from peer feedback than supervisor feedback, such approaches may represent a significant ability to augment and extend what is initiated in face-to-face group supervision. However, such approaches face obstacles from the degree of student acceptance of receiving web-based supervision.

Gainor and Constantine (2002) investigated the effects of web-based versus in-person peer group supervision to foster multicultural counseling skills. Results indicated significantly lower levels of supervisee satisfaction with the web-based format. Furthermore, supervisees assigned to in-person peer group supervision achieved significantly higher scores on a skill measure of multicultural case conceptualization than did those assigned to the web-based supervision. The authors point out that supervisees conceptualization skills did increase significantly in both supervision formats, only more so in the in-person format. They speculate that one major hindrance in learning such skills in group supervision over the web is the lack of non-verbal cues and information, combined with the typical reluctance of supervisees to self-disclose in a group format, in general, as well as their reticence to self-disclose or discuss their reactions to multicultural issues, in particular. This is in contrast to the view that supervisee to supervisor emails appear to foster more disclosure. They concluded that a significant degree of interpersonal intimacy is required for supervision of any type to be effective, let alone supervision focused on multicultural competence, and that training programs should value in-person over web-based group or a combination of the two supervision rather than an exclusively web-based approach.

In a related study, Yeh and colleagues (2008) investigated the process and outcome of an online peer support group for counseling students who were completing clinical field experiences. They found that topics most frequently covered in this group were similar to those covered in face-to-face supervision groups. The authors interpreted their results to suggest that group process occurs in an online peer support group in a manner similar to face-to-face peer, or supervisor-lead group supervision. Interestingly, these researchers also found that students reported that they were more comfortable discussing some topics in the online peer group than in face-to-face supervision. An online group supervision format, therefore, may offer some additional benefits not found in a face-to-face group supervision format. According to Yeh et al. these advantages include: (a) ready availability of feedback and guidance from other members over a relatively long time interval; (b) the ability to get feedback and support for immediate concerns: and, (c) extended time for discussion of student concerns that is not possible in a time-limited face-to-face group.

VIDEO RECORDING & VIDEO CONFERENCING

Audio and visual communication has also seen advances from telephone and voice-only communication with the advent of affordable personal computers and broadband internet connectivity. First, Voice Over Internet Protocol technology services have allowed low cost voice communication over long distances among multiple parties. Most recently audio and visual communication have been linked together in the form of video conferencing technology which has offered a means to deliver individual and group supervision sessions at-a-distance as well as conduct live video observation of a supervisee's clinical work without the full loss of non-verbal/visual data that is inherent in voice only and text-based supervisor mediums. This advancement may represent the strongest strategy to most fully overcome the aforementioned disadvantaged of technology-based supervision and enhance the ability of the supervisor to evaluate supervisee competence.

A primary role of the mental health supervisor is to function as a gatekeeper within their respective profession (Vaccaro & Lambie, 2007). This necessitates adopting evaluation practices that afford the supervisor an opportunity to see valid samples of the clinician's skills in action. Technology has also long been used to produce work samples that can be viewed and evaluated by the supervisor. This includes technologies to aid live supervision such as the aforementioned "bug in the ear" technology, as well technology that allows recording and dissemination of assessment and therapy sessions for review by supervisors and peers. An alternative to the "bug in the ear" approaches to live supervision includes "bug in the eye". Involves placing a computer monitor in the session room behind the client and allowing the supervisor to type text message to the monitor which can only be seen by the clinician (Bernard & Goodyear, 2009; Miller, Miller & Evans, 2002). This also includes the recording of sessions, which presently is almost always done utilizing digital media recordings. In fact, recordings of therapy sessions has been combined with the "bug in the eye" approach to produce tapes that have the "bug in the eye" text submitted by the supervisor inserted as subtitles during the recording of a session (Rosenberg, 2006). If live supervision and recording technology is combined with streaming media over the internet and video conferencing technology the dimension of distance from the supervisor can also be conquered in regards to collecting and disseminating work samples. Lastly, these technological enhancements fundamentally shape the process of supervision. It is likely obvious that supervision takes a different tone when a supervisee knows that a live or recorded sample of their work will be observed by their supervisor, or through the internet observed by a bevy of expert supervisors. This factor may promote increased accountability by all parties, increased professional commitment by the supervisee, and perhaps even increased cohesion and trust in the supervisory relationship.

With the integration of audio and video two-way communication at-a-distance video-conferencing may be the most promising medium for the technologically-based provision of individual and group supervision sessions given its potential ability to allow full verbal and non-verbal communication between multiple parties in real-time. However, VC technology has only recently advanced to the point of being a cost-effective and efficient means of facilitating clinical supervision at-a-distance, and much remains to be discovered in regards to the vagaries of supervision in this format. The VC format has been found to have unique advantages, relative to face-to-face supervision; these include:

a. Ability to present and process both auditory and visual information during interaction, and thereby maintain some of the spontaneity and "realness" present in face-to-face communication (Olson, Russell, & White, 2001)
b. Decreased stress related to traveling to supervision (Marrow, Hollyoake, Hamer, & Kenrick, 2002)
c. Ability to pair supervisor and supervisees working in similar specialties, but who reside in different geographical areas (Marrow, Hollyoake, Hamer, & Kenrick, 2002)
d. Ability of participants to use VC technology with little preparation and training (Garrett, & Dudt, 1998)
e. Fostering clearer and more structured cmmunications between supervisors and supervisees (Gammon et al., 1998)
f. Support real-time interaction between multiple individuals that includes visual and auditory information and with less time lapse between responses by participants

However, VC supervision has also been found to be associated with various drawbacks including:

a. Difficulty accessing and utilizing equipment, particularly when ongoing technical support is lacking (Marrow, Hollyoake, Hamer, & Kenrick, 2002),
b. The tendency for participants to withhold emotionally difficult material for future face-to-face supervision (Gammon et al., 1998),
c. Reduced tolerance for silence by supervisees in the supervision session and a consequent

increase in exaggerated assertive behaviors in attempts to ensure they are heard (Gammon et al., 1998),

d. Concern that the supervisor's ability to maintain a working alliance with supervisees maybe diminished when using VC technology.

Wood, Miller,and Hargrove (2005) have offered a specific model of supervision that includes video-conferencing group supervision as a component. Their model of supervision is intended to offer supervision to mental health professionals working in remote areas and is based on practices established in previous telehealth consultation and supervision models. These authors outline a combination of face-to-face and electronic communication between supervisors and supervisees. They stress the importance in phase one of the model of training all parties in the technology being utilized in order to increase comfort levels and smooth the transition to conducting some supervision over electronic media. Their model includes the use of case studies that are provided to supervisees through a web page, followed by discussion between supervisor and supervisees via email and chat rooms. The third phase of this supervision model involves the provision of group supervision via live video-conferencing. The fourth and final phase involves provision of traditional face-to-face individual supervision. The authors note that telesupervision in general offers the same cost effectiveness found in group supervision, and gives supervisees in remote settings an opportunity they might otherwise not be offered. However, the role of remote technology-assisted supervision is still as an adjunct to some degree of face-to-face supervision in their model.

Gammon et al. (1998) conducted a qualitative study of supervisors and supervisees reactions to VC-based psychotherapy supervision. The study involved 8 participants (2 supervisors and 6 trainees). Interestingly they found that VC supervision had positive effects on supervision such as more structure and more preparation on the part of involved parties for supervision. This was at the cost of less perceived spontaneity and sensed emotional presence of the other. Overall, the participants viewed VC supervision as a potentially useful adjunct to face-to-face supervision, but not as a replacement. Video conferencing has an enormous amount of potential, particularly if it is integrated with other technologies and used as an adjunct to some degree of face-to-face contact.

COMPUTER-MEDIATED VIRTUAL REALITY

Most recently the use of standardized virtual patients has provided a more standardized and reliable method of assessing clinician competency (Srinivasan et al., 2006). This topic is covered more thoroughly in a separate chapter of this text, but deserves a brief mention here. One downside of work samples with actual clients is the lack of standardization of the client responses and behaviors towards the clinician. The creation of "intelligent" virtual clients/patients has allowed supervisors to examine a clinician's responses to a standardized stimuli, which facilitates comparison between supervisees and provides the supervisor with a higher degree of control over the clinical stimuli with which the learner is presented.

COMPUTER/WEB-BASED TRAINING

Lastly, though it is also beyond the scope of this chapter; web-based learning systems have the potential to revolutionize the "training" of MHPs in a variety of models and approaches to clinical service. As mentioned the training or teaching aspect of MHP education is somewhat distinct from the process of clinical supervision. Regardless a authors such as Cucciare, Weingardt and Villafranca (2008) have described how using multiple learning systems including web-based learning systems can enhance the acquisition of evidence based psychotherapy knowledge and skills. Additionally Weingardt (2004) has argued for a closer integration of the fields of mental health and instructional design to aid in the creation of effective training systems that would allow for a long sought improvement of the large scale transfer of research-based knowledge into practice settings. A final example in this area would be the use of virtual reality technology to train MHPs in psychotherapy and assessment skills (Beutler & Harwood, 2004). What follows is a more detailed review of selected technology-based approaches to clinical supervision in the following areas: email, web-based groups, and video-conferencing.

BENEFITS AND RATIONALES FOR TECHNOLOGY-BASED CLINICAL SUPERVISION

While interest appears to be steadily increasing in regards to utilizing technology to deliver supervisory services to MHP trainees, little attention has been paid to how such approaches may fundamentally change how MHP students and supervisors relate and interact with one another. Additionally, technology-based supervision is likely to change a supervisee's relationships with their peers, their clients and with the organizations with which they interact and by which they are employed. To be certain these changes are likely a mixture of disadvantages relative to face-to-face supervision as well as unique advantages relative to traditional supervision paradigms. To this end the chapter will review research and theoretical work in regards to how technology might enhance the practice of supervision while not detracting from the professional skill development of supervisees. We will also attempt to propose what fruitful next steps might be in the application and research of emerging technologies in supervision.

In the field of counselor education Layne and Hohenshil (2005) have argued that the use of technology to serve clients as well as train counselors is here to stay, and that members of the field must adapt to these new technologies. The question is now not *whether* clinical supervisors will adopt features of technology-enhanced supervision, but *how*. Much of this necessity is likely driven by falling budgets in higher education as well as increasing demand for mental health services and consequently demand for more mental health providers. Technology-based training and supervision of MHPs may require less of the supervisor's time and travel and, in theory, allows faculty to deliver more supervision services to larger number of students.

In addition to the acknowledged necessity of utilizing technology in supervision, scholars have noted important functional benefits of integrating technology into clinical training, and weighing those benefits against known costs. Benefits of technology-enhanced clinical supervision that potentially are present in regards to educational institutions, supervisors, supervisees, and to the consumers in the mental health system at large. Consumers may benefit by technology's ability to allow for training of mental health professionals working in rural and remote mental health services with populations that are historically underserved and have poor access to care (Olson, Russell, & White, 2001). Supervisees also may experience reduced costs associated with travel to face-to-face supervision (Olson, Russell & White, 2001). Consumers may also benefit if technology allows for increased dissemination and implementation of evidence based approaches which are likely to work better than the status quo approaches to treatment in the field (Weingardt, 2004). Benefits to the learner include accessing more specialized and "master" supervisors who may be geographically remote (Janoff & Schoenholtz, 1999), and having the content of supervision communications available for a longer period of time, which might enhance reflection and synthesis of knowledge (Hara, Bonk, & Angeli, 2000). This ability to overcome geography is perhaps the most often cited rationale and benefit of technology-based supervision. An emerging consensus is present in mental health that technology-assisted training and supervision has its own unique advantages and disadvantages from face-to-face supervision and can serve, at least, as a useful adjunct to traditional face-to-face supervision (Olson, Russell, & White, 2001; Wood, Miller, & Hargrove, 2005).

LEGAL AND ETHICAL CONCERNS

Perhaps chief argument or concerns regarding technology based supervision is the same concern most often cited regarding the technology-based mental health services—the potential loss of client confidentiality. By using email, threaded discussions, chat or videoconferencing supervisors and supervisees run the risk of having client data shared in supervision become compromised. In addition to statutes that give privileged communication status to information shared with mental health professionals and ethical code requirements that all client information is kept confidential; the Health Insurance Portability and Accountability Act now requires significant safeguards be implemented when communicating about clients across electronic formats, in particular the use of password protected computing stations, steps to ensure the identity of recipients of electronic communication and the use of encryption technology to render the electronic data transmitted impenetrable to those seeking to compromise such data.

In general the internet cannot be viewed as a secure or private medium for communication. However, Kanz argued in 2001 that encryption technology had advanced greatly, and at present many computer networks and online communication software systems do allow for a greatly increased assurance of privacy. Secure encryption has become a primary means of protecting client data and has also become more available at low costs across a wide range of software from email to web-based social groups and video conferencing software. Even if the communication is encrypted there are still requirements that the identity of the information recipient's identity be verifiable. Other steps typically taken to keep supervisory data confidential include the use of regularly changing passwords to access web-based supervision resources and deidentifying any client data transmitted electronically (Janoff & Schoenholtz, 1999). Supervisors should seek consultation on such matters from both other mental health professionals as well as technology experts and make every effort to both institute practices that will protect client confidentiality as well as provide appropriate informed consent to supervisee's clients as to the supervisory process, specifically how their private data is being disseminated electronically, the risks posed by such dissemination and the steps that are being taken to protect such data (Olsen, Russell, & White, 2001).

Another ethical concern is how crisis events are adequately addressed through the use of technology to provide supervision at-a-distance. This concern would typically necessitate that a clinician-in-training have some level of available face-to-face supervisory oversight if working at a site physically remote from the supervisor of record for their clinical work, and have the ability to access modes of communication such as a cell phone that are faster than is found on web-based modes of communication (Janoff & Schoenholtz, 1999). This concern is typically allayed by having immediately available on-site supervision in addition to remote electronic supervision, i.e. multiple layers of supervision.

Legal arguments and cautions against technology-based supervision have been offered in regards to how supervision delivered remotely via technology impacts the supervisor's degree of liability for the services delivered to clients by the supervisee. The primary question here is what is the nature of the supervisor-supervisee relationship when it is constituted over a virtual technological medium? Scholars have argued when health services or supervision are delivered through a remote technology-based medium the provider or supervisor may be less liable than if they were delivered face-to-face. This is because the technological medium creates a perception of a less intimate and less clear set of obligations between physician and patient or supervisor and supervisee (Granade & Sanders, 1996). Related to this concern is a simpler question of whether supervisor liability insurance policies clearly and adequately cover supervision delivered over a virtual electronic medium (Panos et al., 2002). Lastly, if supervisors deliver supervision services across state lines they may be practicing in their respective MHP without a license in that a license typically is only valid for the state the supervisor resides in and sought licensure (Bernard & Goodyear, 2009).

Another concern regarding technology-based supervision is in regards to the competence with which supervisors and supervisees are able to utilize tools such as email, web-based groups, and video-conferencing. This concern links to the ability to supervise and practice ethically as well (Vaccaro & Lambie, 2007). Barak (1999) noted that supervisor and supervisees who do not understand the capacities and limitations of technology may unwittingly compromise client data, e.g. sending emails to the wrong recipient or posting data on a web-group that is not deidentified or rely on technology to meet clinical requirements for which the technology is inappropriate, e.g. sending an email to a supervisor to address a crisis. These lapses would not necessarily be due to poor ethical comprehension, but a lack of adeptness with the technology itself.

EPISTEMOLOGIES IN CLINICAL SUPERVISION

Within supervision are goals for supervisee learning that fall within both positivist and constructivist epistemologies. As Berger (2004) notes technology-based learning systems can serve as both a "tutoring system" to facilitate the acquisition of objective knowledge, as well as a "interactive learning environment" that facilitates the construction of knowledge. While supervision does involve, in part, "teaching" the supervisee pieces of "objective" knowledge about psychological disorders, treatment techniques, ethical precepts etc.; the endeavor also inherently leads to co-construction of knowledge. This second aspect of supervision occurs in the context of the supervisory relationship, in which the supervisee and supervisor work together to produce a case conceptualization, diagnosis, treatment plan and then proceed in the interpersonal task of helping the client recover and make changes. This set of tasks involves a blending of objectivist/positivist epistemology with constructivist epistemology as the pathway during supervision through which the clinician translates nomothetic concepts gleaned from such sources as scientific research, expert opinion, and best practices based on professional consensus with idiographic data gleaned from both the supervisory relationship as well as the clinician-client relationship. This idiographic data includes the particular values, skills, and limitations of all parties involved. Thus supervision aided by technology such as web-based textual communication, video-conferencing or telephone communication must be able to allow for sufficient exchange of a range of discrete information as well as interpersonal information between supervisor and supervisee so that the more nuanced co-construction of clinical knowledge in a given case can occur.

IMPACT OF TECHNOLOGY ON INTERPERSONAL RELATIONSHIPS IN CLINICAL SUPERVISION

At the heart of supervision as well as all clinical interventions are the supervisor-supervisee relationship and the clinician-client relationship respectively. Mental health is a field that generally values the interpersonal dimensions of service delivery. In fact outcome research suggests that the therapeutic relationship accounts for a moderate but consistent amount of the variance in treatment outcomes (Norcross & Lambert, 2006). The supervisory relationship is frequently viewed as crucial in the practice of clinical supervision as it is in the practice of assessment and psychotherapy (Bernard & Goodyear, 2004). Concerns exist regarding the impact of technology-based communication upon the supervisory relationship primarily due to the potential lack of sufficient face-to-face contact (Barak, 1999). This may be reduced with the use of video conferencing approaches, but until such technologies are ubiquitous, text-based electronic communications are likely to be widely relied upon when web-based supervision is undertaken. The fear is that primarily text-based electronic communication will reduce the full range of verbal and non-verbal information shared in supervisor-supervisee interactions and inhibit the conveyance of more complex and subtle meanings when discussing clinical work (Vaccaro & Lambie, 2007). Ultimately this could impede a clinician's professional development and ultimately place an upper limit on the quality of the services they deliver to clients. In a sense one of the dominant epistemologies within supervision practice is a view that the relationship yields insights, ways of knowing and "truths" that are an outgrowth of the relational frame provided by face-to-face interaction with a supervisee over time.

While web-based supervision allows those interested in the clinical training of mental health professionals to transcend many of the limitations of distance, such approaches may also fundamentally alter the interpersonal factors present between supervisee and supervisor. Interestingly research has shown that these interpersonal changes do not appear necessarily deleterious. For example Janoff and Schoenholtz (1999) examined a combined face-to-face and computer-mediated group supervision format and found that group members with a high degree of status and power were less likely to steer the content of the dialogue in computer-mediated group supervision. Men and women were equally likely to initiate discussion points in a computer-mediated group, perhaps because the inability to see one another may reduce the pressure to conform to gender roles triggered by visual cues. Group supervisees in such a format are more likely to generate a diversity of perspectives when the pressure to conform or avoid negative social consequences is attenuated. The downside to this lack of non-verbal information is that participant's may be more easily offended due to the ambiguity of text-only computer-mediated communication. Similarly, Conn, Roberts and Powell (2009) examined a hybrid model of counseling supervision with school counselors and found no differences in the perception of the quality of a face-to-face supervision paradigm vs. a mixed face-to-face and web-based paradigm. Though, there was a significant trend for self-reported comfort with technology to correlate with reported satisfaction with the hybrid model. Such research is a first step in assessing whether web-based distance supervision has a necessarily deteriorating impact upon the supervisory relationship and/or the relationship between supervisees.

Despite such preliminary finding of certain unique advantages of web-based supervisory environments a common thread in the literature is to assert that web-based supervision is a useful adjunct, but not replacement for face-to-face supervision (Janoff & Schoenholtz-Read, 1999). The basis for such a sentiment lies in the limitations technology-based supervisory mediums place upon communication and interpersonal relationships. In general, online relationships are viewed as circumscribed forms of actual face-to-face relationships (Kanz, 2001). Miller and Gergen (1998) argued that virtual, online communities decrease the level of interpersonal accountability among participants in a group. Participants receive little immediate feedback, and are unlikely to get useful feedback about the impact they have upon other members in groups that exist only in a virtual space. Gammon et al. (1998) has further argued that the loss of non-verbal cues in many forms of electronic communication leads to a task-oriented, depersonalized approach that lacks spontaneity or authenticity. Also, without other confirming evidence, the level of authenticity inherent in a participant's responses is essentially unknowable to members of the group. Thus, participants have little ability to gauge whether a response is congruent with the respondent's inner state and values (i.e. how genuine is the responder). As a consequence, comments by participants may have a diminished or unintended impact upon other group members, and thereby limiting how cohesive the group can become. Given the challenges of fostering a full and textured relationship between a supervisor and supervisee in text-based electronic communication; the task of facilitating such a relationship with and between members of a training group is significantly complicated.

Many of the limitations noted above may be at least partially overcome by video conferencing (VC) based supervision. However, VC technology is the youngest communication technology and still more expensive than other technologies. Supervisees may find that technical limitations of computing equipment make VC supervision less then desirable (Walter, Rosenquist & Bawtinhimer, 2004). Also, as Gammon et al.'s (1998) early study of VC-based psychotherapy supervision revealed supervisees typically still view VC as an adjunct, not a replacement, for face-to-face supervision. That said, a clear case can be made that when face-to-face supervision, particularly with supervisees working in isolated or remote areas or when the services of a geographically distant expert supervisor is needed, would not otherwise be possible; VC-based supervision would provide significant "add-on" benefits and replicate face-to-face group supervision reasonably well. An example of this is present in research by Panos (1010) who delivered VC supervision to social work field students working in remote international areas. In such a scenario where face-to-face supervision with a known supervisor is not possible VC technology provides an opportunity to deliver supervision and guidance that would otherwise not be possible.

CONCLUSION & FUTURE DIRECTIONS

The application of technology, particularly web-based groups and videoconferencing, to clinical supervision of mental health services has offered intriguing possibilities for improved training of supervisees in remote/rural areas and early research suggests that such an approach has advantages above and beyond its cost effectiveness. The text-based medium of web groups appears to provide a forum where concerns that would likely not normally be voiced are put forth and different interpersonal processes of an egalitarian nature may be easier to facilitate than in face-to-face supervision. The primary concerns that linger in regards to technology-based supervision are outlined below. Those who are in the position of designing MHP training programs, and who are providing supervision must content with these questions if they take up the gauntlet of leveraging technology to enhance and extend traditional face-to-face supervision.

The first lingering question is whether virtual supervision replace face-to-face supervision? The immediate sentiment appears to be a resounding no in mental health given the increasing interest in hybrid forms of supervision that mix face-to-face with technology-enhanced. Such an approach leverages the strengths of both and minimized the weaknesses of both. One of the primary concerns within this question is the threat to the supervisory relationship or alliance posed by virtual supervision. Also, a basic guiding idea here is that technology-based supervision is used when a clear unique benefit is provided by doing so, i.e. supervision via internet, video conferencing is needed because it offers an opportunity that without utilizing such methods supervision would be fundamentally compromised if not impossible. Where face-to-face supervision is possible, it should probably constitute at least part of the supervision practice.

Second, how does a supervisor best protect the confidentiality of client data when conducting technology-based supervision? Encryption technology appears to have the potentially to most solidly answer this question, though issues of existing and not yet foreseen federal laws, and client subjective reactions to virtual supervision may present continued obstacles.

Third, will the proliferation of virtual supervision ultimately add to the overall supervisory workload of faculty and site-based supervisors and thereby reduce the quality of clinical supervision particularly by the deleterious effects this might have to the supervisory relationship. Here the ethical priorities and professional identities of clinical supervisors may come in conflict with the legitimate requirement for higher education administrators to look for and exploit cost saving measures in an era of falling budgets in colleges and universities. More than ethical concerns there is the fear that such technology fueled proliferation of supervision will add to the threats to the unique nature of the supervisory relationship by reducing the degree of trust, intimacy and disclosure in supervisory contexts. The end result could be not just a change in how supervision is conducted to a more technically-oriented objectivist endeavor, but also a rippling effect in which the identity of mental health professionals, the culture of the mental health professions and the relationships between provider and client are all similarly changed.

REFERENCES

Barak, A. (1999). Psychological applications on the internet: A Discipline on the Threshold of a New Millennium. *Applied & Preventive Psychology*, *8*, 231–245. doi:10.1016/S0962-1849(05)80038-1

Berger, T. (2004). Computer-based technological applications in psychotherapy training. *Journal of Clinical Psychology*, *60*(3), 301–315. doi:10.1002/jclp.10265

Bernard, R., & Goodyear, J. (2009). *Fundamentals of Clinical Supervision* (4th ed.). Boston: Allyn & Bacon.

Beutler, L. E., & Harwood, T. M. (2004). Virtual reality in psychotherapy training. *Journal of Clinical Psychology*, *60*(3), 317–330. doi:10.1002/jclp.10266

Caspar, F. (2004). Technological developments and applications in clinical psychology and psychotherapy: Introduction. *Journal of Clinical Psychology*, *60*(3), 221–238. doi:10.1002/jclp.10260

Clingerman, T. L., & Bernard, J. M. (2004). An investigation of the use of e-mail as a supplemental modality for clinical supervision. *Counselor Education and Supervision*, *44*, 82–96.

Craig, J., & Patterson, V. (2005). Introduction to the practice of telemedicine. *Journal of Telemedicine and Telecare*, *11*, 3–9. doi:10.1258/1357633053430494

Cucciare, M. A., Weingardt, K. R., & Villafranca, S. (2008). Using blended learning to implement evidence-based psychotherapies. *Clinical Psychology: Science and Practice*, *15*(4), 299–307. doi:10.1111/j.1468-2850.2008.00141.x

Falender, C. A., & Shafranske, E. P. (2004). *Clinical Supervision: A Competency-Based Approach*. Washington, D.C.: American Psychological Association. doi:10.1037/10806-000

Gainor, K., & Constantine, M. (2002). Multicultural group supervision: A comparison of in-person versus web-based formats. *Professional School Counseling*, *6*(2), 104–111.

Gammon, D., Sørlie, T., Bergvik, S., & Høifødt, T. S. (1998). Psychotherapy supervision conducted via videoconferencing: A qualitative study of users experiences. *Nordic Journal of Psychiatry*, *52*(5), 411–421. doi:10.1080/08039489850139445

Garrett, J. L., & Dudt, K. (1998). Using videoconferencing to supervise student-teachers. *Technology and Teacher Education Annual*, 1084-1088.

Graf, N. M., & Stebnicki, M. A. (2002). Using E-mail for clinical supervision in practicum; A qualitative analysis. *Journal of Rehabilitation*, *68*(3), 41–49.

Granade, P. F., & Sanders, J. H. (1996). Implementing telemedicine nationwide: Analyzing the legal issues. *Defense Counsel Journal*, *63*, 67–73.

Harvey, V. S., & Carlson, J. F. (2003). Ethical and professional issues with computer-related technology. *School Psychology Review*, *32*, 92–104.

Hilty, D. M., Alverson, D. C., Alpert, J. E., Lowell, T., Sagduyu, K., & Boland, R. J. (2006). Virtual reality, telemedicine, web and data processing innovations in medical and psychiatric education and clinical care. *Academic Psychiatry*, *30*(6), 528–533. doi:10.1176/appi.ap.30.6.528

Hilty, D. M., Luo, J. S., Morache, C., Marcelo, D. A., & Nesbitt, T. S. (2002). Telepsychiatry: An overview for psychiatrists. *CNS Drugs*, *16*(8), 527–548. doi:10.2165/00023210-200216080-00003

Janoff, D. S., & Schoenholtz-Read, J. (1999). Group supervision meets technology: A model for computer-mediated group training at a distance. *International Journal of Group Psychotherapy*, *49*(2), 255–272.

Kanz, J. E. (2001). Clinical-supervision.com: Issues in the provision of online supervision. *Professional Psychology, Research and Practice*, *32*(4), 415–420. doi:10.1037/0735-7028.32.4.415

Ladany, N., Friedlander, M. L., & Nelson, M. L. (2005). *Critical Events in Psychotherapy Supervision: An Interpersonal Approach*. Washington, DC: American Psychological Association. doi:10.1037/10958-000

Lambie, G. W., Sias, S. M. (2009). An integrative psychological development model of supervision for professional school counselors-in-training. *Journal of Counseling & Development, Summer,* (87), 349-356.

Layne, C. M., & Hohenshil, T. H. (2005). High tech counseling: Revisited. *Journal of Counseling and Development*, *83*(2), 222–226.

Marrow, C. E., Hollyoake, K., Hamer, D., & Kenrick, C. (2002). Clinical supervision using video-conferencing technology: A reflective account. *Journal of Nursing Management*, *10*, 275–282. doi:10.1046/j.1365-2834.2002.00313.x

Miller, K. L., Miller, S. M., & Evans, W. J. (2002). Computer-assisted live supervision in college counseling centers. *Journal of College Counseling*, *5*, 187–192.

Myrick, R. D., & Sabella, R. A. (1995). Cyberspace: New place for counselor supervision. *Elementary School Guidance & Counseling*, *30*(1), 35–45.

Norcross, J. C., & Lambert, M. J. (2006). The Therapy Relationship. In Norcross, J. C., Beutler, L. E., & Levant, R. F. (Eds.), *Evidence-Based Practices in Mental Health: Debate and Dialogue on the Fundamental Questions*. Washington, DC: American Psychological Association. doi:10.1037/11265-000

Ohler, J. (2010). The power and peril of web 3.0: It's more than just semantics. *Learning and Leading with Technology*, (May): 14–17.

Olsen, M. M., Russell, C. S., & White, M. B. (2001). Technological implications for clinical supervision and practice. *The Clinical Supervisor, 20*(2), 201–215. doi:10.1300/J001v20n02_15

Panos, P. T., Panos, A., Cox, S. E., Roby, J. L., & Matheson, K. W. (2002). Ethical issues concerning the use of videoconferencing to supervise international social work field practicum students. *Journal of Social Work Education, 38*, 421–430.

Parker-Oliver, D., & Demiris, G. (2006). Social work informatics: A new specialty. *Social Work, 51*(2), 127–134.

Parrott, L., & Madoc-Jones, I. (2008). Reclaiming information and communication technologies for empowering social work practice. *Journal of Social Work, 8*(2), 181–197. doi:10.1177/1468017307084739

Rosenberg, J. I. (2006). Real-time training: Transfer of knowledge through computer-mediated, real-time feedback. *Professional Psychology, Research and Practice, 37*, 539–546. doi:10.1037/0735-7028.37.5.539

Srinivasan, M., Hwang, J., West, D., & Yellowless, P. M. (2006). Assessment of clinical skills using stimulator technologies. *Educational Assessment, Interventions, and Outcomes, 30*(6), 505–515.

Stedmon, J., Wood, J., Curle, C., & Haslam, C. (2006). Development of PBL in the training of clinical psychologists. *Psychology Learning & Teaching, 5*(1), 52–60.

Strehle, E. M., & Shabde, N. (2006). One hundred years of telemedicine: Does this new technology have a place in paediatrics? *Archives of Disease in Childhood, 91*, 956–959. doi:10.1136/adc.2006.099622

Trepal, H., Haberstroh, S., Duffey, T., & Evans, M. (2007). Considerations and strategies for teaching online counseling skills: establishing relationships in cyberspace. *Counselor Education and Supervision, 46*, 266–279.

Trolley, B., & Silliker, A. (2005). The Use of WebCT in the supervision of counseling interns. *Journal of Technology in Counseling, 4* (1). Retrieved from http://jtc.colstate.edu/Vol4_1/Trolley/Trolley.htm on 4/15/10

Vaccaro, N., & Lambie, G. W. (2007). Computer-based counselor-in-training supervision: Ethical and practical implications for counselor educators and supervisors. *Counselor Education and Supervision, 47*, 46–57.

Walter, D. A., Rosenquist, P. B., & Bawtinhimer, G. (2004). Distance learning technologies in the training of psychiatry residents: A critical assessment. *Academic Psychiatry, 28*(1), 60–65. doi:10.1176/appi.ap.28.1.60

Weingardt, K. R. (2004). The role of instructional design and technology in the disseminatin of empirically supported, manual-based therapies. *Psychology: Science and Practice, 11*(3), 313–331. doi:10.1093/clipsy/bph087

Wood, J. A. V., Miller, T. W., & Hargrove, D. S. (2005). Clinical supervision in rural settings: A telehealth model. *Professional Psychology, Research and Practice, 36*(2), 173–179. doi:10.1037/0735-7028.36.2.173

Yeh, C. J., Change, T., Chiang, L., Drost, C. M., Spelliscy, D., Carter, R. T., & Chang, Y. (2008). Development, content, process and outcome of an online peer supervision group for counselor trainees. *Computers in Human Behavior, 24*, 2889–2903. doi:10.1016/j.chb.2008.04.010

KEY TERMS AND DEFINITIONS

Telemedicine: The practice of delivering direct or ancillary health care services and sharing health care information through electronic communication, particularly interactive audio and visual electronic communication.

Clinical Supervision: Supervision is an intervention provided by a more senior member of a profession to a more junior member or members of that same profession. This relationship: (a) is evaluative and hierarchical, (b) extends over time, and, (c) has the simultaneous purposes of enhancing the professional functioning of the more junior person(s); monitoring the quality of professional services offered to the clients that she, he, or they see; and serving as a gatekeeper for those who are to enter the particular profession.

Mental Health Professional: A cluster of professions including psychiatry, psychiatric nursing, professional counseling, clinical social work, clinical/counseling/ school/combined-integrated psychology and marriage/family therapy, all of which focus on delivering assessment, diagnosis, and intervention services to individuals living with mental, emotional and behavioral problems.

Video-Conferencing Supervision: A set of technologies that allow real-time interaction through cameras linking two locations with both audio and visual information. Video conferencing can be used to facilitate the delivery of health and mental health services as well as clinical supervision and consultation with mental health professionals in training at-a-distance.

Live Supervision: The practice of the supervisor observing a supervisee's clinical work sample in real-time either through a two way mirror or through a video link. Live supervision is often enhanced with "bug in the ear" and "bug in the eye" technologies which allow for the supervisor to communicate with the supervisee as they are interacting with the client either through, respectively, auditory means using a speaker in the supervisee's ear or through visual means through displaying text messages on a screen that sits behind the client.

Email Supervision: The practice of conducting the interactions between supervisor and supervisee via email messages. Typically this method is not used to deliver all of the supervisory services, rather only as a means to further supervisory communication in the interim period between face-to-face individual or group supervision meeting.

Web-Based Group Supervision: The practice of delivering group and peer supervision through web-based platforms that allow for asynchronous text-based communication via threaded discussions and email as well as synchronous text communication via chat and instant messaging. This approach also allows for the uploading of work samples such as case reports, treatment plans, videos of client sessions, etc. Such methods allow a group of supervisors and supervisees to discuss and provide feedback without the obstacle of time or space.

Chapter 10
Enhancing Clinical Education for Healthcare Professionals through Innovative Pedagogy, Advanced Technologies, and Design Research

Thomas C. Reeves
University of Georgia, USA

Patricia M. Reeves
University of Georgia, USA

ABSTRACT

Clinical education is a major component of higher education programs for healthcare professionals in fields such as medicine, nursing, pharmacy, public health, and social work. The increasing complexity of performance in these fields demands new approaches to clinical education and training. The reform of clinical education in colleges and universities must be driven first and foremost by innovative pedagogy (e.g., authentic tasks and case-based learning models) rather than advanced technologies alone (e.g., 3D immersive simulations and social networking tools). The overall transformation of clinical education and training would be best guided by a design research approach.

INTRODUCTION

In June 2009, the United Nations (U.N.) Food and Agricultural Organization (http://www.fao.org/) announced a grim milestone. Hunger, defined by the U.N. as the consumption of fewer than 1,800 calories a day, was being experienced by one in every six people on earth. Exacerbated by factors such as the global financial crisis, climate change, and political instability, serious hunger is a daily

DOI: 10.4018/978-1-60960-147-8.ch010

experience for one billion people. As terrible as the hunger tragedy is, it is just one aspect of a global crisis in public health which also includes the prevalence of disease, the lack of effective medical care, and widespread ignorance of basic health promotion activities (Bywaters, McLeod, & Napier, 2009; Garrett, 2000).

Competent healthcare professionals are essential to resolving this global crisis. They must possess competencies specific to their disciplines as well as general (often called "core") competencies. In recent years, various national and international health agencies have attempted to define the core competencies of healthcare professionals. For example, in the United States, the Council on Linkages between Academia and Public Health Practice (http://www.phf.org/) has defined core competencies (i.e., the set of skills, knowledge, and attitudes necessary for the broad practice of public health) in eight key domains:

- Analytic/Assessment Skills
- Policy Development/Program Planning Skills
- Communication Skills
- Cultural Competency Skills
- Community Dimensions of Practice Skills
- Basic Public Health Sciences Skills
- Financial Planning and Management Skills
- Leadership and Systems Thinking Skills

Clinical education is a major component of all higher education programs related to healthcare, such as medicine, nursing, pharmacy, public health, and social work. In most healthcare education programs students spend some period of time studying core subjects (e.g., the first two years of medical school) and then spend a defined period of time in clinical training (e.g., the second two years of medical school) where they actually work with real clients (e.g., patients in a teaching hospital associated with a medical school). In other healthcare education programs such as social work, core education and clinical training are interwoven with students spending part of each week in core courses and another part in field placements. However, the separation of core education and clinical training is still the dominant approach in higher education related to the healthcare professions. For example, although a few medical schools have adopted some form of problem-based learning model (Barrows, 1986, 2003), wherein students begin to see patients much earlier in their programs, most still follow the traditional model whereby core subjects must be mastered before clinical experience begins.

Traditional instructional methods are no longer adequate in the healthcare professions for several reasons. According to a U.S. National Institute of Medicine report edited by Greiner and Knebel (2003):

Education for the health professions is in need of a major overhaul. Clinical education simply has not kept pace with or been responsive enough to shifting patient demographics and desires, changing health system expectations, evolving practice requirements and staffing arrangements, new information, a focus on improving quality, or new technologies. (p. 1)

A primary rationale for the reform of clinical education arises from the degree to which the sheer complexity of performance in the healthcare professions has increased. Consider the core competency of communications skills. Gawande (2009) described how miscommunication among surgical teams consisting of surgeons, nurses, anesthesiologists, and others is a primary cause of complications during surgery, with the result that "at least seven million people a year are left disabled and at least one million dead – a level of harm that approaches that of malaria, tuberculosis, and other traditional public health concerns" (p. 87). Healthcare professionals must develop strong expertise related to teamwork, communications, and other social skills, and these are best learned within the context of clinical education.

Wodehouse (2007) argued convincingly that healthcare educators must adopt new educational methods in the 21st Century such as small group learning, problem-based learning, case-based methods, story-telling, experiential learning, and inquiry-based learning, but there is little evidence that this is happening on a wide scale. If clinical training for healthcare professionals is going to be reformed, three things must happen. First, there must be a shift from traditional didactic teacher-centered pedagogy to innovative alternative student-centered pedagogy. Second, there must be widespread adoption of new technologies that enable implementation of these innovative pedagogies. Third, the whole reform enterprise must be driven by a design research approach. The purpose of this chapter is to outline this three-pronged approach to reforming clinical education in the 21st Century.

THE ROLE OF PEDAGOGY

Over the last 25 years, preparing people for success in the various healthcare professions has undergone what some experts have called a "paradigm shift" represented by a general change from a focus on training to a focus on learning (Stolovitch & Keeps, 2002). Within the broader context of higher education in the USA, Barr and Tagg (1995) described this paradigm shift as moving from a view of a university or college as "an institution that exists to provide instruction" to "an institution that exists to produce learning" (p. 12).

One of the primary drivers for the new or renewed emphasis on learning is the desire to ensure that the content and activities of higher education programs for healthcare professionals focus on relevant and active learning rather than the transmission of inert knowledge. Traditional educational programs in the health professions all too often separate knowing and doing. The instructors in these traditional programs frequently teach principles, concepts, and facts in abstract, de-contextualized ways, e.g., through lengthy PowerPoint presentations during which they merely read the bullet points on the slides to their students. Students in courses dominated by this "stand and deliver" pedagogy seek to capture the information in these classroom lectures by taking notes (or alternatively by purchasing the notes from note-taking services). But regardless of how information is "transmitted" to students, unless they have opportunities to apply new knowledge, it will likely remain inert. Instead of developing robust knowledge and skills that can applied to real-world problems, students often recall just enough information to pass tests and exams within the context of a specific course, rarely retaining the information for more than a few weeks, much less developing the capacity to transfer the knowledge and skills to a meaningful context of use (Hersch & Merrow, 2005; McDaniel, 1988; Zemsky, 2009). In a scathing critique of higher education in America, Bok (2006) wrote:

...many professional school faculty have long believed [that] passive lecturing and drill can help students memorize rules and concepts and apply them to a limited range of problems similar to those covered in class, but they do little to equip undergraduates to apply their knowledge to new problems. (p. 116)

Another reason for the emphasis on learning is that the range and depth of outcomes expected to be achieved by graduates of healthcare education programs today is more complex than in the past. At least three types of cognitive outcomes must be considered in contemporary clinical education: (1) knowledge and skills, (2) mental models, and (3) higher-order outcomes.

The first type of outcome is knowledge and skills. Cognitive psychology has enriched our understanding of the mental states that result from learning to include constructs such as concepts (e.g., pharmacy students understanding purity, potency, safety and efficacy in relationship to commercial drugs), schema (e.g., pharmacy students developing abstract mental structures that represent their understanding of chemical compounds), rules (e.g., pharmacy students learning to always dispense short-dated pharmaceuticals first), and skills (e.g., pharmacy students learning to communicate clearly with elderly clients) (Winn & Snyder, 1996).

Mental models, the second type of outcome, are the mental structures we use to "understand systems and solve problems arising from the way systems work" (Winn & Snyder, 1996, p. 123). It may seem strange to separate "mental models" from other types of knowledge and skills, but developing robust mental models (e.g., the complex nature of drug interactions) is such an important outcome in the healthcare professions today that it deserves special attention. Healthcare professionals must be able to activate appropriate mental models, use them to interpret new information, assimilate new information back into those models, reorganize the models in light of the newly interpreted information, and use the newly strengthened mental models to explain, interpret, or infer new knowledge (Johnson-Laird, 2009; Norman, 1983).

The third type of outcome is higher order outcomes. Although many healthcare educators remain concerned primarily with the transmission of existing knowledge and skills in their respective disciplines, others also intend for their students to develop higher-order outcomes such as problem-solving abilities, creativity, intellectual curiosity, and the desire for lifelong learning. A list of higher order outcomes for healthcare programs in higher education might include the capacity to:

- Recognize and solve ill-structured problems;
- Engage in sustained reasoning about complex phenomena;
- Navigate, locate, evaluate, and organize information from diverse sources;
- Collaborate with people from diverse backgrounds;
- Communicate with multiple audiences at appropriate levels; and
- Anticipate changes in regulations, technology, and other factors that influence professional practice.

The types of pedagogical strategies used in the education of healthcare professionals depend largely on the view of learning held by the instructors who plan the instructional programs. In recent years, there has been a fundamental change in our understanding of how human learning occurs. The traditional view of learning is that it involves moving information from working (short-term) memory to long-term memory. From this perspective, learning is a process of knowledge acquisition that results from the efficient presentation of information and the mental encoding process involved in moving information from the sensory memory (where it is perceived) and working memory (where it is processed) into the long-term memory (where it is stored) of the brain. According to Jonassen (2009), "most formal educational institutions measure knowledge in terms of what students are able to recall from long-term memory when given an examination" (p. 15), and thus there remains an emphasis on transmitting information to students in many colleges and universities.

An alternative view of learning is that it is much more complex than simple long-term storage and retrieval of information. Learning from the point of view known as the constructivist perspective is not just stored "in" the brain, but is much more complex, often found within the context of social interactions (Brown & Duguid, 2000). Jonassen (2009) described nine types of knowledge that must be learned, with each having a different function in the capacity of healthcare professionals to be successful practitioners of their given discipline:

- **Declarative knowledge:** the type of information stored in long-term memory (facts, concepts, principles), e.g., a public health student learning that the CDC was established in 1946.
- **Structural knowledge:** relates to how concepts within a discipline (e.g., public health) are interrelated, e.g., understanding how various data points are used to determine the likelihood of a global influenza outbreak.
- **Conceptual knowledge:** relates to higher levels of integration of declarative knowledge as in a mental model, e.g., a mental model of the HIV pandemic.
- **Procedural knowledge:** the step-by-step knowledge required to complete a task, e.g., how to apply biostatistical skills in the context of an epidemiology study.
- **Situational knowledge:** relates to understanding of problems, their contexts, and feasible solutions, e.g., knowledge of the public health threats likely to arise under flood conditions.
- **Strategic knowledge:** relates to the web of mental strategies required to perform a task and monitor its effective completion, e.g., debriefing a public health team after a disease outbreak has been controlled.
- **Tacit (Implicit) knowledge:** what we know but cannot tell, e.g., the intuitive recognition that data from a given geographical region is unreliable.
- **Sociocultural knowledge:** the world view, belief systems, attitudes, and socially shared knowledge within a specific culture, e.g., knowledge of how people from different cultures communicate about public health issues.
- **Experiential (Episodic) knowledge:** the stories we remember that allow us to interpret our personal and interpersonal experiences, e.g., how we reacted to the H1N1 vaccination campaign of 2009-2010.

Instructors in healthcare fields who view learning primarily in terms of the acquisition of the contents of long-term memory are likely to design and deliver instruction based upon a set of beliefs about the nature of pedagogy such as:

- Direct instruction whereby people are told or shown what to do is the most effective method of teaching.
- Complex knowledge and skills can be broken down into constituent simpler parts and taught one by one.
- Knowledge and skills can be learned independently outside of a realistic context of use.
- Simpler concepts and skills must be learned before more complex concepts and skills can be learned.
- The instructor should be the most active person in a course because the instructor must transmit information clearly and fill the minds of the learners with new knowledge.

By contrast, instructors in healthcare fields who view learning primarily as the construction of a complex web of different types of knowledge, skills, attitudes, and intentions are likely to design and deliver instruction based upon a different set of beliefs about the nature of pedagogy such as:

- Learners should be the most active people in a course because they must try to do challenging things, make mistakes, and then try again for meaningful learning to occur.
- Learning is derived from trying to solve complex, difficult problems rather than passively attending to messages transmitted by an instructor.
- Learners are not empty bins to be filled with knowledge, but active minds that already possess considerable prior knowl-

edge and experience that must form the foundation of new knowledge.

- Knowledge and skills should be learned in a context similar to the ones in which the knowledge and skills will eventually be applied if the learning is not to be inert.
- Transfer of learning from one context to another is very difficult and, therefore, learners must apply their knowledge and skills in multiple realistic contexts.
- The primary role of the instructor is to "scaffold" students as they construct new knowledge. Scaffolding involves providing learners with just enough of the help they need to succeed in a new context (akin to training wheels on a bike) and then gradually removing the support as they make progress toward professional proficiency.

It is our belief that for substantive learning to occur, students must be actively engaged in meaningful interactions that support their learning. Different types of activities support different types of learning. For example, Herrington, Reeves, and Oliver (2010) describe an "authentic tasks" based model for teaching that is especially effective in helping students develop knowledge, skills, and attitudes that can be applied in real-world contexts. One of the challenges of designing activities that support learning beyond simple memorization is that it is often difficult to get students to accept alternative instructional methods. Generally, students seem to prefer traditional instructional strategies over innovative ones. For example, Bower, Girard, Wessel, Becker, and Choi (2008) found that when they surveyed 755 physicians concerning their preferred instructional methods, the first choice was "large group lecture" rather than more effective strategies such as small group interactive sessions. Most healthcare professionals like to stay in their comfort zones and thus take a somewhat passive role in learning scenarios. As a result, one of the biggest challenges faced by advocates of healthcare education reform is getting students to open up to alternative pedagogical methods.

Those who desire to reform clinical education for healthcare professionals must strive to design different learning activities to match the learning needs within a specific healthcare education program or course. There are numerous learning activities from which to choose including: lecture, reading, discussion, demonstration, drill and practice, sharing personal experiences, debate, games and simulations, brainstorming, guided imagery, authentic tasks, role playing, skits, peer teaching, reflection, concept mapping, quizzes, and video. Unfortunately, educational research has not yielded a perfect match between different types of instructional activities and different types of learning outcomes, but there are design principles that can help instructors and instructional designers choose more effective activities. For example, students are much more likely to retain what they have to figure out for themselves or have opportunities to apply. Some form of teaching by telling, perhaps through a brief lecture or a video, is often necessary, but any telling activities should be followed up with more engaging activities that require hands-on, minds-on interactions among the learners (Bransford, Brown, & Cocking, 2000; Brown, Collins, & Duguid, 1989). Evidence-based teaching is especially important in healthcare because of the growing emphasis on evidence-based practice in healthcare disciplines (Petty, 2009).

THE ROLE OF ADVANCED TECHNOLOGIES

For several decades, Clark (1983, 2001) has been trying to get educators at every level to understand that the most important thing about technology is that it does not directly influence learning. Those who seek to enhance education for healthcare professionals with educational technologies such as online courses, podcasts, and virtual worlds must recognize that although technology and media can support teaching and enable learning, they are only vehicles for instructional methods that more directly influence the learning accomplished by students. Decades of media comparison research studies indicate that different delivery modalities (e.g., a classroom-based course versus an online course) yield similar results (Bernard, Abrami, Lou, Borokhovski, Wade, Wozney, Wallet, Fiset, & Huang, 2004; Hattie, 2009; Tallent-Runnels, Thomas, Lan, Cooper, Ahern, Shaw, & Xiaoming, 2006). What really makes a difference in student achievement and outcomes is the instructional design or pedagogical dimensions of the learning environment. If the same instructional design is delivered via two different modalities, it makes no sense to expect different outcomes. (However, one modality may be preferred over another for other reasons such as differences in cost, accessibility, and efficiency.)

Similar to most higher education practitioners, healthcare educators have not been immune to the temptation to adopt new technologies in the belief that they will automatically transform education. These initiatives are well intentioned, but unless the use of technology is driven by careful instructional design, there is little likelihood of transformational change.

There are examples of the integration of effective pedagogy with innovative technology in higher education for healthcare professionals. For example, Heinrichs, Youngblood, Harter, and Dev (2008) described the use of the *Second Life* virtual world to help students in clinical education programs concerned with critical medical care learn to manage clinical cases effectively as a member of a team. Boulos and Wheeler (2007) illustrated how popular Web 2.0 applications such as wikis, blogs and podcasts are being used in social work and public health education to help students engage in reflective metacognition and refine their communications skills. Nehring and Lashley (2009) delineated how increasingly sophisticated computer-based games and simulations have been applied in basic and clinical nursing education for more than 40 years.

As innovative as these and similar adaptations of new technologies to clinical education for healthcare professionals have been, none has provided unequivocal evidence supporting their efficacy in comparison to traditional education methods (Cuban, 2001). As Reeves and Reeves (2008) emphasized, effective use of technology in healthcare education requires more than a mere shift from one medium to another. The critical dimensions of the learning environment must be accounted for in any innovation, and these dimensions must be carefully aligned (Reeves, 2006). At a minimum, they include eight interlinked factors: (1) goals, (2) content, (3) instructional design, (4) learner tasks, (5) instructor roles, (6) student roles, (7) technological affordances, and (8) assessment.

The massive online multi-player simulations, virtual environments, social networking websites, and other interactive tools provided by today's Web 2.0 technologies are enticing, but they must be viewed as secondary to pedagogy or instructional design. Each new technology has unique affordances, e.g., the interaction possibilities posed by avatars and objects in online virtual worlds. The affordances of new technologies to support learning in the healthcare professions are noteworthy, but evidence for their efficacy is still weak. For example, in the preface to their edited book *Computers Games and Team and Individual Learning*, O'Neil and Perez (2008) stated:

While effectiveness of game environments can be documented in terms of intensity and longevity of engagement (participants voting with their quarters or time), as well as the commercial success of games, there is much less solid empirical information about what learning outcomes are systematically achieved by the use of individual and multiplayer games to train adult participants in acquiring knowledge and skills. (p. ix)

THE ROLE OF DESIGN RESEARCH

There is a long history of media comparison studies in the field of educational technology through which researchers have sought to demonstrate the relative effectiveness of innovative and traditional course delivery modalities (Clark, 1983), and it continues to this day (Reeves, 2009). The bulk of published research indicates that training delivery modalities such as online learning versus classroom instruction yield similar results (Bernard et al., 2004; Tallent-Runnels et al., 2006; Hattie, 2009). But is "just as good" really the best we can expect with regard to innovative approaches to clinical education for healthcare professionals?

A more effective research agenda would focus on identifying specific design principles that could guide the development of enhanced pedagogy and interactive learning technologies in ways that would best match the learning needs of students in the healthcare professions. The most appropriate methodology for this research agenda is educational design research (van den Akker, Gravemeijer, McKenney, & Nieveen, 2006).

Design research is distinctly different from the quasi-experimental methods that have most often been applied in media comparison studies. First and foremost, design research addresses critical complex problems in real-world contexts, problems that are identified in close collaboration with practitioners (e.g., educational researchers working with medical educators to address the shortage of primary care physicians willing to work in rural areas). Second, design research integrates known and hypothetical design principles with technological affordances to render plausible solutions to these real world problems (e.g., the design of online tools that support the refinement of self-regulated learning skills among medical students so that they can be better prepared for lifelong professional development). Third, design research requires iterative cycles of rigorous and reflective inquiry to test and refine innovative learning environments as well as to identify and refine new design principles (e.g., a multi-year effort to develop a clinical skills simulation based upon advanced learning designs and the affordances of virtual worlds).

RECOMMENDATIONS

The challenge of enhancing the quality and effectiveness of the clinical education offered by higher education institutions is enormous, but the challenge can be met if administrators, faculty members, accrediting agencies, professional organizations, foundations, and others collaborate in large-scale reform initiatives. To begin this process, we recommend the following:

- Within the context of accreditation or other forms of self-study, the articulation of a program's clinical education with the core competencies of 21st Century healthcare professionals should be carefully examined and realigned as needed.
- Faculty members involved in clinical education and training should actively engage in professional development activities related to innovative pedagogy and advanced learning technologies. These activities should be designed to provide them firsthand experience with alternative pedagogies and diverse learning activities. Campus-wide or college-specific instructional design and technology experts should be recruited to collaborate in the provision of these professional development opportunities.
- Educational researchers should be engaged in long-term design research initiatives with faculty members and students in clinical education programs with the two-fold goal of enhancing clinical education programs and identifying reusable design principles for subsequent enhancement of these programs.

CONCLUSION

The reform of clinical education and training for healthcare professionals will not be achieved by simply adopting new technology or by conducting the kinds of simplistic quasi-experiments that have characterized much of the educational technology research in this area. Without better instructional design and new design-oriented approaches to educational research, healthcare educators will continue to fail in their attempts to employ educational technology to reform teaching and learning in their respective disciplines. In light of the increasing complexity of professional performance in healthcare, new ways of teaching and learning must be developed in clinical higher education. Improving healthcare is a global challenge, and a large component of any initiative to meet this challenge must involve enhancing clinical education of healthcare professionals. Gawande (2009) described in shocking detail the evidence of how slow healthcare professionals have been to adapt more effective communications and better teamwork strategies to reduce "the extraordinary high rate at which care for patients is duplicated or flawed or completely uncoordinated" (p. 59). The time for reform is now.

REFERENCES

Barr, R. B., & Tagg, J. (1995). From teaching to learning – a new paradigm for undergraduate education. *Change*, *27*(6), 12–25.

Barrows, H. S. (1986). A taxonomy of problem-based learning methods. *Medical Education*, *20*(1), 481–486. doi:10.1111/j.1365-2923.1986.tb01386.x

Barrows, H. S. (2003). *Problem-based learning applied to medical education*. New York: Springer.

Bernard, R. M., Abrami, P. C., Lou, Y., Borokhovski, E., Wade, A., & Wozney, L. (2004). How does distance education compare to classroom instruction? A meta-analysis of the empirical literature. *Review of Educational Research*, *74*(3), 379–439. doi:10.3102/00346543074003379

Bok, D. (2006). *Our underachieving colleges: A candid look at how much students learn and why they should be learning more*. Princeton, NJ: Princeton University Press.

Boulos, M. N. K., & Wheeler, S. (2007). The emerging Web 2.0 social software: An enabling suite of sociable technologies in health and health care education. *Health Information and Libraries Journal*, *24*(1), 2–23. doi:10.1111/j.1471-1842.2007.00701.x

Bower, E. A., Girard, D. E., Wessel, K., Becker, T. M., & Choi, D. (2008). Barriers to innovation in continuing medical education. *The Journal of Continuing Education in the Health Professions*, *28*(3), 148–156. doi:10.1002/chp.176

Bransford, J. D., Brown, A. L., & Cocking, R. R. (2000). *How people learn: Brain, mind, experience, and school*. Washington, DC: National Academy Press.

Brown, J. S., Collins, A., & Duguid, P. (1989). Situated cognition and the culture of learning. *Educational Researcher*, *18*(1), 32–42.

Brown, J. S., & Duguid, P. (2000). *The social life of information*. Boston: Harvard Business School Press.

Bywaters, P., McLeod, E., & Napier, L. (Eds.). (2009). *Social work and global health inequalities: Practice and policy developments*. Portland, OR: The Policy Press.

Clark, R. E. (1983). Reconsidering research on learning with media. *Review of Educational Research*, *53*(4), 445–459.

Clark, R. E. (2001). *Learning from media: Arguments, analysis and evidence*. Greenwich, CT: Information Age Publishers.

Cuban, L. (2001). *Oversold and underused: Computers in the classroom*. Cambridge, MA: Harvard University Press.

Garrett, L. (2000). *Betrayal of trust: The collapse of global public health*. New York: Hyperion.

Gawande, A. (2009). *The checklist manifesto: How to get things right*. New York: Metropolitan Books.

Greiner, A. C., & Knebel, E. (2003). *Health professions education: A bridge to quality*. Washington, DC: National Academies Press.

Hattie, J. A. C. (2009). *Visible learning: A synthesis of over 800 meta-analyses related to achievement*. New York: Routledge.

Heinrichs, W. L., Youngblood, P., Harter, M., & Dev, P. (2008). Simulation for team training and assessment: Case studies of online training with virtual worlds. *World Journal of Surgery*, *32*(2), 161–170. doi:10.1007/s00268-007-9354-2

Herrington, J., Reeves, T. C., & Oliver, R. (2010). *A guide to authentic e-learning*. New York: Routledge.

Hersch, R. H., & Merrow, J. (2005). *Declining by degrees. Higher education at risk*. New York: Palgrave Macmillan.

Johnson-Laird, P. (2009). *How we reason*. New York: Oxford University Press.

Jonassen, D. H. (2009). Reconciling a human cognitive architecture. In Tobias, S., & Duffy, T. M. (Eds.), *Constructivist theory applied to instruction: Success or failure?* New York: Routledge.

McDaniel, M. A. (1988). Transfer: Rediscovering a central concept. In Roediger, H. L. III, Dudai, Y., & Fitzpatrick, S. M. (Eds.), *Science of memory: Concepts* (pp. 267–270). New York: Oxford University Press.

Nehring, W. M., & Lashley, F. R. (2009). Nursing simulation: A review of the past 40 years. *Simulation & Gaming*, *40*(4), 528–552. doi:10.1177/1046878109332282

Norman, D. A. (1983). Some observations on mental models. In Gentner, D., & Stevens, A. L. (Eds.), *Mental models* (pp. 7–14). Hillsdale, NJ: Lawrence Erlbaum Associates.

O'Neil, H. F., & Perez, R. S. (2008). *Computer games and team and individual learning*. Boston: Elsevier.

Petty, G. (2009). *Evidence-based teaching: A practical approach* (2nd ed.). Gloucestershire, UK: Nelson Thornes.

Reeves, P. M., & Reeves, T. C. (2008). Design considerations for online learning in health and social work education. *Learning in Health and Social Care Journal*, *7*(1), 46–58. doi:10.1111/j.1473-6861.2008.00170.x

Reeves, T. C. (2006). How do you know they are learning? The importance of alignment in higher education. *International Journal of Learning Technology*, *2*(4), 294–309. doi:10.1504/IJLT.2006.011336

Reeves, T. C. (2009). E-Learning in Asia: Just as good is not good enough. *International Journal on E-Learning*, *8*(4), 577–585.

Stolovitch, H. D., & Keeps, E. J. (2002). *Telling ain't training*. Alexandria, VA: American Society for Training and Development.

Tallent-Runnels, M. K., Thomas, J. A., Lan, W. Y., Cooper, S., Ahern, T. C., Shaw, S. M., & Xiaoming, L. (2006). Teaching courses online: A review of the research. *Review of Educational Research*, *76*(1), 93–135. doi:10.3102/00346543076001093

Van den Akker, J., Gravemeijer, K., McKenney, S., & Nieveen, N. (Eds.). (2006). *Educational design research*. London: Routledge.

Winn, W., & Snyder, D. (1996). Cognitive perspectives in psychology. In Jonassen, D. H. (Ed.), *Handbook of research for educational communications and technology* (pp. 112–142). New York: Macmillan.

Wodehouse, J. (2007). *Strategies for healthcare education: How to teach in the 21st Century*. Oxford, UK: Radcliffe Publishing.

Zemsky, R. (2009). *Making reform work: The case for transforming American higher education*. Piscataway, NJ: Rutgers University Press.

KEY TERMS AND DEFINITIONS

Advanced Technologies: Refer to interactive tools, programs, and systems that can be used to provide learning opportunities to students. Advanced technologies include 3D immersive virtual worlds, podcasts, social networking tools, and web-based conferencing, among others.

Clinical Education and Training (CET): Are those portions of education and training programs during which students actually work with real clients. CET is often contrasted with traditional coursework in a degree program or leader-led training.

Core Competencies: Are the key or essential abilities and capacities that characterize the performance of professionals within a given discipline. For example, the core competencies of social workers include assessing client needs, planning interventions, advocating for clients, and pursuing lifelong learning.

Design Research: An innovative approach to educational research that has two primary goals: enhancing practice in a specific context and refining reusable design principles related to theory. Design research emphasizes close collaboration between researchers and practitioners.

Innovative Pedagogy: Refers to alternative instructional models to the dominant traditional, lecture-based models used in most education and training programs. Alternative pedagogical methods include authentic tasks, case-based learning, inquiry-based learning, and problem-based learning, among others.

Instructional Design: (also referred to as Instructional Systems Design): The systematic process of developing effective instruction to enable students to learn. Instructional design is often represented in five phases with the acronym ADDIE (analysis, design, development, implementation, and evaluation).

Learning Activities: Are specific instructional events including: lecture, reading, discussion, demonstration, drill and practice, sharing personal experiences, debate, games and simulations, brainstorming, guided imagery, role playing, skits, peer teaching, reflection, concept mapping, quizzes, and video.

Chapter 11
Educational Technology in the Medical Industry

Keith B. Hopper
Southern Polytechnic State University, USA

Carol L. Johns
Upson Regional Medical Center, USA

ABSTRACT

The enormous U.S. medical industry is a rich laboratory and think tank for technology integration. Higher education in the medical industry is comprised of a large number of professional training programs as well as formidable continuing medical education. Continuing education for medical professionals is inconsistent and flawed. Technology integration in medical fields has mirrored the false starts and frustrations seen generally in higher education. There are promising areas of investigation such as high-fidelity patient simulators and incorporation of wireless handheld devices for point-of-care reference information and best practices. Widespread adoption of electronic medical records may allow medical education researchers to link instructional practices to eventual patient outcomes, with implications for higher education.

"It was the best of times, it was the worst of times..." Charles Dickens, A Tale of Two Cities

INTRODUCTION

This chapter introduces the issues, needs, history and challenges of higher education in the medical industry, including continuing medical education (CME). The scope of this important industry and the unique training and retraining needs of medical professionals are discussed. Exciting advances and applications in educational technology in medical applications are addressed and real world experiences of representative learners are presented in detail.

The enormous U.S. medical industry is a rich laboratory and think tank for information and communication technology, as well as technology

DOI: 10.4018/978-1-60960-147-8.ch011

applications in teaching and learning. With 14.3 million wage and salary workers, healthcare is one of the largest and fastest growing industries (U.S. Bureau of Labor Statistics, 2009). U.S. graduates in professional medical programs granting a bachelor's degree or higher total about 160,000 each year (National Center for Education Statistics, 2008), with a larger number in associate degree and certificate programs (National Center for Education Statistics, 2009). Healthcare is the most common field of study in subbaccalaureate programs. Many leaders in higher education and educational technology credit a background in a medical field for their inspiration and accomplishment. A great deal of innovative thinking, research, and application in progressive instructional approaches in higher education is grounded in the pressing need to train, assess, retrain, and sustain clinicians in a bewildering variety of specialties in a vast industry serving virtually the entire population. Consider the educational challenges of the medical arena, including:

- Primary training of hundreds of thousands of practitioners per year in approximately 50 fields and specialties.
- Credentialing and recredentialing of clinicians and technicians for competency, from cardiologists to registered nurses to pharmacy technicians.
- Continuous in-service education requirements, mandated for virtually every medical field, and requiring extensive preparation, delivery, verification, and documentation of instruction.
- Dissemination of new knowledge and skills in medical practice, some of it evolving and expanding at a dizzying rate.

Indeed, to choose a medical career is to personify the dusty high school admonition to be a lifelong learner, for a clinician who does not diligently learn and relearn throughout his or her career may become unemployable, if not dangerous.

But the medical industry is an often enigmatic mix of innovation and tradition, of reaching toward an innovative, often technology-based instructional future while holding to traditional, time-worn attitudes and practices. Technology integration in education has generally been technology-driven, faddish, expensive, at times frenetic, and with generally unsatisfying outcomes (Ely, Foley, Freeman, & Scheel, 1995; Reiser, 2002; Salomon, 2002). Ten years ago we described educational technologies as generally "expensive, fragile and stupid" (Hopper, 1999, p. 52). One researcher described the online instruction phenomenon as a "frenzied drive toward the Web-based cliff " (Harmon & Jones, 1999, p. 28). So has it been in the medical industry (Williams & Dittmer, 2009). Added to this is the natural rivalry among medical specialties for status, professional practice turf, and compensation. It has been only within the past quarter century that intensive care nurses and respiratory therapists dared carry a visible stethoscope to the hospital cafeteria; though this item of time worn technology is indispensible in their work, it is an icon of medical prowess and stature that was strictly reserved for physicians. While leaders in public education sometimes compare educational innovation and reform to the challenge of redesigning an airplane in flight, medical industry education might be compared to navigating a speedy ship with an entire crew of captains, each with a somewhat different course and destination in mind. The result in the medical industry is a bewildering range and variety of technology applications in teaching and learning, a crazy quilt with hues ranging from intensive, innovative technology integration to near-zero change in decades.

While higher education and educational technology scholars and researchers have led the theoretical dialogue and debate on bedrock cognitive principles applied to teaching and learning, with positivist underpinnings seeming to steadily give ground to constructivist thought, this discussion finds pressing purpose in the medical industry where it is of profound, immediate importance to define and measure learning. Perhaps in no other setting does Dewey's (1933) admonition, "To know is to do" assume greater urgency.

Consider the challenge of measuring clinical competency to credential practitioners in highly complex medical specialties such as cardiology, radiology, or neonatology. Can this, should this be done using a multiple-choice exam, or does this require an actual or simulated clinical assessment component? What if there are thousands or hundreds of thousands of practitioners to be assessed and periodically reassessed, and the quality and safety of patient care, with attending legal issues, hangs in the balance? What about expense to practitioners, credentialing agencies, and employers? Similarly, the medical industry endows questions of media and efficacy with new urgency. While the "no significant difference" (Clark, 1983; Russell, 1999) stance may satisfy in ordinary contexts, is this satisfactory in the medical arena? Is a physical therapy assistant competently trained in a partially online hybrid program? A fully online program? What about a nurse, pharmacist, therapist, or surgeon? Will a physician trained largely by multimedia technologies and online instruction be accepted by her peers? Trusted by her patients? Credentialed by state medical review boards? Compensated by medical insurers?

Integrating technology in the medical arena involves a degree of risk unseen in the general case of higher education, that technically simple technology "bugs" and glitches may cause a critical training or evaluation system to fail utterly (Ellaway, 2007), and this gives pause to technology champions in medical fields. Just as higher education in general calls for technology applications beyond collections of PowerPoint presentations, so it is in the medical industry (Ellaway, 2008). Medical education visionaries have called for the same level of rigor in instructional approach demanded in medical scientific research (Harris & Simpson, 2005).

Nearly every medical field is required to document minimal standards of CME. As this is for adult learners and is an extension of education and training received mostly in college, this is sensibly characterized as a category of higher education. With or without technology, the current state of CME in the U.S. is disturbing. The CME system is characterized as deeply flawed and criticized for failing to provide the consistent, comprehensive system of continuing education needed to permit effective healthcare and to ensure patient safety (Institute of Education Sciences Institute of Medicine, 2010). Specific shortcomings identified in CME include:

- There is a fragmented, underdeveloped underpinning science in the general approach to delivering and evaluating CME.
- Health professionals and their employers focus on meeting regulatory requirements rather than authentically assessing and addressing learning needs.
- Didactic learning methods dominate in a hands-on industry.
- There is little credible basis for choosing effective CME offerings.
- CME providers cannot evaluate efficacy of instruction.
- Corporate (primarily pharmaceutical companies) dominate financing and research on CME for important fields.
- Regulations vary widely by medical specialty and by state.

These issues confound medical educators who debate with peers, employers, students, various governmental and credentialing entities, and other medical fields to find satisfying answers. Although there are few ultimate answers to these complex questions, the topic of technology in the medical industry has prompted fascinating development and discussion. On the whole, this has been healthy and productive, resulting in across-the-board attention to education in the medical arena.

A BELLWETHER FIELD

Among U.S. medical fields, respiratory care has traditionally served a bellwether role in technology integration in teaching. Respiratory care is a large medical field with a sixty-year evolutionary history beginning with crude oxygen delivery technologies and dubious positive pressure breathing therapies, progressing to its current status as a respected, technology-oriented innovator in both medical and educational arenas. According to the American Association for Respiratory Care, the field employs about 145,000 clinicians, far below the large number of registered nurses, which has more than 2.5 million practitioners, but roughly the number of dental hygienists, physical therapists, emergency medical technicians, and radiologic technologists (U.S Bureau of Labor Statistics, 2009). Respiratory care employs sophisticated technology applications in adult and neonatal-pediatric mechanical ventilation, cardiopulmonary testing, sleep study, drug administration, oxygen and hyperbaric therapies, and delivery of various medical interventions and modalities in all venues from the intensive care unit to the home. Respiratory care is distinguished by the formidable clinical analysis and decision requirements of its practitioners. These are often associated with potentially dire consequences when clinical situations are not quickly, accurately assessed or interventions are not judiciously applied. Respiratory care practitioners must think fast and act skillfully, making this field uniquely well suited to technology applications in classroom, laboratory, and clinical teaching.

Similarly, the strong technology orientation of the field has fostered a great deal of innovation in educational technology (Hopper, 2004), often in advance of larger, older medical professions. A distinguishing characteristic of the field is that its practitioners and teachers have traditionally embraced and exploited technology. Indeed, the survival of the field of respiratory care has likely depended on its culture of innovation in technology applications, including teaching and learning. In the 1960s and 1970s the medical industry became fascinated with innovative new methods to assess clinical competence of physicians and other clinicians, leading to the ground-breaking, energetic work of self-styled education mavericks such as Christine McGuire (Harris & Simpson, 2005; C. H. McGuire, 1995). Among a number of insightful and pioneering advances in the training and assessment of healthcare providers, McGuire championed the development of text-based clinical simulations, story problems based on best practices involving cycles of information gathering and decision making. Formerly using an inefficient, brutal and widely criticized form of oral examination (Kernaghan, 1978), respiratory care adopted simulation methodology, incorporating branching-logic clinical simulations in the credentialing testing of respiratory therapists beginning in 1979. The field continues to use clinical simulations, now computer-managed, in combination with a traditional multiple-choice examination. But the 1979 implementation of clinical simulations serendipitously matched the introduction of the Apple microcomputer, which was immediately recognized as a near perfect match of methodology and technology. The result was explosive commercial development of microcomputer-managed clinical simulations, as well as tutorials and drill and practice programs. More so than many other medical fields, respiratory care embraced technology delivered instruction and testing, which became integral to the field's culture and practice.

Respiratory care was a pioneering medical field in educational teleconferencing, initiating national "Professor's Rounds" teleconferencing in 1990 (Hopper, 2004). In the first year, an estimated 10,000 healthcare practitioners from 350 institutions participated. These live sessions were recorded for later review for CME purposes, but the "same time, different place" aspect was an obstacle to widespread implementation. Webcasting technology more recently resolved this issue, accommodating larger numbers of live users and providing ready access to high-fidelity archives accessed online. Telecasts were replaced by webcasts beginning in 2003. Telecasts and webcasts were/are not free, but institutional licensing can provide CME for staff for a relatively low cost per participant.

Respiratory care's innovative culture has at times backfired, as in the case of early endorsement of postal correspondence-school training, long before the advent of the Internet and online education. This has been criticized as lending a correspondence-school stigma to a field contending with issues of credibility and professional image (Hopper, 2000). But respiratory care educators are accomplished, widely published professional teachers, with influence across the medical industry and in higher education.

A national survey of respiratory care managers and educators (Hopper & Johns, 2007) provides a picture of technology's role in a medical field, some of it surprising, with insights that are representative of the educational technology experience across the medical industry. Respiratory care training program directors and clinical managers, primarily hospital based, were polled using online research tools and techniques. The study reports that educational technologies play an important role in initial therapist training, continuing education, and advanced education for graduate clinicians (Many respiratory therapists earn an associate degree.) Educators and managers are heavy users of office productivity applications; many use personal digital assistants (PDAs), sometimes in educational roles, and often rely on technology-delivered instruction. But few report technology uses that would be considered exotic or cutting edge, such as virtual reality clinical simulations or computer-managed patient simulators. Computer-managed clinical simulations, text-based (as described above) are a staple in the schools and clinics alike.

Three-quarters of the respiratory care programs offer no fully online courses, but a majority delivers at least one hybrid (Internet supported) course, and most educators and managers report a high level of confidence in these courses. Significantly, while managers consider continuing education delivered by the Internet, such as professional webcasts, to be appropriate, one-third report that they will not hire a therapist trained by distance learning. Both educators and managers hold strongly to the view that face-to-face instruction in distance learning training is essential. Compared to earlier studies in the field, this study found an overall improving attitude toward distance learning and that this is most significant in educators or managers who have themselves taken a course by distance learning. Many respondents have taken fully online courses (20% to 40% of managers and educators, respectively) with a lesser number having earned a degree online (15% to 20%, respectively). The study resulted in telling comments, including:

"I think advanced courses are appropriate, but face-to-face learning with hands-on professors for entry-level and initial courses is crucial to patient care."

"Our students enrolled in distance learning have done well, but state [that] they prefer instructors face-to-face."

The overall picture of technology in a teaching role in this medical field is conservative and bland. But the technology fascination characteristic of respiratory therapists leads many to leadership roles in technology innovation, often in collaboration with other medical specialties. Interspersed in the national field are pockets of remarkable technology applications in teaching and learning, and these may be harbingers of exciting things to come.

For example, Al Moss, program director of the respiratory care program at Kalamazoo Valley Community College, Kalamazoo, Michigan, exudes enthusiasm for his program's current and historical use of technology in teaching and learning, and describes an extraordinary vision of the near future. In 28 years of teaching in respiratory care, Moss relates a technology focus beginning with delivering commercial text-based clinical simulations by Apple II microcomputer, writing and coding in-house simulations using various authoring systems and programming applications, and progressing through the evolution of learning management systems. All courses in the program are now Internet-supported, although there are no fully online courses, and students routinely collect course notes and materials, access drill and practice resources, take practice exams, and view clinical performance records on standardized Moodle course management sites. Students are required to routinely use email and program websites for communication and housekeeping purposes, making phone calls and office visits infrequent. Although not required, many respiratory care instructors and students carry PDAs such as Apple's iTouch, which they use to access commercial bedside references and tools such as for pharmacology information and clinical practice calculations. Student clinical evaluations and records are posted entirely online for student access and for monitoring and evaluation by faculty using DataArc (www.dataarc.ws) a commercial database service for biomedical education. But Moss's rich experience has persuaded him that there are limits to applying technology in the clinical arena, declaring, "Bringing a laptop to the bedside doesn't work."

Moss describes all this as a major break in program management attitudes and practices compared to a pre-Internet time.

"We've always been on the 'bleeding edge' of technology, and just when we get good at something it becomes obsolete so we start over," Moss reports, showing his wide experience in technology adoption in medical education and training. He describes a daunting series of technologies that he and his faculty labored to master but can no longer justify due to its time commitment, now relying on commercially prepared offerings. But Moss says this without bitterness or discouragement and in the next breath gushes over his program's adoption of high-fidelity patient mannequins. On his campus, respiratory care shares a simulation lab with the emergency medical services (EMS) program. Using sophisticated new hands-on training technology such as the SimMan advanced simulator (www.laerdal.com), EMS and respiratory care students experience intensely challenging clinical simulations in emergency care, such as airway assessment and management with endotracheal intubation, cardiopulmonary resuscitation and Advanced Cardiac Life Support (ACLS) procedures, capnography (monitoring of exhaled carbon dioxide), and hemodynamic monitoring.

"These are so good that we achieve what Disney terms 'dispelling of disbelief' in our simulation exercises," Moss maintains. Working independently, in pairs or teams with other students in respiratory care or EMS, students become emotionally involved in the simulated dramas and this can equal the stress experienced in the clinic with real patients. But unlike training experience in a clinical setting, where it is impossible to schedule the optimal mix of experiences and to distribute this fairly among students, high-fidelity simulations can be scheduled, self-evaluated and assessed by instructors for immediate feedback, repeated for mastery, and done without risk to patients. Moss is intrigued by the efficiency and effectiveness these technologies seem to offer. His institution plans to build a simulation center that will serve these two medical programs as well as others on campus.

True to his technology innovation in heritage and background, Moss reports that his program modifies and extends these commercial simulators to customize them for his program's needs. For example, he has incorporated sophisticated test lung technology, designing a custom interface, so that various lung injuries and disease states can be faithfully simulated. But this level of sophisticated technology integration is not typical of medical program offerings in his area, and Moss perceives that his program and field often serve as early adopters (Rogers, 1995) and that other fields profit from this and follow his lead but slowly.

MEDICINE

Medical education and clinical training have powerful historic roots, but these are giving ground to technology mediated innovations, which are modifying the traditional staples of rigorous study and grueling residency. Seasoned physicians share a training heritage largely consisting of "see one, do one" or "see one, do one, teach one" (Wang et al., 2008, p. 1051) but recent technology affordances seem to promise a clinical training experience that is significantly richer. Medical school curricula and pedagogy have been remarkably resistant to persistent criticisms of disconnect between teaching and testing conventions from the real world expectations of practitioners in the clinics (C. H. McGuire, 1995). Some researchers describe organizational political resistance to innovations in teaching with technology but also a tendency for innovative faculty and students to find or create digital resources and bypass the boundaries of host institutions (McGee & Begg, 2008). Issues of authority and control have only begun to be addressed. Even so, participative Web 2.0 technologies such as wikis, blogs, YouTube, and social networking websites are increasingly used by many medical students and some faculty. A cultural obstacle to innovation in teaching in medical programs is the bedrock reliance on the "dose-effect" paradigm in Western medicine, applied to teaching and learning (Hopper, 2004) and even to literal exposure to caregivers (Brooten & Youngblut, 2006). That is, while the traditional pedagogy of lecture and regurgitation of facts goes largely unexamined, innovations in teaching in medical programs are often subject to an expectation of statistical proof as if a teaching approach were comparable to a specific drug administered for a specific ailment. The complexities of pedagogy, cognition, personality variations, and a blizzard of contributing factors make this an untenable standard of evidence.

A compelling focus of technology integration in medical education and training is the recent explosive interest in high-fidelity simulators (Issenberg et al., 2002; Okuda et al., 2008; Scalese, Obeso, & Issenberg, 2008; Taylor, 2007; Wang, et al., 2008; Wayne et al., 2006). Described in a *Time* magazine article in 1967, computer-managed human body mannequins have reached a startling level of sophistication, as Voelker (2009) describes:

They have multiple detectable blood pressure points, pupils that respond to light, pores and hair follicles, heart and bowel sounds, breathing lungs, and chests that flail. They can cry, urinate, bleed, respond to chest compressions, suffer a collapsed lung, have a seizure, develop drug allergies, and give birth to an infant simulator. (p. 2,190)

Complex and expensive, patient simulators are best suited to emergency and intensive care areas of training and practice, such as anesthesiology, emergency medicine, cardiology, and obstetrics. Simulation allows residents and other health care students and practitioners to practice high-risk but low-incidence interventions and to provide this in a safe, expert-guided but realistic setting without the "arguably unethical" (Scalese, et al., 2008, p. 46) practice of subjecting patients to training perils. Faculty can monitor and assess and document practice to mastery. Beyond technical skills, simulators can facilitate team performance learning between residents and also with other healthcare practitioners in the typical medical environment.

The current place of technology in education and in the professional lives of physicians is nicely revealed in interviews of two practicing physicians in the same community, one a veteran of more than twenty years clinical experience, the other a recent graduate. Both are in practice at Upson Regional Medical Center, Thomaston, Georgia.

Dr. Louis Mameli, MD began professional practice more than twenty years ago. A native of New York, Mameli graduated from a prestigious metropolitan medical school. Asked about the role of technology in medical school and residency, he reports simply: "nothing." He recalls a strictly traditional academic and clinical training without computer-based-instruction, computer-managed simulations or tutorials, laser disk resources, technology-mediated instruction of any kind, or even significant use of instructional videotapes. His educational experience is typical of his peers and consisted of lecture, lab, clinical exposure, and the requisite grueling clinical residency.

"There were no personal computers anywhere in this," he says bluntly, and his subsequent continuing medical education for more than a decade consisted only of periodic travel to professional conferences and, most heavily, regular journal reading. His first personal computer experience was a home computer he purchased for word processing, occasional scientific-educational reference mostly for personal interest, and because he felt that he needed to explore the PC's potential. He shared the device with his family and was largely self-taught. Computing technology also entered his workplace at this time but was used only by staff, primarily for billing and accounting.

In Dr. Mameli's office, the absence of a laptop or desktop computer or monitor is conspicuous. He does not use a handheld device nor a Blackberry, reports his first Internet experience to have been in about 1999, and began to use email only within the past five years, mostly for personal use. He does not use podcasts but does refer patients to various online informational resources, some provided by his medical specialty society. His practice has a high bandwidth Internet connection, used mostly for business communications but not for instructional purposes. Technology in the practice is almost entirely in the hands of staff.

But Mameli is no Luddite. He speaks with anticipation of a forthcoming rollout of electronic medical records to be harmoniously linked to nearby Upson Regional Medical Center. This will allow physicians and others to instantly access copious medical record data both in the practice clinic and the hospital, using the same interface. Mameli sees profound positive potential in reducing manual record keeping, eliminating duplication of data, and reducing practice and billing errors. He is aware of new technologies with potential in bedside practice, such as drug information for physicians delivered in handheld devices and updated wirelessly, but has not taken the time to explore these.

Mameli notes that the past few years have brought a dramatic change in how he receives CME content and credit from his professional society. More than half of his materials are delivered electronically, and the increased CME requirements to maintain certification are largely met with online technologies. However, Mameli declines live and archived webcasts in favor of traditional journal reading verified and documented by online multiple-choice testing. This is primarily a matter of expediency. He appreciates online offerings with narration, high-quality graphics, and video, but cannot spare the time, which would erode his personal life because online training could not be accommodated in his work day. Asked his opinion of the efficacy of online instruction, Mameli acknowledges that it is likely effective but also feels that there is "something missing" compared to live, face-to-face instruction.

Mameli knows that like most of his colleagues, he is a busy professional and that "this is a business." He has a shrewd view of the evolution of technologies, noting how expensive they tend to be, how much frustration and time they involve, and how quickly they evaporate. Clearly in the late majority category (Rogers, 1995) of technology adopters, Mameli takes a pragmatic, hard-nosed stance regarding instructional and other technologies. He feels that even if he champions technology use, colleagues who hope to retire before adopting new technologies will balk.

Asked his views on new technologies in his profession, such as the prospect of telemedicine in OB-GYN practice, Mameli states strongly that while exciting and promising, it should be employed strictly in consulting roles and that the locus of authority must remain with the bedside physician. His succinct explanation is that no matter the level of expertise of a distant physician in telecommunication, "You're not here."

Dr. John Jenkins, MD completed residency and entered professional practice two years ago. A Georgia native who attended Medical College of Georgia, he approximates Prensky's (2007) description of the "digital native" and describes a profoundly different relationship with technology than his older colleague, a "digital immigrant." Jenkins recalls his introduction to computer technology in early high school, learning to program at his home on an Apple II microcomputer. While still in high school, he became a heavy Internet user and enthusiastically adopted online scholarly databases, such as University System of Georgia's marvelous Galileo system (www.galileo.usg.edu). Jenkins vividly recalls the tedium of searching for articles and books using traditional catalog card library resources, and how dramatically online technologies improved on this.

When Jenkins began undergraduate study, his college provided email service and required students to use it. This was his introduction to information and communication technologies in an instructional role, and many classes provided support materials online. Many campus classes were very large and PowerPoint visuals were a staple, along with student copies of DVDs such as pathology slides for study and reference. Jenkins views these technologies as eminently useful in his professional preparation. He has never taken a fully online course but expresses no skepticism about their efficacy or suitability in the medical industry. Jenkins describes a central role of high-fidelity simulation mannequins in his residency, describing them as highly realistic, sophisticated, and very important. The simulators allowed residents to practice to mastery, provided a range of infrequent but important clinical events, and were readily available.

Jenkins used branching-logic patient management problems (PMPs) to prepare for board exams and encountered them in the exams themselves, describing these as text-based but graphics-rich. Similar to clinical simulation long used by respiratory care, these simulations permit open-ended typing instead of multiple-choice items in a story problem. Jenkins describes his overall impression of this and other technologies in highly positive terms, noting that he "learned how to find answers" and that this is far more important than "trying to learn everything."

Like his colleague Dr. Mameli, Dr. Jenkins still relies on medical journals for current content in his medical practice and earns CME credit online by taking online quizzes. But Jenkins also accesses online content in various forms, finds it useful and competently done, and appreciates the savings in time and travel expense. He shared an insight in online video on clinical topics, making an analogy with television football. "It's good to be in the stadium but you really get a better view watching the game on TV."

Jenkins relies on medical reference resources and various applications for calculations performed on a handheld device. He routinely updates content wirelessly and heavily uses his Blackberry and a clinic PC to access current literature and online resources. For example, Jenkins consults a digital Physicians Desk Reference and uses the Epocrates (http://www.epocrates.com) application to access drug information such as dosages, drug interactions, cautions, and pricing.

Curiously, Jenkins ranks himself as average to low in technology acumen among his peers, maintaining that other residents in his training were more advanced.

The technology experience reported by these two practicing physicians suggests a marked difference in attitudes and practices in the span of a single generation. While both physicians are clearly competent and diligent, the younger physician's understated comfort and self-efficacy in technology integration seems remarkable, and may portend the sort of technology "sea change" that Dede and Prensky seek. Clearly, introducing online learning as a dominant practice for older physicians must address technical training needs and the intimidation factor inherent in new technologies. The exigencies in shrinking healthcare funding may move physicians with a preference for travel and traditional face-to-face instruction to reconsider technology-mediated alternatives.

OTHER FIELDS

A sampling of technology integration queries in other medical fields indicates a similarly spotty pattern. Registered nursing, the largest U.S. healthcare occupation with 2.6 million jobs (U.S. Bureau of Labor Statistics, 2009), is arguably the largest consumer of educational and information technologies in the medical industry. Lacking a tradition of heavy technology use, nurses nonetheless are required to employ a bewildering array of technologies in their everyday work and in continuing education. Since 1994, nurse licensure candidates have taken the National Council Licensure Examination (NCLEX) on test center computers (National Council of State Boards of Nursing, 2010). This is a computerized, variable length, adaptive testing methodology primarily using multiple choice questions. A recent international survey of technology in nursing (McGillivray, Yates, & McLister, 2007) finds widespread concerns about technology training, the effect of technology on workload, and reliability and accessibility issues. Perhaps most telling in the survey is that the survey invitation was declined by nurses and nursing administrators from several countries, including the U.S., most typically due to heavy workload. This hints at a galling issue in technology integration in the medical industry, that of being "too busy mopping up the water to turn off the faucet." Even so, there are remarkable recent initiatives in technology applications in nursing, such as "telenursing" (Lorentz, 2008) to help care for geographically distant patients and to better distribute medical assistance at reduced cost. Nursing is involved in the industry-wide recognition that best practices in patient care ought to be evidence-based and is exploring ways to better integrate health information technology in clinical practice (Szydlowski & Smith, 2009). Some nursing programs are aggressively innovating with technology, such as the nursing program at University of Medicine and Dentistry of New Jersey, which requires students to use handheld devices (e.g., Apple iTouch and Palm Centro) in the clinics. Nursing students download and use EpocratesRX and DynaMed (http://www.ebscohost.com/dynamed/) for current drug information and evidence-based content (Williams & Dittmer, 2009), respectively.

This aggressive use of handheld devices is not yet the norm in nursing preparation. Paula Brown, a senior nursing student at University of West Georgia, Carrollton, Georgia, reports buying an Apple iTouch and using it heavily in her clinical rotations. She accesses the Internet via hospital wireless systems and searches for drug and pathology information simply using Google. Mostly commonly she finds this information on WebMD (http://www.webmd.com/) but also uses a commercial iPod app to look up unfamiliar words in a medical terminology dictionary. Previously banned from the clinics, such handheld devices are now permitted but not formally supported. Some faculty are following suit, using Blackberry cell phones for Internet access in the clinics.

Most medical fields publish experiential reports of technology integration. For example, pharmacy education is implementing required mobile computing in many schools (Cain, Bird, & Jones, 2008) and the field of public health is finding increased student interaction and learning by using participative seminar blogs (Goldman, Cohen, & Sheahan, 2008). Some fields have found startling applications of technology in teaching, such as virtual slide telepathology in laboratory medicine, which may soon lead to the abandonment of glass slides in U.S. medical schools (Weinstein, 2008). This digital technology permits centrally located pathologists to directly interact with larger numbers of medical students, and even suggests the potential of recording eye movements of seasoned pathologists to precisely define and compare the techniques of experts versus students.

THE FUTURE

"I know of no way of judging the future but by the past." Patrick Henry

As Bates and Poole (2003) noted, "The paradox of technology enhanced education is that technology changes very rapidly and human beings change very slowly" (p. xiii). This is painfully so in the medical industry, perhaps partially due to the medical culture but also due simply to the fact that medical professionals are extraordinarily busy people. Observe a skilled intensive care nurse caring for multiple critically ill patients and it becomes easy to understand why there is little time for serene reflection on cognitive theory.

Dede (2007), in a stirring introduction to the recent ECAR (Educause Center for Applied Research) study of undergraduate students and information technology (Salaway, Caruso, & Nelson, 2007), describes the beginnings of a "sea change" in technology integration in higher education. Although we do not share Dede's perception regarding technology in the general case of higher education (Hopper & Hendricks, 2008), we do suspect that the medical industry may be on the brink of a "sea change" of a somewhat more dramatic nature. The medical industry may be the perfect research and development venue for exciting and bold work in applied educational theory, with or without technology. Only in recent decades have we seen a wholesale shift toward student-centered, rather than teacher-centered, instruction. This was prompted in large part by the bandwidth limitations of early online courses, necessitating adoption of more collaborative, discussion oriented approaches. As many researchers have noted, attention to online pedagogy tends to diffuse into campus teaching improvements as well.

We see three compelling areas of significant technology integration potential in the medical industry:

1. High-Fidelity Simulations

This exciting technology may soon reach a point of critical mass, propelling this learning approach to a prominent, widespread place in the training and maintenance of healthcare professionals. Medical journal research articles, well known for understatement and conservative tone, are using phrases such as "significantly and substantially different" to describe measured results of simulation training, and boldly stating, "Educational interventions using simulation technology that engage learners in deliberate practice of clinical skills produce large improvements in a relatively short time, with little faculty involvement" (Issenberg, et al., 2002, p. 224). The promises of efficacy and efficiency are too potent to ignore.

For example, the Johns-Hopkins Simulation Center (http://www.hopkinsmedicine.org/simulation_center/) declares that learners "practice on plastic" to learn diagnostic procedures and communication skills before working with patients. A central theme is that learners have "permission to fail." This simulation unit houses a simulated operating room, two simulated intensive care units, and 12 exam rooms for high-fidelity simulators as well as human actors who play specific patient roles. The center delivers training for nearly 500 medical students per year, provides orientation and annual review of skills for a respiratory care staff of about 120, and also serves nursing, pharmacy, and house-staff. The center serves both a training/retraining role and offers certification or credentialing required by various regulatory bodies. The Johns-Hopkins Simulation Center also fulfills an important role in simulation research as well as research in important areas such as resuscitation.

Credentialing of medical professionals by simulation was the vision expressed by McGuire (1973) decades ago, as she contended with the disconnect between medical education and examination consisting mostly of isolated facts and having little connection to the real expectations of clinical practice (C. H. McGuire, 1995). Her incisive comment rings true, "...if you want to know can someone do something, ask him (to do it)" (Harris & Simpson, 2005, p. 73). Her seminal work on patient management problems, largely text-based, may now be realized in full bloom in the marvelous simulation technologies available today.

2. Synthesis of Medical Information and Instructional Data

The 2009 American Recovery and Reinvestment Act calls for electronic medical records for all patients by 2014, and substantial funding for physicians and medical practices will be provided to support this aggressive initiative. The act strengthens patients' privacy rights with civil monetary penalties for people who disclose confidential information, while facilitating information exchange between hospitals and physicians and medical staffs.

An unanticipated potential affordance of this technology is that it may realize McGuire's dream of linking pedagogical practices not just to competency measures in students but to eventual patient outcomes. This may address the issue of the "very long chain of inference" (Harris & Simpson, 2005, p. 74) McGuire described, commenting that the intended outcome of medical education is not pleasing examination scores, it is effective health care. As she astutely pointed out, our attention has been focused on production when it should be on outcomes. That is, while it is helpful to deliberately modify teaching design and style to deliberately involve students, this is not an ultimate goal, especially in the professional preparation of students in higher education, in the medical industry or in other areas. Improvements in student critical thinking and problem-solving are what performance technologists term "fuzzy goals" (Gilbert, 1996; Mager & Pipe, 1997), which are difficult to define and nearly impossible to measure. We really need to know if this affects learners in their vocations. More precisely, does it positively affect the subjects (patients, students, clients) the educational effort and expense seeks to eventually serve? The ultimate goal in the preparation of medical professionals is that patients are better served with demonstrably better outcomes.

It may become possible to digitally synthesize data from instructional practices, information technologies, and electronic medical records to reveal efficacy of educational approaches and elements. This has profound implications. It may move us beyond heady theoretical discussions of the merits of one instructional practice or educational technology, until now examined only in a narrow, piecemeal fashion, and actually demonstrate outcomes linked to best teaching practices. And these findings will likely be meaningful across higher education.

3. Facilitating Evidence-Based Practice

Medical professions in general have embraced a paradigm shift toward evidence-based practice, where current research and literature on best practices are routinely accessed and applied at the point of care. Practical obstacles of time, convenience, and availability of information may now be overcome by wirelessly connected handheld devices described above and by partnerships between fields such as nursing and library services

(Pochciol & Warren, 2009). This initiative has profound implications not only for quality of healthcare delivery but also for issues of authority. This shifts the locus of knowledge authority from the hands of a few institutional faculty or clinical supervisors to individual practitioners, and threatens the traditionally hierarchical social structure of the medical industry. Note that in some instances, students are championing wireless access to medical information in the clinics. And just as bedside caregivers can now instantaneously access the latest information on pathology, pharmacology, or treatment, so can patients. Imagine the scenario of a "technosavvy" patient consulting a wireless handheld device to check off clinical practice guidelines during a diagnostic or therapeutic procedure. From the bedside, the patient could then email a credible evaluation of care to a hospital administrator or an attorney.

"I MUST HURRY AFTER THE OTHERS, FOR I AM THEIR LEADER" — A TECHNOLOGY PRESCRIPTION

Though seemingly chaotic, technology integration in the medical industry suggests patterns and insights that might be heeded by medical profession training programs on and off college campuses, by credentialing bodies, and by hospitals and other employers. Perhaps most important is that stemming, controlling or ignoring the flood of information technology adoption is futile and that institutions and educators who wish to maintain credibility must adopt a position of adaptability. The wise captain does not fight wind and current but rather adjusts sails and rudder. Students and clinicians are adopting technology in spite of institutional attitudes and policies, and it is no longer possible to control or even monitor this. Better to embrace technology's manifest usefulness in supporting evidenced-based medical care and address pressing needs to prepare students and bedside caregivers to be critical evaluators of online literature and resources, accepting the inherent shift of authority. If we are not proactive in guiding students to reputable resources they will find their own and we must hope that they have critical thinking skills to discern this knowledge as factual, researched, and true.

The explosion of medical simulation development and the astonishing effectiveness reported in the medical literature may present an opportunity to address some major shortcomings in CME. Training, credentialing, and retraining of medical practitioners must move aggressively toward authentic simulation and away from marginally relevant multiple-choice testing, computerized or not. The headlong adoption of electronic medical records must be exploited to make connections between how we teach, how we test, and how we practice in the clinics. Our ultimate goals must be efficacy and efficiency in delivery of healthcare, and judicious use of educational technologies can help. In the same sense, medical professional training programs must attend to fundamentals of informatics and computer technology for all students.

CONCLUSION

This chapter is an overview of the present state of educational technology integration in the medical industry in general and by examining several representative fields. Technology integration in the medical industry is in an intensive state of innovation, application, and evaluation while at the same time stalled by obstacles of time and tradition. There is concentrated focus on improving medical education and training and on continuing medical education. Technology applications may be expected to play a major role by offering unique affordances and potential cost effectiveness.

REFERENCES

Bates, T., & Poole, G. (2003). *Effective teaching with technology in higher education: Foundations for success* (1st ed.). San Francisco: Jossey-Bass.

Brooten, D., & Youngblut, J. M. (2006). Nurse dose as a concept. *Journal of Nursing Scholarship, 38*(1), 94–99. doi:10.1111/j.1547-5069.2006.00083.x

Cain, J., Bird, E. R., & Jones, M. (2008). Mobile computing initiatives within pharmacy education. *American Journal of Pharmaceutical Education, 72*(4), 76–76.

Clark, R. E. (1983). Reconsidering research on learning from media. *Review of Educational Research, 53*(4), 445–459.

Dede, C. (2007). Introduction: A sea change in thinking, knowing, learning, and teaching--The ECAR study of undergraduate students and information technology, 2007. *Educause Center for Applied Research Key Findings,* (September 2007). Retrieved from http://www.educause.edu/ir/library/pdf/ers0706/rs/ers07062.pdf

Dewey, J. (1933). *How we think, a restatement of the relation of reflective thinking to the educative process*. Boston: D.C. Heath and company.

Ellaway, R. (2007). eMedical Teacher. Beware of passive attitudes to e-teaching and e-learning and be more aware of the fundamental effects of technology (and its failure) on the psychological health of your organisation! *Medical Teacher, 29*(5), 519–520. doi:10.1080/01421590701557059

Ellaway, R. (2008). eMedical Teacher. *Medical Teacher, 30*(7), 734–735. doi:10.1080/01421590802356351

Ely, D. P., Foley, A., Freeman, W., & Scheel, N. (1995). Trends in educational technology. In Anglin, G. J. (Ed.), *Instructional Technology Past, Present and Future* (pp. 34–60). Englewood, CA: Libraries Unlimited, Inc.

Gilbert, T. F. (1996). *Human competence: Engineering worthy performance* (Tribute ed.). Silver Spring, MD: International Society for Performance Improvement.

Goldman, R. H., Cohen, A. P., & Sheahan, F. (2008). Using seminar blogs to enhance student participation and learning in public health school classes. *American Journal of Public Health, 98*(9), 1658–1663. doi:10.2105/AJPH.2008.133694

Harmon, S. W., & Jones, M. G. (1999). The five levels of web use in education: Factors to consider in planning online courses. *Educational Technology, 39*(6), 28–32.

Harris, I. B., & Simpson, D. (2005). Christine McGuire: At the heart of the maverick measurement maven. *Advances in Health Sciences Education : Theory and Practice, 10*(1), 65–80. doi:10.1007/s10459-005-2339-8

Hopper, K. B. (1999). Mastering the invisible technologies in education: Who are the real technology prodigies among college teachers? *Educational Technology, 39*(1), 50–56.

Hopper, K. B. (2000). Are online distance learners learning or just distant? [letter]. *Respiratory Care, 45*(4), 432–434.

Hopper, K. B. (2004). Education, teleconferencing, and distance learning in respiratory care. *Respiratory Care, 49*(4), 410–420.

Hopper, K. B., & Hendricks, R. (2008). Technology integration in the college classroom—A baker's dozen frugal but promising strategies. *Educational Technology, 48*(5), 10–17.

Hopper, K. B., & Johns, C. L. (2007). Educational technology and distance learning in respiratory care: Attitudes and practices. *Respiratory Care, 52*(11), 1510–1524.

Institute of Education Sciences Institute of Medicine. (2010). *Redesigning continuing education in the health professions*. Preproduction Copy, Available from http://www.iom.edu/Reports/2009/Redesigning-Continuing-Education-in-the-Health-Professions.aspx.

Issenberg, S. B., McGaghie, W. C., Gordon, D. L., Symes, S., Petrusa, E. R., & Hart, I. R. (2002). Effectiveness of a cardiology review course for internal medicine residents using simulation technology and deliberate practice. *Teaching and Learning in Medicine*, *14*(4), 223–228. doi:10.1207/S15328015TLM1404_4

Kernaghan, S. G. (1978). Clinical Simulation: The profession's new tool for registry evaluation. *Respiratory Care*, *23*(6), 570–576.

Lorentz, M. M. (2008). Telenursing and home healthcare. The many facets of technology. *Home Healthcare Nurse*, *26*(4), 237–243. doi:10.1097/01.NHH.0000316702.22633.30

Mager, R. F., & Pipe, P. (1997). *Analyzing performance problems, or, you really oughta wanna: How to figure out why people aren't doing what they should be, and what to do about it* (3rd ed.). Atlanta, GA: Center for Effective Performance.

McGee, J. B., & Begg, M. (2008). What medical educators need to know about "Web 2.0". *Medical Teacher*, *30*(2), 164–169. doi:10.1080/01421590701881673

McGillivray, R., Yates, S., & McLister, B. (2007). Nurses and technology: An international survey. *Biomedical Instrumentation & Technology / Association For The Advancement. Medical Instrumentation*, (Suppl), 19.

McGuire, C. H. (1973). Diagnostic examinations in medical education. *Public Health Papers*, (52): 59–69.

McGuire, C. H. (1995). Reflections of a maverick measurement maven. *JAMA: The Journal Of The American Medical Association*, *274*(9), 735–740. doi:10.1001/jama.274.9.735

National Center for Education Statistics. (2008). *Digest of education statistics*. Retrieved 1/10/2010, from U.S. Dept. of Education Institute of Education Sciences: http://nces.ed.gov/programs/digest/d08/tables/dt08_275.asp

National Center for Education Statistics. (2009). *Changes in postsecondary awards below the bachelor's degree*. Retrieved 1/10/2010, from U.S. Dept. of Education Institute of Education Sciences: http://nces.ed.gov/pubs2010/2010167.pdf

National Council of State Boards of Nursing. (2010). *2010 NCLEX examination candidate bulletin*. Retrieved from https://www.ncsbn.org/2010_NCLEX_Candidate_Bulletin_Ata-Glance.pdf

Okuda, Y., Bond, W., Bonfante, G., McLaughlin, S., Spillane, L., & Wang, E. (2008). National growth in simulation training within emergency medicine residency programs. *Academic Emergency Medicine*, *15*(11), 1113–1116. doi:10.1111/j.1553-2712.2008.00195.x

Pochciol, J. M., & Warren, J. I. (2009). An information technology infrastructure to enable evidence-based nursing practice. *Nursing Administration Quarterly*, *33*(4), 317–324.

Prensky, M. (2007). New issues, new answers--Changing paradigms. *Educational Technology*, *47*(4), 64.

Reiser, R. A. (2002). A history of instructional design and technology. In Reiser, R. A., & Dempsey, J. V. (Eds.), *Instructional Design and Technology* (pp. 26–53). Upper Saddle River, NJ: Merrill Prentice Hall.

Rogers, E. M. (1995). *Diffusion of Innovations* (4th ed.). New York: Free Press.

Russell, T. L. (1999). *The no significant difference phenomenon: As reported in 355 research reports, summaries and papers*. North Carolina: North Carolina State University.

Salaway, G., Caruso, J. B., & Nelson, M. R. (2007). The ECAR study of undergraduate students and information technology, 2007. *Educause Center for Applied Research Key Findings,* (September 2007). Retrieved from http://www.educause.edu/ir/library/pdf/ers0706/rs/ers07062.pdf.

Salomon, G. (2002). Technology and pedagogy: Why don't we see the promised revolution? *Educational Technology*, *42*(2), 71–75.

Scalese, R. J., Obeso, V. T., & Issenberg, S. B. (2008). Simulation technology for skills training and competency assessment in medical education. *Journal of General Internal Medicine*, *23*(Suppl 1), 46–49. doi:10.1007/s11606-007-0283-4

Szydlowski, S., & Smith, C. (2009). Perspectives from nurse leaders and chief information officers on health information technology implementation. *Hospital Topics*, *87*(1), 3–9. doi:10.3200/HTPS.87.1.3-9

Taylor, C. (2007). The wave of the future, or just fun and games? Virtual training for healthcare workers. *Biomedical Instrumentation & Technology / Association For The Advancement. Medical Instrumentation*, (Suppl), 57–59.

Voelker, R. (2009). Medical simulation gets real. *JAMA: Journal of the American Medical Association*, *302*(20), 2190–2192. doi:10.1001/jama.2009.1677

Wang, E. E., Quinones, J., Fitch, M. T., Dooley-Hash, S., Griswold-Theodorson, S., & Medzon, R. (2008). Developing technical expertise in emergency medicine--The role of simulation in procedural skill acquisition. *Academic Emergency Medicine*, *15*(11), 1046–1057. doi:10.1111/j.1553-2712.2008.00218.x

Wayne, D. B., Butter, J., Siddall, V. J., Fudala, M. J., Wade, L. D., & Feinglass, J. (2006). Mastery learning of advanced cardiac life support skills by internal medicine residents using simulation technology and deliberate practice. *Journal of General Internal Medicine*, *21*(3), 251–256. doi:10.1111/j.1525-1497.2006.00341.x

Weinstein, R. S. (2008). Time for a reality check. *Archives of Pathology & Laboratory Medicine*, *132*(5), 777–780.

Williams, M. G., & Dittmer, A. (2009). Textbooks on tap: Using electronic books housed in handheld devices in nursing clinical courses. *Nursing Education Perspectives*, *30*(4), 220–225.

ADDITIONAL READING

Brooten, D., & Youngblut, J. M. (2006). Nurse dose as a concept. *Journal of Nursing Scholarship*, *38*(1), 94–99. doi:10.1111/j.1547-5069.2006.00083.x

Clark, R. E. (1983). Reconsidering research on learning from media. *Review of Educational Research*, *53*(4), 445–459.

Clark, R. E., & Feldon, D. F. (2005). Five common but questionable principles of multimedia learning. In Meyer, R. E. (Ed.), *The Cambridge Handbook of Multimedia Learning* (pp. 97–115). New York: Cambridge University Press.

Dede, C. (2007). *Introduction: A sea change in thinking, knowing, learning, and teaching--The ECAR study of undergraduate students and information technology, 2007*. Educause Center for Applied Research Key Findings, (September 2007). Retrieved from http://www.educause.edu/ir/library/pdf/ers0706/rs/ers07062.pdf

Dewey, J. (1933). *How we think, a restatement of the relation of reflective thinking to the educative process.* Boston: D.C. Heath and company.

Harris, I. B., & Simpson, D. (2005). Christine McGuire: at the heart of the maverick measurement maven. *Advances in Health Sciences Education : Theory and Practice*, *10*(1), 65–80. doi:10.1007/s10459-005-2339-8

Hopper, K. B., & Johns, C. L. (2007). Educational technology and distance learning in respiratory care: Attitudes and practices. *Respiratory Care*, *52*(11), 1510–1524.

Institute of Education Sciences Institute of Medicine. (2010). *Redesigning continuing education in the health professions. Preproduction* Copy, Available from http://www.iom.edu/Reports/2009/Redesigning-Continuing-Education-in-the-Health-Professions.aspx

McGuire, C. H. (1995). Reflections of a maverick measurement maven. *JAMA: The Journal Of The American Medical Association*, *274*(9), 735–740. doi:10.1001/jama.274.9.735

Rogers, E. M. (1995). *Diffusion of innovations* (4th ed.). New York: Free Press.

Scalese, R. J., Obeso, V. T., & Issenberg, S. B. (2008). Simulation technology for skills training and competency assessment in medical education. *Journal of General Internal Medicine*, *23*(Suppl 1), 46–49. doi:10.1007/s11606-007-0283-4

KEY TERMS AND DEFINITIONS

Clinician: Physician, therapist, technician or other medical field professional who works directly in patient care areas, such as hospitals or laboratories.

Continuing Medical Education (CME): Sometimes referred to as in-service education, annual requirements for updated information and skills training mandated by credentialing bodies and various government entities.

Credentialing: Practice of certifying competency as sanctioned by a local, state, or national agency with authority over practitioners in a field.

Residency: Period of medical training following graduation from medical school, involving direct patient care in a medical specialty.

Simulation: Expertly prepared exercise for student learning or testing, employing one of a variety of techniques to realistically represent circumstances and choices encountered in clinical patient care. Simulations range in sophistication to simple story problems to high-fidelity computer-managed models. Simulations aim to require knowledge mastery, critical thinking skills, and other aspects of competent clinical care.

Telemedicine: Use of telephone or teleconferencing technology to provide assessment or treatment functions, usually by a physician.

Training: Intentional preparation for skills, which are specific and likely to be implemented soon.

Chapter 12
Mobile Computing in Higher Education

Raymond S. Pastore
University of North Carolina Wilmington, USA

Susan M. Land
Pennsylvania State University, USA

Eun Ju Jung
Pennsylvania State University, USA

ABSTRACT

This chapter examines research on mobile learning, its impact in higher education, and the technologies being used as mobile learning devices. Mobile learning includes devices that have the capability to be site and/or job specific, such that learners can access content immediately regardless of their location. Mobile learning is being successfully employed in many higher education classrooms throughout the world, as it enables new methods of learning and for redefining learner interactions. New teaching methods may now be possible that allow for exchange and creation of information in novel learning contexts. Social and organizational issues of mobile learning are analyzed and presented.

INTRODUCTION

Over the past decade, the use of mobile technology has increased dramatically both within and outside of higher education. This increase has been caused by a need to communicate through wireless technologies, such as the mobile phone, as well as the proliferation of portable media players such as the iPod. These devices are no longer seen as solely communication media; more recently, they have also been used in the classroom for learning. In fact, a market research study conducted by Ambient Insight, LLC estimates that 246.9 million dollars will be spent on mobile learning technology by 2011 (Brown & Metcalf, 2008, p. 1). Due to this popularity and growth, it is expected that mobile technology will soon become a common learning tool, utilized by both corporate and academic institutions. As such, there is a great need to examine both the potential and difficulties this technology may have on learning within these environments.

DOI: 10.4018/978-1-60960-147-8.ch012

This chapter will examine current research on mobile learning, its impacts in academia, and the technologies being used as mobile learning devices. The chapter begins by describing and defining mobile learning. Then, the technologies, research, and specific examples for each mobile technology will be presented. The chapter concludes with a discussion of implications of mobile computing on social and organizational aspects in higher education.

What is Mobile Learning?

While many researchers have discussed and defined mobile learning (mLearning), the concept of mobile learning remains less clear (Traxler, 2007). Mobile learning has emerged to encompass multiple technologies, which are discussed further in this chapter. As a result, research is generally limited to features or technologies only contained in one device rather than all of the devices that can be used in a mobile learning environment. Thus, the research on mLearning is device and feature dependent, which makes it difficult to generalize findings across technology devices.

Defining mLearning can be a complicated task, as the boundaries separating different technology applications are blurred. The literature often defines mLearning by comparing it to eLearning, which shares many of the same characteristics. Elearning most often refers to learning that takes place on a computer, in an online environment, where information is sent or received instantly (Rosenberg, 2001). Research on mobile learning (Caudill, 2007; Kukulska-Hulme, 2005; Peters, 2007; Traxler, 2007) depicts it as an extension of eLearning that includes the use of technology that can be carried easily in a pocket or purse, used 'on the go' (on the job or en route), turned on instantly without the need to boot up, is internet capable through a service or wifi connection, and has other identifiable features such as word processing ability, html browser, SMS messaging, Camera, MP3 player, GPS, etc.

In addition to technology features, Klopfer, Squire, and Jenkin (2008) have identified several functions unique to mlearning that include social interactivity, context sensitivity, connectivity, individuality, and portability. Social interactivity refers to the popularity of texting, social sites such as Facebook and Twitter, and social interactions that take place in real time. Context sensitivity refers to the ability to gather real-time data in a unique environment and location. Connectivity, through handhelds, provides the ability to connect to databases, networks, computers, and other mobile users. Individuality provides students with self-directed learning opportunities to explore on their own. Portability refers to devices that are portable and can fit into your pocket that can be used in real time or 'on the go'.

Each of these features and uses help to create a clear line that separates mLearning from eLearning. The major difference is that eLearning involves a desktop or laptop computer whereas mLearning utilizes a mobile device. These mobile devices include cell phones, PDAs, iPods, portable GPS units, as well as other types of mobile technologies. Thus, the standard desktop computer and laptop are not considered mobile learning technologies due to the fact that they need to be booted up, cannot fit into a pocket, and cannot be used on the go (Caudill, 2007).

Additionally, mobile learning includes devices that have the capability to be site and/or job specific, such that learners can access materials immediately regardless of their location. For instance, if you were in a museum and wanted more information on a particular piece of art you were viewing, you could simply look it up. Another example includes making electronic comments or notes about a lecture that is currently taking place. Elearning does not always offer these same functionalities.

MOBILE LEARNING TECHNOLOGIES: CURRENT APPLICATIONS

Mobile devices are unique and differ from their traditional desktop cousins. They share many similarities such Internet connections, access to word processing software, and camera and video technologies. They can also be used to view or send content or email, participate in discussion forums, submit assignments, and send/receive feedback (Rekkedal & Dye, 2007). Additionally, in higher education, mobile technologies are being used for enrolling in courses, communication, texting, and emergency warning systems. The technologies differ from standard desktop computers in that they are mobile and thus can be used on the go or at the point of demand. However, this portability, while advantageous, does carry its disadvantages. Rekkedal and Dye (2007) explain that these devices have small screens that are sometimes difficult to see, have limited web capabilities, and generally have slow Internet connections. While these limitations are being updated with each new generation of device, they remain tied to device size and portability.

Generating clear guidelines for instructional designers and faculty to use mobile devices in higher education is challenging, due in part to the fact that applications tend to be compartmentalized around specific technology devices (e.g., I-pods vs. handhelds). To illustrate the range of mobile learning applications in higher education, the following section describes specific mobile devices, the technology used for each, and cases illustrating how they have been used within university classroom contexts.

Podcasting

The term podcasting is derived from both "i-Pod" and "broadcast" and is typically composed of several technologies such as MP3 files and players, RSS, and blogs. Specifically, podcasting is "the process of capturing an audio event, song, speech, or mix of sounds and then posting that digital sound object to a Web site or blog in a data structure called an RSS 2.0 envelope or feed" (Meng, 2005, p. 1). Adam Curry, often known as "the podfather," developed a podcatching software and began a podcasting service on the website Odeo, which enables users to create podcasts easily (Campbell, 2005). Beginning with Odeo, Apple's iTunes hastened the development and influence of podcasting, along with the RSS functionality. The RSS feed removes time-consuming work by allowing users to subscribe to podcasts and download the subscribed podcasts automatically upon new release. The main features of podcasting can be summarized in three words: time, place, and portability (Cebeci & Tekdal, 2006; Evans, 2008). Specifically, people can listen to a podcast while participating in other activities, such as jogging and household affairs, without inconvenience. Moreover, users pause and replay podcasts at their leisure. The strengths of podcasting are the low economic cost to develop a podcast compared to other mediums, and the simpler technological expertise required to produce it.

Initial interest in podcasting within higher education started with Duke University. In 2004, Duke provided 1,600 20GB Apple iPods to freshmen. This project aimed to explore the effectiveness of iPods in the learning environment for both faculty and students (Belanger, 2005). iPods were integrated within at least 15 fall courses and 33 spring courses, including foreign language and social science. Although researchers expected the audio playback function of iPods to be used most frequently, an evaluative survey revealed that recording was most popular. Sixty percent of the iPods were utilized as recording devices for interviews, field notes, small group discussion, and preparation for oral assignments. Besides recording, iPods were also used as tools for course content and dissemination, study support, and file storage and transferring.

Since Duke University began its widespread integration of podcasting into college classrooms, the University of Washington also executed a pilot podcasting program in 2005 (Lane, 2006). Four fall courses provided podcasting to 668 students. The next academic quarter, 4,128 students in 13 courses were provided with podcasting. The University conducted a survey of 41 students about their listening habits and attitude towards podcasting. One finding was that students used podcasting to improve course comprehension by replaying lectures before or after class. In addition, students used podcasting to prepare for tests, analyze lectures and take notes. These results coincide with Duke University's reports. Two educational functions of podcasting can be inferred from these cases: Instructors enhance their classroom practices by providing class material via podcasting, and students can generate their own podcasts of book summaries, opinions, and class discussions. Institutional support of podcasting is becoming more commonplace, with Stanford University, Drexel University, University of Michigan, University of Dayton, Pennsylvania State University, and Virginia Tech also offering podcasting to students to support classroom learning.

Podcasting provides students with ubiquitous learning opportunities through innovative distribution (Bongey, Cizadlo, & Kalnbach, 2006; Dale, 2007; Kurtz, et al., 2007; Lonn & Teasley, 2009). While the distribution technology of podcasting offers new opportunities for learner-content interactions, audio is not new to education. Manning explains the strength of listening as the following: "What one hears through the speaker's intonation, diction and inflection conveys a richer understanding not only of the content, but of the speaker. Listeners connect to that voice and may feel less isolated" (Manning, 2005, p. 2). According to a series of studies, podcasting can be used instructionally to achieve four primary purposes: to alleviate student anxiety, to increase course satisfaction (Miller & Piller, 2005), to improve course comprehension (Grabe, 2005), and to expand and connect classroom to society (Blaisdell, 2006).

Cell Phones

The use of cell phones in recent years has grown widely. In fact many people could not imagine life without them. According to Gartner Inc., 555.2 million cell phones were sold worldwide in the first half of 2009 (Gartner Press Release, 2009). As a result of this popularity and growth, cell phones have the potential to change the way we learn, in the same way they have changed the way we communicate with one another. When cell phones were first introduced to the global market, they were simply used for speaking. However, most recently, mobile phones are used for texting, otherwise known as SMS messaging, or the ability to send text messages to and from a mobile phone. Additionally, these devices now have the ability to access the Internet via html web browsers. They have features such as GPS, email functionality, cameras, mp3 players, calendars, clocks, and the ability to open documents in Word, PowerPoint, and PDF formats. Some models even have a miniature QWERTY keyboard and touch screen capabilities. As demand for features increases, companies have aimed to make cell phones as powerful as desktop computers. These new, powerful cell phones are referred to as smartphones, which carry the ability to download software programs called 'apps' and connect users to their computer workstations. As a result, these devices are functioning less like mobile phones of the past and more like portable computers.

Although these devices are owned by many people and used in their daily lives, they are just beginning to be used in learning environments. It wasn't until cell phones began to include functions other than just speaking that their true potential for learning was recognized. Currently, cell phones, like other mobile devices are new learning tools, so clear guidelines for their use in education have yet to emerge (Holzinger, Nischelwitzer, and

Meisenberger, 2005). However, they carry many features that can aid the learning process and give learners new ways of interacting and learning in everyday and classroom contexts.

The literature has shown that users are often skeptical at first when introduced to cell phones as a learning tool. This section describes two studies that highlight initial findings on cell phone use in a college classroom. A study by Seppala and Alamaski (2003), at the University of Helinski in Finland, took place in the spring of 2002 with 11 students, 5 of whom were teachers. Each student was given a mobile phone and digital camera. They were asked to discuss teaching issues during the supervisor teaching process via SMS messages and to take pictures where necessary. These messages and images would then be used to discuss learners' actions, teaching techniques, and training events. Results of the study were analyzed via a survey that asked participants why and where they used the devices, situations where they used them, and how they felt during use. The responses were broken into three categories based on Kynaslahti (2003), which consisted of convenience, expediency, and immediacy. For convenience, the participants indicated that they were able use them anywhere, such as on the train to and from home or work. For expediency, they could use them when they actually needed the information. For immediacy, they could get the information immediately when they needed it. They also reported that they liked to communicate when traveling and enjoyed that if they did something, such as take a picture, they could get feedback immediately.

Similar conclusions were made by Shen, Wang, Pan, and Xiaoyan (2008), who conducted a study at the e-Learning lab of Shanghai Jiaotong University, where they developed a class that could be conducted via a mobile phone. The system was developed to support communications to and from the instructors and students. The course was comprised of a classroom, a server, and mobile phones. The classroom computer was used to send and receive information from the students' cell phones. This computer would track activities such as learning progress, polls, and questions. For course access, students simply needed to install a software program onto their phones. Once enrolled in the course, they could choose whether they wanted to view it via text, audio and video, video only, or text only. However, students' cell phone features limited what they could view. The system was tested on 1000 students in a Social English class and included eight class quizzes. The instructor provided classroom materials and quizzes via cell phones, and they evaluated responses using their cell phones. Students were sent surveys at the beginning and end of the course to measure how they felt about the use of mobile phones in a learning environment. Five hundred twenty-six students responded to the pre course survey and 735 responded to the post course survey. In the pre-survey, 85% reported they did not want to use their cell phone for the class. Post survey revealed that 92% were satisfied with the class format. They indicated that they enjoyed the 24/7 access to materials and flexibility. The unsatisfied students reported they could not keep up with the speed of text messaging.

As was demonstrated in both of the cases presented above, learners tended to be skeptical when cell phones were first introduced into their learning environment. However, after the novelty and uncertainty pass, they enjoyed the experience. The participants in these cases identified that instant access to their class anywhere/anytime was the main reason they enjoyed the technology. It is important to note that some learners indicated they had problems keeping pace with the SMS (texting) messages in the class. This is something to keep in mind if trying to implement this technology especially with users whom have little experience using the texting feature on mobile phones and/or phones that do not have a QWERTY keyboard. Overall, the use of mobile phones in the classroom is still a new idea but is something that may be implemented more over time and as mobile phone technology improves. However, a number of institutional and organizational barriers exist to implementation of mobile phones in college classrooms, a point that will be discussed later in this chapter.

Wireless Handheld Devices

Handheld devices include a range of technologies such as personal digital assistants, cell phones or iPod Touch systems, global position systems (GPS), or portable gaming devices (Wagner, 2008). Most utilize wireless capabilities, enabling them access to the Internet and/or to share files, data, or information. Wireless handheld devices (WHDs) have been used to support mobile learning in higher education both within and outside of the classroom. Within classrooms, WHD examples might include audience response systems to encourage participation or formative assessment in real time within large, lecture classes (Evans & Johri, 2008). The pragmatic constraints of teaching within large lecture halls limit both instructional and assessment activities. Using audience response systems, faculty can design activities that poll students on an opinion or question, and then display the aggregated data for purposes of discussion. Use of handheld technology to enable formative feedback is not limited solely to the large lecture classroom. Ducut and Fontelo (2008) describe using handhelds as polling devices in medical education. By polling students during class, medical educators can adjust classroom teaching based on the deficiencies of students. This type of technology can very efficiently provide feedback to instructors about how well students understand complex material, and whether or not more class time is needed to work through knowledge deficiencies.

Given the portability of WHDs, new opportunities are created through technology for engaging the world outside of the college classroom. We briefly discuss three different approaches to supporting field-based learning using WHDs: (a) portable information repositories; (b) real-world data collection devices; (c) augmented environments/simulations. All three approaches share the common goal of enabling learning in context. Hence, students are supported to participate in real-world practices that are shared by, or consistent with, a given community of practitioners. This can include field-based data collection, or access to information in real-time that will enable knowledgeable participation in field-based or clinical practices.

For instance, handheld devices can be used as *portable information repositories* to help students to participate knowledgeably in clinical or practicum activities on demand. Ducut and Fontelo (2008) note that PDA's have been used for more than a decade to aid medical students to manage the growing amount of information needed to perform effectively, especially at the point of care. Handheld devices serve as "mobile libraries" (Ducut & Fontelo) to enable medical information on demand with access medical texts, reference tools, and calculation programs to augment their performance within the real world context of patient care. Similar functions of handhelds can be used to support a variety of clinical or practicum experiences of college students, ranging from law to engineering.

A second use of handheld devices in field studies is *portable real-world data collection devices*. For instance, undergraduate genetics students at Cornell University used mobile devices to explore corn genotype (Rieger & Gay, 1997). With portable computers and probe-enabled data collection devices, students collected data on conditions such as plant height, soil pH, or temperature for ten varieties of corn. Data were then used for classroom discussion and more detailed analyses. Similar projects involve using probes connected to handheld computers to collect and aggregate stream quality or air quality data (Dieterle et al., 2007). Probe-enabled portable computers provide opportunities to move students out of the lecture hall and into their environment to collect and explore real world phenomena. Similar activities can be supported through field-based surveys, where students use handhelds to interview others around campus, and upload data to be analyzed as a class (Dieterle et al.).

A final approach to using handheld devices to enable field-based learning is through *augmented environments/simulations*. Augmented reality environments create contrived scenarios for learners to explore a topic within a place-based context (Rogers et al., 2004). Klopfer et al (2008) created the *Environmental Detectives* simulation, which placed students in the hypothetical role of environmental scientists investigating toxins in the water supply on the MIT campus. As students moved about campus, their GPS-enabled handhelds relayed their location, allowing them to collect simulated field data based on their location and their role. Students could access sample concentrations of the groundwater, depending on their location. At certain points on campus, virtual characters/experts would provide place-specific information about the problem. Teams then compiled their data and performed further analyses. In augmented reality environments, students don't collect "real" data; instead, a game or simulation is created that relies on context- or place-sensitive information to provide a more immersive learning experience.

Netbooks, Laptops, and Other Portable Computers

While laptops are capable of working without plugging into a power source and can utilize wireless networks, they are not devices that people can carry everywhere and quickly access at any time due to their size, configuration, and the time required to boot up and shut down. For instance, while you may have your laptop with you on a train, you might not have it in the grocery store when you need to access the Internet to find the ingredients to a recipe. As a result, laptops are not considered mobile learning technologies. However, the recent surge in popularity of a new type of laptop, called a netbook may change this.

Netbooks are small portable laptops that are generally 7-10 inches in size making them nearly half the size of the standard laptop and significantly less expensive. Some manufactures are trying to make them even smaller. The key trait making netbooks so popular is that they perform all of the same functions as a laptop, thus, they are considered mini laptops. However they differ from laptops because they are limited in their RAM and processing capacity (Descy, 2009). They currently can run Windows XP, Windows 7 and Linux operating systems. However, due to their small size, they are difficult to type on as the QWERTY keyboard is not regular size. As a result, some view these as inconvenient and feel that they might as well use their mobile phone and/or laptop because the netbook does not replace either. However, recent trends indicate that people are buying these devices. It is commonplace to walk into a college classroom and see more netbooks than laptops. Additionally, cell phone carriers, such as Verizon Wireless ™ are offering these devices with service coverage similar to that of a cell phone, so that they can access the Internet anywhere regardless of wifi hotspots. At this point, the service is relatively slow and expensive, but that will likely improve as demand for wireless devices increases. Additionally, in the future, these devices will be able to make calls like a cell phone as trends show a merging of netbooks and mobile devices together.

However, the question remains as to whether these are separate from laptops, which are not considered part of the mobile learning trend. These devices are small and thus they can be carried anywhere. However they are not as small as a cell phone and do require time to boot up. Thus, based on the definition of mobile learning as noted above, these should not yet be considered mobile learning devices, but rather just smaller laptops. However as technology advances netbooks will soon be a part of the mobile learning world as boot up becomes instant, they become more ergonomically friendly and easier to carry around, bearing closer resemblance to smart phones.

HUMAN, SOCIAL, AND ORGANIZATIONAL ASPECTS

Mobile technology has yet to make a clear impact on higher education. There is little research on the topic (Zhang, 2008) and wide scale implementation in higher education is difficult to achieve due to "... resources (that is, finance and money but also human resources, physical estates, institutional reputation, intellectual property, and expertise) and culture (that is, institutions as social organizations, their practices, values and procedures, but also the expectations and standards of their staff, students and their wider communities, including employers and professional bodies)." (Troxler, 2007, p. 9-10). The following section discusses a variety of human, social, and organizational aspects as they relate to implementing mobile technology into higher education.

Human and Social Aspects

Implementing technology into an academic institution can prove to be a daunting task. This has been demonstrated many times as new technologies such as websites and course management systems are introduced into university settings (Kronen, 2003). It is no different with mobile learning. What separates mobile learning from other technology implementations is the fact that the everyone involved in the process has used mobile devices on some level for personal use. However, while those involved are familiar with mobile devices, they are not necessarily familiar with using them in a learning environment (Hulme & Pittit, 2008). As a result, it is important to examine the effects of this implementation on faculty and students.

When implementing any technology into an institution, examining past cases and experiences in order to help ensure success is very helpful. Generally, technology users are comprised of innovators, early adopters, early majority, late majority, and laggards (Rogers, 1995). The innovators and early adopters are the first to experiment with the technology and develop best practices. Once the technology is established and design guidelines are in place, the majority will accept and embrace it. The laggards either will not adopt it or will accept it only when forced to do so.

In addition to types of users in the system, social aspects of adopting technology in the classroom are highlighted in the literature. For instance, Straub (2009) discusses three social aspects: complexity of implementation, individuals' unique perspectives that affect their adoption decisions, and the cognitive, emotional, and contextual concerns of its users. Technology adoption can be seen as a complex process due to the fact that it not only involves buying a technology and implementing it, but also training for the users, adoption/acceptance by the users, faculty incentives, and maintenance/support. Individuals construct unique opinions on the technology, and thus training must address these issues to ensure that both faculty and students are comfortable using it in the classroom. Additionally, successful implementation must address internal and external concerns for stakeholders and users of the system in order to be effective.

As was discussed earlier, over 500 million cell phones were sold worldwide in the first half of 2009 (Gartner Press Release, 2009). Nearly all students, faculty, and administrators in higher education have used this technology for personal use. However, classroom use of this technology presents unique challenges not encountered in personal use. Higher educators are already encouraged to use many technologies such as course management systems, Blogs, wikis, plagiarism assessment systems, and so on. Hence, it is reasonable to ask questions about the practicality of introducing new mobile technologies for classroom teaching. For instance, do faculty have time to learn how to use another technology for learning? Will it be a benefit to them and the learning process? Who will buy this technology? Will students be required to enter programs with mobile devices? Will instructors be forced to purchase them or use them in their classroom? Widespread incorporation of mobile technologies will require system-wide infrastructure and change. Earle (2002) stresses that in order for technology implementation to be successful, changes must be systemic rather than temporary. Thus, in order for successful implementation to take place, all stakeholders (administrators, faculty, students) need to be involved in the process and in the end, satisfied with the technology.

For instance a study by Nicolle and Lou (2008) found that involving faculty stakeholders in the implementation significantly helped them learn and adopt new technologies. Similar conclusions were drawn by Lewis and Starsia (2009) whom identified three lessons learned from implementing technology into higher education institutions: (a) define the core business; (b) invest in infrastructure; and (c) resist the tendency to allow budget to become the driving force in strategy decisions. This suggests that solutions need to benefit students as the core business consideration, but that all key stakeholders should be involved in the implementation process. By generating strategies that consider more than cost as the primary consideration in strategic planning, a greater focus can be made on investing in the infrastructure to develop and maintain buildings, mainframes, or computers to best meet learning needs. This will help save time and money in the future.

Organizational Aspects

Introducing mobile technology to an academic institution is different from other technology implementations, such as course management systems, and has thus far proved to be a difficult task (Wagner 2008). Since the pedagogy associated with the technology is new, there have yet to be clear implementation guidelines on its use. Additionally, certain concerns or issues are device dependent, such as the service charge for a cell phone. However, there are a host of concerns identified in the literature on mobile learning that all mobile implementations will need to address (Driscoll & Carliner, 2005). These include policy issues such as security, cost, and maintenance.

Additionally, a number of issues can be identified from the faculty's perspective with regards to organizational constraints. For instance, some faculty and administrators are concerned that podcasting might boost opportunities to skip a class if students access the lectures online. According to podcasting studies about students' attendance, podcasting does not appear to lead students to miss classes (Blaisdell, 2006; Bongey, et al., 2006; Grabe, 2005). In fact, students view podcasts as supplemental material, not a replacement to lectures (Pastore, 2008). Other issues remain regarding incentive structures for faculty to adopt or use technologies in the classroom, most namely, promotion and tenure requirements. Top-down mandates for integrating mobile technology are not ideal, given the specialized teaching needs of Colleges and Departments across the University as well as academic freedom of faculty designing their courses. Hence, faculty adoption of these technologies remains primarily a function of individual faculty interests or willingness to explore use of the technology. With budget restrictions on how university funds can be used for purchase of mobile devices like cell phones, widespread adoption will necessarily be limited to those with the personal inclination towards innovation or those who explore external funding opportunities. Nonetheless, the type of implementation will greatly effect how these issues are handled.

Implementation issues arise from lack of experience with these types of technologies. Such issues include deciding which devices to support and how to address technology that is rapidly changing. The following considerations have been consistently mentioned throughout the literature on mobile learning implementation: devices, system, training, incentives, maintenance, security, cost, on-the-go learning, and small screen size.

(Cobcroft, Towers, Smith, & Bruns, 2006; Keegan, 2005; Shih and Mills, 2007). Deliberation on these issues lead naturally to questions about whether users will be required to purchase specific devices, features, or use specific wireless service carriers. The extent to which users' existing devices can be integrated into a mobile wireless system without compromising security and effectiveness will affect the success of the implementation.

Incentives for faculty to learn and use new technologies are important considerations that will need to be transparent during training/adoption. More staff may be needed to maintain networks, provide technical support, and ensure devices are suitable for use. Since the technology is new, security measures for large numbers of devices are not likely standardized, and policies are not likely in place to handle the implications of lost devices. In addition, costs and screen size need to be considered at each level of implementation. High costs associated with service and maintenance fees could be limiting factors.

Mobile devices are becoming better and more powerful and at a very rapid rate. The technology to take pictures, videos, and send/receive information is changing quickly and is different from device to device. Additionally, new devices are incorporating features such as GPS, and facial recognition software. It is unclear at this time whether these features will be important to the faculty and learners. Once organizational aspects are addressed, it becomes apparent that implementing this technology into the classroom is no easy feat. Small screen size may limit content that can be displayed and may be difficult for users not accustomed to mobile devices

Given these challenges at multiple levels of the organization, it might be more advantageous to begin using mobile technology as an alternative way to access the classroom and use that time as a trial-and-error period to discover what is needed to implement organization wide. Owen and Demb (2004) conducted a study on technology implementation at the college level and found that encouragement for innovation must come from top-level administrators. Forging strategies should provide incentives and financial support to faculty for implementing new technology. Identifying champions and the early adopters will encourage research and development for technology in teaching. Additionally, the University's vision and goals should stress the need for technological innovation. Faculty innovation needs to be supported through the availability of financial resources, increased support for innovating projects, and acknowledgement and reward of achievements.

There will always be early adopters of technology. As a result, universities need to demonstrate to faculty how and why this technology is of benefit. They will also need to support faculty if they want them to adopt this innovation. That support will include training, cost, technical help, and incentives. There is a general trend in higher education to give faculty the tools necessary to perform their jobs and allow them to choose how and if to use it in their classroom (Anderson et al, 2007). However, research will need to show clear learning benefits, not just improvements in efficiency or convenience.

CLOSING

The popularity of mobile devices is increasing at a rapid pace. This fact has correspondingly increased their use in education, as many types of mobile devices are being used as learning tools. This chapter examined various aspects of mobile learning (mLearning). As was shown, mLearning is difficult to define due to the many different devices it encompasses. However, specific features of those devices and associated pedagogy are beginning to emerge. Each mobile device described in this chapter is currently being used in higher educational institutions today. Implementation affects both the users, such as faculty and students, as well as the organizational structure. Some researchers argue that wide-scale implementation is not an easily accomplished task (Troxler, 2007). This stems from multiple reasons including money, incentives, training, lack of resources, maintenance issues, and user adoption. However, despite these challenges, mobile learning is being successfully explored in many higher education classrooms throughout the world. It carries with it a potential for new methods of learning and for redefining learner interactions. New teaching methods may now be possible that allow for exchange and creation of information outside the classroom and computer lab. We have just begun to explore mobile technology in higher education, and we have yet to feel its impacts.

Future research on this topic needs to address multiple issues. On the forefront, clear guidelines for implementation within higher education need to be made. This will provide educators with the necessary knowledge to make mobile learning a successful classroom practice. Research needs to also examine the types of technology and applications being made available and how they impact the classroom. For instance, podcasts are seen as great supplements to lectures, however, we have yet to fully understand many of the mobile technologies' potential. This will help alleviate faculty fears that this technology is a means to replace them. Additionally, learners' perceptions of mobile learning and their needs for it need to be considered.

REFERENCES

Alexander, B. (2004). Going nomadic: Mobile learning in higher education. *EDUCAUSE Review*, *39*(5), 28–35.

Belanger, Y. (2005). *Duke University iPod first year experience final evaluation report*. Durham, NC: Duke University.

Blaisdell, M. (2006). Academic MP3: Is it time yet? *Campus Technology*. Retrieved December 1st, 2009 from http://campustechnology.com/articles/2006/02/special-double-feature-academic-mp3s--is-it-itime-yet.aspx.

Bongey, S. B., Cizadlo, G., & Kalnbach, L. (2006). Explorations in course-casting: Podcasts in higher education. *Campus-Wide Information Systems*, *23*(5), 350–367. doi:10.1108/10650740610714107

Brown, J., & Metcalf, D. (2008). Mobile Learning Update. *Learning Consortium Perspectives*. Retrieved March 17, 2009 from http://www.masie.com.

Campbell, G. (2005). There's something in the air: Podcasting in education. *EDUCAUSE Review*, *40*(6), 32–47.

Cangialosi, G., Irelan, R., Bourquin, T., & Vogele, C. (2008). *The business podcasting book*. Burlington, MA: Elsevier, Inc.

Caudill, J. G. (2007). The growth of m-Learning and the growth of mobile computing: Parallel developments. *International Review of Research in Open and Distance Learning*, *8*(2).

Cebeci, Z., & Tekdal, M. (2006). Using podcasts as audio learning objects. *Interdisciplinary Journal of Knowledge and learning objects, 2*, 47-57.

Cobcroft, R. S., Towers, S. J., Smith, J. E., & Bruns, A. (2006). *Mobile learning in review: Opportunities and challenges for learners, teachers, and institutions*. InOnline Learning and Teaching (OLT) Conference 2006, 26 September 2006, Queensland University of Technology, Brisbane, Australia

Dale, C. (2007). Strategies for using podcasting to support student learning. *Journal of Hospitality, Leisure, Sport and Tourism Education*, *6*(1), 49–57. doi:10.3794/johlste.61.155

Descy, D. E. (2009). Netbooks: Small but powerful friends. *TechTrends*, *53*(2).

Dieterle, E., Dede, C., & Schrier, K. (2007). Neomillennial learning styles propagated by wireless handheld devices. In Lytras, M., & Naeve, A. (Eds.), *Ubiquitous and pervasive knowledge and learning management: Semantics, social networking and new media to their full potential* (pp. 35–66). Hershey, PA: Idea Group, Inc.

Ducut, E., & Fontelo, P. (2008). Mobile devices in health education: Current use and practice. *Journal of Computing in Higher Education, 20*, 59–68. doi:10.1007/s12528-008-9003-2

Earle, R. S. (2002). The integration of instructional technology into public education: Promises and Challenges. *Educational Technology, 42*, 5–13.

Evans, C. (2008). The effectiveness of m-learning in the form of podcast revision lectures in higher education. *Computers & Education, 50*, 491–498. doi:10.1016/j.compedu.2007.09.016

Evans, M., & Johri, A. (2008). Facilitating guided participation through mobile technologies: Designing creative learning environments for self and others. *Journal of Computing in Higher Education, 20*, 92–105. doi:10.1007/s12528-008-9004-1

Gartner Press Release. (2009). Retrieved December 1st, 2009 from http://www.gartner.com/it/page.jsp?id=1126812.

Gartner Press Release. (2009). Retrieved December 1st, 2009 from http://www.gartner.com/it/page.jsp?id=985912.

Georgiev, T., Georgieva, E., & Smrikarov, A. (2004). *M-Learning: A new stage of E-Learning*. Paper presented at the International conference on computer systems and technologies.

Grabe, M. (2005). Voluntary use of online lecture notes: correlates of note use and note use as an alternative to class attendance. *Computers & Education, 44*, 409–421. doi:10.1016/j.compedu.2004.04.005

Holzinger, A., Nischelwitzer, A., & Meisenberger, M. (2005). Mobile phones as a challenge for m-learning: Examples for mobile interactive learning objects (milos). *Pervasive Computing and Communications Workshops, IEEE International Conference*, 307-311.

Keegan, D. (2005). *The incorporation of mobile learning into mainstream education and training.* Mobile Technology: The future of learning in your hands, Cape Town, 65-70.

Klopfer, E., Squire, K., & Jenkin, H. (2008). Environmental Detectives – The development of an Augmented Reality Platform for Environmental Simulations. *Educational Research Technology and Development, 56*(2), 1042–1629.

Kronen, E. (2003). The website as a catalyst for change: Developing and implementing a content management system at Southern Cross University. CAUDIT *Australasian Information Technology Award*, 1-6.

Kukulska-Hulme, A. (2005). Introduction. In Kukulska-Hulme, A., & Traxler, J. (Eds.), *Mobile learning: A handbook for educators and trainers* (pp. 1–6). London: Routledge.

Kynaslahti, H. (2003). In search of elements of mobility in the context of education. In Kynaslahti, H., & Seppala, P. (Eds.), *Mobile Learning* (pp. 41–48). IT Press, Helinski.

Lane, C. (2006). *Podcasting at the UW: An evaluation of current use*. Retrieved December 1st from http://www.washington.edu/lst/research_development/papers/2006/podcasting_report.pdf.

Lewis, B., & Starsia, G. (2009). Challenges in technology implementation for learning spaces in higher education. *EDUCAUSE Quarterly, 32*(1).

Lonn, S., & Teasley, S. D. (2009). Podcasting in higher education: What are the implications for teaching and learning. *The Internet and Higher Education, 12*, 88–92. doi:10.1016/j.iheduc.2009.06.002

Manning, S. (2005). The promise of podcasting. *Pointers & Clickers*, *6*(2), 1–6.

Meng, P. (2005). *Podcasting & vodcasting: Definitions, discussions & implications (a White paper): IAT Services at University of Missouri*. Retrieved December 1st from http://www.wssa.net/WSSA/SocietyInfo/ProfessionalDev/Podcasting/Missouri_Podcasting_White_Paper.pdf.

Miller, M., & Piller, M. (2005). *Principal factors of an audio reading delivery mechanism: Evaluating educational use of the iPod*. Paper presented at the World Conference on Education Multimedia, Hypermedia & Telecommunications, and Chesapeake, VA.

Nicolle, P. S., & Lou, Y. (2008). Technology adoption into teaching and learning by mainstream university faculty: A mixed methodology study revealing the "How, when, and why not". *Journal of Educational Computing Research*, *39*(3), 235–265. doi:10.2190/EC.39.3.c

Owen, P. S., & Demb, A. (2004). Change dynamics and leadership in technology implementation. *The Journal of Higher Education*, *75*(6), 636–666. doi:10.1353/jhe.2004.0037

Pastore, R. S. (2008). Students' perceptions of podcasting in the classroom. *International Journal of Instructional Technology and Distance Learning*, *5*(12), 55–62.

Peters, K. (2007). m-Learning: Positioning educators for a mobile, connected future. *International Review of Research in Open and Distance Learning*, *8*(2).

Reiser, R. A. (2001). A history of instructional design and technology: Part I: A history of instructional media. *Educational Technology Research and Development*, *49*(1), 53–64. doi:10.1007/BF02504506

Rekkedal, T., & Dye, A. (2007). Mobile Distance Learning with PDAs: Development and testing of pedagogical and system solutions supporting mobile distance learners. *International Review of Research in Open and Distance Learning*, *8*(2).

Rieger, R., & Gay, G. (1997). Using Mobile Computing to Enhance Field Study. In R. Hall, N. Miyake & N. Enyedy (Eds.), *Computer Supported Collaborative Learning* (Proc. 2nd Conf., Toronto, Ontario, December) (p. 215-223). Mahwah, NJ: Erlbaum & Assoc.

Rogers, E. M. (1995). *Diffusion of innovations* (4th ed.). New York: Free Press.

Rogers, Y., Price, S., Fitzpatrick, G., Fleck, R., Harris, E., Smith, H., et al. (2004). Ambient wood: designing new forms of digital augmentation for learning outdoors. *Proceedings of the 2004 Conference on Interaction Design and Children: Building a Community* (p. 3-10). Maryland.

Rosenberg, M. J. (2001). *e-Learning: Strategies for delivering knowledge in the digital age*. New York: McGraw Hill.

Seppala, P., & Alamaki, H. (2003). Mobile learning in teacher training. *Journal of Computer Assisted Learning*, *19*, 330–335. doi:10.1046/j.0266-4909.2003.00034.x

Shen, R., & Wang, M., Pan, & Xiaoyan, P. (2008). Increasing interactivity in blended classrooms through a cutting-edge mobile learning system. *British Journal of Educational Technology*, *39*(6), 1073–1086. doi:10.1111/j.1467-8535.2007.00778.x

Shih, Y. E., & Mills, D. (2007). Setting the new standard with mobile computing in online learning. *International Review of Research in Open and Distance Learning*, *8*(2).

Traxler, J. (2007). Defining, Discussing, and Evaluating Mobile Learning. *International Review of Research in Open and Distance Learning*, *8*(2).

Wagner, E. D. (2008). Realizing the promises of mobile learning. *Journal of Computing in Higher Education, 20*, 4–14. doi:10.1007/s12528-008-9008-x

KEY TERMS AND DEFINITIONS

E-Learning: Learning that takes place on a computer, in an online environment, where information is sent or received instantly (Rosenberg, 2001).

Mobile Learning: An extension of eLearning that includes the use of technology that can be carried easily in a pocket or purse, used 'on the go' (on the job or en route), turned on instantly without the need to boot up, is internet capable through a service or wifi connection, and has other identifiable features such as word processing ability, html browser, SMS messaging, Camera, MP3 player, GPS, etc (Caudill, 2007; Kukulska-Hulme, 2005; Peters, 2007; Traxler, 2007).

Podcasting: Electronic files comprised of audio, audio with images, or video that have been posted online to a web site or blog, can be downloaded to a mobile device, and may be available via RSS (Pastore, 2008; Meng, 2005).

Netbooks: Small portable laptops that are generally 7-10 inches in size making them nearly half the size of the standard laptop and significantly less expensive. They can perform all of the same functions as a laptop. However, they differ from laptops because they are limited in their RAM and processing capacity (Descy, 2009).

Wireless Handheld Devices (WHDs): Devices (iPods, GPS, Gaming) that utilize wireless capabilities, enabling them access to the Internet and/or to share files, data, or information.

On-theGo Learning: Learning on the job or en route to school, home, or other location.

Smart Phones: Mobile phones that carry the ability to download software programs called 'apps' and connect users to their computer workstations.

SMS Messaging: The ability to send/receive text messages to and from a mobile phone.

Chapter 13
Impact of Web 2.0 on Higher Education

Nada Dabbagh
George Mason University, USA

Rick Reo
George Mason University, USA

ABSTRACT

The chapter addresses the impact of Web 2.0 on higher education institutions. Using Christensen's theory of disruptive innovations, the authors ask whether Web 2.0 is a sustaining innovation that is creating incremental changes in higher education practices as older technologies have, or if Web 2.0 is a disruptive innovation that is slowly easing its way to meet the needs of specialized audiences but ultimately may drive out the conventional education model or turn it on its head. To tackle this question, the authors briefly review the current state of Web 2.0 in higher education, discuss related issues and controversies, and then focus on the impact of Web 2.0 on human, social, and organizational aspects of higher education institutions.

OVERVIEW OF WEB 2.0

Web 2.0 is as much a concept as it is a technology. As a concept, Web 2.0 characterizes themes such as openness, personalization, customization, collaboration, social networking, social presence, user-generated content, the people's Web, read/write Web, and collective wisdom (Alexander, 2006; Jones, 2008; Lindstrom, 2007; Norton & Hathaway, 2008; O'Reilly, 2005; Sessums, 2006). As a technology, Web 2.0 represents a qualitative shift in how information is created, delivered, and accessed on the web. For example, a wiki is an extremely flexible Web 2.0 technology that enables anyone with an Internet connection and a web browser to create, access, and edit a website, and to determine the degree of control that users can have over the content of this website (Rosen & Nelson, 2008). Web 2.0 as a technology is interchangeable with terms like social software

DOI: 10.4018/978-1-60960-147-8.ch013

and social media which are broadly defined as technologies that extend and enhance human communication capabilities (Anderson, 2005; Rollette, Lux, Strohmaier, Dösing, & Tochterman, 2007). Web 2.0 technologies support social interaction and collaboration through various processes and strategies such as the ability to express individual identity, gain awareness of the presence of others, establish meaningful relationships, form purposeful or goal-oriented groups, and share experiences and resources publicly (Dabbagh & Reo, 2011).

Examples of Web 2.0 technologies include experience- and resource-sharing tools such as Delicious, WordPress, and Twitter that enable online/social bookmarking, blogging, and microblogging respectively; wiki software such as PBworks that enables the creation of collaborative workspaces; media sharing tools such as Flickr and YouTube that enable social tagging (Peterson, 2006; VanderWal, 2005); and social networking applications such as Facebook and LinkedIn that enable sociosemantic networking (Seldow, 2007). The proliferation of Web 2.0 technologies is affording the creation of networked learning experiences that foster the characteristics of Web 2.0 as a concept resulting in new social behaviors and pedagogical practices (Alexander, 2006; Cormier, 2008; Carroll, 2008).

The question we address in this chapter is how significant of an impact Web 2.0 will have on higher education institutions. More specifically, is Web 2.0 a *sustaining innovation* (Christensen, Horn, & Johnson, 2008) that is creating incremental changes in higher education practices as older technologies have, or, is Web 2.0 a *disruptive innovation* (Christensen, Horn, & Johnson, 2008) that is slowly easing its way to meet the needs of specialized audiences but ultimately may drive out the conventional education model or turn it on its head? To tackle this question, we briefly review the current state of Web 2.0 in higher education, discuss related issues and controversies, and then focus on the impact of Web 2.0 on human, social, and organizational aspects of higher education institutions.

CURRENT STATE OF WEB 2.0 IN HIGHER EDUCATION

Web 2.0 is having a pervasive impact on the university as a system as well as on its constituents, i.e., faculty, students, and administrators. For example, studies show that undergraduate students are simultaneously learning and using Web 2.0 technologies and that this state of affairs is affecting students' academic performance even though students are not deliberately or strategically using Web 2.0 technologies for learning (Smith, Salaway, & Borreson Caruso, 2009; Solomon & Schrum, 2009). Rather, such effects represent changes that stem from independent and grassroots activity of students and faculty and may also arise out of enterprise level administrative decisions to implement Web 2.0-enabled applications in specialized needs areas. Research also shows that faculty are increasingly using Web 2.0 technologies to support teaching and learning activities (EDUCAUSE Learning Initiative, 2007). For example, some faculty are using Skype (a Web 2.0-enabled communications tool) in the classroom to enable students to participate first hand in interviews with domain experts, while others are encouraging students to use blogging software (e.g., WordPress) as a platform for the development of e-portfolios which have become an important performance-based assessment tool in higher education (Rosen & Nelson, 2008). Some faculty are also using wiki software (e.g., PBworks) to engage students in collaborative projects that support the creation, editing, and management of content and enable peer and expert feedback (Hazari, North, & Moreland, 2009). Furthermore, the use of online bookmarking technology (e.g., Delicious) is gaining ground as a tool that can help students organize and categorize course information in meaningful ways using tags (keywords or descriptors), and share their bookmarks with others to create folksonomic (organic or grassroots) classification of course content or resources (Solomon & Schrum, 2007; Schachter, 2008). These practices support the Web 2.0 characteristic of filtering and remixing content dynamically and organically which was not possible with Web 1.0 technology.

Despite these efforts, most universities have made only small accommodations to integrate Web 2.0 technologies into the institution's infrastructure. In fact, these efforts are perceived to be occurring largely in isolated pockets and only on some campuses which supports the concept of disruptive innovations (Fletcher, 2009). Christensen (1997) describes disruptive innovations as a new product, process, or service that initially may not be perceived as effective as the current product, process, or service, but over time, it becomes more responsive and evolves to meet the need of a broader audience driving out the standard or current product. While some believe that Web 2.0 is behaving like a disruptive innovation, others perceive Web 2.0 as a continuation of a broad class of older computer-mediated communication tools (Dabbagh & Reo, 2011) creating incremental changes in higher education practices and hence behaving more like a sustaining innovation. We discuss this controversy and related issues next.

ISSUES AND CONTROVERSIES SURROUNDING WEB 2.0

Web 2.0 is impacting all sectors of society but many academics are unaware of the prospects this holds for higher education. Several researchers, visionaries, and technology evangelists (e.g., Davidson & Goldberg, 2009; Katz, 2008; Wiley & Hilton, 2009) are predicting that immediate and large scale changes are in store for educational institutions because of the emergence of Web 2.0. Others believe that Web 2.0 will have the most impact on the business sector and yet others believe that Web 2.0 will lead to a fundamental epistemological change. Katz (2008) suggests that we are in an "interregnum" – a transition period between the 1000 year reign of the current scholastic educational system and a new one waiting to be born. Hilton (2006) reminded us that we have a choice of how to view the disruptions precipitating this transition, we can see it as a *perfect storm* that will negatively impact the future of higher education, or we can see it as the beginning of a new era of possibilities (p.59).

Numerous educational and IT leaders have begun to wrestle with these lofty and knotty issues and many believe that higher education is under siege (Fletcher, 2009). Questions such as: is higher education on the verge of significant change similar to what Web 2.0, digital media, and the Internet did to the recording (music) or newspaper industry, and, will top tier schools emerge unscathed while others lower on the totem pole be forced to restructure, are but a few of the questions that are on the minds of educational and IT leaders and administrators. Furthermore, cloud computing, which describes a paradigm shift in the way a wide range of IT services are provided to organizations, is adding to the issues and controversies surrounding Web 2.0 and could even be representative of a disruptive innovation in and of itself. For example, Katz (2008, p. xiv) asks "What is the role of the *institution*, in a world where *individuals* are empowered to seek solutions anywhere in the network cloud?" The cloud is a metaphor for outsourced, and often virtualized, Internet services typically hosted on servers that are external to the organization's local infrastructure and delivered based on a customized need. Although cloud computing is not the main focus of this chapter, it is important to note that many cloud services host Web 2.0 technologies as well as non-Web 2.0 technologies and applications such as learning management systems, e-mail, and others.

Web 2.0 has empowered the masses to take charge of their own learning or meaning making, or what Siemens (2009) refers to as "sense making". Many young social media enthusiasts interpret this to mean that there is no arbiter of their knowledge, work, publication, thinking, etc., which begs the question: Should higher education institutions make pedagogical changes to mitigate these perceptions? Hilton (2009) believes that higher education is being challenged by such perceptions and that technological innovations are at the heart of such challenges. More specifically, Hilton perceives the image of "the lone scholar tolling away in isolation" as fading and giving way to "globally connected scientists and scholars working collaboratively on massive data sets with shared technologies" (¶ 1).

However many scholars still view Information and Communication Technologies (ICT) merely as tools with little strategic value. As Edelson (2001) suggested, this may be because ICT are often made available in educational institutions without a plan to associate them with the curriculum or research. Additionally, supporters of these views believe that technological changes impacting higher education are developmental in nature or evolutionary rather than revolutionary (Dabbagh & Reo, 2011). Subsequently, Web 2.0 technologies are perceived as a sustaining innovation premised on the continuation of a tradition of ICT, which began with a focus on augmenting human thinking and progressed to computer-mediated communication, group collaboration, and eventually collective intelligence, a characteristic of Web 2.0 as a concept. Despite this evolutionary trend, there is ample evidence to suggest that Web 2.0 has radically changed the nature of communication and social interaction resulting in new socio-pedagogic affordances that may have significant implications on higher education particularly as this relates to human and social aspects of the academic experience. We elaborate on this next.

IMPACT OF WEB 2.0 ON HUMAN AND SOCIAL ASPECTS OF HIGHER EDUCATION

Disruptive innovations like the Internet and the Web are transformational in that they are capable of producing a radical or qualitative change to the status quo. However, innovations in online activity in the era of the early web (Web 1.0) were not as transformational as the second generation of the web (Web 2.0). Online activity in the Web 1.0 phase resulted in terms prefixed with "e" such as eLearning, eCommerce, eCommunity, eBooks, etc., while online activity in the Web 2.0 phase resulted in terms suffixed with "2.0", such as Library 2.0, Classroom 2.0, or Pedagogy 2.0. While the "e" represented perhaps an easy way to distinguish online from face-to-face or non-electronic activities, the "2.0" label arguably demarcates areas of higher education where a potentially significant transformation of practice is underway. The 2.0 suffix is used in the following section headings to emphasize this point.

FACULTY 2.0

How is Web 2.0 affecting the role of faculty? In some respects, the faculty role has been evolving from sage on the stage to guide on the side since the advent of eLearning - well before Web 2.0 appeared. However Web 2.0 has contributed enabling factors for repositioning this role even further off stage. For example, new faculty roles related to the academic experience began emerging to include designer, co-designer, moderator, co-learner, critic, co-producer and others. McLoughlin and Lee (2008) posit that while "the directive for the teacher to be a guide on the side as opposed to a sage on the stage has been with us for many years, Web 2.0 equips us with new ways in which to realize this goal while continuing to recognize the role of the teacher as an expert" (p. 5).

A related Web 2.0 concept that is impacting faculty role is openness which is associated with concepts such as open content, open source, open access, and open education among others. Individual faculty at various higher education intuitions are embracing openness without waiting for their programs or institutions to do so (Wiley & Hilton, 2009). For example, Dr. Mark Sample, assistant professor at George Mason University in Fairfax, Virginia, describes his academic practice as an open source professor and shares the tenets of open source in his work (Sample, 2009). He makes two key points. The first is that the open professor can share and take a more open or transparent attitude to research without the fear of others usurping his/her work and publishing his/her ideas. The second is that faculty should take an open approach to intellectual property since in many fields the discoveries are so incremental and infinitesimal that the value of the small insights that any single researcher contributes do not warrant strong protections and competition.

Openness with regard to sharing content is also having an impact on how faculty disseminate teaching or educational materials (Wiley, 2006a). Wiley (2006b) suggests that there are about 175 universities worldwide participating in programs that enable them to provide free and open access to course content for over 2,000 university courses with the MIT Open Courseware initiative leading the way. Furthermore, other types of educational resources (e.g., small learning modules) are also being shared through collaborative online projects such as MERLOT (Multimedia Educational Resource for Learning and Online Teaching). Are these open access practices threatening faculty jobs? Wiley (2006a) argues that effective teaching encompasses much more than the transmission of information and that open content is no more a threat to faculty than the traditional library system.

In addition to openness, Web 2.0 with its spirit of customization, personalization, social interaction, and collaboration is creating qualitatively new ways of teaching and learning. Educational researchers and leaders (e.g., Anderson, 2008; Dede, 2006; Weigel, 2002; Siemens & Tittenberger, 2009; Katz, 2008) argue that Web 2.0 technologies are precipitating a pedagogical transformation that can be perceived as pedagogy 2.0. For example, Siemens (2005) describes this new pedagogy as connectivism, a new learning paradigm resulting from the convergence of constructivism, social media and networked interaction. Others refer to it as a "rhizomatic model of education" in which "the community is the curriculum" and "not the path to understanding or accessing the curriculum" (Cormier, 2008, p.1&3). Social learning can also be perceived as a more generic or broad term to refer to learning activity that is enabled by Web 2.0 technologies.

Pedagogy 2.0 harnesses the principles of social learning in an unprecedented fashion. Pedagogy 2.0 is enabling the creation of personal and social learning spaces and experiences that are stretching the scope and deepening the interconnectedness of learning activities often blurring the lines between faculty and students. Knowledge in these learning spaces is perceived as belonging to, and distributed in, communities of practice or *environments of participation* in which the learner practices the patterns of inquiry and learning, and the use of shared resources is part of the preparation for membership in a particular community (Anderson, 2005; Firdyiwek, 1999). Higher education institutions should seriously consider the impact of pedagogy 2.0 and adapt to the fact that Web 2.0 is slowly but surely leveling the playing field between the wisdom of the crowds and traditional authority.

STUDENT 2.0

According to Weigel, James, and Gardner (2009, 29) most attempts to characterize the "impact of the engagement of youth with digital media" are short-sighted. The notion of student 2.0 as a term to characterize the impact of Web 2.0 on students treads the same thin line as trying to characterize young people's digital mindset with terms like digital natives (Prensky, 2001) and net gens (Tapscott, 1998). Similar to these characterizations, which were meant to herald a generational shift in thinking due to increased access and use of digital media by a small demographic of young people, we intend student 2.0 to refer to a general preference to use social media as a result of ubiquitous access to Web 2.0 technologies. Student 2.0 represents a profile of students who, surrounded by or immersed in Web 2.0 technologies, are used to communicating and collaborating online, tagging and sharing content, using smart phones and social networks, blogging, twittering, etc. (Johnson, Levine, Smith, & Stone, 2010). These Web 2.0-enabled social behaviors are accompanying students to campus and to the classroom, setting new expectations of the academic experience.

But the reality is that students of varying ages are being variously transformed by using digital media. Dede (2005, p. 15.2) sees a continuum of cognitive styles across learners of all ages ranging from less technical "traditionals" to "millenials" whose style is oriented toward emerging learning technologies to "neo-millenial learning style" with a strong preference for immersive learning experiences. The "neomillenial learning style" emphasizes "immersive presence" as the quality par excellence which Dede (2005, p. 15.16) speculates will impact higher education and suggests strategic changes are needed to "physical plant, technology infrastructure, and professional development" to make institutions competitive. He sees the neomillenials as having a preference for learning experiences that are distributed across multiple platforms, learning spaces, and activities. Thus, Web 2.0 social experiences shape cognitive orientation which in turn requires concomitant changes to the teaching and learning environments.

Brill and Park (2008, p.70) found that the student 2.0 mindset can be harnessed for engaged learning when pedagogically grounded learning designs are aligned with Web 2.0 tool affordances. Weigel, James, and Gardner (2009, 31) "operate on the assumption that NDM [New Digital Media] contain affordances that, if leveraged properly, could create future learning environments and cultures in which the promises of constructivist, social, situated, and informal learning are realized." We agree with these authors and think that new digital media aka Web 2.0 tools have the potential to transform both teaching and learning practices, and thereby, what it means to be a student in the 21st century. Students shape and are shaped by their learning environments. Higher education institutions should recognize these new socio-pedagogic affordances and provide guidance to develop these affordances into discipline-specific pedagogical practices and competencies.

Not all students who use Web 2.0 technologies expect to have more choice in the direction of their learning. In fact, the opposite may be true. For example, most students in large lecture general education courses are content to sit passively in class and do what is needed to earn a good or passing grade. Some faculty are responding to this inherently problematic pedagogic situation by leveraging Web 2.0 technologies to try to engage students in large lecture environments. While some students will not find this approach useful, Web 2.0-enabled students hold promise for a re-engagement in large classrooms. This situation lends some credence to the theory of disruptive innovation since big changes are triggered at weak points in the educational system. There is also a need to reconcile the impact of Web 2.0 on off campus/out-of-classroom and in-classroom experiences as well as the online/offline experience. We discuss this next.

CLASSROOM 2.0

Evidence of the impact of Web 2.0 on higher education can also be seen in a transformed classroom. Students are coming into the classroom with wireless laptops and smart phones capable of running web applications and interfacing with learning platforms. However it is what students are doing with these devices in the classroom that are presenting challenges. Some students use these mobile devices as distractions (e.g., checking Facebook feeds or texting friends), others use them for taking notes or finding class related information online, and yet others use them for multitasking (e.g., learning and social connectivity). Some faculty welcome these devices in their classrooms, others passively permit them, and yet others restrict them.

Faculty who are embracing the classroom 2.0 concept are leveraging these digital devices for learning. For example, Twitter is a Web 2.0 technology that many faculty see as having potential uses in the classroom. Twitter is a combination of texting, IM, microblogging, and social networking that works well on laptops or smart phones (EDUCAUSE Learning Initiative, 2007). There are a variety of ways Twitter can be used in and out of the classroom however not all instructional uses of Twitter have been successful. For example, the summer 2009 Twitter Experiment conducted by Dr. Rankin at the University of Texas resulted in limited success based on stated goals to engage students (Rankin, 2009). The experiment which required a TA and numerous workarounds for the instructor did not appear scalable or sustainable as a means of conducting in-class discussions. Despite these initial research findings, there are many ways of using Twitter to stimulate student engagement in the classroom that do not require so much effort by the instructor. Figure 1 depicts a matrix of instructional uses of Twitter ranging from low engagement/low faculty effort such as course information broadcasting, to high engagement/high faculty effort such as in-class or out-of-class discussions.

Smart phones and cell phones present yet another challenge in the classroom. How does a faculty member adjust to students who respond to cell phone calls or text messages? With weather alerts and disaster notifications becoming institutional policy for security and safety reasons, these devices tacitly encourage students to keep connected in the classroom. The use of smart phones is also having a significant impact off campus or outside the classroom. According to the 2010 Horizon Report (see Johnson, Levine, Smith, & Stone, 2010) and the BECTA TechNews Report (Sept., 2009), many older students own smart phones and will increasingly expect to use them to access educational content. This suggests that colleges will need to plan to support a more diverse range of devices for home and remote learning.

Classroom 2.0 also comes with a variety of new media equipment for presentation, recording, and networked connectivity. For example, electronic whiteboards permit the capture of hand written notes, dual projectors allow the instructor to present from multiple media, wired and wireless networks afford faculty and student connection to global resources, and lecture capture systems simplify the recording of classroom lectures and some lecture capture systems may include one click publishing options to make this available to public and limited access audiences easily (Kim, 2009).

Figure 1. Instructional uses of Twitter

HIGHER	In-class Back Channel	Out-of-Class Discussion	In-class Guided Discussion
Student Engagement	Low Threshold Activities	People/Topical Tracking Activities	Metacognitive Activities
	Institutional communication	Instructor communication	Pedagogical Communication
LOWER	**Instructor Time and Effort**		**HIGHER**

IMPACT OF WEB 2.0 ON ORGANIZATIONAL ASPECTS OF HIGHER EDUCATION

Web 2.0 is not hyperbole propagated by an irrationally exuberant technology business sector; rather, it was derived from business observations of a trend toward renewed patterns of success in high tech industries that was then popularized by the media. Since commercial interests are a driving force of the Web 2.0 movement, it makes sense to draw on economical models to help understand its impact on higher education as an organization or system. In this section, an economic model of disruptive innovation will be offered as a way of framing or structuring the debate about the future of higher education. It provides a way to understand changes that are affecting other organizations and puts in the light a natural process that has some dimensionality of perspective, forecasting, and results that can accommodate human interventions.

Christensen (1997) developed the idea of disruptive innovation to describe the way new business markets (products/processes) come to displace existing ones whose products no longer provide the best performance, cost effectiveness, quality, or fill a need. This may happen by establishing an entirely new niche of consumers or by innovating improvements to incumbent markets that change them. Thus, a disruptive innovation has the potential to radically alter the market demand for an existing product or process. A sustaining innovation does not; rather, it supports the status quo market. Disruptive innovation is a potential consequence of the integration of Web 2.0 style technologies and approaches into the creation and delivery of higher education systems. Just like Web 2.0 disrupted the music recording and publishing industries (Katz, 2008; Hilton, 2006), it has the potential to radically change higher education models or systems.

Hilton (2006) observed that the role of higher education was being "fundamentally redefined" and he laid out four disruptive forces that are involved: unbundling, demand pull, ubiquitous access, and rise of pure property view of ideas. Unbundling, refers to the disintermediation of the services and products of traditional educational institutions such that they can be broken down into sub-packages that can be re-bundled in various ways by nontraditional online education providers or universities that need to restructure to stay competitive. Demand pull, refers to the reversal of consumer role from passive recipient of information to active chooser and avid producer. Ubiquitous access implies persistent, reliable, and 360° access to people and resources. And, the rise of pure property view of ideas manifests in various reactions to overly strict copyright laws. Hilton sees the legal system's viewing of ideas as "intellectual" property as limiting the original purpose of copyright which is to improve access to and sharing of ideas and therefore to support learning from them. This situation has prompted a global response in terms of open access/open content initiatives. Web 2.0 as a concept and as a technology is an enabler of these four disruptive forces.

Christensen's notion of disruptive innovation serves as a way to view a combination of factors that coalesce under the umbrella of Web 2.0 and dominate a description of the dynamic state of higher education: (1) Web 2.0-style customization of user experiences, (2) Open access, open content initiatives to provide broad access and availability to high quality, on-demand curricular and co-curricular tools, content, and resources (Wiley & Hilton, 2009), and (3) improved online pedagogy (pedagogy 2.0), i.e., leaner-centered, online strategies that increase access, quality, and reach beyond traditional offerings. Thus, Web 2.0 joins forces with open access/open content and improved online pedagogy to produce a real watershed moment in higher education in terms of prompting serious changes at the institutional level. The combination of well designed learner-centered pedagogy with Web 2.0 delivery and open collaboration tools helps flatten the playing field for the rise of innovative online learning organizations that can target new market niches and provide a more cost effective and customized learning experience than traditional institutions—that's the disruptive innovation.

For example, corporate or government universities (e.g., Defense Acquisition University and IBM University) have for years found it more efficient and convenient to manage their workforce learning needs by developing their own curriculums, credentials, and courses, rather than depending on local universities. For-profit universities such as University of Phoenix and Strayer University are leveraging a global business model, capitalizing on the power of distance learning to attract students. And more recently, not-for-profit universities such as University of the People (Wiley & Hilton, 2009), a UN-backed initiative to offer free education in emerging markets, is using the power of distance learning and virtual collaboration to offer degrees to a global audience.

The point here is that distance education is considered a key battle front where the fight for higher education customers is already being fought. However, Weigel (2002) urges higher education institutions to strategically differentiate themselves via value added services unique to their strengths before jumping on the distance education bandwagon. Wiley and Hilton (2009) employ Hagel and Brown's (2005) concept of dynamic specialization in the context of open education to describe a future in which higher education institutions will have to choose to take fewer and more focused roles that differentiate their mission. Hilton (2009), who believes Web 2.0 changes the rules of operation for essential IT services, suggests universities leverage Web 2.0 disruptions against IT initiatives in such a way that their distance learning strategy benefits. The IT organization plays a tactically significant role in this fight.

In addition to distance education, IT leaders identified 10 top issues that higher education institutions should focus on for strategic success (Scrivener Agee, Yang, & the 2009 EDUCAUSE Current Issues Committee, 2009). Of the 10 issues, five mentioned Web 2.0 or cloud computing as an important facet of the issue. Specifically, issue #1, Funding IT, contained the most references to Web2.0 factors and indicated that Web 2.0 may have the most to offer in terms of providing a way out of financial challenges many institutions are facing. Examples of how this could be achieved included optimizing the infrastructure through virtualization strategies which is tied to cloud or grid computing and enhancing learning experiences by integrating mobile platforms, virtual worlds, and social media sites with institutional systems such as the enterprise learning management systems or eLMS.

ENTERPRISE LEARNING MANAGEMENT SYSTEM 2.0

The enterprise level LMS or eLMS is a bastion of institutional control and convenience for teaching online within higher education (Dron, 2007). With the advent of Web 2.0, some are advocating the redesign of the eLMS while others are pursuing alternative learning platforms that have more interactive or learner-friendly features like those found in blogs, wikis, and social networking sites. While redesign efforts are leading to improvements, they are largely incremental and hence can be perceived as sustaining innovations in terms of improving the learning experience. The Web 2.0 alternatives also lack features that higher education still depends on, such as a gradebook, security, privacy, and the ability to provide a single familiar institutional interface. Nevertheless, Web 2.0 alternatives, whether highly structured as a stand-alone LMS or "loosely joined" into a make-shift LMS represent a disruptive innovation for the traditional institutional LMS.

In a recent ECAR bulletin, Niall Scalter (2008) assessed the value and future of eLMSs compared to Web 2.0 social networking platforms. Scalter's assessment suggested that eLMS are still a valuable and viable tool despite the rise in popularity of social networking platforms. We agree with Scalter's assessment and add that eLMS are not destined to go away anytime soon especially given concerns about privacy and security which inhibit most universities from adopting Web 2.0 or open source platforms for teaching and learning. However there are exceptions. For example, Athabasca University has adopted a social networking learning platform called Me2U, which has strong privacy controls. Me2U was not set up to replace Athabasca's eLMS, rather it is being used in conjunction and as an alternative Web 2.0 learning environment that is part of a design research experiment (Anderson, 2008, p.236).

The future eLMS will need to foster pedagogy 2.0, in part by adopting the benefits of Web 2.0 tools that enable social networking activities and group collaboration. A hybrid approach that marries the best of eLMS with student-centered tools may be more likely to occur before a new type of eLMS is realized. One way this could play out for some institutions is to develop a hybrid technology integration strategy that begins instruction in an eLMS and gradually relinquishes control of the learning to students in more personalized learning environments (PLEs) that are built on externally hosted (in-the-cloud) Web 2.0 tools/services designed to help students aggregate and share resources, participate in collective knowledge generation, and manage their own meaning making (Dron, 2007). As the example of Athabasca's Me2U illustrates, universities are experimenting with social networking platforms to do a better job creating student centered learning environments or experiences. The open source LMS Moodle can also be perceived as an effort in this direction (Siemens, 2009).

CONCLUSION

Weigel (2002) points out that technology is a disruptive force that more often than not brings about organizational change rather than "enhances the status quo" (p.39). In the face of Web 2.0, higher education institutions across the tiers are beginning to see the potential for their own strategic interests and make choices. Katz, Goldstein, and Yanosky (2009) talk about this as a time for structural change for colleges and universities and questions if each knows this, and what and which infrastructural changes are important. Power shifts are the main impediment to change (Couros, 2006; Katz, Goldstein, & Yanosky, 2009). When the recording (and now the publishing) industry faced disruption from Web 2.0 technologies, music companies that embraced innovation were transformed and prospered while those that were not as forward-thinking disappeared. Web 2.0 technology is transforming people's access to learning and slowly altering their perception of the role of higher education institutions as a purveyor of lifelong learning. Higher education is certainly not destined to follow the same path that Web 2.0, digital media, and the Internet brought to the music industry. But some mainstream higher education institutions that don't distinguish their name brand, differentiate their specialized roles, or globalize their products or processes may be at risk. Maybe the best of breed colleges are safe, but the low tier schools whose customers (markets) can get their educational needs met better by other means will disappear or be absorbed, as the theory of disruptive innovation suggests.

Disruptive innovation encapsulates a view of Web 2.0 as a dominate force acting on higher education, prompting potentially significant changes at the institutional level, and flattening the playing field for the rise of innovative online learning organizations that provide both a more cost effective and customized learning experience than traditional institutions. How the institution responds to Web 2.0 adoption and incorporates it into existing processes will determine the positive impact of this disruptive innovation that strengthens the institution, makes its mission relevant, and keeps it competitive.

REFERENCES

Alexander, B. (2006). Web 2.0: A new wave of innovation for teaching and learning? *EDUCAUSE Review*, *41*, 32–44.

Anderson, T. (2008). *The theory and practice of online learning (2nd ed.)*. Edmonton, AB: Athabasca University (AU) Press.

Anderson, T. (2005). Distance learning – Social software's killer ap? *The Open & Distance Learning Association of Australia*. Retrieved July 2, 2008, from http://auspace.athabascau.ca:8080/dspace/bitstream/2149/2328/1/distance_learning.pdf

BECTA. Tech News Report: 1-46, (2009). Retrieved September 30, 2009, from http://emerging-technologies.becta.org.uk/upload-dir/downloads/page_documents/ research/technews/sept09.pdf

Brill, J., & Park, Y. (2008). Facilitating engaged learning in the interaction age: Taking a pedagogically–disciplined approach to innovation with emergent technologies. *International Journal of Teaching and Learning in Higher Education, 20*(1), 70-78. Retrieved April 1, 2010, from http://www.isetl.org/ijtlhe/pdf/IJTLHE474.pdf

Carroll, D. (2008). Dorion Carroll: Technorati. In Jones, B. L. (Ed.), *Web 2.0 heroes: Interviews with 20 web 2.0 influencers* (pp. 55–78). Indianapolis: Wiley.

Christensen, C. M., Horn, M. B., & Johnson, C. W. (2008). *Disrupting class: How disruptive innovation will change the way the world learns*. New York: McGraw-Hill.

Christensen, C. M. (1997). *The innovator's dilemma: When new technologies cause great firms to fail*. Boston: Harvard Business School Press.

Cormier, D. (2008). Rhizomatic education: Community as curriculum. *Innovate* 4(5). Retrieved July 2, 2008, from http://innovateonline.info/pdf/vol4_issue5/Rhizomatic_Education-__Community_as_Curriculum.pdf

Couros, A. (2006). *Examining the open movement: Possibilities and implications for education.* Unpublished doctoral dissertation, University of Regina, Saskatchewan. Available from http://www.scribd.com/doc/3363/Dissertation-Couros-FINAL-06-WebVersion?autodown=pdf

Dede, C. (2005). Planning for neomillenial learning styles: Implications for investments in technology and faculty. In D. G. Oblinger and J. L. Oblinger (eds), *Educating the net generation.*, (pp. 15.1–15.22). Retrieved April 1, 2010, from EDUCAUSE: http://net.educause.edu/ir/library/pdf/pub7101o.pdf

Dede, C. (2006). *Online professional development for teachers: Emerging models and methods (ed.).* Cambridge, MA: Harvard Education Press.

Dabbagh, N., & Reo, R. (2011). Back to the future: Tracing the roots and learning affordances of social software. In Lee, M. J. W., & McLoughlin, C. (Eds.), *Web 2.0-based e-Learning: Applying social informatics for tertiary teaching* (pp. 1–20). Hershey, PA: IGI Global.

Davidson, C. N., & Goldberg, D. T. (2009). The future of learning institutions in a digital age. *The John D. and Catherine T. McArthur Foundation Reports on Digital Media and Learning.* Cambridge, MA: MIT Press. Retrieved November 13, 2009, from http://mitpress.mit.edu/books/full_pdfs/Future_of_Learning.pdf

Dron, J. (2007). *Control and constraint in e-learning: Choosing when to choose.* Hershey, PA: Idea Group.

Edelson, D. C. (2001). Design research: What we learn when we engage in design. *Journal of the Learning Sciences, 22*(1), 105–121.

EDUCAUSE Learning Initiative (ELI). (2007). *The seven things you need to know about ....* Retrieved January 15, 2008, from http://www.educause.edu/7Things

Firdyiwek, Y. (1999). Web-based courseware tools: Where is the pedagogy? *Educational Technology, 39*(1), 29–34.

Fletcher, G. (2009, September). Disruptive innovation. *Campus Technology, 23*(1), 6.

Hagel, J., & Brown, J. (2005). *From push to pull – Emerging models for mobilizing resources.* Retrieved January 15, 2010, from http://www.johnhagel.com/paper_pushpull.pdf

Hazari, S., North, A., & Moreland, D. (2009). Investigating pedagogical value of wiki technology. *Journal of Information Systems Education, 20*(2), 187–198.

Hilton, J. (2006). The future for higher education: Sunrise or perfect storm? *EDUCAUSE Review*, (March/April): 59–71.

Hilton, J. (2009). Essential versus strategic IT investments. *EDUCAUSE Review*, (July/August): 8–9.

Johnson, L., Levine, A., Smith, R., & Stone, S. (2010). *The 2010 Horizon Report*. Austin, TX: The New Media Consortium.

Jones, B. L. (2008). *Web 2.0 heroes: Interviews with 20 Web 2.0 influencers*. Indianapolis, IN: Wiley.

Katz, R. (2008). The gathering cloud: Is this the end of the middle? In R. Katz (Ed.), *The tower and the cloud: Higher education in the age of cloud computing (pp. 2-42)*. Available from EDUCAUSE: http://educause.edu/books

Katz, R. (2008). *The tower and the cloud:Higher education in the age of cloud computing* (Ed.). Available from EDUCAUSE: http://educause.edu/books

Katz, R., Goldstein, P., & Yanosky, R. (2009). Demystifying cloud computing for higher education. *EDUCAUSE Center for Applied Research (ECAR)*. Available from http://www.educause.edu/ecar

Kim, J. (2009). Capturing lectures: No brainer or sticky wicket? *EDUCAUSE Center for Applied Research (ECAR)*. Available from http://www.educause.edu/ecar

Lindstrom, P. (2007). Securing "Web 2.0" technologies. *In-Depth Research Report, The Burton Group*. Retrieved February 3, 2008, from EDUCAUSE Center for Applied Research (ECAR): http://www.educause.edu/ecar

McLoughlin, C., & Lee, M. (2008). Future learning landscapes: Transforming pedagogy through social software. *Innovate, 4*(5). Retrieved July 2, 2008, from http://www.innovateonline.info/pdf/vol4_issue5/Future_Learning_Landscapes-__Transforming_Pedagogy_through_Social_Software.pdf

Norton, P., & Hathaway, D. (2008). On its way to K-12 classrooms, web 2.0 goes to graduate school. *Computers in the Schools, 25*, 163–180. doi:10.1080/07380560802368116

O'Reilly, T. (2005, October 10). Web 2.0: Compact definition? *O'Reilly Radar*. Retrieved July 23, 2006, from http://radar.oreilly.com/archives/2005/10/ web_20_compact_definition.html

Peterson, E. (2006). Beneath the metadata: Some philosophical problems with folksonomy. *D-Lib Magazine, 12*(11). Retrieved March 16, 2007, from http://www.dlib.org/dlib/november06/peterson/11peterson.html

Prensky, M. (2001). Digital natives, digital immigrants. *On the Horizon, 9*(5). Retrieved November 2, 2009, from http://www.twitchspeed.com/site/Prensky%20-%20Digital%20Natives,%20Digital%20Immigrants%20-%20Part1.htm

Rankin, M. (2009). *Some general comments on the "Twitter Experiment"*. Retrieved July 25, 2009, from http://www.utdallas.edu/~mar046000/usweb/twitterconclusions.htm

Rollette, H., Lux, M., Strohmaier, M., Dösing, G., & Tochterman, K. (2007). The web 2.0 way of learning with technologies. *The International Journal of Learning Technology, 3*(1), 87–107. doi:10.1504/IJLT.2007.012368

Rosen, D., & Nelson, C. (2008). Web 2.0: A new generation of learners and education. *Computers in the Schools, 25*, 211–225. doi:10.1080/07380560802370997

Sample, M. (2009). *The open source professor: Teaching, research, and transparency*. Slideshare presentation. Retrieved January 4, 2010, from http://www.slideshare.net/samplereality/the-open-source-professor-teaching-research-and-transparency

Schachter, J. (2008). Delicious. In Jones, B. (Ed.), *Web 2.0 heroes: Interviews with 21 Web 2.0 influencers* (pp. 169–175). Indianapolis, IN: Wiley Pub.

Scalter, N. (2008). *Web 2.0, personal learning environments, and the future of learning management systems. EDUCAUSE Center for Applied Research* (ECAR). Available from http://www.educause.edu/ecar

Scrivener Agee, A., & Yang, C.The 2009 EDUCAUSE Current Issues Committee. (2009). Top-ten IT issues, 2009. *EDUCAUSE Review, 44*(4), 44–59.

Seldow, A. (2007). *Social tagging in education and the workplace*. Paper presented at the 3rd annual Innovations in E-Learning Symposium. George Mason University, Fairfax, VA.

Siemens, G. (2005). Connectivism: A learning theory for the digital age. *International Journal of Instructional Technology and Distance Learning, 2*(1). Available from http://www.itdl.org/Journal/Jan_05/article01.htm.

Siemens, G., & Tittenberger, P. (2009). *Handbook of emerging technologies for learning*. Retrieved from http://umanitoba.ca/learning_technologies/cetl/HETL.pdf

Siemens, G. (2009, November 13). *Moodle - the wrong tool for the job?* Retrieved December 30, 2009, from http://www.learningconversations.co.uk/ main/index.php/2009/11/13/moodle-the-wrong-tool-for-the-job?blog=5

Sessums, C. (2006, January 21). *Notes on the significance of the emergence of blogs and wikis*. Retrieved October 12, 2006, from http://eduspaces.net/csessums/weblog/6172.html

Smith, S. D., Salaway, G., & Borreson Caruso, J. (2009). The ECAR study of undergraduate students and information technology. *EDUCAUSE Center for Applied Research (ECAR)*. Available from http://www.educause.edu/ecar

Solomon, G., & Schrum, L. (2007). *Web 2.0: New tools, new schools*. Washington, DC: International Society for Technology in Education.

Tapscott, D. (1998). *Growing up digital: The rise of the net generation*. New York: McGraw-Hill.

Vander Wal, T. (2005). *Folksonomy definition and Wikipedia*. Retrieved March 14, 2007, from http://www.vanderwal.net/random/entrysel.php?blog=1750

Weigel, V. (2002). *Deep learning for a digital age: Technology's untapped potential to enrich higher education*. San Francisco: Jossey-Bass.

Weigel, M., James, C., & Gardner, H. (2009). Learning: Peering backward and looking forward in the digital era. *International Journal of Learning and Media,* 1 (1) 1-18. Retrieved April 1, 2010, from Massachusetts Institute of Technology Press: http://www.mitpressjournals.org/doi/full/10.1162/ijlm.2009.0005

Wiley, D. (2006a). Open source, openness, and higher education. *Innovate, 3* (1). Retrieved January 9, 2010, from http://innovateonline.info/pdf/vol3_issue1/Open_Source,_Openness,_and_Higher_Education.pdf

Wiley, D. (2006b). *The current state of open educational resource.* Retrieved February 3, 2007, from http://opencontent.org/blog/archives/247

Wiley, D., & Hilton, J., III. (2009). Openness, dynamic specialization, and the disaggregated future of higher education. *The International Review Of Research In Open And Distance Learning, 10*(5). Retrieved January 3, 2010, from http://www.irrodl.org/index.php/irrodl/article/view/768

KEY TERMS AND DEFINITIONS

Sustaining Innovation: Innovations in products, processes, or services that create incremental changes in existing practices and behaviors (e.g., moving from Windows XP to Windows Vista).

Disruptive Innovation: Innovations in products, processes, or services that initially may not be perceived as effective as the current product, process, or service, but over time, become more responsive to meet the need of a broader audience driving out the standard or current product, process or service (e.g., the Internet and the World Wide Web).

Folksonomy: or **Folksonomic Classification:** A system of classification of content based on collaborative tagging. Also known as, social classification, social indexing, and social tagging.

Connectivism: A learning theory for the digital age developed by George Siemens and Stephen Downes to explain the effect technology has had on how we live, how we communicate, and how we learn

Rhizomatic Education: A model of learning that supports knowledge as a process of construction and negotiation rather than as a curriculum predefined by experts. The community acts as the curriculum, spontaneously shaping, constructing, and reconstructing itself and the subject of its learning.

Web 2.0: A popular term characterizing an expansive range of innovative capabilities that have emerged from technological advances that make up the 21st century web as a medium of social exchange. The term embodies ideas such as openness, personalization, collaboration, social networking, user-generated content, and collective intelligence. Web 2.0 as a technology is interchangeable with terms like social software and social media.

Social Software: An older term used to refer to emergent, networked applications used to extend and enhance human communication and collaborative capabilities, and is often interchangeable with the terms Web 2.0 and social media.

Social Media: A 21st century term used to broadly define a variety of networked tools/technologies that emphasize the social aspects of the Internet as a channel for communication, collaboration, and creative expression, and is often interchangeable with the terms Web 2.0 and social software.

Openness: An attribute of Web 2.0 that describes tools and services designed to make available or expose a variety of information to discovery, public access, and reuse.

Cloud Computing: A paradigmatic way to use the Internet to host a wide array of IT services or virtualized resources that offer as-needed and on-demand cost efficiencies.

PLE (Personal Learning Environments): A type of social software-based learning environment that supports a learner-centered pedagogy—designed to help learners aggregate and share the results of learning achievements, participate in collective knowledge generation, and manage their own meaning making.

Chapter 14
Assistive Technology in Higher Education

Susan B. Asselin
Virginia Tech, USA

ABSTRACT

Assistive technology makes a task possible for an individual with a disability, while technology makes a task easier for a non-disabled person. Increasing enrollments of students with disabilities have challenged our institutions to provide opportunities to participate in higher education by having access to assistive technologies and universally designed instruction. Provision of accessible learning environments is a shared responsibility between disability services, information technology, and faculty. College students find themselves in an environment where they encounter negative attitudes and a need to self advocate for critical support services to insure access to learning. Recent trends hold promise for removing these barriers including universal design in instruction, mandated web accessibility, multiple technologies for e-learning, universal accessibility of learning tools, and opportunities for professional development of faculty and staff.

INTRODUCTION

Access to postsecondary education for learners with disabilities can best be achieved through partnerships between students, disability service providers and instructional technology professionals. It is critical that these partners work collaboratively to promote positive academic and career outcomes. Growing numbers of college students with disabilities challenge our institutions to find ways to use technology to create more inclusive learning environments. This chapter will explore how the use of assistive technology in higher education offers students with disabilities opportunities to participate and benefit from an education. While access to the college is enhanced

DOI: 10.4018/978-1-60960-147-8.ch014

by assistive technology, there are potential barriers that must be addressed in the academic environment. Solutions to access include implementing universal design in instruction, designing accessible information technology and e-learning, and delivering professional development. Finally, innovations and trends in assistive technology will raise the bar and continue to challenge higher education.

BACKGROUND

Colleges and universities are serving an increasing number of diverse students, including learners with disabilities. An estimated 11% of undergraduate and 7% of graduate students attending college report having a disability. The largest enrollments are among students with learning disabilities, attention deficit hyperactivity disorders and returning veterans with newly diagnosed disabilities. Of these students, 21.9% had mental illness or related disorders, 25.4% had physical disabilities, 17.3% had health impairments, 11% had attention deficit disorder, 7.5% had a learning disability, 5% had hearing impairments, 3.8% had visual impairments and 7.8% were listed as other disabilities (National Center for Education Statistics, 2008). In the past, higher education served primarily individuals with sensory or mobility needs, however these data represent a student population with a wider range of disabilities, many who have "hidden" or cognitive disabilities (Horn & Berktold, 1999).

The Government Accountability Office (2009) reported an increasing number of students with autism, medical conditions and returning veterans with traumatic brain injury, post-traumatic stress disorders and mobility impairments. Another population expected to grow will be students with intellectual disabilities seeking a non-degree program focusing on life and functional skills. Growing numbers of students with invisible learning disabilities led to a focus on individual learner strengths and compensation for limitations (Scherer, Sax, Vanbiervleit, Cushman & Scherer, 2005; Peterson-Karlan & Parette, 2005). The introduction of accommodations that focus on characteristics is a more person centered approach since regardless of diagnostic labels, individuals with disabilities may experience other limitations, vary in functioning levels, and need different supports across settings.

Legislation

Historically, individuals with disabilities were stigmatized in our society and institutions. Prior to the passage of the 1973 Rehabilitation Act, participation was viewed less favorably in our schools, colleges and communities. Hallmark federal legislation broke down barriers and reduced the social stigma attached to a disability. The Americans with Disabilities Act (ADA) of 1990, extended protections against discrimination and mandated full access in employment, communications, transportation, recreation and facilities. The ADA further clarified the definition of a disability as a "physical or mental impairment that substantially limits one or more major life activities." This mandate reflected a shift from focusing on disabilities as a deficit to recognizing disability as a normal part of life.

Over the past, thirty years the percentage of students with disabilities entering colleges and universities has more than tripled. Institutions of higher education are required to insure that individuals with disabilities are not discriminated against and are offered opportunities to benefit from and participate in a full range of services, including reasonable accommodations. Unfortunately the outcomes for students with disabilities are not as positive as their peers since they still lag behind in completion of a college degree (Murray, Goldstein, Nourse, & Edgar, 2000; Stodden, 2001). Without a postsecondary education, individuals are at a distinct disadvantage in the job market, reducing their ability to earn an adequate salary and contribute to society. If we create more inclusive learning communities in higher education, students with disabilities will experience increased opportunities for success.

Assistive technology is increasingly available to college students, thus enabling them to participate and benefit from higher education. As early as 1973, Section 504 of the Rehabilitation Act defined assistive technology as an auxiliary aid. Initially, assistive technology devices served primarily individuals with sensory and physical disabilities; however, these devices can help an even wider range of individuals to compensate for their disabilities. If institutions of higher education received federal funds they were required to provide accommodations and accessible programs. The 1990 Americans with Disabilities Act and subsequent amendments extended protections against discrimination and influenced growing opportunities to participate in higher education.

Assistive Technology

While the definition of assistive technology has evolved over time, The 1988 Technology-Related Assistance for Individuals with Disabilities Act or Tech Act definition is currently accepted by professionals in education, rehabilitation and labor. Assistive technology includes items, devices, equipment, or products which may be commercially available, customized, or adapted to help a person with a disability to function or to improve, maintain or increase their capacity to function (Technology Related Assistance for Individuals with Disabilities Act, 1988). Assistive technology includes a broad range of devices from computer based, high technology to low cost, readily available technology. Examples of assistive technology devices for education, work, or independent living, may include but are not limited to:

- Computer based software for reading or writing
- Environmental controls for lighting
- Adapted computer controls for mobility and access
- Hearing aids or devices
- Augmentative communication devices
- Facility modifications like ramps, automatic doors or stair lifts
- Modified work sites for height, physical access, or equipment for scanning text

The definition for assistive technology goes beyond just devices and includes services for access and training to use the devices. Assistive technology services include help in selecting, acquiring or using technology, and evaluating individual characteristics to match device functions to needs. Services may also involve adapting or customizing an existing device, and repair and maintenance of devices. An important distinction between technology and assistive technology needs to be made. Technology can make a task easier for all persons, while assistive technology makes a task possible for an individual with a disability.

The Americans with Disabilities Act, Title II and Section 504 of the Rehabilitation Act, prohibit discrimination against individuals with disabilities in all postsecondary institutions, including colleges, universities, vocational and adult education programs that receive federal financial assistance. Section 504 of the Rehabilitation Act further delineates that students with disabilities must not be discriminated against because of the absence of auxiliary aids.

The purpose of these aids and services provides individuals with disabilities equal opportunities to participate and enjoy benefits of programs, services or activities by postsecondary institutions; in other words, aids make learning possible. Aids and services must be provided in a timely manner. Colleges do not have to provide the most sophisticated assistive technology devices, however they must be appropriate and meet the needs of the students after consulting with the student. Institutions that offer assistive devices and services meet the intention of this basic civil rights legislation (US Department of Education, 2010).

ACCESS AND THE COLLEGE ENVIRONMENT

Accommodations

Prior to moving from high school to college, students are provided with assistive technology device or service as an accommodation for their disability if they help the individual accomplish functional skills. The Individuals with Disabilities Education Improvement Act of 2003 (IDEIA) mandates that assistive technology be "considered" in the development of a student's individualized education program. Assistive technology in secondary education applies to improving access to education as well as life or independent living or a 504 accommodation plan is updated in their last year of high school.

Students with disabilities are obligated to provide information about their disability and identify appropriate accommodations once they reach higher education (Burgstahler, 2003). Common college accommodations include electronic texts, readers, adapted equipment, note-takers, extended time on tests or sign language interpreters. These accommodations may include assistive technology, if students disclose their disabilities and present appropriate documentation of needs.

University policies for assistive technology supports vary from college to college. Two year colleges provide a wider range of supports, while large public universities may offer more services. On campus offices for students with disabilities are the most common source of assistive technology supports or in departments with assistive technology programs (Stodden, Roberts, Picklesimer, Jackson & Chang, 2006). College disability service providers may work with vocational rehabilitation counselors who can offer assistive technology assessments and resource referrals, however, the institution is responsible for providing the assistive technology unless they can prove it would cause an undue financial burden.

It is assumed that students have been exposed to various assistive technologies before they enter college. Unfortunately, variables such as cost, preferences of the user, expert opinions and knowledge, and level of training impact a student's decision to use assistive technology. If students have not been provided with accessible technologies while in high school, it is increasingly difficult to acquire information and training in higher education. There are several issues related to access and assistive technologies, but the biggest barrier is negative attitudes due to limited knowledge about the needs and capabilities of individuals with disabilities. Without this knowledge, the potential and versatility that technology offers learners is often unrealized.

Social Stigma

Students with disabilities continue to encounter attitudinal barriers in higher education. They report that the most frequently encountered unintentional barrier is lack of awareness of disabilities by faculty. Some faculty question the very existence of disabilities, especially those "hidden" disabilities such as learning disabilities or attention deficit disorders. Other faculty relate that they feel that accommodations provide an unfair advantage to other students in their classes (Shannon, Tansey & Schoen, 2009).

Students with disabilities are concerned about negative stereotypes, and believe faculty make assumptions that they are not competitive with their peers and those accommodations are unfair. New experiences and challenges in the college environment also impact students' level of anxiety, avoidance of uncomfortable situations, and lack of self confidence (Trammel, 2009; Wong, Chan, Cardoso, Lam, & Miller, 2004). It is important that higher education personnel understand learning needs and the potential impact of these barriers to their success.

Estimates show that only about one-fourth of entering college students with previously identified disabilities actually disclose a disability. As a result these students are reluctant to seek critical accommodations and support services which impact college retention and completion of degrees (National Center for Education Statistics, 2008). If universities and faculty create a welcoming and inclusive environment students will have an opportunity to benefit from participating in higher education along with their non-disabled peers.

Students who do use assistive technologies may encounter negative attitudes and acceptance by professionals and their peers due to struggles in keeping up with assignments. If students do not feel disability services staff understand and support the potential of assistive technology for access and independence, students are more likely to abandon the device. Students also encounter barriers if disability services staff are unwilling to provide assistive services due to perceived costs, maintenance, or lack of familiarity with emerging technologies. Some institutions of higher education are reluctant to convert course materials to Braille due to the time and costs, especially for mathematical equations, graphics, and foreign languages (Government Accountability Office, 2009). In addition to social and emotional needs, students with disabilities are faced with challenges to learning. Research demonstrates that assistive technologies hold promise for and contribute to the completion of a college degree, which increases the success of students with disabilities (Getzel, McManus & Briel, 2001).

Microsoft (2004) commissioned Forrester Research to conduct a study of computer use among individuals with disabilities to determine awareness, knowledge and use of computers and assistive technology. A comparison of users with and without disabilities revealed that fewer individuals with disabilities used computers (84% to 74%). As our population ages and the population of individuals with disabilities increases, it is important to insure accessibility of technology for 38% of our working- age adult population. A significant finding revealed that 57% of computer users with disabilities are likely to benefit from using assistive technology regardless of the severity of their disability. Consumers are more likely to use accessible features if they make computing easier, more convenient, and comfortable. In addition, individuals with disabilities are more likely to use technologies that are readily available to the general population including built in accessibility, input devices magnification and voice recognition.

Instructional Tools

If universities employ instructional strategies that are already "built-in" and universally accessible, then students with disabilities are more likely to succeed. Assistive technology tools offer faculty opportunities to increase accessibility of instruction and engage students in active learning. Assistive technology also provides accommodations for learning challenges such as memory, organization, reading, math, communication, and writing skills. At the same time technology can compensate or enhance functioning of cognitive, sensory, language, and motor skills. Students with disabilities challenge educators to closely examine the capacity that technology offers for inclusive practices in teaching and learning.

Higher education has traditionally used text-based learning tools and lectures. Learners are required to read, write, analyze and interpret written information. Unfortunately, text-based materials do not recognize functional strengths in language, sensory, motor or cognitive skills of individuals. Sole reliance on one tool and one mode of learning limits learner's performance of academic tasks of reading, writing or listening due to disability related barriers (Bryant, Bryant & Rieth, 2002). For example, the printed text is often inaccessible for learners with language based learning limitations however, the use of text to speech software, a multimedia technique, offers students another way to access the written word. This shift from students as passive to active learners has potential to transform higher education instruction.

Universal Design

One of the trends in higher education is the implementation of universal design for instruction. The CAST Center and the North Carolina State University, Center for Universal Design have provided the impetus to improve the learning environment for diverse learners, including those with disabilities and cultural differences. All learners possess functional strengths and limitations that determine how they acquire information and demonstrate content mastery (Meyer & Rose, 2005). Implementation of universal design in learning is critical to providing diverse learners with multiple means to access information, express knowledge and be engaged through use of digital media, multimedia and multiple methods. Learning technologies in higher education focus on increasing the quality of instruction to maximize the learning environment for all learners.

The basic premise of universal design is creation of a flexible curriculum through varied methods and materials that enhance learning for ALL students. The Higher Education Opportunity Act (2008) identified *Universal Design for Learning* as a research based intervention in colleges and universities. This act affirms the definition found in Section 3 of the Assistive Technology Act of 1998.

The *Universal Design for Learning (UDL)* framework contains three principles:

- Multiple methods of presentation
- Flexible methods of expression
- Flexible methods of engagement

The first principle, *multiple methods of presentation*, supports learners who have preferred modes of accessing and acquiring knowledge. For example, students may learn best by reading, listening, participating in hands-on demonstrations or simulations, or using manipulatives. The second principle, *flexible methods of expression*, recognizes that students use a variety of strategies to process knowledge. Learners need a variety of learning strategies to interact with content and assign meaning. The third principle, *flexible methods of engagement*, relates to individual levels of motivation and involvement in learning. Learners demonstrate that they know the content thru visual, written, oral, or modeling modes (Rose & Meyer, 2002).

While the UDL framework focuses on the learner, a postsecondary model, *Universal Design for Instruction (UDI)*, approaches access to the instructional environment as proposed by the Center for Postsecondary Education and Disability (McGuire, Scott and Shaw, 2003). Faculty designed instruction for a wide range of diverse learners is a ubiquitous approach that benefits learners with disabilities by offering multiple ways to access learning materials and methods. While this model does not reduce the need for assistive technologies in higher education, it may reduce the number of accommodations and provide a more seamless approach for learners with disabilities.

There are considerations in implementing principles of universal design that are distinct to higher education. These principles are not prescriptive but rather serve merely as examples of inclusive teaching. Faculty may be surprised to learn that applying these principles for effective instruction may be easily integrated into course design. The principles of UDI include:

- Flexibility and choice of materials and methods
- Equitable use or access
- Simple, predictable and straightforward language

- Perceptible information to meet diverse sensory or cognitive strengths and needs
- Tolerance for error through pacing, feedback and practice
- Low effort either physical or attention
- Size and space for reach and mobility
- Community of learners to enhance communication and networks
- Instructional climate that is welcoming and inclusive

Electronic Information

The Internet and access to the World Wide Web is becoming an integral part of our society. Web based information is fast replacing traditional resources and service delivery. Since we are using the Web to deliver and receive information, it is critical that individuals with disabilities be provided with equitable access and opportunity to benefit from and participate fully in our society. Section 508 of the Rehabilitation Act of 1973 mandated equal access to communication, information and services, while the 1998 amendments included all electronic and information technology. Accessibility applies to all aspects of procurement, developing, maintaining and using technology. Technology covers a wide range such as computers, software, electronic office equipment, all training programs, World Wide Webpages and web based instruction. The Americans with Disabilities Act also mandated that barriers to print, audio and visual media be removed to insure individuals are discriminated against in education and communication. The Rehabilitation Act and ADA provided the impetus for institutions of higher education to adopt information technology accessibility policies to insure people with disabilities have equal access.

The Web is an opportunity to increase an individual's opportunities to interact socially, communicate with friends and family, and participate in the workplace. Gray, Silver-Pacuilla & Saucer (2008) highlight the benefits of participation in social media to connect persons with disabilities through online communication and collaboration tools. The growth of Web enabled technologies – blogs, wikis, social networking sites, photo and video sharing sites and gaming offer great potential to remove barriers of geography, and disability. Guidelines for accessible design were developed by individuals with disabilities, researchers, government and technology professionals to meet the sensory, cognitive, physical and language needs and abilities of users. The guidelines address how technology can reach a maximum number of people by offering a variety of outputs such as presenting auditory and visual information. Another guideline addresses using a variety of inputs such as keyboards, alternative mice, switches or voice controls. Physical access can be approached by designing various ways to manipulate the environmnent, structures and locations in a safe and hazard free manner. Documentation to operate the devices needs to be offered in variety of formats to meet the sensory and cognitive needs of individuals (Vanderheiden & Vanderheiden, 1992).

Assistive technologies and implementation of universal design can enhance access to all university services and academic instruction (Web Accessibility Initiative, 2010). Students increasingly rely on computers to access information but they may also have to use assistive technology such as software or electronic equipment to be successful. Online university services to all students makes information more readily accessible. Computers are used to register for classes, search for library resources, check course grades and transcripts, receive campus news, pay bills, and manage schedules. Computer mediated communication helps students with disabilities feel included, enhances social interaction and increases autonomy and independence. In addition computer access can reduce barriers of time, schedules, transportation and distance (Burgstahler & Cronheim, 2001).

E-Learning and distance education can mediate some of these barriers to instruction and provide opportunities to use computer assistive technology, often unrealized in traditional classroom settings. Adaptive input devices such as headsticks, keyboards and magnifiers, reading and writing software, e-texts, captioned videos, large print materials or electronic materials remove barriers to student learning. Text to speech, magnification and FM listening systems were also in the most frequently used devices. These devices are accommodating a wider range of individuals than they were originally designed to serve. Some of the barriers to using technologies include cost, ease of use, obsolescence and changing needs of student learners (Fichten, Asuncion, Barile, Genereux, Fossey, Judd, Robillard, DeSimone & Wells, 2001). If colleges and universities implemented universal design principles, they could make all technologies accessible by using assistive technologies.

At the same time, Web based instruction can present barriers even with the presence of assistive technology. Faculty and instructional designers without knowledge of universal design principles or Web accessibility can create barriers to learning. Examples of barriers include Webpages that have graphics without text descriptions, cluttered screens, confusing page navigation with text to voice software, audio content without captioning or transcripts, and confusion caused by magnification of small portions of Webpages. Furthermore, videoconferencing, synchronous chats and discussions might be too slow or difficult to follow visual or auditory information (Web Accessibility Initiative, 2010). Universal design principles and the World Wide Web Consortium (2008) call for Web content that is perceivable (alternatives to text), easy to navigate and operate, understandable (clear, concise language), and robust (compatible with for assistive technologies). When these principles are applied in Web course design, they will assist all learners, especially those with language, cognitive, sensory, and physical disabilities.

Professional Development

Educators can make full use of technology if they are provided with intensive training and best practices for integrating technology to meet the needs of diverse learners. Training must be delivered by experts with technical knowledge and learners must have multiple opportunities to use the technology. Successful targeted training not only provides initial instruction but offers ongoing, technical support to increase skills and adoption of technology. Professionals who are confident in their abilities to use technology will make technology an important teaching tool. Assistive technology devices are often specialized to particular types of learning needs, so the development of tutorials, forums and face to face instruction is more successful approach to adopting new technologies (National Center for Technology Innovation, 2009).

Understanding the potential that assistive technology offers students as an accommodation most often rests with university disability services offices. Unfortunately, students with disabilities encounter barriers to acquiring needed accommodations due to inadequate knowledge of disability services personnel regarding appropriate assistive technology and Web accessibility (Burgstahler & Moore, 2009). Students with disabilities entering higher education have encountered similar barriers in high school due to lack of knowledge about assistive technology and limited training of teachers even though most students are included in general education settings (Parette, Peterson-Karlan, Smith, Gray, & Silver-Pacuilla, 2006). Secondary educators and disability services providers need to work closely together with technology support personnel about how AT can meet the learning needs of students and provide training.

As higher education continues to transform organizational structures and academic environments to meet needs of students with disabilities they must initiate campus wide training and professional development. Disability issues have been addressed by disability services offices, however they have inadequate knowledge about technology resulting in limited input into technology decision making. Faculty, disability service providers and instructional designers could benefit from a collaborative training to implement universal design instructional strategies. When these professionals participate in collaborative training programs, students with disabilities are the ones who benefit when faculty and services providers are knowledgeable about the potential of technology and universal design (Finn, Getzel, Asselin & Reilly, 2008). Providing universally designed technology increases access for all learners, and levels the playing field for those with disabilities.

ASSISTIVE TECHNOLOGY TRENDS

Innovations in technology hold promise for enhancing access for learners with disabilities to fully participate in higher education. The consumer electronics and technology industry is moving towards software as a service rather than an application on a device. Software applications through the internet and cloud computing offer assistive technologies on any computer, so individuals do not have to be tied to a dedicated machine. This ubiquitous approach provides individual users with software licenses or portable software such as a jump drive that can be used on any internet supported computer. Eventually, the need for specialized assistive technology labs in colleges and universities will be eliminated (Gray, Pacuilla & Overton, 2009). Vanderheiden (2008) was a proponent of leveling the playing field so individuals with disabilities can access accessibility features on any computer by thinking about ubiquitous accessibility, features that are accessed over the Internet instead of specialized software and devices resident with stationary computer stations.

As assistive technology tools are designed they to need provide flexibility so individuals can use them in their homes, school, communities and the workplace. Technology offers the potential for sharing information across platforms, integrated data management systems, and application across multiple settings (National Center for Technology Innovation, 2009).We are still in the early stages of determining the best way for assistive technology to follow students as they make these life changing transitions.

Technology opens doors to a more global society for individuals with disabilities as we prepare individuals for success in the 21st century. The National Center for Technology Innovation recommends AT developers and service providers have a global view of the potential that assistive technology offers individuals with disabilities. Specifically, they suggest that assistive technology tools need to a) serve as quality of life tools, b) maximize access to open source and Web 2.0 tools, c) be more accessible in partnership with consumer marketing of products, and d) include universally designed solutions (Gray, Pacuilla & Overton, 2009). As individuals with disabilities are recognized as potential consumers, technology staff and learning specialists need to think more globally to insure all consumers have access to our increasingly competitive economy. As we create technological innovations to make consumer's lives *easier*, we must recognize that these same innovations make participation and living life to its fullest *possible* for persons with disabilities.

Equitable access for learning as one of life's major activities for people with disabilities is a legal and moral imperative. Higher education must recognize that creating an accessible learning environment is a shared responsibility. An increasing number of universities have advisory committees composed of disability service providers, information technologies, Americans with Disability Act directors, and professional development professionals to deal with accessibility of computer technology. Thompson (2005) studied best practices in higher education and accessibility and found that a little over half of the institutions provided had a Web accessibility policy or dedicated staff. Fewer institutions provided accessible instructional technology and recognized the need to provide professional development opportunities. It is unfortunate that at most institutions, all accessibility of information technology is left up to the disability services offices while the accessibility of college or university Webpage creates the first impression of the campus climate for individuals with disabilities.

Disability service providers and instructional technology professionals must collaborate with departments and programs across their campuses to insure instructional materials and methods, equipment and services meet the needs of individuals with disabilities. Knowledge about learner needs, the process for documenting needs and legal obligations under the Americans with Disabilities Act are shared by disability specialists. Information technology professionals are charged with faculty training and support and can help faculty implement principles of universal design in the classroom and increase familiarity with assistive technology devices. Disability specialists can also have input into policies on Web accessibility and implementation of Section 508 of the Rehabilitation Act regulations. If higher education is serious about creating equitable access it must address campus barriers and create collaborative partnerships (Asuncion, Fichten, Barile, Fossey & Robillard, 2004).

Disability and information technologists can form partnerships to insure that all students benefit from and successfully participate in higher education. It is important to understand the learning characteristics of individuals with disabilities and select assistive technology devices and provide services that meet their needs.

CONCLUSION

Technology can free people by extending their abilities, managing their lives, and helping them to be more effective in work. Innovations in technology offer users smaller, lighter weight, more affordable and powerful devices and software in a rapidly changing field. As the person's needs and life responsibilities evolve, so will the assistive technology. It is critical that individuals with disabilities express these changes and be their own self advocate as they seek and use assistive technology.

Now that we have legislation and policies to promote use of assistive technology, inclusion and participation in all aspects of our society, we have an opportunity to focus on a social model rather than the medical model of services. We no longer need to "fix" the person with a disability which was the view of our society before the 1970s, but rather examine the environment and offer accommodations (Scherer, 2005). With the current person-centered approach, these individuals have opportunities to self-advocate and work with providers to determine the potential that technologies offer to improve their quality of life. As we enter the 21st century people with disabilities feel less stigmatized, and see themselves as having differences as an accepted way of life. It is up to our institutions of higher education to value these differences and support our students, faculty and employees with accommodations based on their needs.

Institutions of higher education are required, by law, to break down social and academic barriers. Universal design in instruction, accessible information technology, and accessible learning systems are promising practices. The overall impact of creating an inclusive learning environment significantly enhances financial independence, employment opportunities and career satisfaction of individuals with disabilities. As a result of the shift in policies that prevent discrimination, offer opportunities for participation, and willingness to integrate accessible practices, individuals with disabilities can be successful as a valued member of society.

REFERENCES

Americans with Disabilities Act of 1990, U.S.C. §12, 101-112, 213.

Bryant, B. R., Bryant, D. P., & Rieth, H. J. (2002). The use of assistive technology in higher education. In Brinckerhoff, L. C., McGuire, J. M., & Shaw, S. T. (Eds.), *Postsecondary education and transition for students with learning disabilities*. Austin, TX: ProEd.

Burgstahler, S. (2003). The role of technology in preparing youth with disabilities for postsecondary education and employment. *Journal of Special Education Technology*, *18*(4), 7–19.

Burgstahler, S., & Cronheim, D. (2001). Supporting peer-peer and mentor-protégé relationships on the internet. *Journal of Research on Technology in Education*, *34*(1), 59–74.

Burgstahler, S., & Moore, E. (2009). Making student services welcoming and accessible through accommodations and universal design. *Journal of Postsecondary Education and Disability*, *21*(3), 155–174.

Center for Applied Special Technology (CAST). (2009). *Universal design for learning: New directions in higher education.* Retrieved from http://www.cost.org/pd/institute/june8.html

Fichten, C. S., Asuncion, J. V., Barile, M., Genereux, C., Fossey, M., & Judd, D. (2001). Technology integration for students with disabilities: Empirically based recommendations. *Educational Research and Evaluation*, *7*, 185–221. doi:10.1076/edre.7.2.185.3869

Finn, D., Getzel, E., Asselin, S., & Reilly, V. (2008). Incorporating universal design applications across campus. In Burgstahler, S., & Cory, R. (Eds.), *Universal Design of Postsecondary Education: From Principle to Practice*. Boston: Harvard Education Press.

Getzel, E. E., McManus, S., & Briel, L. (2001). *An effective model for college students with learning disabilities and attention deficit hyperactivity disorders*. Research to Practice, National Center on Secondary Education & Transition.

Government Accountability Office. (2009). *Higher education and disability. GAO-10-33*. Washington, DC: Author.

Gray, J. T., Pacuilla, H. S., & Overton, C. (2009). *Learning and assistive technology: Thriving in a global marketplace*. Washington, DC: American Institutes for Research, National Center for Technology Innovation.

Gray, J. T., Silver-Pacuilla, H., & Saucer, M. (2008). *The power of social media to provide assistive and learning technologies*. Washington, DC: American Institutes for Research.

Higbee, J. L., Bruch, P. L., & Siaka, K. Disability and diversity: Results from the multicultural awareness project for institutional transformation. In Higbee, J.L. & Goff, E. (Eds.) (2008). *Pedagogy and student services for institutional transformation: Implementing universal design in higher education*. University of Minnesota, Center for Research on Developmental Education and Urban Literacy.

Higbee, J. L., & Goff, E. (Eds.). (2008). *Pedagogy and student services for institutional transformation: Implementing universal design in higher education*. University of Minnesota, Center for Research on Developmental Education and Urban Literacy.

Higher Education Opportunity Act. 20 U.S.C § 1001 et seq.(a)23.

Horn, L., & Berktold, J. (1999). *Students with disabilities in postsecondary education: A profile of preparation, participation, and outcomes (Report No. NCES 1999-187)*. Washington, DC: United States Department of Education, National Center for Education Statistics.

Individuals with Disabilities Education Improvement Act of 2004, U.S.C. § 300 *et seq.*

McGuire, J. M., Scott, S. S., & Shaw, S. F. (2003). Universal design for instruction: The paradigm its principles, and products for enhancing instructional access. *Journal of Postsecondary Education and Disability*, *17*(1), 11–21.

Meyer, A., & Rose, D. (2005). *The future is in the margins: The role of technology and disability in educational reform.* Paper presented to the American Institute for Research, US Department of Education, Office of Educational Technology.

Microsoft Corporation. (2004). *Accessible technology in computing: Examining awareness, use, and future potential.* Cambridge, MA: Forrester Research, Inc.

Murray, C., Goldstein, D. E., Nourse, S., & Edgar, E. (2000). The postsecondary school attendance and completion rates of high school graduates with learning disabilities. *Learning Disabilities Research*, *15*, 119–127. doi:10.1207/SLDRP1503_1

National Center for Education Statistics. (2008). *Digest of education statistics: 2008*. Washington, DC: US Department of Education, Institute for Education Sciences.

National Center for Technology Innovation. (2009). *Unleashing the power of innovations for Assistive Technology. Author*. Washington, DC: American Institutes for Research.

Parette, H. P., Peterson-Karlan, G. R., Smith, S. I., Gray, T., & Silver-Pacuilla, H. (2006). The state of assistive technology: Themes from an outcomes summit. *Assistive Technology Outcomes and Benefits*, *3*(1), 15–33.

Peterson-Karlan, G., & Parette, P. (2005). Millennial students with mild disabilities and emerging assistive technology trends. *Journal of Special Education Technology*, *20*(4), 27–38.

Rose, D. H., & Meyer, A. (2002). *Teaching every student in the digital age: Universal design for learning*. Alexandria, VA: Association for Supervision and Curriculum Development.

Scherer, M., Sax, C., Vanbiervliet, A., Cushman, L., & Scherer, J. (2005). Predictors of assistive technology use: The importance of personal and psychosocial factors. *Disability and Rehabilitation*, *27*(21), 1321–1331. doi:10.1080/09638280500164800

Scherer, M. J. (2005). *Living in the state of stuck*. Brookline, MA: Brookline Books.

Shannon, C. D., Schoen, B., & Tansey, T. N. (2009). The effect of contact, context, and social power on undergraduate attitudes towards persons with disabilities. *Journal of Rehabilitation*, *75*(4), 11–18.

Sitlington, P. L. (2003). Postsecondary education: The other transition. *Exceptionality*, *11*(3), 103–113. doi:10.1207/S15327035EX1102_05

Stodden, R. A. (2001). Postsecondary education supports for students with disabilities: A review and response. *Journal for Vocational Special Needs Education*, *23*(2), 4–11.

Stodden, R. A., Roberts, K. D., Picklesimer, T., Jackson, D., & Chang, C. (2006). An analysis of assistive technology supports and services offered in postsecondary institutions. *Journal of Vocational Rehabilitation*, *24*, 111–120.

The Rehabilitation Act of 1973, U.S.C. §94(d)

The Technology Related Assistance for Individuals with Disabilities Act of 1988, U.S.C. § 2201,2202.

Thompson, T. (2005). Information technology accessibility in higher education. EDUCAUSE *Center for Applied Research Bulletin, 2005(12).*

Trammel, J. (2009). Postsecondary students and disability stigma: Development of the postsecondary student survey of disability-related stigma (PSSDS). *Journal of Postsecondary Education & Disability.*, *22*(2), 106–113.

United States Access Board. (2010). Retrieved from http://www.access-board.gov/

U.S. Department of Education, Office of Civil Rights. *Auxiliary aids and services for postsecondary students with disabilities.* Retrieved from http://www.ed.gov/print/about/offices/list/ocr/docs/auxaids.html

Vanderheiden, G.C. (2008). Ubiquitous accessibility, common core and micro assistive technology. *ACM Transactions on Accessible Computing, 1*(2), 10.1-10.7.

Vanderheiden, G. C., & Vanderheiden, K. R. (1992). *Guidelines for the design of consumer products to increase their accessibility to people with disabilities or who are aging* (Working draft 1.7). Madison WI: Trace Research and Development Center. Retrieved from http://trace.wisc.edu/docs/consumer_producxts_guidelines/toc.html

Web Accessiblity Initiative. (2010). *How people with disabilities access the Web.* Cambridge MA: World Wide Web Consortium. Retrieved from http://www.w3.org/WAI/WCAG20/quickref/

Wong, D. W., Chan, F., Cardoso, E. D., Lam, C. S., & Miller, S. M. (2004). Rehabilitation counseling students; attitudes towards people with disabilities in three social context: A joint analysis. *Rehabilitation Counseling Bulletin, 47*, 194–204. doi:10.1177/00343552040470040101

World Wide Web Consortium. (2008). *Web content accessiblity guidelines (WCAG) 2.0: W3C Recommendations.* Cambridge MA: Author. Retrieved from http://www.w3.org/TR/WCAG20/

KEYWORDS AND DEFINITIONS

Americans with Disabilities Act: federal legislation extending protections against discrimination and full access in employment, communications, transportation, recreation and facilities and provides the definition for disability

Assistive Technology Devices: items, devices, equipment, or products which may be commercially available, customized, or adapted to help a person with a disability to function or to improve, maintain or increase their capacity to function

Assistive Technology Services: selecting, acquiring or using technology and individual evaluation to match characteristics and functioning needs to devices. Services may also involve adapting or customizing an existing device, and repair and maintenance of devices

Disability: physical or mental impairment that substantially limits one or more major life activities

Disability Services: higher education professionals responsible for documentation and reasonable accommodations for learners with disabilities

Information Technology: computers, hardware, software, computer accessories, procedures, support services and related resources including communication products

Universal Design for Instruction: a postsecondary model that offers principles for effective instruction for diverse learners

Universal Design for Learning: an approach that focuses on the learner by creating a flexible curriculum with varied methods and materials

Chapter 15
Affect-Sensitive Virtual Standardized Patient Interface System

Thomas D. Parsons
University of Southern California, USA

ABSTRACT

Virtual Standardized Patients (VSPs) are advanced conversational virtual human agents that have been applied to training of clinicians. These interactive agents portray standardized patient scenarios involving VSPs with clinical or physical conditions. VSPs are capable of verbal and nonverbal interaction (receptive and expressive communication) with a clinician in an effort to enhance differential diagnosis of psychiatric disorders and teach interpersonal skills. This chapter describes the design and development of both software to create social interaction modules on a VSP platform and individualized affective models for affect recognition. This author describes clinically relevant scenarios for affect elicitation and protocols for reliable affect recognition. Further, there is an elucidation of a VSP interface system that has the capacity to monitor the trainee's affective response using physiological signals. Research findings will be summarized from studies on (1) the usability and applicability of VSPs with training clinicians on various mental health disorders (e.g., adolescent male with conduct disorder; adolescent female who has recently been physically traumatized); and (2) preliminary use of the affect-sensitive system to systematically assess and manipulate aspects of VSPs to more fully develop cognitive and affective models of virtual humans with pathological characteristics.

INTRODUCTION

Traditional approaches to training clinicians in the interpersonal communication skills needed for assessment, diagnosis, and interview performance rely upon a combination of classroom learning and role-playing with human standardized patients. The importance of interpersonal communication is reflected in recent requirements

DOI: 10.4018/978-1-60960-147-8.ch015

for communication evaluation in medical schools. The Accreditation Council for Graduate Medical Education (ACGME; 2007) has emphasized the importance of interpersonal and communication skills in training clinicians. Residents are expected to: (1) create and sustain a therapeutic and ethically sound relationship with the patient; (2) use effective listening skills, eliciting and providing information using effective nonverbal, explanatory, questioning, and writing skills; and (3) work in an efficient manner with others. However, evaluation studies have revealed methodological deficiencies in many cases (Chant et al., 2002) and limited positive training effects (Hulsman et al., 1999). In an effort to increase interpersonal communication assessment, standardized patients (paid human actors) have been recruited and trained to exhibit the characteristics of an actual patient, thereby affording novice clinicians a realistic opportunity to practice and to be evaluated in a mock clinical environment. Although a valuable training approach, there are limitations with the use of human standardized patients that can be mitigated through simulation technology. For example, human standardized patients are expensive and cost several thousand dollars per student. Further, given the fact that there are only a handful of sites (for over 130 medical schools in the U.S.) providing standardized patient assessments of the clinician in training's communication ability as part of the U.S. Medical Licensing Examination (USMLE), the current model provides limited availability. Another concern is the issue of standardization. Despite the expense of standardized patient programs, the standardized patients themselves are typically unskilled actors. As a result of common turnover, administrators face considerable challenges for offering psychometrically reliable and valid interactions with the training clinicians. A related issue is the limited scope that the actors are able to portray. As a result, there tends to be an inadequate array of developmentally, socially, and culturally appropriate scenarios. For example, when a clinician has a pediatric focus and needs access to children, it is difficult for the clinician to pretend that the actor is a child. Finally, many clinical cases (e.g., traumatic brain injury) have associated physical symptoms and behaviors (e.g., dilated pupils, spasms, and uncoordinated movements) that simply cannot be accurately portrayed by human actors.

Design and Simulation of Pathologies

One proposed answer to some of the difficulties inherent in training persons with standardized patients, hence human actors, is to use virtual humans as patients. Virtual humans (VH) are developing into powerful interfaces that can enable greatly increased intuitive human like interactions. These virtual human systems consist of characters that have realistic appearances, can think and act like humans, and can express themselves both verbally and non-verbally. Additionally, these virtual humans can listen and understand natural language and see or track limited user interactions with speech or vision systems. Advances in simulated virtual humans afford the possibility of virtual standardized patients that reduce cost, ensure standardization and faithfully model physical symptoms. Virtual standardized patients (VSPs) are artificially intelligent (AI) virtual human agents that control computer generated bodies and can interact with users through speech and gesture in virtual environments (Gratch, et al., 2002). Advanced virtual humans are able to engage in rich conversations (Traum et al., 2008), recognize nonverbal cues (Morency et al., 2008), analyze social and emotional factors (Gratch and Marsella, 2004) and synthesize human communication and nonverbal expressions (Thiebaux et al., 2008). Building virtual humans requires fundamental advances in AI, speech recognition, natural language understanding and generation, dialog management, cognitive modeling and reasoning, virtual human architectures and computer graphics and animations. All of these technologies need to be integrated together into a single system that can work in unison, be expandable, flexible and plug-and-play with different components.

The University of Southern California's Institute for Creative Technologies (USC/ICT) is a world-recognized leader in virtual-human research. The VH work at USC/ICT offers an interactive experience. Further, our virtual humans are capable of listening to users, reasoning about the situation at hand based on sensor input and the situational context and choosing appropriate dialog and actions and delivering those actions in generated verbal output that is synchronized to realistic human like non-verbal animations.

The virtual human systems we develop include complex cognitive agents, question response agents, and culturally specific characters. These virtual characters have beliefs, desires and intentions, as well as daily routines that can be carried out within virtual worlds. These agents are based around a set of distributed components that communicate with each other and perform specific tasks (e.g. speech recognition). Although these agents do require time and effort for adequate development, we have tried to address this with a distributed underlying virtual human architecture. Given the distributed nature of the architecture, we are able to replace components without large integration efforts, which reduces the time needed to build or expand a given application. Additionally a set of tools is continually being developed to ease the task of creating these characters. The major components in the system, as seen in Figure 1 are:

- **Speech Recognition:** digitizes the user's speech and produces a string of words as output.
- **Natural Language Understanding and Dialogue Management:** parses the word string produced by speech recognition and extracts meaning and concepts to form an internal semantic representation.
- **Intelligent Agent:** reasons about plans and generates actions based on its internal state and the input from the verbal text or other multi-modal devices. Complex agents can be created using a cognitive architecture that reason about plans and actions and integrate a dialog manager and emotion model. Simple agents can be created with

Figure 1. Virtual patient data flow diagram

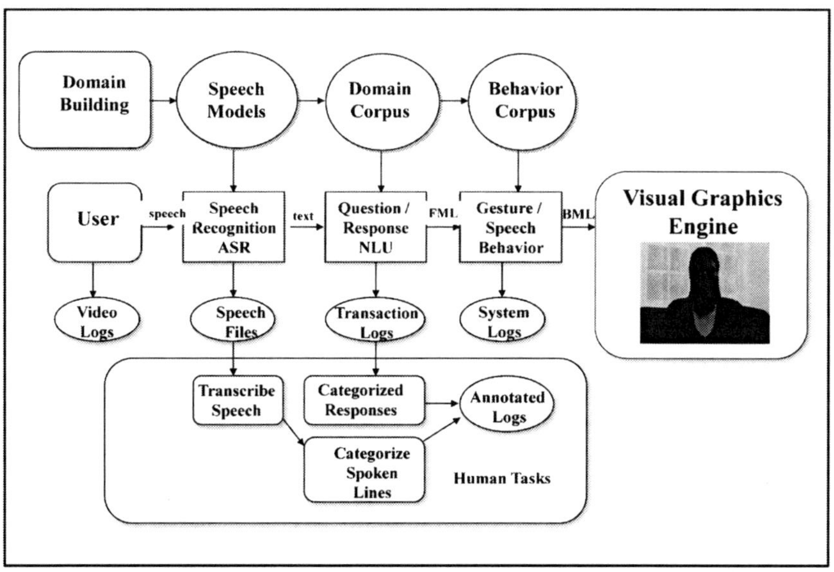

a question response system that picks a response based on statistical analysis of the input text. The output of the agent is a response output string and actions.

- **Non-Verbal Behavior Generation:** takes the response output string and applies a set of rules to select gestures, postures and gazes for the virtual characters.
- **Procedural Animation System:** synchronizes speech output with gestures and other non-verbal behavior to control the characters in the virtual environment.
- **Speech Generation:** performs speech synthesis from the text generated by the agent. Or alternatively a set of pre-recorded voice strings can be used as the speech.
- **Game Engine Graphic Display:** is the current underlying graphics engine used to display the character and virtual environment.

Building on the VH technology, VSPs fulfill the role of standardized patients by simulating a particular clinical presentation with a high degree of consistency and realism (Stevens et al., 2005). There is a growing field of research that applies VSPs to training and assessment of bioethics, basic patient communication, interactive conversations, history taking, and clinical assessments (Bickmore &Giorgino, 2006; Bickmore et al., 2007; Lok et al., 2006; Parsons et al., 2008). Results suggest that VSPs can provide valid and reliable representations of live patients (Kenny et al., 2007; Triola et al., 2006; Andrew et al., 2007). Additionally VSPs enable a precise presentation and control of dynamic perceptual stimuli; along with conversational dialog and interactions, they have the potential to provide ecologically valid assessments that combine the veridical control and rigor of laboratory measures approaching a verisimilitude that reflects real life situations (Parsons et al., 2008; Andrew et al., 2007).

Herein the reader will find a description of attempts in this author's lab to advance the state of the art in VSPs. Prototypes have been developed for mental health assessment (Kenny et al., 2007; Kenny et al., 2008a; Kenny et al., 2008b; Kenny et al., 2009; Parsons et al., 2009a) and extended the behavioral fidelity necessary to support such diagnoses (e.g., physical appearance, gestures and facial expressions, reactions to pain, sweating, etc.).

VIRTUAL STANDARDIZED PATIENT

The general architecture supports a wide range of VHs from simple question/answering to more complex ones that contain cognitive and emotional models with goal oriented behavior. The architecture is a modular distributed system with many components that communicate by message passing. Interaction with the system works as follows: the trainee talks into a microphone which records the audio signal that is sent to a speech recognition engine. The speech engine converts the signal into text. The text is then sent to a statistical natural language system that matches the input text to a question/answer pair which selects an answer. The answer is sent to a non-verbal module which applies rules to create the appropriate gestures and behaviors. A procedural animation system then synchronizes the gestures, speech and lip synching and plays a pre-recorded or generated voice of the input text for the character for final output to the screen. The user then listens to the response and asks more questions to the character.

Design and Simulation of Pathologies

One of the challenges of building complex interactive VSPs that can act as simulated patients has been in enabling the characters to act and carry on a dialog like a real patient that has the specific mental condition in the domain of interest. Additional issues involve the breadth and depth of expertise required in the psychological domain to generate the relevant material for the character and dialog.

Virtual Standardized Patient: Conduct Disorder

Teaching interviewing skills with VHs and VSPs is still a young discipline. There are no standard methods and metrics. The larger problem of teaching general interviewing skills is even less distinct as there are many techniques and it is not well understood how to properly implement those with a VSP. To alleviate this problem this author's lab at USC/ICT is concentrating on teaching skills required to diagnose a particular disorder. For example, we have developed a VSP with conduct disorder. Through an iterative process a proficient training set was developed. The first project involved the construction of a natural language-capable VSP named "Justin." The clinical attributes of Justin were developed to emulate a conduct disorder profile as found in the Diagnostic and Statistical Manual of Mental Disorders (DSM IV-TR). Justin (see Figure 2) portrays a 16-year old male with conduct disorder who is being forced to participate in therapy by his family. Justin's history is significant for a chronic pattern of antisocial behavior in which the basic rights of others and age-appropriate societal norms are violated. He has stolen, been truant, broken into someone's car, been cruel to animals, and initiated physical fights (see Figure 2). Our goal was to obtain objective data from an initial intake interview. This was accomplished by evaluating the questions asked by the trainee to the VSP and the corresponding answers.

The trainee's interview questions were guided by the need to determine if the patient is internalizing or externalizing behaviors and for eliciting information regarding the four general symptom categories prevalent in conduct disorder:

- **Aggressive behavior:** fighting, bullying, being cruel to others or animals
- **Destructive behavior:** arson, vandalism
- **Deceitful behavior:** repeated lying, shoplifting, breaking into homes or cars
- **Violation of rules:** running away, engaging in non appropriate behavior for age

The VSP system is designed to provide answers to questions that target each of these categories and

Figure 2.

will respond to a variety of questions pertinent to these areas. Some responses by the VSP may be on target, off target, involve "brush away" responses, and in some cases, they may be irrelevant replies. The probability of a specific response being emitted is rated to the question asked. For example if the trainee asks: "How are things going at home" or "Are you having any problems at home" or "How are things going?". The system will respond with "My parents think I messed up." Further questions will lead to finding out that the patient has been running away. This will lead to marking one of the above categories true for the diagnosis in the trainees' interview. In order for the trainee to pass it will require responses in all of the categories. The total set of questions and responses are extracted from role playing exercises, initial subject testing, interviews with doctors and common sense for specific responses. In total a question set would consist of over 100-200 lines of text. The matching of questions to responses is a manual process with automated learning techniques to generate probability values.

Research has been completed to assess the system by (1) experimenter observation of the participants as they communicated with the VSP; and (2) questionnaires. To adequately evaluate the system, a number of areas were determined that were believed needed in the questionnaires:

- **Consistency:** The behavior of the VSP should match the behavior one would expect from a patient in such a condition (e.g. verbalization, gesture, posture, and appearance)
- **Adequacy:** The discourse between the VSP and the participants should provide adequate verbal and nonverbal communication
- **Proficiency:** The clarity, pace, utility of VSPs discourse with the participant
- **Quality:** The quality of the speech recognition of utterances spoken.

Basic usability findings revealed that the VSP had high-quality overall system performance. Participants reported that the system (1) simulated real-life experience; and (2) the verbal and nonverbal behavior was satisfactory. However, results also revealed that some participants found aspects of the experience "frustrating". For example, some participants complained that they were receiving anticipated responses and the system tended to repeat some responses too frequently. This was due to the speech recognition's inability to evaluate certain of the stimulus words. Further, there were too many "brush off" responses from the VSP when participant questions were outside the VSP's dialog set.

Although in the early stages of system development, initial outcomes have been favorable. We have collected (and continue to collect) quantitative and qualitative results. The VSPs fit well into usability testing. The clinicians in training were videotaped as they performed the interview with the VSP and this recording was stored for later analyses of their verbal communication, nonverbal behavior (e.g., gaze), and overall reaction to their interaction with the VSP. Ultimately, this reflects a general construct of believability. The construct of believability is typically understood as the extent to which data is regarded as true and credible. Among other factors, it may reflect an individual's assessment of the credibility of the data source, comparison to a commonly accepted standard, and previous experience (Magnenat-Thalmann et al., 2005). For the VSP work, this means that the clinicians compared their experience with the VSP to their general experience with human standardized patients and actual patients they see as a part of their clinical training. Findings suggested that the clinicians in training had positive response to the VSP and behaved as they normally would during a clinical encounter. However, two issues remain: (1) what was the phenomenological experience of these training clinicians as they interacted with the VSPs; and (2) how adequate are the appraisal models used in virtual human research at generating cognitive and emotional models (see discussion below: "2.2 Psychophysiology to enhance cognitive and affective models of virtual humans"). While the latter is lends itself well to a psychophysiological assessment approach (see discussion below: "2.2 Psychophysiology to enhance cognitive and affective models of virtual humans"), a review of the literature reveals that the former lends itself to theoretical speculation of the phenomenological experience of the clinician in training.

Phenomenonology of Clinical Encounters with Virtual Standardized Patients

The task of a clinician is exceedingly multi-faceted, involving concurrent awareness of the patient's verbal and nonverbal communication, self-regulation of the clinician's own observation and management of countertransference reactions (Sternberg, 2000). The training of the clinician grows out of, and is governed by, therapeutic experience. To focus on a clinical encounter with a virtual standardized patient, then, is to focus on a complex context characterized by the clinician in training as he or she interacts with the simulation. For the clinician in training, the VSP will need to aid their commitment to the integrity of the context within which each novice clinician encounters the VSPs and that is organized around certain determinable constitutive features. The phenomenological approach taken in this author's lab reflects the four phenomenological areas postulated by Zaner (2006) for phenomenologicaly addressing the therapeutic relation: (1) **Immersion:** attainment of clinical knowledge by a trainee requires that the novice clinician put out of action all the convictions he or she has been accepting up to now; (2) **Reflective-Attentive shift:** herein reflection involves a shift of focal attention from active involvement in clinical cases for their own sake, to considering them as examples of the practice; (3) **Appeal to Evidence:** regardless of the clinician in training's desire for "Immersion" and "Reflective-Attentive shift", there still needs to be a judgment on the basis of soundest available evidence; and (4) **Clinical Ethics:** to consult as an "ethicist" on a simulated case means that the training clinician be focused on the simulated situation (e.g. context, persons simulated, issues, etc.) itself, for its own sake.

It seems apparent that virtual patients will play an important role in the future of psychotherapy education for psychiatry residents and psychology trainees. The use of virtual patients could be implemented in several ways. For example, virtual patients could be developed to recognize the essential features and common pitfalls of an initial psychotherapy interview so that they could give more specific, relevant, and reliable verbal feedback to the residents involved. In addition, the use of virtual patients illustrating common problems such as acting out, transference, intrusive questions, or seductive behavior would allow residents to have an experience with these anxiety provoking situations in a simulated setting before they occur in their practice. Finally, performance in virtual patient scenarios could be used as an additional source of data for the assessment of resident competency in the psychotherapy domain.

An issue that is bound to come up when discussing the training of clinicians using a simulated patient is the resident's perception of being assessed against a non-human agent. For this author's work, this issue is understood as a phenomenological issue inherent in any therapeutic relation. Following Zaner's (2006) phenomenological approach (mentioned above), there are four areas of interest for the novice clinician's interaction with the virtual patient. First, there is the issue of "Immersion" and the extent to which the clinician in training immersible. This is an important issue, because this author's own research has found that the extent to which a participant is capable of "absorption" and "hypnotism" are very important for social science research using virtual reality. The propensity of participants to get involved passively in some activity and their ability to concentrate and block out distraction are important factors to consider when conducting a study. Likewise, evidence suggests that immersiveness and hypnotizability play a role in the outcome of studies using virtual environments. Research into these moderating individual traits is of value because such research may augment participant selection (Macedonio et al., 2007). Second, there is the related issue of the "Reflective-Attentive shift", in which the clinician's acceptance of a virtual patient approach may be limited by the extent to which the trainee is able to shift attention from active involvement in clinical cases with virtual standardized patients, to considering them as examples of the practice. Of course, there is still the issue of the "Appeal to Evidence" and this is where the simulation really needs to present a very plausible and believable scenario so that the clinician in training is able to offer a judgment on the basis of soundest available evidence. Finally, it will be up to the trainer to help the novice clinician understand that the interaction with the scenarios involves an ethical focus that "suspends belief" in the fidelity of the graphics so that the focus can be on a potential real life scenario.

Virtual Standardized Patient: Trauma Exposure

For the next VSP, this author's lab constructed an adolescent female character called Justina that had been the victim of an assault and showing signs of PTSD (see Figure 3). The technology used for the system is based on the virtual human technology developed at USC and is the same as what was used with the previous VSP 'Justin'.

PTSD Domain

The experience of victimization is a relatively common occurrence for both adolescents and adults. However, victimization is more widespread among adolescents, and its relationship to various problem outcomes tends to be stronger among adolescent victims than adult victims. Whilst much of the early research on the psychological sequelae of victimization focused on general distress or fear rather than specific symptoms of PTSD, anxiety, or depression, studies have consistently found significant positive correlations between PTSD and sexual assault, and victimization in general and violent victimization in particular (Norris et al., 1997). Although there

Figure 3.

are a number of perspectives on what constitutes trauma exposure in children and adolescents, there is a general consensus amongst clinicians and researchers that this is a substantial social problem (Resick & Nishith, 1997). The effects of trauma exposure manifest themselves in a wide range of symptoms: anxiety, post-trauma stress, fear, and various behavior problems. New clinicians need to come up to speed on how to interact, diagnose and treat this trauma.

According to the most recent revision to the American Psychiatric Association's DSM Disorders (2000), PTSD is divided into six major categories; refer to the DSM-IV category 309.81 for a full description and subcategories;

A. Past experience of a traumatic event and the response to the event.
B. Re-experiencing of the event with dreams, flashbacks and exposure to cues.
C. Persistent avoidance of trauma-related stimuli: thoughts, feelings, activities or places, and general numbing such as low affect and no sense of a future.
D. Persistent symptoms of anxiety or increased arousal such as hyper vigilance or jumpy, irritability, sleep difficulties or can't concentrate.
E. Duration of the disturbance, how long have they been experiencing this.
F. Effects on their life such as clinically significant distress or impairment in social or educational functioning or changes in mental states.

Diagnostic criteria for PTSD includes a history of exposure to a traumatic event in category A and meeting two criteria and symptoms from each B (i.e., re-experiencing), C (i.e., avoidance), and D (i.e., hypervigilance). The duration of E (i.e., duration of disturbance) is usually greater than one month and the effects on F (i.e., social functioning) can vary based on severity of the trauma. Effective interviewing skills are a core competency for the clinicians, residents and developing psychotherapists who will be working with children and adolescents exposed to trauma. A clinician needs to ask questions in each of these categories to properly assess the patient's condition.

We aimed primarily to evaluate whether a VSP generate responses that elicit user questions relevant for PTSD categorization. Findings suggest that the interactions between novice clinicians and the VSP resulted in a compatible dialectic in terms of rapport, discussion of the traumatic event, and the experience of intrusive recollections. Further, there appears to be a satisfactory amount of discussion related to the issue of avoidance. These results comport well with what one may expect from the VSP (Justina) system.

In some of our earlier work, we found that the individual characteristics of study participants may impact the immersiveness and subsequent findings of a given study. Of primary importance is the extent to which a participant is capable of "absorption" and "hypnotism." Hence, individual differences may moderate presence and confound findings. The propensity of participants to get involved passively in some activity and their ability to concentrate and block out distraction are important factors to consider when conducting a study. Likewise, evidence suggests that hypnotizability plays a role in the outcome of studies using VR. Research into these moderating individual traits is of value because such research may augment participant selection.

We applied these findings to our work with VSPs to investigate the relationship between a number of psychological variables and the resulting VSP responses. The primary goal in this study was evaluative: can a virtual standardized patient generate responses that elicit user questions relevant for PTSD categorization? Findings suggest that the interactions between novice clinicians and the VSP resulted in a compatible dialectic in terms of rapport, discussion of the traumatic event, and the experience of intrusive recollections. Further, there appears to be a fair amount of discussion related to the issue of avoidance. These results comport well with what one may expect from the VSP (Justina) system. Much of the focus was upon developing a lexicon that, at minimum, emphasized a VSP that had recently experienced a traumatic event and was attempting to avoid experienced that my lead to intrusive recollections. However, the interaction is not very strong when one turns to the issue of hyper-arousal and impact on social life. While the issue of impact on social life may simply reflect that we wanted to limit each question/response relation to only one category (hence, it may have been assigned to avoidance instead of social functioning), the lack of questions and responses related to hyper-arousal and duration of the illness reflects a potential limitation in the system lexicon. These areas are not necessarily negatives for the system as a whole. Instead, they should be viewed as potential deficits in the systems lexicon.

A secondary goal was to investigate the impact of psychological variables upon the VSP Question/Response composites and the general believability of the system. After controlling for the effects of these psychological variables, increased effects were found for discussion of the traumatic event, avoidance, individualized models for affect recognition hyper-arousal, and impact on social life. Further, the impact of psychological characteristics revealed strong effects upon presence and believability. These findings are consistent with other findings suggesting that hypnotizability, as defined by the applied measures, appears moderate user reaction. Future studies should make use of physiological data correlated with measures of immersion to augment and quantify the effects of virtual human scenarios.

There are several modalities such as facial expression, vocal intonation, gestures, and postures that are regularly used to evaluate and model the affective states of individuals interacting with a virtual human. In this author's lab, there is an attempt to take a take a multimodal approach that builds on the work of virtual human researchers, but extends the cognitive and affective modeling through the incorporation of psychophysiological data. This is done for the following reasons: (1) Psychophysiology is an important component left out of many cognitive and affective models used in virtual human research; and (2) physiological signals are continuously available and are arguably not directly impacted by technological limitations inherent in virtual human assessment of facial expression, vocal intonation, gestures, and postures.

Psychophysiology to Enhance Cognitive and Affective Models of Virtual Humans

Current cognitive and affective models found in virtual human research tend to use appraisal models that specify how events, agents and objects are used to elicit an emotional response depending on a set of parameters (e.g., goals, standards and attitudes) representing the subject. In principle, it is possible to model appraisal processes using classical symbolic AI techniques (Picard, 1997; Chwelos & Oatley, 1994). However, cognitive and affective models of virtual humans do not generally account for neurophysiological data (Fellous, Armony, & LeDoux, 2003). Further, as Magnenat-Thalmann and Thalmann (2005) have pointed out in their review of virtual human research, virtual human models of emotional responses tend to be generated from a cognitive point of view and do not adequately take into account the psychophysiological response. Although appraisal does play a role in many current theories of emotion, most contemporary psychologists studying emotion emphasize the importance of psychophysiological arousal and that emotions are to be understood as cognitive appraisals and are accompanied by autonomic nervous system activity.

Although many appraisal models contend that cognitive processes (e.g., sensory perception) present verification for the preeminence of appraisal in emotion, other theorists indicate that appraisal processes occur following perception and represent a separate cognitive process (Izard, 1993). Of course, while most would agree that perception is a necessary part of any sensory experience, it is not known whether perceptual processes are the foundation of cognitive models of emotion or if these emotions are concerned with higher order cognitive appraisals that assign meaning and valence (Eckhardt, Norlander, & Deffenbacher, 2004).

A major limitation to many appraisal models found in virtual human research is that they follow outdated appraisal models that assert specific patterns of physiological changes that may be observed in affect occurrence after the subjective experience of affect. Research in psychophysiology has not supported these cognition first models (Cox & Harrison, 2008). In fact, a common frustration to attempts at developing an adequate scientific approach to emotion has been focus upon constructing theories of the subjective appraisals. Again studies of the neural basis of emotion and emotional learning have instead focused on how the brain detects and evaluates emotional stimuli and how, on the basis of such evaluations, emotional responses are produced (Magnenat-Thalmann & Thalmann, 2005).

This author believes that a preferred approach to developing cognitive and emotional virtual human models would include psychophysiological inputs from the humans to the virtual humans during interactions. It is believed that these additional inputs can be developed into affect-sensitive VSP interfaces that go beyond conventional virtual human models designed by pure (i.e., devoid of psychophysiological metrics) cognitive appraisal principles. The resulting affect-sensitive VSP interfaces would be similar to brain-based-devices (BBDs) that are being designed based on biological principles and are programmed to alter their behavior to the environment through self-learning (Edelman, 2006). An example of such research is found in work to develop intelligent robots. A series of devices with sensors and computer-simulated brains have been built in Gerald Edelman's (2006) Neurosciences Institute in La Jolla. The brains are modeled on human anatomy, complete with versions of visual cortex, inferotemporal cortex, and hippocampus. They are not pre-programmed, but evolve neuronal connections in response to experience. These devices can learn to recognize patterns and navigate novel environments.

Although the development of such computational models for virtual humans would be difficult, researchers (Magnenat-Thalmann & Thalmann, 2005) have pointed out that computational approaches to emotional processing are both possible and practical. In the following, there is a description of preliminary attempts at incorporating psychophysiological metrics into an affect-sensitive VSP interface system. Our goal is to first develop the interface and then build upon the interface to model affect and enhance the VSPs' cognitive and affective models.

Psychophysiology to Enhance Cognitive and Affective Assessment of User

The tendency of virtual human researchers to rely upon modalities such as facial expression, vocal intonation, gestures, and postures results in limitations due to "communicative impairments" (both nonverbal and verbal) inherent in the technology. This is very much the case regarding expression of affective states. Although these vulnerabilities place limits on traditional conversational and observational methodologies found in much virtual human research, psychophysiological signals are (1) continuously available; and (2) are arguably not directly impacted by these difficulties. As a result, psychophysiological metrics may proffer an approach for gathering robust data despite potential virtual human technology limitations. Furthermore, there is evidence that psychophysiological activity of persons immersed in virtual environments is associated with (1) trait differences (immersability; Macedonio, 2007) and (2) state differences (intensity of the environment; Parsons et al., 2009b, Parsons et al., 2009c; Meehan et al., 2005). These findings from virtual reality research reflect the finding that transition from one affective state to another is accompanied by dynamic shifts in indicators of autonomic nervous system activity (Bradley, 2005).

Psychophysiologically-Driven Interfaces for Adaptive Virtual Standardized Patients

According to Fairclough (2009), the next generation of intelligent technology will be characterized by increased autonomy and adaptive capability. Such intelligent systems need to have ample capacity for real-time responsivity (Aarts, 2004). For example, to decrease the intensity of a simulation if a user is overloaded by stimuli within a learning environment, or to make the simulation more challenging if the user is bored. The psychophysiological computing approach proffers the VSP a means of monitoring, quantifying, and representing user context and adapt in real-time.

A primary focus of the work described herein is the development of VSPs that are capable of real-time adaptive responding to affective processing of novice clinicians during clinical training paradigms and to enhance cognitive and affective models of virtual human technology. In what follows, there is a description of the current VSP task design and affective modeling techniques that are used during studies of interactions between novice clinicians and VSPs. The biocybernetic adaptation (Pope et al., 1995) of the affect-sensitive VSP system during interaction with a novice clinician can be summarized as follows: First, psychophysiological signals from the novice clinician are recorded while she is interacting with the VSP system. Next, the psychophysiological signals are filtered and quantified to operationalize relevant psychological constructs (e.g., frustration, user engagement, alertness) for incorporation into a unique psychophysiological profile for that user. 3) The psychophysiological profile is input into a database that has been developed from expert opinion, psychophysiology literature, and multimodal data (facial expression, vocal intonation, gestures, postures, dialectical interactions, and psychophysiology) gleaned from previous subjects interacting with VSPs (Kenny et al., 2007; Kenny et al., 2008a; Kenny et al., 2008b; Kenny et al., 2009; Parsons et al., 2009a). The VSP system next finds the best matching stimuli from its databases with respect to the intensity level of an affective state. An assessment of user state may be achieved via the development of discriminant algorithms (Liu, Rani, & Sarkar, 2005) or neural networks (Gevins et al., 1998; Laine et al., 2002). Finally, the system adapts the VSP's representation of the interaction and behavior accordingly.

Psychophysiology and Affect Modeling

Individual (Parsons et al., 2009b) and cohort (Parsons et al., 2009d) differences have been shown to impact results gleaned from psychophysiological assessments using virtual environments, which reflects the need for psychophysiological assessment of persons interacting with VSPs. In addition to extending the validation of VSPs, this author's lab uses psychophysiological metrics to develop a psychophysiological interface for VSPs that can adapt VSP scenarios to the user's psychophysiological processing of information. More specifically, psychophysiological measures such as heart rate, skin conductance responses, facial electromyographic response recordings, respiration, electroencephalographic recordings, and eyetracking can be continuously recorded while subjects interact with the VSP. These recordings can be processed in real time to gain information about the user's current state of emotional and cognitive processing. This information can then be relayed to the virtual environment in order to change for example, the behavior of the VSP. If the user is distressed by the current state of the interaction, a psychophysiological pattern of increased heart rate, increased skin conductance levels, a more rapid rate of respiration, increased corrugator muscle activity, decreased alpha wave activity and diversion of gaze may develop. Allowing for access to this information about the user's current emotional state offers the VSP an increased capability to understand the dynamics of the current interaction and develop a context appropriate response or behavior change.

In order to have reliable reference points, this author's lab has been running subjects through a protocol in which they interact with our VSPs. A primary goal has been to develop a reference knowledge database that is based on relevant data from literature, expert consensus, and actual psychophysiological data gleaned from persons interacting with VSPs.

Virtual Standardized Patient: Assessing Bias

Data for the reference knowledge database is initially being modeled off of data from previous experiments. In addition to the experiments mentioned above, this author's lab has also run subjects through protocols in which we measured the activation and control of affective bias using 1) startle eye blink responses; and 2) self-reports as human participants interacted with VSPs representing both the human's race and another race (Parsons et al., 2009a). We also assessed the differences in psychophysiological responses of humans interacting with VSPs representing same and different sex groups. By measuring eyeblink responses to startle probes occurring at short and long latencies following the onset of same compared with other ethnicity VSPs, we were able to examine affective processes associated with both the activation and potential control of bias.

A number of studies have used startle eye blink to successfully detect positive and negative affective responses (Blascovich, 2000; Lang, 1995). Startle eye blink has been found to adequately detect implicit affective race bias (Amodio, Harmon-Jones, & Devine, 2003). Part of the reason that the startle response is a good choice for this research is that a relatively simple and brief, but intense stimulus (i.e., usually a 100 db, 50 ms burst of static) can result in a primitive, defensive reflex. In previous studies, researchers have found that the startle response is increased or potentiated by stimuli that evoke a negative affective response and decreased or inhibited by stimuli that evoke a pleasant affective response or appetitive stimuli (Lang, 1995). The startle response has also been shown to be effective in predicting affective reactions to people of a particular race (Amodio et al., 2004).

Individual differences in levels of bias were predicted using E. A. Plant and P. G. Devine's (1998) Internal and External Motivation to Respond without Prejudice scales (IMS/EMS). Since participants with varying levels of IMS and EMS may differ in their responses to general affective stimuli unrelated to ethnicity, we presented general affective pictures from the International Affective Picture System (IAPS; Lang, Bradley, & Cuthbert, 2005). Finally, we obtained participants' responses to the Attitude Toward Blacks/Whites scale to compare the predictive ability of both the VSP interaction and the IMS–EMS with a traditional attitude measure of prejudice.

Eye blinks were collected and scored as electromygraphic (EMG) activity of the orbicularis oculi muscle of the left eye according to standard procedures (Blumenthal et al., 2005; Biopac, Santa Barbara, CA). One small (4 mm) silver-silver chloride (Ag-AgCl) electrode was placed on the left eyelid directly below the pupil while a second 4 mm electrode was placed approximately 1 cm lateral to the first. The impedance between the two electrodes was measured and deemed acceptable if below 10 KΩ. A large (8 mm) Ag-AgCl electrode was placed behind the left ear to serve as a common ground. Startle blinks were identified in each portion of the recordings as follows:

an interval (from 20 to 150 ms) adjacent to each startle probe was searched for the largest spike whose absolute value exceeds a high threshold (of 150 μV).

A difference score between the median blink amplitude to African American VSPs and Caucasian VSPs was determined. The difference score was then analyzed in terms of IMS and EMS scores. As all participants reported similar levels of internal motivation to respond without racism, they were separated into two groups of higher and lower external motivation scores. A one-way ANOVA was performed to determine if high vs. low external motivation related to physiological responses to different racial groups of virtual patients. The difference score tended to be lower in those with high external motivation to behave in a non-racist manner. Those who were lower in external motivation had a larger difference score between startle amplitudes while looking at African American vs. Caucasian VSPs.

The larger difference score reflects larger startle amplitudes to African American VSPs, suggesting an implicit negative bias towards that group. The difference between the low EMS and high EMS groups was not significant but suggests need for future analyses into the ways in which motivations can influence behavior at even automatic levels.

While the findings of the study are interesting, our current interest in this dataset is the modeling of user representation. We are currently running additional subjects to enhance the modeling through the inclusion of other modalities such as facial expression, vocal intonation, gestures, and postures, which may be amalgamated with psychophysiology to increase the complexity of the user representation.

Psychophysiological Computing as a Means of Providing User Context

Psychophysiological computing represents an innovative mode of human computer interaction (HCI) where system interaction is achieved by monitoring, analyzing and responding to covert psychophysiological activity from the user in real-time (Parsons et al., 2009a; Parsons et al., 2009c; Plant & Devine, 1998; Allanson & Fairclough, 2004). These systems operate by transforming psychophysiological data into a control signal (or an input to a control signal) without a requirement for any overt response from the user.

Psychophysiological computing captures spontaneous and subconscious facets of user state, opening up bandwidth within the HCI by enabling an additional channel of communication from the user to the VSP. As such, information exchange between human and VSP is rendered symmetrical as the psychophysiological interface constructs, consults and responds to a dynamic representation of the user.

Psychophysiological Assessment

We are collecting psychophysiological (e.g. heart rate; skin conductance; respiration; etc) data from users at USC via Biopac sensors. These data are being filtered and quantified to operationalize relevant psychological constructs (e.g., frustration, user engagement, alertness). These data will be correlated with other metrics (e.g. verbal and nonverbal receptive language) to enhance user interactions with the VSP. Specifically, we aim to gain psychophysiological data that we will analyze in order to quantify or label the state of the user so that we may develop an affect-sensitive VSP interface system. Following Fairclough (2009), we envision user state assessment as something being made with reference to absolute (e.g., heart rate exceeds 80 percent of normal baseline) or relative criteria (e.g., heart rate has risen 20 percent since the previous data collection epoch); alternatively, the assessment provided by the system may be categorical in nature (e.g., pattern of heart rate activity and changes in skin conductance level indicate that the person is in a negative rather than a positive emotional state). Based upon the user's psychophysiological responses to interacting with the VSP, enhancements may be made to the VSP's interactivity.

Psychophysiological Validity

As part of our ongoing data collection and data analytic process, we are endeavoring to validate the psychophysiological protocol: 1) Content validity is being established through careful selection of psychophysiological variables based on a review of existing literature (i.e., that a precedent exists for specific variables to tap those psychological constructs targeted by the system designer); and 2) Concurrent validity of the psychophysiological interface (i.e., degree to which a particular psychophysiological measure(s) can be demonstrated to predict the target psychological dimension). Further, we are establishing the reliability of the psychophysiological inference across a range of representative test conditions (e.g., high vs. low levels of operator stress) and individual differences among users.

VIRTUAL STANDARDIZED PATIENTS FOR TECHNOLOGY INTEGRATION IN HIGHER EDUCATION

Although traditional approaches to training clinicians in the interpersonal communication skills currently include a combination of classroom learning and role-playing with human standardized patients, there are limitations that can be mitigated through the integration of simulation technology. For example, while human standardized patients are expensive and cost several thousand dollars per student, the integration of virtual patient technology into the curriculum would be relatively inexpensive because it would require a one time programming cost. Further, given the fact that there are only a handful of sites (for over 130 medical schools in the U.S.) providing standardized patient assessments of the clinician in training's communication ability as part of the U.S. Medical Licensing Examination (USMLE), the current model provides limited availability. The integration of virtual patient technology would allow for the exact same virtual patient technology to be integrated and implemented at multiple locations. Another concern is the issue of standardization. Despite the expense of standardized patient programs, the standardized patients themselves are typically unskilled actors. As a result of common turnover, administrators face considerable challenges for offering psychometrically reliable and valid interactions with the training clinicians. The integration of virtual patients would allow for a standardized administration, standardized scoring, and standardized interpretation of the novice clinicians learning across multiple presentations and interactions. A related issue is the limited scope that the actors are able to portray. As a result, there tends to be an inadequate array of developmentally, socially, and culturally appropriate scenarios. For example, when a clinician has a pediatric focus and needs access to children, it is difficult for the clinician to pretend that the actor is a child. Finally, many clinical cases (e.g., traumatic brain injury) have associated physical symptoms and behaviors (e.g., dilated pupils, spasms, and uncoordinated movements). While these signs and symptoms simply cannot be accurately portrayed by human actors, they are a relatively straightforward programming issue for use with a virtual standardized patient.

As discussed above there are a number of ways in which the integration of virtual standardized patient technology can enhance clinical training in communication. The contribution of a virtual standardized patient to increased doctor patient communication is important and may enhance multifarious aspects of health outcomes. For example, increased doctor patient communication has been found to offer elevated compliance (Cegala, 2000), improved health outcomes (Stewert et al., 1995), increased patient satisfaction (Jackson, 2001), and a decrease in malpractice risk (Levinson and Roter, 1997). Given a virtual standardized patient's ability to simulate a particular clinical presentation with a high degree of consistency and realism, a virtual standardized patient may increase communication skills. Further, virtual standardized patients can be developed for special populations (e.g., children; octogenarians; neurological disorders) that cannot be adequately represented by a human actor (human standardized patient). Hence, a virtual standardized patient may help clinicians, educators, and health service administrators better understand clinician-patient communication that is unique.

CONCLUSION

In this chapter, there was a discussion of the ways in which advanced technologies (i.e., virtual standardized patients can move beyond traditional approaches to training clinicians in assessment, diagnosis, interviewing and interpersonal communication. The traditional approaches rely upon a combination of classroom learning and role-playing with human standardized patients. Much of this work is done with actors that have been recruited and trained to exhibit the characteristics of an actual patient, thereby affording novice clinicians a realistic opportunity to practice and to be evaluated in a mock clinical environment. Although a valuable training approach, there are limitations with the use of human standardized patients that can be mitigated through simulation technology. For example, human standardized patients are expensive and cost several thousand dollars per student. Further, given the fact that there are only a few sites providing standardized patient assessments as part of the U.S. Medical Licensing Examination, the current model provides limited availability.

In addition to issues of availability of trained actors, there is the issue of standardization. Despite the expense of standardized patient programs, the standardized patients themselves are typically unskilled actors. As a result of common turnover, administrators face considerable challenges for offering psychometrically reliable and valid interactions with the training clinicians. A related issue is the limited scope that the actors are able to portray. As a result, there tends to be an inadequate array of developmentally, socially, and culturally appropriate scenarios. For example, when a clinician has a pediatric focus and needs access to children, it is difficult for the clinician to pretend that the actor is a child. Finally, many clinical cases (e.g., traumatic brain injury) have associated physical symptoms and behaviors (e.g., dilated pupils, spasms, and uncoordinated movements) that simply cannot be accurately portrayed by human actors.

In this chapter a series of experiments were described to elucidate the usefulness and effectiveness of an affect-sensitive VSP Interface System. While self- report data are widely used in virtual human research, they are susceptible to modification by a participant's awareness of the social desirability of particular responses, reducing the sensitivity of the measures, implicit behavioral and psychophysiological responses are automatic and thus considered less susceptible to self-conscious influences (Schwarz, 1999). A further issue discussed in this paper was that the current cognitive and affective models found in virtual human research tend to use appraisal models generated from a cognitive point of view and do not adequately take into account the psychophysiological response.

It was contended that a preferred approach to developing cognitive and emotional virtual human models would include psychophysiological inputs from the humans to the virtual humans during interactions. It is believed that these additional inputs can be developed into affect-sensitive VSP interfaces that go beyond conventional virtual human models designed by pure (i.e., devoid of psychophysiological metrics) cognitive appraisal principles. The resulting affect-sensitive VSP interfaces would be similar to brain-based-devices (BBDs) that are being designed based on biological principles and are programmed to alter their behavior to the environment through self-learning.

In summary, effective interview skills are a core competency for training clinicians. Although schools commonly make use of standardized patients to teach interview skills, the diversity of the scenarios standardized patients can characterize is limited by availability of human actors. Further, there is the economic concern related to the time and money needed to train standardized patients. Perhaps most damaging is the "standardization" of standardized patients—will they in fact consistently proffer psychometrically reliable and valid interactions with the training clinicians. Virtual Human Agent technology (e.g., virtual standardized patients) has evolved to a point where researchers may begin developing mental health applications that make use of virtual reality patients for training.

REFERENCES

Aarts, E. (2004). Ambient intelligence. A multimedia perspective. *IEEE MultiMedia, 11*, 12–19. doi:10.1109/MMUL.2004.1261101

Accreditation Council for Graduate Medical Education. ACGME Outcome Project.(2010). Retrieved December 5, 2007 from www.acgme.org/Outcomes.

Allanson, J., & Fairclough, S. H. (2004). A research agenda for physiological computing. *Interacting with Computers, 16*, 857–878. doi:10.1016/j.intcom.2004.08.001

Amodio, D. M., Harmon-Jones, E., & Devine, P. G. (2003). Individual differences in the activation and control of affective race bias as assessed by startle eyeblink responses and self-report. *Journal of Personality and Social Psychology, 84*, 738–753. doi:10.1037/0022-3514.84.4.738

Amodio, D. M., Harmon-Jones, E., Devine, P. G., Curtin, J. J., Hartley, S. L., & Covert, A. E. (2004). Neural signals for the detection of unintentional race bias. *Psychological Science, 15*, 88–93. doi:10.1111/j.0963-7214.2004.01502003.x

Andrew, R., & Johnsen, K. (2007). Comparing Interpersonal Interactions with a Virtual Human to those with a Real Human. *IEEE Transactions on Visualization and Computer Graphics, 13*, 443–457.

Bickmore, T., & Giorgino, T. (2006). Health Dialog Systems for Patients and Consumers. *Journal of Biomedical Informatics, 39*, 556–571. doi:10.1016/j.jbi.2005.12.004

Bickmore, T., Pfeifer, L., & Paasche-Orlow, M. (2007). Health Document Explanation by Virtual Agents. *Lecture Notes in Computer Science, 4722*, 183–196. doi:10.1007/978-3-540-74997-4_18

Blascovich, J. (2000). Psychophysiological methods. In Reis, H. T., & Judd, C. M. (Eds.), *Handbook of research methods in social and personality psychology* (pp. 117–137). Cambridge, UK: Cambridge University Press.

Blumenthal, T. D., Cuthbert, B. N., Filion, D. L., Hackley, S., Lipp, O. V., & van Boxtel, A. (2005). Committee report: Guidelines for human startle eyeblink electromyographic studies. *Psychophysiology, 42*, 1–15. doi:10.1111/j.1469-8986.2005.00271.x

Bradley, M. (2000). Emotion and motivation. In Cacioppo, J. T., Tassinary, L. G., & Berntson, G. (Eds.), *Handbook of Psychophysiology*. New York: Cambridge University Press.

Cegala, D. J., Marinelli, T., & Post, D. (2000). The effects of patient communication skills training on compliance. *Archives of Family Medicine, 9*, 57–64. doi:10.1001/archfami.9.1.57

Chant, S., Jenkinson, T., Randle, J., Russell, G., & Webb, C. (2002). Communication skills training in healthcare: A review of the literature. *Nurse Education Today, 22*, 189–202. doi:10.1054/nedt.2001.0690

Chwelos, G., & Oatley, K. (1994). Appraisal, Computational Models, and Scherer's Expert System. *Cognition and Emotion, 8*, 245–257. doi:10.1080/02699939408408940

Cox, D. E., & Harrison, D. W. (2008). Models of anger: contributions from psychophysiology, neuropsychology and the cognitive behavioral perspective. *Brain Structure & Function, 212*, 371–385. doi:10.1007/s00429-007-0168-7

DSM, American Psychiatric Association. (2000). *Diagnostic and statistical manual of mental disorders (4th edn, text revision)*. Washington, DC: American Psychiatric Press, Inc.

Eckhardt, C. I., Norlander, B., & Deffenbacher, J. (2004). The assessment of anger and hostility: a critical review. *Aggression and Violent Behavior, 9*, 17–43. doi:10.1016/S1359-1789(02)00116-7

Edelman, G. M. (2006). *Second Nature: Brain Science and Human Knowledge*. New Have, CT: Yale University Press.

Fairclough, S. H. (2009). Fundamentals of physiological computing. *Interacting with Computers, 21*, 133–145. doi:10.1016/j.intcom.2008.10.011

Fellous, J.-M., Armony, J. L., & LeDoux, J. E. (2003). *Emotional Circuits and Computational Neuroscience. The Handbook of Brain Theory and Neural Networks* (pp. 398–401). Cambridge, MA: The MIT Press.

Gevins, A., Smith, M. E., Leong, H., McEvoy, L., Whitfield, S., & Du, R. (1998). Monitoring working memory load during computer-based tasks with eeg pattern recognition models. *Human Factors, 40*, 79–91. doi:10.1518/001872098779480578

Gratch, J., & Marsella, S. (2004). A domain independent framework for modeling emotion. *Journal of Cognitive Systems Research., 5*, 269–306. doi:10.1016/j.cogsys.2004.02.002

Gratch, J., & Rickel, J. (2002). Creating Interactive Virtual Humans: Some Assembly Required. *IEEE Intelligent Systems*, (July/August): 54–61. doi:10.1109/MIS.2002.1024753

Hulsman, R. L., Gos, W. J. G., Winnubst, J. A. M., & Bensing, J. M. (1999). Teaching clinically experienced physicians communication skills: A review of evaluation studies. *Medical Education, 33*, 655–668. doi:10.1046/j.1365-2923.1999.00519.x

Izard, C. E. (1993). Organizational and motivational functions of discrete emotions. In Lewis, M., & Haviland, J. M. (Eds.), *Handbook of emotions*. New York: Guilford Press.

Jackson, J. L., Chamberlin, J., & Kroenke, K. (2001). Predictors of patient satisfaction. *Social Science & Medicine, 52*, 609–620. doi:10.1016/S0277-9536(00)00164-7

Kenny, P., Parsons, T. D., Gratch, J., Leuski, A., & Rizzo, A. A. (2007). Virtual Patients for Clinical Therapist Skills Training. *Lecture Notes in Artificial Intelligence, 4722*, 197–210.

Kenny, P., Parsons, T. D., Gratch, J., & Rizzo, A. A. (2008b). Evaluation of Justina: A Virtual Patient with PTSD. *Lecture Notes in Artificial Intelligence, 5208*, 394–408.

Kenny, P., Parsons, T. D., Pataki, C. S., Pato, M., St-George, C., Sugar, J., & Rizzo, A. A. (2008a). Virtual Justina: A PTSD Virtual Patient for Clinical Classroom Training. *Annual Review of Cybertherapy and Telemedicine, 6*, 113–118.

Kenny, P., Parsons, T. D., & Rizzo, A. A. (2009). Human Computer Interaction in Virtual Standardized Patient Systems. *Lecture Notes in Computer Science, 5613*, 514–523. doi:10.1007/978-3-642-02583-9_56

Kenny, P., Rizzo, A. A., Parsons, T. D., Gratch, J., & Swartout, W. (2007). A Virtual Human Agent for Training Novice Therapist Clinical Interviewing Skills. *Annual Review of Cybertherapy and Telemedicine*, *5*, 81–89.

Laine, T. I., Bauer, K. W., Lanning, J. W., Russell, C. A., & Wilson, G. F. (2002). Selection of input features across subjects for classifying crewmember workload using artificial neural networks. *IEEE Transactions on Systems, Man, and Cybernetics. Part A, Systems and Humans*, *32*, 691–704. doi:10.1109/TSMCA.2002.807036

Lang, P. J. (1995). The emotion probe: Studies of motivation and attention. *The American Psychologist*, *50*, 372–385. doi:10.1037/0003-066X.50.5.372

Lang, P. J., Bradley, M. M., & Cuthbert, B. N. (2005). *The International Affective Picture System (IAPS)*. University of Florida.

Levinson, W., & Roter, D. L. (1997). Physician-patient communication: The relationship with malpractice claims among primary care physicians and surgeons. *Journal of the American Medical Association*, *277*, 553–559. doi:10.1001/jama.277.7.553

Liu, C., Rani, P., & Sarkar, N. (2005). An empirical study of machine learning techniques for affect recognition in human-robot interaction. *Paper presented at the IEEE Conference on Intelligent Robots and Systems.*

Lok, B., Ferdig, R., Raij, A., Johnsen, K., Dickerson, R., & Coutts, J. (2006). Applying Virtual Reality in Medical Communication Education: Current Findings and Potential Teaching and Learning Benefits of Immersive Virtual Patients. *Journal of Virtual Reality.*, *10*, 185–195. doi:10.1007/s10055-006-0037-3

Macedonio, M., Parsons, T. D., & Rizzo, A. A. (2007). Immersiveness and Physiological Arousal within Panoramic Video-based Virtual Reality. *Cyberpsychology & Behavior*, *10*, 508–516. doi:10.1089/cpb.2007.9997

Magnenat-Thalmann, N., Kim, H., Egges, A., & Garchery, S. (2005). Believability and Interaction in Virtual Worlds. *Proceedings of the 11th International Multimedia Modelling Conference* (pp. 2-9).

Magnenat-Thalmann, N., & Thalmann, D. (2005). Virtual Humans: Thirty Years Of Research, What Next? *The Visual Computer*, *21*, 1–19. doi:10.1007/s00371-004-0243-5

Meehan, M., Razzaque, S., Insko, B., Whitton, M., & Brooks, F. P. Jr. (2005). Review of four studies on the use of physiological reaction as a measure of presence in stressful virtual environments. *Applied Psychophysiology and Biofeedback*, *30*, 239–258. doi:10.1007/s10484-005-6381-3

Morency, L.-P., & de Kok, I. (2008). Context-based Recognition during Human Interactions: Automatic Feature Selection and Encoding Dictionary. *10th International Conference on Multimodal Interfaces*, Chania, Greece, IEEE.

Norris, F. H., Kaniasty, K., & Thompson, M. P. (1997). The psychological consequences of crime: Findings from a longitudinal population-based study. In Davis, R. C., Lurigio, A. J., & Skogan, W. G. (Eds.), *Victims of Crime* (2nd ed., pp. 146–166). Thousand Oaks, CA: Sage Publications Inc.

Parsons, T. D., Cosand, L., Courtney, C., Iyer, A., & Rizzo, A. A. (2009c). Neurocognitive Workload Assessment using the Virtual Reality Cognitive Performance Assessment Test. *Lecture Notes in Artificial Intelligence*, *5639*, 243–252.

Parsons, T. D., Courtney, C., Cosand, L., Iyer, A., Rizzo, A. A., & Oie, K. (2009d). Assessment of Psychophysiological Differences of West Point Cadets and Civilian Controls Immersed within a Virtual Environment. *Lecture Notes in Artificial Intelligence*, *5638*, 514–523.

Parsons, T. D., Iyer, A., Cosand, L., Courtney, C., & Rizzo, A. A. (2009b). Neurocognitive and Psychophysiological Analysis of Human Performance within Virtual Reality Environments. *Studies in Health Technology and Informatics*, *142*, 247–252.

Parsons, T. D., Kenny, P., Cosand, L., Iyer, A., Courtney, C., & Rizzo, A. A. (2009a). A Virtual Human Agent for Assessing Bias in Novice Therapists. *Studies in Health Technology and Informatics*, *142*, 253–258.

Parsons, T. D., Kenny, P., Ntuen, C., Pataki, C. S., Pato, M., & Rizzo, A. A. (2008). Objective Structured Clinical Interview Training using a Virtual Human Patient. *Studies in Health Technology and Informatics*, *132*, 357–362.

Picard, R. W. (1997). *Affective Computing*. Cambridge, MA: M.I.T Press.

Plant, A. E., & Devine, P. G. (1998). Internal and external motivation to respond without prejudice. *Journal of Personality and Social Psychology*, *75*, 811–832. doi:10.1037/0022-3514.75.3.811

Pope, A. T., Bogart, E. H., & Bartolome, D. S. (1995). Biocybernetic system evaluates indices of operator engagement in automated task. *Biological Psychology*, *40*, 187–195. doi:10.1016/0301-0511(95)05116-3

Resick, P. A., & Nishith, P. (1997). Sexual assault. In Davis, R. C., Lurigio, A. J., & Skogan, W. G. (Eds.), *Victims of Crime* (2nd ed., pp. 27–52). Thousand Oaks, CA: Sage Publications Inc.

Schwarz, N. (1999). Self-reports: How the questions shape the answers. *The American Psychologist*, *54*, 93–105. doi:10.1037/0003-066X.54.2.93

Sternberg, R. J. (2000). Images of mindfulness. *The Journal of Social Issues*, *56*, 112–126. doi:10.1111/0022-4537.00149

Stevens, A., Hernandez, J., et al. (2005). The use of virtual patients to teach medical students communication skills. *The Association for Surgical Education Annual Meeting*. New York, NY.

Stewart, M., Brown, J. B., & Donner, A. (2000). The impact of patient-centered care on outcomes. *The Journal of Family Practice*, *49*, 796–804.

Thiebaux, M., Marshall, A., et al. (2008). SmartBody: Behavior Realization for Embodied Conversational Agents. *International Conference on Autonomous Agents and Multi-Agent Systems*. Portugal.

Traum, D., Gratch, J., et al. (2008). Multi-party, Multi-issue, Multi-strategy Negotiation for Multi-modal Virtual Agents. *8th International Conference on Intelligent Virtual Agents*. Tokyo, Japan:Springer

Triola, M., & Feldman, M. (2006). A randomized trial of teaching clinical skills using virtual and live standardized patients. *Journal of General Internal Medicine*, *21*, 424–429. doi:10.1111/j.1525-1497.2006.00421.x

Zaner, R. M. (2006). The phenomenon of vulnerability in clinical encounters. *Human Studies*, *29*, 283–294. doi:10.1007/s10746-006-9028-3

KEY TERMS AND DEFINITIONS

Standardized Patient: Actor that has been trained to act as a real patient in order to simulate a set of symptoms or problems.

Virtual Human: Embodied agent with a graphical front-end that is capable of engaging in conversation with humans employing the same verbal and nonverbal means that humans do (e.g., gesture, facial expression).

Virtual Standardized Patients: Advanced conversational virtual human agents programmed to portray standardized patient scenarios (e.g., mental or physical conditions) for the training of clinicians.

Immersion: State of consciousness where a person immersed in a virtual environment has diminished awareness of physical self due to his or her being surrounded in an engrossingvirtual environment

Psychophysiology: Domain of psychology that is emphasizes the physiological bases of psychological processes

Psychophysiological Computing: Computer system that can recognize, interpret, and process real-time psychophysiological activity and use it as input data

Affect Modeling: Detection of emotional information using sensors that capture data about the user's physical state or behavior. Recognizing emotional information requires the extraction of meaningful patterns from the gathered data (e.g., parsing the data through various processes such as speech recognition, natural language processing, or facial expression detection)

Validity: Extent to which a concept, conclusion or measurement is well-founded and corresponds accurately to the real world.

Chapter 16
The Impact of Technology on Assessment and Evaluation in Higher Education

James P. Van Haneghan
University of South Alabama, USA

ABSTRACT

This chapter explores the impact of technology on assessment and evaluation in higher education. The impacts on classroom, program, and organizational assessment are discussed. Both formative and summative assessments in classrooms have been impacted by emerging technologies. However, the impact of many of the technological tools developed by measurement specialists has not been as widespread as one would expect given the age of many assessment technologies. Nevertheless, there remains a great potential for new measurement technologies to significantly improve classroom assessment practices. Technology for organizational assessment has continued to boom in light of the dual push for both accountability and continuous improvement by accreditors. The social impacts and burden of organizational assessment and evaluation are discussed. Overall, it is concluded that in order to evaluate the impact of technology, attention needs to be paid to the consequences of both classroom and organization assessment.

INTRODUCTION

There is no question that new technologies for assessment and evaluation in higher education have impacted students, faculty, and administrators. It has created more options for creating assessments that can be used to improve student learning. Additionally, it has created more efficient ways to assess more complex and authentic academic products like projects and portfolios that students can create. Further, new technologies have created new kinds of products that could be used as alter-

DOI: 10.4018/978-1-60960-147-8.ch016

natives for assessing students. For instance, Web quests (Dodge, 1995), blogs, presentations done with PowerPoint, web page development, evaluation of student reasoning in threaded discussions are just a few of the kinds of products that have been used as alternatives to traditional products like essays, speeches, tests, projects, simulations, and other traditional assessment tools. Technology has facilitated the discussion of performance and alternative assessments that claim better validity than traditional forms of assessment (Frederiksen & Collins, 1989). So technology can make the assessment activities that people have traditional engaged in more efficient, can change the media for presenting them, or can transform the way assessment occurs by introducing new forms of assessment activities.

It is not possible to talk about assessment without addressing evaluation activities based on assessments. Evaluation involves making judgments of merit or worth about the work of a student, a program, a unit, or even the institution. Evaluation can be formative, providing provisional knowledge that can be helpful for improvement, or summative, providing grounds for deeming worthy or unworthy a student's work, a program, or what ever entity that is being evaluated. These more summative evaluation judgments can have significant impacts on the individual or organization being evaluated. A student might be dismissed from a program, a program might be funded at a higher or lower level, a unit or even an institution might be closed down. These kinds of consequences point toward the importance of what Messick (1994) called consequential validity. In looking at any assessment activity, it is important to consider whether the use for an assessment will yield valid conclusions that lead to appropriate consequences. Hence, when examining the impact of assessment activities on people in higher education, the focus will be on the issue of consequential validity.

To help frame the discussion of this issue it is also helpful to think of assessment and evaluation as a process of communication (Van Haneghan, 2009). Generally, assessment situations are aimed at providing someone with some kind of information. It could be a professor providing a student with information about their success or failure in a course. It could be a professor learning that the students leaving his or her program are unable to meet the competencies he or she has taught. The meaning of that information is subject to a variety of different interpretations. For example, a student might view failure in the course as meaning he or she does not have the ability to succeed. Alternatively, he or she could interpret failure as a sign that the professor was not a very good teacher, or that the assessment was unfair. The professor might attribute the failure of students in a program to variety of factors. For example, the professor might attribute the student failure to changes in student selection into the program rather than to problems with his or her teaching.

Also, just like any other communication, it generally has an intended message, but the intended message is not always understood. For example, often the purpose of student assessments is to provide feedback for performance improvement. However, that purpose is often missed in the concern students have over grades. They may see the information as having summative purposes and not cull out information that could lead to better performance on later assignments or on ways to improve their skills in the future. Likewise, program assessments may be viewed as busy work by faculty rather than opportunities to improve the program.

Also, just like any other communication it is subject limitations of what people can comprehend. For example, feedback from a professor might be too complex for students to understand given their level of expertise. Further, given the limits to working memory capacity and the way information is presented, the amount of assessment information might simply be too much to process in working memory (Van Haneghan, 2008). If students have not had prior experience with electronic portfolio assessments, or the use of rubrics, they may need further instruction on how to understand them and thereby benefit from the information they provide.

Finally, just like any other communication, the relationships between people make a difference in how that communication is interpreted (Van Haneghan, 2009). For example, a faculty member who does not "buy in" to the administration's assessment program may view the assessment information provided by such a program as lacking validity. Hence, when asked to carry out an assessment that is part of the program that faculty member might only do a cursory assessment rather than an in depth one that would provide more valuable information. Likewise, students might not learn from formative assessment information because they are intimidated by a professor. These examples illustrate how complex social processes are associated with both student and institutional assessment. The remainder of this chapter will further elaborate the elements of student and institutional assessment.

This chapter will be organized into two sections. The first section will examine classroom assessment and the second section will examine program and institutional assessment. Although these will be discussed separately, they are becoming more and more connected. For example student performance on capstone projects (often viewed as a program learning outcome), provides information to students about their competency, but also provides feedback to the program about what students did or did not learn from program coursework. Within each section, impacts created by using technology for activities that have been part and parcel of assessment at universities will be explored. Then, the transformative impacts of technology on assessment activities will be discussed.

IMPACTS OF TECHNOLOGY ON CLASSROOM ASSESSMENT

Impact of Technology on Traditional Assessments

As noted above, technology has both changed how we carry out traditional assessment and has transformed assessment in classes. Perhaps the simplest way technology has improved assessment has been to make it easier to create and score multiple choice examinations. For instance, the ability to develop sheets to scan test answers is a very simple and now very old established technology has become easier and easier to carry out. For example, there are software packages like Remark Office OMR (Remark Products Group, 2009) that can make plain paper forms for scanning. Likewise most all instructors' manuals are available on computer disks with test construction software for selecting items and building exams. Exams can also be constructed easily and given online within most distance education shells. On the scoring side, scanned and computer-based scoring often includes classic test item analysis statistics like difficulty and discrimination indices. Given that professors use such information, they can get some basic estimates of how well items operate. More sophisticated models for items can be developed through the use of Item Response Theory (IRT) models. Given enough items and the appropriate model, item difficulty and ability levels required to successfully master items can be used to generate tests that can discriminate between students of different levels of competency. Further IRT analyses can be easily used to develop computer adaptive tests that allow instructors to more efficiently test student competency levels. Computer adaptive tests (CAT) involve administering a starting item, then changing the difficulty level up or down depending upon the correctness of the response. The subsequent questions move up or down until a level where the student is likely to get questions correct is established. This usually happens with many fewer items than a traditional test. The use of IRT and CAT require either skill in using technology or at least access to someone to help in the development process. Hence, one potential benefit of technology for professors is the ability to do traditional testing more efficiently and effectively. These benefits need to be weighed against the cost of developing and implementing these kinds of systems. While CAT and IRT based assessment systems have been developed for admissions tests and placement tests, the frequency of their implementation for classroom testing has not been widespread as of yet.

For students, these efficiencies can make it easier for them to get feedback about their test scores. Not only might they quickly learn what items they missed, but also some systems are set up to provide students with feedback about why other answers were wrong and the correct answer was right. Because most CAT and IRT applications involve extensive item analysis and are set up to provide a system for assessment, the quality of the feedback is potentially better. The properties of the items and the level of expertise they represent need to be well defined to use them in such models. Computer adaptive tests provide students with an interesting way to quickly gauge there skill, although the difference in how the test is generated might cause students some unease about the validity of the score. For example, Lilley, Barker, and Britton (2004) examined students' perception of a computer adaptive test for English language learners and found that students were somewhat positive about computer adaptive tests, but had some concern over test lengths and stopping rules. Tonidandel, Quinones, and Adams (2002) found that the difficulty of the first item had an impact on the subsequent items completed by test takers. As the initial item went from easy to hard, the number of questions answered correctly went down. These two studies suggest that student ideas about CAT tests are important to their successful implementation.

These technologies can be fruitful, but as noted above they have not been widely used. One reason for the limited use is that the development of such systems is expensive (Drasgow, Luecht, & Bennett, 2006). Another problem is that there are not enough people with in-depth knowledge of these approaches (IRT and CAT) who can develop or train people to use such systems (Herszenhorn, 2006). Thus without higher budgets and better trained people to develop these systems, they will not flourish. The irony is that these technologies are hardly new anymore. From my point of view there has just been gulf between practice and the state of the art.

Lastly, one issue that needs to be addressed with the widespread use of testing on computers, and especially over the internet, is test security concerns (Drasgow et al., 2006). Problems in securing test items, the inability to track students who are working on-line to determine whether they are the actual person who should be assessed, issues with students using the internet or cell phones to find information, and the need to create enough alternative forms to avoid leakage of test information all present problems that are not easy to solve. They can in some cases lead instructors to seek alternative approaches to assessment especially in the online environment. For example, as an instructor in an online course, I use open-book essay exams that require thinking and not simply rote memorization to succeed.

Another classroom assessment activity, scoring and reviewing papers, has also been made easier by technology. First, electronic copies can be scanned for spelling and grammatical errors. While spelling and grammar checkers are not always perfect, they do catch the majority of errors. Feedback, editing, and comments can be easily dealt with through the use of track changes and comments in Microsoft Word. There have even been systems developed that purportedly can automate scoring of essays via computer (e.g., Attali & Burstein, 2006) with promising results. However, automated essay scoring is still an experimental rather than widespread practice. The ability to check for plagiarism has also increased. For example, "Turnitin.com" allows professors the opportunity to check whether students plagiarized their work from others. In the past, professors had to be skilled in examining student work for odd patterns of writing or writing that appeared to be indicative of greater expertise than a student has shown in the past. Sites such as "Turnitin" provide data to support or refute claims of plagiarism.

Transformation of Assessment by Technology

Along with improvements in how prior assessment activities have been carried out, technology and new ideas about assessment have provided an impetus for more focus on "authentic" performance assessments and formative assessment of student work (Frederiksen & Collins, 1989). Although work on formative assessment initially was aimed toward P-12 education (e.g., Black & William, 1998), the principles of formative assessment are applicable in higher education as well. Technology has provided the basis for complex tutoring systems that provide formative assessment information that can be used to tailor instruction to student needs. Simulations using multimedia and/or Web-based platforms can allow students to engage in performances that would not be easily possible previously. The ease of creating and storing electronic documents and media has led to the emergence of the electronic portfolio as a tool for assessment in the university as well. While in the past, paper portfolios could be completed with a great deal of effort, electronic systems for capturing artifacts are easy to use and provide opportunities and space for reflection making the portfolio easier to create and edit. These systems allow for easy development of rubrics for scoring. A rubric is typically defined by a series of scoring levels that indicate various levels of expertise on a particular artifact or the entire portfolio. More will be said below about rubrics because they represent a different way of thinking about assessment than numeric grading.

The benefits of electronic portfolios have been touted by a number of educators (e.g., Holtzman & Dagavarian, 2007) but the evidence base needs more high quality studies (Tochel et al., 2009). The major benefits touted by proponents are the ease of creating and including multiple types of artifacts, the ability to see growth and learning through student self-reflection, and the ability of faculty to more easily provide formative feedback and score a body of student work. Portfolios have the potential for providing a holistic picture of a student's competencies. However, there are technical issues that sometimes complicate the use of these portfolio systems. For example, some studies report that students and faculty have difficulties understanding their purposes, feel unprepared to use the technology, and sometimes do not see their value (Luyegu, 2009;Ntuli, Keengwe, & Kyei-Blankson, 2009; Swan, 2009). Further, these systems are not always used with the self-reflective and formative purposes in mind. For example, while we in our college use an electronic portfolio system to track student scores on indicators of state standards, the number of standards (160 or more) that need to be scored makes tracking growth and creating a holistic understanding of a student's level of competence difficult. Ntuli et al. (2009) and Swan both point out the importance of faculty "buy-in" in the success in using portfolios. Portfolios need coherent frameworks, reliable and valid scoring, and thoughtful faculty feedback to work (Meeus, Van Petegem, & Engels, 2009). When there have been problems, these elements have not been in place. Meeus et al. (2009) report that because purposes and contents of portfolios are so varied, no general statement about their reliability and validity can be made. They do suggest that they can be examined for reliability and validity, although the subjective nature of the scoring of portfolios sometimes makes reliability evidence difficult to evaluate.

Technology introduces new kinds of educational products, and instructors are required to develop valid ways to grade these new kinds of products. Evaluating student performance on a simulation, grading a student created blog, or a web-page are tasks that are somewhat different from the traditional essays and tests that instructors have given in the past. Further, there are often concerns with these performance assessments in determining whether student success is related to skill with a particular technology rather than their knowledge of the content domain. Messick (1994) described construct irrelevant variance in performance assessments. Construct irrelevant variance concerns differences in performance on an assessment that are related to factors other than the construct or factor of interest. For instance, students assessed on their knowledge of history based on their construction of a Web page may fail because of their technology skills rather than their knowledge of history. Their acumen with the technology presents construct irrelevant variance associated with the medium of response rather than history knowledge per se. This issue is not totally unique to technology use. For example, the dilemma of determining how to score an essay where writing is technically correct, but the content weak, is one example of how this was manifest before these new technologies arrived. On the other hand, there is at least a "folklore" about some students being far better able to produce Web pages or multimedia presentations than recognize or recall material on exams or write essays. Consequently one advantageous element of allowing students to work with alternative technologies for producing projects may be that they could choose a media that was their strong suit rather than one where they were less creative or capable. Such flexibility must be handled with care, however, because there may be issues about the equivalence of the evaluations associated with different types of products created by students (Lane & Stone, 2006).

As noted earlier, performance assessments that are facilitated by technology often use rubrics for scoring student success and failure. Most college or university instructors, except perhaps in selected areas, have had little training in assessment other than scoring tests or essays. Rubrics typically use a short numeric scale (e.g., 1 to 4) with descriptors of performance at different levels of expertise. Ideally, as Lane and Stone (2006) note, rubrics should not be so task specific that they do not clearly measure the more general constructs that students are to learn and transfer beyond that specific situation. The development of a rubric is not a simple task. There needs to be a well developed model of expertise in order to create a valid rubric. For example, one popular approach used in higher education is to use the SOLO (Structure of the Observed Learning Outcome) taxonomy to indicate different levels of expert performance (e. g., Biggs, 1999). At lower levels in the taxonomy student knowledge consists of isolated facts. As students reach higher levels they show evidence of integrating information and understand the underlying structure of a domain. Expertise in many academic fields grows in this way, so the taxonomy provides a useful framework. On the other hand, there are aspects of expertise in specific fields that general taxonomies like SOLO are not capable of capturing. In such cases, measures of growing levels of competency need to be developed using acceptable criteria that fit with the particular domain of expertise. As noted above, rubrics are often the scoring choice for portfolio assessments. Hence, as noted above, the reliability and validity of rubrics are highly dependent on the nature of the field and the quality of the model of expertise developed by the creators of the rubric.

Another technology for formative and summative assessment that has taken hold involves the use of so-called "clickers" or personal response systems. In most systems the clickers are wirelessly linked to a computer that can record multiple choice or very short answers to questions that are posed as a professor lectures. The systems can also be used for quizzes and attendance in classes. One advantage of these systems includes the ability to learn quickly what students know and make adjustments in instruction to fix gaps or misconceptions that students have before they are more formally assessed. Another possible advantage is that students can get quick feedback on quizzes and tests, and professors get another quick way to score multiple choice questions.

There has been some research on clickers with many studies reporting positive effects on learning and/or motivation. For example, a quasi-experimental study by Mayer et al. (2009) found that clickers led to better performance in large educational psychology classes than paper and pencil questions, or no questioning. Hence, they were useful in providing formative feedback and elaboration that led to better performance. On the other hand, Morgan (2008) did not find them to be helpful, finding no difference in course grades or attrition in favor of classes using clickers. To some extent, the success or failure of clickers is largely a function of the how they are used. For example, if the questions professors ask from them are simple fact questions, they may not be helpful. However, when questions are crafted to get at conceptual misunderstanding they can be a quite powerful formative tool. Further, inclusion of questions included just to use the technology may not prove beneficial. They may disrupt the flow of a lecture, distract students, and lead students to dismiss the technology. For instance, in Morgan's study, she found that the clicker classes sometimes did not complete as much material. Just like any other technology, the clicker technology is only works if the underlying use is based in a valid educational purpose.

The ability to engage in similar kinds of formative activities can also be carried out online and through computer assisted instruction (CAI) that embeds questions and provides feedback, or through intelligent tutoring systems that identify student conceptions (e.g., Steinberg, 1991) CAI is a relatively old technology now, but has the potential to continue to serve the function of providing formative assessment data for students to monitor their learning and instructors to monitor their instruction. What has changed is the platform we use (web versus mainframe, versus PC based) to deliver that instruction and the degree that it can be done with richer media. Black and William (1998) and others (e.g., Pellegrino, Chudowsky, & Glaser, 2001; Shute, 2008) report on the robustness of formative assessment across a wide range of disciplines and technology. Any technology that facilitates formative feedback provides a potential to enhance learning and merits consideration by faculty in higher education.

Virtual reality environments, simulations, and games also provide another mechanism for providing students with formative and summative assessments. Simulations and games as assessments have been around for a great deal of time (e.g., Thorton III & Mueller-Hanson, 2004), but technology has made the fidelity and richness of such simulations much better. The use of virtual reality for instruction and assessment has been particularly prolific in medical education where there is little room for formative feedback with live patients. Virtual reality simulations allow for students to make errors and improve their skills without the risks associated with errors of practice (Cosman, Cregan, Martin, & Cartmill, 2002). Cosman et al., (2002) report that the use of such simulations requires validating performance in the virtual environment with the performance in the real world. In other domains, and with other forms of performance assessments (real, virtually real, or contrived) validity evidence for the generalizability of performance assessments still serves as an important impediment to further use of these tools. As professors and instructors look to using virtual reality settings like "Second-Life" to assess students' performance, there is a need to consider issues of validity and generalizability outside such contexts.

Summary of Section on Classroom Assessment

Both faculty and students have seen both an improvement in the efficiencies of carrying out assessment activities and the development of new forms of assessment that are facilitated by computer technology's ability to create virtual environments that mimic activities that are present in the world outside of the classroom. In many cases technologies that improve testing and assessment practices has been highly developed but not used much by faculty. On the other hand, sometimes the implementation of new technologies has preceded their rigorous testing. For instance, Mayer et al. (2009) report that most of the early studies with the clickers were poorly designed and did not test out the impact of clickers on learning. Only recently have quasi-experimental and experimental (Campbell & Mayer, 2009) studies been done to establish effectiveness. Corresponding to new technologies has been recognition of the importance of formative assessment in education (Black & William, 1998; Bransford, Brown, & Cocking, 1999). The effectiveness of formative assessment on classroom performance is well documented, and there is a clear literature concerning the conditions for creating feedback that works (Shute, 2008). The greater the emphasis on formative assessment, the greater the likelihood is that a technological advance will improve assessment within a domain.

Impact of Technology on Program and Institutional Assessment

Technology has created an ability to implement assessment systems for continuous improvement and accountability purposes for institutions of higher learning. Accreditation agencies like the National Council for Accreditation of Teacher Education (NCATE), the Accreditation Board for Engineering and Technology (ABET), and other regional accreditation boards (e.g., Southern Association of Colleges and Schools, SACS) require assessment systems as part of their continued accreditation.. While these organizations have always required some kind of assessment, these organizations have become more data driven at least partially because technology helps make data collection and analysis much simpler. Generally there are three major purposes to assessment systems that are created for accreditation organizations. One is to help provide evidence that the organization meets the standards the agency sets for programs and institutions. A second is for public accountability purposes. Data collected for accreditation purposes is publicly shared so that policy makers, funders, and other stakeholders are aware of the successes or failures of organizations. Finally, a third reason for development of organizational assessment systems is for devising and setting up a system for continuous improvement of programs and the organization. For example, organizations that notice drops in graduation rates, or programs that notice a drop in the quality of their graduates on program assessments would use such information to make improvements in program successes. These systems influence not only faculty and administration, but students too. Students are often assessed in new or additional ways and sometimes required to purchase licensing for electronic portfolio software.

The work that has focused on improvement has been driven by notions of the learning organization (Argyris, 1991, 2004). Some improvement systems are driven by business models like Six Sigma (e.g., see Murphy, 2009) and the Baldridge plan (Satterlee, 1996). Educational organizations use data driven systems to help their organizations better meet goals and serve their students. Technology helps make the process of strategic planning and data collection easier. Software for strategic planning typically provides a data base for goals, evidence, and plans for improvement. Such software helps organize cycles of planning, evaluating, and action. Departments, programs, colleges or other units within a college or university set goals and/or objectives, identify or create assessment data to determine whether the goal or objective was met, then determine actions to carry out if the objective was not met. For example, a program might want to meet a minimum criterion for student success on a licensing exam. If the criterion is not met, program changes that address areas where students were more likely to fail could be implemented and the impact of the changes then can be tracked in a future cycle. A department might set minimum publication expectations for faculty, determine whether that expectation is met, and then make changes if it is not. For example, faculty might get changes in their course loads, the department might set up a subject pool for research, more productive senior faculty might be used to mentor younger faculty members, or a variety of other professional development activities could be undertaken. The ability to track these kinds of changes and interventions is facilitated through technology by having a central location in a database where the process can be made public. Such a system can also be advantageous for accreditation because almost all accreditation agencies look for evidence that institutions use data for program improvement.

However, the use of technology does not handle a large number of issues that are important elements to assessment systems. First, people still need to make the plans. Assessment plans that are not well thought out can create problems in implementation, data collection, and data analysis. Further, the nature of the data is really important. The data need to be reliable and valid and often the goal is provide data that are quantitative in nature so that change can be measured. However, there are some things do not lend themselves to easy quantification and most individuals who work as university professors have little training in what it means to state that a measure is reliable and valid, never mind going through a process to validate a measure.

Along with assessment for continuous improvement, there are assessments that are done for accountability purposes. For example, NCATE and state departments of education require teacher education programs to meet certain standards to maintain their accreditation. If programs do not meet certain standards, then programs risk losing such accreditation. The loss of accreditation might have significant negative consequences on enrollment, the ability of graduates to find positions, and may even endanger the program's existence. State legislators, parents, and other groups are often concerned about graduation rates. Data showing low graduation rates for institutions, especially state funded institutions, has led legislators to enact laws or make funding contingent upon meeting certain standards. Technology increases the reach of accountability measures. National data bases such as the IPEDS (Integrated Postsecondary Education Data System) allow easy comparison of institutions and provide a basis for asking questions about such issues as graduation rates. In teacher education, accountability data systems are starting to hold schools of education in some states accountable for the success of their graduates in teaching students. For example, Noell & Burns (N.D.) report on a system in Louisiana where teacher education programs are evaluated on whether there graduates show evidence that they can help students learn. The ability to tag the teacher's training program in the data base of student test scores shows that the reach for accountability data can extend well beyond graduation rates, and success on professional tests. It can reach into the on-the-job success of candidates. Modern information technology makes such analyses possible with very little effort other than entering a field in a database.

So with all of these changes and the emphasis on accountability, what impacts have there been on faculty, students, and administrators in higher education? How have these different groups been influenced by the new technologies associated with assessment and accountability in higher education? Below are some issues related to accountability and assessment systems that may influence how people interact with them.

First, there is a need to consider how such systems fit into the existing work that people do. For example, in my college, a state mandated assessment for teacher education candidates required faculty to give scores on around 160 or so indicators of state teaching standards on a four point rubric. While technology has helped us to develop a system for collecting these data, there is faculty time in developing assessments for each of these indicators, linking the scoring rubric to the specific standards, checking reliability of assessments, and many other tasks that create additional work for faculty members. Given additional demands on their time, some faculty members are likely to take the path of least resistance, doing as little as possible to meet the demands of the system. So, rather than focus on carrying out the assessments to help with continuous improvement, the assessments become a check mark that they need to enter so that they can get on with their other work. Thus, the continuous improvement element of the assessment system gets lost in the amount of time and effort needed to work the system effectively

Another issue that plays a role is that educational institutions often do not view themselves like business organizations. The model taken from business does not always easily fit educational institutions, especially public institutions. For example, many regional state universities have fairly low admissions standards that allow some students in who may not be university ready. Access to institution means entering students are not always at highest levels of academic performance. In the business model if the inputs are weak, you simply get them from a different supplier or use a tougher standard. Such an option is not a politically viable one for state institutions that are publicly funded.

While elite institutions can be selective and thereby show better graduation rates, public institutions cannot just decide to accept fewer people. While studies (e.g., the Documenting Effective Educational Practice [DEEP] study, Kuh, Kinzie, Schuh, & Whitt, 2005) show that there are some less selective universities that can show better than expected graduation rates, the evidence still shows that by and large that less selective public institutions have lower graduation rates. Sometimes institutions can be more stringent, but most times there is a tradeoff for public institutions between selectively and access. Most people would argue that state colleges and universities were designed to provide access to the public to higher education that would otherwise be limited to the rich and academically elite. Hence, public institutions are given the difficult task of changing their performance without the selectivity of some elite institutions.

What also may be problematic for implementing systems designed in the business world is that faculty enter academia with a view that the "Academy" does not operate like the business world. Most enjoy the flexibility, freedom, and creativity of working in an institution of higher education. An accountability system that may open up their work to scrutiny could be perceived as threatening that autonomy.

Another disadvantage that may limit the applicability of business-based quality improvement systems are the organizational structures of universities. For instance, the concept of tenure limits changes that can be made in personnel that might be warranted based on assessment data. This is not to say that improvement plans are a bad idea or that no changes can be made, but that differences in organizational structure may limit how these more business oriented models can apply.

Assessment Meaning and Burden in Institutional Assessment Systems

As noted earlier, one impact of new assessment systems is that they may provide more actual work. Faculty need to learn to use the technology and sometimes add to their grading. They may change how they work. For instance, in implementing a new system of assessment, faculty may abandon old approaches. In our system in the college of education, faculty required to assess state standards might change their assignments and grading criteria shifting from tests and traditional assignments to performance assessments that work with the rubric that they are required to use. However, in focusing solely on the rubric they might abandon otherwise valid assessment strategies that are perhaps more accurate. Thus there are both positive and negative influences of implementing new systems.

If assessment planning works right, it can serve as a way of improving performance of the individual students, faculty members, and the organization. If it is perceived as the "make me more work more when I do not have any spare time already plan" rather than the plan for continuous improvement, there will be problems with buy in and acceptance. What potential concerns like this suggest is that the meaning of assessments to those involved in giving them is crucial to their success. Assessments have within them many layers of meaning to people who are involved in receiving, giving, and mandating them. One of the difficulties in implementing a system of continuous improvement is that there is a need for people to perceive the system in a constructive way rather than as a personal indictment of their competency as a professional. As Argyris (1991) points out in his analysis of high level consultants, people who are generally very successful, often have difficulties dealing with critical analysis of their work. Just like high level consultants, university faculty members have been at least successful enough in their field to get a doctoral level degree. Hence, they may have a difficult time accepting an institutional assessment system that is often designed by others to point out what they would perceive as purported flaws their work.

Assessment systems involve power relations between people, and their meaning to people can have a great impact on how they are perceived (Simola & Rhinne, 2008; Van Haneghan, 2009). For example, assessment systems mandated by accreditation agencies hold power over an institution's ability to operate on many levels, and hence, investments in meeting standards are important to university administrations. As noted earlier, this focus on meeting accreditation may threaten some faculty members who view it as taking away their academic freedom and disrespecting their expertise. On the other hand, as Van Haneghan (2008) points out, the system can be viewed in a positive light as a system for continuous improvement that can only enhance one's abilities as a faculty member and improve the programs that faculty are part of at their institution.

Not only are issues of the meaning of institutional assessment multifaceted for faculty, but students as well. Luyegu (2009) examined the implementation of an electronic portfolio system set up to assess state teacher education standards in a college of education. She found some confusion surrounding the system. Some students did not understand its purpose, and other students, like faculty members, felt that the expense and burden of the system was thrust upon them in an already busy curriculum.

Van Haneghan (2008) coined the term "assessment burden" to describe how people perceive assessment systems. Assessment burden is a complex notion that assessments or systems of assessment are perceived as burdensome. Assessments can be seen as burdensome when, as noted above, such systems are viewed as a threat. However, there are legitimate aspects of assessment systems that can create burden. For example, the working memory load (Sweller, 2006) associated with understanding the results of assessments, or figuring out a complex scoring system add legitimately to the work load of faculty members. Likewise, students who have to deal with a complex electronic portfolio system may be overwhelmed with understanding it.

Technology serves as a double-edged sword in that it can lessen the legitimate burden associated with assessment and accountability. On the other hand, it can also create burden because of its power as a data collection tool. Just because data can be collected on something does not mean it always should or need be collected. For instance, collecting data on 160 standards in a program may mean that there is little opportunity for formative assessment that can help students improve their skills. Simola and Rhinne (2008) suggest that assessment systems can have unintended negative consequences. In implementing these systems accreditation agencies, university administrations, state departments of educations, and others need to think through these consequences.

Another issue that arises in considering assessment systems is that institutions of higher education are often have to balance the needs and wants of multiple accrediting agencies and regulators. For example, a college of education will have to deal with NCATE, state departments, professional specialty organizations, and regional accreditation agencies. All of these groups may have interests in an assessment system that addresses their standards. The unit has to coordinate all of these different standards into an assessment system. Sometimes that means duplication effort or setting up separate assessments that add further to the burden of assessment and evaluation.

Finding Balance

As can be seen, technology has brought both exciting advances in assessment technologies that allow instructors and institutions to assess more accurately, more efficiently, and in new ways. However, with the power of new technologies comes the possibility of unintended consequences that are not always positive. The impacts of technology range from changing classroom assessments to creating very complex systems of assessments for evaluating programs and institutions. These complex systems can create assessment burden for faculty and institutions. After a number of years of No Child Left Behind, there is a sense that k-12 education systems are beginning to realize too much time has been taken up by standardized assessments. Institutions of higher learning, their accreditors, and governing bodies need to look closely at the lessons learned in k-12 education and move to develop accountability systems that help improve their institutions while not creating undue burden on faculty and students. Assessment and evaluation can create positive influences on students, faculty, and institutions. The goal is to find the right balance so that assessment systems can improve student performance and help programs and institutions continue to improve.

REFERENCES

Argyris, C. (1991). Teaching smart people how to learn. *Harvard Business Review*, *69*(3), 99–109.

Argyris, C. (2004). Reflection and beyond in research on organizational Learning. *Management Learning*, *35*(4), 507–509. doi:10.1177/1350507604048276

Attali, Y., & Burstein, J. (2006). Automated essay scoring with e-rater® V.2. *Journal of Technology, Learning, and Assessment*, *4*(3). Available from http://www.jtla.org.

Biggs, J. (1999). What the student does: teaching for enhanced learning. *Higher Education Research & Development*, *18*(1), 57–75. doi:10.1080/0729436990180105

Black, P., & William, D. (1998). Inside the black box. *Phi Delta Kappan*, *80*, 139.

Bransford, J. D., Brown, A. L., & Cocking, R. R. (1999). *How people learn: Brain, mind, experience, and school*. Washington, DC: National Academy Press.

Campbell, J., & Mayer, R. E. (2009). Questioning as an instructional method: Does it affect learning from lectures? *Applied Cognitive Psychology*, *23*, 747–759. doi:10.1002/acp.1513

Cosman, P. H., Cregan, P. C., & Martin, C. J., & Cartmill. (2002). Virtual reality simulators: current status in acquisition and assessment of surgical skills. *ANZ Journal of Surgery*, *72*, 30–34. doi:10.1046/j.1445-2197.2002.02293.x

Dodge, B. J. (1995). WebQuests: A structure for active learning on the World Wide Web. *The Distance Educator,* 1(2).

Drasgow, F. Luecht, R. M., & Bennett, R. E. (2006). Technology and testing. In R. L. Brennan (Ed.), *Educational Measurement (4th* Ed., pp. 471-515). Westport, CT: Praeger.

Frederiksen, J., & Collins, A. (1989). A systems approach to educational testing. *Educational Researcher*, *18*(9), 27–32.

Herszenhorn, D. M. (2006). As test-taking grows, test makers grow rarer. *New York Times*, May 5, 2006. Retrieved online February 15, 2010 from http://www.nytimes.com/2006/05/05/education/05testers.html?_r=1

Holtzman, D., & Dagavarian, D. (2007). The use of electronic portfolios in assessing student learning outcomes. *Journal of Continuing Higher Education*, *55*(1), 65–69.

Kuh, G. D., Kinzie, J., Schuh, J. H., & Whitt, E. J. (2005). *Student success in college: Creating conditions that matter*. New York: Jossey-Bass.

Lane, S., & Stone, C. A. (2006). Performance assessment. In Brennan, R. L. (Ed.), *Educational Measurement* (4th ed., pp. 387–431). Westport, CT: Praeger.

Lilley, M., Barker, T., & Britton, C. (2004). The development and evaluation of a software prototype for computer adaptive testing. *Computers & Education Journal*, *43*(1-2), 109–123. doi:10.1016/j.compedu.2003.12.008

Luyegu, E. A. (2009). *Students' perceptions of assessment and the electronic portfolio project in the College of Education.* Unpublished Dissertation, University of South Alabama.

Mayer, R., Stull, A., DeLeeuw, K., Almeroth, K., Bimber, B., & Chun, D. (2009). Clickers in college classrooms: Fostering learning with questioning methods in large lecture classes. *Contemporary Educational Psychology*, *34*(1), 51–57. doi:10.1016/j.cedpsych.2008.04.002

Meeus, W., Van Petegem, P., & Engels, N. (2009). Validity and reliability of portfolio assessment in pre-service teacher education. *Assessment & Evaluation in Higher Education*, *34*(4), 401–413. doi:10.1080/02602930802062659

Messick, S. (1994). The interplay of evidence and consequences in the validation of performance assessment. *Educational Researcher*, *23*(2), 13–23.

Morgan, R. (2008). Exploring the Pedagogical Effectiveness of Clickers. *InSight: A Journal of Scholarly Teaching, 3*31-36.

Moss, P. A. (2003). Reconceptualizing validity for classroom assessment. *Educational Measurement: Issues and Practice*, *22*(4), 13–25. doi:10.1111/j.1745-3992.2003.tb00140.x

Murphy, S. (2009). Leveraging lean Six Sigma to culture, nurture, and sustain Assessment and change in the academic library environment. *College & Research Libraries*, *70*(3), 215–225.

Noell, G., & Burns, J. (n.d.). *Value added teacher preparation assessment: Overview of 2007–8 study.* Baton Rouge, LA: Louisiana Board of Regents. Retrieved May 11, 2010, from http://www.regents.louisiana.gov/Academic/TE/2008/Overview%20of%202007-08%20Value%20Added%20Teacher%20Preparation%20(12.03.08).pdf

Ntuli, E., Keengwe, J., & Kyei-Blankson, L. (2009). Electronic portfolios in teacher education: A case study of early childhood teacher candidates. *Early Childhood Education Journal, 37*(2), 121–126. doi:10.1007/s10643-009-0327-y

Pellegrino, J. Chudowsky, N, & Glaser, R. (2001). *Knowing what students know: The science and design of educational assessment*. Washington, DC: National Academies Press.

Satterlee, B. (1996). *Continuous improvement and quality: Implications for higher education.* Retrieved from ERIC database (ED399845).

Shute, V. J. (2008). Focus on formative assessment. *Review of Educational Research, 78*, 153–189. doi:10.3102/0034654307313795

Simola, H., & Rinne, R. (2008). Researching the political effects of quality assurance and evaluation (QAE) in education – Reflections on some comparative issues in sociology and the politics of education in the audit society. In Pereyra, M. A. (Ed.), *Changing knowledge and education: communities and new policies in global societies* (pp. 171–183). Frankfurt am Main: Peter Lang.

Steinberg, E. R. (1991). *Computer-assisted instruction: A synthesis of theory, practice, and technology*. Hillsdale, NJ: Erlbaum.

Swan, G. (2009). Information systems in teacher preparation programs: What can we learn from a 5-Year longitudinal case study of an electronic portfolio database? *Journal of Educational Computing Research, 41*(4), 431–451. doi:10.2190/EC.41.4.c

Sweller, J. (2006). Discussion of 'emerging topics in cognitive load research: Using learner and information characteristics in the design of powerful learning environments'. *Applied Cognitive Psychology, 20*, 353–357. doi:10.1002/acp.1251

Thorton, G. C. III, & Mueller-Hanson, R. A. (2004). *Developing Organizational Simulations*. Mahwah, NJ: Lawrence Erlbaum and Associates.

Tochel, C., Haig, A., Hesketh, A., Cadzow, A., Beggs, K., Colthart, I., & Peacock, H. (2009). The effectiveness of portfolios for post-graduate assessment and education: BEME Guide No 12. *Medical Teacher, 31*(4), 320–339. doi:10.1080/01421590902883056

Tonidandel, S., Quiñones, M. A., & Adams, A. A. (2002). Computer adaptive testing: The impact of test characteristics on perceived performance and test takers' reactions. *The Journal of Applied Psychology, 87*, 320–332. doi:10.1037/0021-9010.87.2.320

Van Haneghan, J. P. (October, 2008). *Assessment burden: When does the burden of assessment and evaluation outweigh the benefit?* Paper presented at the National Evaluation Institute, Wilmington, NC.

Van Haneghan, J. P. (2009). Validating assessment for learning: Consequential and systems approaches. *Journal of Multidisciplinary Evaluation, 6*(12), 23–31.

Chapter 17
Enterprise Resource Planning Systems in Higher Education

Melissa J. Haab
Alabama Southern Community College, USA

Sharon F. Cramer
Buffalo State College, USA

ABSTRACT

Since most higher education institutions have, or will, implement enterprise resource planning systems (Cramer, 2005), it is important to understand how such an implementation will have an impact throughout an institution. In this chapter, enterprise resource planning systems will be defined, and the benefits to the various constituents of the institution will be described. Barriers (and strategies for overcoming them) will be identified, specifically administration-related barriers, resource allocation barriers, time barriers, barriers related to campus policies, human barriers, and product specific barriers. Leaders of institutions at the crossroads, who are determining whether or not to implement an integrated ERP, can better understand the social implications of such projects as a result of consideration of the key issues raised within this chapter.

INTRODUCTION

Innovation depends on technology, yet many times technology drives innovation. As business practices in personal and professional endeavors become increasingly dependent upon access to the internet and online services, higher education has been forced to become more and more technologically advanced. With the evolution of online learning and distance learning opportunities, those institutions that can meet the needs of a potential pool of applicants who are willing to "shop around" to get the best "deal" are more likely to attract qualified students. In many ways, "students" have become "customers." Colleges and universities are forced to become both more accountable and responsive to an impatient and fickle customer base. Unhappy customers can

DOI: 10.4018/978-1-60960-147-8.ch017

easily find another institution that will meet their needs, and these customers are willing to transfer if another institution meets their needs faster and more efficiently. Higher education has become an industry.

With constantly emerging technology advances, customer service in higher education has been redefined from face-to-face interactions during business hours to 24/7/365 online services. Where the pressure for smiles, efficiency and friendly service used to be a priority to attract prospective students and parents, the pressure now is to respond first, and give the customer exactly what they request -- many times with real time, personalized electronic contact, and no face-to-face time. Customers in higher education include community members, prospective students, parents, current students, alumni, faculty, staff, and donors. Additional groups of interest include board members, state and federal agencies, and policy makers. All of these constituents have grown to expect real-time service and accurate data at their immediate disposal. Any error in data could defer funding or provide embarrassment in the public arena.

Prospective and current students want to complete transactions (including advising, transcript requests, registration and fee payment) in the privacy of their home and sometimes at unconventional times of day, week or year (e.g., services over holidays are becoming increasingly common, at times when institutions used to see as "down time" for many staff members). Institutions feel a sense of pressure from these constituents to increase online services, especially as education has become more global. Students are shopping around for low cost online courses that offer flexibility in order to meet their academic (or non-academic) goals. Enterprise Resource Planning systems have become the vehicle that can help institutions to meet these goals.

DEFINITION OF ENTERPRISE RESOURCE PLANNING

Shoemaker (2003) defines an Enterprise Resource Planning (ERP) as an "integrated software application that supports the core business processes of a firm by handling and integrating most of the intra-firm business practices in real time" (p. 69). This type of system, usually implemented in modules, forces an integrated and real-time student information system to provide information to policy makers, administrators, recruiters, advisors, teachers, fundraisers, students and staff members alike. Since all constituents feel that their own needs supersede those of others, and demand instant and accurate information, implementing such a complex system requires decision makers and project managers to carefully consider current (and future) calendars, project timelines, and team assignments. Lack of attention to detail during implementation can have disastrous effects on an institution post-implementation.

HISTORY OF ERPS IN HIGHER EDUCATION

Many institutions adopted ERPs in the mid to late 1990s to handle the Y2K changeover, as well as retirements of those who had created and maintained home grown systems. As these employees faced retirement age, institutions were faced with the challenge of trying to train newer employees on old technology, or moving to a system that could deliver the integrated processes that were needed. Home grown systems were dependent upon those employees that had basically grown up with and had written systems which had logic limitations. As fears mounted in regards to Y2K, many institutions were forced to purchase ERPs that would prevent what was considered to be a potential disaster at the turn of the twenty-first century.

Concurrently, the world-wide web was gaining presence in business and educational settings. What had once been used by scientists and esoteric researchers became part of the educational landscape. Simultaneously, online services and distance education began to gain momentum. Students were becoming more interested in searching for information and comparing institutions via electronic means. Colleges and universities began to place more emphasis on the look and feel of their websites, and began to market themselves through electronic services as well as print media. Students who had extensive experience with online resources developed by sophisticated vendors expected similar options as they searched for post-secondary education. Institutions quickly found that their website was attracting or deterring prospective students. Changes in the web presence were linked to other institutional activities- admissions, billing, payment, change-of-major, etc. And the ERP options- with conflicting pros and cons of each option- are ones campus leaders then explored.

As funding issues become more and more dominant, accountability for institutions has also increased. Transparency and accountability have become key issues for fundraisers and policy makers. Institutions are becoming more specific and public in how funds are gathered and spent. ERPs also provide a solution for alumni donations and capital campaigns to identify potential donors, collect contributions and maintain human interest connections, and communicate, with interested parties. Linking data across units via the ERPs can enable institutions to coordinate information in ways that was previously impossible.

IMPLEMENTATION DRIVERS

The decision to implement an ERP is not an easy one. The most obvious deterrent is that ERPs are expensive to purchase and implement. The process of implementation is labor intensive; few institutions are able to face implementations easily, as in most cases staff needs are already lean. The process of implementation forces rethinking of business practices that can be extremely painful. Technology might drive changes in policy because of limitations with the purchased ERP system. Customization can cause future problems when the ERP is upgraded. The implementation process also forces departments that could normally work in "silos" to learn to work together, and incorporate cross-training into job descriptions. This forced communication can also create many problems because departments' business practices (previously independent) must now be coordinated, and in some cases become interdependent. Policies and practices that were idiosyncratic to the unit, and could be modified or manipulated as needed, now require shared decision making before changes can be made.

In spite of all these difficulties, the benefits of implementing an enterprise resource planning system far outweigh the decision to maintain a non-integrated system. Driven by customer service, administrators have an expectation of data for planning purposes, including enrollment, space utilization and building needs. Not only have customer and internal expectations become dependent on the integrated systems, but institutional effectiveness and accountability have become staple priorities for accreditation and state and federal reporting. Accountability to state and federal agencies providing grants (and other types of aid) relies upon the ability to provide data on demand. All constituents demand real time access in order to research a particular department, and download personal information (i.e. transcripts or tax deductable receipts). Federal reporting requires common elements to be collected and shared. Consistent reporting among schools that share a common board is another reason to implement.

BENEFITS FOR STAKEHOLDERS OF INSTITUTIONS

Administration. Administrators and decision makers can expect more integration with an ERP system, with greater likelihood of accurate and current information. For example, there would be only one access point for name and address information, and all modules will access these data resources from a common source (rather than each department maintaining its own "shadow system" with updates performed intermittently, if at all). The benefit of an integrated system is that information is only updated in one place in the database. A specific office is designated to be responsible for creating the record and maintaining the changes. Although reporting is more complex, the staff members throughout the institution become more adept at meeting the requirements. For example, data definitions become more specific and reporting needs are carefully considered. Institutions become better able to allow the public access to published reports.

Students. The individuals who benefit the most from an integrated system are the students, as students demand the greatest accessibility. The point of entry for potential students can begin with the first inquiry and a single sign-on can be created. As the potential students enroll and eventually take on new roles as student worker, faculty, staff, alumni or donor (or as employees become students – or students become employees), access to different modules can be granted.

Students have access to their own personal information, as well as being able to view current and historical information including programs of study, current and past catalogs, course schedules and unofficial transcripts. Academic advising becomes not only more automated, (since students can complete "what-if" scenarios in order to determine if a change of major is plausible) but more accurate, containing updated information about policy changes that advisors may not have been told, or if told, may not remember. Students can become more self-sufficient as they research questions about their programs and degree requirements.

Faculty. Faculty members have much to gain from an integrated system. They can access information about students in their classes and their advisees, to form better, more accurate images of their students. If granted access, they can view historical data about the students (i.e., transcripts and other academic information) as well as demographic data that can give them a better idea on how to plan for classroom management (number of students as registration occurs, male/female ratio, age of students, majors and non-majors, etc.) Faculty can begin to communicate prior to a semester beginning and can clearly outline what is expected prior to the first class meeting. If the student permits access to personal information to faculty and staff, advisors, needing to communicate with students, can have up-to-date telephone numbers, facilitating easier communication regarding program planning.

Some institutions have chosen to utilize ERP solutions as a catalyst for curriculum changes. Computer Information Science academic departments and business colleges have considered incorporating ERP problem solving into the course curriculum. This provides two benefits (1) to teach and reinforce ERP systems and concepts, and (2) better prepare the CIS graduates for job opportunities making use of this knowledge in higher education settings.

Staff. The greatest pressure for data accuracy falls on data entry staff members. Once a record is created, employees can potentially view the record and information could impact local, state and federal reporting. Specific guidelines have to be considered for when and how records are created and maintained, and who will have access to the information. Duplication of records needs to be carefully avoided in order to reduce inconsistencies between records, although it is understood that this is impossible to completely prevent. Training of staff is a critical part of the implementation process, both in terms of procedures and the rationale behind each procedure, so that staff members carefully perform all data entry.

Alumni. Alumni can stay connected to an institution in a seamless and active manner. Since the system is integrated, the single point of entry will stay consistent, even though the role of the individual may change. Alumni may not be able to register for classes (unless they reapply for a new program), but they can conveniently do many things, such as (1) view historical academic information (i.e. unofficial transcripts), (2) maintain relationships within the system, and (3) easily make donations (depending upon how the institutional advancement module is set up). Alumni can maintain their student email address (depending upon the policies within the institution), maintain electronic portfolios, make use of the career development center within their institution, and/or update all contact information for future communication with the institution. Alumni interested in a specific aspect of their former institution (e.g., musical performances, sports, academic achievements of their favorite faculty members) can easily remain connected.

Community. Depending on the demands from the local, state and federal communities that an institution serves, access can be created for constituents outside the institution of higher education. Reporting can become automated, and interested parties can have online access to various data and reports. Local boards, Boards of Trustees, and/or other interested parties can be granted online services and/or access to real time data. Discussions between the individuals in the institution involved in security of the ERP system and the community members seeking access can result in creation of roles that are satisfactory to all concerned.

BARRIERS TO IMPLEMENTATION AND STRATEGIES TO OVERCOME THEM

ERPs remain at the top of the agendas for IT departments in higher education, coming in as the Number 2 IT issue for 2009 (*Educause Review, 44*(6), 2009). As institutions of higher education embark upon investments of time and resources in implementing and maintaining ERPs, they are wise to examine other major campus-wide initiatives that have been recently undertaken. These other initiatives may be harbingers of the kinds of cross-campus cooperation, as well as turf battles, that might be encountered along the way, as the ERP is incorporated into the norms of the campus. The challenges facing campuses, and their IT departments, continue to be explored as opportunities for innovation; at the same time, practical considerations for the allocation of resources that will advance the campus (e.g., Collins, et al., 2009) must be taken into account. Participation by as many employees as possible would be ideal, but not cost effective or an efficient use of time; therefore, strategies must be developed to have facilitation, representation and collaboration (Haab & Surry, 2009) to create a positive environment for implementation.

In a research project in which 179 individuals who had previously been involved in implementation initiatives were queried, Ensminger, et al. (2003) identified four factors that accounted for 73% of the variance of factors influencing implementation success; these were (1) managed change (accounting for 25.3% of the variance), (2) performance efficacy of the individuals, and their belief that they had the skills needed to implement change effectively (accounting for 19.8% of the variance), (3) external rewards (meaning that team members "will be more likely to participate in the implementation process if they receive some recognition or reward for using the innovation" p. 69), accounting for 14.2% of the variance) and (4) resources, accounting for 14%

of the variance ("equipment, finances, personnel and other resources are in place and easily accessible before implementing an innovation" p. 69). Each of these factors is examined within the latter portion of this chapter.

Few initiatives have the potential for impacts as far-reaching as an ERP. Few have the possibilities for positively transforming the interactions within the campus. In this section of the chapter, specific types of barriers campus members are likely to face are identified, along with strategies for overcoming barriers. While the RIPPLE (Resources, Infrastructure, People, Policies, Learning, Evaluation and Support) model (Surry, 2002; Surry, et al., 2005) identifies for consideration of integration of most instructional technologies into higher education settings has many overlaps with the discussion below, some considerations are unique to implementation and use of an ERP.

Administration-Related Barriers

The momentum required to commit major budget resources to an ERP almost always includes the need to "sell" the local campus administration, Board of Trustees, and/or other governing bodies on the rationale for such an investment. As campus administrators describe their visions of new opportunities for connectedness and efficiencies, the tendency to minimize the potential barriers exists. Anticipation of, and incorporating discussion of, these barriers into all presentations will lead to a more successful implementation and use of the ERP overall. Ferrell (2007) examines how the higher education institution can examine, as part of its ERP usage, a broader consideration of its services to students, taking advantage of ways to look at service delivery in many ways.

Strategies for overcoming Administrator related barriers: When implementing an enterprise resource planning system, it is important to understand the dynamics of organizational change. In a change of this magnitude, the implementation will force all its members to examine the practices within the institution, and eventually challenge every existing policy and procedure. This change should be viewed not as an event, but rather a process. In the Concerns-Based Adoption Model (CBAM), twelve principles are identified as important when implementing school change (Hall & Hord, 2001). Administrators who understand the dynamics of such change and develop a plan for addressing the known issues will be able to facilitate and champion the change process.

Resource Allocation Barriers

Resource allocations include more than just funding for the product itself. The institution must consider resources (in addition to actual cost of the product) such as consulting packaging, cost to finance personnel to handle the day-to-day operations while staff is involved in the implementation process (backfill), annual fees associated with continued use of the product, and the cost of employee time.

Cost Barriers: Multi-year budget allocation is essential for the implementation and maintenance of an ERP system. Generally, such an investment is an allocation that dwarfs nearly all other IT commitments (and campus commitments, with the exception of new buildings). The costs of consultants, the product itself, and equipment replacements (or upgrades) quickly balloon to a proportion of the overall campus budget that is guaranteed to create "sticker shock" for members of campus budget committees. As such, the CIO or other administrator in charge of the allocation may be tempted to underestimate costs, in order to make them more palatable, especially in a time of austerity and economic downturn on campuses (Goldstein, 2008). The need for transparency of budgets in the current climate of campus norms can make that temptation even more appealing.

Strategies for Overcoming Cost Barriers: Avoid the siren song of under-estimating the cost of ERPs. Budget adjustment is a less painful process if the rationale for each budget item can not only be explained with facts, but with details about the consequences of reducing the budget by elimination of that item from the budget. Dialogue with peer institutions that have implemented similar ERPs can provide clarification of the need for some of the more costly, less easily understood items. Many, for example, question the cost of consultants – usually including not only extraordinary hourly charges, but lodging and travel. For the typical campus budget committee, composed of faculty members and professional staff, as well as members of the budget staff, these numbers are astonishing. Mahon (2008) describes recommendations for developing and sharing budget information.

Preparation for the presentation of the ERP budget (whether purchase, implementation, upgrade or maintenance) should assume a need for an acclimation of neophytes who are unfamiliar with proposed allocations with so many zeros. Include an explanation of the budget items in terms of what "typical" costs are for ERP implementation and maintenance (available through EduCause or AACRAO). Additionally, the cost of *not* making use of these resources (e.g., of the potential for failure, or for extending the timeline) needs to be made clear.

Involving individuals associated with the project, as well as others across campus indirectly involved with the project, in understanding the development of the budget, and the value of items included, can enable all to become more sensitive to the need for cost savings in other areas. For example, the increased frugality that is imposed on other parts of the campus can be better understood when a contingency budget is explained. Additionally, the decision to not embark on other costly projects (cost in terms of time or funds) during turning points of the ERP implementation or upgrade can be better accepted if campus members have been educated. Although time-consuming, these explanations to the relevant groups involved with budget oversight can yield understanding, if not support, in the long run. These explanations, when shared with the budget committee of the Board of Trustees (or College Council), can also yield benefits; since there is a risk of providing too much detail at quarterly meetings, the on-going discussions with the budget committees can maintain open dialogue. The information flow is two way, allowing for time for questions as well as progress updates. When budget corrections must be made, the foundation for such changes has been laid.

Backfill Barriers. During an ERP implementation or upgrade, after careful review of the milestones to be accomplished, potential team members are identified. Likely, the list includes key people who must be directly involved in ERP day-to-day activities, not just the occasional meeting. Generally, these are lynch-pin people who serve in vital roles in other parts of the institution. The question of how to make the decision to backfill these individuals must be answered on a case-by-case basis. However, the following problems emerge exist when the backfill option in not selected:

- Individuals cannot perform 100% of their regular duties while dealing with the pressures and crises associated with ERPs. Some slippage is inevitable.
- Individuals become demoralized and overwhelmed when recognizing that dual work responsibilities have become the norm. They sense that the initial unrealistic expectations for overtime, and the unpredictable crisis becoming the norm, will be ongoing throughout the ERP project. Many involved realize that such conditions are likely to only become more intense as the ERP timeline of implementation, upgrade, or product change takes place.
- Failure to take the time for cross training can mean that the institution becomes overly dependent on crucial people. When illness, life events, or departure for a new employment opportunity comes along,

emergencies tap the resources of individuals who are already stretched too thin.

Strategies for Overcoming Backfill Barriers. The use of backfill can appear difficult both in terms of cost and replacement of vital people. However, by talking with counterparts at peer institutions where the backfill option was not chosen, the problems associated with that choice become clear. With careful planning in terms of cross-training, time line, and budget, the backfill option can become a reality. The benefits that occur in terms of morale, efficiencies, and depth of trained personnel in key areas can enable campuses to benefit tremendously from what looks initially to be costly and optional.

Time Barriers. A perennial problem with all ERP efforts is aptly depicted in the title of Green's 2007 article, "Prodding the ERP turtle." "Why is this taking so long?" is a question frequently asked by members of the campus community. "With all these resources, can't you speed things up?" The second temptation, following closely after the seductive thoughts of reducing the ERP budget, is to provide a timeline that is overly optimistic.

In developing a project timeline, the project managers often will neglect to include the "black out dates" during which members of the campus (often, even those involved on the project with backfill) must have their time and energy redirected to normal campus operations (such as end-of-semester tasks, preparation for registration, graduation checks, etc.). Depending upon the size of the campus, and the number of faculty and staff members involved in the ERP work, these predictable events vary in terms of the amount of time consumed. When creating a project timeline, therefore, the extended amount of time to be used for all major ERP-associated is often seen as a barrier. Interestingly, the extended involvement of the entire campus to maintain the ERP system is necessary: "technology staff cannot maintain new systems alone. Just as the initial implementation team required a user-driven, collaborative effort with IT, so too does ongoing systems maintenance. This need has also caught most institutions by surprise" (Goldstein, 2006, p. 54). From the point of committing to an ERP, the allocation of time is necessary.

Strategies regarding the use of Time. The campus community should be kept well informed of the progress of the project, as well as the "windows of opportunity" for when certain key activities can take place (generally between major campus events, such as extended on-line registration, or posting grades). The use of ERP project web sites can provide those individuals who are most interested with information about progress, including specific problems that have arisen, and how they are being addressed.

The major success strategies for campuses in "use of time" is to make sure that there are regularly scheduled open dialogues with key campus stakeholders. Open reporting opportunities (e.g., open meetings, presentations at planning councils or meetings of the College Senate) can facilitate understanding, and derail energy that might otherwise go toward suspicion or criticism related to the ERP. These types of conversations would be part of the campus communication plan for the ERP. As Fowler & Gilfillan (2003) recommend, the broader the stakeholder involvement, the better.

There should be no surprises when a deadline is missed. The campus community, if kept informed about the commitment of the ERP team to waiting until all testing has been done, and the implementation of only an error-free product, will come to understand that not all deadlines can absolutely be fixed in advance. Only a well informed campus will understand, and quietly accept, changes in decisions. Such acceptance reflects an on-going commitment to the ERP.

Barriers Related to Campus Policies

The use of an ERP system often requires the scrutiny of many long-standing policies, due to "the need for organizational policies and procedures to adapt to new technologies. Many organizational policies, especially those in relatively stable, long-term businesses such as higher education, were developed before technology became a common tool in the workplace" (Surry, 2002). Whether these are easily changed (e.g., instead of approval of calendars one year ahead of time, the approval of calendars two years ahead becomes a necessity when on-line grading and registration are implemented), or more complex (e.g., the implementation of a new designation in the grading process to denote judicial misconduct), policies intrude into the established ERP system. Changes to the system, reflecting changes to policies. must be incorporated into the ERP plan.

It is often the case that policies impacted by the ERP system have not been updated for decades. The surprise with which the conflict between technology and policy is discovered is often followed swiftly by the urgent need for a solution. When under pressure to resolve a conflict quickly, decisions can be made that are not fully analyzed, leading to additional policy modification, following further panic about the incomplete nature of the policy change. This crisis cycle undermines the careful policy review/revision process, and gives many people reason to doubt the care being taken with the ERP process.

Goldstein (2006) identifies the necessity of changing the ways of doing business due to the need to participate in on-going work of ERPs:

"The phenomenon of continuous implementation has had four broad impacts on institutions. It has:

- Created a need for more active and integrated systems governance
- Necessitated a continual commitment to operations improvement
- Altered the traditional boundaries between IT and user areas in systems management
- Given rise to the need for a new user skill set" (p. 54)

The work of the campus involves developing new practices, as well as new ways to meet all the responsibilities associated with the ERP.

Suggestions for Overcoming Policy Barriers. Concurrent with the start of the ERP implementation or upgrade, it is extremely beneficial to bring together a diverse group of stakeholders. Look for members who meet one or more of these characteristics: (a) familiar with campus policies, (b) involved in examining the functionality of the ERP system, or (c) involved with the campus structure for policy revision. This Policy Review group can prioritize policies that will be most pertinent to the ERP, and begin a slow, thoughtful discussion of them. In so doing, the need for revision of specific policies may be highlighted. The membership of this policy group can be a key factor in the success the group will have in being realistic, and systematically draft revisions of relevant policies. Follow Mahon's advice: "Do not pave the cow path" (2009, p. 7).

The group is the first to explore these policies, and may work in an advisory capacity with the relevant campus administrator(s) or governance body. In some cases, exploratory discussions with peer institutions can reveal that the ERP product has the capacity to implement existing policies. In other cases, a domino effect of new options made available by the ERP system may lead to streamlining policies that were in place for the wrong reasons. New policies that address long standing concerns, but were out of reach of a non-integrated system, may be one of the unexpected outcomes of implementing the ERP system. Making use of the ERP implementation for policy review is at the heart of turning a technology implementation into a campus-wide change management effort (e.g., Scott, 2003).

Consideration of the campus climate (technological and cultural) when the policies were developed can lead to understanding of whether or not it is time for a policy change. Consider the standard keyboard, and how out-of-date/dysfunctional it is. When the location of keys on a standard keyboard (for a manual typewriter) was designed, the prime rationale was not efficiency. Instead, the little fingers used for important letters and punctuation were chosen to slow the typist down, to prevent typewriter keys from getting entangled. Such a need has long been obsolete. However, all efforts to move to newer, more efficient keyboard layouts have been consistently rejected with the explanation that "people are accustomed to the keyboard" and "it would be too hard to change." Good reasons to leave things as they are? Not really. Is this analogy relevant to campus ERP usage? Absolutely.

The policies at many institutions of higher education were designed around human needs (e.g., end-of-semester grading window was designed around the need for the Registrar's office to manually enter grades in advance of holiday breaks, time to mail probation letters, or preparation of diplomas for commencement). The options provided by technology allow for new policies as well as practices.

Human Barriers

To successfully make use of an ERP system, care must be taken to identify and overcome people-based barriers. While some of the individuals who are impediments to an ERP are uninformed about the rationale for, and usage of, the ERP, others have personality traits which cannot be eliminated by sharing information. The discussion below clarifies some of the barriers to take into consideration with the ERP usage that will enhance ERP usage.

Barriers in the form of burnout and discouragement of the Project Team. As members of the project team work longer and harder on the ERP, they can get more and more discouraged. Perhaps the product fails to live up to expectations. Unexpected turnover within the project team (having nothing to do with the project) or the need for development of new skills without proper preparation or training can demoralize the individuals who are directly involved with implementing and maintaining the ERP.

Strategies to overcome burnout and discouragement. Each of the following can give the team members a sense that their work is not being ignored:

- One-time support in the form of an honorarium, compensatory time, or access to a campus resource that would otherwise cost money (e.g., campus health club, lecture series, music series)
- Periodic pats on the back (in the form of e-mails, letters to file, hand-written communication) from different individuals on campus (administration, enrollment management), beneficiaries of ERP (students, alumni) or vendor, or regularly scheduled compensatory time
- Promotions
- Funding and time to attend conferences or institutes that address general ERP issues, as well as on campus or off campus training relevant to skills specific to the ERP
- Participation in publication or presentation by others on campus reporting on ERP at local or national conference
- Improvement of own skill set (e.g., presentation skill training, writing training)

Personal characteristics that work against the ERP. There are at least four responses that you might hear from your campus community during the implementation process:

- "It was a lot easier in the old days." (Response 1)
- "If you wait long enough, this fad will pass, too." (Response 2)
- "Why doesn't anyone know what they are doing around here?" (Response 3)
- "When will things get back to normal?" (Response 4)

Each of these responses identifies a different barrier that individuals involved with ERPs are likely to encounter from members of their campus community.

Nostalgia. On many campuses, individuals look back to the previous way of doing business (e.g., Response 1). Either the "pre computer" era, or the previous technology solution, is seen as the "right" way to do things. These individuals often have very convenient memories, evoking recollections of benefits that may have previously been overlooked.

Suspicion and skepticism. Some individuals (e.g., Response 2) have found that many campus solutions (technology and otherwise) disappear before they become fully integrated into the campus business models. As a result, willingness to "wait out" nearly all initiatives has led some campus members to successfully predict the failure of the latest endeavor. They may wait to board the ERP train, perhaps hoping to stall indefinitely.

Criticism and finger pointing. Because the ERP will require a combination of change of structure and a technological solution, individuals who are quick to accuse others of incompetence (e.g., Response 3) are likely to accurately criticize once in a while. Depending upon the visibility and credibility of these nay-sayers, the ERP project members can lose time while informing and/or placating them.

Resistant to Change. While less is heard lately about "change management" at technology conferences, there are many candidates for change management boot camp (Response 4). The lessons most campuses have learned in ERP implementations and upgrades are the "new normal" – the ERP goes on forever, and there is no freedom from change. It becomes the responsibility of leaders on campus to guide the entire campus community toward this understanding: patience and joint ownership of the challenges ERPs pose will be required.

Strategies for overcoming Personal Characteristic Barriers. A campus-wide understanding of the human components of ERP success will lead to an investment of time and creativity in all aspects of the ERP. Instead of limiting time prior to a campus change of the ERP product to only regression testing, or end-user training, successful campuses invest time and resources in assisting campus members who are not on board with the ERP. This investment can look like development and use of one or more of the following:

- **Campus Communication Plan.** A communication plan is an essential part of the ERP implementation. A plan that highlights how the new product is an improvement over previous service delivery models can do more than just communicate information. In many cases, while the previous systems may have been convenient for the back office staff, there may be new recipients of the functionality of the new ERP product (e.g., students, alumni, department secretaries) who will have new or improved access. An effective communication plan takes advantage of many different formats for information sharing, evaluation, and consideration of next steps. The best plans have mechanisms incorporated that solicit and use feedback from campus members regarding the recent technological innovation clarifying the use, or modification, of suggestions made. Members of the campus have different priorities for what is most important about the implementation (Cramer, Tetewsky, & Marczynski, 2010). Attuning communications to a wide range of concerns (e.g., student benefits, pragmatic, economic) will ensure broader connections with campus members.
- **Change Management Plan.** Making use of the opportunity for cross-functional groupings for reflection and planning (e.g., co-mingling the enrollment management units and the academic units, involving the IT staff members not just in training but in

demonstrations of the functionality of the product) can give all on campus an understanding of the range of services available via use of the ERP. This diminishes the silo mentality. A mind-shift can occur when individuals have new perspectives about the results of resource allocation to the ERP initiative. Integration of change management into a technological innovation (e.g., Shohan & Perry, 2009) is an investment that expands the likelihood that the initiative will be successful. Scott (2003) thoughtfully explores patterns of change pertaining to incorporation of technology into student learning, with many parallels to the ERP process.

- **Two-to-two dialogues.** Although the last thing individuals deeply involved in an ERP project may want to do is meet with the highly negative campus members, such meetings can be productive. Have two members of the project team meet with the difficult person, and encourage the difficult person to bring along a colleague so there are even numbers for the discussion. This prevents the two people from getting stuck, and not listening to each other. Provide time for the critics to speak their minds, and also have a chance to learn more than would be possible in a more generalized campus information format (whether web-based, or town hall meeting format).
- **Reinforce shared ownership of the ERP effort.** The method of giving the entire campus a way to participate in the design and success of an ERP may go from the trivial (contest to select the name) to the most complex (open forums that offer opportunities to hear details of the ERP's potential from the campus team involved in the implementation, and/or individuals from other campuses who have been directly involved with the same product). Instead of standing outside the initiatives, and looking in, all members of the campus community have been invited to be involved (e.g., Hanna, 2003).

Interpersonal Barriers

Campus Specific. The difficulties on campus that occur as a result of warring factions, each attempting to orient the ERP toward their own unit's needs, can be highly disruptive. Time and resources often must be channeled to transform silo thinking into a cooperative effort oriented toward student access or improved information-sharing across units. The turf battles that prevent effective problem solving often shift the focus away from "what might be done" toward "what has gone wrong," or "what has been inefficient."

At times, this can be a function of members of top campus management having very different views of the potential benefits of the ERP. Usage may be redefined to meet the needs of one group, at the expense of another. Inadequate support from key campus administrators (or weakened positions of the administrator who is the ERP champion) can force protracted discussions of matters that would be otherwise settled simply. A campus might take multiple semesters to phase in use of a particular feature (e.g., use of a PIN number for advisement by volunteer departments) when a decision by the President could bring all on board at once.

Strategies to address campus-specific interpersonal barriers. When planning meetings to develop the ERP project timeline, risk analysis and charter, invite individuals who have had a wide range of experiences with the campus – some long-term members, as well as some new ones. Make sure to include a facilitator who is good at keeping all options open, and encourages the sharing of many ideas. Make use of the same monitoring mechanisms successfully used in previous campus efforts (e.g., the strategic plan, advancement of the assessment of general education), so that it will be possible to determine whether maximum progress is being made in a timely way. Additionally, providing those involved in development of sufficient information so that an effective timeline can be developed can increase the likelihood of the success of the plan (Surry & Ensminger, 2002). This can give the campus a way to recycle strategies that have been effective in the past, and to prevent the waste of time and energy on weakness or dysfunction.

Leadership has been identified (e.g., Cramer, 2005; Cramer, 2003) as an essential feature of technology implementations – both within the team and in commitment of campus administrators to the initiative. Leading in difficult times is especially challenging (Goldstein, 2008), but essential. Hawkins (2007) describes it in this way:

For IT to make a difference on campus, the key is not having the greatest technology but, rather, having a collaborative team that envisions and sets a goal within an organizational context. The key is having a strong leader at the helm who has the courage to take a risk and who can marshal other leaders on campus to believe that this is a desirable risk to take. (p. 62)

Campuses can develop their own standards for leadership which enable dialogue to precede risk taking. Invite the informal and formal campus leaders to develop routines for setting and monitoring technology-specific goals. Welcoming this involvement may feel counter-intuitive, but such participation can lead to greater investment in the implementation.

Consultant Specific. The use of consultants is the norm for nearly all ERPs, since the highly technical nature of the ERP products makes reliance exclusively on implementation documentation very time-consuming. However, not all consultants are right for every campus. In some cases, the consultant lacks depth in an area of expertise the campus expects. In other cases, the consultant's interaction style is problematic. Because the campus is highly vulnerable, and less familiar with the product than the consultant purports to be, it often takes a while for a campus to realize that a problem exists.

Strategies to address consultant-specific barriers. Develop a mechanism to assess satisfaction with each consultant, and put that process in place within the first few weeks of the start of each consultant working on the ERP. The support of effective consultants can illustrate to all what is going right, and firing/rejecting a consultant who has been offered by a firm can put the company on notice about campus standards for consultants. Firing a consultant can go a long way toward getting higher caliber consultants throughout the ERP project.

Product-Specific Barriers and Solutions

One of the most discouraging experiences campuses can have is when the implementation of an ERP is unsuccessful because the product lacks necessary functionality. Prevent this before it becomes a problem by thoroughly researching the product, talking with peer institutions using the product under consideration, as well as other products. Avoid this problem so that it does not disrupt the potential benefits of using an ERP to improve business practices on campus.

During implementation, institutions should try to minimize customization of the ERP solution. Any customization of a current version will involve future customizations (and costs) with every patch and upgrade. Reporting capability should be increased, but the difficulty comes with trying to define reports, and being very clear about the purpose of certain reports. The institution must develop a common vocabulary across departments. The use of the word "petition" may be uniquely defined within five or six different department, but the ERP will require a single meaning. This can be an especially difficult aspect of implementations at larger (or multi-campus) institutions. Some departments may have a long history of not working together, and now are forced to use the common terminology. Attentive leadership, and sharing the vision of the potential benefits of the ERP, may bring down the walls that have prevented collaboration in previous decades.

CONCLUSION

In an effort to become more effective and efficient, institutions will continue to implement ERPs, either by upgrading a current product or seeking a better solution. Successful projects must begin with a clear rationale for the change, a widely targeted communication plan, and a well-led change management vision. Assuming that these are carried out with a realistic timeline, there should be a paradigm shift on campus towards a culture of change rather than a one-time implementation event. The social and organizational implication is that the institution will have survived a transition that will make it more productive and better equipped to serve all of the campus constituents. The institution will also have a history of success that can be replicated with other challenges – whether technological or system-wide in non-technological ways.

The key to a successful post-implementation is the structure of the implementation teams and the institution's approach to decision making and training. One of the concurrent pro and con to implementing an ERP system is that the institution is forced to rethink current business practices along the lines of the system's architecture. Since the modules within an ERP are integrated, decisions that are made within one team may drastically affect the policy and practices of another. This forces conversations between offices within an institution that may have never had to interact in the past. Some processes will be easy to implement into the new system. However, many practices will have to be re-negotiated based on limitations of the system. These negotiations can bring about policy change. During the negotiations, teams will begin to take sides and it will feel as if there is a "winner" and a "loser" for the decision. It is important that these decisions do not hinder communication and progress for the institution.

Usually an implementation involves a strategic plan for "going live" with different modules in a specified order. As modules are added, communication and accountability are especially crucial. Departments that may not have had to interact previously will now understand each other more intimately than ever before. For example, student records that are created when a prospective student makes initial inquires to the institution will be the same record that eventually will be used by the alumni association when asking for a large donation, decades after the individual graduated. Naming conventions, data standards and maintenance of personal and student information could impact the likelihood of an alumni donation, so these guidelines must be decided prior to data collection. Project managers and implementation team leaders must carefully control these decision-making opportunities, reminding everyone to discern best decisions for the institution.

Colleges and universities all share a common goal: to recruit, enroll, and graduate students, and to maintain relationships with alumni. The process of implementation will change the campus climate and campus culture, and the implemented ERP should enhance the ability to better educate and serve the campus community.

REFERENCES

Collins, S.Educause Evolving Technologies Committee. (2009). What technology? Reflections on evolving services. *EDUCAUSE Review*, *44*(6), 60–76.

Cramer, S. F. (2003). Challenging core assumptions: Integrating transformative leadership models into campus-wide implementation activities. *College and University Journal*, *79*(1), 15–22.

Cramer, S. F. (2005). *Student Information Systems: A Guide to Implementation Success*. Washington, D.C.: American Association of College Registrars and Admissions Officers.

Cramer, S. F. (2006). Student information system implementations: A context for campus change. *College and University Journal, 81*(2), 21–33.

Cramer, S. F., Tetewsky, S. J., & Marczynski, K. S. (2010). What facilitates and impedes collaborative work during higher education software implementation projects? *Journal of Educational Change, 11*(4), 457–486..doi:10.1007/s10833-010-9142-x

Ensminger, D. C., Surry, D. W., Porter, B. E., & Wright, D. (2004). Factors Contributing to the Successful Implementation of Technology Innovations. *Journal of Educational Technology & Society, 7*(3), 61–72.

Ferrell, G. (2007). Enterprise approaches to information and learning technologies. *Perspective, 11*(1), 12–17.

Fowler, A., & Gilfillan, M. (2003). A framework of stakeholder integration of higher education information systems projects. *Technology Analysis and Strategic Management, 15*(4), 467–489. doi:10.1080/095373203000136051

Goldstein, P. J. (2006). Implementation never ends! The post-implementation organizational and operational implications of ERP. *New Directions for Higher Education, 136*, 53–68. doi:10.1002/he.239

Goldstein, P. J. (2008). *Managing the Funding Gap: How Today's Economic Downturn Is Impacting IT Leaders and Their Organizations*. An EDUCAUSE

Green, K. C. (2007). Prodding the ERP Turtle. *EDUCAUSE Review, 42*(6), 148–149.

Haab, M., & Surry, D. W. (2009). *Implementation of ERP systems in higher education: Relationship between modes of participation and satisfaction with implementation of enterprise resource planning systems in higher education*. Saarbrucken, Germany: VDM-Verlag.

Hall, G. E., & Hord, S. M. (2001). *Implementing Change: Patterns, Principles, and Potholes*. Boston: Allyn and Bacon.

Hanna, D. E. (2003). Building a leadership vision: Eleven strategic challenges for higher education. *Educause Review, 38*(4), 24-28 and 30-34.

Hawking, P., McCarthy, B., & Stein, A. (2004). Second wave ERP education. *Journal of Information Systems Education, 15*(3), 327–332.

Hawkins, B. L. (2007). Winds of change: Charting the course for IT in the twenty-first century. *EDUCAUSE Review, 42*(6), 54, 56–70.

Lozinsky, S. (1998). *Enterprise-wide software solutions: Integration strategies and practice*. Reading, MA: Addison-Wesley.

Mahon, M. (2009). Implementing an ERP on time and on budget: An innovative and inclusive approach. Educause Center for Applied Research, *Research Bulletin, 2009, (*10), 1-13 (complete). n. n. (2009). Recommended resources for the top ten IT Issues. *EDUCAUSE Review, 44*(6), 102–103.

Scott, G. (2003). Effective change management in higher education. *EDUCAUSE Review, 38*(6), 64–80.

Shohan, S., & Perry, M. (2009). Knowledge management as a mechanism for technological and organizational change management in Israeli universities. *Higher Education, 57*(2), 227–246. doi:10.1007/s10734-008-9148-y

Surry, D. W. (2002). *A model for integrating instructional technology into higher education.* Paper presented at the American Educational Research Association Conference, April, 2002, New Orleans, LA.

Surry, D. W., & Ensminger, D. C. (2002). *Perceived Importance of Conditions that Facilitate Implementation.* Paper presented at the American Educational Research Association Conference, April, 2002, New Orleans, LA.

Surry, D. W., Ensminger, D. C., & Haab, M. (2005). A Model for Integrating Instructional Technology into Higher Education. *British Journal of Educational Technology, 36*(2), 327–329. doi:10.1111/j.1467-8535.2005.00461.x

White Paper from the December 2008 ECAR Symposium.

KEY TERMS AND DEFINITIONS

Backfill: The process of filling the daily jobs of key stakeholders that hold prominent roles during implementation while their time is allocated to the project.

Barriers: The factors that serve as impediments to the implementation process.

Enterprise Resource Planning (ERP): Shoemaker (2003) defines an **ERP** as an "integrated software application that supports the core business processes of a firm by handling and integrating most of the intra-firm business practices in real time" (p. 69).

Go-Live: This is the date that is assigned when a module will be "turned on" for constituents to utilize. For example, a "registration go live" date would be when the students begin registration on the new system (advisors will access, students will register, administration will monitor head count, etc.).

Pre-Implementation: The time frame that begins with the decision to explore the possibility of replacing an existing student information system with an enterprise resource planning system.

Implementation: The time frame that succeeds ERP selection and the launching of the campus communication and change management plan through the "go live" date.

Post-Implementation: This is the time frame that exists after a "go-live" event. Since most ERPs are implemented in modules, different departments/offices could be various stages of the implementation process. Processes move into a maintenance stage and periodic reviews of the progress should continue.

Section 3
Evolving Impacts of Technology

Chapter 18
Toward a New Standard of Quality in Online Learning:
Critical Interaction and the Death of the Online Instructor

Robert Gray
University of South Alabama, USA

James Dwight
Lancaster Theological Seminary, USA

ABSTRACT

This chapter explores how Barthes's concept of writerly/readerly texts can be applied to enrich our understanding of interaction in online courses. Writerly texts are texts that require the reader to actively participate in the production of the text's meaning, whereas readerly texts offer only a limited number of possible interpretations. Barthes privileges the writerly text because it pictures the reader in an active posture, in the role of co-writer, jointly producing meaning rather than passively receiving it. The authors argue that the writerly/readerly opposition provides a powerful tool with which we can reconceptualize the relationship between the instructional content of online courses and the students who encounter them. Such an approach will allow us a fuller understanding of not only the interpretive nature of the learning process, but also of the advantages inherent in empowering students in that process. Furthermore, this approach will allow us to better understand and measure quality in online courses.

Without Contraries is no progression.

William Blake (1793/1988, p. 34)

DOI: 10.4018/978-1-60960-147-8.ch018

INTRODUCTION

Online learning has evolved considerably over its first decade and a half of existence, but many of the major issues facing it at its inception still remain.

While technologies continue to improve and the numbers of courses and participating institutions continue to grow, the question of quality in online courses has never been adequately addressed, perhaps because doing so would require a task of unimaginable complexity. One of the chief causes of this is simply the difficulty in defining what constitutes quality and what it would really mean to measure something that is so elusive and contested in a way that is not ultimately too simplistic or reductive. While thousands of articles, hundreds of books, and countless conference presentations have all attempted to explore the subject of quality in online learning, there does seem to be a general consensus among commentators on what constitutes good practice in the online classroom, and no one would argue—regardless of their ideological, philosophical, political, or even commercial perspective—that online learning is "good enough" in its current state; therefore much work is left to be done in developing a richer understanding of the possibilities afforded by ever-improving instructional technologies and pedagogical practices.

While the digital campus could never fully replicate the traditional environment of the college campus—and this is true on many levels: socially, instructionally, developmentally, even aesthetically—the same can be said for the online classroom. Regardless of one's particular attitude toward online learning, however, we must recognize that, at least for the foreseeable future, it is not going to go away for a variety of reasons. While the ramifications of its continued presence and growth are open to debate, whether or not it threatens the core of what we consider to be of most value about the university, it is the responsibility of the university to ensure that what online learning does in the name of the university is not a travesty.

That is not to say that the online classroom should seek merely to replicate the traditional classroom. It is highly unlikely that the best classroom practice can be replicated online, but it is equally unlikely that these best practices can be widely replicated in the traditional classroom either. Even more unlikely is the notion that we could ever clearly identify any kind of replicable essential element that makes the "best" practices best. The presumed existence of this sort of *je ne sais quoi*, and more importantly the qualities that make it unknowable, is behind much of the difficulty in establishing a universally effective model for online teaching and learning. This mystical reality, this essence of good teaching, is simply not something that can be reduced to a dependent variable; nor is it translatable into any kind of statistical formulae or, for that matter, into theoretical exposition. Therefore, the comparison between traditional and online learning is at best problematic, especially when we recognize that virtually all of the education research outside of that which focuses on the online classroom tends to be fairly critical of the quality of instruction in the traditional classroom, particularly at the higher education level. One need not look far to find that the fetishism of this traditional classroom is merely an unfounded rumor.

Our search for this *je ne sais quoi* that represents the "best" of educational practice also demonstrates the value of a postmodern or poststructuralist approach to education. Through the lens of poststructuralism, we can recognize the search for a reified "best of" as a demonstration of the metaphysics of presence, a search for a transcendental signified. While we believe that there can be quality online courses, such quality cannot be easily quantified or automatically implemented. More importantly, the best university education experiences, whether online or in the classroom, are experiences that allow the student/reader an opportunity to participate dialogically in the production of meaning in the classroom. First, however, we must look at the concept of interaction.

INTERACTION

From the time online learning first hit the mainstream in higher education, interaction has been considered by most authorities to be one of the chief indices of quality in online learning (Moore et al., 2001; Palloff & Pratt, 1999; Wallace, 2003), and interaction as an activity, even as an abstract entity, has received a considerable amount of attention in the literature. In order to take full advantage of the educative benefits provided by interaction, however, we need to develop a richer understanding of interaction that goes beyond simplistic adaptations of communication theory, untested decade-old assumptions, and even mathematical analysis. We need a more sophisticated understanding of interaction, as well as of what interaction can be. We need to move beyond mere interaction to what might be called critical interaction.

One place to start developing such an understanding is through the language of literary theory. Literary theory has a long and rich history of exploring the relationship between writers, readers, and texts, and most contemporary literary theory derives from the same theoretical and philosophical traditions that have shaped sociology, anthropology, and qualitative education research. These traditions—poststructuralism, semiotics, reader-response theory, cultural studies, Marxism, and Feminism—can give us considerable insights into how we view all aspects of online learning from course materials to curriculum. It is important to note that rethinking our concept of interaction will involve a radical challenge to traditional concepts of online course pedagogy.

The primary advantage of literary theory is that it will provide the tools necessary to reconceptualize online courses as "texts," which will allow more sophisticated modes of analysis of the teaching and learning process. While our first instinct may be to take "online course texts" to mean the instructor-written portions of a course, the term "text" here is something much larger. A text is any combination of "signs" that convey meaning, and if we are to improve our understanding of online courses, we will need to adopt the Derridean stance that "everything is a text" (quoted in Rawlings, 1999). This theoretical frame will make every aspect of an online course available for analysis and inclusion: from written text from the instructor; to written text from other content experts outside of the course (e.g., textbooks, articles, external websites, etc.); to audio or video from the instructor; to audio or video from others (e.g., guest lectures, commercial videos, etc.); to written text or audio from students. Furthermore, the "text" can take place anywhere, from the content page of the course proper, to discussion boards, chat rooms, and emails, as well as images, videos, and other multimedia objects. Therefore, when we consider online courses as texts, we consider not only the instructors' written materials, although these are certainly included in that term, but also the complex web of signifiers and signifieds that are produced by and within the online course as a whole. It is important to note students in the online environment are an important portion of that textual web as well, not only in the form of their contributions to discussions and chats, but also in that they become embodied texts themselves, actual avatars writing the course in active collaboration.

DEFINING INTERACTION

Before we can turn radically in a new direction, however, we must first look at the development of the concept of interaction. Interaction has been a major part of the conversation concerning online learning from the beginning, and Moore's (1989) definition of three primary types of interaction has remained the standard for most treatments of interaction in online courses:

- Learner-content interaction
- Learner-instructor interaction

- Learner-learner interaction

All three of these are important in virtually any educational endeavor (Moore et al, 2001; Sims, 2003), but for most of the conversation regarding online courses, learner-learner interaction seems to have gotten the most play. This is particularly important in that Moore's list "affirms the value of student-to-student exchanges, thus making a key addition to the traditional, instructor-centered view of instruction" (Roblyer & Wiencke, 2003, p. 80). However, Moore asserts that educators should thoughtfully and appropriately apply all three types of interaction in their teaching to "ensure maximum effectiveness" (1989, p. 5).

Of course, there are several other types of interaction that could and need to be explored, and a better model of interaction should incorporate more of the multiplicity of factors that actually mediate any kind of interaction. Thus, a typical string of actions might comprise the following events:

student↔computer↔instructor↔computer↔
computer↔society↔computer↔student

It is worth noting that most views of interaction tend to focus on concrete things rather than relations, but real interaction, perhaps, is what occurs in the arrows.

The most important (and overlooked) aspect of understanding interaction is that it must be understood as (at the very least) a two-way phenomenon. Very early in the interaction literature, Herring (1987) defines interaction as "reciprocal events that require at least two objects and two actions, and...occur when these objects and events mutually influence one another" (quoted in Wagner, 1994, p. 13). This fundamental, seemingly clear statement is at the heart of what is potentially valuable about interaction in online learning, but it also subtly reveals what most of the literature on the subject often fails to consider. It is the "mutual influence" that defines interaction, where the learner influences the educational experience reciprocally, where the dialogics of learning are strived for and achieved, and are not simply a subtly hegemonic gesture.

LEARNER-CONTENT INTERACTION

While most of the attention in the interaction literature is given to learner-instructor and learner-learner interaction, learner-content interaction is arguably the most important kind in an educational context. Even so, it is necessary to point out that information is not learning (Shank, 1998), that "good teaching involves more than the distribution of information" (Noble, 1998, quoted in Vess, 2004, p. 385). In this regard, it is worth noting that while a library is an important feature of a university, and while that library contains an appropriate amount of "knowledge" or information from which an enterprising student could appropriate a sufficient learning base equivalent to what could be learned in a classroom course, or even an entire degree program, there is no one who would argue that the library threatens to render the rest of the university obsolete. In other words, the library is not the university. Instruction has as much to do with the provider and provision—as well as with the receiver and reception—of instruction as it does with the actual content to be learned. Of course, learning can occur wherever information exists, and there is potential for learner-content interaction when a properly trained and motivated student intellectually interacts with information. However, the potential for learning does not necessarily constitute learning. Its legitimacy as teaching could be called into question as well.

Moore lists learner-content interaction as the first type of interaction for a reason. Without it, he explains, there "cannot be education, since it is the process of intellectually interacting with content that results in changes in the learner's understanding, the learner's perspective, or the cognitive structures of the learner's mind" (1989, p. 2). This is an important start, but to a great extent, at this level the interaction is still largely one-way. We need to find ways to make this kind of interaction more dialogic, to make it achieve Herring's (1987) test of "mutual influence." Furthermore, to recognize that learners and instructors, and perhaps even content, are mutually influencing is not going far enough. A course's content, in the interactive processes of teaching and learning, becomes a distillation of the traditional texts, the instructor's goals and experiences, and the students' various writings upon and within the content. Moreover, to take a Foucauldian turn, the institution at the macro and micro levels influences the content. For instance, someone who has taught literature in a Catholic high school and in a state university will quickly recognize that those institutions play a large role in the scope of what is taught and the methods that can be employed. The content is no longer a discreet entity, but rather a distillation of many factors. It is nebulous as it is so differently understood by all the participants, and transitory as it is constantly in a state of flux. To avoid this dangerous kind of dualism (Dewey, 1902), we must develop a more complex understanding of what interaction is.

POSTSTRUCTURALISM AND HYPERTEXT

One area where sophisticated theory is being applied in the learner-content literature is hypertext. Hypertext is simply the ability provided by electronic texts, particularly web-based texts, to be linked together through hyperlinks. One example might be that if this text were published on the Internet, we could make the word "hypertext" in the previous sentence a link that, if clicked, would trigger a pop-up window containing a definition of "hypertext." Or, it could lead to another document about hypertext, opening new paths for readers to pursue. Dwight and Garrison (2003), drawing in part from the work of poststructuralist theorists like Jacques Derrida and Roland Barthes, see hypertext as the new frontier in online pedagogy. In "A Manifesto for Instructional Technology: Hyperpedagogy" (2003), they make a powerful case for the possibilities that hypertext offers learning by opening new pathways for learner-content interaction. They point out the monologic character of traditional pedagogy and see hypertext as a means to dialogism, as a way to "decentralize learning by allowing more voices to join the conversation." Perhaps more importantly, they seek to expose two fundamental errors of conventional curriculum theory and instructional design: to assume "we can determine the "objectives" of learning before curriculum development" (2003, p. 703) and to privilege "learning goals, objectives, and standards defined by the designer as opposed to the needs, interests, and purposes of the student" (2003, p. 704). These possibilities are vital to democratic education.

While various writers have bandied about the term democracy in conjunction with education, it cannot be seen as a vaguely heart-warming term with little appreciable meaning. As George Orwell warned in "Politics and the English Language" (1946), what democracy entails in computer mediated communication (CMC) and online learning environments is a lived praxis, not simply an ideological term. If education is growth, as John Dewey posited in *Democracy and Education* (1916), then room should be given for a variety of means for growth. Dewey perceived education much like life, as a self-sustaining process that requires both nurture and freedom for individual growth. Therefore, democracy in education is not freedom from responsibility for one's learning, but rather a requirement that learners are more responsible for the direction and shape of their learning. As such, loosely defined learning environments, such as class-created wikis and blogs, can prompt greater learner ownership of students' own learning. Instead of perceiving learning as a data input/output exercise, a recreation of the instructor's teleological goals, learning can be a manifestation of mutual strands of content coming together as a shared matrix.

Certainly, instructors should have course goals and provide much of the content as the content area expert, but students, as people attempting to become conversant in the content area, should play an active role in co-creating the content along with the instructor. Democracy in CMC and online learning environments, therefore, entails a great deal of interaction in which all parties listen to one another. Dialogue is highly valued in that meaning is created in a dialectic sense of shared meanings being constantly rewritten and multiply appreciated. Therefore, the use of CMC and online learning has a potential for democratic education by inspiring active learner engagement in a multiplicity of texts, non-linear and with loose boundaries.

A more democratic education, however, necessitates a shift in metaphysics as well. As Dwight and Garrison (2003) point out, we need to move our consciousnesses out of the nineteenth century, away from our fixed and centered teleological notions that have been systematically dismantled by the progression of twentieth-century philosophy. Almost a hundred years ago, John Dewey claimed that we need to learn the lessons of Darwin, and, as Dwight and Garrison point out, "Instructional technologists have yet to learn Darwin's lessons, so they harness post-modern technology to ancient and medieval metaphysics" (p. 711).

Where hypertext really becomes important, however, is in its decentering of the text. As Landow points out, hypertext allows each reader to choose her own pathway through the experience of the text, which means she "is not locked into any kind of particular organization or hierarchy" (1997, p. 38). One of the biggest steps we can take is to move beyond the "limitations of print culture, the culture of the book" (Landow, 1997, p. 46), to free our minds from the ways of books and embrace the textual possibilities—on screen, page, or consciousness—of hypertext.

In order to make this move beyond the book, or the lecture, or any other kind of centralizing "text," we must first recognize how these seemingly natural products are actually cultural products that have been naturalized over time. The maturation of the Internet (and hypertext) has, to an extent, already decentered the book, but it has not yet succeeded in decentering instructional authority, particularly in the traditional classroom, and most notably in terms of the lecture.

Conceptualizing online courses as texts, and more importantly as decentered texts, can lead to a new kind of interaction, to a new way of learning. For Dwight and Garrison (2003), students should become not only active readers, but active co-writers of the course content, so that students' roles will be more like that of the teacher, which would then diminish "the sense of otherness that often discourages our best efforts to instill values predicated on self-worth and democratic agency" (p. 717). This line of thinking brings us to a point where new theoretical directions must be considered. Landow (1997) and Dwight and Garrison (2003) introduce poststructuralist theory into the arena of online learning, but there is much work left to do, particularly in how we incorporate these theories into the conceptualization, evaluation, and ultimately the production of online course texts.

Furthermore, we cannot adequately appraise the quality, nor even the potential, of online learning until we have come to better understand course development as a process of textual production. By reconceptualizing courses as texts, new tools and theoretical frameworks for analysis emerge. Landow (1997) and Dwight and Garrison (2003) have provided a glimpse of how poststructuralist theory can help us rethink the meaning and possibilities of interaction through the use of hypertext, but that is only a start. Their theoretical discussions need to be augmented and applied to practice through an extensive consideration of how poststructuralism and other schools of thought can conceptualize and improve online learning. Literary theory incorporates powerful and sophisticated mechanisms for analysis that promise to revolutionize the way we view and measure the quality of interaction.

ROLAND BARTHES AND "WRITERLY" TEXTS

One place to start this new work is to look at Roland Barthes's concept of the "writerly" text (Barthes, 1974). In his influential essay, *S/Z* (1970/1974), Barthes considers how texts can legitimately be evaluated:

The primary evaluation of all texts can come neither from science, for science does not evaluate, nor from ideology, for the ideological value of a text (moral, aesthetic, political, alethiological) is a value of representation, not of production (ideology "reflects," it does not do work). Our evaluation can be linked only to a practice, and this practice is that of writing. On the one hand, there is that what it is possible to write, and on the other, what it is no longer possible to write: what is within the practice of the writer and what has left it: which texts would I consent to write (to re-write), to desire, to put forth as a force in this world of mine? What evaluation finds is precisely this value: what can be written (rewritten) today: the writerly. Why is the writerly our value? Because the goal of the literary work (of literature as work) is to make the reader no longer a consumer, but a producer of the text. (pp. 3-4)

This passage is instructive for several reasons. First, Barthes supplies us with the powerful recognition that evaluation must be linked to practice. Science (e.g., quantitative statistical methods) is no more able to determine quality in online courses than it is the value of a work of art. We must look to the practice of writing, of meaning making, to fully evaluate online courses. Barthes privileges the writerly text because it pictures the reader in an active posture, in the role of co-writer, jointly producing meaning rather than passively receiving it.

This insight becomes even more telling for education when we consider the continuation of Barthes's paragraph:

Our literature is characterized by the pitiless divorce which the literary institution maintains between the producer of the text and its user, between its owner and its customer, between its author and its reader. This reader is thereby plunged into a kind of idleness—he is intransitive; he is, in short, serious: instead of functioning himself, instead of gaining access to the magic of the signifier, to the pleasure of writing, he is left with no more than the poor freedom either to accept or reject the text: reading is nothing more than a referendum. (p. 4)

This passage displays many of Barthes's major themes; from "*jouissance*," which means the bliss or ecstasy of the text, to "the magic of the signifier," to "the pleasure of writing," to commercial concerns about the text industry itself (Allen, 2002). He also promotes his concept of "play," as suggested by its contrary, the word "serious."

What is most interesting about this passage, however, is that one could easily substitute the concepts of "teaching" for "literature" and "student" for "reader" in the above paragraph, and the statement would have equal import and relevance for schooling. For example:

Our modern teaching practice is characterized by the pitiless divorce which the education establishment maintains between the provider of instruction and its receiver, between the school and its customer, between the teacher and the student. This student is thereby plunged into a kind of idleness—she is intransitive; she is, in short, not playful: instead of functioning herself, instead of gaining access to the magic of the signifier, to the pleasure of learning, she is left with no more than the poor freedom either to accept or reject the curriculum: learning is nothing more than a vote on acceptance. (p. 4)

The kind of text described in Barthes's original paragraph is the opposite of the writerly text: the "readerly" text. Readerly texts are "what can be read, but not written…They are products (and not productions)" (pp. 4-5). In short, readerly texts offer a limited number of interpretations and discourage (even disable) any kind of active or critical reading. Unfortunately, as Barthes points out, readerly texts constitute the great majority of all texts, not only literary texts, but educational texts as well, including everything from textbooks to the "spoken texts" of live classroom teaching, audio recordings, and streaming video lectures. This is unfortunate, both for online and traditional learning.

One could easily argue that the vast majority of all educational texts, from textbooks to spoken lectures to online course texts, would be characterized as readerly. These texts typically presume to have the answers, to hold full authority, and the student's role is then to receive the message uncritically, exactly in the form in which it was coded. However, if we are ever to achieve an understanding of what can be considered meaningful and educative, in other words, critical interaction, we must strive to make our educational texts more writerly, where learners interact with the content at the level of meaning and meaning making, where interaction is a full participation in the production of a lesson's meaning. It is this aim of co-producing a course's meaning which should be considered the true objective of learning. If we are to have critical interaction, it should happen at all levels of the course and allow, as mentioned earlier, the freedom of textual production to lead in new directions, directions not foreseen by the instructor at the time the content and objectives were created. Currently, many instructors intentionally try to create their online course materials in the form of declarative lectures and explanations. These well-intended efforts, however, produce only what can be read, when instead they need to create the beginnings of their students' writing.

A year after publishing *S/Z*, Barthes carried these ideas a little further in his essay, "From Work to Text" (1971). He does not use the binary of writerly/readerly in this essay, rather the terms "Text" and "work." Yet "Text" (note the capital "T") and "work" operate in much the same way. For Barthes, a work is a reified object, something that sits on a shelf. A Text, on the other hand, is a living thing that comes alive with each reading: "*the Text is experienced only in an activity, a production*" (p. 237, emphasis in original). This leads Barthes to a conclusion that is central to all of his writing:

The Text requires an attempt to abolish (or at least to lessen) the distance between writing and reading, not by intensifying the reader's projection into the work, but by linking the two together in a single signifying process. (p. 79)

Barthes's work on privileging the reader has tremendously rich potential in its applicability to educational theory and practice. Privileging the student in a way that abolishes (or at least lessens) the distance between teaching and learning can cause a fundamental shift in the way we think about not only online learning, but also the concept of active learning. In order to do this, however, we must rethink the role of the teacher in the signifying (i.e., teaching) process.

THE DEATH OF THE AUTHOR, OR, THE DEATH OF THE ONLINE INSTRUCTOR

Barthes opens his famous essay, "The Death of the Author" (1968) with a series of questions about Balzac's short story, "Sarrasine" (which is also the primary focus of *S/Z*). He asks who is speaking a particular line. Is it the hero in the story? The author as an individual? The author as the author?

Universal wisdom? Or even Romantic psychology? He then concludes that we can never know because once language becomes writing, it loses all function except its own signification, so that "this gap appears, the voice loses its origin, the author enters into his own death, writing begins" (p. 1131). Or, more directly, "it is language which speaks, not the author" (p. 1131). As Umberto Eco (1979) claims, the author is "a mere metaphor for «textual strategy»" (p. 11). Also, Barthes argues that to give a text an Author is to "impose a brake on it, to furnish it with a final signified, to close writing" (p. 1132).

The concept of the death of the Author deals not only with how the reader can become the central figure in the drama, but also with how shifting some of the agency in the process of textual (or semantic) production away from the author to social discourses renders the text a composite "of multiple writings, proceeding from several cultures and entering into dialogue, into parody, into contestation." Barthes continues,

there is a site where this multiplicity is collected and this site is not the author, as has hitherto been claimed, but the reader: the reader is the space in which are inscribed, without any of them being lost, all the citations out of which a writing is made; the unity of a text is not in its origin but in its destination. (pp. 1132-1133)

And then ultimately, "the birth of the reader must be requited by the death of the Author" (p. 1133). This is also to say that the birth of the online student comes at the cost of the death of the online instructor. Educationally, the birth of the student, or at least the recognition of the centrality of the student, is what is most important. We must keep in mind that with this conception of the reader/student, "the text and the meaning of the text are dynamic, constantly changing, in the process of becoming, not something fixed, or static" (Sheriff, 1989, p. 22). The instructive utterance of the teacher, in whatever form, cannot then be considered final, or even, ultimately, authoritative. Certainly this conceptual shift not only involves the pedagogic revolution of teacher-centered to student-centered classrooms, but also the dissolution of the division between the two. It also involves an epistemological change of agency in which instructors' ownership of the material, even their authority, comes into question in order to make room for the constructive role of the student/reader.

BENEFITS OF WRITERLY COURSES

The potential benefit of reconceptualizing online courses through a writerly/readerly lens is remarkable, far beyond even hypertext's provision of "the presence of multiple reading paths" (Landow, 1997, p. 25). The online learning literature is full of calls for interaction and the use of active learning strategies (Moore, 1989; Moore et al., 2001; Palloff & Pratt, 1999). However, virtually all of these recommendations concern the creation of student activities or the shift of the online instructor from the role of lecturer to that of facilitator. And while all of these recommendations are valuable, none of them offer a sophisticated analysis of the conceptualization, production, and presentation of course content. If online courses become more writerly, particularly in terms of content produced by the instructor in the initial development, as well as by the instructor and students during the course itself, the notion of interaction can be expanded tremendously. If this expansion can go beyond the realm of pedagogical critique, such a reconstruction will foster a philosophical reconsideration of the purpose of online education itself.

Such a shift, however, will require the translation of these theoretical explorations into real educational practice, which, in turn, will demand a considerable amount of effort, experimentation, and evaluation by online faculty and course designers everywhere. The primary shift required in this process, however, is not so much in practical applications as in the way that instructors approach their instruction. In other words, there is no recipe for making online courses more writerly; a writerly course does most of the same things that a readerly one does. The difference is the way those things are done.

For instance, instructors who were planning on lecturing in their readerly course can still lecture in their writerly one. However, planning that lecture with an awareness that their lecture will not be passively received as the final word, but rather actively interpreted (and even rewritten) by their students, will in itself change the way they approach the lecture process. This awareness will enable students to benefit more from (and carry more away from) the lecture by actively participating in the generation of meaning from those words. All that is required to accomplish this kind of writerliness, or at least the first step toward it, is a willingness to keep things open or dialogic.

For a lecture that is normally an hour long in the classroom and primarily monologic and declarative in nature, the instructor should first of all identify that which that can only come from his or her unique knowledge and perspective, and then have students fill in the gaps by giving them something active to do with the missing content. This can be done by having students find answers to specific or implied questions either in other texts or through some other process of discovery. It could be done either individually or in cooperation with one or more classmates. Such activities could range from a thought provoking threaded discussion topic to a well-crafted WebQuest (Dodge, 1995, 2001). Other ideas might include conceptualizing the lecture as a blog (whether the lecture be text, audio, or video) where students are encouraged or required to comment at the end. Yet another strategy might be to construct a class wiki where the students literally participate in the writing of the course's meanings. Care should be taken, however, to make sure that students are involved in multiple parts of the wiki writing process so that they do not simply write their part and ignore the rest. The important thing is for instructors to always keep in mind that they are striving for the writerly.

MAKING THE SHIFT: HOW TO ACHIEVE WRITERLINESS IN THE ONLINE CLASSROOM

A course is a text in itself as the multiple coordination of a matrix of texts, including instructor supplied texts, instructor's lectures and musings on the content, the tradition of the content, the lived experiences of the instructor, the institutional ethos, the provided online learning environment, and what is the most overlooked text: the students. The students are themselves individually texts of multiple intersections (e.g. familial, ideological, social, psychological and physiological statuses, the contexts in which the content is interfaced, etc.), each a lived nexus, if you will, that forms aspects/parts of the nebulous whole of a class text. An intentionally writerly text, therefore, can (and in our opinion should) be predicated on multiplicities of voices, what Bakhtin called heteroglossia (Bakhtin, 1981).

To achieve this, however, a fine line between cacophony and orchestra needs to take place in which the instructor coordinates the voices towards a greater appreciation of the content, but it is important to note that the instructor does not dominate the direction. Imagine an online instructor as a pilot of a ship in a storm. The pilot wants to take the ship to a destination, but the course must take into account the weather, wind direction and strength, tides, the topography of the ocean bottom, wave direction and size, and the abilities and temperaments of the crew. A ship in a storm can be steered in such a way that a beautiful and awesome coordination of these various elements can take place. Or it can run into dangerous shoals breaking apart at the seams. It is also quite possible that the ship will arrive, unexpectedly, at an unintended destination, one far richer than the one originally planned.

In on-line environments, instructors can plan for play using the elements that online communication provides. Students create a reimagined text when interacting reciprocally with the course content as digitized paper text (e.g., textbooks, articles, diagrams, videos, etc…). Moreover, courses can provoke students to share their understandings of the texts via blogging or text-trees using course management systems such as Blackboard or Moodle. And students should be compelled to read and evaluate other entries to blogs/trees. As such, the text's inherent multiplicities are appreciated by more than an instructor evaluating individual student responses to assigned texts. Students can also research topics and present their findings to one another to further broaden the understanding of class materials as text. Students, therefore, become co-creators of content along with the instructor (or perhaps instructors). The instructor is not merely a first among equals, to borrow Caesar Augustus' paradoxical phrase, but rather a coordinator of signification, of meaning-making.

Therefore, learning in the online classroom becomes more than an act of reading and rewriting. It becomes a social act. And as these active textual learning experiences become a standard element of one instructor's online classroom, the process of intertextuality, through the agencies of both students and instructors, will carry these learning processes into other instructors' classrooms, and eventually into traditional classrooms, until writerly course texts will pervade the entire institution as a transformative force. And then the process will find its way to other institutions.

CONCLUSION

When viewing online courses as writerly texts, particularly when we consider the writerly our "value," the act of teaching becomes an act of writing. When we design our course content, we must become aware of when we are trying to be exhaustive and when we are intentionally leaving gaps, and perhaps more importantly, of when we are planting the seeds of suggestiveness. It is this kind of reflexivity that will prove most fruitful in our reconceptualization of online learning.

By rethinking online courses as texts, and by then reconceiving those courses as what we have described as "writerly" texts, we can not only improve the level of interaction in the online classroom, but also improve the quality, as well as the perception of quality, of that classroom. Therefore, the concept of writerly texts becomes a powerful tool for the analysis and development of interaction in online courses by allowing us a fuller understanding of not only the interpretive nature of the learning process, but also of the advantages inherent in empowering students in that process. Furthermore, by providing students the agency to complete the content of their lessons, online learning can open new avenues to learning and student achievement. It can move toward a practice where education is not merely a measurable process but rather to new productions that can be meaningfully contemplated and utilized.

In conclusion, true, critical interaction should not be seen as a back-and-forth, but rather as a moving forward, or as Blake would put it, a progression.

REFERENCES

Allen, G. (2002). *Roland Barthes: S/Z. The literary encyclopedia.* Retrieved March 7, 2005, from http://www.litencyc.com/php/sworks.php?rec=true&UID=10346.

Bakhtin, M. M. (1981). *The dialogic imagination.* Austin, TX: University of Texas Press.

Barthes, R. (1968/1992). The death of the author. In Adams, H. (Ed.), *Critical theory since Plato* (*revised edition*, pp. 1130–1133). Fort Worth, TX: Harcourt Brace Jovanovich.

Barthes, R. (1971). From work to Text. In Barthes, R. (Ed.), *Image-music-text. Heath, S. (Trans.)*. New York: Noonday.

Barthes, R. (1974). *S/Z. Miller, R. (Trans.)*. New York: Farrar, Straus & Giroux.

Blake, W. (1988). The marriage of heaven and hell. In Erdman, D. V. (Ed.), *The complete poetry and prose of William Blake* (pp. 32–44). New York: Doubleday. (Original work published 1793)

Dewey, J. (1902). *The child and the curriculum*. Chicago: University of Chicago Press.

Dewey, J. (1916). *Democracy and education*. New York: Macmillan.

Dodge, B. (1995). WebQuests: a technique for internet-based learning. *Distance Education*, *1*(2), 10–13.

Dodge, B. (2001). Focus: five rules for writing a great WebQuest. *Learning and Leading with Technology*, *28*(8), 6–9, 58.

Dwight, J., & Garrison, J. (2003). A manifesto for instructional technology: Hyperpedagogy. *Teachers College Record*, *105*(5), 699–728. doi:10.1111/1467-9620.00265

Herring, R. (1987, March). *Looking at interaction*. Paper presented at the Annual Meeting of the National Society for Performance and Instruction, San Antonio, TX.

Landow, G. P. (1997). *Hypertext 2.0*. Baltimore, MD: Johns Hopkins University Press.

Moore, G. S., Winograd, K., & Lange, D. (2001). *You can teach online: Building a creative learning environment*. Boston, MA: McGraw-Hill.

Moore, M. G. (1989). Three types of interaction. *The American journal of distance learning* 3(2), 1-6.

Orwell, G. (1946/1950). Politics and the English language. In *Shooting an elephant and other essays*. London: Secker and Warburg.

Palloff, R. M., & Pratt, K. (1999). *Building learning communities in cyberspace: Effective strategies for the online classroom*. San Francisco: Jossey-Bass.

Rawlings, J. (1999). *Jacques Derrida*. Stanford University, Stanford Presidential Lectures in the Humanities and Arts. Retrieved March 24, 2005 from http://prelectur.stanford.edu/lecturers/derrida/.

Roblyer, M. D., & Wiencke, W. R. (2003). Design and use of a rubric to assess and encourage interactive qualities in distance courses. *American Journal of Distance Education*, *17*(2), 77–98. doi:10.1207/S15389286AJDE1702_2

Shank, R. (1998). Horses for courses. *Communications of the ACM*, *41*(7), 23–25. doi:10.1145/278476.278482

Sheriff, J. K. (1989). *The fate of meaning: Charles Peirce, structuralism, and literature*. Princeton, NJ: Princeton University Press.

Sims, R. (2003). Promises of interactivity: Aligning Learner Perceptions and Expectations with Strategies for Flexible and Online Learning. *Distance Education*, *24*(1), 87–103. doi:10.1080/01587910303050

Wagner, E. D. (1994). In support of a functional view of interaction. *American Journal of Distance Education*, *8*(2), 6–29. doi:10.1080/08923649409526852

Wallace, R. M. (2003). Online learning in higher education: A review of research on interactions among teachers and students. *Education Communication and Information*, *3*(2), 241–280. doi:10.1080/14636310303143

ADDITIONAL READING

Barone, T. (2000). *Aesthetics, Politics, and Educational Inquiry: Essays and Examples*. New York: P. Lang.

Bondanella, P. (1997). *Umberto Eco and the open text*. New York: Cambridge University Press. doi:10.1017/CBO9780511581755

Bowers, C. (2000). *Let them eat data: How computers affect education, cultural diversity, and the prospects of ecological sustainability*. Athens, GA: University of Georgia Press.

Cooper, S. (2002). *Technoculture and Critical Theory: In the Service of the Machine?* New York: Routledge. doi:10.4324/9780203167021

Derrida, J. (1966). Structure, sign, and play in the discourse of the human sciences. *Writing and difference* (pp 278-294). Bass, A. (Trans.). London: Routledge

Eagleton, T. (1983). *Literary theory: An introduction*. Minneapolis, MN: University of Minnesota.

Eco, U. (1962/1989). *The open work. Cancogni, A. (Trans.)*. Cambridge, MA: Harvard University Press.

Feenberg, A. (1999). *Questioning technology*. New York: Routledge.

Hall, S. (1973/1980). Encoding/decoding. In Hall, S. (Ed.), *Culture, media, language: Working papers In Cultural Studies, 1972-79* (pp. 128–138). London: Unwin Hyman.

Holquist, M. (1990). *Dialogism: Bakhtin and his world*. New York: Routledge. doi:10.4324/9780203330340

Iser, W. (1971). Indeterminacy and the reader's response. In *Prospecting: From reader response to literary anthropology. (1989)*. Baltimore, MD: Johns Hopkins Press.

Iser, W. (1980). Interaction between text and reader. In *Prospecting: from reader response to literary anthropology. (1989)*. Baltimore, MD: Johns Hopkins Press.

Maeroff, G. (2003). *A classroom of One*. New York, NY: Palgrave MacMillan.

Marshall, J. (1999). The mode of information and education: Insights on critical theory from Michel Foucault. In Popkewitz, T. (Ed.), *Terrains of knowledge and politics* (pp. 141–163). New York: Routledge.

McKnight, D. (2004). Task of the teaching life: Self through Bakhtinian dialogue and ideological engagement. *Interchange, 35*(3), 281–302. doi:10.1007/BF02698878

Romiszowski, A. J., & Cheng, E. (1992). Hypertext's contribution to computer-mediated communication: in search of an instructional model. In Giardina, M. (Ed.), *Interactive multimedia learning environments*. Berlin: Springer-Verlag.

Sedgwick, E. K. (1990). *Epistemology of the closet*. Berkeley, CA: University of California Press.

Sidorkin, A. M. (1999). *Beyond discourse: Education, the self, and dialogue*. Albany, NY: SUNY Press.

Wegerif, R. (2007). *Dialogic education and technology: Expanding the space of learning*. New York: Springer. doi:10.1007/978-0-387-71142-3

KEY TERMS AND DEFINITIONS

Democratic Education: The intentional practice of learners taking responsibility for the direction and shape of their learning. Instead of perceiving learning as a data input/output exercise, a recreation of the instructor's teleological goals, learning can be a manifestation of mutual strands of content coming together as a shared matrix.

Dialogism: Often misunderstood as a fancy term for dialogue, but it actually concerns the interplay of voices and perspectives. It can be present in written texts, or rather, in the reading of written texts, where there is conversation between the text and reader, where meaning is negotiated, translated, and appropriated.

Hypertext: The ability to link multiple texts together through the use of hyperlinks. Most commonly seen in electronic texts, hypertext in education enables students to forge their own individualized learning paths of investigation and experience. Hypertext decenters the typical linear text of traditional instruction and increases both agency and democracy in the learning process.

Interaction: The reciprocal and mutually influential interplay between instructors, learners, and content in the learning process. Interaction involves the intersection of teachers and students with a multiplicity of texts and contexts, where the dialogics of learning are strived for and achieved, and are not simply a subtly hegemonic gesture.

Intertextuality: The conscious and unconscious interplay between multiple texts. No text can exist in isolation. Therefore any text, whether written, spoken, or otherwise, pulls from and contributes to a multiplicity of other texts for its production of meaning.

Meaning: In its loosest sense, is the end product of language and/or language acts. Meaning is often understood to be a straightforward relationship between language and its intent, but it is, in actuality, a profoundly complex interplay between the writer/speaker/originator of the language and its reader/hearer/interpreter. Meaning is not a reification of living language into a fixed understanding; rather, it is dynamically negotiated between the writer and reader, and it resides as much in the response of the reader as in the intention of the writer.

Poststructuralism: A loosely connected school of thought best characterized by the work of late twentieth-century French theorists Jacques Derrida, Michel Foucault, Roland Barthes, Jacques Lacan, and Julia Kristeva. Most poststructuralist thought is based on the rejection of structuralist linguistic theory and holds that the relationship between a signifier and its signified is arbitrary, that the meaning of a text is inherently unstable and cannot be located in the author, and that individual subjectivity is constituted by social discourses.

Texts: Traditionally thought of as written documents, but a text is any collection or combination of signs that can potentially communicate interpretable meaning.

Writerly: Writerly texts are texts that require the reader to actively participate in "writing" the meaning of the text, where the act of reading is essentially an act of [re]writing. Roland Barthes privileged writerly texts over readerly texts, which offer only a limited number of possible interpretations and therefore place the reader in a passive position.

Chapter 19
The Right to Technology in Education

Donovan Plumb
Mount Saint Vincent University, Canada

ABSTRACT

Following the lead of geographer, David Harvey (2008), this chapter argues that many contemporary trends in the use of technology in higher education prevent the development of capacities for critical democratic citizenship. Too often, technology is deployed in a top-down fashion to shape student learning. Thus, to enhance the full emergence of students as active, engaged, critical citizens, it is crucial that they be granted access to the right to technology in education.

INTRODUCTION

Unlike many other chapters in this volume, which deal more with the specific challenges of creating, developing, and implementing educational technologies, this chapter attempts a much broader assessment of the place of technology in higher education contexts. It argues that, despite a growing rhetoric of student centeredness in higher education supported by burgeoning social networking technologies, the prime purpose of technology in education is still to control student learning to meet definitive learning objectives. Formal education contexts remain dominated by a knowledge transmission/reception notion of learning that conceives of learners as passive vessels and educators (and, increasingly, education managers) as powerful possessors of privileged knowledge. Rather than being an open-ended, creative, and collaborative process, university educators see learning as a realm to be controlled to meet specific ends. For the most part, educational technologies serve educators to determine, shape and measure learning processes. Although students can possess advanced tools to aid them in internalizing new knowledge, for the most part,

DOI: 10.4018/978-1-60960-147-8.ch019

educational technologies remain in control of educators. My main contention in this paper is that to enhance the full emergence of students as active, engaged, critical citizens, it is crucial that they be granted, what following David Harvey (2008) I will term, the right to technology in education. This right assures them power to guard against imperial uses of technology over their learning and to use technology in creative and critical ways to participate in convivial and collaborative teaching/learning relations with others.

"THE RIGHT TO THE CITY" AND "THE RIGHT TO TECHNOLOGY IN EDUCATION"

In a recent article, geographer David Harvey (2008) argues that widespread liberal promotion of human rights has done little to address rising social inequalities throughout the world. Harvey is particularly concerned that contemporary trends in urban development are generating social spaces within which democratic decision-making is increasingly difficult. In a vicious circle, declining capacities for democratic participation creates even more opportunities for a powerful few to develop urban contexts that serve their narrow economic and political interests. Harvey contends that a first step towards seriously addressing human rights requires establishing what he calls "the right to the city." Increasing democratic participation in urban development (both its material and social aspects), Harvey contends, is the only way to generate contexts that can support further democratic participation. For Harvey, struggling for "the right to the city" is a powerful first step towards building a democratic society capable of resisting the imperatives of a runaway global economic system.

Working the same vein as Harvey, I would like to suggest that, just as trends in urban development are making democratic engagement more difficult, many contemporary trends in the use of technology in higher education are restricting opportunities for people to develop capacities for critical democratic citizenship. Just as in the case with urban development, when opportunities for critical learning decline, it reduces democracy in education. This, in turn, results in ever fewer resources for critique. In an escalating downward spiral, teachers and learners lose their capacity to resist an even more destructive intrusion of controlling forms of technology into the learning context. Only by establishing the right to technology in higher education, by reclaiming, refurbishing, and developing techniques for participating in collaborative learning can students and teachers acquire capacities for participating in robust, democratic learning contexts.

Following Harvey's lead, in this chapter, I call on teachers and students to reclaim "the right to technology in higher education" as a way to build capacities for critical democratic citizenship. I argue that, although people can learn teaching techniques to interrupt, deflect, and control the learning of others in ways that benefit privileged social groups at the expense of the common good, they can also learn techniques that can enable them to participate in collaborative learning in communities of practice. Reclaiming the right to technology in education, I suggest, requires that we stop viewing teaching and learning as a process that allows one person to use technology to transfer knowledge into the mind of another person. It also requires us to refuse the view of technology as a body of freestanding and politically neutral tools, machines and processes that can be uncritically used in educational contexts. Finally, and perhaps most importantly, it necessitates that we remain wary of ideological justifications of new technologies (especially social networking technologies) as enhancing capacities for critical democratic citizenship. While it may seem that these technologies support more student engagement, used uncritically, these educational technologies can exacerbate the individualization of learners and deepen cultural commodification.

In short, reclaiming a right to technology in higher education requires the ongoing enskillment of teachers and learners to join with one another in shared contexts of collaborative learning.

As a critical geographer, Harvey is very conscious of the mutually influencing (he describes it as "dialectical") relationship that exists between humans and their surroundings (Harvey, 1996, 2009). Harvey argues that our sense of our world is deeply conditioned by our entwinement in its structures. The human mind is not, as Descartes described it, divisible from our bodies or separable from the world. Harvey rejects the positivist view that it is possible to attain an objective and detached view of the world. Rather, our perceptions and knowledge of the world come from being embedded in it. Our participation in the practices of our culture and society indelibly condition our sense of what works, what is ethical, and what is beautiful. As Pierre Bourdieu (1977), describes it, our participation with others in social practices shapes our minds and bodies to fit the material, social and cultural contours of the world. As we engage in the structures of our world, we develop a "habitus," which, like the feel of the game of a soccer player, allows us to engage (and often restricts or constrains our engagement) with the flows of life.

Harvey is no determinist, however. He is also very conscious of how, even when social practices shape the material world into imposing structures that constrain possibilities for action (Harvey focuses on streets and buildings but we can easily extend these to technologies), these structures do not determine what we can become (Harvey, 2000). All too often, he observes, socially constructed structures appear as a natural and determining force over which we have little or no sway. Although it is true that social structures deeply condition our potentials and powers as human agents, they do not, in the end, eliminate our capacity to act in ways that can transform these structures. Claiming the right to technology in education, I suggest, acknowledges and works to expand our capacity to resist the taken-for-granted sense we have of current controlling uses of technology in education.

TEACHING AND LEARNING IN COMMUNITIES OF PRACTICE

Although it is not a path followed by Harvey, I have found that focusing on the nature of human learning, particularly as it transpires in the throes of the natural and social worlds, provides insight into the ways social structures (including technologies) constrain, but do not determine, our capacities for social action. Recent practice-based theories of human learning and its role in the production and reproduction of social and cultural structures offer an especially important view (Chaiklin & Lave, 1996; Ingold, 2000; Lave, 1988; Lave & Wenger, 1991; Rogoff, 1984, 1991; Wenger, 1999).

For example, in their influential book, *Situated Learning: Legitimate Peripheral Participation* (1991), Jean Lave and Etienne Wenger are critical of prevailing conceptions of learning as a process through which an external and largely freestanding body of knowledge is transmitted into the mind of a learner. According to Lave and Wenger, "all theories of learning are based on fundamental assumptions about the person, the world, and their relations" (p. 47). "Conventional conceptions," they argue, "view learning as a process by which a learner internalizes knowledge, whether 'discovered,' 'transmitted' from others, or 'experienced in interaction' with others." They suggest that, such a view of learning assumes a separation of person from their context, divides inside from outside, posits "knowledge as largely cerebral," and presumes that it is within the individual person that the learning process transpires. Although this view of learning can help us understand some dimensions of human learning (for example, how human brains might form memories or process perceptions), it is far from sufficient. Its tight focus on the isolated and solitary mind blinds it to the distinctly situated and cultural nature of human learning. As anthropologist Tim Ingold (2004) observes, "a fundamental insight of [these] studies of learning is that knowledge is not transmitted across generations as a ready-made corpus of information, but rather undergoes continual regeneration in the contexts of learners' practical engagement with their surroundings."

Rather than being a process where an individual internalizes knowledge, practice-based theorists of learning (such as Lave and Wenger) describe learning as a situated and largely social process that transpires when people engage with each other in what they call, "communities of practice." Developmental psychologist, Michael Tomasello (Tomasello, 1999, 2008, 2009), provides further insight into the nature of communities of practice as distinctive human learning contexts.

According to Tomasello, humans possess a unique capacity for collaborative learning that comes from our ability to join with others in contexts of shared attention. This inimitable skill is rooted in our capacity to perceive other humans as possessing minds like our own. Unlike other animals who are restricted to a rather egocentric view of the world, a human being can imagine him or herself in the place of another person. This opens a capacity to forge a common perspective on the world, share intentions, participate together in joint projects, build common understandings, and develop bonds of understanding and solidarity unique to our species. Over time, humans who are linked together in learning can begin to amass a common repertoire of understandings that contribute to effective joint action. For example, shared understandings enable people to work together to affect their surroundings in ways impossible for a person alone. A common repertoire of understandings helps make interactions predictable and opens new possibilities for bonds of trust and care. As well, when newcomers join the shared learning context, they too can be included and, through a process of what Lave and Wenger call legitimate peripheral participation, intertwined in the practices of the learning collective.

According to Tomasello, the emergence of capacities for collaborative and cultural learning was momentous for humans. It made it possible for humans to collaborate in remembering, sharing, and reproducing cultural practices through time. Each iteration of cultural learning also provided opportunities to elaborate the complexity, to add to the effectiveness, or deepen the meaning of existing social practices. As Tomasello (2005) relates, the advent of collaborative learning gave rise to the "ratchet effect" of culture that, generation after generation, gradually added to the capacity of humans to adapt to shifting environments (p. 6). Human history, from this view, is the story of the effects of this capacity. In the end, the acquisition and development of complex tools; the growth and development of gestural, spoken, and written language; the elaboration of ever more sophisticated social structures; and the proliferation of diverse cultural ways of life all hinge on the ability of humans to join with each other in existing but ever-shifting patterns of practice through a process of cultural learning in communities of practice.

The powerful message of theorists like Tomasello and Lave and Wenger is that learning and teaching transpire much more broadly than is commonly understood. Rather than being confined to formal educational institutions, learning is a bedrock human capacity that transpires in communities of practice that pervade our entire lives. From birth, we are enwrapped in a culture that nurtures our participation in collaborative learning. As we live our lives we move into, participate within, and move out of communities of practice. We learn to harmonize our thoughts and actions as we enter the flows of practices unfolding in our communities. We acquire identities, contribute to the formation and propagation of cultural meanings, acquire capacities for effective action, and form bonds of solidarity with others. Moreover, our collective participation in collaborative learning is the very mechanism that produces and reproduces social and cultural structures. Given the vast richness of the cultural storehouse of meanings, roles, institutions, technologies, religions, languages, art, cities, and so on generated throughout history in contexts of collaborative learning, this small and everyday power is very impressive, indeed.

There is another important element to add to this story: the role of teaching. The development of our capacity to understand other people as having minds like our own gave rise to a growing interest in intervening in the lives of others so that they might share our perspectives, skills, or knowledge. According to Tomasello (1999), although some higher primates sometimes (rarely) behave as if they have an interest in imparting information or sharing skills with others, only humans deliberately teach each other. This is particularly apparent in the relationships between adults and children. For the most part, the learning of children happens without plan as an outcome of their engagement with their natural and social environments. Often, however, an adult will interfere directly with the learning context of the child, shaping aspects of the learning situation to make it easier for a child to fall into pace with the elements of a particularly complex skill, social role, concept, story, and so on. To do this, however, requires a growing sense of what best supports the learning of the child. Moreover, it requires a developing repertoire of specific practices (techniques like scaffolding, for instance) to ease the learning of difficult things.

Using a variety of techniques, one person in the role of teacher can shape the ways another person participates in and entwines with flows of social practices. In everyday contexts, people in interaction often flip from being in the role of teacher to assuming the role of learner. This is most obvious, for example, in conversations between social equals striving to negotiate a common understanding. Even in contexts where participants possess different levels of social power, between adults and children for instance, turn taking in teaching and learning often prevail. Although a parent might spend more time in the role as teacher – helping a child to say a new word by using a technique like speaking the word slowly or emphasizing a difficult consonant or to drink from a cup by partially filling it or guiding the child's hands – children, too, are encouraged to refine practices for teaching the adult about the child's world. Teaching a child to speak, for instance, entails deliberately placing oneself in a position of listener (or learner) so the child can develop capacities for shaping the practices of others. In important respects, engaging in collaborative learning contexts presumes that, to some extent or another, all participants develop skill in using techniques for teaching.

THE EVERYDAY TECHNIQUES OF TEACHING IN COMMUNITIES OF PRACTICE

What might some of these techniques be like? Michael Tomasello (1999) provides insight into some of the more powerful techniques a teacher (and this included people even fleetingly in the teaching role) can use to influence (or, to use a more provocative term offered by Tim Ingold (2000), to "reveal" a path of collaborative learning. According to Tomasello, one of the first things humans must do to learn collaboratively is to establish a point of shared attention. Gestures like pointing are extremely important as they serve to turn the attention of others to something specific in the world, something to be shared and engaged in together. Techniques for keeping focus by reducing distractions (simply facing a person, for instance, is a simple and effective strategy for reducing competing social demands) are also very important as these techniques provide more time for learners to engage in shared practices related to whatever is holding their attention. According to Wenger, these particular techniques aim to increase participation in shared learning contexts.

Their purpose is to reveal an aspect of the world to our collective scrutiny and action.

Drawing attention and preventing distractions can have an opposite effect as well. At the same time as they open a point of focus for learners, these techniques also place a range of other phenomena in the background, out of the focus of concern. Thus, at the same time as an act like pointing can open an aspect of the world to shared scrutiny, it actively prevents other elements from appearing as salient. Over time, using teaching techniques, a person can structure a desired path of attention, switching from point to point of concern, that actively privileges certain elements of the joint attentional scene and (just as actively) suppresses other elements. Like a shuttle in a loom, these techniques help weave learners in select ways into the tapestry of social practices unfolding in the world. While Ingold (2004) is correct in suggesting that we learn as an outcome of our engagement in natural and social contexts, it is important to remember that, in many cases, this engagement does not go unmediated. In fact, of all of the cultural practices devised by humans – including those as impressive as fashioning and using tools, communicating with language, and living in social institutions – the deliberate practices of teaching must count amongst the most important. They not only serve to enhance our overall entwinement in the world, but, for good or for ill, also influence the path of our learning, and, as a consequence, the production and reproduction of the social order.

TECHNOLOGY AND THE ABSENCE OF THE SOCIAL

Not all techniques that shape, deflect, or interfere with the flows of collaborative learning are as fleeting as pointing a finger or guiding a hand. Even more importantly, not all aim to enhance our shared capacities for collaborative learning. At the same time as certain teaching techniques can enable us, in general, to join with others in collaborative learning, when embedded in inequitable social relationships, teaching techniques can also provide a basis for controlling the specific path of learning (and hence, the production and reproduction of social forms). This is particularly true when, as has happened in modernity, the link between technique and social power becomes obscured.

Sometimes, deliberate teaching practices aim to produce substantial changes in the material and social world that affect the ways learners engage with their surroundings, sometimes far into the future. This is particularly true when, in the role of teachers, people develop tools, processes, techniques, and environments to deliberately condition the flow of participation in communities of practice. While we tend to think of educational technologies in terms of advanced information and computer technologies, it is important to understand that humans have used various teaching techniques (including remarkably simple techniques like pointing) from the very moment cultural learning emerged as a unique human capacity.

Think, for example, about the spatiality of the traditional school classroom. In this instance, educators interested in controlling learning to produce specific outcomes shaped a space that could discipline and regulate the ways students participate in collaborative learning. The context is very familiar. Educators enclosed students in walled rooms that confined and regulated their body movements (very different, for example, than the fields, forests, or neighborhoods they might otherwise inhabit). They sat students at desks or on benches that regulated their interactions with their peers. The room was designed to make it easy for a teacher to observe students at all times and, perhaps more importantly, difficult for students to observe or talk with each other. Educators equipped the room with tools like chalkboards, textbooks, writing tablets, and maps and constrained students to quiet practices like listening, reading, writing, and calculation. Students learned "subjects" like literature, mathematics, or science in time-periods punctuated by the ringing of a bell.

Interestingly, once they have stabilized, contexts and technologies shaped by social action often lose their socially constructed feel. Instead of experiencing the spatiality of the classroom as a construct produced by an historical array of social practices, teachers and students experience it as they might other natural surroundings or phenomena. The classroom becomes a taken-for-granted context that constrains the flow of subsequent social practices.

The same must be said for other less material but equally taken-for-granted technologies. As Michel Foucault (1977) details, in the modern era, a growing cadre of educators achieved social discipline through the assembly and deployment of a range of small techniques and strategies for controlling the actions and interactions of human beings. The emerging science of psychology, especially its behaviorist and cognitivist variants, provided educators with knowledge and skills to maximize knowledge transfer. At the same time as this new science largely ignored the substantial capacities of students for collaborative learning, they elevated the important role of educators to both hold and transmit privileged social knowledge. Educators extolled these techniques as ways to effectively transmit progressive knowledge into the minds of individual learners. For Foucault (1977), this included strategies for individualizing and objectifying students, establishing behavioral norms, conducting surveillance, and assessing performance. Schools began to test, measure, diagnose, sort, pass, and fail individual students.

Thus, the immediate and most visible actions of educators to interfere with learning are far from being the main force that conditions the learning of students in formal education contexts. Far more important are the broad, socially constructed, technologies of education that, largely without our even knowing it, deflect, restrict, and condition the flows of human participation and learning. Now, with some kind of hindsight, it is possible for us to distance ourselves from the taken-for-granted feel, for example, of the school classroom. In fact, for many liberal-minded educators, the classroom now can be critically understood as a technology that served to help reproduce the hierarchical social and cultural structures of the 19th and 20th centuries (to the point that radical critic Ivan Ilich (Illich, 1971, 1977) can contend that social justice can only be achieved if we "deschool society").

While this critique of older, more industrial-like educational technologies is important, it is perhaps even more important to try to understand the ways new technologies also might be being used to interfere with collaborative learning processes, and, in pernicious ways, producing or maintaining a less than desirable social order. In David Harvey's (2008) view, despite the rhetoric of human rights, we do not live in a time of increasing social justice. In fact, he and many others offer powerful reasons to question the current leanings of our society. In this context, we must struggle to keep from falling prey to the sense of contemporary technologies as something neutral or something that must determine our actions, including our participation in collaborative learning contexts. The shape of our current world, including the wonders of ever more powerful technologies, seems so pervasive, however, that it is extremely difficult to see them once again as the socially constructed outcomes of particular historical patterns of social practice.

There is a deep struggle required, akin to the struggle Harvey suggests with his notion of the right to the city. To have any hope of fostering democratic educational contexts that focus more on releasing our unique capacity for collaborative learning than on controlling it, educators must find ways to democratically extend the right to use technology in teaching/learning contexts beyond the narrow cadre of elite professionals currently in place in institutions of higher education. For this to happen, however, educators must achieve a deeper understanding of ways technology currently shapes learning in our increasingly unsustainable global economic and political system.

NEOLIBERALISM, AUDITING, AND TECHNOLOGY IN EDUCATION

David Harvey (2005, 2006, 2007) provides some sense of how we might begin to understand the current place of technology in higher education. Over the past several decades, he argues, powerful social groups around the world have implemented an effective political economic campaign, now commonly called neoliberalism, to free the global economy from the strong state interference that had arisen in the decades following the Great Depression. For several decades during the middle of the 20th century, governments around the world, including the New Deal governments of the United States, used strong measures to regulate private enterprise and to redistribute economic wealth. As Naomi Kline (2008) relates, "To make products affordable, politicians fixed prices; to make workers less exploited, they set minimum wages; to make sure everyone had access to education, they kept it in the hands of the state" (p. 61). Welfare state policies resulted in "social security in the U.S., public health care in Canada, welfare in Britain, workers' protections in France and Germany" (p. 63). A key initiative of welfare state governments around the world was a massive expansion of post-secondary education institutions. In the U.S., for instance, the "G.I. Bill" provided WWII veterans with generous support for higher education. Educational institutions grew quickly to accommodate an influx of students from social classes and groups previously excluded from college education. Governments kept tuitions low and developed student loans and bursary schemes to maintain open access.

By the end of the 1970s, however, neoliberal political pressure began to curtail government commitment to higher education. Whereas, previously, governments provided strong state funding for expanding higher education institutions, beginning in the 1980s, government funding began to tail off. According to the neoliberal view, most public institutions, including universities, had become large and inefficient bureaucracies with low accountability and credibility. Thus, a decline in government funding was accompanied by pressure for universities and colleges to adopt new management strategies modeled strongly on those already in use in private enterprise, especially newly emerging or recently revamped corporations in high technology sectors (Deem, 2001; Deem & Brehony, 2005; Shore & Wright, 1999). A ubiquitous feature of these new management strategies was the deployment of new systems for observing and controlling institutional outcomes. In particular, as Michael Power (1999) relates:

During the late 1980s and early 1990s, the word 'audit' began to be used ... with growing frequency in a wide variety of contexts. In addition to the regulation of private company accounting by financial audit, practices of environment audit, value for money audit, management audit, forensic audit, data, audit, intellectual property audit, medical audit, teaching audit, and technology audit emerged and, to varying degrees, acquired a degree of institutional stability and acceptance. (p. 3).

Higher education managers, with their preexisting concern for controlling learning outcomes, were especially willing to accept and champion, what Power describes as the underlying normative or "programmatic" assumptions of the "rituals of verification" espoused by neoliberals (p. 14). Moreover, they were also open to adopting newly developing technologies to help this happen. By the 1980s, universities, especially in the Western world, were already high-tech institutions. It was a small step for them to begin to deploy technologies in new ways to observe and control an expanding array of institutional practices. This was particularly true as information technologies increased the power of managers for data collection and storage, information distribution, student surveillance, and so on.

The growing prevalence of auditing practices collectively account for a substantial portion of the technological change that has taken place in day-to-day teaching and learning contexts in higher education institutions. This is particularly apparent when it comes to measuring the outcomes of learning. Standardized testing and customizable test-item banks that accompany many university textbooks are broadly seen as viable "rituals of verification" that university professors, departments, and institutions can use to assert accountability. Student surveillance technologies to guard against cheating and plagiarism, information delivery technologies that can record student utilization and engagement with materials (both in class and in the library), automated student feedback systems that can be used to rate professors, and so on, open ways for universities (and governments that fund them) to assess the performance of pedagogical contexts. Faced with pressure to meet 'best practice' standards, over the last few years education managers have striven to develop more effective mechanisms for meeting educational benchmarks, including instituting new, low-cost systems for course delivery (many of these, like video-recorded lectures, podcasts, discussion forums, course websites, were forged in departments of distance learning but are now being deployed to augment on-campus courses).

For the most part, the prime motive for technological change in universities and colleges has been the desire to *assert their legitimacy* as effective and trustworthy producers of student learning (and, thus, to garner more student tuitions and government funding). In an increasingly neoliberal context, however, this has meant abandoning all pretence to broad notions of what might count as valuable learning. Instead of viewing learning as a ubiquitous process through which people entwine themselves and others into their natural, social and cultural worlds in emergent, unanticipated and creative ways, learning is reduced to a process of knowledge transfer that can be specified in advance, manipulated along the way, and measured at the end. According to Michael Power (1999), the capacity of auditing to convey legitimacy derives more from our willingness to accept its underlying instrumental presuppositions than its actual ability to disclose meaningful and important things about an institution's accomplishments.

This harkens back to Martin Heidegger's famous critique of technology (Heidegger, 1982). In Heidegger's view, the danger of technology does not lie in any particular power that a device may have to shape our world. The danger, he insists, is the larger supposition that underlies technology, that it is possible to impose our will on the world (including on each other). It is our technological mind set, our hubris, that Heidegger protests, a hubris that blinds us from seeing and prevents us from being comfortable with things in the world that are not in our control. The desire of institutions to assert their legitimacy leads them to adopt technologies that allow them to display the ways they are in control of the production of significant student learning. The supreme irony, here, is that, to the extent that they strive to control and struggle to show that they are in control, higher education institutions actually imperil learning.

The ultimate outcome of neoliberal, new management pressures is the deployment of a technological regime in higher education institutions that variously neglects, curtails, deflects, and interferes with collaborative learning processes of students in communities of practice so that definable and quantifiable institutional objectives can be attained. Despite all kinds of rhetoric that the purpose for introducing new educational technologies is to help students achieve in higher education contexts, in the vast majority of cases, what counts as achievement is not in the students' hands. The interests of students are served, in this context, only to the extent that students themselves accept the instrumental values of their school and allow their free-ranging, open-ended, collaborative, and uncontrollable cultural learning processes to be one-sidedly guided by educational technologies down a narrow and specific path.

THE RIGHT TO TECHNOLOGY IN EDUCATION

To this point, I have offered a rather one-sided perspective on technology in higher education institutions. Universities and colleges are complex contexts rift by contradicting forces, including, notably, groups strenuously opposed to neoliberal values, policies and practices; groups deeply skeptical of the value of modern technology in teaching/learning contexts; and groups genuinely interested in the potential use of technology to enhance collaborative learning processes. Despite the struggles of these groups to broaden both conceptions of learning and the uses of technology, I suggest that, at the current juncture, the state of technology in higher education remains, in the main, much like I have described above.

This, I think, is Harvey's (2008) perspective, too. He characterizes contemporary cities as shaped by the same overarching forces as those shaping higher education contexts and, although his characterization of cities as contexts that constrain the critical and democratic capacities of citizens over generalizes, it does, for the most part, capture the broad state of things. Harvey's key point, and the one I want to carry forward here, is that, within an urban context so dominated by structures that direct and control peoples' everyday practices in ways beyond their choosing, even small changes that can begin to provide people with a sense of their right to the city can have large consequences.

My contention is similar. Within higher education contexts like I have described above, where peoples' learning is so deeply shaped by powerful technologies (both old, like traditional classrooms, and new, like online course management systems), the smallest experience of the right to technology in education can have large consequences. The more we offer opportunities for ourselves and others to sense our shared right to technologies that enhance our longstanding cultural and collaborative learning capacities, the more new opportunities for developing as yet unforetold supportive technologies will be possible. Of course, given what I have said above, in our daily lives we already enjoy a rich panoply of simple and convivial tools for supporting rich teaching/learning processes (Illich, 2001). To a large extent, these small things, like turn taking when talking and listening, showing and watching, doing and waiting, are the very processes that are inhibited in formal learning contexts (teachers talk, show, and act; students listen, watch, and wait). Although it is important to try to recover even these basic elements of shared learning, given the powerful suppressive force of contemporary technology enhanced pedagogical practices, the right to technology in higher education requires more deliberate support.

Take, for example, my recent use in my own class of the 20-sided polygon, the icosahedron, as a model for regulating class discussion amongst my students. According to cybernetics theorist, Stafford Beer (Beer, 1994, 1995), the icosahedron is an ideal model for fostering, what he called, "syntegrity," that is, a powerful, yet unpredictable, means for stimulating group creativity and fostering group consensus. I introduced it to my students as a way they might share work in which they investigated contemporary ideas about lifelong learning. For the icosahedron to really help them, though, students felt they needed to adapt our course website to facilitate the flow of teaching/learning transactions recommended by the icosahedron. While the result of the experiment was far from perfect, we all ended up thinking that Beer's rather strange ideas actually worked pretty well. Interestingly, one of the things the students most valued about the process was the critical insight they gained into the ways prevailing strategies for fostering class discussion inevitably ended up dominated either by the teacher, a few powerful students, or by a search for the "right" answer. The icosahedron generated a very different set of dynamics that could easily be enhanced by small changes to current technology to produce interesting forms of shared learning. Experiencing this new way of learning together had the effect of revealing heretofore unseen limitations of other discussion facilitation techniques.

Despite its quirky appeal, it might be thought that this little innovation cannot constitute any serious example of how we might assert any student right to technology in education. Well, in part, this is true. Stafford Beer's innovation is too small on its own to be much of a force for shifting the current state of technology in higher education (although, it must be noted that, at one point, with a much more elaborated version of his little innovation at hand, Stafford Beer, himself, was retained by the Chilean government of Salvadore Allende to develop a large-scale mechanism for controlling the entire economy of Chile (Bechler, 2002)).

My contention, however, is that, whatever innovations are developed to make this change, they will probably mostly be small and unassuming like Beer's icosahedron. Although institutional change can be inspired, and certainly is better supported, from the top down by big, institution-wide initiatives, the kinds of changes that need to take place in higher education, the kind consistent with my call for a struggle for the right to technology in education, must inevitably come from small instances like my class experiment. Thus, despite what might appear as naïve idealism, our way forward with this must be to pursue modest means for our students to sense their right to technology in education. We should provide opportunities, for example, for them to modify a social networking technology, to commandeer and adapt a web discussion board, to shift chairs, to hold a pot luck in class, to design their own exam, to develop a wiki or blog, and so on. Small steps like these have the potential to engage students in collaborative learning. Even the smallest increase in their native capacity to integrate technology in equitable, sustainable, and mutually supportive ways into their collaborative teaching and learning relations will provide a basis for ever greater and more influential expansion of their right to technology in higher education.

REFERENCES

Bechler, R. (2002, November 7). Stafford Beer: The man who could have run the world. *OpenDemocracy.net*. Retrieved from www.cybsoc.org/contacts/opendrunworld.pdf

Beer, S. (1994). *Beyond Dispute: The Invention of Team Syntegrity* (1st ed.). San Francisco: Wiley.

Beer, S. (1995). *Designing Freedom* (1st ed.). San Francisco: Wiley.

Bourdieu, P. (1977). *Outline of a Theory of Practice*. New York: Cambridge University Press.

Chaiklin, S., & Lave, J. (1996). *Understanding Practice: Perspectives on Activity and Context*. New York: Cambridge University Press.

Deem, R. (2001). Globalisation, New Managerialism, Academic Capitalism and Entrepreneurialism in Universities: is the local dimension still important? *Comparative Education*, *37*(1), 7–20.. doi:10.1080/03050060020020408

Deem, R., & Brehony, K. J. (2005). Management as ideology: the case of 'new managerialism' in higher education. *Oxford Review of Education*, *31*(2), 217–235..doi:10.1080/03054980500117827

Foucault, M. (1977). *Discipline and punish: the birth of the prison* (1st ed.). New York: Pantheon Books.

Harvey, D. (1996). *Justice, nature, and the geography of difference*. Cambridge, MA: Blackwell Publishers.

Harvey, D. (2000). *Spaces of Hope* (1st ed.). Berkeley, CA: University of California Press.

Harvey, D. (2005). *The New Imperialism*. Oxford, UK: Oxford University Press.

Harvey, D. (2006). *Spaces of Global Capitalism: A Theory of Uneven Geographical Development* (1st ed.). London: Verso.

Harvey, D. (2007). *A Brief History of Neoliberalism*. Oxford, UK: Oxford University Press.

Harvey, D. (2008). The Right to the City. *New Left Review, 53*, Retrieved from http://www.newleftreview.org/?view=2740.

Harvey, D. (2009). *Cosmopolitanism and the Geographies of Freedom*. New York: Columbia University Press.

Heidegger, M. (1982). The question concerning technology. In *The Question Concerning Technology, and Other Essays*. New York: Harper Perennial.

Illich, I. (1971). *Deschooling society* (1st ed.). New York: Harper & Row.

Illich, I. (1977). *Disabling professions*. London: M. Boyars.

Illich, I. (2001). *Tools for Conviviality*. London: Marion Boyars.

Ingold, T. (2000). *The perception of the environment essays on livelihood, dwelling & skill*. London: Routledge. doi:10.4324/9780203466025

Ingold, T. (2004). *Learning though doing and understanding in practice*. Retrieved January 29, 2010, from http://www.c-sap.bham.ac.uk/resources/project_reports/findings/ShowFinding.asp?id=113

Klein, N. (2008). *The shock doctrine: the rise of disaster capitalism* (1st ed.). New York: Picador.

Lave, J. (1988). *Cognition in Practice: Mind, Mathematics and Culture in Everyday Life*. New York: Cambridge University Press. doi:10.1017/CBO9780511609268

Lave, J., & Wenger, E. (1991). *Situated Learning: Legitimate Peripheral Participation* (1st ed.). New York: Cambridge University Press.

Power, M. (1999). *The Audit Society: Rituals of Verification* (2nd ed.). New York: Oxford University Press, USA.

Rogoff, B. (1984). *Everyday cognition: its development in social context*. Cambridge, MA: Harvard University Press.

Rogoff, B. (1991). *Apprenticeship in Thinking: Cognitive Development in Social Context. New York*. USA: Oxford University Press.

Shore, C., & Wright, S. (1999). Audit Culture and Anthropology: Neo-Liberalism in British Higher Education. [doi]. *The Journal of the Royal Anthropological Institute*, *5*(4), 557. doi:10.2307/2661148

Tomasello, M. (1999). *The cultural origins of human cognition*. Cambridge, MA: Harvard University Press.

Tomasello, M. (2008). *Origins of human communication*. Cambridge, MA: MIT Press.

Tomasello, M. (2009). *Why we cooperate*. Cambridge, MA: MIT Press.

Wenger, E. (1999). *Communities of Practice: Learning, Meaning, and Identity* (1st ed.). New York: Cambridge University Press.

Chapter 20
The Future of Online Learning in Higher Education

Marshall G. Jones
Winthrop University, USA

Stephen W. Harmon
Georgia State University, USA

ABSTRACT

This chapter addresses the future of online learning and online learning technologies in higher education. Our understanding of the use of future technologies can be aided by a better understanding of how we have addressed the use of technologies in our past and in our present. A brief history of the use of technology in teaching and learning serves as a catalyst for a discussion of the near term, mid-range and far term technologies and possible issues associated with them. The authors propose that keeping the focus on human learning instead of specific tools will help higher education take full advantage of online learning in the near and far term future.

INTRODUCTION

When we first started talking about the future of online learning for this chapter, we did a number of things. First, we looked at where technology may be headed. We regularly follow online and print-based sources to see what technologies are on the horizon and how we might use them in teaching and learning. We consulted sites such as http://slashdot.com, http://technorati.com/technology/, and the ubiquitous Google Lab (http://www.googlelabs.com/). We looked at the Horizon Reports for 2009 (http://net.educause.edu/ir/library/pdf/CSD5612.pdf) to see what they were tracking. We looked at what futurists were writing about technology and society in general (e.g. Kurzweil, 2005). Additionally, we considered the history of the field of Educational Technology (Ely & Plomp, 1996; Saettler, 1990). We have met much change in technology and its impact on education over time and we feel it is important to look at our history so that we are

DOI: 10.4018/978-1-60960-147-8.ch020

not doomed to repeat it, if you will. To distill much of the reading and discussions we have had both in preparation to write this chapter, and in our ten plus years of research and writing about online learning (Harmon & Jones, 1999, Jones & Harmon, 2002; Jones & Harmon, 2006; Jones & Harmon, 2009), we can say conclusively and without reservation, that as to the future of online learning: it depends.

But make no mistake. The future of higher education will be inextricably intertwined with the Internet, or whatever the Internet becomes. Whether or not you support online learning, it will become a part of our future in higher education. As society embraces these technologies, we in higher education will find it impossible to ignore them. We see these changes already in everything from how students turn in assignments (in digital drop boxes) to how they obtain their course readings (as digital downloads to eBooks). And as a generation of web savvy- FaceBook-tweeting-texting students prepare to enter higher education in the immediate future, we will either embrace these technologies also, or be steamrolled by them. In this chapter we plan to speak briefly about our past experiences dealing with the future, the near term future, the far term future and how we should be preparing for them.

A BRIEF HISTORY OF THE FUTURE

Suffice it to say that we in education have a rocky relationship with technology. Saettler (1990) who wrote the book, both figuratively and literally, on the history of American Educational Technology, details how various technologies have, over the years, been presented to educators as revolutionary and bound to change education as we know it. Moving from Edison's introduction of film, to radio, television, computer-based education, to online learning and everything in between, technology has been heralded as both a savior to education and, in many cases, as a replacement for teachers. After a few decades of this, teachers at all levels became, rightfully in our opinion, somewhat nervous about technology. While it seems unlikely that technology will replace teachers (at least anytime soon), at present we agree with the widely attributed saying "any teacher who can be replaced by technology should be." And even if technology is not going to replace teachers, but "merely" revolutionize education, professional educators have a vested interest in what happens with technology.

As a society, we have watched our schools spend millions of dollars on technology to improve teaching and learning. From film strips to broadband to interactive whiteboards, we have put a considerable amount of technology into classrooms, and some would argue, to little or no positive effect (e.g. Postman, 1993; Oppenheimer, 2003; Cuban, 2001). Of course those of us who work in the learning technologies world know that technology isn't the answer in and of itself. No single technology will solve our problems. What will solve our problems is first defining them and then applying research-based strategies to them. The question then becomes, which problems will a technology solve, and how will it solve them? Norman (1988) popularized the work of Gibson (1977) on the concept of affordances. The basic idea being that different technologies have different strengths and weaknesses. The trick is to leverage the strengths and avoid the weaknesses. Historically, we have not been particularly good at this. PowerPoint is a good example. Yes, PowerPoint.

Back in the day, we used overhead transparencies to provide visual information to learners during instruction. And in the days before computers enabled us to make compelling transparencies easily and affordably, creating overhead transparencies was quite resource intensive. For example, to letter a bulleted list in a professional font (e.g. not hand written) you needed quite a bit of time and patience. This might have meant rub-off letters, or tracing stencils to create a professionally produced transparency. If it took that kind of effort to create a single slide, then you were not likely to create many of them. At the risk of sounding like we are waxing poetic about the good old days (because they aren't all that old, and they weren't all that good), you had to make your visuals matter.

PowerPoint changed all of that. Suddenly, it was remarkably easy to create slides. You could put images and text together in a matter of minutes. And here is what that meant: a thirty minute presentation, back in the day, might have six slides, or five minutes per slide. Today a thirty minute presentation may have thirty visuals or more. We have all been exposed to such slide whippings, and perhaps some of us are guilty of inflicting them.

Many in higher education looked to the inclusion of PowerPoint in classes as proof positive that technology was being used in teaching and learning. We would argue that this was a gross overstatement. More to the point, PowerPoint became used solely as a lecture support tool, and much of that support took the form of a lot of bulleted lists. So many people today don't really think about PowerPoint's ability to provide ease of creation or its beautifully transparent method of chunking information, or even its functionality as a media development tool. What they remember are the tedious presentations of slide after bulleted list slide that they have had to endure. PowerPoint's unfortunate legacy is impacted by implementation. We raise this point because we feel that implementation of online learning will be paramount to its future success in higher education. To avoid a future much like our past, where web-based learning is seen not for its strengths but only its weaknesses, it will be important not just to learn the technology from a technical standpoint, but it will be important to learn the technology from a learning impact standpoint.

ONLINE LEARNING: THE NEAR FUTURE

In looking at the future of online learning, people are often restricted by the scope of their view. For some, the fine granularity provided by specific tools may be seen as the key to the future. For example the tools of social networking in its varied manifestations (e.g. FaceBook or Twitter) are seen as being a positive step in the future of web-based learning. Recognizing the power of social networking, some have sought the best tool to use in social networking. And there are many options, such as http://facebook.com, http://twitter.com, http://ning.com and http://edmodo.com.

Social networking allows for shared knowledge. We firmly believe that there exists within a group of people working toward a common goal shared knowledge. Further we believe that, if this shared knowledge is harnessed and managed, it can be far superior to the single perspective of any one instructor, regardless of how good an instructor they are. The combined knowledge and skill of a classroom full of dedicated, intelligent students is a powerful thing. All of us are smarter than any of us. As Alan Kay (1989, p.6) was fond of saying "perspective is worth 80 IQ points." For an example of how we might harness this we turn to *folksonomies*. (Rethlefsen, 2007; Wu, Zubair, & Maly, 2006).

Taxonomies are classification systems created by an expert; folksonomies are classification systems created by groups of users (Reflesen, 2007). Folksonomies are often represented as the tags associated with a video on http://youtube.com or a picture on http://www.flickr.com/ (Wu, Zubair, & Maly, 2006). When communities of users gather to describe or comment on a phenomenon, the phenomenon begins to take on a more relevant description than that being provided by a single instructor. While an individual instructor may have one or two examples of a difficult concept, a group of learners may be able to provide scores of examples, often annotated with links. Those examples and links are a manifestation of the concept of folksonomies. The advantage of folksonomies is that they support the "long tail" (Anderson, 2006) which describes the large number of users who may search using low-frequency keywords that may not have been included in a taxonomy (Wu, Zubair, & Maly, 2006). The disadvantage of folksonomies is that they are often filled with meta noise, which is created by idiosyncratic tagging in a document (Wu, Zubair, & Maly, 2006). Currently, meta noise can make the use of folksonomies more trouble than they are worth. But promising research has made it possible to filter out much of the meta noise to focus on the elements of the folksonomy that may be useful. Wu, Zubair, and Maly (2006) have modified search engine algorithms to help develop an ontology, or hierarchy, of a document or other taggable object, based on user generated tags. Research like this has the potential to make the vast amount of data associated with web-based information infinitely more useable.

Through the use of taggable media, the concept of folksonomies can be manifested in most social networking environments and most media sharing environments. Focusing on the larger concept of folksonomies rather than which tool provides for it best seems to us to be a key component to maximizing the current potential of online learning. Recognizing the larger trends would be an area that will be rife with research opportunities as we move forward. While there are many trends we need to be preparing for, two of the trends that we need to be ready for in the near future are Synchronous Online Learning Environments (SOLE's) (Jones & Harmon, 2009) and Virtual Worlds.

SOLEs provide the ability for a class to interact online much the same way they would in a face to face class. Through the use of microphones, headphones, and, increasingly, web cams, teachers and students can talk to each other in real time. For better or worse, many of the same instructional strategies that are employed in a face to face class can be recreated in a SOLE. SOLEs also offer the opportunity for ancillary communication (Jones and Harmon, 2006) which provides for multiple channels of communication, such as audio, text-based chats, white board presentations and real time Internet searches to be used to support instruction concurrently. SOLEs are possible through commercially available products, such as Elluminate (http://elluminate.com) or free through such tools as SKYPE (http://skype.com). Because of the similarities of SOLEs with face to face classes, in the near future, higher education will need to determine whether an online class and a face to face class should even be considered differently at all. More to the point, for the purposes of accreditation, should a synchronous online class be considered online at all? The online designator was created originally for asynchronous types of classes. In a SOLE students and teachers may still be meeting for the same contact hours, still interacting in class in much the same way they would for a traditional class. Will we still consider this an online class? If so, the distinction is a thin one, based solely on the communication medium.

Similarly, Virtual Worlds provide for people to interact in real time, or synchronously if you will, through the use of avatars, or digital representations of the real person. Second Life (http://secondlife.com) is the best known example of this at the moment. Interest in the use of Virtual Worlds for learning is growing considerably. In the near future we will need to be considering what types of instructional strategies will make sense in this type of learning environment. Indeed it is entirely possible that the most important thing we will have to do in the near future with respect to learning technologies is to attend to instructional strategies. But even in this, we can take our cue from our history.

THE FUTURE OF TEACHING

There are two things that people with no practical experience or formal training are absolutely convinced they can do. The first is Coach and the second is Teach. One of the reasons for this idea that anybody can teach is the falsely held notion that teaching is primarily about presenting information. Gagne (1985) proposed nine distinct events of instruction to best facilitate the nine internal processes of learning. These are, using Gagne's numbers, (1) gaining attention, (2) informing learners of the objective, (3) stimulating recall of prior learning, (4) presenting the stimulus, (5) providing learning guidance, (6) eliciting performance, (7) providing feedback, (8) assessing performance, and (9) enhancing retention and transfer.

Gagne said that for effective instruction to happen, all nine of these things need to happen. They don't necessarily have to happen in this order, but if people are going to learn, we need to be accounting for these events. In looking at the events we would like to point out that only one of them, event number 4, deals with presenting information. Teaching is not simply telling. What often happens in many classes in higher education, though certainly not all, is that faculty will provide for events 1, 2, 4 and 8. For example, a professor will greet the class (event 1), remind them of what is on the syllabus for that day (event 2), lecture to them (event 4), and give them a test (event 8). What many people recognize as instruction is presenting the information, often through the use of a compelling lecture. Gagne calls this presenting the stimulus.

The Teaching Company (http://www.teach12.com/) sells higher education courses by compelling lecturers. And they tell us on their website that their "Great Courses" series gets an 8.97 out of 10 satisfaction score from their customers. And this is good. But it is one part of teaching, the telling part. And while that can be important, it is not the only part of good instruction, and it may not even be the most important part of good instruction. We argue that good instruction is about presenting information, to be sure, but it is also about providing learners with multiple examples and with significant opportunities to work with complicated content in a safe environment that provides informative feedback before learners are assessed. This is true for face to face classes and for online classes. The difference between them may have more to do with information presentation than anything else.

From module-based, self-paced asynchronous learning (Harmon & Jones, 1999) to synchronous online learning environments (SOLE) (Jones & Harmon, 2009) there continues to be a focus on information presentation. And we continue to think of the instructor as being responsible for information presentation. Even in online classes it is up the instructor to define the curriculum and provide for content. It is hard to find fault with this idea. After all, if that is not what we are doing, then why should there be a teacher in the first place? While not having faculty would certainly reduce the cost of higher education, we believe that it would also negatively impact the quality of higher education. But we may be biased. A class of twenty years ago may have had a required text or two or some other readings, but largely the role of the professor was to be the synthesizer of a vast amount of content acquired during their own education and honed over a long career. This is no longer the case. A quick Google search can yield more information than a faculty member would have read in his or her career.

We argue that the future of online learning is not in didactic information presentation, but rather in the use of online learning to create more user centered, generative, constructivist learning environments. And we believe that the way to do this is to attend to the details of good instruction. Indeed there is some suggestion that online teaching in higher education can actually help somebody become a better teacher in a traditional classroom (Kolwich, 2009). It is not that teaching online makes you a better teacher, according to Kolwich (2009), it is rather that paying attention to teaching makes you a better teacher. Even senior faculty with years of teaching experience in face to face classes found that developing online learning made their face to face classes stronger (Kolwich, 2009). We are not surprised by this. Because if we have learned anything from the media in teaching debate (Clark, 1983; Kozma, 1991) it is that good instruction is good instruction regardless of how it is delivered. And even as we prepare for the near term future and the long term future, we would do well to remember that it will be our attention to sound, content specific and technology relevant instructional strategies that will have the most positive impact on web-based learning.

ONLINE LEARNING: THE MID-RANGE FUTURE

Just a bit farther out two additional trends seem likely to have an influence on online learning. First is the concept of informal learning. Already, we see quite sophisticated structures in place to provide instruction on a wide variety of topics. Instruction that was once the purview solely of formal educational institutions and structures, now has become commonplace on a vast variety of topics and themes. The notion of just-in-time training has extended to include just-in-time learning. Take, for example, the popular multiplayer online role-playing game, and virtual world, *World of Warcraft*. Players have a vast variety of characters, classes, occupations, and other knowledge to master in order to successfully play the game. To our knowledge, there is as yet no formal *World of Warcraft* training Institute. Yet, there are multitudes of websites, blogs, wiki's, and even old-fashioned printed texts that teach players how to master the intricacies of the game. While most of these are offered freely, some people have created businesses to teach people how to play the game (http://www.zygorguides.com/?hop=mmktggrp). There are even businesses that will train you how to write a World of Warcraft training guide.(ie. http://www.warcraftaffiliates.com/). Similar training networks exist for dozens of games.

It's not only games that spawn such informal learning opportunities. Excellent online training modules exist for just about every hobby or interest you can think of. From woodworking to guitar playing, from cooking to camping, there are multitudes of online instructional modules. Most of these are available for free. For example, the website http://www.ehow.com offers over 1 million articles and around 170,000 videos instructing people how to do just about anything. We are not sure why people create these online learning opportunities; perhaps it's that humans have an innate desire to share what they know. Regardless of the reason, it seems likely that the number of these informal teaching and learning opportunities will increase in the future.

Higher Education may find increasing competition from free resources available on the Internet. It could be that the role of educational institutions in the future may be more that of a certifying body as opposed to an educating body. People will get their education informally from a wide variety of online sources and then attend a formal institution in order to gain the credential that shows they have mastered the content.

The second concept that seems likely in the midrange future is that of distributed problem solving (DPS) also known as crowdsourcing (Howe, 2006). In much the same way that cloud computing is currently evolving so that networked computers manage and distribute data, DPS involves networks of people all working on small pieces of the same problem. Nearly two decades ago the US Department of Labor (SCANS, 1991) issued a report calling for schools to prepare students to work better collaboratively. In traditional education students learn to work as individuals. They are given individual assignments, complete them independently, and are penalized if they are seen working in a group. Yet, few businesses work in this manner. In most corporate organizations teams, or even groups of teams, all work together to solve problems. Today, this concept is evolving even further. Now, temporary distributed teams come together to work on large problems and then disband. New teams are forming and dissolving all the time. The people in the teams may not know each other and may never see each other again. The best example of this comes from Amazon's Mechanical Turk project.

The Mechanical Turk project (https://www.mturk.com/mturk/) allows people to post any problem requiring human intelligence on a common discussion board. Anyone on the Internet can then access and work on that problem, receiving micro-payments ranging from a few cents to a few dollars for each aspect of the problem they complete. In this way the problem poster can virtually and effortlessly recruit hundreds or even thousands of people to complete a task that a single person might take years to accomplish. In another example, the Galaxy Zoo project recruits volunteers to classify nearly a million photographs of galaxies recorded by the Sloan Digital sky survey. During the first year of the project nearly 150,000 people made nearly 50 million classifications of galaxies (http://www.galaxyzoo.org/).

It seems likely that as society continues to adapt to distributed problem solving, learning and instruction will need to adapt as well. Higher Education may need to focus on preparing students to break problems into small parts suitable for distribution, recruiting a crowd of workers to solve each small part, and then assembling the individual solutions into one overall solution to the problem. If distributed problem solving becomes a standard mode of work, it may be that education will need to focus as much on management processes as on learning processes.

THE FARTHER FUTURE OF LEARNING AND TECHNOLOGY

Much further out than inevitable, possible futures blossom like the dogwoods in the spring. The future of learning and technology is inextricably tied to the future of society in general. Some futurists project a markedly different world than that which we have today. Most notable among these is Ray Kurzweil who has examined technology trends for the last couple of hundred years. He has come up with what he calls "the law of accelerating returns." Kurzweil (2005) holds that the rate of progress is an exponential function, not a linear one. That is, the rate of acceleration is itself accelerating. This means that if you consider the rate of technology progress today as a stable non-changing rate, then 100 years of progress will take 100 years. However, because the rate of technology progress is itself accelerating we may expect that what would be 100 years of progress at today's rate could happen in as few as 25 years. Kurzweil suggests that this has profound implications for society. Two of them stand out.

First, he predicts that by around the year 2040 computers will be sentient. Moreover, he predicts that society will then begin designing even more advanced computers that will soon pass beyond human ken. He calls this moment of time the singularity. Just as at the event horizon of a black hole, the point at which light can no longer escape is known as the singularity, Kurzweil (2005) argues that the future beyond this point is essentially unknowable, in our present state. The notion of our present state is important because, second, Kurzweil holds that at about the same time humans will begin downloading their minds into computers. We will, in effect become digital beings.

What do learning and instruction mean to a digital being? We can only speculate at this point, but it seems reasonable that at least some of what we already know about learning will still apply. For example, the role of Gagne's (1985) fourth event of instruction will be diminished. Digital learners (in the sense of humans whose conscious exists in a digital medium) will be able to access the universe of content knowledge in much the same way as we flesh and blood humans access our own long-term memory. Digital humans will be able to "recall" the collected content of human thought, even if they have never "learned" it to begin with. In fact, learning for digital humans could precipitate a stunning turnaround (if you are keeping score at home) in the hierarchy of the nine events of instruction. Event 4, "presenting the stimulus" which has long enjoyed prominence as the central (and in some cases the only) event of teaching, may no longer be needed for digital humans. Instead, the other 8 events become critical. As we are already realizing from our current experience with Google and other search engines, merely having access to information is, not in and of itself, sufficient. Digital humans will still need to know that they need the information they are seeking to recall, and they will need to know how to find it. We must also be able to assimilate that information with what we already know in order to use it.

Learning basic content knowledge (the accretion of discrete facts that would today be stored in declarative memory) may become obsolete. Instead, learning in the future of digital humans may focus on what we think of today as higher order learning practices involving re-organization of knowledge. Gagne's (1985) fifth domain of learning "Cognitive Strategies" may supplant "Intellectual Skills" as the focus of formal education as we seek to enhance digital humans' epistemological capacity. How we think about things will become at least as important (if not more so) as what things we think about. We suggest that the basic educational curriculum for higher education in this future may focus on the following capabilities:

1. The ability to identify a problem (defined here as an opportunity to apply knowledge);
2. The ability to determine what knowledge and information is needed to solve the problem;
3. The ability to find that information;
4. The ability to evaluate the value of the information found;
5. The ability to assimilate the information found with existing knowledge;
6. The ability to formulate a solution based on the assimilated information;
7. The ability to implement the solution;
8. The ability to evaluate the results of the implementation.

Indeed, these capabilities could be said to represent much of what is important in learning today, but we list them here to emphasize the future diminished role of memorizing content as the dominant conception of learning.

Of course the future of digital humans still seems like something of a long shot from our current perspective. While it may eventually be possible to become digital, we think that the people of a society unwilling to give up SUV's, cigarettes, or talk radio may have a hard time giving up their bodies. At present it seems more likely that the future will come from a different direction. Ultimately, we believe that the future of technology and learning lay in neuroscience.

Perhaps the Holy Grail of cognitive neuroscience is to understand human thought at the level of the neuron. If we were able to recognize a bit of information by the arrangement and signaling pattern of a neuron then we would physically be able to manipulate what has up to now been strictly mental. Teaching, at that point, may once again gain dominance over learning as a way by which information and knowledge is passed along. Learning may become a passive act in which the learner sits comfortably in a chair while the teacher physically manipulates the learner's neurons to instill a new set of knowledge. While this does sound somewhat far out, we do seem to be making progress toward this end. For example, *Sony*, has patented a device for direct neural stimulation of a person's senses (Hogan & Fox, 2005). If they are able to do what the patent says, the person wearing the device would actually see, hear, touch, taste, smell, and feel things that do not exist in the real world. Imagine being chased by a dinosaur through a dense jungle in a Jurassic Park video game. On second thought, you wouldn't have to imagine it because with this technology you would actually experience it. Perhaps this will be a key selling point for the *PlayStation 300*.

We do seem to be heading in a direction which makes direct neural manipulation (DNM) seem plausible. Researchers at Microsoft have developed a means for tagging images people view on the World Wide Web by measuring electroencephalogram brain waves as they surf the Internet (Kapoor, Shenoy & Tan, 2008). The participants do not need to actually think about the image they view, they merely passively watch and the software tags the image with an appropriate label with up to 90% accuracy. More recently, neuroscientists at Case Western Reserve University have managed to isolate rat short-term memory cells and represent information in them in vitro (Larimer & Strowbridge, 2009). So while the idea of DNM as a mechanism of instruction is certainly a long-way off at best, we at least appear to be on a track that could lead there.

If DNM does become possible the role of instructional technologists may change dramatically. First, the skills of task analysis may become paramount. Determining the exact content to be implanted neurally will become a highly specialized, and no doubt highly remunerated skill. Developing job/task algorithms could become a highly competitive arena in which designers could sell algorithms for any desired task. These could be standard "off-the-shelf" packages or individualized "designer" skill sets. There could be a wide range of quality/price-point skill sets available, with established upgrade paths for each. Even if this were possible it still seems likely there will be a need for assimilation and integration of new content with existing knowledge. This integration may occur more easily than we expect today.

Recent findings by researchers at EPFL in Lausanne, Switzerland determined that perceptual learning—like learning how to detect anomalies on medical images that are extremely hard to detect for untrained people—can proceed just as effectively through mental imagery (imagination) as through exposure to real data. This research suggests that there is a threshold quantity of information that needs to be soaked up in a given domain, after which significant gains might be made simply through advanced internal simulation, analysis, and "practice." (Anissimov, 2009, np.)

In other words, the assimilation and integration of new knowledge with old may be possible through simply thinking about it. Once the task analysis and skill-set design are complete, "programmers" would then convert the algorithms to neurally implantable signals and then neurologists would implant them. Neurologists might then be thought of as what we call today professional trainers. In this future, teaching would be much more similar to what we think of as programming today. The old notion of tabula rasa may come again to the fore and the learner as a passive recipient of knowledge may be the desired state.

SOLUTIONS AND RECOMMENDATIONS

There are likely no real solutions for the future, and specific recommendations for higher education are varied and likely specific to individual campuses, but we suggest professional development, the campus experience and a focus on emerging technologies as common areas of concern for all learning organizations.

From expanded summer schedules to meeting the needs of working students, many schools are expanding their online options. A brick and mortar campus that wishes to expand their online education mission needs to provide adequate resources to help faculty learn to teach online. This may mean expanded responsibilities for academic support centers or it may mean the creation of new organizations to help handle training and support. Training and support should not be in technology alone, but should also include instruction in appropriate instructional strategies for online courses (Harmon & Jones, 1999; Jones & Harmon, 2009). Many institutions are good at providing technical support for online classes, but pedagogical support needs to be provided as well. Specifically, support needs to be provided in how to create learning environments that provide for increased interactions between students and students and faculty and students. Professional development on how to provide for learning guidance within an online classroom is also needed. We feel that any campus engaged in online learning should provide human and capital resources to stay current not only in technology, but in instructional strategies specific to online learning as well. As we stated early on in this chapter: our focus should always be on advancing human learning.

While watershed moments do happen with technology, most change is incremental. Organizations need to be involved in "environmental scanning" or looking at the current landscape in order to spot future trends. Other chapters in this book would be a good place to look for what is happening today and what we may expect in the future. We regularly consult sites such as http://slashdot.com, http://technorati.com/technology/ and Google Labs (http://www.googlelabs.com/). Additionally, we advise an annual reading of the excellent collaboration of the New Media Consortium and Educause, *The Horizon Reports* (http://www.nmc.org/horizon). But beyond that every campus should develop a culture of looking forward. Rather than reacting to technologies, as we are currently doing on many campuses to mobile phones, we should be looking at them in a proactive manner to see how they can help us advance human learning. Teams should be developed that include technical expertise, Instructional Technologists and teaching faculty to be preparing campuses, be their physical or virtual, for advances in technology.

Understanding how online communities fit into your campus will be crucial in the near and far term future. Higher education focuses not only on the education of the student, but also on the experience of the student. While classes are important, we also want our students to have a positive experience that helps them become well rounded citizens. We encourage our students to build relationships with others and to become involved in their communities. There exists, at times, an uncomfortable dynamic between the students and the faculty in higher education as it relates to online learning and online communities. For faculty of a particular mindset, relationships and learning environments are built and maintained through proximate interactions. But for many students, and for an increasing number of faculty, relationships and learning happen not only in proximate relationships, but also in online communities. It is not uncommon to hear a faculty member speak of an online community as virtual. But to students, these are not virtual environments at all. They are real. They are tangible. It would serve us well to learn why online relationships are real to our students and to help leverage that understanding to make the campus experience more valuable to the student. For the completely virtual campus this will help make the campus experience, and not just the classes, useful to learners. For brick and mortar campuses, this will help to expand and strengthen the scope and mission of the university.

CONCLUSION

While it sounds trite to say that the future of web-based learning in higher education is ours to write, it is still true. As we have discussed in this chapter, the future of web-based learning for higher education in the near term depends on a careful attention to its affordances. We will keep our competitive edge by focusing on advancing human learning and the needs of learners rather than focusing on specific online tools. By paying attention to sound instructional design principles we can use online learning effectively and let it be known for its benefits and not its weaknesses. In the far term, we must not simply wait and see. We must step forward to greet the future and integrate it with our present. Because the future does not simply occur overnight, it is built by all of us with each advance that we discover and share. We are building the future today; we would do well to remember this.

REFERENCES

Anderson, C. (2006). *The long tail: How endless choice is creating unlimited demand.* London: Random House.

Anissimov, M. (2009, December 14). *The benefits of a successful singularity.* Retrieved from http://www.good.is/post/The-Benefits-of-a-Successful-Singularity/

Clark, R. E. (1983). Reconsidering research on learning from media. *Review of Educational Research, 53*(4), 445–459.

Cuban, L. (2001). *Oversold and underused: computers in the classroom.* Cambridge, MA: Harvard University Press.

Ely, D., & Plomp, T. (1996). *Classic writings on Instructional Technology.* Englewood, CO: Libraries Unlimited.

Gagne, R. (1985). *The conditions of learning* (4th ed.). New York: Holt, Rinehart & Winston.

Gibson, J. J. (1977). The theory of affordances. In Shaw, R., & Bransford, J. (Eds.), *Perceiving, acting, and knowing.* Hillsdale, N.J.: Erlbaum.

Harmon, S. W., & Jones, M. G. (1999). The five levels of web use in education: Factors to consider in planning an online course. *Educational Technology, 6*(39), 28–32.

Hogan, J., & Fox, B. (2005, April 7). Sony patent takes first step towards real-life Matrix. *New-Scientist,* (2494). Retrieved from http://www.newscientist.com/article/mg18624944.600.

Howe, J. (2006). The rise of crowdsourcing. *Wired Magazine 14*(6). Retrieved from http://www.wired.com/wired/archive/14.06/crowds_pr.html.

Jones, M. G. & Harmon, S. W. (2002). What professors need to know about technology to assess online student learning. *New Directions for Teaching and Learning.* Fall (91). (pp. 19-30).

Jones, M. G., & Harmon, S. W. (2006). Intentional instructional strategies for mobile learning environments. In Isaias, P., Kommers, P., & Sanchez, I. A., (Eds.). *Proceedings of the IADIS international conference mobile learning.* (Pp. 222-226) IADIS Press.

Jones, M. G., & Harmon, S. W. (2006). Ancillary communication as an intentional instructional strategy in online learning environments. In M. Simonson, & M. Crawford (Eds.). *Proceedings of the 2006 international conference of the Association of Educational Communications and Technology, (2).* (pp 194-199).

Jones, M. G., & Harmon, S. W. (2009). Instructional strategies for teaching in synchronous online learning environments (SOLE). In Yang, H., & Yuen, S. (Eds.), *Collective intelligence and E-Learning 2.0: Implications of web-based communities and networking* (pp. 78–93). Hershey, PA: IGI Publishing.

Kapoor, A., Shenoy, P., & Tan, D. S. (*2008*). Combining brain computer interfaces with vision for object categorization. *IEEE CVPR.* Retrieved from http://research.microsoft.com/pubs/64264/cvpr2008-bciandvision.pdf.

Kay, A. C. (1989). Predicting the future. *Stanford Engineering, 1(1), Autumn, pg 1-6.* Retrieved from http://www.ecotopia.com/webpress/futures.htm.

Kolowich, S. (2009, December 7). Learning from online. *Inside Higher Education*. Retrieved from http://www.insidehighered.com/news/2009/12/07/online/

Kozma, R. (1991). Learning with media. *Review of Educational Research, 61*(2), 179–211.

Kurzweil, R. (2005). *The singularity is near: When humans transcend biology*. New York: Penguin Group.

Larimer, P., & Strowbridge, B. W. (2009, December 27). Representing information in cell assemblies: persistent activity mediated by semilunar granule cells. *Nature Neuroscience*. Retrieved from http://www.nature.com/neuro/journal/vaop/ncurrent/abs/nn.2458.html.

Norman, D. (1988). *The design of everyday things*. New York: Doubleday.

Oppenheimer, T. (2003). *The flickering mind: the false promise of technology in the classroom, and how learning can be saved*. New York: Random House.

Postman, N. (1993). *Technopoly: The surrender of culture to technology*. New York: Vintage.

Rethlefsen, M. (2007). Chief thingamabrarian. [Retrieved from Health Source: Nursing/Academic Edition database.]. *Library Journal, 132*(1), 40–42.

Saettler, P. (1990). *The evolution of American educational technology*. Englewood, CO: Libraries Unlimited.

The Secretary's Commission on Achieving Necessary Skills (SCANS). (1991). *What work requires of schools: A SCANS report for America 2000*. Washington, DC: U.S. Department of Labor.

Wu, H., Zubair, M., & Maly, K. (2006). Harvesting social knowledge from folksonomies. *Proceedings of the 17th Conference on Hypertext and Hypermedia*. Odense, Denmark. (pp. 111-114).

KEY TERMS AND DEFINITIONS

Asynchronous Online Learning: Planned learning that uses online materials and resources. Learning happens within a learning community without the constraints of time and place. Often referred to as "anytime, anywhere" learning or "on demand" learning.

Crowdsourcing: Also known as distributed problem solving (DPS). A technique for solving complicated problems by having individuals or groups of individuals work on a single component of the problem and then combining all of the work into a single solution.

Direct Neural Manipulation (DNM): The ability to interact with digital objects mentally and not physically.

Folksonomies: Classification systems created by users. Typically created through meta tags of digital objects.

Formal Learning: Planned learning events that are created and managed by a sanctioned or accredited learning agency, instructor or group of instructors.

Informal Learning: Unplanned learning that happens outside the boundaries of a sanctioned or accredited learning organization.

Synchronous Online Learning: Planned learning that occurs through computer mediated communications and occurs through the use of real time interactions between teachers and students and students and students.

Virtual Worlds: Online environments where users exist in a computer generated setting and interact with each other through the use of avatars.

Chapter 21
Viability, Sustainability, Scalability and Pedagogy: Investigating the Spread of Real-time, Rich Media Technologies in Australian Universities

Robyn Smyth
University of New England, Australia

Deborah Vale
University of New England, Australia

Trish Andrews
University of New England, Australia

Richard Caladine
University of Wollongong, Australia

ABSTRACT

In a two year project called the Leading Rich Media project, the implementation of rich media technologies in Australian universities was investigated from the standpoints of viability, sustainability, scalability and pedagogy. Over half of all universities responded with several respondents from each institution providing rich data concerning how implementation is planned, funded, maintained and administered. The silences in the investigation were interesting, with the project team discovering a surprising lack of current scholarly publications available to inform their work. Other silences in the data led them to conclude that there is a policy and strategic planning void in many institutions which could threaten best use of emerging rich media technologies such as desktop videoconferencing and other synchronous communications technologies.

DOI: 10.4018/978-1-60960-147-8.ch021

INTRODUCTION

In Australian higher education institutions technology in teaching, learning, administration and research is washing over the sector in ever diverse waves. Since the onset of the initial online learning wave earlier in the last decade, we have seen increasing use of the internet in Australian universities for teaching and learning, research and administration. Most recently, there have been increasing uses of multi-media and social networking technologies and rising demand for synchronous communications. However, little evidence is available to show how the adoption of synchronous technology is strategically planned for positive impact on organisational efficiency as well as to enhance the social experience of staff and students.

Our *Leading Rich Media Project* (Funded by ALTC, The Australian Learning and Teaching Council) has begun to unpack this context by investigating the implementation of real-time, rich media, communications technologies from points of view around sustainability, viability, scalability and pedagogy. The project is founded in educational change theory and practice. It uses the concept of the 'professional community' as a support structure for the project. The mediating variables which are critical to mobilising the sector for change are the shared knowledge and expertise of the existing stakeholders and others in universities, partner institutions and the corporate sector, nationally and internationally.

Thus, the project team set out with the intention to form a community of practice comprising technicians and others using the technology, to quantify how Australian universities plan for and implement technologies, and to investigate emerging pedagogies.

The project methodology is based in the educational change literature because the generalised failure of educational change initiatives over the last 30 years (Fullan, 2007), shows us that a strong basis in educational change theory and practice provides a useful lens through which to analyse the adoption of rich media technologies. The approach to managing the project uses Sergiovanni's (1998) concept of the 'professional community' as its conceptual framework because his notions of community encapsulate the values required for success: expertise, collegiality, professional obligations, norms and conduct to leverage deep and enduring change. The shared knowledge and expertise of the stakeholders is utilised through a virtual community of practice which includes a wide range of staff in universities and partner institutions, particularly the Australian Academic Research Network (AARNet Pty Ltd). In order to operationalise this proposal the project leaders chose to assume the role of integrators in the Competing Values Framework devised from the substantial body of work in management literature, most recently by Vilkinas and Cartan (2006). The project leaders oversee the project from this perspective in order to support and expand a functioning professional community which can support sustained change. Thus, their roles include aspects of each of the elements within the four foci of the framework: people, task, external and internal. Using this framework in the hope of success, the project leaders have consciously dealt with change through regular videoconference meetings, collaborated to obtain resources and attempted to look after the people who are the community of practice while getting the job done (Vilkinas & Cartan, 2006).

The evaluators for the project have been involved regularly throughout the life of the project and provided expertise from methodological and technological perspectives derived from their expertise nationally and internationally. The project leaders have been grateful for their engagement and acknowledge this. Similarly, the support and collaboration of AARNet management and members of the AARNet videoconferencing network has been ongoing since their early work on videoconferencing futures which preceded the project (AARNet Pty Ltd, 2006).

Data emerging about user uptake and knowledge of the rapidly changing technology show the next big challenges facing universities relate to demands for mobility and personal real-time, rich media communications technologies. This could easily see pressure from students to communicate with fellow students and teachers from their mobiles or computers either at home or work. At first glance this looks to be a worthwhile step for reasons of environment and convenience but it becomes difficult when class numbers are high. For example to communicate with 5 others requires six video windows to be open on a computer screen as each participant appears in their own window. While this is manageable with number say up to ten what happens with classes of 100 students? How will technology serve these needs well?

BACKGROUND

Although there have been many papers published in the last decade which take the form of case studies into a particular use of rich media technologies (Acar, 2007; Blair, 2007; Bloomberg, 2007; Colbert, 2005; Finley, 2005; Hernandez-Ramos, 2007; Hron, Cress, Hammer, & Friedrich, 2007; Kidd & Stamatakis, 2006; Kinnear, McWilliams, & Caul, 2002; Lynar, 2005; Penniston, 2005; Pomales-Garcia, Rivera, & Chamoun, 2009; Saw et al., 2007; Sheikh, 2006; Shen, Wang, & Pan, 2008; Skeekey, 2005; Wang, Shen, Novak, & Pan, 2008; Williams, 2007) there is a paucity of recent scholarly writing on the implementation of rich media technologies in higher education and only a small number of authors have attempted to research the benefits of rich media technological use in teaching and learning (Caladine, 2008a; Gillies, 2008; Hedestig & Kaptelinin, 2005; Knipe & Lee, 2002; Smyth & Zanetis, 2007). The pace of technological change, which is revealed to some extent in the chronology of the literature, makes research into the advantages and disadvantages of particular technologies very difficult to evaluate. New technologies are being used before any serious research is published on the former versions and searching for scholarly investigation, theorising or reporting of practice yielded considerable manufacturer generated information or industry reports (Greenberg, 2008) but little that was directly relevant in the easily accessible academic literature. Some pedagogy-related thinking is emerging slowly and we have contributed to this, but rich media technologies still seem to be the 'elephant-in-the-room' as far as strategic well founded research is concerned (Andrews, Caladine, Smyth, Tynan, & Vale, 2008; Bossu, Stein, Smyth, & Shanahan, 2006; Smyth, 2005, 2009a).

Thus, the project team completed its own literature search as well as engaging a consultant to complete a global review on our behalf. The parameters for this review (Greenberg, 2009) were to investigate trends in 1) technology; 2) policy and governance; and 3) research. In addition, we commissioned a business analyst to survey Australian institutions who have adopted rich media technologies with a view to gathering exemplars of best practice integration or implementation and the financial planning associated with these. Despite his deep government and corporate sector links, this consultant experienced a similar dearth of published literature other than industry generated reports and promotional materials, reinforcing the team's experience. Nevertheless, significant information was gathered as data and in reports as well as the ongoing scanning of academic and other relevant literature.

In order to focus the project and to effectively interpret the data, the team needed to define the technologies accurately and to determine the boundaries for the investigation. In an early meeting the scope of technologies and affordances to be included and excluded led to defining the form and type of technologies to be scrutinised. The current versions of these are included here to guide the reader although there is a sense in which they will continue to evolve for the life

Table 1. A taxonomy of communications technologies

	COMMUNICATIONS TECHNOLOGIES			
	ONE WAY		TWO WAY	
	asynchronous	synchronous	asynchronous	synchronous
Rich Media	*Podcasts* *Vodcasts* Video recorded to media such as DVD, Blu-Ray or tape. Video can also be hosted on a website. Recorded Presentations Several products are available for the automated recording of presentations or lectures. These include Lectopia (previously known as iLectures).	*Broadcasts.* For example television and radio (satellite or terrestrial). Webcasts	*Voicemail* (when two way)	*iVC or Internet Visual Communications.* For example Skype (video), MSN messenger, Windows Live Messenger, Apple iChatAV *Videoconference.* For example appliance-based systems such as Tandberg, Polycom and Lifesize etc. *Web Collaboration.* For example Webex, Ellunimate, Marratech, Cisco Meetingplace, Adobe Connect (Breeze) *Access Grid.* Dedicated high speed and bandwidth videoconferencing where multiple users interact simultaneously to create common objects collaboratively.
AUDIO ONLY	*Voicemail*		*Voicemail* (when two way)	Telephony The plain old telephone system. teleconference For example a telephone conference call
Text	*Email* (electronic mail) *Letter* (print or snail mail)		*Wiki* *Email* (exchanges) *CMC* *Letters* (exchanges) (print or snail mail)	*IM* (Instant Messaging) Text based. Also known as Chat. For example IRC (Internet Relay Chat) SMS exchanges Short Message Service

of the project and beyond via interactivity to be encouraged through the forthcoming project web site: www.richmedia.edu.au.

Rich media is defined as media which approximates the immediacy of face-to-face communication where participants read non-verbal cues such as vocal inflection and body language (93% of all communication) to increase understanding and obtain rapid feedback (Daft and Lengel 1986, p. 560 cited in Baecker, 2003). Thus, rich-media technologies include those affordances which promote technology enhanced learning through real-time, face-to-face dialogue with authentic interaction occurring over the internet between distributed participants. They are further defined as those videoconferencing technologies which facilitate interactive communication between users, who can see, hear and interact with multiple communication streams synchronously or access them asynchronously (AARNet Pty Ltd, 2006). They currently include videoconferencing, personal webconferencing, Access Grid and the like (Berriman, 2007). The term 'rich media' is not intended to delimit particular affordances currently available so should be seen as an indicator of any emerging affordances which promote synchronicity.

The taxonomy below is a simple conceptualisation developing from our collective experience and research to guide the work of the *Leading Rich Media* project which is centred on emerging two-way synchronous technologies shown in the shaded column in Table 1.

The question arising from the project team's thinking and literature searching is not so much: *What is the benefit to students of rich media technologies*? It appears to be fairly obvious that distance education students will benefit from interaction with their lecturer, tutors, and other students. The real question appears to be: *How*

Figure 1. Rich media technologies in use as reported by respondents to the survey

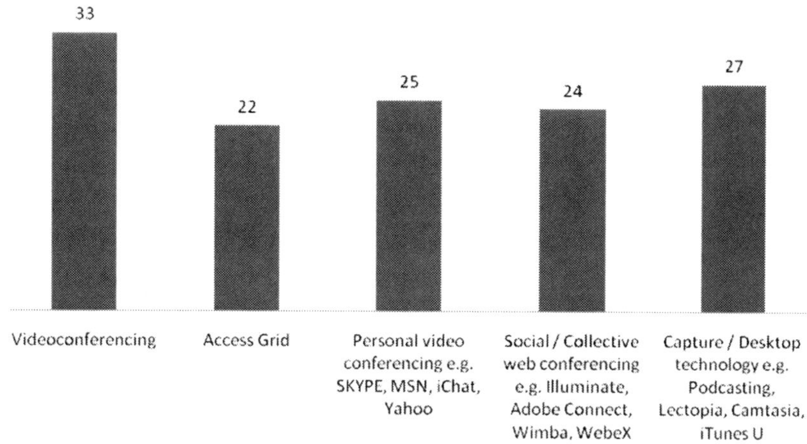

will institutions make decisions on which technologies to use to aid student teaching and learning and how will such decisions be effectively implemented and sustained?

PROJECT FINDINGS, ISSUES AND DISCUSSION

In order to obtain as much information about how Australian universities use and plan to implement rich media technologies in their institutions the project leaders decided to survey as many staff as possible in the universities who had some involvement in these kind of decision making processes. Letters inviting participation in the project, including information sheets for participants, were sent to every Vice-Chancellor at an Australian university, asking them to nominate up to five staff members from their institution, and offering them the results of the project in the form of business plans and professional development units which should be of great use to them when planning and instigating rich media in their institution. The variety of contacts requested was to allow the researchers to obtain different viewpoints from each institution. Replies were received from 22 of the 38 Australian Universities naming 76 contacts in total. This was a reasonable response rate from which to begin (Vale, 2009). (We should note that data charted and quoted below is derived from the analyses reported for the project reported by Vale (2009). This report included an extensive chronological literature review as well as analyses of data gathered.)

How do Australian Higher Education Institutions Use Rich Media Technologies?

The majority of respondents came from institutions with multiple campuses (86%), and 36% of respondents represented institutions involved in distance education. All of the universities responding to the survey used videoconferencing. Access Grid was the least used technology with 14 of the institutions (22 respondents) reporting its use.

The use of personal video conferencing (18 universities) and capture/desktop technologies (20 universities) reflects the changing nature of rich media within higher education institutions. Greenberg and others (Greenberg, 2008) predict that the desktop type of rich media technologies will overtake the use of videoconferencing within the next few years.

Figure 2. Rich media technologies planned to be introduced to Australian universities

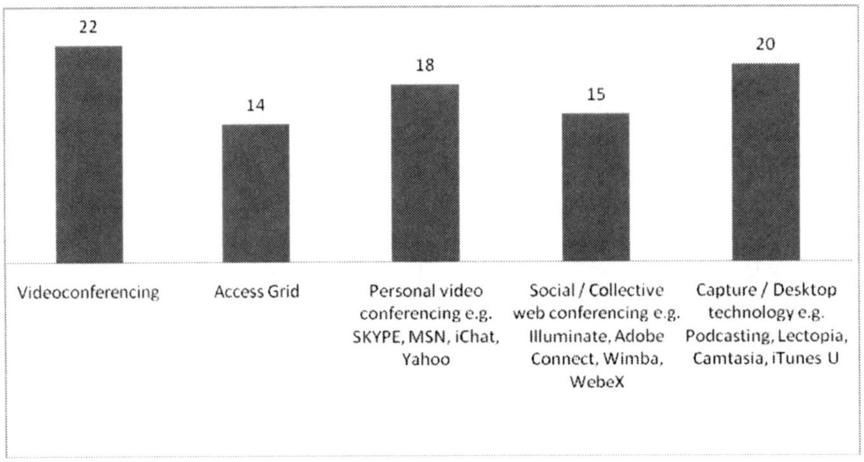

Although 14 of the institutions were planning to increase their use of videoconferencing and 13 their use of Access Grid, the most increase in rich media technological use was in personal web conferencing (77%) and video streaming, both asynchronous and synchronous (73%). These responses are in keeping with research by the Wainhouse Research group who predict that the use of web conferencing and video streaming would increase greatly in the next three years (Greenberg, 2009) in higher education and more broadly.

The respondents were also asked if any other technologies not listed were planned for their institution. Only five of the universities planned to implement the unified and mobile types of technologies. One university was planning to implement Optiportal, live DVN (digital video network) capability, and another was planning Elluminate. One said that they were making significant investment into mobile technologies

Figure 3. The variety of uses made of rich media technologies (grouped by institution)

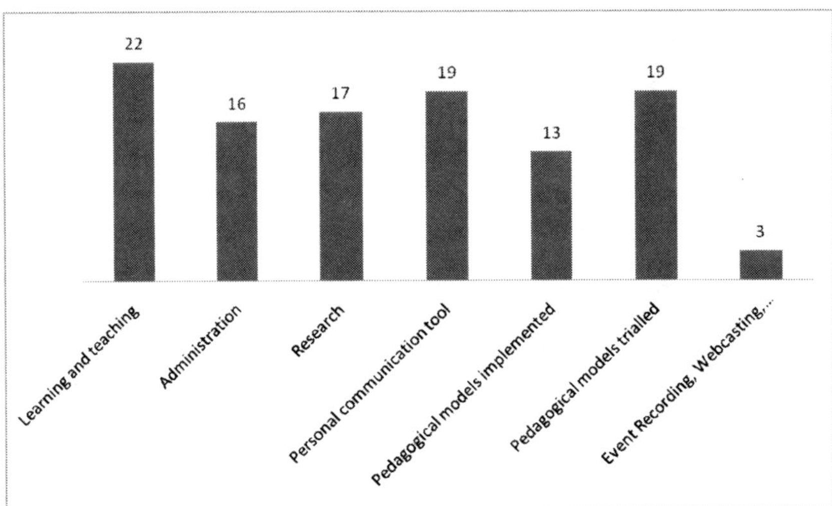

as a part of their institution's vision, and another said WEB 2.0 technology.

In our survey, the respondents identified uses in administration (73%), and research (77%), and three of the institutions reported that rich media technologies were being used in widely ranging fields such as event recording, webcasting, training, and for engaging with prospective students and community outreach projects. Nineteen of the institutions (86%) had trialled pedagogical models for using rich media technology and twelve of the institutions (59%) participating in the survey had implemented pedagogical models. However, none supplied policy or other documents to substantiate or exemplify these claims.

None of the respondents reported that they were planning more use of social software such as Twitter or Facebook, or virtual world types of technology such as Second Life, though the use of these technologies is set to increase in the next three years (Greenberg, 2009; Johnson, Levine, Smith, Smythe, & Stone, 2009). In their report to the *Leading Rich Media* Project Wainhouse Research noted that a survey of over 300 educators and administrators in a large U.S. western state, one that is highly rural and struggles with many geographical obstacles similar to those found in Australia (long distances, sparse rural populations), found that the use of social software or virtual world technologies was expected to more than double in the next three years. This is not reflected in the responses of the Australian universities participating in the survey.

This is perhaps as Caladine (2008b) found, in a survey of Australian universities on the use of peer-to-peer real time communications, that most institutions may allow the use of these technologies on their networks. However, more than half imposed restrictions or warnings on their use, and some attempted to manage or restrict the use of the technologies. The emerging uses for the technologies were for learning and teaching and as a personal communication tool.

Responsibility for Rich Media Technologies

A series of questions in the survey required the participants to check boxes indicating who was responsible for maintenance, bookings, policy and facilities at their institution. They were given choices for indicating the areas of responsibility – Information Technology Departments (ITD), Teaching and Learning Centre (TLC), Library or Faculties, and also given the option of checking a box headed 'none' or 'various'. The project researchers wished to ascertain if there were any consistencies across the institutions represented and how rich media technologies are managed by the universities.

Respondents reported (Table 2) that the responsibility for rich media management fell to multiple departments in most of the universities responding to the survey with responsibility for maintenance falling solely upon ITD departments in 10 institutions, though t12 said that various departments were responsible for maintenance. When it came to booking the use of the equipment only six institutions nominated ITD departments as the sole provider of bookings, and three said

Table 2. Summary of responses regarding responsibility for rich media technologies

	ITD	TLC	Library	Faculties	None	Various:
Maintenance	18	7	2	4		4
Bookings	12	7	3	7		9
Policy	12	13	5	5	2	11
Facilities	13	5	4	8		8

that their TLC had sole responsibility. The other 13 institutions nominated various or multiple responsibilities for booking the use of rich media equipment. The responsibility for policy and facilities were even less clear according to the respondents to the survey. Most institutions (20) nominated multiple or various responsibility for policy whilst only one said the ITD departments and one said that no-one was responsible for policy on the use of rich media. The ITD department claimed sole responsibility for the management of facilities housing rich media technology hardware in four of the institutions responding to the survey, and the remaining eighteen institutions reported multiple or various departments claiming responsibility. One of the interesting conclusions from this level of analysis is that none of the Directors of the ITD departments believed that the sole responsibility for policy development regarding rich media technologies should reside in their own departments preferring to share this responsibility across numerous institutional departments.

The confusion evident in the data seems symptomatic of the lack of planning indicated by the literature and consultants' reports. The respondents were asked to provide the URL to their policies governing use of rich media technologies at their institution. Eleven of the responding institutions did not supply an URL to their institutional policy on the use of rich media, and of these three replied that they did not have any policy on the use of the technologies. Analysis of the URLs supplied showed that policies thought to relate to rich media technologies were actually more generic IT policies. Eleven (50%) of the responding institutions spoke of rich media technologies being aligned with their Institutional Strategic Plan through supporting teaching and learning, and eight (36%) of the institutions said it aligned with their plan for research. Six (27%) of the institutions cited flexibility in the delivery of teaching programs, and five (23%) supporting multi-campus and/or distance education as being a part of their Strategic Plan and that rich media technologies enhanced these aims. Four (18%) of the institutions said that it was an aim of their strategic plan to be more responsive to students' needs, and two (9%) thought that the use of rich media technologies aligned with their desire to form a community of learning. Potentially this situation will hinder the speed of implementation and opportunities for new implementations.

Drivers for Adoption

Most of the respondents believed that the adoption of rich media technologies was being driven by student demand (83%), followed closely by demand by the staff at their university (78%). Reducing travel budgets was also seen as a driver by 28 of the

Figure 4. Individual respondents' about drivers for adoption of rich media technologies at their institutions

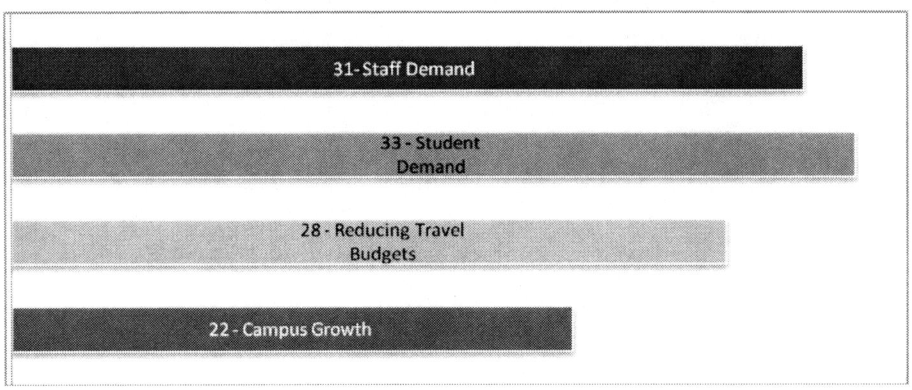

respondents (70%). These drivers fit with broader trends (Greenberg, 2009) worldwide, particularly in Europe and the USA. A recent evaluation of the implementation of desktop videoconferencing in the Regional Institute of Technical and Further Education, South Australia (TAFE SA) (Smyth, 2009b) confirms these drivers as significant.

Where the geographic spread of universities affects their day-to-day business, technology has been adopted as a means to increase viability by reducing costs e.g James Cook University in far north Queensland has two campuses in Townsville and Cairns, one in Brisbane and five satellites separated from each other by at least 200kms so videoconferencing, is a core technology as it is for the University of Wollongong with its five satellite campuses and Access Centres on the NSW south coast. Similarly, the Joint Medical Program established between the University of New England and the University of Newcastle is premised on sharing staff and the problem-based learning curriculum as well as using rich media technologies to facilitate learning when students are situated in rural and remote clinical settings. Interestingly, the University of Melbourne, an urban institution, is one of the first to indicate adoption of rich media technologies as a core plank of its strategic planning. Some of the more innovative intentions for rich media technologies derived from various universities strategic plans include: encouraging community participation in university events, maximising access to scholarly expertise and cultural collections, and fostering community outreach.

Sources of Funding

For the initial purchase of the equipment the source of funding was most likely to be a project specific grant or source of funding, as well as capital pool development funding or the purchase being funded from central university funds.

Questions inquired into the institutional plans for on-going funding of rich media technology with the majority of respondents indicating that the ongoing funding of rich media technologies relied on central funding (55%), and external or internal grants and project based grants (27%). One of the universities said that they had no plans for on-going funding and two did not answer the question. Four of the institutions responding to the survey said that costs may be carried by faculties or departments (18%). Other forms of funding for rich media technologies included a bidding system, annual infrastructure submissions and capital development pools.

Figure 5. Sources for funding for rich media technologies (number of responses)

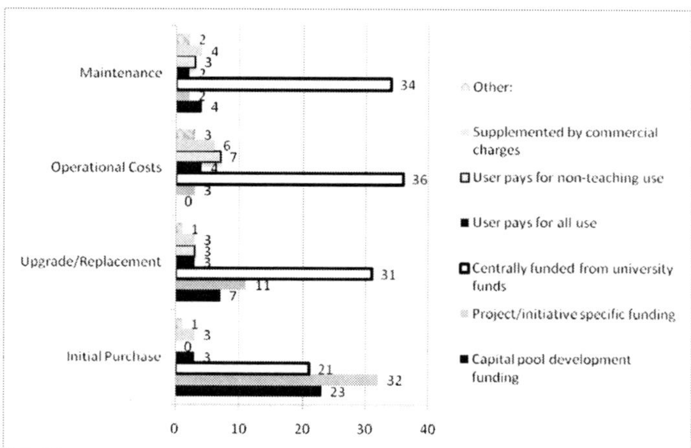

In addition, one university respondent indicated that on-going funding would be dependent on the success of the implementation of rich media technologies, though they did not say how this would be quantified. Another respondent said that funding would be dependent on 'structural cost reductions combined with growth in revenues from higher enrolments' while a colleague from a different institution said that funding for all technology was currently under review in the overall university budget.

For all of the other categories, upgrade/replacement, operational costs and maintenance the respondents thought that the funds for these, on the whole, were sourced from central funding from university funds.

Business Planning

A second online survey was conducted by the Project's business analyst with Chief Operating Officers from the 13 universities who responded to a financial survey that focused on core linkages between their university's strategic business goals for campus wide teaching and learning and the degree of integration of the business planning processes adopted by them for the acquisition of rich media technologies and lifecycle support services to underpin or assist their university's delivery of teaching and learning. In particular, this online survey was seeking to uncover exemplars of 'best practice' in fiscal policy in an era of increasing expenditure demand and the need to consider sustainability, viability and scalability when planning technology acquisitions. Global foci on reducing greenhouse gases and climate change are beginning to exert pressure on many private and public institutions to reduce carbon footprints will become a driver of great influence, if manufacturer's claims are to be believed (http://www.tandberg.net/).

Although only three of the thirteen respondents acknowledged that they had a master plan for campus wide implementation of rich media technologies, there was a strong correlation between this group and the maturity and integration of the business planning processes that directly link to their university's strategic goals for teaching and learning. This group had formal processes for investment evaluation and funding the acquisition and life cycle support services and all respondents from this group stated that they their plans incorporate the concept of unifying communications and that their plans were underway. From the survey results there is evidence that these universities have a more centralised approach to the business planning process and the role of ITD is central to technology policy and strategy in planning for acquisition of rich media technologies where rich media technologies are just one element of the overall university technology plan. What is not certain from the survey results is whether the decision to adopt the concept of unifying communications has been a driver for the centralised approach to business planning or whether it is more likely to be an outcome of the centralised approach to business planning which is more closely aligned to the overall university strategic goals. Either way, the potential here is that these three institutions will become lighthouses for other adopters to imitate.

Barriers to Adoption

Most respondents thought that the lack of financial support would be the greatest barrier to their institution taking up more rich media technologies. The area which was seen as the least problem was network capacity. These findings align well with the results of the survey carried out by Greenberg (2009) who asked respondents to rate ten barriers to the adoption of rich media technologies. The greatest barrier in this survey was also funding, while network/bandwidth capacity rated ninth (Greenberg 2009). The difficulties in coordination and sharing of technology in large institutions, which has been shown through the answers the survey respondents' gave credence to questions on policy and administration of rich media technologies in their institution.

Some of the other barriers to the adoption of rich media technologies foreseen by Greenberg (2009) are also listed by the survey respondents. However, they seem to add even more barriers than Greenberg had foreseen:

- Compliance with restrictive copyright regulations for digital content
- Silos [of activity within the institution]
- Achieving consistency in relevant hardware
- Skills and engagement of academic staff
- Lack of staff resources to support new technologies
- Policy support to establish remote end-points in Sydney and other capitals where staff would willingly video conference to students
- Rapid change in technology.

The other side of the coin to barriers is pre-conditions to implementation. Not surprisingly, we discovered rich detail of issues that will be needed to be addressed before rich media technology can synchronise with the everyday business of an Australian university (Vibert & Place, 2006). It was curious that five (23%) of the participating universities said that there were no pre-conditions to their uptake of rich media technologies but perhaps this is from ignorance or lack of recognition of the potential issues. Seven (32%) of the institutions said that there would need to be more training and professional development for their staff and only four (18%) said that they would require more funding. Five (23%) institutions said that they would have to ensure that the technology would enhance teaching and learning in their institutions. Interestingly, many concerns were raised regarding technical aspects of using rich media technologies. Some spoke of co-ordination and uniformity across all of their campuses, and others felt that infrastructure and networks would need to be upgraded even though earlier data found that network capacity was not an issue.

Our finding is that the primary preconditions required to support the implementation of rich media technologies were

- Coherent institutional policies
- Network infrastructure
- Staff awareness and preparedness
- Provision of technical support
- Ongoing financial support
- Innovation in pedagogy.

These primary preconditions were found to be strengths of the TAFE SA adoption. In particular, appropriate technical and staff support was essential (Smyth, 2009b).

Support for Staff

Twenty-six respondents (70%) thought that professional development and seminars and/or workshops would be suitable tools for assisting staff in learning to use rich media technologies. Professional development is a very broad term and could perhaps encompass all of the other options, so it is surprising that all of the respondents did not choose this option. The next most popular choice for staff training in using rich media technologies was seed funding and online learning (46%). The least popular option was a formal course (19%), perhaps because of the already heavy workloads carried by academic staff. Five respondents (13%) said that their institution had no plans for staff development in the use of rich media technologies. Information about plans for technical support was a silence in the data.

Solutions and Recommendations

The *Leading Rich Media* project has provided very useful lens through which to analyse information about the uses, viability, scalability and sustainability of rich media technologies. As a result,

Figure 6. How the survey respondents thought their institution would support staff in experimenting with rich media technologies – by position in the institution

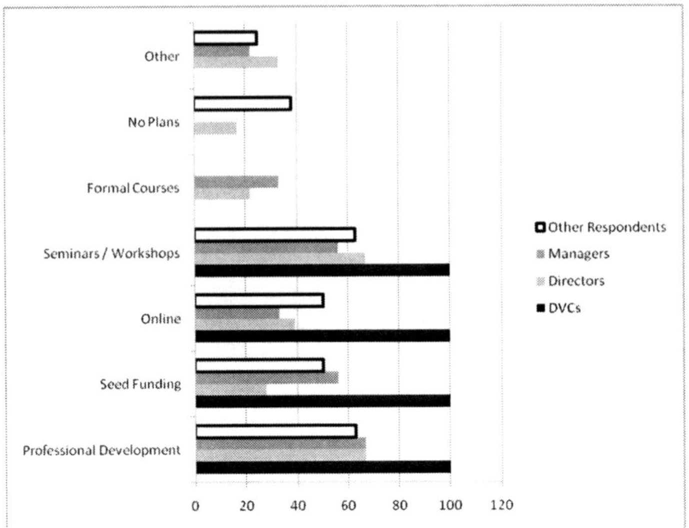

we have discovered that much of the information concerning organisational policy and practice indicates a significant lack of strategic vision and planning in most institutions. Similarly, much of the available literature is vendor generated or limited in research rigour and provides little useful guidance for organisations intending to adopt rich media technologies. Such a picture illustrates some of the preconditions for implementation failure predicted by the change management literature so more research is required.

Drawing on the data obtained in the study and the suggestions above, we recommend the need for planning and policy about the use of rich media technologies as a critical aspect of the successful adoption and sustainable use of these technologies. Policy on the use of rich media technologies appears to be lagging behind the use of the technology. Many institutions rely on grant types of funding to provide the infrastructure for the technology, resulting in issues relating to medium and long term sustainability. The e-learning scene is changing so rapidly and all of the institutions participating in the survey are endeavouring to provide their students with the best possible means of enhancing their teaching and learning experience. They may however, need to allow more time for the development and implementation of policy regarding the use of rich media technologies to successfully integrate these technologies into their programs and courses. Institutions may also need to allow time to examine how these technologies rate in the importance of enhancing teaching and learning in their institutions, what staff and technical support should included as budget items and to plan for their continued use and upgrade of equipment. Viability, sustainability, scalability and pedagogical concerns can be discussed during planning processes, therefore, reducing risk of inappropriate implementation. From the TAFE SA evaluation potential for success is increased if these issues underpin planning decisions (Smyth, 2009b).

FUTURE RESEARCH DIRECTIONS

From the *Leading Rich Media* Project, we suggest that there are needs for scholarly work to inform policy development and practice in the use of rich media technologies. It may be possible to build upon the work already completed in the e-learning arena. After studying why some e-learning programs in Europe had failed Kegan and colleagues (2007) made five major 'conclusions and recommendations that are characteristic of all or nearly all of the initiatives, that were closed because they failed to reach targeted goals':

- 'Hard-nosed market research is essential for the success of any e-learning initiative;
- E-learning initiatives should plan carefully for and control carefully their revenue and expenses. Seeding funding dries up quickly;
- Choice of courses and its accreditation is crucial;
- It is important that those planning e-learning initiatives should define precisely the relationships of their initiative to existing providers and define precisely the institutional model they will adopt;
- E-learning initiatives should plan carefully to manage both their educational and business activities.' (Keegan et al., 2007).

In our view, these recommendations highlight the silences in our own data and so could be used for further research to support technology planning in higher education. After all, such implementations are significant change initiatives and the educational change literature has told us for 30 years now that preconditions to success include adequate vision building, collaborative planning with stakeholders, financial and personal support. Technology implementations are large scale educational change projects so require adequate change management, planning and financial commitment (Vibert & Place, 2006)!

CONCLUSION

What is emerging is a picture which is more complex than anticipated and yet has clear pointers to the changing roles of staff, practices and pedagogies as the recurrent waves of technological innovation wash over higher education. One surprising outcome of our investigations into a broad church of related literature is the sparseness of scholarly output concerning pedagogy, implementation strategies and business case development. Our investigation shows that there are many instances of innovative practice to celebrate in individual institutions and that the use of rich media technologies is diverse across the sector reflecting the individual characteristics of the 22 institutions which responded and represent 58% of the sector. Thus, no one approach to implementation is common. However, the lack of policy and strategy in all but three institutions which are planning for rich media technologies as a core infrastructure is a common concern emerging from the data.

So, how are rich media technologies changing social and organisational practices in higher education? The greatest impact seems to be in its use for administration, multi and cross campus/institutional teaching and research. Here, organisations are not maximising the potential financial and social benefits of the technology for the betterment of the organisation. From our business modelling, it is becoming apparent that savings in terms of administration costs could potentially be a significant driver for many institutions, particularly regional ones where travel budgets require significant airline travel and where staff are suffering burnout from too much travel. Evidence of the positive impact of rich media technologies on organisations in these ways is yet to emerge but the tide is also rising in terms of environmental accountability across the university sector in Australia so if the vendor hype about greenhouse savings is realisable then this will provide further impetus for adoption, stimulating creative social and organisational uses for synchronous communications tools.

Overall, the *Leading Rich Media* project has shown that rich media technologies have had, at best, limited ad hoc impact on organisations and their staff and students but we remain confident that they are useful tools which can impact positively on the social and organisational aspects of universities. The positive impact of rich media technologies should, therefore, translate into increased institutional viability and sustainability. To date, scalability has yet to become a particular driver but interest in engaging more closely with students at a personal level seems to be on the rise. This will force new pedagogy for the adoption of personal rich media technologies.

REFERENCES

AARNet Pty Ltd. (2006). *The results of the AARNet Survey on Video over IP in the Australian Academic & Research Sector*. Canberra: AARNet. July.

Acar, A. (2007). Teaching languages from a distance through multipoint videoconferencing. *Foreign Language Annals*, *40*(2), 311–319. doi:10.1111/j.1944-9720.2007.tb03203.x

Andrews, T., Caladine, R., Smyth, R., Tynan, B., & Vale, D. (2008). *Rich media technologies and uncertain futures – developing sustainable, scalable models*. Paper presented at the Hello! Where are You in the Landscape of Educational Technology? Conference, Melbourne, 30th November -3rd December, ASCILITE.

Baecker, R. (2003). *A principled design for scalable internet visual communications with rich media, interactivity, and structured archives.* Paper presented at the Proceedings of the 2003 conference of the Centre for Advanced Studies on Collaborative research IBM Press, Toronto, Ontario, Canada, pp. 16-29 Available from Berriman, A. (2007, 14/02/2007). *Visual Communications: Transformational possibilities vs incremental realities.* Paper presented at the Wainhouse Research Collaboration Summit, Wainhouse Research, Sydney, pp. 1-60. Available from http://www.wainhouseresearch.com/sydney07/presentations

Blair, K. J. (2007). Telemedicine, urban style. *Distance Learning*, *4*(3), 59–63.

Bloomberg, L. D. (2007). Culture and community: case study of a video-conferenced graduate distance education program. *Journal of Distance Education*, *22*(1), 41–58.

Bossu, C., Stein, S. J., Smyth, R., & Shanahan, P. (2006). *Internet-based videoconferencing for distance teaching and professional development.* Paper presented at the Improving University Teaching Conference, 2006, University of Otago, Dunedin, New Zealand. Available from Caladine, R. (2008a). *Enhancing E-Learning with Media-Rich Content and Interactions*. London: Information Science Publishing.

Caladine, R. (2008b). *An Evaluation of the use of Peer to Peer Real Time Communications Applications within the Australian Academic and Research Community.* Wollongong, Australia: Australian Academic and Research Network (AARNet)

Colbert, R. (2005). New technologies for the education market smash barriers in distance learning. *Distance Learning*, *2*(4), 7–8.

Finley, B. (2005). the AVCs of display. *Video systems, 31* (8), 44.

Fullan, M. (2007). *The NEW Meaning of Educational Change* (4th ed.). New York: Teachers' College Press.

Gillies, D. (2008). Student perspectives on videoconferencing in teacher education at a distance. *Distance Education*, *29*(1), 107–118. doi:10.1080/01587910802004878

Greenberg, A. (2008). The Distance Education and e-Learning Landscape.: *Vol. 2. Videoconferencing, Streaming and Capture Systems for Learning (Segment Report)*. Brookline, MA: Wainhouse Research November.

Greenberg, A. (2009). *The Leading Rich Media Project (Consultation Report)*. Brookline, MA: Funded by The Australian Learning and Teaching Council. Wainhouse Research. September.

Hedestig, U., & Kaptelinin, V. (2005). Facilitator's roles in a videoconferencing learning environment. *Information Systems Frontiers*, *7*(1), 71–83. doi:10.1007/s10796-005-5339-6

Hernandez-Ramos, P. (2007). Aim, shoot, ready! Future teachers learn to 'do' video. *British Journal of Educational Technology*, *38*(1), 33–41. doi:10.1111/j.1467-8535.2006.00600.x

Hron, A., Cress, U., Hammer, K., & Friedrich, H. F. (2007). Fostering collaborative knowledge construction in a video-based learning setting: effects of a shared workspace and a content-specific graphical representation. *British Journal of Educational Technology*, *38*(2), 236–248. doi:10.1111/j.1467-8535.2006.00619.x

Johnson, L., Levine, A., Smith, R., Smythe, T., & Stone, S. (2009). *The Horizon Report: 2009 Australia–New Zealand Edition*. Austin, TX: The New Media Consortium.

Keegan, D., Lõssenko, J., Mázár, I., Michels, P. F., Paulsen, M. F., Rekkedal, T., et al. (2007). *E-learning initiatives that did not reach targeted goals* (No. 3). Bekkestua, Norway: Megatrends Project 2007. N. P. House. Retrieved from http://www.nettskolen.com/in_english/megatrends/Book3.pdf

Kidd, R. S., & Stamatakis, M. K. (2006). Comparison of students' performance in and satisfaction with a clinical pharmacokinetics course delivered live and by interactive videoconferencing. *American Journal of Pharmaceutical Education*, *70*(1), 1–6.

Kinnear, H., McWilliams, S., & Caul, L. (2002). The use of interactive video in teaching teachers: an evaluation of a link with a primary school. *British Journal of Educational Technology*, *33*(1), 17–26. doi:10.1111/1467-8535.00235

Knipe, D., & Lee, M. (2002). The quality of teaching and learning via videoconferencing. *British Journal of Educational Technology*, *33*(3), 301–311. doi:10.1111/1467-8535.00265

Lynar, C. (2005). Saving lives with teletrauma: Vermont trauma surgeons provide consultative services to rural communities using state-of-the-art videoconferencing technology. *Distance Learning*, *2*(6), 29–30.

Penniston, P. (2005). Creative solutions for distance administration of TVI and O & M services. *RE:view*, *37*(3), 118–119.

Pomales-Garcia, C., Rivera, M., & Chamoun, D. (2009). *Best practices and assessment process for an engineering course through videoconference*. Paper presented at the 2009 Industrial Engineering Research Conference. Conference, Saw, K. G., Majid, O., Ghani, N. A., Atan, H., Idrus, R. M., Rahman, Z. A., et al. (2007). The videoconferencing learning environment: technology, interaction and learning intersect. *British Journal of Educational Technology, 39* (3), 475-485.

Sergiovanni, T. (1998). Market and Community as Strategies for Change. In Hargreaves, A., Lieberman, A., Fullan, M., & Hopkins, D. (Eds.), *International Handbook of Educational Change* (*Vol. 1*, pp. 576–595). Dordrecht, Netherlands: Kluwer Academic Publishers.

Sheikh, F. (2006). Canadian telehealth project aims to build capacity in Middle East. *Technology in Government*, *13*(3), 6.

Shen, R., Wang, M., & Pan, X. (2008). Increasing interactivity in blended classrooms through a cutting-edge mobile learning system. *British Journal of Educational Technology*, *39*(6), 1073–1086. doi:10.1111/j.1467-8535.2007.00778.x

Skeekey, J. (2005). The jury's in: videoconferencing is invaluable to the legal profession. *Distance Learning*, *2*(5), 38–39.

Smyth, R. (2005). Broadband videoconferencing as a tool for learner-centred distance learning in higher education. *British Journal of Educational Technology, 36*(5), 805–820. doi:10.1111/j.1467-8535.2005.00499.x

Smyth, R. (2009a). Enhancing learner-learner interaction using video communications in higher education: Implications from theorising about a new model. *British Journal of Educational Technology*..doi:10.1111/j.1467-8535.2009.00990.x

Smyth, R. (2009b). *Evaluation Report: The TAFE@ Your PC CleverNetworks Project of the Regional Institute of TAFE SA*. Armidale: Technical and Further Education South Australia. Robyn Smyth Consulting.

Smyth, R., & Zanetis, J. (2007). Internet-based videoconferencing for teaching and learning: a Cinderella story. *Distance Learning, 4*(2), 61–70.

Vale, D. (2009). *Report on the Survey of the Use of Rich Media Technologies in Australian Universities*. Armidale: Australian Learning and Teaching Council Funded Leadership Grant.

Vibert, C., & Place, C. (2006). Technology and Change in Higher Education. In Hunt, L., Bromage, A., & Tomkinson, B. (Eds.), *The Realities of Change in Higher Education: Interventions to Promote Learning and Teaching* (pp. 115–127). London: Routledge.

Vilkinas, T., & Cartan, G. (2006). The integrated competing values framework: its spatial configuration. *Journal of Management Development, 25*(6), 505–521. doi:10.1108/02621710610670092

Wang, M., Shen, R., Novak, D., & Pan, X. (2008). The impact of mobile learning on students' learning behaviours and performance: report from a large blended classroom. *British Journal of Educational Technology*. Retrieved from http://www3.interscience.wiley.com/journal/120119993/abstract. doi:.doi:10.1111/j.1467-8535.2008.00846.x

Williams, W. (2007). Connecting the docs. *Behavioral Healthcare, 27*(4), 39.

KEY TERMS AND DEFINITIONS

Rich Media Technologies: Comprise synchronous communications technologies which enable participants to see and hear each other in real time.

Distance Education: The practice of studying when the student and teacher experience geographical separation.

Grant Funding: Money received from government by a competitive application process.

Australian Learning and Teaching Council: An Australian Government agency set up to promote excellence in learning and teaching in higher education.

Access Grid: Dedicated high speed and bandwidth videoconferencing rooms where multiple users interact simultaneously to create common objects collaboratively, often using electronic whiteboards as well as high definition videoconferencing.

Chapter 22
Adoption of Technologies in Higher Education:
Trends and Issues

John Nworie
Independent Researcher and Consultant, USA

ABSTRACT

The impact of digital technology and the resulting change has impacted society and every aspect of life, including higher education. Technology has affected every area of operation in higher education, dramatically changed the way work is performed, and enhanced productivity and efficiency levels. While the efforts of higher education institutions to adopt new technological innovation are laudable, it is worth noting that such adoption has not been even across campuses. Technology use has not been consistent due to a number of factors, including adoption and integration approaches, resistance, budget allocations, institutional priorities, shifting student demographics, organizational cultures, leadership issues, and failure to apply systemic approaches to adoption, among others. This chapter examines how higher education has responded to the adoption of digital technologies, reviews some of the existing issues and challenges, and identifies areas that need to be addressed to further the use of technology to improve instructional and administrative practices in higher education.

INTRODUCTION

The past few decades have witnessed the impact of the rapid growth of digital technology on the society and every aspect of life. Every sphere of society has been touched by technology including higher education (Kozeracki, 1998; Milet, 1996). Technology has affected every area of operation in higher education and has dramatically changed the way work is performed, enhancing productivity

DOI: 10.4018/978-1-60960-147-8.ch022

and efficiency levels in many cases. For a long time higher education was known for its delayed response to change and adoption of innovations, but the current computer technology revolution has significantly diminished that stereotype.

The long held view in higher education of technological and scientific innovation as the exclusive province of academic research has changed; it is now being used to support the business and administrative processes and operations of colleges and universities, for research, and to improve teaching and learning. In their efforts to equip college graduates with the skills needed to compete in the emerging knowledge economy, academic institutions are using existing and emerging technologies, as employers look for technologically savvy graduates (Chisholm, Carey, & Hernandez, 2002). There are now many administrative, research, communication, interactive, teaching and learning, and assessment technologies. Faculty members are employing existing and emerging technologies technology to conduct research and collaboration with colleagues globally. The field of distance education has exploded, largely due to information technology.

While the adoption and integration of technologies is evident on campuses, such adoption has not been even across campuses and results have not been consistent due to a number of factors, including adoption and integration approaches, resistance, budget allocations, institutional priorities, shifting student demographics, organizational cultures, institutional and technology leadership issues, change management abilities, and failure to apply systemic approaches to adoption, among others. The digital divide resulting from socioeconomic inequities, adoption processes, resistance, costs, organizational culture, as well as Internet security-related issues have contributed to limiting the wider spread and even diffusion of information technology on campuses.

This chapter examines how higher education has responded to the adoption of digital technologies, reviews some of the existing issues and challenges, and identifies areas that need to be addressed for maximum benefit in the use of technology to improve the academy.

ADOPTION, INTEGRATION, AND DIFFUSION OF TECHNOLOGY IN HIGHER EDUCATION

The adoption, integration, and diffusion of technological innovation by higher education has been influenced by different models and theories of adoption, integration, and diffusion of innovation and has been explored by many authors (Burkman, 1987; Celsi & Wolfinbarger, 2002; Ellsworth, 2000; Hall & Hord, 1987; Hooper & Rieber, 1995; Hord, Rutherford, Huling-Austin, & Hall, 1987; Massy & Wilger, 1998; Rieber & Welliver, 1989; Rogers, 1995, 2003; Sherry, 1998; Stockdill & Morehouse, 1992; Surry 1997; Surry & Brennan, 1998; Zaltman, Duncan, & Holbeck, 1973). Some models examine the source of the innovation (Sauer and Anderson, 1992), while others focus on the development, application, and the nature of innovation (Axtell, Holman, Unsworth, Wall, Waterson, & Harrington, 2000). The investigations of diffusion of innovation involve efforts in determining the nature and rate at which innovations and technology diffuse within organizations or cultures.

Rogers (1995, 2003) diffusion of innovation theory has been widely used to provide framework for the discussion, adoption, and diffusion of innovation on many campuses. Rogers provides a generally used definition of adoption of innovation and describes the processes involved and also explains why certain innovations are successfully adopted and others are not. Rogers (1995) defines diffusion as "the process by which an innovation is communicated through certain channels over time among the members of a social system" (p. 5), adding that communication with regard to innovation is essential because the messages being transmitted concern a new idea. Zaltman and Duncan (1977) also define innovation as "any idea, practice, or material artifact perceived to be new by the relevant unit of adoption" (p. 12). Some authors suggest that the term innovation can also refer to an old idea that is applied in a new setting (King & Anderson, 2002).) The process of adopting innovation is gradual and occurs over time Surry (1997).

In many instances, adoption and integration processes in higher education have not been systemic or systematic and have been devoid of well-defined intended outcomes. As diffusion and adoption processes continue, it is important for higher education to pay attention to how the innovation is adopted and diffused and subsequently institutionalized (Surry & Ely, 2002). Successful implementation of technology must be holistic and target members of the institution to ensure that they find value in the innovation and are committed to its consistent use. Unplanned implementation could lead to failure to reap the benefits of technology innovation. Failure to derive maximum gains that accrue from the adoption of innovation could be more of a result of failure to implement than failure of the innovation itself (Klein & Sorra, 1996).

Adoption, integration, and diffusion processes continue to evolve in higher education as institutions are at varying stages of adoption and integration of technology, especially as new technologies continue to emerge.

Higher Education Response to Technology Adoption

Computer technology, obviously, is not the first technological innovation in higher education. Technology has been present in higher education since the lantern slide was developed in the mid-1800s. Over the years several technologies have found their way into higher education. In the early twentieth century, some of the media used in education included films, slides, and photographs (Saettler, 1990). In 1910, the University of Texas established a bureau of visual instruction. From the early 1920s schools increasingly used visual materials, such as pictures and lantern slides (Reiser, 2002). The introduction of film and radio as educational tools led to the name change from visual instruction to audiovisual instruction (McCluskey, 1981). Over time, photography, overhead projectors, slide projectors and other early forms of technology were introduced, along with television and video, which received widespread adoption and were ubiquitous on campuses. While useful, these earlier technologies did not transform higher education as some had predicted.

Higher education's adoption of computer technology has been gradual. The mid '80s to early '90s still saw a gradual approach to adoption as potential users were faced with apprehension, reluctance, skepticism, and apathy. At the onset, many institutions did not have any adoption and implementation strategies, goals, or consolidated plans. The earlier adopters and innovators (Rogers, 1995) were the trailblazers on campuses and were often asked to lead technology-adoption efforts. Some of the initial attempts at adoption were the result of bandwagon effect as institutions followed trends that were in vogue at other institutions. Some institutions succumbed to the wooing of technology vendors to acquire new technology without adequate plan for the use. The acquisition and use of technology in higher education became a yardstick that institutions used to measure and demonstrate how competitive they are and their technology leadership (Henriksen & Soule, 1998), and was also used to attract new students.

Many approaches to instruction have not taken full advantage of the inherent and latent abilities of today's technologies to transform teaching and learning. For the most part, efforts appear to be disjointed, with technology appended to existing teaching and learning methods (Zemsky & Massey, 2004).

Accruing Benefits

Nonetheless, many successes have been achieved and accruing benefits are evident on campuses as a result of technology adoption. While the impact of technology on teaching and learning in higher education has not reached a stage that many expect, progress has been made over the years. Institutions have in a few short decades moved towards developing infrastructure and support services, including creating information technology units, faculty development offices, instructional technology centers, digital libraries, technology committees, distance education units, and offering extended helpdesk support.

Information Technology Units

University information technology (IT) units have a short history in higher education, but since their inception they have successfully taken up diverse information technology initiatives. IT units have been instrumental in managing enormous technology budgets, acquiring new technologies, and setting up and enforcing technology policies and standards. They have successfully wired campuses, built vast network systems and infrastructures, implemented course management systems (CMS), developed and installed student registration and admission systems, created financial management systems, managed robust electronic systems, provided institution-wide technology training, supported research technologies, provided 24/7 security protection on networks and technology assets, and provided helpdesk and technology support. IT units have successfully migrated from mainframe computers to powerful mini servers, desktop computers, and portable systems. Their operations are ubiquitous and, most often, run smoothly. Many transactions that were formerly paper-based are routinely conducted electronically.

Libraries

Technology has forever changed libraries and the way librarians serve their patrons. Librarians have played a key role in technology adoption and application on campuses and have kept up with changes in technology. Academic libraries were among the first units on campus to recognize the potentials of the digital technologies and to and embraced. This, perhaps, could be attributed to successful adoption of earlier technologies in the libraries. In libraries, sophisticated information management systems have replaced card catalogs, digital resources and electronic formats are available to users, digital media has replaced aging materials, research databases are frequently updated, and institutional repositories are created, and online services are available, making it possible for patrons to be served virtually. Automation has made it possible for patrons to interact with online systems and require less dependence on library staff.

Instructional Technology Centers

Instructional technology centers are often the first port of call for faculty members when they have questions on issues relating to technology application to instruction. The centers have contributed technology adoption and in supporting faculty in the areas of pedagogy and in the use of technology and media. Along with other faculty support groups, instructional technology centers provide technology workshops, teaching and learning workshops, instructional resources, and consultative support to faculty members. Instructional technology centers conduct research on emerging technologies to evaluate their suitability for application to instruction. The centers have advised and supported faculty members in the use of various media and technologies, the integration of pedagogy and technology, use of simulations, use of CMS for hybrid and fully online instruction, the establishment and maintenance of "smart classrooms," the application of multimedia to instruction, and the use of social networking technologies such as virtual worlds, social bookmarking, video-sharing sites, tweeting, wikis, blogs, mash-ups, folksonomies, crowdsourcing, and other Web 2.0 technologies for instruction. The efforts of the instructional technology center staff have contributed to the use of technology in teaching and learning and to course improvement initiatives.

Distance Education

Distance education has rapidly gained ground in higher education and has become a testament to the impact and benefit of digital technologies. In its early days, distance education took the form of textbook-based correspondence courses before the adoption and use of radio, television, and video as delivery methods. The early formats were slow and lacked effective communication, interaction, and collaboration systems. Current technologies have added some dynamism and drastically reshaped distance education. The increasing popularity of the World Wide Web, development of the course management system, and developments in digital technologies resulted in increase in the popularity of distance education. The development and use of CMS improved distance education, making it possible for students to take courses from any location in the world once they have access. Students can communicate, collaborate, and interact with content, the instructor, and fellow students; access multimedia resources; complete their assignments; and document their progress in digital portfolios. Online and hybrid courses are in the forefront of innovative and effective pedagogy and technology adoption.

Administrative and Research Processes

Enterprise resource planning (ERP) systems are in place at many institutions to provide a process for managing tangible assets, enhancing operational productivity, and supporting efficient use of resources including financial resources, business services, admission processes, student services, and human resources. ERPs facilitate the flow of information among business operations within institutions as well as manage relationships with external stakeholders. These systems are typically supported by the IT units.

LINGERING ISSUES

Funding

The fast pace of technological advancements and the need to adopt new technologies or upgrade existing systems places college administrators in a difficult position in an era of diminishing government and private sector funding. Administrators stretch limited funds by deciding which emerging technologies support the core functions of their institutions and which show the greatest promise for successful adoption, while avoiding the problems of campus technology infrastructure becoming obsolete.

In the past three decades, colleges and universities have made significant investments in new information technologies. In the 1980s, institutions spent billions of dollars on computer technology acquisition (Hirschbuhl & Faseyitan, 1994). According to Geoghegan (1994a), colleges and universities in the United States spent about $70 billion in information technology goods and services during the previous decade and a half. Many institutions have doubled their investment in information technology in the last decade (Office of Higher Education, 2001).

As technology infrastructure costs continue to soar, budget allocation and funding will remain major administrative issues. Expenditures for technology acquisition, upgrades, and licensing fees present a big challenge for institutions that want to sustain technology gains; continue to adopt viable technologies as they evolve; and remain competitive, especially as for-profit institutions gain ground in the academic marketplace. Funding IT was first on the Educause list of top ten IT issues of 2009. It has remained a key issue in K. C. Green's campus computing surveys.

Systemic Approach to Adoption of Technological Innovation

Higher education has for a long time struggled with the challenge of taking a systemic, institution-wide approach towards technology adoption. Adoption processes have largely centered on individual or departmental levels, which results in few incremental gains, slowed diffusion processes, and unintended results. This has been more evident in the adoption and integration of technology in teaching and learning. With computer technologies, as was with earlier technologies, there has been expectation that technology would transform teaching and learning (Geoghegan, 1994b; Gilbert, 1994).

The current approach to the adoption of instructional technology too often falls on departments or on individual faculty members who are left to choose the technology they want to use in their courses. This reliance on faculty initiative does not achieve a robust and institution-wide result. Already stretched to the limit with teaching assignments, research and publication requirements, conferences presentations, need to serve on committees, and expectation to engage in service to the institution and the community, faculty members lack the time, and sometimes support, to adequately use technology. When they find time and opportunity to attend workshops that demonstrate technology for teaching and learning, faculty may not be able to apply the knowledge that they gain immediately to improve their courses because they are already in the middle of the term. Successful adoption and integration of technology and pedagogy requires a considerable expenditure of time and that faculty members rethink how the technology fits into their instructional strategies.

Improving the Instructional Processes

Integration of the Instructional Processes

Part of the challenge many institutions face in the application of technology to improve teaching and student learning is on the isolation of the departments involved in the support of teaching, learning, and technology. Currently, much of the instructional process is fragmented at many institutions. Technology training and support are often available through one department while curriculum development, instructional development, teaching and learning support, instructional technology, faculty development, and assessment are supported by different departments or offices on a campus. Accreditation is looked at as yet another isolated process. Often, there is no coordination of efforts among the departments. Why must there be separate offices on one campus for instructional development, faculty development, curriculum development, assessment, accreditation, instructional technology, and media services?

What happens when all of these units, which may be spread across campus, try to support an individual faculty member in course or curricular design, technology application, or course improvement? Will the faculty member be directed to different buildings? These are not disparate and independent units; they maintain some relationships. In simple terms, the curricular and instructional development processes includes setting instructional goals and objectives; the goals and objectives help to identify the appropriate media and technology and selection of instructional strategies and delivery methods needed to achieve learning outcomes. Evaluation and assessment processes are integrated to help determine if the goals and objectives were met and if learning occurred. Having these units together in one department or structuring the different service units to maintain close relationships is essential for streamlining the development process and in achieving successful course development or improvement.

A systemic and systematic course and curricular development process supports an integrated approach in which technology is not just an add-on and assessment is not an after-thought. The units that support these endeavors better when together; if that is not possible due to administrative or organizational culture issues, the units need to be organized to work together on course and curriculum development projects. The integrated instructional development process can also aid in creating the necessary documentation and artifacts required for accreditation purposes. Until higher education begins to view instructional process from an integrated, systemic, and systematic perspective, and bring together all the related support units, it will be difficult to have a cohesive approach to further improve teaching and learning.

Technology in Teaching and Learning

Instructional Technology

Educause (2009) included teaching and learning with technology as one of the top ten technology issues. In spite of decades of instructional technology's presence on campuses, the prevalence of technologies, increasing familiarity with technology by faculty and staff, and institutions' enormous investments in technology, most agree that technology has not been integrated into teaching and learning to the degree that had been anticipated (Albright & Graf, 1992; Geoghegan, 1994b; Hartman, 2008; Massy & Wilger, 1998; Massy & Zemsky, 1995). Some contend that the use of technology for instructional purposes has not kept pace with other uses of technology in higher education (Murray, 2008; National Science Foundation, 2008). Many authors have speculated on the reasons for the slow response to the use of instructional technologies (Bauer & Kenton, 2005; Hartman, 2008; Levin & Wadmany, 2008; Nichols, 2008; Rogers, 2000; Sahin & Thompson, 2007; Surry, 1997; Twigg, 2000). One reason alluded to earlier was that by the time faculty members attend a workshop to learn about a new technology for use in instruction, the term/semester may be half-way over. At that point, they have already prepared their syllabi, adopted an instructional strategy and gone far in their teaching. Another reason for slow adoption of instructional technologies points to is the practice of depending on the individual faculty initiative, which, in addition to being time consuming, results in an inability to obtain consistent outcomes, replicate results, and disseminate best practices (Bates, 2000). This is more glaring in the design and development of distance education courses, where the faculty is often the sole developer.

A serious issue related to the use of instructional technology is the over-emphasis on technology hardware and software while neglecting the process aspect. The focus on hardware and software ignores the fact that they are tools designed to support the teaching and learning process. The process aspect of technology is the key to transforming teaching and learning. Reiser's (2001) definition of instructional technology includes "the use of media for instructional purposes" and "the use of systematic instructional design procedures (often simply called instructional design)" (p. 54). The Association for Educational Communications and Technology (AECT), the foremost association for instructional technologists, provides a definition which states that instructional technology is the "study and ethical practice of facilitating learning and improving performance by creating, using, and managing appropriate technological processes and resources" (AECT 2004). These definitions include the process aspect of instructional technology, an instructional design approach, which includes assessment, design, development, instruction, media and technology integration, and evaluation.

The Spellings Commission (2006) suggests developing "new pedagogies, curricula, and technologies to improve learning," establishing "course redesign programs using technology-based, learner-centered principles," and implementing "new models of curriculum development and delivery." The focus on the process aspect of instructional technology provides structure and a systematic approach to the design of instruction. Approaches to teaching and learning need to be restructured to be learner-centered (Barr & Tagg, 1995; Boettcher, 1999; Dede, 1999; Sprague & Dede, 1999; Twigg, 2000).

Applying technology hardware and software solutions are akin to the "maintenance service" approach to technology application to teaching and learning, whereby there are "fixes" here and there and every now and then. The process aspect of instructional technology offers a systemic and systematic approach to the application of technology to teaching and learning and is likely to yield the desired outcomes. The right approach to course design or redesign and application of relevant media and technology can yield benefits to the institutions, faculty, and students (Albright, 1997; Barr & Tagg, 1995; Twigg, 2000) and save costs (Twig, 2005).

Team Approach

The team approach is a development process requiring team effort in course development and technology integration in teaching and learning. Its use can lead to the elimination of the reliance on individual faculty members' efforts on course development, assure the effective application of technology, provide consistent results, encourage a systemic and systematic approach to course development, and ensure appropriate time investment. A team approach will seamlessly integrate the instructional design aspect of instructional technology in the course development process. As Hartman (2008) points out, there are many technologies to choose from and many ways to use them. This presents a confusing landscape for faculty who can't be expected to know about all the available technologies, what they do, and how to use them effectively. Similarly, it may not be realistic to expect faculty members to be experts on all pedagogical issues. Applying the team approach enables academic departments and course instructors to set goals and measure the attainment of the goals at desired intervals, measure student learning outcomes, and ensure that the technologies used, instructional strategies employed, and delivery methods used are all working in concert to deliver content and engage students in the learning process.

The team approach to instructional development has been used successfully in different settings in the past. The approach involves the inclusion of other experts, who are knowledgeable in pedagogy, learning theories, technology use, multimedia development, and other key areas, to work with course instructors. While the instructor serves as the content expert, the expertise of instructional designers, curriculum specialists, assessment specialists, librarians, media specialists, and computer technology support staff are all involved. The goal is not to take away the instructors' authority over the courses they teach, but rather to provide the assistance they need to improve their courses. The team approach lifts much of the burden of course development and technology application from the course instructors; it provides the expertise that faculty members may not have, frees up their time, and approaches course development from a holistic perspective. Technology integration, assessment and evaluation, or media selection are not treated as add-ons, ensuring that the best possible product is created, outcomes are measured uniformly, and progress and outcomes that could meet other requirements, including accreditation, are documented.

Instructional Approach

The use of a team approach that includes instructional designers will assist in incorporating appropriate pedagogy and learning theories. The past three decades have witnessed a resurgence of interest in social constructivism and other learning theories that are believed to work well with current technologies. Recently, there has been a shift towards student-centered learning which is supported by constructivist principles to teaching and learning and today's technologies. Applying constructivist principles will encourage the application of student-centered learning approaches that engage students in the learning process. Barr and Tagg (1995) published a seminal piece on student-centered learning that has continued to generate interest on the subject.

Applying constructivist principles to teaching and learning or restructuring the course and curricular development processes to incorporate technologies will require institutional efforts and direction, buy-in and behavior change by faculty, sufficient time, and professional guidance. The faculty member needs to be sufficiently prepared as the role of the instructor shifts to facilitation in constructivist learning environments (Sprague & Dede, 1999). The instructional designer in a team approach can determine how best to support aspects of constructivist principles with the appropriate technology to facilitate student engagement, interaction, collaboration, communication, and learning.

The systemic approach is not recommended for application in only one or a few particular technologies. It is recommended for improving teaching and learning processes with technologies that have broad application within institutions. Effective planning as well as the use of effective processes is critical to success. As rightly noted by Spitzer (1987), the field of educational technology is replete with failed initiatives, rejected tactical approaches, and inappropriate media, hardware, and software. Spitzer argues that without a grand design, it will be difficult for technology to succeed.

Supporting Instructional Technology

Important characteristics of successful implementation of technology in teaching and learning include providing consistent and effective support to faculty members, providing access to relevant technologies and resources, establishing process for course improvement, having the institutional ability to forge a positive relationship between IT and instructional technology units, and establishing the right leadership for the technology support units (Albright & Nworie, 2008; Hartman, 2008). A positive relationship between the technology support units and the institutional leadership is needful to assure that IT and instructional technology leaders align their services with the mission, goals, strategic plans, and objectives of the institution's academic programs and strategic plans. The technology support units need adequate staffing and funding to be able to support faculty members.

Success in instructional technology adoption and diffusion requires course restructuring, systemic change, changes in attitudes, understanding of the benefits of innovative use of technology, faculty support, and buy-in from all the stakeholders. Institutions will need to review course and curricular development processes in light of current instructional approaches and emerging technologies and devise strategies to improve courses. Institutions will also need to take a look at faculty reward systems, including recognition and compensation (Cole, Simkins, & Penuel, 2002). Few institutions provide meaningful recognition or have reward systems that include faculty course improvement efforts and technology use in tenure and promotion requirement, for the extra effort and time faculty members expend in learning new technologies and applying them to their courses. Issues related to release time needs to be revisited as faculty members need time for course improvement and technology application. According to Backhouse (2003), faculty need time to prepare for teaching and to attend to various other duties and extracurricular activities. Similarly, faculty spend substantial amount of time on conferences, research and publications, and on committee work.

Institutions will also need to provide meaningful recognition to faculty members for successful innovative use of classroom technologies that enhance faculty performance and productivity and student learning. To be perceived as valuable, such recognition must be included as part of the tenure and promotion requirements (Caffarella & Zinn, 1999; Massy & Wilger, 1998; Rao & Rao, 1999).

Administrative Technology

Technology applications for business and administrative operations has been adopted and implemented by many institutions while others continue their investigations to determine which systems will best suit their institutions and their budgets. For several years now, ERP systems have been major technology projects on college and university campuses, the most popular being Oracle, SCT (Banner), PeopleSoft, and SAP. These ERP systems have expanded their range of functionality in recent years to include more applications, such as grants management, marketing automation, electronic commerce, student systems, and supply chain systems.

ERP projects provide software solutions that integrate information and business processes that facilitate the sharing of resources throughout the institution, improving workflow and efficiency in administrative and academic offices. The challenges and issues facing the adoption of ERPs include the substantial outlay of money and time at the implementation phase, incorrect use of the systems, strain on IT personnel, the recurring need for upgrades, and lack of institution-wide use.

IT units also struggle with issues of funding and recruitment and retention of staff in order to offer sufficient resources to meet campus demands. Institutions face the challenge of developing effective IT policies that can meet institutional needs and accommodate evolving technologies (Reid, 1999).

Student Technology Use

There is general belief that students arriving on campuses in recent years are knowledgeable about technologies and that they learn differently (Anson, 1999; Kaminski, Seel, & Cullen 2003; McCormick, 1999). Extant literature suggests that students favor learning methods that are supported by technology (Lowerison, Sclater, Schmid, & Abrami, 2006; Milliken & Barnes, 2002). However, the assumption that all students arriving on college campuses are technologically savvy might be misleading as all students are not knowledgeable about every technology. The problems of the digital divide, gender gaps, and racial inequities still exist, and results in students not having access to technology at school or at home and, therefore, lack sufficient knowledge of technology (Cooper, 2006; Mullis, Mullis & Cornille, 2007; Parker, 2001; Parker, 2007). Insufficient computer literacy plagues both traditional students and returning adult students who have not had consistent access and exposure to technologies prior to arriving on campus. In addition to problems of computer literacy, many students continue to face problems of information and media literacy. Faculty members often report that they spend valuable time teaching basic computer skills to students instead of concentrating on the course content.

An institution-wide approach will require having information technology and information literacy competency standards for all students, so that by the time they graduate, they have gained the desired competencies at the required levels. Students who take courses online or via videoconferencing need instruction on the technologies that will be used in course delivery, before they start, to enable them successfully navigate through the course. Similarly, students need orientation to the technologies that will be used in hybrid or traditional classroom environments. With the shift in instruction moving from teacher-centered approaches to student-centered strategies, students need the requisite technology skills as technology will be used extensively to engage students in the learning process (Rutherford & Grana, 1995).

Sustaining Gains

The issue of sustainability deserves attention in the adoption of technology in teaching and learning in higher education as there is need to sustain the gains made over the years. While the desired level of assimilation of technological innovation in teaching and learning has not yet been realized, there exists some degree of progress that has been made and best practices that should be preserved. Some individual faculty members, administrators, and institutions have learned new lessons, acquired new experiences, and made some gains in the application of various administrative and instructional technologies. Sustainability in this respect refers to the ability to prolong, reinforce, and maintain over time the dynamism and valuable segments of a project, learned lessons, or best practices so they may be preserved or supported for continued utilization in different ways. For the years that higher education has experimented with administrative and academic technology applications, there have been cases of innovative individual or institutional applications that have exceeded expectations. Such outstanding cases need to serve as models to other individuals and institutions, be replicated, and further improved for future use. For example, an enterprise-wide model of systemic course and curricular transformation that improves teaching and learning processes needs to be preserved and shared.

Successful innovative practices need to be "recycled" for the benefit of other individuals and institutions. To be considered as sustainable, innovative practices must be of high quality and independently vetted through peer-review processes. Information management systems can be created as repositories for the storage, retrieval, and easy access of the best practices. Such systems must be searchable and the entries must be tagged with metadata to facilitate easy access, retrieval, and reuse. Potential users need to be made aware of the existence of the repositories.

Sustainability of best practices extends to successful projects. For instance, there are instances where external grants funded excellent programs that purchased computers and other essential resources. Though successful, the projects were allowed to atrophy because no sustainability plans were in place to continue to fund and support the projects. In some cases, successful programs became victims of internal politics, in others, applications developed by faculty and students that could have been of value to the institution and others outside the institution are lost when there are no plans in place to adopt and support such innovative applications.

Unintended Consequences

Institutions need to be aware of unintended consequences that may result in the process of adopting technologies for various campus applications. When new technologies or innovations are adopted, they are intended to serve specific purposes. However, in the adoption and diffusion processes other results that were not intended become evident, as unanticipated results can follow the introduction or implementation of innovations. Blumenfeld, Fishman, Krajcik, Marx, & Soloway (2000) suggest that new solutions to problems could result in unexpected consequences or even introduce unintended results in situations that did not have problems previously. These unforeseen and unplanned results are outside of, but not always opposite to the intended purpose, and can distract from or disrupt the intended outcomes (Nworie and Haughton, 2008).

The introduction of technologies on campuses has had some unintended results while meeting the intended goals. Some unintended results include distractions and disruptions in learning environments as students use digital technologies to send text messages, play games, check their email, shop online, blog, answer cell phone calls, or read the latest news or check sports scores during class time. Cell phones can go off, disrupting class sessions.

Students have been known to use digital devises to cheat during tests. There have been reports of increasing number of students buying term papers online or downloading materials created by others without permission or attribution. The availability of online materials poses additional risks for students who download inaccurate information. Online technologies have made it easy to engage in copyright infringements. Discourteous behavior among students is on the increase in online environments due to the anonymity provided by online technologies.

Despite these unintended consequences, computer technologies have had positive effects, generally, in achieving the intended results. The purpose of discussions about unintended consequences is to draw attention to the fact that unintended consequences can follow the adoption of innovation and also to highlight the need to plan to respond promptly when unintended outcomes are detected to minimize their effects. Identifying unintended consequences early and responding appropriately is essential to counteract negative effects that could impede the intended outcomes.

Managing Institutional Knowledge

Higher education has, over the years, generated or acquired a large amount of information that exists in different formats and in different locations. Data is generated by various campus sources including academic units and administrative offices. This information is gathered from institutional effectiveness data, assessment, institutional research, human resources, admissions, student services, business and financial services, assessment data, academic data, student data, and other areas and is stored in different offices, and often there is duplication of efforts among departments as they may be unaware of existing data sources. Despite the availability of sophisticated computer systems, advanced network, and communication infrastructures, and data management programs, many institutions lack systems to support the storage, retrieval, and reuse of the knowledge that is available to them. As a result, decisions makers are not always aware of available data and where it resides.

While gathering and managing explicit knowledge has not received enough attention, retrieving tacit knowledge held by the human capital in higher education remains mostly untouched. There are learning objects, best practices, and instructional artifacts that could be stored and reused for instructional purposes within the institution, but often there are no systems in place to harness and leverage institutional knowledge for instructional and institutional improvement and advancement (Nworie & Dwyer, 2004). Knowledge management is a growing field, but higher education has not fully embraced it or its technologies.

Social Issues

Institutions are part of society. People who work in the institutions are also part of society and are social beings. It is inevitable that technological change will bring about social change. In institutions as in the larger society, ownership, access, and knowledge of technologies are often not distributed equitably. Socioeconomic status affects the ability to acquire technology and have access to information, knowledge, and power. Therefore, the social context of higher education should not be ignored in the adoption, integration, and diffusion phases of technology (Stockdill & Morehouse, 1992; Surry & Farquhar, 1996). Social factors vary from institution to institution and include institutional culture, user demographics, organizational capacity, access to technology support, and vendor influence. Tessmer (1991) emphasizes the importance of analyzing the environment in which the technology will be used, including identifying the relevant physical and user characteristics. Stockdill and Morehouse (1992) suggest that adopters conduct a complete analysis of educational needs and user characteristics as they relate to the relevant features of the new educational technology.

Effective institution-wide integration of technology into administrative processes, research, and teaching and learning requires that the vital elements of resources, infrastructure, people, policies, processes, environment, and support issues must be taken into consideration throughout the adoption and integration processes (Surry, Ensminger, & Jones, 2007).

Technology has affected the social nature of transactions on campuses. It has made it possible for students to enroll in college and university programs electronically and to take classes online in both traditional mode institution and virtual campuses. The technologies used in online learning environments enable students to interact and collaborate with other students virtually. Faculty members interact with colleagues around the world, and administrators are able to schedule virtual face-to-face meetings using online and videoconferencing technologies. Campus purchasing offices, bookstores, and offices engage in e-commerce, conducting transactions from their desktops. Potential students and their families can see campuses without leaving their homes. While these have been successful outcomes, the intrinsic blend of social interactions that are inherent in such exchanges—the eye contact, smiles, hugs, handshakes, and other non-verbal cues that serve to warm-up or extend relationships—are missing.

Technology has also affected social relationships on campuses. Cell phones have altered the original function of phones as they now support digital imaging, texting, and a host of other applications. Cell phones are extensively used in texting and have become students' preferred mode of communication. Texting has turned into a fast-paced communication method that condenses and transforms thoughts and messages into short phrases and abbreviations. It has had a significant impact in the way students communicate and interact and spurred a whole new lingo that most parents, faculty, and administrators find difficult to decipher. The growing use and popularity of social networking technology applications in teaching and learning environments and social interactions have created the potential for distractions in classrooms, caused lack of proper decorum in communication, as well as increase the opportunity for students to withdraw from personal interactions. Many students will prefer to text each other than meet in person to socialize and some will choose to retrieve class materials posted online. In some instances, students in traditional mode institutions choose to download podcasted lectures or lectures packaged in other media instead of attending classes.

A positive aspect of social networking is the growing interest by institutions to use blogs, Facebook, YouTube, Wikis, Flickr, MySpace, and homegrown networking sites to reach potential students and to communicate with students on campus. This opportunity has become a challenge to administrators to learn the social networking technology and determine how best to target students as they do not all flock to one particular technology.

Leadership Issues

Higher education is a dynamic environment that requires strong leaders with good decision-making skills. Institutional leaders have the level of authority required to authorize and manage change in the adoption and diffusion of technology. The position of institutional leaders requires that they have information that will guide them in making decisions. When making decisions that relate to technology issues, institutional leaders need to have access to all relevant information and cautiously weigh the impact of their decisions on their internal constituencies and stakeholders, including staff, faculty, and students.

One of the organizational implications for successful adoption of new technologies is that the process requires vision of technology provided by institutional leaders, a systematic approach, and well-grounded infrastructure. As discussed earlier, technology diffusion in teaching and learning will not achieve the desired results if institutional leaders do not address the issues of faculty recognition, rewards and incentives, promotion and tenure, intellectual property rights, release time, as they spend time to learn new technologies and rethink how to use them to improve their courses, and the application of systemic and systematic approaches to course and curricular development. The decision to effect campus-wide technological change can only come from institutional leaders. Continued support of technology adoption and diffusion require administrative awareness and engagement. Similarly, effective faculty professional development is essential in technology use and requires the support of administrators.

CONCLUSION

Despite the diverse views about its ultimate value and different reactions to its presence, information technology has become entrenched in the academy and higher education now relies heavily on it to control almost every function of its operations and services; however, the level of diffusion that some desire has not been attained.

Though higher education has traditionally been perceived as slow to adopt innovations, it has boldly embraced IT. Computer technologies abound on campuses, in the libraries, staff and faculty offices, open labs, and smart classrooms. Sophisticated technology systems are available for research in different academic fields, data analysis, simulations, and projections. Technology has made in-roads in teaching and learning processes in both virtual and traditional classroom environments. Some believe that the level of impact in teaching and learning is below what is anticipated. To improve the situation, current practices in the adoption and use of instructional technologies which are still based on the individual efforts of faculty members needs to be revisited.

A systemic, institution-wide approach to adoption and implementation might benefit higher education. Senge, Kleiner, Roberts, Ross, and Smith (1994) suggest that systems thinking can be successful in achieving organizational change. Careful planning and strategic decision-making, an integrated approach, faculty cooperation, collaboration with support units, and institutional commitment will also be required to reach the desired levels of diffusion and transformation. The outcome of successful technology implementation will impact an institution's internal constituencies, including faculty, students, administrators and staff; and external oversight agencies, such as federal and state governments, quality assurance and performance improvement agencies, and accrediting agencies that seek information on the performance of institutions and academic programs.

REFERENCES

Albright, L. P. (1997). The information technology imperative for higher education: A report. *Library Acquisitions: Practice and Theory*, *21*(3), 268. doi:10.1016/S0364-6408(97)00022-7

Albright, M. J., & Graf, D. L. (1992). Instructional technology and the faculty member. In M. J. Albright & D. L. Graf (Eds.), *Teaching in the information age: The role of educational technology. New Directions for Teaching and Learning* (no. 51, pp 7-16). San Francisco: Jossey-Bass.

Albright, M. J., & Nworie, J. (2008). Rethinking Academic Technology Leadership in an Era of Change. *EDUCAUSE Quarterly*, *31*(1), 14–23.

Anson, C. M. (1999, January). Distant voices: Teaching and writing in a culture of technology. *College English*, *61*(3), 261–280. doi:10.2307/379069

Association for Educational Communications and Technology. (n.d.). *Definition and Terminology Committee*. Retrieved March 28, 2010, from http://www.aect.org/about/div_.asp?DivisionID=18.

Axtell, C. M., Holman, D. J., Unsworth, K. L., Wall, T. D., Waterson, P. E., & Harrington, E. (2000). Shopfloor innovation: Facilitating the suggestion and implementation of ideas. *Journal of Occupational Psychology*, *73*, 265–285. doi:10.1348/096317900167029

Backhouse, B. (2003). Information and communication technology integration: Beyond the early adopters. *TechTrends*, *47*(3), 5–8. doi:10.1007/BF02763468

Barr, R. B., & Tagg, J. (1995, November/December). From teaching to learning – A new paradigm for undergraduate education. *Change*, *27*(6), 12–25.

Bates, A. W. (2000). *Managing technological change: Strategies for college and university leaders*. San Francisco: Jossey-Bass.

Bauer, J., & Kenton, J. (2005). Toward technology integration in the schools: Why it isn't happening. *Journal of Technology and Teacher Education*, *13*(4), 519–546.

Blumenfeld, P., Fishman, B. J., Krajcik, J., Marx, R. W., & Soloway, E. (2000). Creating usable innovations in systemic reform: Scaling up technology-embedded project-based science in urban schools. *Educational Psychologist*, *35*(3), 149–164. doi:10.1207/S15326985EP3503_2

Boettcher, J. (1999, August). The shift from a teaching to a learning paradigm. *Syllabus*, *13*(1), 50–51.

Burkman, E. (1987). Factors affecting utilization. In Gagne, R. M. (Ed.), *Instructional technology: foundations*. Hillsdale, NJ: Lawrence Erlbaum.

Caffarella, R. S., & Zinn, L. F. (1999). Professional development for faculty: A conceptual framework of barriers and supports. *Innovative Higher Education*, *23*(4), 241–254. doi:10.1023/A:1022978806131

Celsi, R. L., & Wolfinbarger, M. (2002). Discontinuous classroom innovation: Waves of change for marketing education. *Journal of Marketing Education*, *24*(1), 64–72. doi:10.1177/0273475302241008

Chisholm, I. M., Carey, J., & Hernandez, A. (2002). Information technology skills for a pluralistic society: Is the playing field level? *Journal of Research on Technology in Education*, *35*(1), 58–79.

Cole, K., Simkins, M., & Penuel, W. R. (2002). Learning to teach with technology: Strategies for inservice professional development. *Journal of Technology and Teacher Education*, *10*(3), 431–455.

Cooper, J. (2006). The digital divide: The special case of gender. *Journal of Computer Assisted Learning*, *22*, 320–334. doi:10.1111/j.1365-2729.2006.00185.x

Educause. (2009, November/December). Recommended resources for the top ten IT issues. *EDUCAUSE Review*, *44*(6).

Ellsworth, J. B. (2000). *Surviving change: A survey of educational change models*. Syracuse, NY: Eric Clearinghouse on Information & Technology.

Ely, D. P. (1999). Conditions that facilitate the implementation of educational technology innovations. *Educational Technology*, *39*(6), 23–27.

Geoghegan, W. (1994b). Stuck at the barricades: Can information technology really enter the mainstream of teaching and learning? *AAHE Bulletin*, *47*(1), 13–16.

Geoghegan, W. H. (1994a, July 17-20). *Whatever happened to instructional technology?* (Reaching Mainstream Faculty). Paper presented at the 22nd Annual Conference of the International Business Schools Computing Association, Baltimore, MD.

Gilbert, S. W. (1994). If it takes 40 or 50 years, can we still call it a revolution? *The Educational Record, 75*(3), 19–28.

Green, K. C. (2010). *The National Survey of Information Technology in US Higher Education*. The Campus Computing Project. Available at http://www.*campuscomputing*.net/summaries/2009.

Hall, G. E., & Hord, S. M. (1987). *Change in schools: Facilitating the process*. New York: SUNY Press.

Hartman, J. L. (2008, November/December). Moving teaching and learning with technology from adoption to transformation. *EDUCAUSE Review, 43*(6).

Henriksen J., & Soule, A. (1998). Sources and information: Identifying and implementing technologies for higher education. *New Directions for Community Colleges, 101 (spring)*, 91-98.

Hirschbuhl, J. J., & Faseyitan, S. O. (1994). Faculty uses of computers: Fears, facts and perceptions. *T.H.E. Journal, 21*(9), 64.

Hooper, S., & Rieber, L. P. (1995). Teaching with technology. In Ornstein, A. (Ed.), *Teaching: theory into practice* (pp. 154–170). Needham Heights, MA: Allyn and Bacon.

Hord, S. M., Rutherford, W. L., Huling-Austin, L. L., & Hall, G. E. (1987). *Taking charge of change*. Austin, TX: Southwest Educational Development Laboratory.

Kaminski, K., Seel, P., & Cullen, K. (2003). Technology literate students? *EDUCAUSE Quarterly*, (3): 35–40.

King, N., & Anderson, N. (2002). *Managing Innovation and Change: A Critical Guide for Organizations* (2nd ed.). London: Thomson.

Klein, K. J., & Sorra, J. S. (1996). The challenge of innovation implementation. *Academy of Management Review, 21*(4), 1055–1080. doi:10.2307/259164

Kozeracki, C. (1998). Managing organizational change in the community college. *ERIC Digest*. (ERIC Reproduction Service No. ED424-884). http://www.ed.gov/databases/ERIC_Digests/ed424884.html

Levin, T., & Wadmany, R. (2008). Teachers' Views on Factors Affecting Effective Integration of Information Technology in the Classroom: Developmental Scenery. *Journal of Technology and Teacher Education, 16*(2), 233–263.

Lowerison, G., Sclater, J., Schmid, R. F., & Abrami, P. C. (2006). Are we using technology for learning? *Journal of Educational Technology Systems, 34*(4), 401–425. doi:10.2190/ER58-3H7P-Y8FK-U8F7

Massy, W. F., & Wilger, A. K. (1998). Technology's contribution to higher education productivity. *New Directions for Higher Education, 26*(3), 49–59. doi:10.1002/he.10304

Massy, W. F., & Zemsky, R. (1995). Using information technology to enhance academic productivity. Presented at the *1995 CAUSE Conference*. http://www.educause.edu/nlii/keydocs/massy.html

McCluskey, F. D. (1981). DVI, DAVI, AECT: A long view. In Brown, J. W., & Brown, S. N. (Eds.), *Educational media yearbook: 1981*. Littleton, CO: Libraries Unlimited.

McCormick, S. (1999). The case for visual media in learning. *Syllabus*; 4-6.

Milet, L. K. (1996, April 11-14). Organizational models for managing technology services: Keeping up with rapid change. *Proceedings of the Consortium of College and University Media Centers*, 29-31. San Diego, CA.

Milliken, J., & Barnes, L. P. (2002). Teaching and technology in higher education: student perceptions and personal reflections. *Computers & Education*, *39*(3), 223–235. doi:10.1016/S0360-1315(02)00042-8

Mullis, R. L., Mullis, A. K., & Cornille, T. A. (2007). Relationships between identity formation and computer use among black and white emerging adult females. *Computers in Human Behavior*, *23*, 415–423. doi:10.1016/j.chb.2004.10.019

National Science Foundation. (2008). Fostering learning in the networked world: The cyber learning opportunity and challenge. *Report of the NSF Task Force on Cyberlearning*. http://www.nsf.gov/pubs/2008/nsf08204/nsf08204.pdf.

Nichols, M. (2008). Institutional Perspectives: The Challenges of E-Learning Diffusion. *British Journal of Educational Technology*, *39*(4), 598–609. doi:10.1111/j.1467-8535.2007.00761.x

Nworie, J., & Dwyer, F. (2004, August). Knowledge management and instructional design: Optimizing organizational knowledge. *Performance Improvement*, *43*(7), 27–32. doi:10.1002/pfi.4140430709

Nworie, J., & Haughton, N. (2008, September). Good intentions and unanticipated effects: The unintended consequences of the application of technology in teaching and learning environments. *TechTrends*, *52*(5), 52–58. doi:10.1007/s11528-008-0197-y

O'Banion, T. (1994, April). Sustaining innovation in teaching and learning. [Mission Viejo, CA: League for Innovation in the Community College.]. *Leadership Abstracts*, *7*(4), 3–4.

Office of Higher Education. (2001, February). 2001). *Higher education on the web. Update*, *7*(1). http://www.nea.org/he/techno.html.

Parker, S. (2001). Searching for the digital divide. *Information Development*, *17*, 205–208. doi:10.1177/0266666014240999

Parker, S. (2007). Editorial: What digital divide? *Information Development*, *23*, 235–236. doi:10.1177/0266666907084758

Rao, P. V., & Rao, L. M. (1999, March). Strategies that support instructional technology. *Syllabus*; 22-24.

Reid, I. C. (1999, May). Beyond models: Developing a university strategy for online instruction. *Journal of Asynchronous Learning Networks*, *3*(1), 19–31.

Reiser, R. A. (2001). A history of instructional design and technology: Part I: A history of instructional media. *Educational Technology Research and Development*, *49*(1), 53–64. doi:10.1007/BF02504506

Reiser, R. A. (2002). A history of instructional design and technology. In Reiser, R. A., & Dempsey, J. V. (Eds.), *Trends and issues in instructional design and technology*. Upper Saddle Creek, NJ: Merrill/Prentice Hall.

Rieber, L. P., & Welliver, P. W. (1989). Infusing educational technology into mainstream educational computing. *International Journal of Instructional Media*, *16*(1), 21–32.

Rogers, E. M. (1995). *Diffusion of innovations* (4th ed.). New York: The Free Press.

Rogers, E. M. (2003). *Diffusion of innovations* (5th ed.). New York: The Free Press.

Rogers, P. L. (2000). Barriers to adopting emerging technologies in education. *Journal of Educational Computing Research*, *22*(4), 455–472. doi:10.2190/4UJE-B6VW-A30N-MCE5

Rutherford, L. H., & Grana, S. J. (1995). Retrofitting academe: Adapting faculty attitudes and practices to technology. *T.H.E. Journal*, *23*(2), 82.

Saettler, P. (1990). *The evolution of American educational technology*. Englewood, CO: Libraries Unlimited.

Sahin, I., & Thompson, A. (2007). Analysis of Predictive Factors that Influence Faculty Members Technology Adoption Level. *Journal of Technology and Teacher Education*, *15*(2), 167–190.

Sauer, J., & Anderson, N. R. (1992). Have we misread the psychology of innovation? A case study from two NHS hospitals. *Leadership and Organization Development Journal*, *13*(2), 17–21. doi:10.1108/01437739210009581

Senge, P. M., Kleiner, A., Roberts, C., Ross, R. B., & Smith, B. J. (1994). *The fifth discipline fieldbook: Strategies and tools for building a learning organization*. New York: Doubleday.

Sherry, L. (1998). An integrated technology adoption and diffusion model. *International Journal of Educational Telecommunications*, *4*(2/3), 113–145.

Spitzer, D. R. (1987). Why technology has failed. *Educational Technology*, *27*(9), 18–21.

Sprague, D., & Dede, C. (1999, September). Constructivism in the classroom: If I teach this way, am I doing my job? *Learning and Leading with Technology*, *27*(1), 6–9, 16–17.

Stockdill, S. H., & Morehouse, D. L. (1992). Critical factors in successful adoption of technology: A checklist of TDC findings. *Educational Technology*, *32*(1), 57–58.

Surry, D. (1997). *Diffusion theory and instructional technology*. Retrieved March 31, 2010, from http://www.gsu.edu/~wwwitr/docs/diffusion/

Surry, D. W., & Brennan, J. P., II. (1998). *Diffusion of instructional innovations: Five important, unexplored questions*. Hattiesburg, MS: University of Southern Mississippi. (ERIC Document Reproduction Service No. ED422892)

Surry, D. W., & Ely, D. P. (2002). Adoption, diffusion, implementation, and institutionalization of instructional design and technology. In Reiser, A., & Dempsey, J. V. (Eds.), *Trends and Issues in Instructional Design and Technology*. Upper Saddle River, NJ: Merrill Prentice Hall.

Surry, D. W., Ensminger, D. C., & Haab, M. (2005). A model for integrating instructional technology into higher education. [Electronic version available at http://iphase.org/papers/RIPPLES.rtf]. *British Journal of Educational Technology*, *36*(2), 327–329. doi:10.1111/j.1467-8535.2005.00461.x

Surry, D. W., & Farquhar, J. D. (1996). Incorporating social factors into instructional design theory. In Bailey, M., & Jones, M. (Eds.), *Work, education, and technology* (pp. 6.1–6.8). DeKalb, IL: LEPS Press.

Tessmer, M. (1991). Back to the future: The environment analysis stage of front end analysis. *Performance and Instruction*, *30*(1), 9–12. doi:10.1002/pfi.4170300104

Twigg, A. C. (2005). Course redesign improves learning and reduces cost. *The National Center for Public Policy and Higher Education*. Retrieved March 31, 2010, from http://www.highereducation.org/reports/pa_core/core.pdf

Twigg, C. (2000). Institutional readiness criteria: Prerequisites to large-scale course redesign. *EDUCAUSE Review*, *35*(2), 42–50.

U. S. Department of Education. (2002). *Findings from the condition of education 2002: Nontraditional undergraduates*. National Center for Education Statistics NCES 2002-012. Retrieved March 28, 2010, from http://nces.ed.gov/pubs2002/2002012.pdf

U. S. Department of Education. (2006, September). *A Test of Leadership: Charting the Future of U. S. Higher Education*, A Report of the Commission Appointed by Secretary of Education Margaret Spellings. Retrieved March 31, 2010, from http://www.ed.gov/about/bdscomm/list/hiedfuture/reports/final-report.pdf

Zaltman, G., & Duncan, R. (1977). *Strategies for planned change*. New York: John Wiley and Sons.

Zaltman, G., Duncan, R., & Holbeck, J. (1973). *Innovations and Organizations*. New York: Wiley.

Zemsky, R., & Massey, W. F. (2004). *Thwarted innovation: What happened to e-learning and why*. West Chester, PA: University of Pennsylvania. [WWW Document] Retrieved from http://www.thelearningalliance.info/Docs/Jun2004/ThwartedInnovation.pdf.

Chapter 23
The Near Future of Technology in Higher Education

Karen L. Rasmussen
University of West Florida, USA

Gayle V. Davidson-Shivers
University of South Alabama, USA

Wilhelmina C. Savenye
Arizona State University, USA

ABSTRACT

Higher education in the 21st century faces a multitude of internal and external challenges. From budget reductions, to globalization, to a new generation of students, the choices that faculty and administrators make about technology will be central to the future success of higher education systems. Technology serves as a tool that students, faculty, and administrators can use to foster innovation through effective and efficient means. For example, emerging technologies, such as those related to social networking and collaboration, enable students and faculty to work together to build new types of learning environments. On the other hand, technology is not the only solution to meet the challenges faced by higher education systems. Careful analyses of problems are necessary to identify appropriate solutions. For purposes of this chapter, best practices in educational technology and in technological integration and use to meet current and near future institutional goals of higher education are presented.

BACKGROUND

It is almost as if there is a "perfect storm" in higher education of the early 21st century. Universities and other post-secondary institutions face an uncertain future as they face challenges posed by internal and external factors. The promise of technology as a supporter of that future is intricately intertwined with the higher education system; technology, itself, plays a critical role in the system from multiple perspectives. The juxtaposition of these factors and technology places higher educational institutions at an interesting crossroad.

In this chapter, the challenges faced by higher education institutions are explored, with particular focus on the consequences of budget reductions,

DOI: 10.4018/978-1-60960-147-8.ch023

accountability, changing demographics, and innovations and uses of technology. A strategy for developing best practices is presented.

Challenges facing Higher Education. Hanna (2003) outlined 11 strategic challenges that higher education faces in the 21st century. The American Association of State Colleges and Universities (AASCU) State Relations and Policy Analysis Team (2010) reported 10 areas of concern that are confronting higher education. In these forecasts, a variety of factors were projected: internal factors included institutional operation, program quality and accountability, faculty and students; external factors included economic concerns, globalization, and competition from for-profit institutions. Globalization and competition from for-profit institutions specifically affect the structure and composition of the future higher education institution (Davidson-Shivers, 2002; Friedman, 2005). Budget concerns, especially at the state level have become a serious issue in 2010 (AASCU Team).

Similarly, issues were also identified in the *Chronicle of Higher Education* (*Chronicle*) on a regular basis in 2009. In a review of *Chronicle* 2009 issues, general trends in higher education regularly covered included:

- Reduced budgets,
- Pressures to increase efficiency, productivity, accountability, and effectiveness,
- Enrollment management, marketing for enhanced enrollments in others, with few increased resources for a number of years to come,
- Students diversity, including generations of students, and concern about underserved students,
- Entrepreneurship and social entrepreneurship,
- Rise of private and for-profit higher education organizations and globalization
- Examination of operations such as scheduling, quarters versus semesters, how student credit hours are generated, tenure, staffing,
- Community engagement and service, including building partnerships across broad sectors of the community, including business, other higher education organizations, non-profits, K-12 schools, government agencies, and even global community partners, and
- Tensions among research, teaching and service.

Two of the trends listed by the *Chronicle* have been occurring, not just in the current economic climate, but for several years: reduced budgets and funding shortfalls, and pressure for accountability and efficiency – an emphasis has been placed on developing a business model for higher education.

Reduced budgets impact higher educational institutions. Considering the recent downturn in the economy, changes to revenue sources of higher education institutions have become necessary. The recession of the early 21st century has placed unprecedented financial strains for most, if not all, U.S. colleges and universities. For example, Diel (2009) reported that Alabama colleges faced severe cuts in state funding and that further cuts in state funding were expected, following the model of other states. The University of Minnesota felt the effects of lack of state funding for the first time in 2009: for the first time tuition provided more revenue than did the state (About Campus, *Minnesota*, 2010). Programs are being eliminated, low-enrollment courses are not being offered, and other reductions in services are being observed in states including Florida, California, Nevada, and Oregon (Clark, K., 2009).

Additionally, the AASCU Team (2010) reported that state support of schools, overall, has been in decline, even before this "Great Recession" occurred. The AASCU Team stated that instead of being *state supported* institutions, universities are moving toward being *state assisted*. These reductions in state support require additional tuition payments from students or require institutions to reduce initiatives, programs or student support. As

Diel (2009) indicated, such tuition increases could make "it harder for students to get into required classes, making it more difficult to graduate in four years" (p. C5), adding time and expense to the higher education experience. Students may not be able to complete their courses in a timely fashion if classes are not offered. Further, students may not be able to take all of the required classes because of additional tuition expenses.

The ramifications of continued and sustained budget shortfalls will impact the mission of higher education institutions and how they operate in the near and distant future. Reactions to, and actions generated for, these challenges have specific implications for higher education administrators, faculty, and students, especially through the lens of technology. Themes that can be generated throughout responses to the challenges often involve technology-related policy, processes, and procedures, especially those elements associated with teaching and learning.

Pressures for accountability and efficiency impact higher education. A second issue or trend found by the ASSCU Team (2010) and in the *Chronicle* 2009 issues related to pressures for accountability and efficiency. While Weidman, Twale, and Stein (2001) suggested that many traditional norms of the academy continue to exist in the early 21st century, at the same time a change is occurring within the collegial culture. According to Weidman et al., Bean "observed that the language of the university has been moving more toward "efficiency, productivity, technology, ... accountability, assessment, ... total quality management ... " (p. 9). Bean (1998) argued that this change related more to an accountability movement (or business model approach) and less about creative activities, scholarship or being a learned community. Bean admitted that while an administration may not be responsible for the actual creation of this movement, practice reinforces its use, especially when an emphasis on quantity becomes the focus rather than quality. With mandates to increase class size and enrollments, generate additional student credit hours, and obtain funding through research grants, faculty are caught in a quality vs. quantity dilemma. Bean also considered faculty culpable by their acceptance of this business model approach and not maintaining the definition of their work in terms of scholarship, education, community, and learning. The culture of accountability is fueled by economic and financial constraints.

The pursuit of a "business" model. Large organizations and higher education institutions are not known for their ability to change without a massive shift in perspective and perception. Accordingly, some advocate that higher education institutions must become nimble to meet the needs of a changing workforce and changing student demographics (AASCU Team, 2010; Hanna, 2003). A business model that focuses on the outcomes – the graduates, the student credit hours – has become the norm in many institutions (or legislated by political agencies). Using a business model, or a bottom-line, maximization of profit approach, forces administrators to emphasize revenue streams, return on investment, production of student credit hours and tangible results, such as awarded grants. In an age of accountability, institutions are evaluated, for example, on graduation rates, time to degree, faculty productivity, income-to-expenses ratios, and tuition generation. Funding, additional resources, and incentives may be tied to performance metrics associated with these evaluation criteria. The return on investment, or what's in it for the institution, becomes critical decision-making criteria.

Yet, there continues to be the concern that such criteria conflict with the nature and mission of higher education institutions – that of being a learned community, focused on teaching, research, knowledge-building, and service. It is this conflict that addresses the core difference between those who focus on the *mission* of higher education and others who focus on the *business* of education. Technology has enabled the collection and analysis of performance metrics or criteria that have become so important to higher education institutions. However, if it is recognized that technology, in and of itself, is not the be all and end all intervention, then pragmatic and appropriate use of technological advances can be an effective business strategy for higher educational institutions to meet financial and other challenges. Technology can be an effective tool to meet and maintain the higher education fundamental and original mission of community, learning and scholarship.

In addition to careful review of funding alternatives and responses to the changing climate or mission of higher institutions, other factors will combine to determine the "successful" institution of the future and pave the way for changes in the teaching and learning processes for those participating in post-secondary education. The challenges facing higher education are daunting and, in many ways, foreign in nature to faculty and administrators. Cocooned in an academic setting, the realities of economies and politics have, in many cases, come as a big, and generally, unpleasant surprise, to students, faculty, and administrators. Institutions and their constituents, however, must face these challenges in a way that facilitates success. Indeed, it is this success that is so important for students, the workforce at large, and society.

THE VIEW OF THE STUDENT

The "face" of the American higher education institution is changing. The "traditional" institution, comprised primarily of 18-22 year olds, has morphed into a new picture, where the traditional student meets the untraditional – the student who has returned to the educational system for professional and career reasons. Students from multiple generations engage in the pursuit of education; baby boomers (born 1943-1960), X-ers (also called 13th Generation; born 1961-1981), and the Millennials (born 1982-2000) form a diverse and varied set of students (Howe & Strauss, 2000).

Students of the 21st century who are X-ers and Millennials have had the opportunity to grow up with technology. From innovation in schools to homes, these students have not experienced a world without technology. For the Millennials, especially, an affiliation for and need of technology is critical to how they view the world. The Millennial generation are digital natives, being reared in an environment where technology in integrated into all aspects of life, especially education and communication (Prensky, 2001).

Digital Natives. The digital natives have entered the world of higher education in full force. In 2004, there were approximately double the numbers of undergraduates as were in higher educational systems in 1970 (National Center for Education Statistics, 2009); the majority of these new traditional undergraduate students are Millennials. These students, born in or after 1982, embrace technology through wide and varied use. One example of the changing student is the popularity of social networking that is facilitated through the ubiquitous use of technology. Facebook, MySpace, YouTube, Flickr, Twitter, blogs, Ning, Second Life, cell phone texting, and instant messaging are examples of tools that students use to interact and communicate in the 21st century. Social networking, collaboration and computer-mediated communication serve as a major way that students of today communicate, work, and play. The general conception that Millennials are technology savvy and always connected, among other characteristics, is widely accepted; however, it is not true of every individual within this generation. Greenhow, Walker, and Kim (2009-10) suggest that low-income students still have limited use of Internet and, indeed, use it for different purposes than other Millennials. Additionally, Millennials may not be that different from other students according to Haney (2007) who suggests that they also like to read books, and have similar interests such as watching TV shows, but use YouTube instead TV. Evans and Po (2007) found that some English students, although they could learn use digital books, couldn't get physically comfortable and did not feel as connected reading hypertext as when they read a printed book. Finally, the question remains as to whether Millennials use (or will use) such technological skills and tools for learning. Professors have reported students, who use labtops in classes, may be checking emails or using Facebook rather than taking notes or attending to class activities (Bauerlein as cited in Cooper, 2009). Haney suggests that like other generations, they will want to use technology in the classroom if the technology is appropriately used by instructors.

Needs of diverse students. A diverse student population brings the need for developmental education in public institutions. While most Millennials are considered to be savvy and heavy technology users, Trenholm (2006), among others, suggests that they may also require remedial or developmental courses. He cited a report by the Fall 2000 National Center for Education Statistics that 97% of public two-year colleges offered remedial math courses. Furthermore, he cited Barnett (2002), reporting that remedial or developmental education comprised one to two percent of the overall expenses of higher education.

These diverse student populations are in pursuit of various educational goals and have various expectations of what they should be learning and doing in the educational environment. Faculty and administrators, who themselves are a diverse group, are attempting to anticipate and meet students' current and future needs and expectations in relation to learning within a changing educational environment. Haney (2007) suggests that "the future is in good hands as long as we give smart students like these what good education has offered students for thousands of years: good teaching, good learning experiences, and respect" (p. B14). Using classroom technology appropriately and with purpose can be a part of the teaching and guidance that Millennials need to succeed in higher education.

THE TECHNOLOGIES

Students, faculty, and administrators access technology through the institutional infrastructure. The infrastructure is comprised of the cables, servers, routers, bridges, and computer systems found in the institution. The infrastructure is extremely costly and requires regular updating and enhancement (Davidson-Shivers, 2002; Davidson-Shivers & Rasmussen, 2006). To continue to meet the needs of students, faculty, and administrators, a commitment to maintain and evolve institutional infrastructure is required to continue to meet those needs of students, faculty, and administrators.

The updating and enhancement of the infrastructure should be a thoughtful, critical series of decisions and events. Technology should not drive the academic decisions; rather, the vision, mission, and goals of the institution, the needs of students, faculty, and administrators should dictate decisions related to technology (Shelly, Cashman, Gunter, & Gunter, 2004). Aligning technology to goals and mission is critical in effectively integrating technology. Integrating new technologies in any system can have the potential of disrupting the environment if the implementation is not well-thought-out. Ensuring that technology serves a function related to the purposes of the institution is critical to the appropriate integration of technology into administration, teaching, and learning.

Technology Integration: The Idea of Doing More with Less

Many organizations, including colleges and universities, explore the use of technology when faced with hard choices such as those required by budget shortfalls. R. E. Clark (2009) observed that colleges are trying to find ways to be cost effective and still provide for quality "student-centered instruction" and "support the learning of underserved minorities" (p. 5). Like other sectors within society (e.g., military, business and industry), higher education is impacted by the ever increasing power and availability of technology and, in many situations, the ultimate result is that the use of technology is a foregone conclusion (Surry, 2008). One way that universities are using technology is to develop and foster online learning environments (Davidson-Shivers & Rasmussen, 2006). Online learning permits institutions to reach a wide audience and the exponential growth of off-campus, distant and virtual campuses has been often discussed and documented (Davidson-Shivers & Rasmussen; Glenn, D'Agostino, & Johnson, 2009).

With the constraints of shortfalls in revenues and pressures of becoming accountable, technology is often seen as the way to do more with less. Garrison and Akyol (2009) warned against being seduced by the promise of technology and suggest that institutions avoid inappropriate uses of technology. Davidson-Shivers and Rasmussen (2006) also suggested that while using virtual and other types of technologies have advantages, there is no guarantee that heavy investments will produce desired results. In other words, technology is not a panacea for solving problems or resolving issues facing higher education and, in some cases, it may exacerbate them. For instance, Steck (2003, cited in Surry, 2008) identified three potential concerns. First, technology may redefine the scope of education in ways not yet fully understood or controlled by individuals. Second, pedagogy may be defined by technology as the driving force rather than being defined in terms of educational and human requirements. [Note: This second concern is similar to Bean's (1998) concerns previously discussed.] The final concern is that heavy financial investments are needed to obtain, maintain and upgrade technology. With limited funding and shortfalls in state revenues, universities may need to draw resources from other areas to maintain up-to-date technology systems.

Although he discussed technology in K-12 schools, Cuban (2005) opined that considerable monies have been spent with little actual use by educators. Cuban was concerned that technologies were not always reliable and there was a lack of technology integration training for educators. These same concerns can be echoed for higher education and must also be addressed for technology to be fully supported and appropriately integrated. Furthermore, emphasis on technology could result in a furthering use of standardized testing, which could lead to problems that are currently being faced by educators in U.S. K-12 schools. Instead of reducing disparities among class, race, and gender groups, there is a possibility that technology could serve to perpetuate or even worsen imbalances and differences (Steck, cited in Surry, 2008). In other words, technology emphasis could increase the digital divide, widening the gap between the "have" and "have nots."

However, Garrison and Akyol (2009) suggested that institution avoidance of inappropriate uses of technology would help mediate some of these concerns. Surry (2008) maintained that what remains missing within higher education is a meaningful dialogue about the appropriate use of technology. Similarly, Garrison and Akyol suggest the best uses of technology are achieved through examination of whether the innovation is based on educational sound ideas and approaches. The key to successful integration and use of technology is alignment.

The development or use of any innovation begins with thorough problem analysis (Rothwell & Kazanas, 2004). By employing such analysis procedures, faculty and administrators can identify root causes of problems and determine how the problem can be resolved. R.E. Clark (2009) proposed that the process should begin with active research on the appropriate use of technology and the decision to make utility decisions should be based on those findings. With either approach, educational soundness becomes the main focus in using technology rather than the focus being only on the capabilities or promise of the technology. In other words, higher educational professionals begin to address not only the question of "can we use technology," but also the questions of "should we use technology," "how should be use the technology," and "how will it be effective?" Through these processes, the chance of enhancing the teaching and learning environment improves.

Our View about the Potential and Power of Technology and Higher Education

As the authors of this chapter looked toward the future of technology in higher education, as might be expected, we were daunted in the charge of writing this chapter. If this chapter were written a few years ago, it would, admittedly, have been much easier to project into the future. As Bugeja (2009) has noted, in the past funding was better for higher education; those were the days of fatter budgets for technology and innovation. However, as we emerge from "The Great Recession," it is expected that most aspects of higher education will not be "business as usual." New pathways will and must emerge for colleges and universities to advance areas of excellence, while still being true to the fundamental mission of teaching, research, knowledge-building, and service.

Colleges and universities empower individuals and hold incredible promise for building a strong nation and world. Von Drehle (2009), writing about Gordon Gee, president of Ohio State University, contended, "In a world were brainpower outstrips muscle power, where innovation trumps conformity, where the nimble and creative stand to inherit the earth, higher education is the key to the next American century" (p. 44). Von Drehle continued, "Classrooms and labs are today what mines and factories were a century ago: America's regional economic powerhouses, [are] one of the few certain engines of growth in good and bad economic times" (p. 46). In addition, universities will continue to be a center for the growth of new knowledge and information and where learning takes place – both inside the U.S. and around the globe.

Hilton (2006) noted, "In today's knowledge economy, the role of higher education is being redefined" (p. 59) and that changes in higher education are significant, in response to what he terms "disruptive forces" that have only grown in scale. Hilton suggested that higher educational professionals can respond to these changes as if they were a negative "perfect storm," or they can "view this time as a dawn of a new day" (p. 59). This choice of response to "Great Recession" must also be made by those others who may have influence and make decisions that impact the welfare of higher education.

People Hold the Key. As many have noted, technology in itself does not have the power for good or evil. It is people who develop, select, and use technologies that make the difference and will build the future. As Von Drehle (2009) stated, "The U.S. needs to step up its game, become more creative, more flexible, more innovative in more ways. Who can take us there if not our educators?" (p. 48). In higher education, the technology wielders and builders, students, faculty and administrators, hold the key to the success of universities and effective technology innovations. Technologies facilitate the interaction and collaboration of these individuals as they design and develop innovations.

Batson (2009a), too, focused on the role of educators in leading educational technology innovation. He contended that, in an era of Web 2.0, virtualization, and cloud computing, educators lead the way, stating, "This moment is for the professoriate. ... Over the past 30 years, faculty have assumed leadership in this new learning era on a number of occasions. ... We faculty have always been the source for innovation in academia and in this renaissance are again" (p. 1). While faculty have the potential to provide leadership in use of technology, this view should be tempered by the reality of trends and other forces that influence the teaching and learning environment.

Forecasting the Near Future: Technology Integration in Higher Education

The students who arrive in colleges and universities may be different for-the-most-part, and are considered more technology-savvy than previous generations. The increasing sophistication of K-12 students in technology skills, especially in the areas of "creation, collaboration, and contribution" (Trendspotter: Next-Geners and Web 2.0, 2009, p. 42) has the potential to affect student expectations for having and using technology in higher education now and in the future.

Web 2.0 tools and resources used by 21st century college students may provide an opportunity for faculty and administration to use those same tools to enhance teaching and learning environments. Web 2.0 tools can be integrated into class environments in ways that promote collaboration, interaction, and social networking (Peacock, 2009). Nagel (2008) described Web 2.0 tools as providing educators with "convenience, collaboration, and convergence" (p. 1). He also, however, noted that issues such as security breaches and other types of vulnerabilities may become a concern to or for educators, pointing out that many schools block social networking sites. Peacock concurred, noting that privacy issues are critical when working with students.

Colleges and universities struggle with issues, such as compliance with FERPA (Family Educational Rights and Privacy Act) regulations. The question becomes: what kinds of information can be distributed and shared in social and collaborative environments. In addition, questionable sites are being blocked from computers in homes and schools (Meeder, 2005). Meeder reported that libraries are required to use filtering software to block questionable sites and be in compliance with the Children's Internet Protection Act (CIPA); however, these blocks "can also prevent students from visiting "clean" sites that discuss controversial, though relevant, topics in an appropriate manner." (p. 56). Again, colleges and universities are working to meet and manage these issues in a responsible manner.

Challenges for the higher education system include, for instance, issues related to ease of online access to information, plagiarism, copyright issues, distractions, cheating, and pressures on faculty time (Glenn, et al., 2009). These challenges focus attention on all stakeholders of the higher education system: students, faculty, and administrators. Hilton (2006) calls for action to be taken take action to ensure that the future is as bright as (higher educational professionals) can make it.

In looking toward the future of technology in higher education worldwide, results of a New Media Consortium survey yield insights (Glenn et al., 2009). A majority (63%) of the 300 executives, with 189 from higher education institutions, indicated that "technology has had - and will continue to have - a significant impact on higher education" (p. 4). Glenn et al. added that "In fact, technology will become a core differentiator in attracting students and corporate partners" (p. 4) and mentioned ways that technology will impact higher education. Their examples included changing course length (variable times, not aligned to a traditional 16- or 10-week schedule) and changing how credit hours are calculated, influencing inter-university collaborations, developing partnerships across colleges and businesses for developing programs, and aiding students in pursuing personalizing degrees.

These executives also found particular value in the wide variety of social and collaborative technologies and strategies (Glenn et al., 2009). Integrating collaborative technologies into teaching and learning environments enables students and faculty to interact in ways that mirror real-world situations. Using social and collaborative technologies can provide a variety of ways that support students as they participate in higher education opportunities.

"Best Practices" for the Future of Educational Technology in Higher Education

As Batson (2009b) noted, faculty do not want to teach their students about technology *per se*, but want to teach well. Interest in the scholarship of teaching and related research focuses on various aspects of the teaching and learning process, including passion for teaching, interaction and engagement with students, structure of the process (e.g., course organization, content knowledge, classroom management, technology integration, mentoring, professional development, assessment, undergraduate research) with a fundamental question: Is teaching a science or an art? (Thomas & Gillespie, 2007; Yair, 2008). One way that faculty, in a desire to deliver high quality instruction, can engage students in teaching and learning processes is through appropriate integration of technology.

If educators, in partnerships, often, with their students, are to be leaders in educational technology innovation, they need support from their institutions. In an environment of lean budgets and increasing political change, the best ways to support the most effective integration of educational technology has four components: lead with vision, encourage and support experimentation, provide streamlined, consistent technology resources and support, and foster quality.

Lead with Vision. Sexton (2009) summarized the key qualities of nine university presidents that make them significant leaders in the U.S. and noted that "one theme unites them: endless innovation" (p. 49). Their innovations cover many areas, but the commonalities among them included: expanding the institution's reach and mission to ensure more students and more types of students have access to higher education.

While speaking at the University of Illinois at Chicago, Vanides (2009) promoted the notion that higher education leaders should forecast a future that included digital initiatives. He proposed a vision of a different type of institution that addressed concerns of types of courses or course credit, personalization of instruction, and, in fact, incorporation of new models for learning. Although difficult at times, university administrators and faculty should work together to meet the challenges that budget shortfalls pose and to integrate appropriate technologies for effective use.

Encourage, and Support Experimentation with Technologies. According to Batson (2009a), it is necessary for faculty to take the lead in innovative new uses of technology; supporting faculty experimentation is one key to success in integrating educational technologies most effectively. Multiple examples outline how faculty continue to innovate with technology. For example, Young (2009a) described how faculty used videoconferencing for meetings and used Twitter for teaching (Young, 2009b). Similarly, Powell (2009) described his experience as a public relations staff member in using Facebook and how he incorporated those experiences into teaching practices. Lang (2009) described how his classes have been improved each time he tries implementing newer technologies. Faculty at East Carolina University used a simple, low-tech approach (low-bandwidth video link and email chat) to link their students with other students overseas (Fischer, 2009). These examples are but a few of the many ways that faculty can use technology in their own educational environments to extend their teaching practices.

One way to support faculty as they learn about new technologies for instruction is through professional development. Nielsen, Strand, Savenye, Spector, Mancilla, and Biggs (2009) developed a systematic and long-term approach to technology integration. They described intensive 2-week summer workshops for faculty where faculty compete for enrollment slots by submitting instructional innovation proposals and receive small stipends for participating. Faculty were trained and supported in designing and building technology-based instructional interventions. They received common training on technology integration and choose to participate in targeted workshops on specific instructional strategies, new methodologies and new and emerging technologies. Shorter, one-two hour workshops were also available for faculty to hone their skills. These strategies enabled faculty to "get their feet wet" and permitted others to learn specific skills and technology they need to accomplish their instructional goals (Nielsen, et al.).

To foster faculty integration of technology in higher education and promotion of technologies that align to institutional goals, continuing support can, and should, be provided. In addition to workshops, another strategy for support is to secure membership in technology consortia, making conferences, training and workshops, especially inexpensive webinars, available to faculty at member institutions. Such organizations and consortia could include, for example, the Association for Educational Communications and Technology (AECT) (2009), EduCause (2009), the New Media Consortium (NMC) (2009), SLOAN-C (2009), and the TLT Group (2009). Faculty can be encouraged to subscribe to relevant educational technology newsletters and listservs such as those of Campus Technology (2009) and Academic Technology (2009), or those related to technology and teaching in their own content areas. Stipends for design development, implementation, and evaluation can provide incentives for faculty to participate in a wide variety of activities and to support their own technology acquisitions.

Provide Streamlined, Consistent Technology Resources and Support. In a time of decreasing budgets, colleges and universities will be increasingly challenged to provide technology support across the campuses. Bugeja (2009) described how his college, with a supportive dean, in a time of decreasing budgets, made hard decisions about efficiencies in technology, with a focus on maintaining good enrollments in courses and maintaining strong student learning. College personnel determined essential technologies and negotiated with vendors for good rates. There was a focus on consolidating the curriculum, and, then, technologies and technology modules were integrated into existing courses, rather than creating new ones. Care was taken so that non-majors were enrolled into larger elective classes, thereby ensuring more-intensive lab courses be open for majors, etc.

Technology implementation, especially for innovative projects, such as simulations, virtual worlds and game-based learning pose challenges for higher education (Foreman, Gee, Herz, Hinrichs, & Prensky, 2004). As Van Eck (2006) noted, challenges of digital game-based learning may include training and technical and financial support. Here again, strategic initiatives, especially those involving partnerships among interdisciplinary departments, funding agencies, businesses, etc., can be scalable and effective. Administrator support of technology implementation enables faculty and student integration of that technology and innovative use of technology.

Issues of what technology should be at large institutions of higher education, especially during challenging budgetary times, are likely to continue to spark quite radical changes. Many institutions are considering, or are already, decreasing support for campus computer labs in favor of student laptop initiatives; many, too, have downsized campus support staff in favor of outsourcing many help services, and have come to rely more and more on cloud computing services rather than purchasing and supporting individual copies of software (cf. Sannier, 2008). Students and faculty may access technology via wireless services rather than wire-based infrastructures. McCrea (2009) indicated some of these trends go beyond "1:1" laptop initiatives and recommended higher education be prepared for students to use more and more applications and devices that go beyond, or mix computing technologies and to support students as they "mash-up" technologies in new ways, such as using online maps that are location-based.

Still, other universities are increasing their support for campus faculty technology labs and services. Nielsen et al. (2009), for instance, describe Instructional Technology Services for faculty in the form of instructional design and technology staff and a faculty computer lab. These support services may also include technology development support for media such as video, graphics, simulations, or games.

Foster Quality. Overall, high quality experiences in higher education are expected by students, faculty, administrators, and accrediting bodies (U.S. Department of Education, 2006). Fostering the quality of higher education programs is critical. With all of the attention of online and distance delivery, quality for these types of environments is particularly relevant to higher education systems and faculty. One approach to promoting the quality of online education has been the enhancement tool and service, *Quality Matters*, developed by the University of Maryland. The rubric and an associated "faculty-centered peer review process is designed to certify online courses and online components" (Maryland Online, 2006, p. 1). Sener (2005) summarized critical aspects of the quality of online courses in the areas of, for instance, the course overview and introduction; course competencies or objectives; assessment; resources; student interaction; technology; support for learners; and compliance with ADA initiatives. Careful attention to quality can facilitate the alignment of relevant and meaningful instructional strategies to appropriate technologies.

Setting the Stage for Best Practices. The stage can be set for the implementation of best practices by using a three-step process: (1) employing needs assessment strategies, (2) engaging stakeholders, and (3) conducting an evaluation. Using a consistent system for the incorporation of technology into teaching, learning, and administrative practices enables a broad and comprehensive perspective.

The process of conducting a needs assessments, or performance analysis, includes the fundamental step of the identification of the actual causes of the problem and, ultimately, the identification of gaps that facilitate the targeting of appropriate interventions for problem resolution (Gano, 2003; Rothwell & Kazanas, 2004). This process provides data that assists in determining what are the best practices and where they are needed. Data can be used for decision making in a way to target the needs of the organization and the stakeholders.

Engaging stakeholders into the implementation of carefully identified best practices can help to build systems that are sustainable (Esque, 2005). Without this stakeholder engagement, the best practice, no matter what it is, is doomed to failure. The idea that the stakeholders (in this case, students, faculty, and administrators) must be active participants in determining best practices and their placement and implementation is critical to the success of the best practice.

A final element of setting the stage for a best practice is the requirement for evaluation. Planning for an evaluation of the best practice facilitates the determining the worth, value, or quality of a best practice was achieved (Guerra-Lopez, 2008). This summative evaluation process permits stakeholders to reflect on the success of the best practice and ensure that the best practice can be used effectively and efficiently. Additionally, as instructional designers ourselves, we subscribe to the idea that formative evaluation must also be included. In formative evaluation, best practices are reviewed and revised accordingly as they are being designed or supplied (i.e., already developed) and implemented into a new environment (Davidson-Shivers & Rasmussen, 2006).

SUMMARY

The issues for stakeholders in colleges and universities are clear. Factors such as reduced funding through a combination of lower state revenue, increased numbers of students, and increased competition, have changed the playing field. There are many different types of technologies that can be integrated into the administrative and teaching and learning environments of the 21st century higher education institution, with distance and online learning being a critical element for many institutions. Higher education institutions must think smart, be smart, and implement innovation in smart ways. A three-step process can be used to prepare higher education for setting the stage for interventions and innovation, with technology being a possible solution.

1. Be smart in conducting needs assessments, or performance analyses, that identify needs or problems, causes and solutions, especially when considering technology as a possible solution. Carefully, accurately, and appropriately align gaps, problems, and solutions to promote institutional goals; judiciously align problems and solutions. Be cognizant of the fact that technology may not always be the best solution. If technology is the appropriate solution, it should then be aligned to meet the institution's mission and goals.
2. Engage stakeholders in the needs assessment and implementation of the intervention or solution. Use a variety of strategies to promote a positive implementation of the intervention, especially technology integration. Keep all stakeholders involved. Provide stakeholders with flexibility and support to encourage innovation.
3. Evaluate the efficiency and effectiveness of the intervention or solution. Target evaluation of technology (equipment, processes, policies and procedures) involved to ensure that the technology has met the institutional goals and has been fully implemented throughout the system. Include the instructional design procedure of formative evaluation as technology-based innovations are being designed or supplied and initially implemented. Such a review and revision opportunity will help sustain the intervention.

The key to successfully integrating educational and instructional technologies into higher education in the future rests upon making good choices about technology selection and interaction. An important component for the success of technology integration is to provide access and, then, to support students, faculty, and administrators. Putting right tools into the hands of the academy enables and facilitates a future that is rich with technology, collaboration, and innovation.

REFERENCES

About Campus (2010, Winter). A cloudy financial outlook. *Minnesota, 109*(2), 12.

Academic Technology. (2009). *Taking Teaching further: Evaluating Emerging Technologies and their Teaching Implications in Higher Education*. Retrieved from http://www.academictechnology.org/

American Association of State Colleges and Universities. (2010, January). *Top 10 Higher Education State Policy Issues*. Retrieved from http://www.congressweb.com/aascu/docfiles/AASCU_Top_Ten_Policy_Issues_2010.pdf

Association for Educational Communications and Technology (AECT) (2009). Retrieved from http://www.aect.org

Barnett, E. (2002). *The costs and benefits of remedial education*. Retrieved from http://occrl.ed.uiuc.edu/Publications/papers/Costs%20Remedial%20Education-%20EB1.pdf

Batson, T. (2009a, December 2). *The Cloud Opens the Floodgates for Faculty Innovation*. Retrieved from http://campustechnology.com/articles/2009/12/02/the-cloud-opens-the-floodgates-for-faculty-innovation.aspx?sc_lang=en

Batson, T. (2009b, October 21). *But I Don't Want to Teach My Students How to Use Technology*. Retrieved from http://campustechnology.com/articles/2009/10/21/but-i-do-not-want-to-teach-my-students-how-to-use-technology.aspx?sc_lang=en

Bean, J. P. (1998). Alternative models of professorial roles: New languages to reimagine faculty work. *The Journal of Higher Education, 69*(5), 496-512. Retrieved from JSTOR databases. URL: http://www.jstor.org/stable/2649107

Bugeja, M. J. (2009, November 9). Reduce the technology, rescue your job. *The Chronicle of Higher Education*. Retrieved from http://chronicle.com/article/Reduce-the-Technology-Resc/49078/

Clark, K. (2009, August 19). Budget Cuts Take Toll on Education: Budget cuts have hit public colleges hard, even as the demand for a well-educated workforce soars. *U.S. News and World Report*. Retrieved from http://www.usnews.com/articles/education/best-colleges/2009/08/19/budget-cuts-take-toll-on-education.html?PageNr=2

Clark, R. E. (2009). Translating research into new instructional technologies for higher education: the active ingredient process. *Journal of Computing in Higher Education, 21*(1), 4–18. doi:10.1007/s12528-009-9013-8

Cooper, K. J. (2009). IT: Intellectually taxing? *Diverse Issues in Higher Education, 26*(3), 11–12.

Cuban, L. (2005). *So much high-tech money invested, so little used: How come?* Retrieved from http://www.edtechnot.com/notarticle1201.html.

Davidson-Shivers, G. V. (2002). Instructional technology in higher education. In, R. A. Reiser. & J. V. Dempsey (Eds.) *Trends and issues in instructional design and technology.* (pp. 256-268). Upper Saddle River, NJ: Pearson/Merrill Prentice Hall.

Davidson-Shivers, G. V., & Rasmussen, K. L. (2006). *Web-based learning: Design, implementation, and evaluation*. Upper Saddle River, NJ: Pearson Merrill Prentice-Hall.

Diel, S. (2009, December 8). Recession puts squeeze on Alabama colleges. *The Mobile Press-Register,* p. C5.

EDUCAUSE Learning Initiative (2009). Retrieved from http://www.educause.edu/eli

Esque, T. (2005). *Making an Impact*. Atlanta, GA: CEP.

Evans, E., & Po, J. (2007). A break in the transaction: Examining students' responses to digital text. *Computers and Composition, 24*, 56–73. doi:10.1016/j.compcom.2006.12.003

Fischer, K. (2009, May 7). East Carolina U. Uses Simple Technology to Link Its Students with Peers Overseas. *The Chronicle of Higher Education*. Retrieved from http://chronicle.com/article/East-Carolina-U-Uses-Simpl/44302

Foreman, J., & Gee, J. P. Herz., J. C., Hinrichs, R., & Prensky, M. (2004, September/October). Game-based learning: How to delight and instruct in the 21st Century. *EDUCAUSE Review, 39*(5), pp. 51–66. Retrieved from http://www.educause.edu/EDUCAUSE+Review/EDUCAUSEReviewMagazineVolume39/GameBasedLearning-HowtoDelighta/157927

Friedman, T. L. (2005). *The world is flat: A brief history of the twenty-first century*. New York: Farrar, Straus and Giroux.

Gano, D. L. (2003). *Apollo Root Cause Analysis*. Yakima, WA: Apollonian Publications.

Garrison, D. R., & Akyol, Z. (2009). Role of instructional technology in the transformation of higher education. *Journal of Computing in Higher Education, 21*(1), 19–30. doi:10.1007/s12528-009-9014-7

Glenn, M. with D'Agostino (Ed.) & Johnson, L. (2009). *The Future of Higher Education: How Technology Will Shape Learning.* A Report from the Economist Intelligence Unit Sponsored by the New Media Consortium. Retrieved from http://www.nmc.org/pdf/Future-of-Higher-Ed-(NMC).pdf

Greenhow, C., Walker, J. D., & Kim, S. (2009-10). Millennial learners and net-savvy teens? Examining Internet use among low-income students. *Journal of Computing in Teacher Education, 26*(2), 63–68.

Guerra-Lopez, I. (2008). *Performance Evaluation: Proven Approaches for Improving Program and Organizational Performance*. San Francisco: Jossey-Bass.

Haney, D. P. (2007, February 2). Millennial, but not really different. *Chronicle of Higher Education, 53*(23), Special Section p. B14.

Hanna, D. E. (2003, July/August). Building a leadership vision: Eleven strategic challenges for higher education. *EDUCAUSE Review, 38*(4), 25–34. Retrieved from http://net.educause.edu/ir/library/pdf/ERM0341.pdf.

Hilton, J. (2006, March/April). The future for higher education: Sunrise or perfect storm? *EDUCAUSE Review, 41*(2), 58–71. Retrieved from http://www.educause.edu/EDUCAUSE+Review/EDUCAUSEReviewMagazineVolume41/TheFutureforHigherEducationSun/158046.

Howe, N., & Strauss, W. (2000). *Millennials rising: The next great generation by Neil Howe and Bill Strauss; cartoons by R.J. Matson*. New York: Vintage Books.

Lang, J. M. (2009, September 17). Teaching resolutions for the new year. *The Chronicle of Higher Education*. Retrieved from http://chronicle.com/article/Teaching-Resolutions-for-th/48379/

Maryland Online, Inc. (2006). *Quality Matters: Inter-Institutional Quality Assurance in Online Learning*. Retrieved from http://www.qualitymatters.org/index.htm

McCrea, B. (2009, December 9). Five Higher Ed Tech Trends to Watch in 2010. *Campus Technology*. Retrieved from http://campustechnology.com/Articles/2009/12/09/5-Higher-Ed-Tech-Trends-To-Watch-in-2010.aspx

Meeder, R. (2005). Access denied: Internet filtering software in K-12 classrooms. *TechTrends, 49*(6), 56–57. doi:10.1007/BF02763732

Nagel, D. (2008, January 16). Web 2.0 in education: Trends for 2008. *Technological Horizons in Education Journal*. Retrieved January 11,2009, from http://thejournal.com/articles/2008/01/16/web-20-in-education-trends-for-2008.aspx

National Center for Educational Statistics. (2009). *The Condition of Education*. Retrieved from http://nces.ed.gov/pubs2009/2009081.pdf

New Media Consortium (NMC). (2009). *Sparking innovative learning and creativity*. Retrieved from http://www.nmc.org/

Nielsen, M., Strand, E., Savenye, W., Spector, M., Mancilla, D., & Biggs, M. J. (2009, October). *Developing Technology-Skilled Faculty across a Large Campus: A Long-Term Technology Integration Program*. Paper presented at the annual meeting of the Association for Educational Communications and Technology, Louisville, KY.

Peacock, K. (2009). *Web 2.0 for Teachers*. Retrieved from http://www.protopage.com/web-2point0forteachers

Powell, R. S. (2009, October 9). Who is on the other end of Facebook? *The Chronicle of Higher Education*. Retrieved from http://chronicle.com/article/Who-Is-on-the-Other-End-of-/48693/

Prensky, M. (2001). Digital natives, digital immigrants. *Horizon, 9*(5), 1–6. Retrieved from http://www.marcprensky.com/writing/Prensky%20-%20Digital%20Natives,%20Digital%20Immigrants%20-%20Part1.pdf. doi:10.1108/10748120110424816doi:10.1108/10748120110424816

Rothwell, W. J., & Kazanas, H. C. (2004). *Improving on-the-job training How to establish and operate a comprehensive OJT program*. San Francisco: Pfeiffer.

Sannier, A. (2008, August 19). *Video Spotlight: Campus Technology 2008 Keynote Address: A 'New' American University for Next-Gen Learners*. Retrieved from http://campustechnology.com/articles/2008/08/video-spotlight-campus-technology-2008-keynote-address.aspx

Sener, J. (2005). The quality matters rubric: A tool for promoting quality improvement in online courses. In *Educational Pathways: Resources for Educators and Learners.* Retrieved from http://www.edpath.com/2005/0205/020504.htm

Sexton, J. (2009, November 23). Nine presidents to watch. One theme unites them: endless innovation. *Time*, 49–51.

Shelly, G. B., Cashman, T. J., Gunter, R. E., & Gunter, G. A. (2004). *Teachers discovering computers: Integrating technology in the classroom*. Boston: Course Technology.

Sloan-C. *A Consortium of Institutions and Organizations Committed to Quality Online Education* (2009). Retrieved from http://www.sloanconsortium.org

Surry, D. W. (2008). Technology and the future of higher education: An Ellulian perspective. In J. Luca & E. R. Weippl (Eds.), *Proceedings of the ED-MEDIA 2008-World Conference on Educational Multimedia, Hypermedia & Telecommunications*. (pp.4901-4906). Chesapeake, VA: Association for Advancement of Computing in Education.

Technology, C. (2009). Retrieved from http://campustechnology.com/home.aspx

The, T. L. T., & the Group. (2009). *Teaching, Learning, and Technology*. Retrieved from http://www.tltgroup.org/

Thomas, E., & Gillespie, D. (2008). Weaving together undergraduate research, mentoring of junior faculty and assessment: The case of an interdisciplinary program. *Innovative Higher Education, 33*, 29–38. doi:10.1007/s10755-007-9060-x

Trendspotter: Next-Geners and Web 2.0 (2009, May). *Campus Technology, 22*(9), 49-51. Retrieved from http://1105production.com/EDU/Campus-Technology/Articles/2009/05/01/Trendspotter.aspx

Trenholm, S. (2006). A study on the efficacy of computer-mediated developmental math instruction for traditional community college students. [RTDE]. *Research and Teaching in Developmental Education, 22*(2), 51–62.

U.S. Department of Education. (2006). *A National Dialogue: The Secretary of Education's Commission on the Future of Higher Education.* Retrieved from http://www2.ed.gov/about/bdscomm/list/hiedfuture/index.html

Van Eck, R. (2006, March/April). Digital game-based learning: It's not just the digital natives who are restless. *EDUCAUSE Review, 41*(2), 17–30. Retrieved from http://www.educause.edu/EDUCAUSE+Review/EDUCAUSEReviewMagazineVolume41/DigitalGameBasedLearningIts-Not/158041.

Vanides, J. (2009, August, 26). *Technology and the (Possible) Future of Higher Education.* Retrieved from http://online/blogs/highered/archive/2009/08/26/technology-and-the-possible-future-of-higher-education.aspx

Von Drehle, D. (2009, November 23). The big man on campus. *Time*, 44–48.

Weidman, J. C., Twale, D. J., & Stein, E. L. (2001). *Socialization of graduate and professional students in higher education: A perilous passage? ASHE-ERIC Higher Education Report, 28(3)* [A. J. Kezar, Series Editor.]. San Francisco: Jossey-Bass.

Yair, G. (2008). Can we administer the scholarship of teaching? Lessons from outstanding professors in higher education. *Higher Education, 55*, 447–459. doi:10.1007/s10734-007-9066-4

Young, J. (2009a, October 18). Beam me to the faculty senate. *The Chronicle of Higher Education*. Retrieved from http://chronicle.com/article/Beam-Me-to-the-Faculty-Sena/48830

Young, J. (2009b, April 10). 10 high fliers on Twitter. *The Chronicle of Higher Education*. Retrieved from http://chronicle.com/article/10-High-Fliers-on-Twitter/16488

ADDITIONAL READING

AASCU State Relations and Policy Analysis Research Team. (2009). *Top 10 State Policy Issues for Higher Education in 2009*. Retrieved from http://www.educational-access.org/Documents/PM-Top10-Jan2009.pdf

Barrett, H. C. (2006). *Authentic Assessment with Electronic Portfolios Using Common Software and Web 2.0 Tools*. Retrieved from http://electronicportfolios.com/web20.html

Bonk, C. J. (2009). *The world is open: How Web technology is revolutionizing education*. San Francisco: Jossey-Bass.

Brown, J. S. (2005). New Learning Environments for the 21st Century. *Aspen Symposium 2005. Forum for the Future of Higher Education*. Retrieved from http://net.educause.edu/ir/library/pdf/ffp0605.pdf

Clarke, J., & Dede, C. (2006, June 22-25). *Robust Designs for Scalability*. Paper presented at the annual Research Symposium of the Association for Educational Communications and Technology, Bloomington, Indiana.

Educause Review (2010). Retrieved from http://www.educause.edu/er

Hanna, D. E. (2000). *Higher education in an era of digital competition: Choices and challenges*. Madison, WI: Atwood Publishing.

Mintz, J. (2009, October 13). *Kindle lightens textbook load, but flaws remain*. Retrieved from http://www.physorg.com/news174670605.html

Moore, J. C. (2005). *The Sloan consortium quality framework and the five pillars*. Retrieved from http://sloan-c.org/publications/books/quality-framework.pdf

Nelson, B., Ketelhut, D., Clarke, J., Bowman, C., & Dede, C. (2005). Design-based research strategies for developing a scientific inquiry curriculum in a multi-user virtual environment. *Educational Technology, 45*(1), 21–27.

Nelson, W. A. (2000). Gagné and the new technologies of instruction. Chapter 9 in R. C. Richey (Ed.) *The Legacy of Robert M. Gagné* (4th ed.). Syracuse, NY: Eric Clearinghouse on Information and Technology. Retrieved from http:www.ibstpi.org/Products/pdf/chapter_9.pdf

Smaldino, S. E., Lowther, D. L., & Russell, J. D. (2008). *Instructional Technology and Media for Learning* (9th ed.). Boston: Allyn & Bacon/Merrill.

KEY TERMS AND DEFINITIONS

Digital Natives: Individuals who have always had access to technology; from a generational standpoint, comprised primarily of individuals who are X-ers (born 1961-1981), and Millennials (born 1982-2000) (Howe & Strauss, 2000; Prensky, M. (2001).

Higher Education: Organizational system that focuses on post-secondary teaching, learning, and research; those institutions commonly thought of as college- or university-level (Davidson-Shivers, 2002)

Millennials: Group of individuals who share common demographic characteristics of being born between 1982 and 2000 (Howe & Strauss, 2000)

Technology Integration: Using technology (processes, procedures, equipment, devices) in various ways to support organizations, in this context, educational institutions in administrative, teaching and learning activities (Davidson-Shivers, 2002; *EDUCAUSE Learning Initiative*, 2009; Shelly, Cashman, Gunter, & Gunter, 2004)

Compilation of References

AAAS. (2008). *Report XXXII: Research and Development FY 2008*. Washington, DC: American Association for the Advancement of Science.

AARNet Pty Ltd. (2006). *The results of the AARNet Survey on Video over IP in the Australian Academic & Research Sector*. Canberra: AARNet. July.

Aarts, E. (2004). Ambient intelligence. A multimedia perspective. *IEEE MultiMedia, 11*, 12–19. doi:10.1109/MMUL.2004.1261101

About Campus (2010, Winter). A cloudy financial outlook. *Minnesota, 109*(2), 12.

About Us. (2010). *About us: Critical Commons.* Retrieved April 30, 2010 from http://criticalcommons.org/about-us

Abrami, P. C., Dehler, C., Schmid, R. F., Bernard, R. M., Lowerison, G., & Tamim, R. M. (2008). Assessing computer use and perceived course effectiveness in post-secondary education. *Journal of Educational Computing Research, 39*(3), 221–234. doi:10.2190/EC.39.3.b

Academic Technology. (2009). *Taking Teaching further: Evaluating Emerging Technologies and their Teaching Implications in Higher Education.* Retrieved from http://www.academictechnology.org/

Acar, A. (2007). Teaching languages from a distance through multipoint videoconferencing. *Foreign Language Annals, 40*(2), 311–319. doi:10.1111/j.1944-9720.2007.tb03203.x

Accreditation Council for Graduate Medical Education. ACGME Outcome Project.(2010). Retrieved December 5, 2007 from www.acgme.org/Outcomes.

Albright, L. P. (1997). The information technology imperative for higher education: A report. *Library Acquisitions: Practice and Theory, 21*(3), 268. doi:10.1016/S0364-6408(97)00022-7

Albright, M. J., & Nworie, J. (2008). Rethinking Academic Technology Leadership in an Era of Change. *EDUCAUSE Quarterly, 31*(1), 14–23.

Albright, M. J., & Graf, D. L. (1992). Instructional technology and the faculty member. In M. J. Albright & D. L. Graf (Eds.), *Teaching in the information age: The role of educational technology. New Directions for Teaching and Learning* (no. 51, pp 7-16). San Francisco: Jossey-Bass.

Alexander, B. (2004). Going nomadic: Mobile learning in higher education. *EDUCAUSE Review, 39*(5), 28–35.

Alexander, B. (2006). Web 2.0: A new wave of innovation for teaching and learning? *EDUCAUSE Review, 41*, 32–44.

Allanson, J., & Fairclough, S. H. (2004). A research agenda for physiological computing. *Interacting with Computers, 16*, 857–878. doi:10.1016/j.intcom.2004.08.001

Allen, G. (2002). *Roland Barthes: S/Z. The literary encyclopedia.* Retrieved March 7, 2005, from http://www.litencyc.com/php/sworks.php?rec=true&UID=10346.

Al-Senaidi, S., Lin, L., & Poirot, J. (2009). Barriers to adopting technology for teaching and learning in Oman. *Computers & Education, 53*(3), 575–590. doi:10.1016/j.compedu.2009.03.015

American Association of University Professors. (2010). *Sample intellectual property policy and contract language.* Retrieved January 10, 2010 from http://www.aaup.org/AAUP/issues/DE/sampleIP.htm

American Association of State Colleges and Universities. (2010, January). *Top 10 Higher Education State Policy Issues*. Retrieved from http://www.congressweb.com/aascu/docfiles/AASCU_Top_Ten_Policy_Issues_2010.pdf

Americans with Disabilities Act of 1990, U.S.C. §12, 101-112, 213.

Amodio, D. M., Harmon-Jones, E., & Devine, P. G. (2003). Individual differences in the activation and control of affective race bias as assessed by startle eyeblink responses and self-report. *Journal of Personality and Social Psychology*, *84*, 738–753. doi:10.1037/0022-3514.84.4.738

Amodio, D. M., Harmon-Jones, E., Devine, P. G., Curtin, J. J., Hartley, S. L., & Covert, A. E. (2004). Neural signals for the detection of unintentional race bias. *Psychological Science*, *15*, 88–93. doi:10.1111/j.0963-7214.2004.01502003.x

Anderson, C. (2006). *The long tail: How endless choice is creating unlimited demand*. London: Random House.

Anderson, T. (2005). Distance learning – Social software's killer ap? *The Open & Distance Learning Association of Australia*. Retrieved July 2, 2008, from http://auspace.athabascau.ca:8080/dspace/bitstream/2149/2328/1/distance_learning.pdf

Anderson, T. (2008). *The theory and practice of online learning (2nd ed.)*. Edmonton, AB: Athabasca University (AU) Press.

Andrew, R., & Johnsen, K. (2007). Comparing Interpersonal Interactions with a Virtual Human to those with a Real Human. *IEEE Transactions on Visualization and Computer Graphics*, *13*, 443–457.

Andrews, T., Caladine, R., Smyth, R., Tynan, B., & Vale, D. (2008). *Rich media technologies and uncertain futures – developing sustainable, scalable models*. Paper presented at the Hello! Where are You in the Landscape of Educational Technology? Conference, Melbourne, 30th November -3rd December, ASCILITE.

Anissimov, M. (2009, December 14). *The benefits of a successful singularity*. Retrieved from http://www.good.is/post/The-Benefits-of-a-Successful-Singularity/

Anson, C. M. (1999, January). Distant voices: Teaching and writing in a culture of technology. *College English*, *61*(3), 261–280. doi:10.2307/379069

Argyris, C. (1991). Teaching smart people how to learn. *Harvard Business Review*, *69*(3), 99–109.

Argyris, C. (2004). Reflection and beyond in research on organizational Learning. *Management Learning*, *35*(4), 507–509. doi:10.1177/1350507604048276

Arthur, W. B. (2009). *The nature of technology: What it is and how it evolves*. New York: Free Press.

Association for Educational Communications and Technology. (n.d.). *Definition and Terminology Committee*. Retrieved March 28, 2010, from http://www.aect.org/about/div_.asp?DivisionID=18.

Association for Educational Communications and Technology (AECT) (2009). Retrieved from http://www.aect.org

Association of Research Libraries. (2009). *Influencing public policies: Copyright & intellectual property policies*. Retrieved December 16, 2009, from http://www.arl.org/pp/ppcopyright/copyresources/copytimeline.shtml

Attali, Y., & Burstein, J. (2006). Automated essay scoring with e-rater® V.2. *Journal of Technology, Learning, and Assessment*, *4*(3). Available from http://www.jtla.org.

Axtell, C. M., Holman, D. J., Unsworth, K. L., Wall, T. D., Waterson, P. E., & Harrington, E. (2000). Shopfloor innovation: Facilitating the suggestion and implementation of ideas. *Journal of Occupational Psychology*, *73*, 265–285. doi:10.1348/096317900167029

Backhouse, B. (2003). Information and communication technology integration: Beyond the early adopters. *TechTrends*, *47*(3), 5–8. doi:10.1007/BF02763468

Baecker, R. (2003). *A principled design for scalable internet visual communications with rich media, interactivity, and structured archives*. Paper presented at the Proceedings of the 2003 conference of the Centre for Advanced Studies on Collaborative research IBM Press, Toronto, Ontario, Canada, pp. 16-29.

Berriman, A. (2007, 14/02/2007). *Visual Communications: Transformational possibilities vs incremental realities.* Paper presented at the Wainhouse Research Collaboration Summit, Wainhouse Research, Sydney, pp. 1-60. Available from http://www.wainhouseresearch.com/sydney07/presentations

Bailey, C. J., & Card, K. A. (2009). Effective pedagogical practices for online teaching: Perception of experienced instructors. *The Internet and Higher Education, 12*(3-4), 152–155. doi:10.1016/j.iheduc.2009.08.002

Bakhtin, M. M. (1981). *The dialogic imagination*. Austin, TX: University of Texas Press.

Barak, A. (1999). Psychological applications on the internet: A Discipline on the Threshold of a New Millennium. *Applied & Preventive Psychology, 8*, 231–245. doi:10.1016/S0962-1849(05)80038-1

Bargh, C., Bocock, J., Scott, P., & Smith, D. (2000). *University Leadership: The Role of the Chief Executive*. Buckingham, UK: SRHE/Open University Press.

Barnett, E. (2002). *The costs and benefits of remedial education*. Retrieved from http://occrl.ed.uiuc.edu/Publications/papers/Costs%20Remedial%20Education-%20EB1.pdf

Barr, R. B., & Tagg, J. (1995). From teaching to learning – a new paradigm for undergraduate education. *Change, 27*(6), 12–25.

Barrows, H. S. (1986). A taxonomy of problem-based learning methods. *Medical Education, 20*(1), 481–486. doi:10.1111/j.1365-2923.1986.tb01386.x

Barrows, H. S. (2003). *Problem-based learning applied to medical education*. New York: Springer.

Barthes, R. (1974). *S/Z. Miller, R. (Trans.)*. New York: Farrar, Straus & Giroux.

Barthes, R. (1968/1992). The death of the author . In Adams, H. (Ed.), *Critical theory since Plato* (*revised edition*, pp. 1130–1133). Fort Worth, TX: Harcourt Brace Jovanovich.

Barthes, R. (1971). From work to Text . In Barthes, R. (Ed.), *Image-music-text. Heath, S. (Trans.)*. New York: Noonday.

Bates, A. (2000). *Managing technological change: Strategies for college and university leaders*. San Francisco: Jossey-Bass.

Bates, T., & Poole, G. (2003). *Effective teaching with technology in higher education: Foundations for success* (1st ed.). San Francisco: Jossey-Bass.

Bates, A. W. (2000). *Managing technological change: Strategies for college and university leaders*. San Francisco: Jossey-Bass.

Batson, T. (2009a, December 2). *The Cloud Opens the Floodgates for Faculty Innovation*. Retrieved from http://campustechnology.com/articles/2009/12/02/the-cloud-opens-the-floodgates-for-faculty-innovation.aspx?sc_lang=en

Batson, T. (2009b, October 21). *But I Don't Want to Teach My Students How to Use Technology*. Retrieved from http://campustechnology.com/articles/2009/10/21/but-i-do-not-want-to-teach-my-students-how-to-use-technology.aspx?sc_lang=en

Bauer, J., & Kenton, J. (2005). Toward technology integration in the schools: Why it isn't happening. *Journal of Technology and Teacher Education, 13*(4), 519–546.

Bays, T., Carchidi, D., Carter-Galvan, S., Chambers, P., Fons, G., Gooding, I., et al. (2009). *Code of best practices in fair use for Opencourseware*. Created for the OCW Consortium. Retrieved January 5, 2010 from http://www.centerforsocialmedia.org/files/pdf/10-305-OCW-Oct29.pdf

Bean, J. P. (1998). Alternative models of professorial roles: New languages to reimagine faculty work. *The Journal of Higher Education, 69*(5), 496-512. Retrieved from JSTOR databases. URL: http://www.jstor.org/stable/2649107

Bechler, R. (2002, November 7). Stafford Beer: The man who could have run the world. *OpenDemocracy.net*. Retrieved from www.cybsoc.org/contacts/opendrunworld.pdf

BECTA. Tech News Report: 1-46, (2009). Retrieved September 30, 2009, from http://emergingtechnologies.becta.org.uk/upload-dir/downloads/page_documents/ research/technews/sept09.pdf

Beer, S. (1994). *Beyond Dispute: The Invention of Team Syntegrity* (1st ed.). San Francisco: Wiley.

Beer, S. (1995). *Designing Freedom* (1st ed.). San Francisco: Wiley.

Belanger, Y. (2005). *Duke University iPod first year experience final evaluation report*. Durham, NC: Duke University.

Bennet, S., Maton, K., & Kervin, L. (2008). The 'digital natives' debate: A critical review of the evidence. *British Journal of Educational Technology, 39*(5), 775–786. doi:10.1111/j.1467-8535.2007.00793.x

Berger, T. (2004). Computer-based technological applications in psychotherapy training. *Journal of Clinical Psychology, 60*(3), 301–315. doi:10.1002/jclp.10265

Bernard, R., & Goodyear, J. (2009). *Fundamentals of Clinical Supervision* (4th ed.). Boston: Allyn & Bacon.

Bernard, R. M., Abrami, P. C., Lou, Y., Borokhovski, E., Wade, A., & Wozney, L. (2004). How does distance education compare to classroom instruction? A meta-analysis of the empirical literature. *Review of Educational Research, 74*(3), 379–439. doi:10.3102/00346543074003379

Berry, B., Hopkins-Thompson, P., & Hoke, M. (2002). *Assessing and Supporting New Teachers: Lessons from the Southeast*. North Carolina: The Southeast Center for Teaching Quality at the University of North Carolina.

Beutler, L. E., & Harwood, T. M. (2004). Virtual reality in psychotherapy training. *Journal of Clinical Psychology, 60*(3), 317–330. doi:10.1002/jclp.10266

Bickmore, T., & Giorgino, T. (2006). Health Dialog Systems for Patients and Consumers. *Journal of Biomedical Informatics, 39*, 556–571. doi:10.1016/j.jbi.2005.12.004

Bickmore, T., Pfeifer, L., & Paasche-Orlow, M. (2007). Health Document Explanation by Virtual Agents. *Lecture Notes in Computer Science, 4722*, 183–196. doi:10.1007/978-3-540-74997-4_18

Biggs, J. (1999). What the student does: teaching for enhanced learning. *Higher Education Research & Development, 18*(1), 57–75. doi:10.1080/0729436990180105

Black, P., & William, D. (1998). Inside the black box. *Phi Delta Kappan, 80*, 139.

Blair, K. J. (2007). Telemedicine, urban style. *Distance Learning, 4*(3), 59–63.

Blaisdell, M. (2006). Academic MP3: Is it time yet? *Campus Technology*. Retrieved December 1st, 2009 from http://campustechnology.com/articles/2006/02/special-double-feature-academic-mp3s--is-it-itime-yet.aspx.

Blake, W. (1988). The marriage of heaven and hell . In Erdman, D. V. (Ed.), *The complete poetry and prose of William Blake* (pp. 32–44). New York: Doubleday. (Original work published 1793)

Blanchard, J. (2009). *The teacher exception under the work for hire doctrine: Safeguard of academic freedom or vehicle for academic free enterprise?*Dordrecht, Netherlands: Springer Netherlands.

Blascovich, J. (2000). Psychophysiological methods . In Reis, H. T., & Judd, C. M. (Eds.), *Handbook of research methods in social and personality psychology* (pp. 117–137). Cambridge, UK: Cambridge University Press.

Blimling, G. S. (2000, September). New technologies: Changing how we work with students. *About Campus*, 3–7.

Block, F., & Keller, M. (2008). *Where do innovations come from? Transformations in the U.S. national innovation system, 1970-2006*. The Information Technology & Innovation Foundation. July 2008. 22pp

Bloomberg, L. D. (2007). Culture and community: case study of a video-conferenced graduate distance education program. *Journal of Distance Education, 22*(1), 41–58.

Blumenfeld, P., Fishman, B. J., Krajcik, J., Marx, R. W., & Soloway, E. (2000). Creating usable innovations in systemic reform: Scaling up technology-embedded project-based science in urban schools. *Educational Psychologist, 35*(3), 149–164. doi:10.1207/S15326985EP3503_2

Blumenthal, T. D., Cuthbert, B. N., Filion, D. L., Hackley, S., Lipp, O. V., & van Boxtel, A. (2005). Committee report: Guidelines for human startle eyeblink electromyographic studies. *Psychophysiology, 42*, 1–15. doi:10.1111/j.1469-8986.2005.00271.x

Boettcher, J. (1999, August). The shift from a teaching to a learning paradigm. *Syllabus, 13*(1), 50–51.

Bok, D. (2003). *Universities in the marketplace: The commercialization of higher education*. Princeton, NJ: Princeton University Press.

Bok, D. (2006). *Our underachieving colleges: A candid look at how much students learn and why they should be learning more*. Princeton, NJ: Princeton University Press.

Bongey, S. B., Cizadlo, G., & Kalnbach, L. (2006). Explorations in course-casting: Podcasts in higher education. *Campus-Wide Information Systems, 23*(5), 350–367. doi:10.1108/10650740610714107

Bossu, C., Stein, S. J., Smyth, R., & Shanahan, P. (2006). *Internet-based videoconferencing for distance teaching and professional development.* Paper presented at the Improving University Teaching Conference, 2006, University of Otago, Dunedin, New Zealand. Available from Caladine, R. (2008a). *Enhancing E-Learning with Media-Rich Content and Interactions*. London: Information Science Publishing.

Boulos, M. N. K., & Wheeler, S. (2007). The emerging Web 2.0 social software: An enabling suite of sociable technologies in health and health care education. *Health Information and Libraries Journal, 24*(1), 2–23. doi:10.1111/j.1471-1842.2007.00701.x

Bourdieu, P. (1977). *Outline of a Theory of Practice*. New York: Cambridge University Press.

Bower, E. A., Girard, D. E., Wessel, K., Becker, T. M., & Choi, D. (2008). Barriers to innovation in continuing medical education. *The Journal of Continuing Education in the Health Professions, 28*(3), 148–156. doi:10.1002/chp.176

Boyer, E. (1990). *Scholarship reconsidered: Priorities of the professoriate*. New York: The Carnegie Foundation for the Advancement of Teaching. John Wiley & Sons.

Bradley, M. (2000). Emotion and motivation . In Cacioppo, J. T., Tassinary, L. G., & Berntson, G. (Eds.), *Handbook of Psychophysiology*. New York: Cambridge University Press.

Bransford, J. B., Brown, A. L., & Cocking, R. R. (Eds.). (1999). *How people learn: Brain, mind, experience, and school*. Washington, DC: National Academy Press.

Brew, L. S. (2008). The role of student feedback in evaluating and revising a blended learning course. *The Internet and Higher Education, 11*(2), 98–105. doi:10.1016/j.iheduc.2008.06.002

Brill, J., & Park, Y. (2008). Facilitating engaged learning in the interaction age: Taking a pedagogically–disciplined approach to innovation with emergent technologies. *International Journal of Teaching and Learning in Higher Education, 20*(1), 70-78. Retrieved April 1, 2010, from http://www.isetl.org/ijtlhe/pdf/IJTLHE474.pdf

Brooks-Young, S. (2009). *Making technology standards work for you: A guide to the NETS-A for school administrators with self-assessment activities* (2nd ed.). Eugene, OR: International Society for Technology in Education.

Brooten, D., & Youngblut, J. M. (2006). Nurse dose as a concept. *Journal of Nursing Scholarship, 38*(1), 94–99. doi:10.1111/j.1547-5069.2006.00083.x

Brown, J. S., Collins, A., & Duguid, P. (1989). Situated cognition and the culture of learning. *Educational Researcher, 18*(1), 32–42.

Brown, J. S., & Duguid, P. (2000). *The social life of information*. Boston: Harvard Business School Press.

Brown, J., & Metcalf, D. (2008). Mobile Learning Update. *Learning Consortium Perspectives.* Retrieved March 17, 2009 from http://www.masie.com.

Bryant, B. R., Bryant, D. P., & Rieth, H. J. (2002). The use of assistive technology in higher education . In Brinckerhoff, L. C., McGuire, J. M., & Shaw, S. T. (Eds.), *Postsecondary education and transition for students with learning disabilities*. Austin, TX: ProEd.

Bugeja, M. J. (2006). Facing the facebook. *The Chronicle of Higher Education, 52*(21), C1–C4.

Bugeja, M. J. (2009, November 9). Reduce the technology, rescue your job. *The Chronicle of Higher Education*. Retrieved from http://chronicle.com/article/Reduce-the-Technology-Resc/49078/

Buggey, T. J. (2000). Accommodating students with special needs in the online classroom. *New Directions for Teaching and Learning, 84*, 41–46. doi:10.1002/tl.846

Burgstahler, S. (2003). The role of technology in preparing youth with disabilities for postsecondary education and employment. *Journal of Special Education Technology, 18*(4), 7–19.

Burgstahler, S., & Cronheim, D. (2001). Supporting peer-peer and mentor-protégé relationships on the internet. *Journal of Research on Technology in Education, 34*(1), 59–74.

Burgstahler, S., & Moore, E. (2009). Making student services welcoming and accessible through accommodations and universal design. *Journal of Postsecondary Education and Disability, 21*(3), 155–174.

Burkman, E. (1987). Factors affecting utilization . In Gagne, R. M. (Ed.), *Instructional technology: foundations*. Hillsdale, NJ: Lawrence Erlbaum.

Bush, V. (1990) [1945]. *Science: The endless frontier*. Washington, DC: National Science Foundation California Administrative Code. 1982. Title 2, R 18705. Filed June 4, 1982.

Bywaters, P., McLeod, E., & Napier, L. (Eds.). (2009). *Social work and global health inequalities: Practice and policy developments*. Portland, OR: The Policy Press.

Caffarella, R. S., & Zinn, L. F. (1999). Professional development for faculty: A conceptual framework of barriers and supports. *Innovative Higher Education, 23*(4), 241–254. doi:10.1023/A:1022978806131

Caffrey, J. G. (1970). *Alternative Models for Higher Education*. Paper presented at the 25th national conference of the American Association for Higher Education, March 3, 1970. Chicago, Illinois.

Cain, J., Bird, E. R., & Jones, M. (2008). Mobile computing initiatives within pharmacy education. *American Journal of Pharmaceutical Education, 72*(4), 76–76.

Caladine, R. (2008b). *An Evaluation of the use of Peer to Peer Real Time Communications Applications within the Australian Academic and Research Community*. Wollongong, Australia: Australian Academic and Research Network (AARNet)

Cambridge, D., Kaplan, S., & Suter, V. (2005). *Community of practice design guide A step-by-step guide for designing & cultivating communities of practice in higher education*. Washington, DC: EDUCAUSE National Learning Infrastructure Initiative. Retrieved January 15, 2010 from http://net.educause.edu/ir/library/pdf/NLI0531.pdf

Campbell, G. (2005). There's something in the air: Podcasting in education. *EDUCAUSE Review, 40*(6), 32–47.

Campbell, J., & Mayer, R. E. (2009). Questioning as an instructional method: Does it affect learning from lectures? *Applied Cognitive Psychology, 23*, 747–759. doi:10.1002/acp.1513

Cangialosi, G., Irelan, R., Bourquin, T., & Vogele, C. (2008). *The business podcasting book*. Burlington, MA: Elsevier, Inc.

Carayannis, E. (2008). Knowledge-driven creative destruction or leveraging knowledge for a competitive advantage. *Industry and Higher Education, 22*(6), 343–353. doi:10.5367/000000008787225957

Carnochan, W. B. (1993). *The battleground of the curriculum: Liberal education and American experience*. Stanford, CA: Stanford University Press.

Carroll, D. (2008). Dorion Carroll: Technorati . In Jones, B. L. (Ed.), *Web 2.0 heroes: Interviews with 20 web 2.0 influencers* (pp. 55–78). Indianapolis: Wiley.

Caruso, J. B., Kvavik, R. B., & Nelson, M. R. (2005). *The ECAR Study of undergraduate Students and Information Technology, 2005: Convenience, connection control and learning.* (Research Study, Vol. 6. Boulder, CO: EDUCAUSE http://www.educause.edu/ecar (Retrieved December 2009).

Caspar, F. (2004). Technological developments and applications in clinical psychology and psychotherapy: Introduction. *Journal of Clinical Psychology, 60*(3), 221–238. doi:10.1002/jclp.10260

Caudill, J. G. (2007). The growth of m-Learning and the growth of mobile computing: Parallel developments. *International Review of Research in Open and Distance Learning, 8*(2).

Cebeci, Z., & Tekdal, M. (2006). Using podcasts as audio learning objects. *Interdisciplinary Journal of Knowledge and learning objects, 2*, 47-57.

Cegala, D. J., Marinelli, T., & Post, D. (2000). The effects of patient communication skills training on compliance. *Archives of Family Medicine, 9*, 57–64. doi:10.1001/archfami.9.1.57

Celsi, R. L., & Wolfinbarger, M. (2002). Discontinuous classroom innovation: Waves of change for marketing education. *Journal of Marketing Education, 24*(1), 64–72. doi:10.1177/0273475302241008

Center for Applied Special Technology (CAST). (2009). *Universal design for learning: New directions in higher education.* Retrieved from http://www.cost.org/pd/institute/june8.html

Chaiklin, S., & Lave, J. (1996). *Understanding Practice: Perspectives on Activity and Context.* New York: Cambridge University Press.

Chant, S., Jenkinson, T., Randle, J., Russell, G., & Webb, C. (2002). Communication skills training in healthcare: A review of the literature. *Nurse Education Today, 22*, 189–202. doi:10.1054/nedt.2001.0690

Checkland, P. (1985). Achieving 'Desirable and Feasible' Change: An Application of Soft Systems Methodology. *The Journal of the Operational Research Society, 36*(9), 821-831. Available online at: http://www.jstor.org/stable/2582171 [last accessed 07/04/10].

Chilvers, A. (2000). Critical issues in the use of Soft Systems Methodology: a case study in the long-term management of digital data objects. *Journal of Librarianship and Information Science, 32*(4), 167–177.

Chisholm, I. M., Carey, J., & Hernandez, A. (2002). Information technology skills for a pluralistic society: Is the playing field level? *Journal of Research on Technology in Education, 35*(1), 58–79.

Chism, N. (2004). Using a framework to engage faculty in instructional technologies. *EDUCAUSE Quarterly, 27*(2). Retrieved January 15, 2010 from http://www.educause.edu/EDUCAUSE+Quarterly/EDUCAUSEQuarterlyMagazineVolum/UsingaFrameworktoEngageFaculty/157291

Christensen, C. M., Horn, M. B., & Johnson, C. W. (2008). *Disrupting class: How disruptive innovation will change the way the world learns.* New York: McGraw-Hill.

Christensen, C. M. (1997). *The innovator's dilemma: When new technologies cause great firms to fail.* Boston: Harvard Business School Press.

Chuang, H. H., Thompson, A., & Schmidt, D. (2003). Faculty technology mentoring programs: Major trends in the literature. *Journal of Computing in Teacher Education, 19*(4), 101–106.

Chwelos, G., & Oatley, K. (1994). Appraisal, Computational Models, and Scherer's Expert System. *Cognition and Emotion, 8*, 245–257. doi:10.1080/02699939408408940

Clark, R. E. (1983). Reconsidering research on learning with media. *Review of Educational Research, 53*(4), 445–459.

Clark, R. E. (2001). *Learning from media: Arguments, analysis and evidence.* Greenwich, CT: Information Age Publishers.

Clark, R. E. (2009). Translating research into new instructional technologies for higher education: the active ingredient process. *Journal of Computing in Higher Education, 21*(1), 4–18. doi:10.1007/s12528-009-9013-8

Clark, K. (2009, August 19). Budget Cuts Take Toll on Education: Budget cuts have hit public colleges hard, even as the demand for a well-educated workforce soars. *U.S. News and World Report*. Retrieved from http://www.usnews.com/articles/education/best-colleges/2009/08/19/budget-cuts-take-toll-on-education.html?PageNr=2

Clingerman, T. L., & Bernard, J. M. (2004). An investigation of the use of e-mail as a supplemental modality for clinical supervision. *Counselor Education and Supervision, 44*, 82–96.

Cobcroft, R. S., Towers, S. J., Smith, J. E., & Bruns, A. (2006). *Mobile learning in review: Opportunities and challenges for learners, teachers, and institutions.* InOnline Learning and Teaching (OLT) Conference 2006, 26 September 2006, Queensland University of Technology, Brisbane, Australia

Colbert, R. (2005). New technologies for the education market smash barriers in distance learning. *Distance Learning, 2*(4), 7–8.

Cole, K., Simkins, M., & Penuel, W. R. (2002). Learning to teach with technology: Strategies for inservice professional development. *Journal of Technology and Teacher Education, 10*(3), 431–455.

Collins, S.Educause Evolving Technologies Committee. (2009). What technology? Reflections on evolving services. *EDUCAUSE Review, 44*(6), 60–76.

Cooper, J. (2006). The digital divide: The special case of gender. *Journal of Computer Assisted Learning, 22*, 320–334. doi:10.1111/j.1365-2729.2006.00185.x

Cooper, K. J. (2009). IT: Intellectually taxing? *Diverse Issues in Higher Education, 26*(3), 11–12.

Copyright Act, 17 U.S.C. § 101 *et seq*. (1976).

Copyright Clearance Center. (2009). *The TEACH Act: New roles and responsibilities for academic institutions*. Retrieved December 17, 2009 from http://www.copyright.com/media/pdfs/CR-Teach-Act.pdf

Cormier, D. (2008). Rhizomatic education: Community as curriculum. *Innovate* 4(5). Retrieved July 2, 2008, from http://innovateonline.info/pdf/vol4_issue5/Rhizomatic_Education-__Community_as_Curriculum.pdf

Cornford, J., & Pollock, N. (2003). *Putting the University Online: Information Technology and Organizational Change*. Buckingham, UK: The Society for Research into Higher Education.

Cosman, P. H., Cregan, P. C., & Martin, C. J., & Cartmill. (2002). Virtual reality simulators: current status in acquisition and assessment of surgical skills. *ANZ Journal of Surgery, 72*, 30–34. doi:10.1046/j.1445-2197.2002.02293.x

Cotton, S. R. (2008). Students' technology use and the impacts on well-being. *New Directions for Student Services, 124*, 55–70. doi:10.1002/ss.295

Council on Competitiveness. 1986. http://www.compete.org/. Washington, DC

Couros, A. (2006). *Examining the open movement: Possibilities and implications for education.* Unpublished doctoral dissertation, University ofRegina, Saskatchewan. Available from http://www.scribd.com/doc/3363/Dissertation-Couros-FINAL-06-WebVersion?autodown=pdf

Cox, D. E., & Harrison, D. W. (2008). Models of anger: contributions from psychophysiology, neuropsychology and the cognitive behavioral perspective. *Brain Structure & Function, 212*, 371–385. doi:10.1007/s00429-007-0168-7

Craig, J., & Patterson, V. (2005). Introduction to the practice of telemedicine. *Journal of Telemedicine and Telecare, 11*, 3–9. doi:10.1258/1357633053430494

Cramer, S. F. (2003). Challenging core assumptions: Integrating transformative leadership models into campus-wide implementation activities. *College and University Journal, 79*(1), 15–22.

Cramer, S. F. (2005). *Student Information Systems: A Guide to Implementation Success*. Washington, D.C.: American Association of College Registrars and Admissions Officers.

Cramer, S. F. (2006). Student information system implementations: A context for campus change. *College and University Journal*, *81*(2), 21–33.

Cramer, S. F., Tetewsky, S. J., & Marczynski, K. S. (2010). What facilitates and impedes collaborative work during higher education software implementation projects? *Journal of Educational Change*, *11*(4), 457–486. .doi:10.1007/s10833-010-9142-x

Creative Commons. (2010). *What is creative commons?* Retrieved January 10, 2010 from http://creativecommons.org/about/what-is-cc

Crews, K. (2002). *New copyright law for distance education: The meaning and importance of the TEACH Act*. Created for the American Library Association. Retrieved December 16, 2009 from http://www.ala.org/ala/issuesadvocacy/copyright/activelegislation/distanceed/teachsummary.pdf

Crews, K. (2009). *The TEACH Act and some frequently asked questions*. Created for the American Library Association. Retrieved December 17, 2009 from http://www.ala.org/ala/issuesadvocacy/copyright/activelegislation/distanceed/teachfaq.cfm

Criminal Infringement of a Copyright, 18 U.S.C.§ 2319 (2008).

Criminal Penalties for Copyright Infringement, Pub. L. No. 102-561, 106 Stat. 4233 (1992).

Critical Commons. (2010). *Critical Commons: Faculty members receive grant to promote digital fair use*. Retrieved April 30, 2010 from http://cinema.usc.edu/about/news/critical-commons.htm

Cuban, L. (2001). *Oversold and underused: Computers in the classroom*. Cambridge, MA: Harvard University Press.

Cuban, L. (2005). *So much high-tech money invested, so little used: How come?* Retrieved from http://www.edtechnot.com/notarticle1201.html.

Cucciare, M. A., Weingardt, K. R., & Villafranca, S. (2008). Using blended learning to implement evidence-based psychotherapies. *Clinical Psychology: Science and Practice*, *15*(4), 299–307. doi:10.1111/j.1468-2850.2008.00141.x

Culliton, B. (1984). Biomedical research enters the marketplace. *Hew Eng. J. Med.*, *304*, 1195. doi:10.1056/NEJM198105143042003

Dabbagh, N., & Reo, R. (2011). Back to the future: Tracing the roots and learning affordances of social software . In Lee, M. J. W., & McLoughlin, C. (Eds.), *Web 2.0-based e-Learning: Applying social informatics for tertiary teaching* (pp. 1–20). Hershey, PA: IGI Global.

Dale, C. (2007). Strategies for using podcasting to support student learning. *Journal of Hospitality, Leisure, Sport and Tourism Education*, *6*(1), 49–57. doi:10.3794/johlste.61.155

Davidson, C. N., & Goldberg, D. T. (2009). The future of learning institutions in a digital age. *The John D. and Catherine T. McArthur Foundation Reports on Digital Media and Learning*. Cambridge, MA: MIT Press. Retrieved November 13, 2009, from http://mitpress.mit.edu/books/full_pdfs/Future_of_Learning.pdf

Davidson-Shivers, G. V., & Rasmussen, K. L. (2006). *Web-based learning: Design, implementation, and evaluation*. Upper Saddle River, NJ: Pearson Merrill Prentice-Hall.

Davidson-Shivers, G. V. (2002). Instructional technology in higher education. In, R. A. Reiser. & J. V. Dempsey (Eds.) *Trends and issues in instructional design and technology.* (pp. 256-268). Upper Saddle River, NJ: Pearson/Merrill Prentice Hall.

Davies, J. L. (2001). The Emergence of Entrepreneurial Cultures in European Universities. *Journal of the Programme on Institutional Management in Higher Education*, *13*(2), 25–44.

Davis, B., Sumara, D., & Kapler, R. (2007). *Engaging minds: Changing teaching in complex times* (2nd ed.). Toronto, ON: Routledge.

Davis, U. C. (2007). *University of California, Davis Innovation Access: Connecting Research to Market*. http://innovationaccess.ucdavis.edu. Regents of the University of California, Davis, CA.

Dawley, L. (2007). *The tools for successful online teaching*. Hershey, PA: Information Science Publications.

Deazley, R. (2004). *On the origin of the right to copy: charting the movement of copyright law in eighteenth century Britain (1695-1775)*. Oxford, UK: Hart Publishing.

Dede, C. (2005). Planning for neomillenial learning styles: Implications for investments in technology and faculty. In D. G. Oblinger and J. L. Oblinger (eds), *Educating the net generation.*, (pp. 15.1–15.22). Retrieved April 1, 2010, from EDUCAUSE: http://net.educause.edu/ir/library/pdf/pub7101o.pdf

Dede, C. (2006). *Online professional development for teachers: Emerging models and methods (ed.)*. Cambridge, MA: Harvard Education Press.

Dede, C. (2007). Introduction: A sea change in thinking, knowing, learning, and teaching--The ECAR study of undergraduate students and information technology, 2007. *Educause Center for Applied Research Key Findings,* (September 2007). Retrieved from http://www.educause.edu/ir/library/pdf/ers0706/rs/ers07062.pdf

Deem, R. (2001). Globalisation, New Managerialism, Academic Capitalism and Entrepreneurialism in Universities: is the local dimension still important? *Comparative Education, 37*(1), 7–20. .doi:10.1080/03050060020020408

Deem, R., & Brehony, K. J. (2005). Management as ideology: the case of 'new managerialism' in higher education. *Oxford Review of Education, 31*(2), 217–235. .doi:10.1080/03054980500117827

DeGeorge, R. T. (1997). *Academic freedom and tenure: Ethical issues*. Oxford, UK: Rowman & Littlefield.

Descy, D. E. (2009). Netbooks: Small but powerful friends. *TechTrends, 53*(2).

Dewey, J. (1902). *The child and the curriculum*. Chicago: University of Chicago Press.

Dewey, J. (1916). *Democracy and education*. New York: Macmillan.

Dewey, J. (1933). *How we think, a restatement of the relation of reflective thinking to the educative process*. Boston: D.C. Heath and company.

DfES (Department for Education and Skills). (2003). 'Education and Skills: The Future of Higher Education', *UK Government White Paper*, Cabinet Office, Norwich, UK, pp. 1-23.

Diaz, V., Garrett, P. B., Kinley, E. R., Moore, J. F., Schwartz, C. M., & Kohrman, P. (2009). Faculty development for the 21st century. *EDUCAUSE Review, 44*(3), 46–55.

Dick, W., Carey, L., & Carey, J. O. (2009). *The systematic design of instruction* (7th ed.). Upper Saddle River, NJ: Pearson Education, Inc.

Diel, S. (2009, December 8). Recession puts squeeze on Alabama colleges. *The Mobile Press-Register,* p. C5.

Dieterle, E., Dede, C., & Schrier, K. (2007). Neomillennial learning styles propagated by wireless handheld devices . In Lytras, M., & Naeve, A. (Eds.), *Ubiquitous and pervasive knowledge and learning management: Semantics, social networking and new media to their full potential* (pp. 35–66). Hershey, PA: Idea Group, Inc.

Digital Millennium Copyright Act, Pub. L. No. 105-304, 112 Stat. 2860 (1998).

DIUS. (Department for Innovation, Universities and Skills) (2009). The Learning Revolution. *UK Government White Paper*, The Stationery Office, Norwich, UK, 4.

Dodge, B. (1995). WebQuests: a technique for internet-based learning. *Distance Education, 1*(2), 10–13.

Dodge, B. (2001). Focus: five rules for writing a great WebQuest. *Learning and Leading with Technology, 28*(8), 6–9, 58.

Dodge, B. J. (1995). WebQuests: A structure for active learning on the World Wide Web. *The Distance Educator,* 1(2).

Donahoe, S. S. (1995, February). *Using distance learning and telecommunications to develop strategies of communication for widely diverse populations.* Paper presented at the meeting of American Association of Colleges for Teacher Education, Washington. D.C.

Drasgow, F. Luecht, R. M., & Bennett, R. E. (2006). Technology and testing. In R. L. Brennan (Ed.), *Educational Measurement (4th* Ed., pp. 471-515). Westport, CT: Praeger.

Dron, J. (2007). *Control and constraint in e-learning: Choosing when to choose*. Hershey, PA: Idea Group.

Drucker, P. (1994). *The Post-Capitalist Society*. New York: Harper-Collins.

DSM, American Psychiatric Association. (2000). *Diagnostic and statistical manual of mental disorders* (*4th edn, text revision*). Washington, DC: American Psychiatric Press, Inc.

Ducut, E., & Fontelo, P. (2008). Mobile devices in health education: Current use and practice. *Journal of Computing in Higher Education*, *20*, 59–68. doi:10.1007/s12528-008-9003-2

Dvorak, J. (2005, July 18). Creative commons humbug. *PC Magazine,* Retrieved January 10, 2010 from http://www.pcmag.com/article2/0,2817,1838244,00.asp

Dwight, J., & Garrison, J. (2003). A manifesto for instructional technology: Hyperpedagogy. *Teachers College Record*, *105*(5), 699–728. doi:10.1111/1467-9620.00265

Earle, R. S. (2002). The integration of instructional technology into public education: Promises and Challenges. *Educational Technology*, *42*, 5–13.

Eckhardt, C. I., Norlander, B., & Deffenbacher, J. (2004). The assessment of anger and hostility: a critical review. *Aggression and Violent Behavior*, *9*, 17–43. doi:10.1016/S1359-1789(02)00116-7

Edelman, G. M. (2006). *Second Nature: Brain Science and Human Knowledge*. New Have, CT: Yale University Press.

Edelson, D. C. (2001). Design research: What we learn when we engage in design. *Journal of the Learning Sciences*, *22*(1), 105–121.

Educational Testing Services. (2006). *2006 ICT Literacy Assessment Preliminary Findings.* http://www.ets.org/Media/Products/ICT_Literacy/pdf/2006_Preliminary_Findings.pdf (Retrieved Jan 2010).

EDUCAUSE Learning Initiative (ELI). (2007). *The seven things you need to know about ....* Retrieved January 15, 2008, from http://www.educause.edu/7Things

EDUCAUSE Learning Initiative (2009). Retrieved from http://www.educause.edu/eli

Educause. (2009, November/December). Recommended resources for the top ten IT issues. *EDUCAUSE Review*, *44*(6).

Ellaway, R. (2007). eMedical Teacher. Beware of passive attitudes to e-teaching and e-learning and be more aware of the fundamental effects of technology (and its failure) on the psychological health of your organisation! *Medical Teacher*, *29*(5), 519–520. doi:10.1080/01421590701557059

Ellaway, R. (2008). eMedical Teacher. *Medical Teacher*, *30*(7), 734–735. doi:10.1080/01421590802356351

Ellsworth, J. B. (2000). *Surviving change: A survey of educational change models*. Syracuse, NY: ERIC Clearing House on Information & Technology (ED99CO0005)

Ellul, J. (1967). *The technological society*. New York: Knopf.

Ely, D. P. (1999). Conditions that facilitate the implementation of educational technology innovations. *Educational Technology*, *34*(6), 23–27.

Ely, D., & Plomp, T. (1996). *Classic writings on Instructional Technology*. Englewood, CO: Libraries Unlimited.

Ely, D. P., Foley, A., Freeman, W., & Scheel, N. (1995). Trends in educational technology . In Anglin, G. J. (Ed.), *Instructional Technology Past, Present and Future* (pp. 34–60). Englewood, CA: Libraries Unlimited, Inc.

Ensminger, D. C., Surry, D. W., Porter, B. E., & Wright, D. (2004). Factors Contributing to the Successful Implementation of Technology Innovations. *Journal of Educational Technology & Society*, *7*(3), 61–72.

Esque, T. (2005). *Making an Impact*. Atlanta, GA: CEP.

Euben, D. (2005). Legal watch: Electronic citizenship. *Academe*, *91*(2), 126. doi:10.2307/40253418

European Commission (1996). Living and Working in the Information Society: People First, Directorate-General for Employment and Social Affairs. *Brussels Green Paper, COM(96)*, 389.

Evans, C. (2008). The effectiveness of m-learning in the form of podcast revision lectures in higher education. *Computers & Education*, *50*, 491–498. doi:10.1016/j.compedu.2007.09.016

Evans, M., & Johri, A. (2008). Facilitating guided participation through mobile technologies: Designing creative learning environments for self and others. *Journal of Computing in Higher Education*, *20*, 92–105. doi:10.1007/s12528-008-9004-1

Evans, E., & Po, J. (2007). A break in the transaction: Examining students' responses to digital text. *Computers and Composition*, *24*, 56–73. doi:10.1016/j.compcom.2006.12.003

Fairclough, S. H. (2009). Fundamentals of physiological computing. *Interacting with Computers*, *21*, 133–145. doi:10.1016/j.intcom.2008.10.011

Falender, C. A., & Shafranske, E. P. (2004). *Clinical Supervision: A Competency-Based Approach*. Washington, D.C.: American Psychological Association. doi:10.1037/10806-000

Family Educational Rights and Privacy Act, 20 U.S.C. § 1232g (1974).

Family Educational Rights and Privacy Act, 20 U.S.C. § 1232g (2009 amended) Retrieved December 21, 2009 from http://ecfr.gpoaccess.gov/cgi/t/text/text-idx?c=ecfr;sid=6b7e313020dfabb7caa0216830b2a7d8;rgn=div5;view=text;node=34%3A1.1.1.1.34;idno=34;cc=ecfr

Farnsworth, K., & Bevis, T. B. (2006). *A fieldbook for community college online instructors*. Washington, DC: Community College Press.

Feiman-Nemser, S. (2001). From preparation to practice: Designing a continuum to strengthen and sustain teaching. *Teachers College Record*, *103*(6), 1013–1055. doi:10.1111/0161-4681.00141

Fell, A. (2004). Nothing ventured nothing gained. *UC Davis Magazine*, *21*, 3.

Fellous, J.-M., Armony, J. L., & LeDoux, J. E. (2003). *Emotional Circuits and Computational Neuroscience. The Handbook of Brain Theory and Neural Networks* (pp. 398–401). Cambridge, MA: The MIT Press.

Ferguson, K. (2009.) *Personal communication*. Director of University of South Alabama Technology and Research Park.

Ferrell, G. (2007). Enterprise approaches to information and learning technologies. *Perspective*, *11*(1), 12–17.

Fichten, C. S., Asuncion, J. V., Barile, M., Genereux, C., Fossey, M., & Judd, D. (2001). Technology integration for students with disabilities: Empirically based recommendations. *Educational Research and Evaluation*, *7*, 185–221. doi:10.1076/edre.7.2.185.3869

Finley, B. (2005). the AVCs of display. *Video systems*, *31* (8), 44.

Finn, D., Getzel, E., Asselin, S., & Reilly, V. (2008). Incorporating universal design applications across campus . In Burgstahler, S., & Cory, R. (Eds.), *Universal Design of Postsecondary Education: From Principle to Practice*. Boston: Harvard Education Press.

Firdyiwek, Y. (1999). Web-based courseware tools: Where is the pedagogy? *Educational Technology*, *39*(1), 29–34.

Fischer, K. (2009, May 7). East Carolina U. Uses Simple Technology to Link Its Students with Peers Overseas. *The Chronicle of Higher Education*. Retrieved from http://chronicle.com/article/East-Carolina-U-Uses-Simpl/44302

Fletcher, G. (2009, September). Disruptive innovation. *Campus Technology*, *23*(1), 6.

Foreman, J., & Gee, J. P. Herz., J. C., Hinrichs, R., & Prensky, M. (2004, September/October). Game-based learning: How to delight and instruct in the 21st Century. *EDUCAUSE Review, 39*(5), pp. 51–66. Retrieved from http://www.educause.edu/EDUCAUSE+Review/EDUCAUSEReviewMagazineVolume39/GameBasedLearningHowtoDelighta/157927

Foucault, M. (1977). *Discipline and punish: the birth of the prison* (1st ed.). New York: Pantheon Books.

Fowler, A., & Gilfillan, M. (2003). A framework of stakeholder integration of higher education information systems projects. *Technology Analysis and Strategic Management, 15*(4), 467–489. doi:10.1080/0953732030001360 51

Fox, J. (1984). Patents encroaching on research freedom. *Science, 224*, 1080. doi:10.1126/science.224.4653.1080

Fox, R., & Hermann, A. (2000). Changing Media, Changing Times: Coping with adopting new educational technologies . In Evans, T., & Nation, D. (Eds.), *Changing University Teaching: Reflections on Creating Educational Technologies*. London: Kogan Page.

Frand, J. L. (2000). The information –age mindset. Changes in students and implications for higher education. *EDUCASE Review, 35*(5), 15-24. http://net.educause.edu/ir/library/pdf/erm0051.pdf (Retrieved December 2009).

Frederiksen, J., & Collins, A. (1989). A systems approach to educational testing. *Educational Researcher, 18*(9), 27–32.

Friedman, T. L. (2005). *The world is flat: A brief history of the twenty-first century*. New York: Farrar, Straus and Giroux.

Fry, S. W. (2007). First-Year Teachers and Induction Support: Ups, downs, and in-betweens. *Qualitative Report, 12*(2), 216–237.

Fullan, M. (2007). *The NEW Meaning of Educational Change* (4th ed.). New York: Teachers' College Press.

Gagne, R. (1985). *The conditions of learning* (4th ed.). New York: Holt, Rinehart & Winston.

Gagné, R., Wager, W., Golas, K., & Keller, J. (2005). *Principles of instructional design* (5th ed.). Belmont, CA: Wadsworth/Thompson Learning.

Gainor, K., & Constantine, M. (2002). Multicultural group supervision: A comparison of in-person versus web-based formats. *Professional School Counseling, 6*(2), 104–111.

Gammon, D., Sørlie, T., Bergvik, S., & Høifødt, T. S. (1998). Psychotherapy supervision conducted via videoconferencing: A qualitative study of users experiences. *Nordic Journal of Psychiatry, 52*(5), 411–421. doi:10.1080/08039489850139445

Gano, D. L. (2003). *Apollo Root Cause Analysis*. Yakima, WA: Apollonian Publications.

Garet, M., Porter, A., Desimone, L., Briman, B., & Yoon, K. (2001). What makes professional development effective? Analysis of a national sample of teachers. *American Educational Research Journal, 38*(4), 915–945. doi:10.3102/00028312038004915

Garrett, L. (2000). *Betrayal of trust: The collapse of global public health*. New York: Hyperion.

Garrett, J. L., & Dudt, K. (1998). Using videoconferencing to supervise student-teachers. *Technology and Teacher Education Annual*, 1084-1088.

Garrison, D. R., & Akyol, Z. (2009). Role of instructional technology in the transformation of higher education. *Journal of Computing in Higher Education, 21*(1), 19–30. doi:10.1007/s12528-009-9014-7

Gartner (2007). *Strategic roadmap for your infrastructure — The Gartner infrastructure maturity model*. Retrieved December 1, 2009, from www.microsoft.no/portfolio/Produktivitetsdagen_2007/Gartner_keynote.ppt

Gartner Press Release. (2009). Retrieved December 1st, 2009 from http://www.gartner.com/it/page.jsp?id=1126812.

Gawande, A. (2009). *The checklist manifesto: How to get things right*. New York: Metropolitan Books.

Geoghegan, W. (1994b). Stuck at the barricades: Can information technology really enter the mainstream of teaching and learning? *AAHE Bulletin*, *47*(1), 13–16.

Geoghegan, W. H. (1994a, July 17-20). *Whatever happened to instructional technology?* (Reaching Mainstream Faculty). Paper presented at the 22nd Annual Conference of the International Business Schools Computing Association, Baltimore, MD.

Georgiev, T., Georgieva, E., & Smrikarov, A. (2004). *M-Learning: A new stage of E-Learning*. Paper presented at the International conference on computer systems and technologies.

Getzel, E. E., McManus, S., & Briel, L. (2001). *An effective model for college students with learning disabilities and attention deficit hyperactivity disorders*. Research to Practice, National Center on Secondary Education & Transition.

Gevins, A., Smith, M. E., Leong, H., McEvoy, L., Whitfield, S., & Du, R. (1998). Monitoring working memory load during computer-based tasks with eeg pattern recognition models. *Human Factors*, *40*, 79–91. doi:10.1518/001872098779480578

Gibbons, M. (1998). *Higher Education Relevance in the 21st Century*. World Bank.

Gibson, J. J. (1977). The theory of affordances . In Shaw, R., & Bransford, J. (Eds.), *Perceiving, acting, and knowing*. Hillsdale, N.J.: Erlbaum.

Gikas, J., Penrod, J., Robertson, J. S., & Schaeffer, S. (2005, January 14). *Final report: NLII community of practice project University of Memphis: Technology Fellows Teaching and Learning Collaboration*. Washington, DC: National Learning Infrastructure Initiative. Retrieved January 15, 2009 from https://umdrive.memphis.edu/g-tfp/www/NLIIFinalReportTFP.pdf?uniq=m5tb9g

Gilbert, S. W. (1994). If it takes 40 or 50 years, can we still call it a revolution? *The Educational Record*, *75*(3), 19–28.

Gilbert, T. F. (1996). *Human competence: Engineering worthy performance* (Tribute ed.). Silver Spring, MD: International Society for Performance Improvement.

Gillies, D. (2008). Student perspectives on videoconferencing in teacher education at a distance. *Distance Education*, *29*(1), 107–118. doi:10.1080/01587910802004878

Glazerman, S., Dolfin, S., Bleeker, M., Johnson, A., Isenberg, E., & Lugo-Gil, J. (2008). *Impacts of comprehensive teacher induction: Results from the first year of a randomized controlled study*. Washington, DC: U.S. Department of Education National Center for Education Evaluation and Regional Assistance.

Glenn, M. with D'Agostino (Ed.) & Johnson, L. (2009). *The Future of Higher Education: How Technology Will Shape Learning*. A Report from the Economist Intelligence Unit Sponsored by the New Media Consortium. Retrieved from http://www.nmc.org/pdf/Future-of-Higher-Ed-(NMC).pdf

Goldman, R. H., Cohen, A. P., & Sheahan, F. (2008). Using seminar blogs to enhance student participation and learning in public health school classes. *American Journal of Public Health*, *98*(9), 1658–1663. doi:10.2105/AJPH.2008.133694

Goldstein, P. J. (2006). Implementation never ends! The post-implementation organizational and operational implications of ERP. *New Directions for Higher Education*, *136*, 53–68. doi:10.1002/he.239

Goldstein, P. J. (2008). *Managing the Funding Gap: How Today's Economic Downturn Is Impacting IT Leaders and Their Organizations*. An EDUCAUSE

Goodyear, P., & Ellis, R. A. (2008). University Students' Approaches to Learning: Rethinking the Place of Technology. *Distance Education*, *29*(2), 141–152. doi:10.1080/01587910802154947

Gordon, S. P., & Maxey, S. (2000). *How to help beginning teachers succeed*. Alexandria, VA: Association for Supervision and Curriculum Development.

Government Accountability Office. (2009). *Higher education and disability. GAO-10-33*. Washington, DC: Author.

Grabe, M. (2005). Voluntary use of online lecture notes: correlates of note use and note use as an alternative to class attendance. *Computers & Education*, *44*, 409–421. doi:10.1016/j.compedu.2004.04.005

Grabinger, R. S., Alpin, C., & Ponnappa-Brenner, G. (2008). Supporting learners with cognitive impairments in online environments. *TechTrends*, *52*(1), 63–69. doi:10.1007/s11528-008-0114-4

Graf, N. M., & Stebnicki, M. A. (2002). Using E-mail for clinical supervision in practicum; A qualitative analysis. *Journal of Rehabilitation*, *68*(3), 41–49.

Granade, P. F., & Sanders, J. H. (1996). Implementing telemedicine nationwide: Analyzing the legal issues. *Defense Counsel Journal*, *63*, 67–73.

Grant, M. M. (2004). Learning to teach with the web: Factors influencing teacher education faculty. *The Internet and Higher Education*, *7*, 329–341. doi:10.1016/j.iheduc.2004.09.005

Grant, M. M., & Mims, C. (2009). Web 2.0 in teacher education: Characteristics, implications and limitations . In Kidd, T., & Chen, I. (Eds.), *Wired for learning: An educators guide to Web 2.0* (pp. 343–360). Charlotte, NC: Information Age Publishing.

Gratch, J., & Marsella, S. (2004). A domain independent framework for modeling emotion. *Journal of Cognitive Systems Research.*, *5*, 269–306. doi:10.1016/j.cogsys.2004.02.002

Gratch, J., & Rickel, J. (2002). Creating Interactive Virtual Humans: Some Assembly Required. *IEEE Intelligent Systems*, (July/August): 54–61. doi:10.1109/MIS.2002.1024753

Gray, J. T., Pacuilla, H. S., & Overton, C. (2009). *Learning and assistive technology: Thriving in a global marketplace*. Washington, DC: American Institutes for Research, National Center for Technology Innovation.

Gray, J. T., Silver-Pacuilla, H., & Saucer, M. (2008). *The power of social media to provide assistive and learning technologies*. Washington, DC: American Institutes for Research.

Green, K. (2002). *Campus computing 2002: The campus computing project*. Encino, CA: Author.

Green, K. C. (2007). Prodding the ERP Turtle. *EDUCAUSE Review*, *42*(6), 148–149.

Green, K. C. (2010). *The National Survey of Information Technology in US Higher Education*. The Campus Computing Project. Available at http://www.*campuscomputing.* net/summaries/2009.

Greenberg, A. (2008). The Distance Education and e-Learning Landscape.: *Vol. 2. Videoconferencing, Streaming and Capture Systems for Learning (Segment Report)*. Brookline, MA: Wainhouse Research November.

Greenberg, A. (2009). *The Leading Rich Media Project (Consultation Report)*. Brookline, MA: Funded by The Australian Learning and Teaching Council. Wainhouse Research. September.

Greenburg, D. (2007). *Science for sale: The perils, rewards, and delusions of campus capitalism*. Chicago: The University of Chicago Press.

Greenhow, C., Walker, J. D., & Kim, S. (2009-10). Millennial learners and net-savvy teens? Examining Internet use among low-income students. *Journal of Computing in Teacher Education*, *26*(2), 63–68.

Greiner, A. C., & Knebel, E. (2003). *Health professions education: A bridge to quality*. Washington, DC: National Academies Press.

Guerra-Lopez, I. (2008). *Performance Evaluation: Proven Approaches for Improving Program and Organizational Performance*. San Francisco: Jossey-Bass.

GUIRR. (1984). *The Government University Industry Research Roundtable*. The National Academies. http://sites.nationalacademies.org/pga/guirr/index.htm. Washington, DC.

Gupta, A. (2002). *Management of higher education*. New Delhi: Anmol Publications.

Guston, D., & Keniston, K. (1994). *The fragile contract: University science and the federal government*. Cambridge, MA: MIT Press.

H.R. Conf. Rep. No. 94-1733 (1976).

H.R. Rep. No. 94-1476 (1976).

Haab, M., & Surry, D. W. (2009). *Implementation of ERP systems in higher education: Relationship between modes of participation and satisfaction with implementation of enterprise resource planning systems in higher education*. Saarbrucken, Germany: VDM-Verlag.

Hagel, J., & Brown, J. (2005). *From push to pull – Emerging models for mobilizing resources*. Retrieved January 15, 2010, from http://www.johnhagel.com/paper_pushpull.pdf

Hall, G. E., & Hord, S. M. (2001). *Implementing Change: Patterns, Principles, and Potholes*. Boston: Allyn and Bacon.

Hall, G. E., & Hord, S. M. (1987). *Change in schools: Facilitating the process*. New York: SUNY Press.

Handy, C. (1993). *Understanding Organisations*. Harmondsworth, UK: Penguin.

Haney, D. P. (2007, February 2). Millennial, but not really different. *Chronicle of Higher Education, 53*(23), Special Section p. B14.

Hanna, D. E. (2003, July/August). Building a leadership vision: Eleven strategic challenges for higher education. *EDUCAUSE Review*, *38*(4), 25–34. Retrieved from http://net.educause.edu/ir/library/pdf/ERM0341.pdf.

Hara, N., & Kling, R. (2000). Student distress in a web-based distance education course. *Information Communication and Society*, *3*(4), 557–579. doi:10.1080/13691180010002297

Harmon, S. W., & Jones, M. G. (1999). The five levels of web use in education: Factors to consider in planning online courses. *Educational Technology*, *39*(6), 28–32.

Harper, G. (2001). *Copyright crash course*. Retrieved December 16, 2009 from The University of Texas System, Office of General Counsel Web site: http://www.utsystem.edu/OGC/IntellectualProperty/copypol2.htm

Harper, G. (2009). *Fair use of copyrighted materials*. Retrieved December 16, 2009 from The University of Texas System, Office of General Counsel Web site: http://www.utsystem.edu/OGC/IntellectualProperty/Cprtindx.htm

Harper, G. (2010). *The TEACH Act finally becomes law*. Retrieved January 6, 2010 from The University of Texas System, Office of General Counsel Web site: http://www.utsystem.edu/OGC/IntellectualProperty/teachact.htm

Harris, I. B., & Simpson, D. (2005). Christine McGuire: At the heart of the maverick measurement maven. *Advances in Health Sciences Education: Theory and Practice*, *10*(1), 65–80. doi:10.1007/s10459-005-2339-8

Hartman, J. L. (2008, November/December). Moving teaching and learning with technology from adoption to transformation. *EDUCAUSE Review*, *43*(6).

Harvey, V. S., & Carlson, J. F. (2003). Ethical and professional issues with computer-related technology. *School Psychology Review*, *32*, 92–104.

Harvey, D. (1996). *Justice, nature, and the geography of difference*. Cambridge, MA: Blackwell Publishers.

Harvey, D. (2000). *Spaces of Hope* (1st ed.). Berkeley, CA: University of California Press.

Harvey, D. (2005). *The New Imperialism*. Oxford, UK: Oxford University Press.

Harvey, D. (2006). *Spaces of Global Capitalism: A Theory of Uneven Geographical Development* (1st ed.). London: Verso.

Harvey, D. (2007). *A Brief History of Neoliberalism*. Oxford, UK: Oxford University Press.

Harvey, D. (2008). The Right to the City. *New Left Review*, *53*, Retrieved from http://www.newleftreview.org/?view=2740.

Harvey, D. (2009). *Cosmopolitanism and the Geographies of Freedom*. New York: Columbia University Press.

Hattie, J. A. C. (2009). *Visible learning: A synthesis of over 800 meta-analyses related to achievement*. New York: Routledge.

Hawking, P., McCarthy, B., & Stein, A. (2004). Second wave ERP education. *Journal of Information Systems Education*, *15*(3), 327–332.

Hawkins, B. L. (2007). Winds of change: Charting the course for IT in the twenty-first century. *EDUCAUSE Review*, *42*(6), 54, 56–70.

Hazari, S., North, A., & Moreland, D. (2009). Investigating pedagogical value of wiki technology. *Journal of Information Systems Education*, *20*(2), 187–198.

Hedestig, U., & Kaptelinin, V. (2005). Facilitator's roles in a videoconferencing learning environment. *Information Systems Frontiers*, *7*(1), 71–83. doi:10.1007/s10796-005-5339-6

Heidegger, M. (1982). The question concerning technology . In *The Question Concerning Technology, and Other Essays*. New York: Harper Perennial.

Heidegger, M. (2003). The question concerning technology. In R. C. Scharff & V, Dusek (Eds.). *Philosophy of technology: The technological condition: An anthology* (pp. 252-264). Malden, MA: Blackwell.

Heifetz, R. A., & Laurie, D. L. (1997). *The Work of Leadership*. Boston: Harvard Business Review. [reprint 2001 R0111K]

Heinrichs, W. L., Youngblood, P., Harter, M., & Dev, P. (2008). Simulation for team training and assessment: Case studies of online training with virtual worlds. *World Journal of Surgery*, *32*(2), 161–170. doi:10.1007/s00268-007-9354-2

Hellewell, J. F. (2002). *Globalization and well-being*. Vancouver: UBC Press.

Henkel, M. (2000). *Academic Identities and Policy Change in Higher Education*. London: Jessica Kingsley Publishers Ltd.

Henriksen J., & Soule, A. (1998). Sources and information: Identifying and implementing technologies for higher education. *New Directions for Community Colleges, 101 (spring),* 91-98.

Hernandez-Ramos, P. (2007). Aim, shoot, ready! Future teachers learn to 'do' video. *British Journal of Educational Technology*, *38*(1), 33–41. doi:10.1111/j.1467-8535.2006.00600.x

Herring, R. (1987, March). *Looking at interaction*. Paper presented at the Annual Meeting of the National Society for Performance and Instruction, San Antonio, TX.

Herrington, J., Reeves, T. C., & Oliver, R. (2010). *A guide to authentic e-learning*. New York: Routledge.

Hersch, R. H., & Merrow, J. (2005). *Declining by degrees. Higher education at risk*. New York: Palgrave Macmillan.

Herszenhorn, D. M. (2006). As test-taking grows, test makers grow rarer. *New York Times*, May 5, 2006. Retrieved online February 15, 2010 from http://www.nytimes.com/2006/05/05/education/05testers.html?_r=1

Higbee, J. L., & Goff, E. (Eds.). (2008). *Pedagogy and student services for institutional transformation: Implementing universal design in higher education*. University of Minnesota, Center for Research on Developmental Education and Urban Literacy.

Higbee, J. L., Bruch, P. L., & Siaka, K. Disability and diversity: Results from the multicultural awareness project for institutional transformation. In Higbee, J.L. & Goff, E. (Eds.) (2008). *Pedagogy and student services for institutional transformation: Implementing universal design in higher education*. University of Minnesota, Center for Research on Developmental Education and Urban Literacy.

Higher Education Opportunity Act. 20 U.S.C § 1001 et seq.(a)23.

Hilton, J. (2006). The future for higher education: Sunrise or perfect storm? *EDUCAUSE Review*, (March/April): 59–71.

Hilton, J. (2009). Essential versus strategic IT investments. *EDUCAUSE Review*, (July/August): 8–9.

Hilton, J. (2006, March/April). The future for higher education: Sunrise or perfect storm? *EDUCAUSE Review*, *41*(2), 58–71. Retrieved from http://www.educause.edu/EDUCAUSE+Review/EDUCAUSEReviewMagazineVolume41/TheFutureforHigherEducationSun/158046.

Hilty, D. M., Alverson, D. C., Alpert, J. E., Lowell, T., Sagduyu, K., & Boland, R. J. (2006). Virtual reality, telemedicine, web and data processing innovations in medical and psychiatric education and clinical care. *Academic Psychiatry*, *30*(6), 528–533. doi:10.1176/appi.ap.30.6.528

Hilty, D. M., Luo, J. S., Morache, C., Marcelo, D. A., & Nesbitt, T. S. (2002). Telepsychiatry: An overview for psychiatrists. *CNS Drugs*, *16*(8), 527–548. doi:10.2165/00023210-200216080-00003

Hirschbuhl, J. J., & Faseyitan, S. O. (1994). Faculty uses of computers: Fears, facts and perceptions. *T.H.E. Journal*, *21*(9), 64.

Hogan, R. L., & McKnight, M. A. (2007). Exploring burnout among university online instructors: An initial investigation. *The Internet and Higher Education*, *10*(2), 117–124. doi:10.1016/j.iheduc.2007.03.001

Hogan, J., & Fox, B. (2005, April 7). Sony patent takes first step towards real-life Matrix. *NewScientist*, (2494). Retrieved from http://www.newscientist.com/article/mg18624944.600.

Holtzman, E. (1984). Competition and the marketplace: The need for balance. *Bioscience*, *34*, 349.

Holtzman, D., & Dagavarian, D. (2007). The use of electronic portfolios in assessing student learning outcomes. *Journal of Continuing Higher Education*, *55*(1), 65–69.

Holzinger, A., Nischelwitzer, A., & Meisenberger, M. (2005). Mobile phones as a challenge for m-learning: Examples for mobile interactive learning objects (milos). *Pervasive Computing and Communications Workshops, IEEE International Conference*, 307-311.

Hooper, S., & Rieber, L. P. (1995). Teaching with technology . In Ornstein, A. (Ed.), *Teaching: theory into practice* (pp. 154–170). Needham Heights, MA: Allyn and Bacon.

Hopper, K. B. (1999). Mastering the invisible technologies in education: Who are the real technology prodigies among college teachers? *Educational Technology*, *39*(1), 50–56.

Hopper, K. B. (2000). Are online distance learners learning or just distant? [letter]. *Respiratory Care*, *45*(4), 432–434.

Hopper, K. B. (2004). Education, teleconferencing, and distance learning in respiratory care. *Respiratory Care*, *49*(4), 410–420.

Hopper, K. B., & Hendricks, R. (2008). Technology integration in the college classroom—A baker's dozen frugal but promising strategies. *Educational Technology*, *48*(5), 10–17.

Hopper, K. B., & Johns, C. L. (2007). Educational technology and distance learning in respiratory care: Attitudes and practices. *Respiratory Care*, *52*(11), 1510–1524.

Hord, S. M., Rutherford, W. L., Huling-Austin, L. L., & Hall, G. E. (1987). *Taking charge of change*. Austin, TX: Southwest Educational Development Laboratory.

Horn, L., & Berktold, J. (1999). *Students with disabilities in postsecondary education: A profile of preparation, participation, and outcomes (Report No. NCES 1999-187)*. Washington, DC: United States Department of Education, National Center for Education Statistics.

Howe, N., & Strauss, W. (2000). *Millennials rising: The next great generation by Neil Howe and Bill Strauss; cartoons by R.J. Matson*. New York: Vintage Books.

Howe, J. (2006). The rise of crowdsourcing. *Wired Magazine 14*(6). Retrieved from http://www.wired.com/wired/archive/14.06/crowds_pr.html.

Howland, J., & Wedman, J. (2004). A process model for faculty development: Individualizing technology learning. *Journal of Technology and Teacher Education*, *12*(2), 239–263.

Hron, A., Cress, U., Hammer, K., & Friedrich, H. F. (2007). Fostering collaborative knowledge construction in a video-based learning setting: effects of a shared workspace and a content-specific graphical representation. *British Journal of Educational Technology*, *38*(2), 236–248. doi:10.1111/j.1467-8535.2006.00619.x

Hubbard, G., Lucas, L., Holmes, K., & Hons, P. (1998). Planning the technology infrastructure: General requirements. In *Designing the technology infrastructure for schools*, (2nd. Ed.). (pp. 15-26). Denton, TX: Texas Center for Educational Technology. (Available at http://www.tcet.unt.edu/pubs/telecomm.htm)

Hulsman, R. L., Gos, W. J. G., Winnubst, J. A. M., & Bensing, J. M. (1999). Teaching clinically experienced physicians communication skills: A review of evaluation studies. *Medical Education*, *33*, 655–668. doi:10.1046/j.1365-2923.1999.00519.x

Illich, I. (1971). *Deschooling society* (1st ed.). New York: Harper & Row.

Illich, I. (1977). *Disabling professions*. London: M. Boyars.

Illich, I. (2001). *Tools for Conviviality*. London: Marion Boyars.

Individuals with Disabilities Education Improvement Act of 2004, U.S.C. § 300 *et seq.*

Ingersoll, R. M., & Smith, T. M. (2004). Do teacher induction and mentoring matter? *NASSP Bulletin*, *88*(638), 28–40. doi:10.1177/019263650408863803

Ingold, T. (2000). *The perception of the environment essays on livelihood, dwelling & skill*. London: Routledge. doi:10.4324/9780203466025

Ingold, T. (2004). *Learning though doing and understanding in practice*. Retrieved January 29, 2010, from http://www.c-sap.bham.ac.uk/resources/project_reports/findings/ShowFinding.asp?id=113

Institute of Education Sciences Institute of Medicine. (2010). *Redesigning continuing education in the health professions*. Preproduction Copy, Available from http://www.iom.edu/Reports/2009/Redesigning-Continuing-Education-in-the-Health-Professions.aspx.

Issenberg, S. B., McGaghie, W. C., Gordon, D. L., Symes, S., Petrusa, E. R., & Hart, I. R. (2002). Effectiveness of a cardiology review course for internal medicine residents using simulation technology and deliberate practice. *Teaching and Learning in Medicine*, *14*(4), 223–228. doi:10.1207/S15328015TLM1404_4

Izard, C. E. (1993). Organizational and motivational functions of discrete emotions . In Lewis, M., & Haviland, J. M. (Eds.), *Handbook of emotions*. New York: Guilford Press.

Jackson, J. L., Chamberlin, J., & Kroenke, K. (2001). Predictors of patient satisfaction. *Social Science & Medicine*, *52*, 609–620. doi:10.1016/S0277-9536(00)00164-7

Jameson, J., Davies, S., & de Freitas, S. (2006). Collaborative Innovation: Joint Information Systems Committee Distributed E-learning Program. *British Journal of Educational Technology*, *37*(6), 969–972. doi:10.1111/j.1467-8535.2006.00664.x

Jameson, J., Ferrell, G., Kelly, J., Walker, S., & Ryan, M. (2006). Building Trust and Shared Knowledge in Communities of E-learning Practice: Collaborative Leadership in the JISC eLISA and CAMEL Lifelong Learning Projects. *British Journal of Educational Technology*, *37*(6), 949–968. doi:10.1111/j.1467-8535.2006.00669.x

Janoff, D. S., & Schoenholtz-Read, J. (1999). Group supervision meets technology: A model for computer-mediated group training at a distance. *International Journal of Group Psychotherapy*, *49*(2), 255–272.

Jessmer, S. L., & Anderson, D. (2001). The effect of politeness and grammar on user perceptions of electronic mail. *North American Journal of Psychology*, *3*(2), 331–346.

Johnson, L., Levine, A., Smith, R., & Stone, S. (2010). *The 2010 Horizon Report*. Austin, TX: The New Media Consortium.

Johnson, L., Levine, A., Smith, R., Smythe, T., & Stone, S. (2009). *The Horizon Report: 2009 Australia–New Zealand Edition*. Austin, TX: The New Media Consortium.

Johnson-Laird, P. (2009). *How we reason*. New York: Oxford University Press.

Jonassen, D. H. (2009). Reconciling a human cognitive architecture . In Tobias, S., & Duffy, T. M. (Eds.), *Constructivist theory applied to instruction: Success or failure?* New York: Routledge.

Jones, B. L. (2008). *Web 2.0 heroes: Interviews with 20 Web 2.0 influencers*. Indianapolis, IN: Wiley.

Jones, M. G., & Harmon, S. W. (2009). Instructional strategies for teaching in synchronous online learning environments (SOLE) . In Yang, H., & Yuen, S. (Eds.), *Collective intelligence and E-Learning 2.0: Implications of web-based communities and networking* (pp. 78–93). Hershey, PA: IGI Publishing.

Jones, M. G. & Harmon, S. W. (2002). What professors need to know about technology to assess online student learning. *New Directions for Teaching and Learning.* Fall (91). (pp. 19-30).

Jones, M. G., & Harmon, S. W. (2006). Intentional instructional strategies for mobile learning environments. In Isaias, P., Kommers, P., & Sanchez, I. A., (Eds.). *Proceedings of the IADIS international conference mobile learning.* (Pp. 222-226) IADIS Press.

Jones, M. G., & Harmon, S. W. (2006). Ancillary communication as an intentional instructional strategy in online learning environments. In M. Simonson, & M. Crawford (Eds.). *Proceedings of the 2006 international conference of the Association of Educational Communications and Technology, (2).* (pp 194-199).

Joo, J. E. (1999). Cultural issues of the internet in classrooms. *British Journal of Educational Technology, 30*(3), 245–250. doi:10.1111/1467-8535.00113

Junco, R., & Mastrodicasa, J. (2007). *Connecting to the net generation.* Washington, DC: National Association of Student Personnel Administrators.

Kaminski, K., Seel, P., & Cullen, K. (2003). Technology literate students? *EDUCAUSE Quarterly*, (3): 35–40.

Kanuka, H., & Garrison, D. R. (2004). Cognitive Presence in Online Learning. *Journal of Computing in Higher Education, 15*(2), 21–39. doi:10.1007/BF02940928

Kanz, J. E. (2001). Clinical-supervision.com: Issues in the provision of online supervision. *Professional Psychology, Research and Practice, 32*(4), 415–420. doi:10.1037/0735-7028.32.4.415

Kaplin, W. A., & Lee, B. A. (2006). *The law of higher education: A comprehensive guide to legal implications of administrative decision making* (4th ed.). San Francisco: Jossey-Bass.

Kaplin, W. A., & Lee, B. A. (2009). *A legal guide for student affairs professionals* (2nd ed.). San Francisco: Jossey-Bass.

Kapoor, A., Shenoy, P., & Tan, D. S. (*2008*). Combining brain computer interfaces with vision for object categorization. *IEEE CVPR.* Retrieved from http://research.microsoft.com/pubs/64264/cvpr2008-bciandvision.pdf.

Katz, I. R. (2007). ETS research finds college students fall short in demonstrating ICT literacy: National Policy Council to create national standards. *C&RL News, 68*(1). http://www.hawaii.edu/lilo/fall09/content/reports/ALA%20_%20ETS%20research.pdf (Retrieved January 2010).

Katz, R. (2008). The gathering cloud: Is this the end of the middle? In R. Katz (Ed.), *The tower and the cloud: Higher education in the age of cloud computing (pp. 2-42).* Available from EDUCAUSE: http://educause.edu/books

Katz, R. (2008). *The tower and the cloud: Higher education in the age of cloud computing* (Ed.). Available from EDUCAUSE: http://educause.edu/books

Katz, R., Goldstein, P., & Yanosky, R. (2009). Demystifying cloud computing for higher education. *EDUCAUSE Center for Applied Research (ECAR).* Available from http://www.educause.edu/ecar

Kay, A. C. (1989). Predicting the future. *Stanford Engineering, 1(1), Autumn, pg 1-6.* Retrieved from http://www.ecotopia.com/webpress/futures.htm.

Keegan, D. (2005). *The incorporation of mobile learning into mainstream education and training.* Mobile Technology: The future of learning in your hands, Cape Town, 65-70.

Keegan, D., Lõssenko, J., Mázár, I., Michels, P. F., Paulsen, M. F., Rekkedal, T., et al. (2007). *E-learning initiatives that did not reach targeted goals* (No. 3). Bekkestua, Norway: Megatrends Project 2007. N. P. House. Retrieved from http://www.nettskolen.com/in_english/megatrends/Book3.pdf

Keengwe, J., Onchwari, G., & Wachira, P. (2008). Computer technology integration and student learning: Barriers and promise. *Journal of Science Education and Technology, 17*(6), 560–565. doi:10.1007/s10956-008-9123-5

Keller, J. M. (2008). First Principles of Motivation to Learn and e[superscript 3]-Learning. *Distance Education, 29*(2), 175–185. doi:10.1080/01587910802154970

Kelley, L. M. (2004). Why induction matters. *Journal of Teacher Education, 55*(5), 438–448. doi:10.1177/0022487104269653

Kennedy, G. E., Judd, T. S., Churhward, A., & Gray, K. (2008). First year students' experiences with technology: Are they really digital natives? Australasian . *Journal of Educational Technology, 24*(1), 108–122.

Kenny, P., Parsons, T. D., Gratch, J., Leuski, A., & Rizzo, A. A. (2007). Virtual Patients for Clinical Therapist Skills Training. *Lecture Notes in Artificial Intelligence, 4722*, 197–210.

Kenny, P., Parsons, T. D., Gratch, J., & Rizzo, A. A. (2008b). Evaluation of Justina: A Virtual Patient with PTSD. *Lecture Notes in Artificial Intelligence, 5208*, 394–408.

Kenny, P., Parsons, T. D., Pataki, C. S., Pato, M., St-George, C., Sugar, J., & Rizzo, A. A. (2008a). Virtual Justina: A PTSD Virtual Patient for Clinical Classroom Training. *Annual Review of Cybertherapy and Telemedicine, 6*, 113–118.

Kenny, P., Parsons, T. D., & Rizzo, A. A. (2009). Human Computer Interaction in Virtual Standardized Patient Systems. *Lecture Notes in Computer Science, 5613*, 514–523. doi:10.1007/978-3-642-02583-9_56

Kenny, P., Rizzo, A. A., Parsons, T. D., Gratch, J., & Swartout, W. (2007). A Virtual Human Agent for Training Novice Therapist Clinical Interviewing Skills. *Annual Review of Cybertherapy and Telemedicine, 5*, 81–89.

Kernaghan, S. G. (1978). Clinical Simulation: The profession's new tool for registry evaluation. *Respiratory Care, 23*(6), 570–576.

Kidd, R. S., & Stamatakis, M. K. (2006). Comparison of students' performance in and satisfaction with a clinical pharmacokinetics course delivered live and by interactive videoconferencing. *American Journal of Pharmaceutical Education, 70*(1), 1–6.

Kim, J. (2009). Capturing lectures: No brainer or sticky wicket? *EDUCAUSE Center for Applied Research (ECAR)*. Available from http://www.educause.edu/ecar

King, N., & Anderson, N. (2002). *Managing Innovation and Change: A Critical Guide for Organizations* (2nd ed.). London: Thomson.

Kinnear, H., McWilliams, S., & Caul, L. (2002). The use of interactive video in teaching teachers: an evaluation of a link with a primary school. *British Journal of Educational Technology, 33*(1), 17–26. doi:10.1111/1467-8535.00235

Kirkpatrick, D. L. (2006). Seven keys to unlock the four levels of evaluation. *Performance Improvement, 45*(7), 5–8. doi:10.1002/pfi.2006.4930450702

Kirkpatrick, D. L., & Kirkpatrick, J. D. (2006). *Evaluating training programs: The four levels* (3rd ed.). San Francisco: Berrett-Koehler.

Klein, N. (2008). *The shock doctrine: the rise of disaster capitalism* (1st ed.). New York: Picador.

Klein, K. J., & Sorra, J. S. (1996). The challenge of innovation implementation. *Academy of Management Review, 21*(4), 1055–1080. doi:10.2307/259164

Kline, S. J. (2003). What is technology. In R. C. Scharff & V, Dusek (Eds.). *Philosophy of technology: The technological condition: An anthology* (pp. 210-212). Malden, MA: Blackwell.

Kling, R. (1992). Behind the terminal: the critical role of computing infrastructure in effective information systems development and use . In Cotterman, W. W., & Senn, J. A. (Eds.), *Challenges and strategies for research in systems development* (pp. 365–413). New York, NY: John Wiley & Sons.

Klopfer, E., Squire, K., & Jenkin, H. (2008). Environmental Detectives – The development of an Augmented Reality Platform for Environmental Simulations. *Educational Research Technology and Development, 56*(2), 1042–1629.

Knipe, D., & Lee, M. (2002). The quality of teaching and learning via videoconferencing. *British Journal of Educational Technology*, *33*(3), 301–311. doi:10.1111/1467-8535.00265

Koehler, M. J., Mishra, P., Hershey, K., & Peruski, L. (2004). With a little help from your students: A new model for faculty development and online course design. *Journal of Technology and Teacher Education*, *12*(1), 25–55.

Kolowich, S. (2009, December 7). Learning from online. *Inside Higher Education*. Retrieved from http://www.insidehighered.com/news/2009/12/07/online/

Kowch, E. (2009). New capabilities for cyber charter school leadership: An Emerging imperative for integrating Educational Technology and Educational Leadership knowledge. *TechTrends*, *4*(5), 41–48.

Kowch, E. G. (2005). Do we plan the journey or read the compass? An argument for preparing educational technologists to lead organizational change. *British Journal of Educational Technology*, *36*(6), 1067–1070. doi:10.1111/j.1467-8535.2005.00577.x

Kowch, E. (2003). *Policy networks and communities in three western Canada universities: Neo-institutional responses to a pan-institutional issue*. Unpublished doctoral dissertation, Department of Educational Administration, University of Saskatchewan.

Kozeracki, C. (1998). Managing organizational change in the community college. *ERIC Digest*. (ERIC Reproduction Service No. ED424-884). http://www.ed.gov/databases/ERIC_Digests/ed424884.html

Kozma, R. (1991). Learning with media. *Review of Educational Research*, *61*(2), 179–211.

Kronen, E. (2003). The website as a catalyst for change: Developing and implementing a content management system at Southern Cross University. CAUDIT *Australasian Information Technology Award*, 1-6.

Kuh, G. D. (2003). What we're learning about student engagement from NSSE. *Change*, *35*(2), 24–32. doi:10.1080/00091380309604090

Kuh, G. D., Kinzie, J., Schuh, J. H., & Whitt, E. J. (2005). *Student success in college: Creating conditions that matter*. New York: Jossey-Bass.

Kukulska-Hulme, A. (2005). Introduction . In Kukulska-Hulme, A., & Traxler, J. (Eds.), *Mobile learning: A handbook for educators and trainers* (pp. 1–6). London: Routledge.

Kurzweil, R. (2005). *The singularity is near: When humans transcend biology*. New York: Penguin Group.

Kynaslahti, H. (2003). In search of elements of mobility in the context of education . In Kynaslahti, H., & Seppala, P. (Eds.), *Mobile Learning* (pp. 41–48). IT Press, Helinski.

Ladany, N., Friedlander, M. L., & Nelson, M. L. (2005). *Critical Events in Psychotherapy Supervision: An Interpersonal Approach*. Washington, DC: American Psychological Association. doi:10.1037/10958-000

Laine, T. I., Bauer, K. W., Lanning, J. W., Russell, C. A., & Wilson, G. F. (2002). Selection of input features across subjects for classifying crewmember workload using artificial neural networks. *IEEE Transactions on Systems, Man, and Cybernetics. Part A, Systems and Humans*, *32*, 691–704. doi:10.1109/TSMCA.2002.807036

Laird, T. F., & Kuh, G. D. (2005). Student experiences with information technology and their relationship to other aspects of student engagement. *Research in Higher Education*, *46*(2), 211–233. doi:10.1007/s11162-004-1600-y

Lambie, G. W., Sias, S. M. (2009). An integrative psychological development model of supervision for professional school counselors-in-training. *Journal of Counseling & Development, Summer*, (87), 349-356.

Lan, J. (2001). Web-based instruction for education faculty: A needs assessment. *Journal of Research on Computing in Education.*, *33*(4), 385–399.

Landow, G. P. (1997). *Hypertext 2.0*. Baltimore, MD: Johns Hopkins University Press.

Lane, S., & Stone, C. A. (2006). Performance assessment . In Brennan, R. L. (Ed.), *Educational Measurement* (4th ed., pp. 387–431). Westport, CT: Praeger.

Lane, C. (2006). *Podcasting at the UW: An evaluation of current use*. Retrieved December 1st from http://www.washington.edu/lst/research_development/papers/2006/podcasting_report.pdf.

Lang, P. J. (1995). The emotion probe: Studies of motivation and attention. *The American Psychologist, 50*, 372–385. doi:10.1037/0003-066X.50.5.372

Lang, P. J., Bradley, M. M., & Cuthbert, B. N. (2005). *The International Affective Picture System (IAPS)*. University of Florida.

Lang, J. M. (2009, September 17). Teaching resolutions for the new year. *The Chronicle of Higher Education*. Retrieved from http://chronicle.com/article/Teaching-Resolutions-for-th/48379/

Larimer, P., & Strowbridge, B. W. (2009, December 27). Representing information in cell assemblies: persistent activity mediated by semilunar granule cells. *Nature Neuroscience*. Retrieved from http://www.nature.com/neuro/journal/vaop/ncurrent/abs/nn.2458.html.

Laughlin, G. K. (2000). Who owns the copyright to faculty-created web sites?: The work-for-hire doctrine's applicability to internet resources created for distance learning and traditional classroom courses. *Boston College Law Review. Boston College. Law School, 41*, 549–583.

Lave, J. (1988). *Cognition in Practice: Mind, Mathematics and Culture in Everyday Life*. New York: Cambridge University Press. doi:10.1017/CBO9780511609268

Lave, J., & Wenger, E. (1991). *Situated Learning: Legitimate Peripheral Participation* (1st ed.). New York: Cambridge University Press.

Lawless, K. A., & Pellegrino, J. W. (2007). Professional development in integrating technology into teaching and learning: Knowns, unknowns, and ways to pursue better questions and answers. *Review of Educational Research, 77*(4), 575–614. doi:10.3102/0034654307309921

Layne, C. M., & Hohenshil, T. H. (2005). High tech counseling: Revisited. *Journal of Counseling and Development, 83*(2), 222–226.

Lee, J. (2001). Instructional support for distance education and faculty motivation, commitment, satisfaction. *British Journal of Educational Technology, 32*(2), 153–160. doi:10.1111/1467-8535.00186

Leskovac, H. (1985). *State governance through conflict of interest rules: The California experience. Monograph 85-8*. Institute for Higher Education Law and Governance. University of Houston.

Levin, T., & Wadmany, R. (2008). Teachers' Views on Factors Affecting Effective Integration of Information Technology in the Classroom: Developmental Scenery. *Journal of Technology and Teacher Education, 16*(2), 233–263.

Levinson, W., & Roter, D. L. (1997). Physician-patient communication: The relationship with malpractice claims among primary care physicians and surgeons. *Journal of the American Medical Association, 277*, 553–559. doi:10.1001/jama.277.7.553

Lewis, B., & Starsia, G. (2009). Challenges in technology implementation for learning spaces in higher education. *EDUCAUSE Quarterly, 32*(1).

Leydesdorff, L., & Etzkowitz, H. (1996). Emergence of a triple helix of university-industry-government relations. *Science & Public Policy, 23*, 279–286.

Lilley, M., Barker, T., & Britton, C. (2004). The development and evaluation of a software prototype for computer adaptive testing . *Computers & Education Journal, 43*(1-2), 109–123. doi:10.1016/j.compedu.2003.12.008

Lin, C., & Ha, L. (2009). Subcultures and use of communication information technology in higher education institutions. *The Journal of Higher Education, 80*(5), 564–590. doi:10.1353/jhe.0.0064

Lindstrom, P. (2007). Securing "Web 2.0" technologies. *In-Depth Research Report, The Burton Group*. Retrieved February 3, 2008, from EDUCAUSE Center for Applied Research (ECAR): http://www.educause.edu/ecar

Liu, C., Rani, P., & Sarkar, N. (2005). An empirical study of machine learning techniques for affect recognition in human-robot interaction. *Paper presented at the IEEE Conference on Intelligent Robots and Systems.*

Lok, B., Ferdig, R., Raij, A., Johnsen, K., Dickerson, R., & Coutts, J. (2006). Applying Virtual Reality in Medical Communication Education: Current Findings and Potential Teaching and Learning Benefits of Immersive Virtual Patients. *Journal of Virtual Reality.*, *10*, 185–195. doi:10.1007/s10055-006-0037-3

Lonn, S., & Teasley, S. D. (2009). Podcasting in higher education: What are the implications for teaching and learning. *The Internet and Higher Education*, *12*, 88–92. doi:10.1016/j.iheduc.2009.06.002

Lorentz, M. M. (2008). Telenursing and home healthcare. The many facets of technology. *Home Healthcare Nurse*, *26*(4), 237–243. doi:10.1097/01.NHH.0000316702.22633.30

Lowerison, G., Sclater, J., Schmid, R. F., & Abrami, P. C. (2006). Are we using technology for learning? *Journal of Educational Technology Systems*, *34*(4), 401–425. doi:10.2190/ER58-3H7P-Y8FK-U8F7

Lozinsky, S. (1998). *Enterprise-wide software solutions: Integration strategies and practice*. Reading, MA: Addison-Wesley.

Luckin, R., Shurville, S., & Browne, T. (2006). Initiating E-learning by Stealth, Participation and Consultation in a Late Majority Institution. *Journal of Organizational Transformation & Social Change*, *3*(3), 317–332. doi:10.1386/jots.3.3.317_1

Luyegu, E. A. (2009). *Students' perceptions of assessment and the electronic portfolio project in the College of Education.* Unpublished Dissertation, University of South Alabama.

Lynar, C. (2005). Saving lives with teletrauma: Vermont trauma surgeons provide consultative services to rural communities using state-of-the-art videoconferencing technology. *Distance Learning*, *2*(6), 29–30.

Macedonio, M., Parsons, T. D., & Rizzo, A. A. (2007). Immersiveness and Physiological Arousal within Panoramic Video-based Virtual Reality. *Cyberpsychology & Behavior*, *10*, 508–516. doi:10.1089/cpb.2007.9997

Mager, R. F., & Pipe, P. (1997). *Analyzing performance problems, or, you really oughta wanna: How to figure out why people aren't doing what they should be, and what to do about it* (3rd ed.). Atlanta, GA: Center for Effective Performance.

Magnenat-Thalmann, N., & Thalmann, D. (2005). Virtual Humans: Thirty Years Of Research, What Next? *The Visual Computer*, *21*, 1–19. doi:10.1007/s00371-004-0243-5

Magnenat-Thalmann, N., Kim, H., Egges, A., & Garchery, S. (2005). Believability and Interaction in Virtual Worlds. *Proceedings of the 11th International Multimedia Modelling Conference*(pp. 2-9).

Mahon, M. (2009). Implementing an ERP on time and on budget: An innovative and inclusive approach. Educause Center for Applied Research, *Research Bulletin, 2009, (*10), 1-13 (complete). n. n. (2009). Recommended resources for the top ten IT Issues. *EDUCAUSE Review*, *44*(6), 102–103.

Manning, S. (2005). The promise of podcasting. *Pointers & Clickers*, *6*(2), 1–6.

Marinelli, D., & Pausch, R. (2004). Edutainment for the college classroom. *The Chronicle of Higher Education*, *50*(28), B16–B16.

Marrow, C. E., Hollyoake, K., Hamer, D., & Kenrick, C. (2002). Clinical supervision using video-conferencing technology: A reflective account. *Journal of Nursing Management*, *10*, 275–282. doi:10.1046/j.1365-2834.2002.00313.x

Martin, E. P., Andrews, S. P., & Gilbert, L. S. (2009). New teachers and support: An examination of ratings of significant agents. *Research in the Schools*, *16*(1), 25–31.

Maryland Online, Inc. (2006). *Quality Matters: Inter-Institutional Quality Assurance in Online Learning.* Retrieved from http://www.qualitymatters.org/index.htm

Massy, W. F., & Wilger, A. K. (1998). Technology's contribution to higher education productivity. *New Directions for Higher Education*, *26*(3), 49–59. doi:10.1002/he.10304

Massy, W. F., & Zemsky, R. (1995). Using information technology to enhance academic productivity. Presented at the *1995 CAUSE Conference*. http://www.educause.edu/nlii/keydocs/massy.html

Mayer, R., Stull, A., DeLeeuw, K., Almeroth, K., Bimber, B., & Chun, D. (2009). Clickers in college classrooms: Fostering learning with questioning methods in large lecture classes. *Contemporary Educational Psychology*, *34*(1), 51–57. doi:10.1016/j.cedpsych.2008.04.002

McCluskey, F. D. (1981). DVI, DAVI, AECT: A long view . In Brown, J. W., & Brown, S. N. (Eds.), *Educational media yearbook: 1981*. Littleton, CO: Libraries Unlimited.

McCormick, S. (1999). The case for visual media in learning. *Syllabus*; 4-6.

McCrea, B. (2009, December 9). Five Higher Ed Tech Trends to Watch in 2010. *Campus Technology*. Retrieved from http://campustechnology.com/Articles/2009/12/09/5-Higher-Ed-Tech-Trends-To-Watch-in-2010.aspx

McDaniel, M. A. (1988). Transfer: Rediscovering a central concept . In Roediger, H. L. III, Dudai, Y., & Fitzpatrick, S. M. (Eds.), *Science of memory: Concepts* (pp. 267–270). New York: Oxford University Press.

McGee, J. B., & Begg, M. (2008). What medical educators need to know about "Web 2.0". *Medical Teacher*, *30*(2), 164–169. doi:10.1080/01421590701881673

McGill, T. J., & Hobbs, V. J. (2008). How students and instructors using a virtual learning environment perceive the fit between technology and task. *Journal of Computer Assisted Learning*, *24*, 191–202. doi:10.1111/j.1365-2729.2007.00253.x

McGillivray, R., Yates, S., & McLister, B. (2007). Nurses and technology: An international survey. *Biomedical Instrumentation & Technology / Association For The Advancement . Medical Instrumentation*, (Suppl), 19.

McGuire, C. H. (1973). Diagnostic examinations in medical education. *Public Health Papers*, (52): 59–69.

McGuire, C. H. (1995). Reflections of a maverick measurement maven. *JAMA: The Journal Of The American Medical Association*, *274*(9), 735–740. doi:10.1001/jama.274.9.735

McGuire, J. M., Scott, S. S., & Shaw, S. F. (2003). Universal design for instruction: The paradigm its principles, and products for enhancing instructional access. *Journal of Postsecondary Education and Disability*, *17*(1), 11–21.

McKeachie, W. J. (2002). *McKeachie's teaching tips: Strategies, research, and theory for college and university teachers*. Boston: Houghton Mifflin Company.

McLoughlin, C., & Lee, M. (2008). Future learning landscapes: Transforming pedagogy through social software. *Innovate, 4*(5). Retrieved July 2, 2008, from http://www.innovateonline.info/pdf/vol4_issue5/Future_Learning_Landscapes-__Transforming_Pedagogy_through_Social_Software.pdf

McNaught, C., & Amory, A. (2006). Multicultural issues in the design of learning technologies. *Research and Practice in Technology Enhanced Learning*, *1*(3), 189–193. doi:10.1142/S1793206806000172

McPherson, M. A., & Nunes, M. N. (2006). Organizational Issues for E-learning: Critical Success Factors as identified by HE Practitioners. *International Journal of Educational Management*, *20*(7), 542–558. doi:10.1108/09513540610704645

McPherson, M. A. (2003). Organizational Critical Success Factors for Managing the Implementation of eLearning in Higher Education. In McPherson M.A., Henderson, L. & Kinshuk (Eds.) *Proceedings of the Workshop on The Changing Face of HE in the 21st Century: Critical Success Factors for Implementing eLearning*. Massey University, New Zealand, pp.8-14.

Meeder, R. (2005). Access denied: Internet filtering software in K-12 classrooms. *TechTrends*, *49*(6), 56–57. doi:10.1007/BF02763732

Meehan, M., Razzaque, S., Insko, B., Whitton, M., & Brooks, F. P. Jr. (2005). Review of four studies on the use of physiological reaction as a measure of presence in stressful virtual environments. *Applied Psychophysiology and Biofeedback*, *30*, 239–258. doi:10.1007/s10484-005-6381-3

Meeus, W., Van Petegem, P., & Engels, N. (2009). Validity and reliability of portfolio assessment in pre-service teacher education. *Assessment & Evaluation in Higher Education*, *34*(4), 401–413. doi:10.1080/02602930802062659

Meng, P. (2005). *Podcasting & vodcasting: Definitions, discussions & implications (a White paper): IAT Services at University of Missouri*. Retrieved December 1st from http://www.wssa.net/WSSA/SocietyInfo/ProfessionalDev/Podcasting/Missouri_Podcasting_White_Paper.pdf.

Merrill, M. D. (2002). First principles of instruction. *Educational Technology Research and Development*, *50*(3), 43–59. doi:10.1007/BF02505024

Messick, S. (1994). The interplay of evidence and consequences in the validation of performance assessment. *Educational Researcher*, *23*(2), 13–23.

Meyer, A., & Rose, D. (2005). *The future is in the margins: The role of technology and disability in educational reform*. Paper presented to the American Institute for Research, US Department of Education, Office of Educational Technology.

Microsoft Corporation. (2004). *Accessible technology in computing: Examining awareness, use, and future potential*. Cambridge, MA: Forrester Research, Inc.

Middlehurst, R. (2004). Changing Internal Governance: A Discussion of Leadership Roles and Management Structures in UK Universities. *Higher Education Quarterly*, *58*(4), 258–279. doi:10.1111/j.1468-2273.2004.00273.x

Milet, L. K. (1996, April 11-14). Organizational models for managing technology services: Keeping up with rapid change. *Proceedings of the Consortium of College and University Media Centers*, 29-31. San Diego, CA.

Miller, K. L., Miller, S. M., & Evans, W. J. (2002). Computer-assisted live supervision in college counseling centers. *Journal of College Counseling*, *5*, 187–192.

Miller, M., & Piller, M. (2005). *Principal factors of an audio reading delivery mechanism: Evaluating educational use of the iPod*. Paper presented at the World Conference on Education Multimedia, Hypermedia & Telecommunications, and Chesapeake, VA.

Milliken, J., & Barnes, L. P. (2002). Teaching and technology in higher education: student perceptions and personal reflections. *Computers & Education*, *39*(3), 223–235. doi:10.1016/S0360-1315(02)00042-8

Mims, C., Polly, D., & Grant, M. (2009). Technology integration in K-12. In M. K. Barbour & M. Orey (Eds.), *The Foundations of Instructional Technology*. Retrieved June 29, 2009, from http://projects.coe.uga.edu/ITFoundations/index.php?title=Technology_Integration_in_K-12

Mishra, P., & Koehler, M. J. (2006). Technological Pedagogical Content Knowledge: A framework for teacher knowledge. *Teachers College Record*, *108*(6), 1017–1054. doi:10.1111/j.1467-9620.2006.00684.x

Moore, M. (1989). Editorial: Three types of interaction. *American Journal of Distance Education*, *5*(3), 1–6. doi:10.1080/08923649109526758

Moore, M. (1991). Editorial: Distance education theory. *American Journal of Distance Education*, *53*(3), 1–6. doi:10.1080/08923649109526758

Moore, G. S., Winograd, K., & Lange, D. (2001). *You can teach online: Building a creative learning environment*. Boston, MA: McGraw-Hill.

Moore, M. G. (1989). Three types of interaction. *The American journal of distance learning* *3*(2), 1-6.

Morency, L.-P., & de Kok, I. (2008). Context-based Recognition during Human Interactions: Automatic Feature Selection and Encoding Dictionary. *10th International Conference on Multimodal Interfaces*, Chania, Greece, IEEE.

Morgan, R. (2008). Exploring the Pedagogical Effectiveness of Clickers. *InSight: A Journal of Scholarly Teaching, 3*31-36.

Morrison, D. (2009). The Benchmarking and Pathfinder Programme and its Role in Institutional Transformation. In Mayes, T., Morrison, D., Mellar, H., Bullen, P. & Oliver, M. York (eds.): *Transforming Higher Education through Technology-enhanced Learning*. The Higher Education Academy. Online at: http://www.heacademy.ac.uk/technology [last visited 08/02/10.

Moss, P. A. (2003). Reconceptualizing validity for classroom assessment. *Educational Measurement: Issues and Practice*, *22*(4), 13–25. doi:10.1111/j.1745-3992.2003.tb00140.x

Mouza, C. (2002-2003). Learning to teach with new technology: Implications for professional development. *Journal of Research on Technology in Education*, *35*(2), 272–289.

Mullis, R. L., Mullis, A. K., & Cornille, T. A. (2007). Relationships between identity formation and computer use among black and white emerging adult females. *Computers in Human Behavior*, *23*, 415–423. doi:10.1016/j.chb.2004.10.019

Murphy, S. (2009). Leveraging lean Six Sigma to culture, nurture, and sustain Assessment and change in the academic library environment. *College & Research Libraries*, *70*(3), 215–225.

Murray, C., Goldstein, D. E., Nourse, S., & Edgar, E. (2000). The postsecondary school attendance and completion rates of high school graduates with learning disabilities. *Learning Disabilities Research*, *15*, 119–127. doi:10.1207/SLDRP1503_1

Myrick, R. D., & Sabella, R. A. (1995). Cyberspace: New place for counselor supervision. *Elementary School Guidance & Counseling*, *30*(1), 35–45.

Nagel, D. (2008, January 16). Web 2.0 in education: Trends for 2008. *Technological Horizons in Education Journal.* Retrieved January 11,2009, from http://thejournal.com/articles/2008/01/16/web-20-in-education-trends-for-2008.aspx

Naidoo, R. (2000). The 'Third Way' to Widening Participation and Maintaining Quality in Higher Education: Lessons from the United Kingdom. *Journal of Educational Enquiry*, *1*(2), 24–38.

National Center for Education Statistics. (2008). *Digest of education statistics*. Retrieved 1/10/2010, from U.S. Dept. of Education Institute of Education Sciences: http://nces.ed.gov/programs/digest/d08/tables/dt08_275.asp

National Center for Education Statistics. (2009). *Changes in postsecondary awards below the bachelor's degree*. Retrieved 1/10/2010, from U.S. Dept. of Education Institute of Education Sciences: http://nces.ed.gov/pubs2010/2010167.pdf

National Center for Education Statistics. (2008). *Digest of education statistics: 2008*. Washington, DC: US Department of Education, Institute for Education Sciences.

National Center for Educational Statistics. (2009). *The Condition of Education*. Retrieved from http://nces.ed.gov/pubs2009/2009081.pdf

National Center for Technology Innovation. (2009). *Unleashing the power of innovations for Assistive Technology. Author*. Washington, DC: American Institutes for Research.

National Council of State Boards of Nursing. (2010). *2010 NCLEX examination candidate bulletin.* Retrieved from https://www.ncsbn.org/2010_NCLEX_Candidate_Bulletin_AtaGlance.pdf

National Education Association. (2009). *TEACH Act highlights and resources*. Retrieved December 18, 2009 from http://www.nea.org/home/35377.htm

National Science Foundation. (2008). Fostering learning in the networked world: The cyber learning opportunity and challenge. *Report of the NSF Task Force on Cyberlearning.* http://www.nsf.gov/pubs/2008/nsf08204/nsf08204.pdf.

Nehring, W. M., & Lashley, F. R. (2009). Nursing simulation: A review of the past 40 years. *Simulation & Gaming*, *40*(4), 528–552. doi:10.1177/1046878109332282

New Media Consortium (NMC). (2009). *Sparking innovative learning and creativity*. Retrieved from http://www.nmc.org/

Ngai, P. B. (2003). Linking distance and international education: A strategy for developing multicultural competence among distance learners. *Journal of Studies in International Education*, *7*(2), 157–177. doi:10.1177/1028315303007002004

Nichols, M. (2008). Institutional Perspectives: The Challenges of E-Learning Diffusion. *British Journal of Educational Technology*, *39*(4), 598–609. doi:10.1111/j.1467-8535.2007.00761.x

Nicolle, P. S., & Lou, Y. (2008). Technology adoption into teaching and learning by mainstream university faculty: A mixed methodology study revealing the "How, when, and why not". *Journal of Educational Computing Research*, *39*(3), 235–265. doi:10.2190/EC.39.3.c

Nielsen, M., Strand, E., Savenye, W., Spector, M., Mancilla, D., & Biggs, M. J. (2009, October). *Developing Technology-Skilled Faculty across a Large Campus: A Long-Term Technology Integration Program*. Paper presented at the annual meeting of the Association for Educational Communications and Technology, Louisville, KY.

Niess, M. L. (2005). Preparing teachers to teach science and mathematics with technology: Developing a technology pedagogical content knowledge. *Teaching and Teacher Education*, *21*, 509–523. doi:10.1016/j.tate.2005.03.006

Noell, G., & Burns, J. (n.d.). *Value added teacher preparation assessment: Overview of 2007–8 study.* Baton Rouge, LA: Louisiana Board of Regents. Retrieved May 11, 2010, from http://www.regents.louisiana.gov/Academic/TE/2008/Overview%20of%202007-08%20Value%20Added%20Teacher%20Preparation%20(12.03.08).pdf

Norcross, J. C., & Lambert, M. J. (2006). The Therapy Relationship . In Norcross, J. C., Beutler, L. E., & Levant, R. F. (Eds.), *Evidence-Based Practices in Mental Health: Debate and Dialogue on the Fundamental Questions*. Washington, DC: American Psychological Association. doi:10.1037/11265-000

Norman, D. (1988). *The design of everyday things*. New York: Doubleday.

Norman, D. A. (1983). Some observations on mental models . In Gentner, D., & Stevens, A. L. (Eds.), *Mental models* (pp. 7–14). Hillsdale, NJ: Lawrence Erlbaum Associates.

Norris, F. H., Kaniasty, K., & Thompson, M. P. (1997). The psychological consequences of crime: Findings from a longitudinal population-based study . In Davis, R. C., Lurigio, A. J., & Skogan, W. G. (Eds.), *Victims of Crime* (2nd ed., pp. 146–166). Thousand Oaks, CA: Sage Publications Inc.

Norton, P., & Hathaway, D. (2008). On its way to K-12 classrooms, web 2.0 goes to graduate school. *Computers in the Schools*, *25*, 163–180. doi:10.1080/07380560802368116

Novel (2000). *Standardization of desktops in an enterprise environment*. Retrieved April 1, 2010 from http://www.novell.com/coolsolutions/feature/2940.html

Ntuli, E., Keengwe, J., & Kyei-Blankson, L. (2009). Electronic portfolios in teacher education: A case study of early childhood teacher candidates. *Early Childhood Education Journal*, *37*(2), 121–126. doi:10.1007/s10643-009-0327-y

Nworie, J., & Dwyer, F. (2004, August). Knowledge management and instructional design: Optimizing organizational knowledge. *Performance Improvement*, *43*(7), 27–32. doi:10.1002/pfi.4140430709

Nworie, J., & Haughton, N. (2008, September). Good intentions and unanticipated effects: The unintended consequences of the application of technology in teaching and learning environments. *TechTrends*, *52*(5), 52–58. doi:10.1007/s11528-008-0197-y

Nye, D. E. (2006). *Technology matters: Questions to live with*. Cambridge, MA: The MIT Press.

O'Hanlon, N. O. (2002). Net knowledge: Performance of new college students on an internet skills proficiency test. *The Internet and Higher Education*, *5*, 55–66. doi:10.1016/S1096-7516(02)00066-0

O'Banion, T. (1994, April). Sustaining innovation in teaching and learning. [Mission Viejo, CA: League for Innovation in the Community College.]. *Leadership Abstracts*, *7*(4), 3–4.

O'Connor v. Ortega, 480 U.S. 709 (1987).

O'Neil, H. F., & Perez, R. S. (2008). *Computer games and team and individual learning*. Boston: Elsevier.

O'Reilly, T. (2005, October 10). Web 2.0: Compact definition? *O'Reilly Radar*. Retrieved July 23, 2006, from http://radar.oreilly.com/archives/2005/10/ web_20_compact_definition.html

Oblinger, D. (2003, July). Boomers, gen-xers and millennials: Understanding the new students. *EDUCASE Review*, *38*(4), 37–47.

Office of Higher Education. (2001, February). 2001). *Higher education on the web. Update*, *7*(1). http://www.nea.org/he/techno.html.

Ohler, J. (2010). The power and peril of web 3.0: It's more than just semantics. *Learning and Leading with Technology*, (May): 14–17.

Okuda, Y., Bond, W., Bonfante, G., McLaughlin, S., Spillane, L., & Wang, E. (2008). National growth in simulation training within emergency medicine residency programs. *Academic Emergency Medicine*, *15*(11), 1113–1116. doi:10.1111/j.1553-2712.2008.00195.x

Olsen, M. M., Russell, C. S., & White, M. B. (2001). Technological implications for clinical supervision and practice. *The Clinical Supervisor*, *20*(2), 201–215. doi:10.1300/J001v20n02_15

Oomen-Early, J., & Murphy, L. (2009). Self-actualization and e-learning: A qualitative investigation of university faculty's perceived barriers to effective online instruction. *International Journal on E-Learning*, *8*(2), 223–240.

Oppenheimer, T. (2003). *The flickering mind: the false promise of technology in the classroom, and how learning can be saved*. New York: Random House.

Orwell, G. (1946/1950). Politics and the English language . In *Shooting an elephant and other essays*. London: Secker and Warburg.

Owen, P. S., & Demb, A. (2004). Change dynamics and leadership in technology implementation. *The Journal of Higher Education*, *75*(6), 636–666. doi:10.1353/jhe.2004.0037

Palloff, R. M., & Pratt, K. (1999). *Building learning communities in cyberspace: Effective strategies for the online classroom*. San Francisco: Jossey-Bass.

Panos, P. T., Panos, A., Cox, S. E., Roby, J. L., & Matheson, K. W. (2002). Ethical issues concerning the use of videoconferencing to supervise international social work field practicum students. *Journal of Social Work Education*, *38*, 421–430.

Papastergiou, M. (2006). Course management systems as tools for the creation of online learning environments: Evaluation from a social constructivist perspective and implications for their design. *International Journal on E-Learning*, *5*(4), 593–622.

Parette, H. P., Peterson-Karlan, G. R., Smith, S. I., Gray, T., & Silver-Pacuilla, H. (2006). The state of assistive technology: Themes from an outcomes summit. *Assistive Technology Outcomes and Benefits*, *3*(1), 15–33.

Parker, S. (2001). Searching for the digital divide. *Information Development*, *17*, 205–208. doi:10.1177/0266666014240999

Parker, S. (2007). Editorial: What digital divide? *Information Development*, *23*, 235–236. doi:10.1177/0266666907084758

Parker-Oliver, D., & Demiris, G. (2006). Social work informatics: A new specialty. *Social Work*, *51*(2), 127–134.

Parrott, L., & Madoc-Jones, I. (2008). Reclaiming information and communication technologies for empowering social work practice. *Journal of Social Work*, *8*(2), 181–197. doi:10.1177/1468017307084739

Parsons, T. D., Cosand, L., Courtney, C., Iyer, A., & Rizzo, A. A. (2009c). Neurocognitive Workload Assessment using the Virtual Reality Cognitive Performance Assessment Test. *Lecture Notes in Artificial Intelligence*, *5639*, 243–252.

Parsons, T. D., Courtney, C., Cosand, L., Iyer, A., Rizzo, A. A., & Oie, K. (2009d). Assessment of Psychophysiological Differences of West Point Cadets and Civilian Controls Immersed within a Virtual Environment. *Lecture Notes in Artificial Intelligence*, *5638*, 514–523.

Parsons, T. D., Iyer, A., Cosand, L., Courtney, C., & Rizzo, A. A. (2009b). Neurocognitive and Psychophysiological Analysis of Human Performance within Virtual Reality Environments. *Studies in Health Technology and Informatics*, *142*, 247–252.

Parsons, T. D., Kenny, P., Cosand, L., Iyer, A., Courtney, C., & Rizzo, A. A. (2009a). A Virtual Human Agent for Assessing Bias in Novice Therapists. *Studies in Health Technology and Informatics*, *142*, 253–258.

Parsons, T. D., Kenny, P., Ntuen, C., Pataki, C. S., Pato, M., & Rizzo, A. A. (2008). Objective Structured Clinical Interview Training using a Virtual Human Patient. *Studies in Health Technology and Informatics*, *132*, 357–362.

Pastore, R. S. (2008). Students' perceptions of podcasting in the classroom. *International Journal of Instructional Technology and Distance Learning*, *5*(12), 55–62.

Peacock, K. (2009). *Web 2.0 for Teachers.* Retrieved from http://www.protopage.com/web2point0forteachers

Pellegrino, J. Chudowsky, N, & Glaser, R. (2001). *Knowing what students know: The science and design of educational assessment*. Washington, DC: National Academies Press.

Penniston, P. (2005). Creative solutions for distance administration of TVI and O & M services. *RE:view*, *37*(3), 118–119.

Penuel, W., Fishman, B., Yamaguchi, R., & Gallagher, L. (2007). What makes professional development effective? Strategies that foster curriculum implementation. *American Educational Research Journal*, *44*(4), 921–958. doi:10.3102/0002831207308221

Peters, T. S., & Waterman, R. H. (1982). *In Search of Excellence: Lessons from America's Best Run Companies*. New York: Harper & Row.

Peters, K. (2007). m-Learning: Positioning educators for a mobile, connected future. *International Review of Research in Open and Distance Learning*, *8*(2).

Peterson, E. (2006). Beneath the metadata: Some philosophical problems with folksonomy. *D-Lib Magazine*, *12*(11). Retrieved March 16, 2007, from http://www.dlib.org/dlib/november06/peterson/11peterson.html

Peterson-Karlan, G., & Parette, P. (2005). Millennial students with mild disabilities and emerging assistive technology trends. *Journal of Special Education Technology*, *20*(4), 27–38.

Petty, G. (2009). *Evidence-based teaching: A practical approach* (2nd ed.). Gloucestershire, UK: Nelson Thornes.

Picard, R. W. (1997). *Affective Computing*. Cambridge, MA: M.I.T Press.

Pinch, T. J., & Bijker, W. E. (2003). The social construction of facts and artifacts . In Scharff, R. C., & Dusek, V. (Eds.), *The philosophy of technology: The technological condition: An anthology* (pp. 221–232). Malden, MA: Blackwell.

Plant, A. E., & Devine, P. G. (1998). Internal and external motivation to respond without prejudice. *Journal of Personality and Social Psychology*, *75*, 811–832. doi:10.1037/0022-3514.75.3.811

Pochciol, J. M., & Warren, J. I. (2009). An information technology infrastructure to enable evidence-based nursing practice. *Nursing Administration Quarterly*, *33*(4), 317–324.

Polly, D., & Brantley-Dias, L. (2009). TPACK: Where do we go now? *TechTrends*, *53*(5), 46–47. doi:10.1007/s11528-009-0324-4

Polly, D., & Hannafin, M. J. (2010). Reexamining technology's role in learner-centered professional development. *Educational Technology Research and Development*, *58*(5), 557–571. doi:10.1007/s11423-009-9146-5

Polly, D., Mims, C., Inan, F., & Shepherd, C. E. (2010). Evidence of impact: An analysis of the influence of PT3 Projects designed to transform methods courses and field experiences. *Teaching and Teacher Education*, *26*(4), 863–870. doi:10.1016/j.tate.2009.10.024

Pomales-Garcia, C., Rivera, M., & Chamoun, D. (2009). *Best practices and assessment process for an engineering course through videoconference*. Paper presented at the 2009 Industrial Engineering Research Conference. Conference, Saw, K. G., Majid, O., Ghani, N. A., Atan, H., Idrus, R. M., Rahman, Z. A., et al. (2007). The videoconferencing learning environment: technology, interaction and learning intersect. *British Journal of Educational Technology, 39* (3), 475-485.

Pope, A. T., Bogart, E. H., & Bartolome, D. S. (1995). Biocybernetic system evaluates indices of operator engagement in automated task. *Biological Psychology*, *40*, 187–195. doi:10.1016/0301-0511(95)05116-3

Postman, N. (1993). *Technopoly: The surrender of culture to technology*. New York: Vintage.

Powell, R. S. (2009, October 9). Who is on the other end of Facebook? *The Chronicle of Higher Education*. Retrieved from http://chronicle.com/article/Who-Is-on-the-Other-End-of-/48693/

Power, M. (1999). *The Audit Society: Rituals of Verification* (2nd ed.). New York: Oxford University Press, USA.

Prensky, M. (2005). "Engage me or engrage me" What today's learners demand. *EDUCASE Review*, *40*(5), 60–64.

Prensky, M. (2007). New issues, new answers--Changing paradigms. *Educational Technology*, *47*(4), 64.

Prensky, M. (2001). Digital natives, digital immigrants. *Horizon*, *9*(5), 1–6. Retrieved from http://www.marcprensky.com/writing/Prensky%20-%20Digital%20 Natives,%20Digital%20Immigrants%20-%20Part1.pdf. doi:10.1108/10748120110424816doi:10.1108/10748120 110424816

Press, E., & Washburn, J. (2000). The kept university. *Atlantic Monthly*, *285*, 39–54.

Prowle, M., & Morgan, E. (2005). *Financial management and control in higher education*. London: RoutledgeGalmer. doi:10.4324/9780203416143

Putnam, R., & Borko, H. (2000). What do new views of knowledge and thinking have to say about research on teaching? *Educational Researcher*, *29*(1), 4–15.

Radford University. (2008). *Information technology strategic plan, 2008-2013*. Accessed October 29, 2009 from, http://cio.asp.radford.edu/about/strategicplan.aspx

Rankin, M. (2009). *Some general comments on the "Twitter Experiment*". Retrieved July 25, 2009, from http://www.utdallas.edu/~mar046000/usweb/twitterconclusions.htm

Rao, P. V., & Rao, L. M. (1999, March). Strategies that support instructional technology. *Syllabus*; 22-24.

Rasmussen, K. L., Nichols, J. C., & Ferguson, F. (2006). It's a new world: Multiculturalism in a virtual environment. *Distance Education*, *27*(2), 265–278. doi:10.1080/01587910600789696

Rawlings, J. (1999). *Jacques Derrida*. Stanford University, Stanford Presidential Lectures in the Humanities and Arts. Retrieved March 24, 2005 from http://prelectur.stanford.edu/lecturers/derrida/.

Reeves, P. M., & Reeves, T. C. (2008). Design considerations for online learning in health and social work education. *Learning in Health and Social Care Journal*, *7*(1), 46–58. doi:10.1111/j.1473-6861.2008.00170.x

Reeves, T. C. (2006). How do you know they are learning? The importance of alignment in higher education. *International Journal of Learning Technology*, *2*(4), 294–309. doi:10.1504/IJLT.2006.011336

Reeves, T. C. (2009). E-Learning in Asia: Just as good is not good enough. *International Journal on E-Learning*, *8*(4), 577–585.

Reid, I. C. (1999, May). Beyond models: Developing a university strategy for online instruction. *Journal of Asynchronous Learning Networks*, *3*(1), 19–31.

Reigeluth, C. M., & Duffy, F. (2008). The AECT Futureminds initiative: Transforming America's school systems. *Educational Technology*, (May): 45–48.

Reiser, R. A. (2001). A history of instructional design and technology: Part I: A history of instructional media. *Educational Technology Research and Development*, *49*(1), 53–64. doi:10.1007/BF02504506

Reiser, R. A. (2002). A history of instructional design and technology . In Reiser, R. A., & Dempsey, J. V. (Eds.), *Trends and issues in instructional design and technology*. Upper Saddle Creek, NJ: Merrill/Prentice Hall.

Rekkedal, T., & Dye, A. (2007). Mobile Distance Learning with PDAs: Development and testing of pedagogical and system solutions supporting mobile distance learners. *International Review of Research in Open and Distance Learning*, *8*(2).

Resick, P. A., & Nishith, P. (1997). Sexual assault . In Davis, R. C., Lurigio, A. J., & Skogan, W. G. (Eds.), *Victims of Crime* (2nd ed., pp. 27–52). Thousand Oaks, CA: Sage Publications Inc.

Rethlefsen, M. (2007). Chief thingamabrarian. [Retrieved from Health Source: Nursing/Academic Edition database.]. *Library Journal*, *132*(1), 40–42.

Rieber, L. P., & Welliver, P. W. (1989). Infusing educational technology into mainstream educational computing . *International Journal of Instructional Media*, *16*(1), 21–32.

Rieber, L. P. (2005). Multimedia learning in games, simulations, and microworlds . In Mayer, R. (Ed.), *The Cambridge handbook of multimedia learning* (pp. 549–567). New York: Cambridge University Press.

Rieger, R., & Gay, G. (1997). Using Mobile Computing to Enhance Field Study. In R. Hall, N. Miyake & N. Enyedy (Eds.), *Computer Supported Collaborative Learning* (Proc. 2nd Conf., Toronto, Ontario, December) (p. 215-223). Mahwah, NJ: Erlbaum & Assoc.

Ringle, M., & Updergrove, D. (1998). Is strategic planning an oxymoron? *Cause/Effect, 21(1)* 18-23. Retrieved November 5, 2009, from http://net.educause.edu/ir/library/html/cem/cem98/cem9814.html

Roach, R. (2002). Assistive technology comes into focus. *Black Issues in Higher Education*, *19*(11), 20–24.

Robinson, C. C., & Hullinger, H. (2008). New benchmarks in higher education: Student engagement in online learning. *Journal of Education for Business*, *84*(2), 101–109. doi:10.3200/JOEB.84.2.101-109

Roblyer, M. D., & Wiencke, W. R. (2003). Design and use of a rubric to assess and encourage interactive qualities in distance courses. *American Journal of Distance Education*, *17*(2), 77–98. doi:10.1207/S15389286AJDE1702_2

Rogers, E. M. (2003). *Diffusion of innovations* (5th ed.). New York: Free Press.

Rogers, D. (2000). A paradigm shift: Technology integration for higher education in the new millenium. *AACE Journal*, *1*(13), 19–33.

Rogers, E. M. (1995). *Diffusion of innovations* (4th ed.). New York: The Free Press.

Rogers, P. L. (2000). Barriers to adopting emerging technologies in education. *Journal of Educational Computing Research*, *22*(4), 455–472. doi:10.2190/4UJE-B6VW-A30N-MCE5

Rogers, Y., Price, S., Fitzpatrick, G., Fleck, R., Harris, E., Smith, H., et al. (2004). Ambient wood: designing new forms of digital augmentation for learning outdoors. *Proceedings of the 2004 Conference on Interaction Design and Children: Building a Community* (p. 3-10). Maryland.

Rogoff, B. (1984). *Everyday cognition: its development in social context*. Cambridge, MA: Harvard University Press.

Rogoff, B. (1991). *Apprenticeship in Thinking: Cognitive Development in Social Context. New York*. USA: Oxford University Press.

Rollette, H., Lux, M., Strohmaier, M., Dösing, G., & Tochterman, K. (2007). The web 2.0 way of learning with technologies. *The International Journal of Learning Technology*, *3*(1), 87–107. doi:10.1504/IJLT.2007.012368

Rose, D. H., & Meyer, A. (2002). *Teaching every student in the digital age: Universal design for learning*. Alexandria, VA: Association for Supervision and Curriculum Development.

Rosen, D., & Nelson, C. (2008). Web 2.0: A new generation of learners and education. *Computers in the Schools*, *25*, 211–225. doi:10.1080/07380560802370997

Rosenberg, J. I. (2006). Real-time training: Transfer of knowledge through computer-mediated, real-time feedback. *Professional Psychology, Research and Practice*, *37*, 539–546. doi:10.1037/0735-7028.37.5.539

Rosenberg, M. J. (2001). *e-Learning: Strategies for delivering knowledge in the digital age*. New York: McGraw Hill.

Rossett, A. (1999). *First things fast: A handbook for performance analysis*. San Francisco: Jossey-Bass/Pfeiffer.

Rothstein-Fisch, C., & Trumbull, E. (2008). *Managing diverse classrooms: How to build students' cultural strengths*. Alexandria, VA: Association for Supervision and Curriculum Development.

Rothwell, W. J., & Kazanas, H. C. (2004). *Improving on-the-job training How to establish and operate a comprehensive OJT program*. San Francisco: Pfeiffer.

Rudestam, K. E., & Schoenholtz-Read, J. (Eds.). (2010). *Handbook of online learning* (2nd ed.). Thousand Oaks, CA: SAGE Publications.

Russell, T. L. (1999). *The no significant difference phenomenon: As reported in 355 research reports, summaries and papers*. North Carolina: North Carolina State University.

Rutherford, L. H., & Grana, S. J. (1995). Retrofitting academe: Adapting faculty attitudes and practices to technology. *T.H.E. Journal*, *23*(2), 82.

Saettler, P. (1990). *The evolution of American educational technology*. Englewood, CO: Libraries Unlimited.

Sahin, I., & Thompson, A. (2007). Analysis of Predictive Factors that Influence Faculty Members Technology Adoption Level. *Journal of Technology and Teacher Education*, *15*(2), 167–190.

Salaway, G., Caruso, J. B., & Nelson, M. R. (2007). The ECAR study of undergraduate students and information technology, 2007. *Educause Center for Applied Research Key Findings,* (September 2007). Retrieved from http://www.educause.edu/ir/library/pdf/ers0706/rs/ers07062.pdf.

Salaway, G., Katz, R. N., Caruso, J. B., Kvavik, R. B., & Nelson, M. R. (2006). The ECAR Study of Undergraduate Students and Information Technology, 2006. *Research Study, 7*. Boulder, CO: EDUCAUSE http://www.educause.edu/ecar (Retrieved December 2009).

Salomon, G. (2002). Technology and pedagogy: Why don't we see the promised revolution? *Educational Technology*, *42*(2), 71–75.

Sample, M. (2009). *The open source professor: Teaching, research, and transparency*. Slideshare presentation. Retrieved January 4, 2010, from http://www.slideshare.net/samplereality/the-open-source-professor-teaching-research-and-transparency

Sanger, D. (1982). Business rents a lab coat and academia hopes for the best. *New York Times*, 21 March. p. 7

Sannier, A. (2008, August 19). *Video Spotlight: Campus Technology 2008 Keynote Address: A 'New' American University for Next-Gen Learners*. Retrieved from http://campustechnology.com/articles/2008/08/video-spotlight-campus-technology-2008-keynote-address.aspx

Satterlee, B. (1996). *Continuous improvement and quality: Implications for higher education.* Retrieved from ERIC database (ED399845).

Sauer, J., & Anderson, N. R. (1992). Have we misread the psychology of innovation? A case study from two NHS hospitals . *Leadership and Organization Development Journal*, *13*(2), 17–21. doi:10.1108/01437739210009581

Scalese, R. J., Obeso, V. T., & Issenberg, S. B. (2008). Simulation technology for skills training and competency assessment in medical education. *Journal of General Internal Medicine*, *23*(Suppl 1), 46–49. doi:10.1007/s11606-007-0283-4

Scalter, N. (2008). *Web 2.0, personal learning environments, and the future of learning management systems. EDUCAUSE Center for Applied Research* (ECAR). Available from http://www.educause.edu/ecar

Schachter, J. (2008). Delicious . In Jones, B. (Ed.), *Web 2.0 heroes: Interviews with 21 Web 2.0 influencers* (pp. 169–175). Indianapolis, IN: Wiley Pub.

Schacter, J. (1999). *The impact of education technology on student achievement: What the most current research has to say*. Santa Monica, CA: Milken Exchange on Education Technology.

Scherer, M., Sax, C., Vanbiervliet, A., Cushman, L., & Scherer, J. (2005). Predictors of assistive technology use: The importance of personal and psychosocial factors. *Disability and Rehabilitation*, *27*(21), 1321–1331. doi:10.1080/09638280500164800

Scherer, M. J. (2005). *Living in the state of stuck*. Brookline, MA: Brookline Books.

Schmid, R. F., Bernard, R. M., Borokhovski, E., Tamim, R., Abrami, P. C., & Wade, C. A. (2009). Technology's effect on achievement in higher educaton: A Stage I meta-analysis of classroom applications. *Journal of Computing in Higher Education*, *21*, 95–109. doi:10.1007/s12528-009-9021-8

Schrum, L., Skeele, R., & Grant, M. (2002-2003, Winter). One college of education's effort to infuse technology: A systematic approach to revisioning teaching and learning. *Journal of Research on Technology in Education*, *35*(2), 256–271.

Schwarz, N. (1999). Self-reports: How the questions shape the answers. *The American Psychologist*, *54*, 93–105. doi:10.1037/0003-066X.54.2.93

Scott, G. (2003). Effective change management in higher education. *EDUCAUSE Review*, *38*(6), 64–80.

Scribner, J. P. (1999). Professional development: Untangling the influence of work context on teacher learning. *Educational Administration Quarterly*, *35*(2), 238–266.

Scrivener Agee, A., & Yang, C.The 2009 EDUCAUSE Current Issues Committee. (2009). Top-ten IT issues, 2009 . *EDUCAUSE Review*, *44*(4), 44–59.

Search for Common Ground. (2004). *Resource guide on strategic planning*. Retrieved November 20, 2009, from http://www.sfcg.org/programmes/ilr/stratplan.pdf

Seldow, A. (2007). *Social tagging in education and the workplace*. Paper presented at the 3rd annual Innovations in E-Learning Symposium. George Mason University, Fairfax, VA.

Sener, J. (2005). The quality matters rubric: A tool for promoting quality improvement in online courses. In *Educational Pathways: Resources for Educators and Learners*. Retrieved from http://www.edpath.com/2005/0205/020504.htm

Senge, P. M., Kleiner, A., Roberts, C., Ross, R. B., & Smith, B. J. (1994). *The fifth discipline fieldbook: Strategies and tools for building a learning organization*. New York: Doubleday.

Seppala, P., & Alamaki, H. (2003). Mobile learning in teacher training. *Journal of Computer Assisted Learning*, *19*, 330–335. doi:10.1046/j.0266-4909.2003.00034.x

Sergiovanni, T. (1998). Market and Community as Strategies for Change . In Hargreaves, A., Lieberman, A., Fullan, M., & Hopkins, D. (Eds.), *International Handbook of Educational Change* (*Vol. 1*, pp. 576–595). Dordrecht, Netherlands: Kluwer Academic Publishers.

Sessums, C. (2006, January 21). *Notes on the significance of the emergence of blogs and wikis*. Retrieved October 12, 2006, from http://eduspaces.net/csessums/weblog/6172.html

Sexton, J. (2009, November 23). Nine presidents to watch. One theme unites them: endless innovation. *Time*, 49–51.

Shank, R. (1998). Horses for courses. *Communications of the ACM*, *41*(7), 23–25. doi:10.1145/278476.278482

Shannon, C. D., Schoen, B., & Tansey, T. N. (2009). The effect of contact, context, and social power on undergraduate attitudes towards persons with disabilities. *Journal of Rehabilitation*, *75*(4), 11–18.

Shapiro, W. L. (1998). New ways to link technology and faculty development. *Change*, *30*(5), 50–53. doi:10.1080/00091389809602643

Sheikh, F. (2006). Canadian telehealth project aims to build capacity in Middle East. *Technology in Government*, *13*(3), 6.

Shelly, G. B., Cashman, T. J., Gunter, R. E., & Gunter, G. A. (2004). *Teachers discovering computers: Integrating technology in the classroom*. Boston: Course Technology.

Shen, R., & Wang, M., Pan, & Xiaoyan, P. (2008). Increasing interactivity in blended classrooms through a cutting-edge mobile learning system. *British Journal of Educational Technology*, *39*(6), 1073–1086. doi:10.1111/j.1467-8535.2007.00778.x

Sheriff, J. K. (1989). *The fate of meaning: Charles Peirce, structuralism, and literature*. Princeton, NJ: Princeton University Press.

Sherry, L. (1998). An integrated technology adoption and diffusion model. *International Journal of Educational Telecommunications*, *4*(2/3), 113–145.

Shih, Y. E., & Mills, D. (2007). Setting the new standard with mobile computing in online learning. *International Review of Research in Open and Distance Learning*, *8*(2).

Shohan, S., & Perry, M. (2009). Knowledge management as a mechanism for technological and organizational change management in Israeli universities. *Higher Education*, *57*(2), 227–246. doi:10.1007/s10734-008-9148-y

Shore, C., & Wright, S. (1999). Audit Culture and Anthropology: Neo-Liberalism in British Higher Education. [doi]. *The Journal of the Royal Anthropological Institute*, *5*(4), 557. doi:10.2307/2661148

Shurville, S., & Browne, T. (2006). ICT-Driven Change in Higher Education: Learning from E-learning. *Journal of Organizational Transformation and Social Change*, *3*(3), 245–250. doi:10.1386/jots.3.3.245_2

Shute, V. J. (2008). Focus on formative assessment. *Review of Educational Research*, *78*, 153–189. doi:10.3102/0034654307313795

Siegel, D., Waldman, D., & Link, A. (2003). Assessing the impact of organizational practices on the relative productivity of university technology transfer offices: an exploratory study. *Research Policy*, *32*, 27–48. doi:10.1016/S0048-7333(01)00196-2

Siemens, G. (2005). Connectivism: A learning theory for the digital age. *International Journal of Instructional Technology and Distance Learning*, *2*(1). Available from http://www.itdl.org/Journal/Jan_05/article01.htm.

Siemens, G. (2009, November 13). *Moodle - the wrong tool for the job?* Retrieved December 30, 2009, from http://www.learningconversations.co.uk/ main/index.php/2009/11/13/moodle-the-wrong-tool-for-the-job?blog=5

Siemens, G., & Tittenberger, P. (2009). *Handbook of emerging technologies for learning*. Retrieved from http://umanitoba.ca/learning_technologies/cetl/HETL.pdf

Signer, B. (2008). Online professional development: combining best practices from teacher, technology and distance education. *Journal of In-service Education*, *34*(2), 205–218. doi:10.1080/13674580801951079

Simola, H., & Rinne, R. (2008). Researching the political effects of quality assurance and evaluation (QAE) in education – Reflections on some comparative issues in sociology and the politics of education in the audit society . In Pereyra, M. A. (Ed.), *Changing knowledge and education: communities and new policies in global societies* (pp. 171–183). Frankfurt am Main: Peter Lang.

Sims, R. (2003). Promises of interactivity: Aligning Learner Perceptions and Expectations with Strategies for Flexible and Online Learning. *Distance Education*, *24*(1), 87–103. doi:10.1080/01587910303050

Sitlington, P. L. (2003). Postsecondary education: The other transition. *Exceptionality*, *11*(3), 103–113. doi:10.1207/S15327035EX1102_05

Skeekey, J. (2005). The jury's in: videoconferencing is invaluable to the legal profession. *Distance Learning*, *2*(5), 38–39.

Sloan-C. *A Consortium of Institutions and Organizations Committed to Quality Online Education* (2009). Retrieved from http://www.sloanconsortium.org

Smith, P. L., & Ragan, T. J. (2005). *Instructional design* (2nd ed.). Hoboken, NJ: John Wiley & Sons.

Smith, S. D., Salaway, G., & Borreson Caruso, J. (2009). The ECAR study of undergraduate students and information technology. *EDUCAUSE Center for Applied Research (ECAR)*. Available from http://www.educause.edu/ecar

Smyth, R. (2005). Broadband videoconferencing as a tool for learner-centred distance learning in higher education. *British Journal of Educational Technology*, *36*(5), 805–820. doi:10.1111/j.1467-8535.2005.00499.x

Smyth, R. (2009a). Enhancing learner-learner interaction using video communications in higher education: Implications from theorising about a new model. *British Journal of Educational Technology*. .doi:10.1111/j.1467-8535.2009.00990.x

Smyth, R., & Zanetis, J. (2007). Internet-based videoconferencing for teaching and learning: a Cinderella story. *Distance Learning*, *4*(2), 61–70.

Smyth, R. (2009b). *Evaluation Report: The TAFE@ Your PC CleverNetworks Project of the Regional Institute of TAFE SA*. Armidale: Technical and Further Education South Australia. Robyn Smyth Consulting.

Solomon, G., & Schrum, L. (2007). *Web 2.0: New tools, new schools*. Washington, DC: International Society for Technology in Education.

Soong, B. M. H., Chan, H. C., Chua, B. C., & Loh, K. F. (2001). Critical Success Factors for On-Line Course Resources. *Computers & Education*, *36*(2), 101–120. doi:10.1016/S0360-1315(00)00044-0

Spender, J.-C., & Grant, R. M. (Eds.). (1996). Knowledge and the Firm. *Strategic Management Journal*, *17*(Special Issue), 5–9.

Spil, A. A. M., & Salmela, H. (1999). The Fall of Strategic Information Systems Planning and the Rise of a Dynamic IS Strategy. *Proceedings of the 22nd Information Systems Research Seminar in Scandinavia (IRIS 22): 'Enterprise Architectures for Virtual Organisations'*, Keuruu, Finland, 7-10 August, 1999. Online at: http://citeseerx.ist.psu.edu/viewdoc/summary?doi=10.1.1.9.7273 [last visited 13/02/10].

Spitzer, D. R. (1987). Why technology has failed. *Educational Technology*, *27*(9), 18–21.

Sprague, D., & Dede, C. (1999, September). Constructivism in the classroom: If I teach this way, am I doing my job? *Learning and Leading with Technology*, *27*(1), 6–9, 16–17.

Srinivasan, M., Hwang, J., West, D., & Yellowless, P. M. (2006). Assessment of clinical skills using stimulator technologies. *Educational Assessment, Interventions, and Outcomes*, *30*(6), 505–515.

Stake, R. (1995). *The art of case research*. Thousand Oaks, CA: Sage Publications.

Standish Group. (2001). *Extreme CHAOS*. Online at: http://www.smallfootprint.com/Portals/0/StandishGroupExtremeChaos2001.pdf [last visited 13/02/10].

Stedmon, J., Wood, J., Curle, C., & Haslam, C. (2006). Development of PBL in the training of clinical psychologists. *Psychology Learning & Teaching*, *5*(1), 52–60.

Steinberg, E. R. (1991). *Computer-assisted instruction: A synthesis of theory, practice, and technology*. Hillsdale, NJ: Erlbaum.

Stensaker, B., & Skjerski, S. (2003). Organising ICT Initiatives in Higher Education. In Hansson, H.& Holmberg, C. (Eds.) *Eight Contributions on Quality and Flexible Learning, Sweden, Swedish Agency for Flexible Learning Report 3*, 103-115.

Stephens, K. K., Houser, M. L., & Cowan, R. L. (2009). R U able to meet me: The impact of students' overly casual email messages to instructors. *Communication Education*, *58*(3), 303–326. doi:10.1080/03634520802582598

Sternberg, R. J. (2000). Images of mindfulness. *The Journal of Social Issues*, *56*, 112–126. doi:10.1111/0022-4537.00149

Stevens, A., Hernandez, J., et al. (2005). The use of virtual patients to teach medical students communication skills. *The Association for Surgical Education Annual Meeting*. New York, NY.

Stewart, M., Brown, J. B., & Donner, A. (2000). The impact of patient-centered care on outcomes. *The Journal of Family Practice*, *49*, 796–804.

Stiles, M., & Yorke, J. (2007). Technology Supported Learning – Tensions between Innovation, and Control and Organizational and Professional Cultures. *Journal of Organizational Transformation and Social Change*, *3*(3), 251–267. doi:10.1386/jots.3.3.251_1

Stockdill, S. H., & Morehouse, D. L. (1992). Critical factors in successful adoption of technology: A checklist of TDC findings. *Educational Technology*, *32*(1), 57–58.

Stodden, R. A. (2001). Postsecondary education supports for students with disabilities: A review and response. *Journal for Vocational Special Needs Education*, *23*(2), 4–11.

Stodden, R. A., Roberts, K. D., Picklesimer, T., Jackson, D., & Chang, C. (2006). An analysis of assistive technology supports and services offered in postsecondary institutions. *Journal of Vocational Rehabilitation*, *24*, 111–120.

Stolovitch, H. D., & Keeps, E. J. (2002). *Telling ain't training*. Alexandria, VA: American Society for Training and Development.

Strehle, E. M., & Shabde, N. (2006). One hundred years of telemedicine: Does this new technology have a place in paediatrics? *Archives of Disease in Childhood*, *91*, 956–959. doi:10.1136/adc.2006.099622

Sullivan, R. (2009). Principles for Constructing Good Clicker Questions: Going beyond Rote Learning and Stimulating Active Engagement with Course Content. *Journal of Educational Technology Systems*, *37*(3), 335–347. doi:10.2190/ET.37.3.i

Surry, D. W., Ensminger, D. C., & Haab, M. (2005). A Model for Integrating Instructional Technology into Higher Education. *British Journal of Educational Technology*, *36*(2), 327–329. doi:10.1111/j.1467-8535.2005.00461.x

Surry, D. W., & Farquhar, J. D. (1996). Incorporating social factors into instructional design theory . In Bailey, M., & Jones, M. (Eds.), *Work, education, and technology* (pp. 6.1–6.8). DeKalb, IL: LEPS Press.

Surry, D. W., & Ely, D. P. (2006). Adoption, diffusion, implementation, and institutionalization of educational innovations . In Reiser, R., & Dempsey, J. V. (Eds.), *Trends & issues in instructional design and technology* (2nd ed., pp. 104–111). Upper Saddle River, NJ: Prentice-Hall.

Surry, D. W. (2008a). Impact of technology . In Tomei, L. A. (Ed.), *Encyclopedia of information technology curriculum integration* (pp. 389–394). Hershey, PA: Idea Group Reference.

Surry, D. W. (2008b). Innovations in learning technology . In Tomei, L. A. (Ed.), *Encyclopedia of information technology curriculum integration* (pp. 413–417). Hershey, PA: IGI Global.

Surry, D. W., & Ensminger, D. C. (2009). University 2.0: Human, social, and societal issues . In Yang, H., & Yuen, S. (Eds.), *Collective Intelligence and E-Learning 2.0: Implications of Web-Based Communities and Networking* (pp. 94–108). Hershey, PA: IGI Global.

Surry, D. (1997). *Diffusion theory and instructional technology*. Retrieved March 31, 2010, from http://www.gsu.edu/~wwwitr/docs/diffusion/

Surry, D. W. (2002). *A model for integrating instructional technology into higher education.* Paper presented at the American Educational Research Association Conference, April, 2002, New Orleans, LA.

Surry, D. W. (2008). Technology and the future of higher education: An Ellulian perspective. In J. Luca & E. R. Weippl (Eds.), *Proceedings of the ED-MEDIA 2008-World Conference on Educational Multimedia, Hypermedia & Telecommunications*. (pp.4901-4906). Chesapeake, VA: Association for Advancement of Computing in Education.

Surry, D. W., & Brennan, J. P., II. (1998). *Diffusion of instructional innovations: Five important, unexplored questions*. Hattiesburg, MS: University of Southern Mississippi. (ERIC Document Reproduction Service No. ED422892)

Surry, D. W., & Ensminger, D. C. (2002). *Perceived Importance of Conditions that Facilitate Implementation.* Paper presented at the American Educational Research Association Conference, April, 2002, New Orleans, LA.

Sutrisna, M., & Barret, P. (2007). Applying Rich Picture Diagrams to Model Case Studies of Construction Projects. *Engineering, Construction, and Architectural Management, 14*(2), 164–179. doi:10.1108/09699980710731281

Swan, G. (2009). Information systems in teacher preparation programs: What can we learn from a 5-Year longitudinal case study of an electronic portfolio database? *Journal of Educational Computing Research, 41*(4), 431–451. doi:10.2190/EC.41.4.c

Sweller, J. (2006). Discussion of 'emerging topics in cognitive load research: Using learner and information characteristics in the design of powerful learning environments'. *Applied Cognitive Psychology, 20*, 353–357. doi:10.1002/acp.1251

Szydlowski, S., & Smith, C. (2009). Perspectives from nurse leaders and chief information officers on health information technology implementation. *Hospital Topics, 87*(1), 3–9. doi:10.3200/HTPS.87.1.3-9

Tallent-Runnels, M. K., Thomas, J. A., Lan, W. Y., Cooper, S., Ahern, T. C., Shaw, S. M., & Xiaoming, L. (2006). Teaching courses online: A review of the research. *Review of Educational Research, 76*(1), 93–135. doi:10.3102/00346543076001093

Tapscott, D. (1999). Educating the net generation. *Educational Leadership, 56*(5), 6–11.

Tapscott, D. (1998). *Growing up digital: The rise of the net generation*. New York: McGraw-Hill.

Taylor, P. G. (2000). Changing expectations: Preparing students for flexible learning. *The International Journal for Academic Development, 5*(2), 107–115. doi:10.1080/13601440050200716

Taylor, R. (1980). *The computer in the school: Tutor, tool, tutee*. New York: Teachers College Press.

Taylor, C. (2007). The wave of the future, or just fun and games? Virtual training for healthcare workers. *Biomedical Instrumentation & Technology / Association For The Advancement. Medical Instrumentation*, (Suppl), 57–59.

Technology, C. (2009). Retrieved from http://campustechnology.com/home.aspx

Technology, Education, and Copyright Harmonization Act, Pub. L. No. 107-273, §13301 116 Stat. 1910 (2002).

Tenner, E. (1996). *Why things bite back: Technology and the revenge of unintended consequences*. New York: Alfred A. Knopf.

Tessmer, M. (1991). Back to the future: The environment analysis stage of front end analysis. *Performance and Instruction, 30*(1), 9–12. doi:10.1002/pfi.4170300104

Testa, M. G., & de Freitas, H. M. R. (2003). *Critical Success Factors of E-Learning Programmes: An Exploratory Study in The Brazilian Context*. Online at: http://professores.ea.ufrgs.br/hfreitas/revista/arquivos/80AIM.pdf [last visited 13/02/10].

Texas A&M University System. (2006). *Regents approve Patents and commercialization of research as new considerations for faculty tenure*. Press release. May 26, 2006.

The Rehabilitation Act of 1973, U.S.C. §94(d)

The Secretary's Commission on Achieving Necessary Skills (SCANS). (1991). *What work requires of schools: A SCANS report for America 2000*. Washington, DC: U.S. Department of Labor.

The Technology Related Assistance for Individuals with Disabilities Act of 1988, U.S.C. § 2201,2202.

The, T. L. T., & the Group. (2010). *Definition and Characteristics of a TLT Roundtable*. Accessed November 11, 2009, from http://www.tltgroup.org/TLTR/Characteristics.htm

The, T. L. T., & the Group. (2009). *Teaching, Learning, and Technology*. Retrieved from http://www.tltgroup.org/

Thiebaux, M., Marshall, A., et al. (2008). SmartBody: Behavior Realization for Embodied Conversational Agents. *International Conference on Autonomous Agents and Multi-Agent Systems*. Portugal.

Thomas, E., & Gillespie, D. (2008). Weaving together undergraduate research, mentoring of junior faculty and assessment: The case of an interdisciplinary program. *Innovative Higher Education, 33*, 29–38. .doi:10.1007/s10755-007-9060-x

Thompson, T. (2005). Information technology accessibility in higher education. EDUCAUSE *Center for Applied Research Bulletin, 2005(12).*

Thorton, G. C. III, & Mueller-Hanson, R. A. (2004). *Developing Organizational Simulations*. Mahwah, NJ: Lawrence Erlbaum and Associates.

Titthasiri, W. (2001). Information technology strategic planning process for institutions of higher education in Thailand. *NECTEC Technical Journal*, *III*(11), 153–164.

Tochel, C., Haig, A., Hesketh, A., Cadzow, A., Beggs, K., Colthart, I., & Peacock, H. (2009). The effectiveness of portfolios for post-graduate assessment and education: BEME Guide No 12. *Medical Teacher*, *31*(4), 320–339. doi:10.1080/01421590902883056

Tomasello, M. (1999). *The cultural origins of human cognition*. Cambridge, MA: Harvard University Press.

Tomasello, M. (2008). *Origins of human communication*. Cambridge, MA: MIT Press.

Tomasello, M. (2009). *Why we cooperate*. Cambridge, MA: MIT Press.

Tonidandel, S., Quiñones, M. A., & Adams, A. A. (2002). Computer adaptive testing: The impact of test characteristics on perceived performance and test takers' reactions. *The Journal of Applied Psychology*, *87*, 320–332. doi:10.1037/0021-9010.87.2.320

Tóth. Péter Benjamin (2009), *Creative humbug*. Retrieved January 10, 2010 from www.indicare.org/tiki-read_article.php?articleId=118

Trammel, J. (2009). Postsecondary students and disability stigma: Development of the postsecondary student survey of disability-related stigma (PSSDS). *Journal of Postsecondary Education & Disability.*, *22*(2), 106–113.

Traum, D., Gratch, J., et al. (2008). Multi-party, Multi-issue, Multi-strategy Negotiation for Multi-modal Virtual Agents. *8th International Conference on Intelligent Virtual Agents.* Tokyo, Japan:Springer

Traxler, J. (2007). Defining, Discussing, and Evaluating Mobile Learning. *International Review of Research in Open and Distance Learning*, *8*(2).

Trees, A. R., & Jackson, M. H. (2007). The Learning Environment in Clicker Classrooms: Student Processes of Learning and Involvement in Large University-Level Courses Using Student Response Systems. *Learning, Media and Technology*, *32*(1), 21–40. doi:10.1080/17439880601141179

Trendspotter: Next-Geners and Web 2.0 (2009, May). *Campus Technology, 22*(9), 49-51. Retrieved from http://1105production.com/EDU/Campus-Technology/Articles/2009/05/01/Trendspotter.aspx

Trenholm, S. (2006). A study on the efficacy of computer-mediated developmental math instruction for traditional community college students. [RTDE]. *Research and Teaching in Developmental Education*, *22*(2), 51–62.

Trepal, H., Haberstroh, S., Duffey, T., & Evans, M. (2007). Considerations and strategies for teaching online counseling skills: establishing relationships in cyberspace. *Counselor Education and Supervision*, *46*, 266–279.

Triola, M., & Feldman, M. (2006). A randomized trial of teaching clinical skills using virtual and live standardized patients. *Journal of General Internal Medicine*, *21*, 424–429. doi:10.1111/j.1525-1497.2006.00421.x

Trolley, B., & Silliker, A. (2005). The Use of WebCT in the supervision of counseling interns. *Journal of Technology in Counseling, 4* (1). Retrieved from http://jtc.colstate.edu/Vol4_1/Trolley/Trolley.htm on 4/15/10

Trowler, P. (1998). *Academics Responding to Change: New Higher Education Frameworks and Academic Cultures*. Buckingham, UK: SRHE and Open University Press.

Twigg, C. (2000). Institutional readiness criteria: Prerequisites to large-scale course redesign. *EDUCAUSE Review*, *35*(2), 42–50.

Twigg, A. C. (2005). Course redesign improves learning and reduces cost. *The National Center for Public Policy and Higher Education*. Retrieved March 31, 2010, from http://www.highereducation.org/reports/pa_core/core.pdf

U. S. Department of Education. (2002). *Findings from the condition of education 2002: Nontraditional undergraduates*. National Center for Education Statistics NCES 2002-012. Retrieved March 28, 2010, from http://nces.ed.gov/pubs2002/2002012.pdf

U. S. Department of Education. (2006, September). *A Test of Leadership: Charting the Future of U. S. Higher Education*, A Report of the Commission Appointed by Secretary of Education Margaret Spellings. Retrieved March 31, 2010, from http://www.ed.gov/about/bdscomm/list/hiedfuture/reports/final-report.pdf

U.S. Department of Education, Office of Civil Rights. *Auxiliary aids and services for postsecondary students with disabilities.* Retrieved from http://www.ed.gov/print/about/offices/list/ocr/docs/auxaids.html

U.S. Department of Education. (2006). *A National Dialogue: The Secretary of Education's Commission on the Future of Higher Education.* Retrieved from http://www2.ed.gov/about/bdscomm/list/hiedfuture/index.html

United States Access Board. (2010). Retrieved from http://www.access-board.gov/

United States Copyright Office. (1999). *Statement of Marybeth Peters the Register of Copyrights before the Committee on the Judiciary.* Retrieved December 16, 2009, from http://www.copyright.gov/docs/regstat52599.html

United States Copyright Office. (2009). *United States Copyright Office: A brief introduction and history, Circular 1a.* Retrieved December 16, 2009, from http://www.copyright.gov/circs/circ1a.html

United States v. Angevine, 281 F.3d 1130 (10th Cir. 2002), cert. denied, 537 U.S. 845 (2002)

University of California Davis. (2003). *IT strategic plan—Technology infrastructure*. Accessed November 13, 2009, from http://stuaff.ucdavis.edu/reports/ITinfrastructure_plan.html

University of Texas System. (2009). *Copyright crash course: The TEACH Act finally becomes a law.* Retrieved December 17, 2009 from http://www.utsystem.edu/ogc/intellectualproperty/teachact.htm

USA Patriot Act, Pub. L. No. 107-56, 116 Stat. 272 (2001).

Vaccaro, N., & Lambie, G. W. (2007). Computer-based counselor-in-training supervision: Ethical and practical implications for counselor educators and supervisors. *Counselor Education and Supervision*, *47*, 46–57.

Vale, D. (2009). *Report on the Survey of the Use of Rich Media Technologies in Australian Universities*. Armidale: Australian Learning and Teaching Council Funded Leadership Grant.

Van den Akker, J., Gravemeijer, K., McKenney, S., & Nieveen, N. (Eds.). (2006). *Educational design research*. London: Routledge.

Van Eck, R. (2006, March/April). Digital game-based learning: It's not just the digital natives who are restless. *EDUCAUSE Review*, *41*(2), 17–30. Retrieved from http://www.educause.edu/EDUCAUSE+Review/EDUCAUSEReviewMagazineVolume41/DigitalGame-BasedLearningItsNot/158041.

van Es, E. A., & Sherin, M. G. (2008). Learning to notice in the context of a video club. *Teaching and Teacher Education*, *24*(2), 244–276. doi:10.1016/j.tate.2006.11.005

Van Haneghan, J. P. (2009). Validating assessment for learning: Consequential and systems approaches. *Journal of Multidisciplinary Evaluation*, *6*(12), 23–31.

Van Haneghan, J. P. (October, 2008). *Assessment burden: When does the burden of assessment and evaluation outweigh the benefit?* Paper presented at the National Evaluation Institute, Wilmington, NC.

Vander Wal, T. (2005). *Folksonomy definition and Wikipedia*. Retrieved March 14, 2007, from http://www.vanderwal.net/random/entrysel.php?blog=1750

Vanderheiden, G. C., & Vanderheiden, K. R. (1992). *Guidelines for the design of consumer products to increase their accessibility to people with disabilities or who are aging* (Working draft 1.7). Madison WI: Trace Research and Development Center. Retrieved from http://trace.wisc.edu/docs/consumer_producxts_guidelines/toc.html

Vanderheiden, G.C. (2008). Ubiquitous accessibility, common core and micro assistive technology. *ACM Transactions on Accessible Computing, 1*(2), 10.1-10.7.

Vanides, J. (2009, August, 26). *Technology and the (Possible) Future of Higher Education.* Retrieved from http:// online/blogs/highered/archive/2009/08/26/technology-and-the-possible-future-of-higher-education.aspx

Vescio, V., Ross, D., & Adams, A. (2006). *A review of research on professional learning communities: What do we know?* Retrieved February 16, 2008 from: http:// www.nsrfharmony.org/research.vescio_ross_adams.pdf.

Vibert, C., & Place, C. (2006). Technology and Change in Higher Education . In Hunt, L., Bromage, A., & Tomkinson, B. (Eds.), *The Realities of Change in Higher Education: Interventions to Promote Learning and Teaching* (pp. 115–127). London: Routledge.

Vilkinas, T., & Cartan, G. (2006). The integrated competing values framework: its spatial configuration. *Journal of Management Development, 25*(6), 505–521. doi:10.1108/02621710610670092

Voelker, R. (2009). Medical simulation gets real. *JAMA: Journal of the American Medical Association, 302*(20), 2190–2192. doi:10.1001/jama.2009.1677

Volery, T., & Lord, D. (2000). Critical Success Factors In Online Education. *International Journal of Educational Management, 14*(5), 216–223. doi:10.1108/09513540010344731

Von Drehle, D. (2009, November 23). The big man on campus. *Time*, 44–48.

Wade, W., Hodgkinson, K., Smith, A., & Arfield, J. (1994). *Flexible Learning in Higher Education.* London: Kogan Page.

Wagner, E. D. (2008). Realizing the promises of mobile learning. *Journal of Computing in Higher Education, 20*, 4–14. doi:10.1007/s12528-008-9008-x

Wagner, E. D. (1994). In support of a functional view of interaction. *American Journal of Distance Education, 8*(2), 6–29. doi:10.1080/08923649409526852

Wallace, R. M. (2003). Online learning in higher education: A review of research on interactions among teachers and students. *Education Communication and Information, 3*(2), 241–280. doi:10.1080/14636310303143

Walter, D. A., Rosenquist, P. B., & Bawtinhimer, G. (2004). Distance learning technologies in the training of psychiatry residents: A critical assessment. *Academic Psychiatry, 28*(1), 60–65. doi:10.1176/appi.ap.28.1.60

Wang, E. E., Quinones, J., Fitch, M. T., Dooley-Hash, S., Griswold-Theodorson, S., & Medzon, R. (2008). Developing technical expertise in emergency medicine--The role of simulation in procedural skill acquisition. *Academic Emergency Medicine, 15*(11), 1046–1057. doi:10.1111/j.1553-2712.2008.00218.x

Wang, M., Shen, R., Novak, D., & Pan, X. (2008). The impact of mobile learning on students' learning behaviours and performance: report from a large blended classroom. *British Journal of Educational Technology.* Retrieved from http://www3.interscience.wiley.com/journal/120119993/ abstract. doi:.doi:10.1111/j.1467-8535.2008.00846.x

Watson, P. (2005). *Ideas: A history of thought and invention from fire to Freud.* New York: HarperCollins.

Wayne, D. B., Butter, J., Siddall, V. J., Fudala, M. J., Wade, L. D., & Feinglass, J. (2006). Mastery learning of advanced cardiac life support skills by internal medicine residents using simulation technology and deliberate practice. *Journal of General Internal Medicine, 21*(3), 251–256. doi:10.1111/j.1525-1497.2006.00341.x

Web Accessiblity Initiative. (2010). *How people with disabilities access the Web.* Cambridge MA: World Wide Web Consortium. Retrieved from http://www.w3.org/ WAI/WCAG20/quickref/

Weidman, J. C., Twale, D. J., & Stein, E. L. (2001). *Socialization of graduate and professional students in higher education: A perilous passage? ASHE-ERIC Higher Education Report, 28(3)* [A. J. Kezar, Series Editor.]. San Francisco: Jossey-Bass.

Weigel, V. (2002). *Deep learning for a digital age: Technology's untapped potential to enrich higher education.* San Francisco: Jossey-Bass.

Weigel, M., James, C., & Gardner, H. (2009). Learning: Peering backward and looking forward in the digital era. *International Journal of Learning and Media*, 1 (1) 1-18. Retrieved April 1, 2010, from Massachusetts Institute of Technology Press: http://www.mitpressjournals.org/doi/full/10.1162/ijlm.2009.0005

Weingardt, K. R. (2004). The role of instructional design and technology in the disseminatin of empirically supported, manual-based therapies. *Psychology: Science and Practice*, *11*(3), 313–331. doi:10.1093/clipsy/bph087

Weinstein, R. S. (2008). Time for a reality check. *Archives of Pathology & Laboratory Medicine*, *132*(5), 777–780.

Weitz, R. R., Wachsmuth, B., & Mirliss, D. (2006). The Tablet PC For Faculty: A Pilot Project. *Journal of Educational Technology & Society*, *9*(2), 68–83.

Wenger, E. (1998). *Communities of practice: Learning, meaning, and identity*. Cambridge, UK: Cambridge University Press.

Wenger, E. (1999). *Communities of Practice: Learning, Meaning, and Identity* (1st ed.). New York: Cambridge University Press.

Weston, T. J. (2005). Why faculty did- and did not- integrate instructional software in their undergraduate classrooms. *Innovative Higher Education*, *30*(2), 99–115. doi:10.1007/s10755-005-5013-4

Wheeler, S. (2007). The Influence of Communication Technologies and Approaches to Study on Transactional Distance in Blended Learning. *ALT-J: Research in Learning Technology*, *15*(2), 103–117.

White Paper from the December 2008 ECAR Symposium.

Wiley, D. (2006a). Open source, openness, and higher education. *Innovate, 3* (1). Retrieved January 9, 2010, from http://innovateonline.info/pdf/vol3_issue1/Open_Source,_Openness,_and_Higher_Education.pdf

Wiley, D. (2006b). *The current state of open educational resource*. Retrieved February 3, 2007, from http://opencontent.org/blog/archives/247

Wiley, D., & Hilton, J., III. (2009). Openness, dynamic specialization, and the disaggregated future of higher education. *The International Review Of Research In Open And Distance Learning, 10*(5). Retrieved January 3, 2010, from http://www.irrodl.org/index.php/irrodl/article/view/768

Williams, M. G., & Dittmer, A. (2009). Textbooks on tap: Using electronic books housed in handheld devices in nursing clinical courses. *Nursing Education Perspectives*, *30*(4), 220–225.

Williams, W. (2007). Connecting the docs. *Behavioral Healthcare*, *27*(4), 39.

Wilson, S., & Velayutham, K. (2009). Creating an Innovation-Oriented Technology Strategy. *Horizon*, *17*(3), 245–255. doi:10.1108/10748120910993277

Winn, W., & Snyder, D. (1996). Cognitive perspectives in psychology . In Jonassen, D. H. (Ed.), *Handbook of research for educational communications and technology* (pp. 112–142). New York: Macmillan.

Wise, A., Chang, J., Duffy, T., & Del Valle, R. (2004). The Effects of Teacher Social Presence on Student Satisfaction, Engagement, and Learning. *Journal of Educational Computing Research*, *31*(3), 247–271. doi:10.2190/V0LB-1M37-RNR8-Y2U1

Wodehouse, J. (2007). *Strategies for healthcare education: How to teach in the 21st Century*. Oxford, UK: Radcliffe Publishing.

Wong, D. W., Chan, F., Cardoso, E. D., Lam, C. S., & Miller, S. M. (2004). Rehabilitation counseling students; attitudes towards people with disabilities in three social context: A joint analysis. *Rehabilitation Counseling Bulletin*, *47*, 194–204. doi:10.1177/00343552040470040101

Wood, J. A. V., Miller, T. W., & Hargrove, D. S. (2005). Clinical supervision in rural settings: A telehealth model. *Professional Psychology, Research and Practice*, *36*(2), 173–179. doi:10.1037/0735-7028.36.2.173

World Wide Web Consortium. (2008). *Web content accessiblity guidelines (WCAG) 2.0: W3C Recommendations.* Cambridge MA: Author. Retrieved from http://www.w3.org/TR/WCAG20/

Wu, H., Zubair, M., & Maly, K. (2006). Harvesting social knowledge from folksonomies. *Proceedings of the 17th Conference on Hypertext and Hypermedia.* Odense, Denmark. (pp. 111-114).

Wyatt, S. (2003). Non-users also matter: The construction of users and non-users of the Internet. In Oudshoorn, N., & Pinch, T. (Eds.), *How Users Matter: The Co-construction of Users and Technology* (pp. 67–79). Cambridge, MA: The MIT Press.

Yair, G. (2008). Can we administer the scholarship of teaching? Lessons from outstanding professors in higher education. *Higher Education, 55*, 447–459. .doi:10.1007/s10734-007-9066-4

Yeh, C. J., Change, T., Chiang, L., Drost, C. M., Spelliscy, D., Carter, R. T., & Chang, Y. (2008). Development, content, process and outcome of an online peer supervision group for counselor trainees. *Computers in Human Behavior, 24*, 2889–2903. doi:10.1016/j.chb.2008.04.010

Young, J. (2009a, October 18). Beam me to the faculty senate. *The Chronicle of Higher Education.* Retrieved from http://chronicle.com/article/Beam-Me-to-the-Faculty-Sena/48830

Young, J. (2009b, April 10). 10 high fliers on Twitter. *The Chronicle of Higher Education.* Retrieved from http://chronicle.com/article/10-High-Fliers-on-Twitter/16488

Zagier, A. (2009). *Missouri patent fight shows perils of 'tech transfer.'* Associated Press. Feb. 7, 2009.

Zaltman, G., & Duncan, R. (1977). *Strategies for planned change.* New York: John Wiley and Sons.

Zaltman, G., Duncan, R., & Holbeck, J. (1973). *Innovations and Organizations.* New York: Wiley.

Zaner, R. M. (2006). The phenomenon of vulnerability in clinical encounters. *Human Studies, 29*, 283–294. doi:10.1007/s10746-006-9028-3

Zemsky, R. (2009). *Making reform work: The case for transforming American higher education.* Piscataway, NJ: Rutgers University Press.

Zemsky, R., & Massey, W. F. (2004). *Thwarted innovation: What happened to e-learning and why.* West Chester, PA: University of Pennsylvania. [WWW Document] Retrieved from http://www.thelearningalliance.info/Docs/Jun2004/ThwartedInnovation.pdf.

Zhang, K., & Carr-Chellman, A. (2006). Courseware copyrights: Whose rights are right? *Journal of Educational Computing Research, 34*(2), 173–186. doi:10.2190/AM4M-97MF-FJCV-PA1U

Zhao, Y., & Frank, K. A. (2003). Factors affecting technology uses in schools: An ecological perspective. *American Educational Research Journal, 4*(40), 807–840. doi:10.3102/00028312040004807

About the Contributors

Daniel W. Surry is a Professor in the College of Education at the University of South Alabama. He teaches courses in instructional design, performance improvement, and training systems. He has also taught at the University of Southern Mississippi and the University of Alabama and served as Instructional Technologist at California State University, Fresno. He holds a Doctor of Education in Instructional Technology from the University of Georgia, a Master's of Science in Instructional Design from the University of South Alabama, and Bachelor's of Arts in Mass Communication from the University of Alabama. His research interests focus on the impact of innovation within organizations, especially in higher education

James "Tres" Stefurak is an Assistant Professor in the College of Education at the University of South Alabama. At USA he teaches courses in the Community Counseling M.S. program (for which he serves as the Practicum/Internship Coordinator), the Combined-Integrated Clinical/Counseling Psychology Ph.D. program and the Psychiatry Residency program. He coordinates an active research and clinical service project with a local juvenile court - the Mobile Juvenile Court Collaborative, and has additional research interests in web-based social networking in the training and lifelong development of mental health professionals particularly in terms of the dissemination of evidence-based practice and practiced-based evidence. He also actively researches and publishes in the field of psychology of religion/spirituality. He has previously taught psychology and served as Director of Clinical Training for the M.S. program in Applied Psychology at Auburn University Montgomery. He received his Ph.D. in Counseling Psychology, M.Ed. in Community Counseling, and B.A. in Psychology from the University of Georgia.

Robert M. Gray, Jr. is Director of the Program for the Enhancement of Teaching and Learning at the University of South Alabama. He holds a Ph.D. in Instructional Technology from the University of Alabama and completed his bachelors and masters in English at the University of Alabama and his doctoral coursework in English at Michigan State University. He has taught at the University of Alabama, Michigan State, Troy State, and South Alabama. His research interests include interaction in online instruction, dialogism in teaching and learning, the role of the self in research methodology, and the democratization of education. He has published in the *SAGE Handbook of Mixed Methods in Social & Behavioral Research* and *New Directions for Teaching and Learning*, and has presented at several national and international conferences. He has published two books of poetry, *I Wish That I Were Langston Hughes* and *DREW: Poems from Blue Water.*

* * *

Trish Andrews has worked in the field of higher education since the early 1990's and has considerable experience in the areas of open, distance, flexible, blended and mobile learning. She has extensive experience in supporting innovative curriculum development with a particular focus on integrating technologies into higher education programs. She has had several educational development and research grants including current ALTC grants in the area of rich media and learning spaces and has published widely in the area of educational innovation. Her current activities and research interests include investigating the student voice in relation to ICTs for teaching and learning, the integration of ICTS including rich media into teaching and learning, mobile learning, learning spaces and academic development.

Susan Asselin is Professor and Chair, Department of Teaching and Learning, in the School of Education at Virginia Tech. She offers graduate programs that prepare secondary educators in transition services, assistive technology and diversity issues in education and work. She directs state funded projects that provide technical assistance to support individuals with disabilities to use assistive technology devices and services, especially in work and higher education. She has also coordinates projects to introduce high school students to disability support services including assistive technology and developing curriculum for secondary educators to introduce students with disabilities to technology. She earned an Assistive Technology Applications certificate from California State University-Northridge and participated in a Universal Design for Learning Postsecondary Institute at the Center for Applied Special Technology (CAST). She teaches a graduate course on access, disability and technology.

Richard Caladine is the Head of Learning, Innovation, Facilities and Technologies (LIFT) at University of Wollongong. He is responsible for the operation of University of Wollongong's audio visual and rich media educational systems. These include a videoconference service consisting of over 60 endpoints and a 40 port videoconference Multi Conference unit that connects seven NSW campuses of the University. As well he is responsible for the podcasting, webcasting and streaming services. He is actively involved with the training of staff in the pedagogically appropriate use of these systems and other educational technologies. He has researched the use of rich media in higher education, has published many papers, book chapters and books all on the appropriate pedagogical use of educational technologies. His current area of investigation is talk-based, technology-mediated, visual communications.

Sharon F. Cramer, Ph.D. is a Distinguished Service Professor at Buffalo State College, where she has been a member of the faculty since 1985. She holds a Ph.D. from New York University, a M.A.T. from Harvard University, and a B. A. from Tufts University. From 1999-2004, she was Executive Director of the SABRE Project, campus implementation of the Oracle Student System for web-based delivery of student services. Leadership roles in state and national professional organizations led to receiving the Burton Blatt Humanitarian Award (2003, Council for Exceptional Children), and the Leo D. Doherty Memorial Award for Outstanding Leadership and Service (2008, Northeastern Educational Research Association). Her publications include (2005) *Student Information System: A Guide to Implementation Success* (published by AACRAO in 2005) and two books published by Corwin Press. She has given over 100 presentations and keynotes in 25 states and Canada. She has been listed in *Who's Who in America* and *Who's Who in American Education* since 2006.

Nada Dabbagh, Ph.D., is Associate Professor of Instructional Technology in the College of Education and Human Development at George Mason University in Fairfax, VA. She received her doctorate in Instructional Systems from The Pennsylvania State University in 1996. She also holds a M.S. in Operations Research from Columbia University and a B.A. in Mathematics from Iona College. Her teaching includes courses on learning theory, instructional design, and e-learning design and pedagogy. Her research focuses on the pedagogical ecology of technology-mediated instructional systems with the goal of understanding the cognitive and design characteristics of task structuring as the basis for effective learning designs. She has an extensive presentation and publication record including two co-authored books titled *Online Learning: Concepts, Strategies, and Application* (Prentice Hall, 2005) and *Learning to Learn with Integrative Learning Technologies (ILT): A Practical Guide for Academic Success* (IAP, 2010).

Gayle V. Davidson-Shivers, Ph.D., is a Professor in Instructional Design and Development (IDD) at the University of South Alabama. Her master's and doctoral degrees are in Curricular and Instructional Systems with related fields of management, industrial/organizational psychology, and evaluation from the University of Minnesota -Twin Cities. Her baccalaureate degree is in education from Western Oregon University. She teaches graduate courses on psychology of learning, human performance technology, and developing online instruction. She was first in the IDD program to teach online. She co-authored the book, *Web-Based Learning: Design, Implementation, and Evaluation*. She presents at national and international conferences and publishes in various journals related to instructional design and technology. Her current research focus is on online learning through discussions and interactions. She serves on the Advisory Board for AECT's Training and Performance Division. Her workshops include online instruction, assessing training, learning styles, among other things.

James Dwight received his doctorate in education from Virginia Tech in 2004. He has taught education courses in philosophy of education and educational foundations at Millersville University and English Literature at the high school level. Dr. Dwight's primary focus for research and writing is hyperpedagogy, which seeks to actualize social justice and poststructural pedagogies in digitally enhanced and online learning environments. Hyperpedagogy is both theory and practice. As theory, hyperpedagogy is critical of modernist assumptions for education, particularly educational standardization. As practice, hyperpedagogy fosters loosely bounded and mutually configured learning environments in computer mediated communication and online learning educational settings. Dr. Dwight has published work on hyperpedagogy in *Teachers College Record, E-Learning,* and the *Philosophy of Education Yearbook.* He has also contributed chapters in books on the subject, including *Queering Straight Teachers: Discourse and Identity in Teacher Education* and *The International Handbook of Virtual Learning Environments.*

David Ensminger has worked as a Clinical Assistant Professor for Loyola University Chicago since 2005. During this time he has served as the Graduate Program Director for MEd School Technology program and the Curriculum and Instruction MEd. and EdD programs, He has taught graduate courses in technology integration, instructional design, educational psychology, program evaluation and educational research. His research interests include implementation of innovations, organizational change, technology integration, and research practices. He has a PhD in Instructional Design and Development, and a MA in Psychology. He has work experiences as an instructional designer and performance improvement consultant in industrial, business, military and higher education settings.

Gregory M. Francom is a doctoral student in the Learning, Design, and Technology Program in the Department of Educational Psychology and Instructional Technology at the University of Georgia. His research interests include learning choices, task-centered learning, and fostering learner self-direction.

Joanne Gikas is Director of Online Education at The University of Memphis, where she works with faculty on the design and development of online programs. Prior to this position, Joanne worked in the university's teaching and learning center researching and promoting the effective use of instructional technologies, as well as working closely with faculty in the development of their face-to-face and online courses. Formerly, she was an instructional designer for human resources at the university and a classroom teacher for Memphis City Schools. She is currently a doctoral candidate in Instructional Design & Technology.

Michael M. Grant is an associate professor in the Instructional Design and Technology program at the University of Memphis. His research considers how to best help faculty members implement technology into teaching and learning, as well as how students represent their learning with computer technologies in different ways. He earned his Ph.D. from the University of Georgia in Instructional Technology.

Charles L. Guest, Jr., Ph.D., NCC, LPC is Chair of the Department of Professional Studies in the College of Education at the University of South Alabama and is currently the Chair of the Alabama Board of Examiners in Counseling. He holds a doctorate in Counselor Education from Mississippi State University.

Joyce M. Guest, Ph.D., is the Instructional Designer for the College of Medicine at the University of South Alabama. She holds a doctorate in Instructional Design and Development from the University of South Alabama.

Melissa J. Haab is the Associate Dean of Academic Affairs for Instructional Design at Alabama Southern Community College, where she has been employed since 2007. She holds a Ph.D. from the University of South Alabama, a M.S. from Mississippi State University and a B.A. Mississippi State University. From 2000-2007 she was the Director of Admissions at the University of South Alabama where she was a Team Leader for the campus implementation of SunGard BANNER Enterprise Resource Planning system. Her primary research interest is technology change in higher education. Her dissertation title was titled *Relationship between Modes of Participation and Satisfaction during implementation of Enterprise Resource Planning systems in Higher Education.*

Stephen W. Harmon is the Director of Learning Technologies at Georgia State University and an Associate Professor of Learning Technologies at Georgia State University in Atlanta. He teaches graduate courses in Instructional Design and Technology. His research interests and consulting experience include project evaluation, elearning, Instructional Technology in Developing Countries and hypermedia.

Richard L. Hayes is Dean of the College of Education and Professor of Clinical and Counseling Psychology at the University of South Alabama. His research applies a democratic philosophy of education to group work using a constructivist developmental psychology. Currently, this work is addressed to educational interventions across cultures internationally. Hayes received his bachelor's degree in Biology from Harvard College and his Ed.D. in Counseling Psychology from Boston University. Prior to becoming Dean of the College of Education at USA, Hayes was the chair of the Department of Counseling & Human Development Services at the University of Georgia.

Keith B. Hopper earned his doctorate in instructional technology from Georgia State University after a career as a health professions educator. He is a registered respiratory therapist and Fellow of the American Association for Respiratory Care. He developed and published instructional software for medical fields for seven years (MedSoft Rainer). He is the instructional design-technology specialist for the Southern Polytechnic Information Design and Communication, and Information and Instructional Design graduate programs. He teaches graduate courses in instructional design, project management, performance technology, online instructional development, multimedia and medical communication. He also teaches undergraduate courses in multimedia and technical writing. His research and scholarship focus is technology integration in higher education and the medical industry.

Jill Jameson is Director of Research and Enterprise at the School of Education and Training, University of Greenwich. The author of five books and numerous articles, Jill is a Fellow of the Royal Society, Fellow of the Institute for Learning (FIfL), with a PhD and MA (King's College), MA (Goldsmith's), MA and BA Hons (Cambridge), PGCE (Nottingham) and BA, PG Dip (UCT). Jill is Chair of the International *Society for Research in Higher Education (SRHE) Conference* 2010, Co-Chair, *ALT-C* 2008; Director, JISC eLIDA CAMEL; Director, JISC eLISA; Convenor SRHE HE-FE Network; *AACE Journal* Editorial Board Member; *E-LEARN, BERA, BELMAS, INORMS, QII 2010* and *ALT-C* presenter; Biographee, Marquis Who's Who in the World; Special Editor, *BJET* (2006), Guest Editor, *Alt-J* (2000), and a Series Editor for Continuum Education Books. Jill has over twenty years senior education management experience. She is a UK-wide Leadership Assessor for the LSIS Principals' Qualifying Programme.

Lucas John Jensen is a doctoral student in the Learning, Design, and Technology program in the Department of Educational Psychology and Instructional Technology at the University of Georgia. His research interests include asynchronous education, personal learning environments, and gaming.

Carol L. Johns earned her master's degree in adult education and organizational development at the University of Georgia. She has more than 25 years of healthcare experience including clinical, classroom, and laboratory instruction for the University System of Georgia. She is presently director of physician services at Upson Regional Medical Center, Thomaston, Georgia. She has experience in organizational development, change management and process improvement. Recently she has specialized in development and marketing of hospital departments in the areas of general hospital education, HROD, and leadership development as well as clinical education, cardiac rehabilitation, outpatient radiology and laboratory services. She presently manages hospital-owned medical and specialty physician practices serving seven rural counties in the mid-central region of Georgia, with responsibility for practitioners from front-line office personnel to specialty physicians. An administrator and adult educator, she is actively involved in the changes sweeping healthcare management and health information exchange.

Marshall G. Jones is an Associate Professor of Educational Technology and Director of Graduate Studies in the Richard W. Riley College of Education at Winthrop University in Rock Hill, South Carolina. He teaches graduate courses in Educational Technology and undergraduate courses in technology integration. He was awarded the inaugural Bank of America Professorship of Education in 2004 at Winthrop University to study mobile, ubiquitous learning environments. His research interests and consulting experience include project evaluation, instructional design, mobile learning, elearning, the design and development of constructivist learning environments, emerging technologies and new media.

Eun Ju Jung is a full-time doctoral student of Instructional Systems Program at Penn State University. She finished her master's program in Instructional Technology from the University of Georgia. Prior to attending UGA, she received her B.A. in Christian Education. Her research interest lies in teachers' and students' epistemological beliefs influencing the learning process.

Joél Lewis is a native of Mobile, Alabama, who enjoys spending time with her family, working with youth, and traveling. She received a Bachelor of Science in Human Resource Management, Master of Science and Ph.D.in Instructional Design and Development from the University of South Alabama. She has received awards such as the Lisa Mitchell Bukstein Foundation Scholarship for Developing Faculty in Education , Pillans Middle School Leadership and Service Award, Mortar Board: National College Senior Honor Society – Top Professor Award, Leadership Alabama Initiative Participant, and Mobile Bay Monthly's Forty under Forty Inaugural Class. She is currently an Assistant Professor at the University of South Alabama in Instructional Design and Development. She is a co-chair of the College of Education Diversity Committee and is sponsor of the Instructional Design & Development Graduate Student Association. Her research interests include diversity in instructional design, self-development training, leadership development, and technology integration.

Eugene Kowch researches complex leadership for education transformation. He networks multi-disciplinary domains like educational technology and education administration leadership to better understand today's evolving learning systems. His research is focused on providing evidence-based knowledge for large, financially and socially expensive learning institutions (including governments) who are increasingly struggling to sustain themselves. Many are failing with amazing speed. Many more are slowly failing. Combining professional experience as an engineer, corporate executive and then as a K-12 principal and deputy superintendent of education, he works to prepare leaders who can 'handle' complexity and rapid change - inclusive of a mix of technology, economics and social changes affecting organization work. He believes that a combination of new administration, instructional and organizational design capacities will be new "keys" for leaders in higher education organizations. Our higher education organizations must leave the 'dark ages' and enter the 'information age' – quickly. His graduate students study advanced organization theory, instructional design, performance improvement, organization theory and leadership theory in the Graduate School of Education at the University of Calgary, and at various universities in North America and Europe.

Susan Land is an Associate Professor of the Instructional Systems Program at Penn State University, University Park. She earned her doctorate in Instructional Systems from the Florida State University in 1995. Previously, she worked as a postdoctoral fellow at the University of Georgia's Learning and Performance Support Laboratory and held a faculty position at the University of Oklahoma, Department of Educational Psychology. Her research investigates leaner cognitive engagement, reflection, and collaboration with open-ended, technology-enhanced learning environments. Her current research investigates open-ended learning in everyday contexts that are mediated by technology.

Russ Lea graduated with a bachelor of science degree from the University of Washington in 1975 went on to earn Ph.D.s from Syracuse University and from SUNY College of Environmental Science and Forestry in 1979. He has 20 years of extensive experience in academic research administration. From 2000 to 2007 he served as Vice President for Research for the 16-campus University of North Carolina System, and was responsible for overseeing $1B in annual external research support from federal, state and private sources, as well as promoting innovation for economic development and technology transfer. As Vice President for Research at the University of South Alabama he is the principal spokesperson for research administration programs and services, and engages in strategic planning for University-wide research initiatives. He oversees the activities of the Office of Sponsored Programs, the Office of Grants Administration, Technology Transfer, and provides oversight of the USA Technology and Research Park.

Maggie McPherson is a Senior Lecturer in the School of Education at the University of Leeds. As an author of over 100 papers, reports, book and book chapters, Maggie has been involved in Information Studies, IT Project Management and e-Learning research for over fifteen years. Notable among her extensive publication list is a book entitled *Developing Innovation in Online Learning: An Action Research Framework.*, co-authored with Dr. Miguel Nunes. Currently, Maggie is a non-executive director and chair of Steering Group for Learning Light, a professional association for the e-learning industry. She is also co-chair for the IADIS E-Learning Conference and co-editor for an Emerald journal entitled *Interactive Technology and SMART Education* (ITSE).

John Nworie is an independent researcher and consultant. He has previously held positions as Director of the Center for Innovation in Teaching and Learning at Fayetteville State University, a constituent institution of the University of North Carolina system; Executive Director of Instructional Technology at TRI-C; Academic Technology Consultant; Coordinator of Media and Technology Services; and other similar positions in higher education. He completed his Ph.D. program in Instructional Systems at the Pennsylvania State University, and a graduate certificate in Distance Education. He has published and presented at national and international conferences. He co-authored a publication in EDUCAUSE Quarterly with Michael Albright, entitled *Rethinking Academic Technology Leadership in an Era of Change*, that received EDUCAUSE Quarterly's 2008 Contribution of the Year Award. His areas of interest include distance education, faculty professional development, leadership issues, and technology application to instruction.

Thomas D. Parsons, PhD is a Clinical and Experimental Neuropsychologist, Assistant Research Professor, and Research Scientist at the University of Southern California's Institute for Creative Technologies. He directs the VRCPAT Laboratory, helping to facilitate human-computer interface research. His work with human-computer interfaces began with invasive brain-computer interfaces and the cognitive sequelae of deep brain stimulation. The long-range goal of his laboratory is to develop noninvasive brain-computer interfaces and psychophysiologically adaptive virtual environments that may be used for neuropsychological assessment, stress inoculation, virtual reality exposure therapy, cognitive training, and rehabilitation. This goal is being pursued with a combination of theoretical and experimental approaches at several levels of investigation ranging from the biophysical level to the systems level. In addition to his patents (with eHarmony.com), he has over 100 publications in peer-reviewed journals and other fora.

Raymond S. Pastore has ten years of instructional design and technology experience, which includes extensive corporate and academic experience. His research focuses on multiple representations, mobile learning, gaming, and metacognitive strategies that support learning from a multimedia environment. Ray completed the requirements for his Ph.D. in Instructional Systems with a minor in Educational Psychology at Penn State University in the Summer of 2009 and is currently an Assistant Professor at the University of North Carolina Wilmington

Donovan Plumb is a professor in education in Halifax, Nova Scotia, teaching in adult education, higher education, and studies in lifelong learning. He is deeply interested in human capacities for collaborative learning and, especially, the ways these capacities both shape and are conditioned by the surrounding spatial and material context. As well as teaching in Canada, he teaches regularly in a Studies in Lifelong Learning graduate program his university offers in Kingston, Jamaica. Recently, Mount Saint Vincent University gave him an instructional leadership award in recognition of his contributions to the development of educational technologies.

Drew Polly is an Assistant Professor in the Department of Reading and Elementary Education at the University of North Carolina at Charlotte. His research interests focus on examining how to best teachers' use of learner-centered pedagogies in their classrooms. Drew's main areas of expertise are technology integration professional development and standards-based mathematics instruction. Drew also serves as the co-director of the UNC Charlotte Professional Development School Partnership Program. Drew graduated in 2006 from the University of Georgia with a Ph.D. in Instructional Technology.

Karen Rasmussen is the Chair of the Department of Computer and Engineering Technology and the Department of Instructional and Performance Technology at the University of West Florida. She is a professor and teaches courses in Performance and Instructional Technology. She has co-authored a text on web-based instruction and continues to conduct her research on the variables affecting learning on the web. Her department participates in a variety of innovative teaching and learning strategies, including mobile delivery of instruction for military service members.

Patricia M. Reeves is an Associate Professor in the School of Social Work at the University of Georgia. Her research focuses on the psychosocial issues of individuals living with HIV/AIDS and the protective/risk factors associated with teen dating violence. She is involved with many health-related, multidisciplinary collaborations at UGA including: serving as co-principal investigator of *Healthy Teens*, a large-scale violence prevention initiative funded by the Centers for Disease Control and Prevention (CDC); spearheading development of a dual master's degree program in Social Work and Public Health; serving on the advisory board for the Global Health Initiative, and; collaborating to establish an Evidence-Based Program for Health Professions Education. A Lilly Teaching Fellow and multiple recipient of the Outstanding Teaching Award in the School of Social Work, she teaches courses in human behavior theory, healthcare in social work, and qualitative research methods.

Thomas C. Reeves is a Professor Emeritus of Learning, Design, and Technology in the Department of Educational Psychology and Instructional Technology in the College of Education at the University of Georgia. After completing his Ph.D. at Syracuse University in 1979, he was a Fulbright lecturer in Peru, and he has since worked in 30 other countries. His research interests include evaluation of educational technology, socially responsible educational research, mental models and cognitive tools, authentic learning tasks, and educational technology applications in developing countries. In 2003, he was the first person to receive the AACE Fellowship Award from the Association for the Advancement of Computing in Education. He has published two books, *Interactive Learning Systems Evaluation* book (with John Hedberg in 2003) and *A Guide to Authentic E-Learning* (with Jan Herrington and Ron Oliver in 2010) as well as nearly 200 other publications.

Rick Reo is an instructional designer for the Division of Instructional Technology at George Mason University, where he consults with faculty on course design and development in the Distance Education program. He also leads and supports Web 2.0 initiatives across the university, such as iTunes U, multiuser weblog and wiki systems, and projects related to the pedagogy of social software tools. He has Master's degrees in both Cultural Anthropology and Education (Instructional Design). He is an adjunct instructor at GMU and teaches a variety of graduate Web 2.0 tools courses and undergraduate information technology courses. He was GMU's interim Director for the New Media Consortium and currently serves on the board of the Association of Collegiate Computing Services of Virginia.

Lloyd Rieber is a Professor in the Learning, Design, and Technology Program in the Department of Educational Psychology and Instructional Technology at the University of Georgia. He is interested in visualization and the design of interactive learning environments.

Stephen R. Rodriguez, Ph.D. has worked in educational technology for over twenty years and earned a doctorate in Instructional Systems from Florida State University. Currently Associate Professor at Texas A&M University—Corpus Christi (TAMUCC), he specializes in instructional design, multimedia development, and applications of learning theories. He served as the principal founder of the Master of Science Degree Program in Educational Technology at TAMUCC which was formally established in 1997. He is a frequent presenter at major technology conferences and is a consulting editor for the journal *Educational Technology Research and Development.* He also participated in the Educational Testing Service's Visiting Scholars Program in the summer of 2010. His current research interests center on strategies for effective e-learning, technology integration, applied learning theories, and technology leadership skills.

Wilhelmina Savenye is a Professor of Educational Technology, in the Division of Applied Studies in Learning, Technology and Psychology in Education at Arizona State University and previously taught at The University of Texas at Austin and San Diego State University. Her area of focus is instructional design and evaluation of technology-based and online learning systems. She has published over 70 articles and chapters, made over 140 conference presentations and workshops, been awarded numerous federal and foundation grants, and has produced many digital technology learning programs. Her instructional design and evaluation work has been conducted in such diverse settings as public school districts, museums, botanical gardens, zoos, universities, corporations, and Army tank maintenance training.

Robyn Smyth completed her doctorate at the University of New England, specialising in marine faunal remains from coastal archaeological sites. After working as an archaeologist and palaeoichthyologist in Australia and Central America, she became interested in academic development and completed a number of small research projects for the Teaching and Learning Centre at UNE. She is currently employed as a project officer on ALTC funded projects at UNE, including the Leading Rich Media Project, which is investigating how tertiary institutions use rich media technologies to improve student learning.

James P. Van Haneghan is professor and Director of Assessment and Evaluation in the College of Education at the University of South Alabama. He has several academic interests including program evaluation, student assessment, and institutional assessment. He has also studied problem solving, mathematical thinking, and motivation over the years. He has written numerous articles and chapters, and has been a frequent reviewer for the *Mental Measurements Yearbook*. He is a member of the American Evaluation Association, the American Educational Research Association, and the Consortium for Research on Educational Accountability and Teacher Evaluation.

Index

Symbols

D

E

Breinigsville, PA USA
03 March 2011
256607BV00006BA/1-50/P

9 781609